THE FUTURE OF CHILD
AND FAMILY LAW

Child and family law tells us much about how a society operates, since it touches the lives of everyone living in that society. In this volume, national experts examine child and family law in thirteen countries – Australia, Canada, China, India, Israel, Malaysia, the Netherlands, New Zealand, Norway, Russia, Scotland, South Africa and the United States. Each chapter identifies the imperatives and influences that have prevailed to date, and offers informed predictions of how the law will develop in the years to come. A common chapter structure facilitates comparison of the jurisdictions, and in the Introduction the editor highlights common trends and salient differences. *The Future of Child and Family Law* therefore provides practitioners, academics and policymakers with access not just to an overview of child and family law in a range of countries around the world, but also to insights into what has shaped it and options for reform.

ELAINE E. SUTHERLAND is Professor of Child and Family Law at the School of Law, University of Stirling, Scotland, and Professor at Lewis and Clark Law School, Portland, Oregon, USA.

THE FUTURE OF CHILD AND FAMILY LAW

International Predictions

Edited by

ELAINE E. SUTHERLAND

CAMBRIDGE
UNIVERSITY PRESS

CAMBRIDGE UNIVERSITY PRESS
Cambridge, New York, Melbourne, Madrid, Cape Town,
Singapore, São Paulo, Delhi, Mexico City

Cambridge University Press
The Edinburgh Building, Cambridge CB2 8RU, UK

Published in the United States of America by Cambridge University Press, New York

www.cambridge.org
Information on this title: www.cambridge.org/9781107006805

© Cambridge University Press 2012

First published 2012

Printed and Bound in the United Kingdom by the MPG Books Group

A catalogue record for this publication is available from the British Library

Library of Congress Cataloguing in Publication data
The future of child and family law: international predictions /
edited by Elaine E. Sutherland.
p.   cm.
Includes bibliographical references and index.
ISBN 978-1-107-00680-5 (hardback)
1. Domestic relations.   2. Children–Legal status, laws, etc.   I. Sutherland, Elaine.
K670.F88 2012
346.01′5–dc23   2012015439

ISBN 978-1-107-00680-5 Hardback

Dedicated to Professor Eric M. Clive

CONTENTS

Notes on contributors   *page* ix
Preface   xv

1 Imperatives and challenges in child and family law: commonalities and disparities   1
ELAINE E. SUTHERLAND

2 Australia: the certain uncertainty   47
FRANK BATES

3 Canada: a bold and progressive past but an unclear future   77
CAROL ROGERSON

4 China: bringing the law back in   112
MICHAEL PALMER

5 India: a perspective   144
ANIL MALHOTRA AND RANJIT MALHOTRA

6 Israel: dynamism and schizophrenia   175
RHONA SCHUZ AND AYELET BLECHER-PRIGAT

7 Malaysia: what lies ahead?   205
NOOR AZIAH MOHD AWAL

8 The Netherlands: the growing role of the judge in child and family law   235
PAUL VLAARDINGERBROEK

9 New Zealand: the emergence of cultural diversity   265
BILL ATKIN

10 Norway: equal rights at any cost?   296
TONE SVERDRUP

11   Russia: looking back, evaluating the present and
     glancing into the future   330
     OLGA A. KHAZOVA

12   Scotland: the marriage of principle and pragmatism   363
     ELAINE E. SUTHERLAND

13   South Africa: changing the contours of child and
     family law   398
     JACQUELINE HEATON

14   The United States of America: changing laws for
     changing families   429
     MARYGOLD (MARGO) SHIRE MELLI

     Index   461

CONTRIBUTORS

BILL ATKIN is a professor of law at Victoria University of Wellington, New Zealand. He teaches a wide range of subjects, both undergraduate and postgraduate, including family law, medical law, torts, welfare law and 'law, values and religion'. He contributes to the *Family Law Service* (loose-leaf) and *Fisher on Matrimonial and Relationship Property* (loose-leaf). Among recent books are (with Henaghan) *Family Law Policy in New Zealand*, 3rd edn (2007), (with Parker) *Relationship Property in New Zealand*, 2nd edn (2009), and (with McLay) *Torts in New Zealand: Casebook and Materials*, 5th edn (2012). He has been involved in government reviews on matrimonial property, adoption and assisted reproduction, is a member of the Family Law Section's Policy and Law Reform Committee, and is the General Editor of the International Society of Family Law's *International Survey of Family Law*, published annually.

NOOR AZIAH MOHD AWAL is Associate Professor at the Faculty of Law, Universiti Kebangsaan Malaysia (UKM). She has lectured on child and family law for the past twenty-six years in Malaysia and was a visiting research and teaching fellow at Victoria University of Wellington, New Zealand, in 1999. She specialises in the comparative study of child, women's and family law in accordance with Islamic law and common law. She is currently a council member of the Co-ordinating Council for the Protection of Children, the Syariah Advisor Panel to the Ministry of Women, Family and Community Development of Malaysia and a working committee member of the Child Support Unit, Department of Syariah Judiciary of Malaysia. The author of more than thirty articles and book chapters, her books include *Introduction to Malaysian Legal System*, 3rd edn (2009), *Women and Law*, (2006) and (with Sohor) *Civil Family Law* (2007).

FRANK BATES is Professor Emeritus of Law at the Law School of the University of Newcastle, New South Wales, Australia. He has held visiting positions at Lewis and Clark Law School, Portland, Oregon, USA;

St Mary's University, San Antonio, Texas, USA; The University of East Anglia, UK and the City University of Hong Kong. He has published over two hundred books, chapters, articles and notes internationally as well as having presented numerous papers throughout the world. He has been Vice-President of the International Society of Family Law, a member of the Australian Family Law Council and a Law Reform Commissioner for the State of Tasmania.

AYELET BLECHER-PRIGAT is Senior Lecturer (Associate Professor) and Co-Director of the Centre for the Rights of the Child and the Family at the Sha'arei Mishpat Law School in Israel. She received her JSD (2005) and LL (Kent scholar 1999) from Columbia Law School. Her LLB (*magna cum laude*) is from the Tel-Aviv University (1997). Prior to her academic career, Dr Blecher-Prigat clerked for Israeli Supreme Court Justice Strasberg-Cohen. Dr Blecher-Prigat's research focuses on various aspects of family law and inheritance law and her publications include articles on new families, law and religion in Israeli family law and children's rights in leading journals within and outside Israel. She is also co-editor of *The Family in Law Journal*, a peer-reviewed interdisciplinary journal (in Hebrew). Dr Blecher-Prigat is Academic Director of, and a frequent lecturer at, the Israeli Bar's continuing legal education workshops on inheritance and family law.

JACQUELINE HEATON is Professor of Private Law at the College of Law, University of South Africa, Pretoria, South Africa. She specialises in Family Law, Child Law and the Law of Persons. She is the author/co-author of more than twenty books in these fields of law and has published many articles in law journals. She has presented papers and chaired sessions at national and international conferences, seminars and workshops, and is the co-editor and guest editor of three law journals. Several postgraduate students have completed their dissertations and theses under her supervision. She is the Rapporteur for the Family Law Committee of the International Law Association and has served on the Advisory Committee of the South African Law Reform Commission for *Project 25 Statutory Law Revision*: *Revision of Legislation Administered by Department of Home Affairs*.

OLGA A. KHAZOVA is Professor of Law at the Institute of State and Law of the Russian Academy of Sciences, Moscow. Her Ph.D. is from the same Institute and her LLM is from Cornell University Law School (USA). Her main field of expertise is family law. Apart from teaching, Olga serves as a consultant/advisor on family law, children's rights and human reproduction for governmental bodies, courts and law firms. She is the author of *Marriage and Divorce in Western Family Law* (1998) (in Russian) and of numerous articles on family law published in Russia and abroad. She is a regular speaker at international conferences, symposia and workshops. Her latest book, *The Art of Legal Writing* (2011) (in Russian), was written in collaboration with White & Case LLC. Olga has been a British Academy Visiting scholar and was awarded a Fulbright Program scholarship (USA). She is a member of the Executive Council of the International Society of Family Law. She participated in the drafting of the Russian Family Code 1995 and is currently an expert at the Committee on Child and Family Matters of the Russian Parliament.

ANIL MALHOTRA has been a practising advocate in India since September 1983, specialising in the interpretation and application of foreign court orders on divorce, child abduction, custody, maintenance, adoption and the family-related issues of non-resident Indians. He gained his BSc and LLB (Professional) from the Panjab University, Chandigarh, India, and an LLM from the University of London (1985). He taught civil procedural laws and matrimonial remedies for six years as a part-time lecturer at the Faculty of Laws, Panjab University, Chandigarh, India. He is the co-author of *Acting for Non-Resident Indian Clients* (2005) and has significant papers and conference participations to his credit. In 2007 he was elected to the International Academy of Matrimonial Lawyers. His latest publication 'India, NRIs and the Law' was released in 2009 by the Union Law Minister of India at New Delhi. In 2010 he was nominated as a Member of the International Family Law Committee of the International Law Association.

RANJIT MALHOTRA was the first Indian lawyer to be awarded the prestigious Felix Scholarship to read for the LLM degree at the SOAS, University of London, obtaining his degree, with merit, in 1993. He is a member of the IBA, IAYFJM, ILPA in London, AILA in Washington, Reunite Child Abduction Agency in London, the Indian Council of Arbitration, the IPBA in Tokyo, CLA, ILA in London and Lawasia in Australia. He is also the Deputy Chair of the Family Law Committee of Lawasia. He regularly presents papers at conferences in India, America, England, Canada and Australia. In 2007 he was elected to the International Academy of Matrimonial Lawyers. He specialises in private international law, appears as an expert witness on Indian family law issues in courts in England, renders expert analysis and testimony for family law and immigration cases, advises foreign lawyers, conducts trust and probate litigation and international family law work. He is a principal author of *Acting for Non-Resident Indian Clients* (2005).

MARYGOLD (MARGO) SHIRE MELLI is Voss-Bascom Professor of Law Emerita at the Law School, University of Wisconsin-Madison. A past vice-president and long-serving member of the Executive Committee of the International Society on Family Law, she is also a member of the American Law Institute, a fellow of the American Academy of Matrimonial Lawyers and has served as Chair of the of the National Conference of Bar Examiners. In 1994 the Madison, Wisconsin Legal Association of Women established the Marygold Melli Achievement Award and she has also been honoured by the Wisconsin Law Foundation and the Wisconsin State Bar. Her books include *The Legal Status of Homemakers in Wisconsin* (1977), *Wisconsin Juvenile Court Practice in Delinquency and Status Offense Cases* (1978), (with Simon and Altstein) *The Case for Transracial Adoption* (1994) and (with Oldham) *Child Support: The Next Frontier* (2000).

MICHAEL PALMER is currently Dean, Professor of Law, and Director, Cheung Kong Centre for Negotiation and Dispute Resolution, STU Law School, Shantou, China. He is a former Chair of the Centre of Chinese Studies (CCS), the Centre of East Asian Law (CEAL) and the Law School at the School of Oriental and African Studies (SOAS). He is now Emeritus Professor of Law at the University of London, and a Research Professor at SOAS and the Institute of Advanced Legal Studies. His publications are mainly in the field of comparative law and cover a wide range of areas, including Chinese family law. He is joint editor of the *Journal of Comparative Law* and co-author (with Roberts) of *Dispute Processes* (Cambridge University Press, 2005). He has served as special legal advisor to the Attorney-General of Hong Kong, and has designed and administered a number of important international training programmes for Chinese legal professionals.

CAROL ROGERSON is a professor of law at the Faculty of Law, University of Toronto, Canada. She teaches and researches in the areas of family law, children's law and constitutional law. She has worked with both the federal and provincial governments on issues of family law reform, most recently as co-director of Justice Canada's Spousal Support Advisory Guidelines Project and author (with Thompson) of *The Spousal Support Advisory Guidelines* (2008). Her publications include 'The Child Support Obligation of Step-Parents' (2001); (with Shaffer) 'Contracting Spousal

Support: Thinking Through *Miglin*' (2003), and 'The Canadian Law of Spousal Support' (2004). She is also the executive editor (with Macklem) of *Canadian Constitutional Law*, 4th edn (2010).

RHONA SCHUZ is Senior Lecturer (Associate Professor) and Co-Director of the Centre for the Rights of the Child and the Family at the Sha'arei Mishpat Law School in Israel (formerly lecturer at Bar Ilan University, London School of Economics and Nottingham University). She is also co-editor of *The Family in Law Journal*, a peer-reviewed interdisciplinary journal (in Hebrew). She has written extensively in the areas of family law and private international law, including articles in leading law journals and a book, *A Modern Approach to the Incidental Question* (1997). During the last decade, her research has focused on international child abduction. She has lectured and published widely on this subject and is currently writing a book, *The Hague Child Abduction Convention: A Critical Analysis* (forthcoming 2012). She served as Consultant to the English Law Commission on the Ground for Divorce (1985–1993) and currently sits (by appointment of the Justice Minister) on a Committee to Examine the Law Relating To Maintenance Payments for Children in Israel.

ELAINE E. SUTHERLAND is Professor of Child and Family Law at the Law School, University of Stirling, Scotland, and Professor of Law at Lewis and Clark Law School, Portland, Oregon, USA, spending six months of the year researching, writing and teaching at each. She has lectured on child and family law around the world and has served on the Family Law Committee of the Law Society of Scotland for many years. The author of some eighty articles and book chapters, she contributes the chapter on Scotland for the *International Survey of Family Law* and her books include *Child and Family Law*, 2nd edn (2008), *Family Law*, 2nd edn (2008), (with Cleland) *Children's Rights in Scotland*, 3rd edn (2009), (with Grant) *Scots Law Tales* (2010), and (with Goodall, Little and Davidson) *Law Making and the Scottish Parliament: The Early Years* (2011).

TONE SVERDRUP is Professor of Law at the Faculty of Law, University of Oslo, Norway. She has been an acting Supreme Court Justice in the Supreme Court of Norway for three periods (2006–2009). Her main fields of research are family law and property law. She is the author of several books in family law, among others a monograph on co-ownership in marriage and unmarried cohabitation, *Stiftelse av sameie i ekteskap og ugift samliv* (1997) and (with Lødrup) the textbook on family law used in Law Faculties in Norway, *Familieretten*, 7th edn (2011). She has published articles and book chapters in Norwegian, English and German, is co-editor and co-founder of Norway's leading journal on family law (*Tidsskrift for familierett, arverett og barnevernrettslige spørsmål*), is a member of the Expert Group of the Commission on European Family Law (CEFL) and a member the Executive Council of the International Society of Family Law (ISFL).

PAUL VLAARDINGERBROEK has been Professor of Family and Child Law at the Law School of Tilburg University since 1984, prior to which he served in a Youth Care Agency (from 1975 to 1984). He was awarded his doctoral degree on the subject of legal procedures in family and child law in 1991. He has written many books and articles on family law, child law and penal law. Since 1994 he has been a deputy judge in the district court of Rotterdam and, since 1997, a deputy judge in the court of appeal in Den Bosch. He was President of the International Society of Family Law from 2005 to 2008.

PREFACE

The stimulus for this volume was the realisation that a tribute to the contribution of Professor Eric M. Clive to child and family law – in Scotland and internationally – was long overdue.

Like many with outstanding talent and accomplishments, Eric is modest, preferring to get on with the project at hand with energy and dedication, but without the fanfare that often accompanies the work of those with larger egos. If anything, Eric's very modesty made it all the more important to recognise his contribution. However, it also presented a dilemma: would he be comfortable with a tribute? In the attempt to resolve the dilemma, I approached Eric's wife, Kay, seeking her advice. Her insight proved invaluable since she suggested that he would want any tribute to be 'useful'. Building on that test – usefulness – the idea began to take shape for a book that would assist scholars, policymakers and practitioners around the world in understanding the imperatives and challenges that have driven child and family law to its present position and to offer insights into what was likely to drive it forward in the future.

Happily, such a volume reflects many aspects of Eric's own work: his scholarship; his commitment to law as an instrument for improving the lives of those it serves; his involvement in law reform; and the national and international nature of his contribution.

Eric M. Clive: a brief biography

Born in Stranraer, Scotland, Eric graduated MA, LLB (with distinction) from Edinburgh University and joined the legal profession in Scotland as a solicitor. However, the call of academia was strong and, after an LLM at the University of Michigan Law School, he took up his first appointment in the Faculty of Law at the University of Edinburgh in 1962, becoming Professor of Scots Law in 1977. During this time at Edinburgh, he gained a reputation as a fine scholar, motivating teacher and delightful colleague. He also deepened and broadened his study of law, travelling to the United

States with Kay and their children to earn an SJD from the University of
Virginia Law School. It was at Edinburgh that he wrote the first edition of
his seminal work, *The Law of Husband and Wife in Scotland*.[1]

As many of his early publications reflect,[2] Eric has a passion for
improving the law, something signalled in 'Scottish Family Law', which
appeared in a volume of essays, *Independence and Devolution: The Legal
Implications for Scotland*,[3] in 1976, when a devolved Scotland was only
an aspiration. In his essay he envisaged 'a family law code that would be
the envy of the Western world', being secular, egalitarian and consumer-
oriented.

In 1981 Eric was appointed to the Scottish Law Commission, where he
worked for nineteen years, becoming its longest serving commissioner.
It would be no exaggeration to say that, during this time, he transformed
the face of Scots child and family law, crafting his ideas for law reform into
draft legislation, much of which made its way onto the statute book. His
work ranged widely and included reform of the law on illegitimacy, capacity of children and young people, parental responsibilities and parental
rights, marriage, cohabitation, aliment (maintenance), matrimonial property and divorce.[4] Particularly noteworthy, not least because it is viewed
with such admiration in Scotland and abroad, is the approach he devised
to financial provision on divorce (now applied to civil partnership dissolution as well). While his dream of codification has yet to be realised fully,
the blueprint for a child and family law code that he drafted will doubtless
be used as the foundation of the code that will, in all likelihood, emerge in
the fullness of time.

It was while he was at the Commission that Eric was able to pursue
another passion – improving the content and operation of the law in the

---

[1] 1st edn with John G. Wilson, 1974; 2nd edn 1982; 3rd edn 1992; 4th edn 1997, Edinburgh:
     W. Green.
[2] Two examples are offered by way of illustration. In 'Legal Aspects of Illegitimacy in
     Scotland' 1979 SLT (Notes) 233, Eric demonstrated the injustice and absurdity of
     classifying children as legitimate or illegitimate, something that was to prove instru-
     mental in the eventual abolition of the status of illegitimacy in Scotland. 'Marriage: An
     Unnecessary Legal Concept?' in John M. Eekelaar and Sanford N. Katz (eds.), *Marriage
     and Cohabitation in Contemporary Societies* (London: Butterworths, 1980), pp. 71–81,
     questioned the legal system's need for a concept of marriage, a radical idea in 1980, mak-
     ing this work an essential reference point for subsequent scholarly discussion around the
     world.
[3] John P. Grant (ed.), Edinburgh: W. Green, 1976, pp. 162–74.
[4] This work resulted in Discussion Papers and Reports published by the Scottish Law
     Commission and they can be found at: www.scotlawcom.gov.uk/about-us/. Many of Eric's
     recommendations led, of course, to legislation.

international arena. Again, this aspect of Eric's interests was signalled early in his career when he became a founder member of the International Society on Family Law, contributing the chapters on Scotland for the early volumes of the *International Survey of Family Law* and presenting thought-provoking papers at the Society's international conferences. While at the Scottish Law Commission, Eric also headed the United Kingdom delegation to the Hague Conference on Private International Law, working on what became the Hague Convention on Children[5] and the Hague Convention on the Protection of Adults.[6]

Thus far, Eric's contribution to child and family law has been highlighted, as befits this volume. However, his interests were never confined to these fields and his work has always ranged very much more broadly. In 1965 he had the foresight to realise that journalists might benefit from an accessible explanation of the law and how it affected them and, along with a journalist, he published the first edition of *Scots Law for Journalists*,[7] now in its eighth edition.[8] Nor was his work at the Scottish Law Commission confined to child and family law and he drafted law reform proposals on such diverse matters as contract, succession (inheritance), evidence, sale of goods, unjustified enrichment and leases. He also found time to work on *A Draft Criminal Code for Scotland with Commentary.*[9]

After retiring from the Commission, 'retirement' was simply not an option for Eric and he became a member of the Commission on European Contract Law and chair of the Editing Group for Part III of its 'Principles of European Contract Law'.[10] This led to membership of the Study Group on a European Civil Code where Eric ended up playing a leading role in the drafting and editing process.[11] More recently Eric has been a member of

---

[5] Convention of 19 October 1996 on Jurisdiction, Applicable Law, Recognition, Enforcement and Co-operation in Respect of Parental Responsibility and Measures for the Protection of Children, HCCH No. 34.

[6] Convention of 13 January 2000 on the International Protection of Adults, HCCH No. 35.

[7] With George Watt, Edinburgh, W. Green, 1965. Eric was involved in four further editions of the book.

[8] Rosalind McInnes, *Scots Law for Journalists*, 8th edn (Edinburgh: W. Green, 2010).

[9] With Christopher Gane, Pamela Ferguson and Alexander McCall Smith, published as a consultation paper by the Scottish Law Commission, September 2003, at: www.scotlawcom.gov.uk/publications/consultation-papers-and-other-documents/.

[10] See Ole Lando, Eric Clive, André Prüm and Reinhard Zimmermann, *Principles of European Contract Law Part 3* (Alphen aan den Rijn: Kluwer International, 2003).

[11] See Christian von Bar, Eric Clive and Hans Schulte-Nölke, *Principles, Definitions and Model Rules of European Contract Law (Draft Common Frame of Reference)* Interim Outline edition (Munich: Sellier, 2008); Christian von Bar, Eric Clive and Hans

the European Commission's Expert Group on Contract Law whose work has formed the basis for the Proposal for a Regulation of the European Parliament and of the Council on a Common European Sales Law published by the European Commission on 11 October 2011.[12]

Eric is a fellow of the Royal Society of Edinburgh and, in recognition of his services to law reform, he was made a CBE (Commander of the British Empire) in 1999. He was awarded an honorary doctorate by the University of Osnabrück in 2008. Eric is currently a visiting professor at the School of Law, University of Edinburgh, and continues to research and write. Always a person to move with the times, he is a major contributor to the European Private Law News blog.[13]

The goals and methodology of the volume

The goal of this book, then, was not simply to provide a discussion of the content of child and family law in the various countries and jurisdictions. Rather, contributors were invited to identify the imperatives and challenges that have driven the law to its current position and to offer insights into what is likely to drive it forward in the future. Thus it was that I approached a number of the leading child and family law scholars from around the world, many of them long-standing friends of Eric – in Australia, Canada, China, England and Wales, India, Israel, Malaysia, the Netherlands, New Zealand, Norway, Russia, South Africa and the United States. All welcomed the opportunity to contribute to a volume honouring Eric.

In order to aid comparison between jurisdictions (again, part of being 'useful'), it was important that each chapter should adopt a broadly similar approach. Yet it is a fundamental feature of child and family law that it reflects the society in which it operates and, indeed, one goal of the book was to highlight different imperatives and different solutions to similar challenges, as well as common ground. Accordingly, each contributor was provided with a template, outlining chapter structure and content,

---

Schulte-Nölke, *Principles, Definitions and Model Rules of European Contract Law (Draft Common Frame of Reference)* Outline edition (Munich: Sellier, 2009); and Christian von Bar and Eric Clive, *Principles, Definitions and Model Rules of European Contract Law (Draft Common Frame of Reference)*, 6 volumes (Munich and Oxford: Sellier and Oxford University Press, 2009).

[12] COM (2011) 635 final.

[13] The blog is located on the School of Law, University of Edinburgh website, at: www.law.ed.ac.uk/epln/.

and a worked example of its application in the form of the draft chapter on Scotland, being Eric's (and my own) native jurisdiction. The request to contributors was to aid comparisons by following the template, subject to a degree of latitude that would enable each to exercise discretion in reflecting developments and priorities in the particular jurisdiction. Since academics tend to be fiercely independent, if not downright rebellious, this approach involved something of an act of faith. Any (slight) fears proved to be unfounded since the contributors accepted the reasons behind the *modus operandum* and embraced the task enthusiastically. Sadly, personal circumstances prevented completion of the chapter from England and Wales.

Thanks

My heartfelt thanks go to all the contributors for giving of their time and very considerable talents in writing chapters that I hope will be landmarks in their own countries and serve the international community well. That they did so with such grace and efficiency is a tribute to their professionalism.

I am enormously grateful to all the staff at Cambridge University Press and, in particular, to Finola O'Sullivan for having faith in the project and for her support and guidance throughout the process of bringing it to fruition.

For my part, it has been a privilege and an honour to have the opportunity to pay tribute to one aspect of Eric's career to date and to do so in cooperation with such a wealth of talent from around the world. In the process I have learned an enormous amount, not simply about the substantive law in the respective jurisdictions, but, perhaps more significantly and in line with the goals of the volume, have gained valuable insights into how it came to take its present form and the imperatives that are likely to shape it in the years ahead.

Doubtless there will be other tributes to Eric's work in the future. For now, I hope that he will regard this volume as recognition of his work in a field to which he has made such an enormous contribution and that he will judge it as passing the crucial test: that it is 'useful'.

1

Imperatives and challenges in child and family law

Commonalities and disparities

ELAINE E. SUTHERLAND

1.1   The goal of this volume is to explore the development of child and family law in a number of countries around the world – Australia, Canada, China, India, Israel, Malaysia, the Netherlands, New Zealand, Norway, Russia, Scotland, South Africa and the United States[1] – in the attempt to identify the imperatives and challenges that have driven it to its current position and those that are likely to determine its future direction. Each chapter is contributed by a leading child and family law scholar with expertise in the country under examination. In order to aid comparison, each contributor has adopted a common chapter structure.

1.2   Implicit in such a work is the rejection of any notion that child and family law is unsuited to comparative analysis. That notion has its roots in the very close connection between this area of the law and the moral, social, cultural, political and religious beliefs of the society in which it operates. Because of the particularly strong impact of these factors on child and family law, in contrast to, say, commercial law, a 'cultural constraints argument' is sometimes made, suggesting that child and family law in one society cannot be compared meaningfully with that in another.[2] Yet the problems of family life arise out of the nature of human relationships,

My thanks go to Craig Callery for his invaluable research assistance with this chapter.

[1] Sadly, personal circumstances prevented completion of the chapter on England and Wales. On occasion, developments there will be referred to in this chapter.

[2] W. Müller-Freienfels, 'The Unification of Family Law' (1968) 16 *American Journal of Comparative Law* 175, 175 ('family law tends to become introverted because historical, racial, social and religious considerations differ according to country and produce different family law systems'); D. Bradley, 'A Note on Comparative Family Law: Problems, Perspectives, Issues and Politics' (2005) 6 *Oxford University Comparative Law Forum* 4 (asserting that 'family law is political discourse' and pointing to 'variations in social and economic policy', reflecting 'differences in political culture and processes').

not out of nationality, domicile or place of residence.[3] Comparing how different legal systems address the creation, functioning, dissolution and ongoing interactions of families may tell us much about the nature of the societies in which they operate, their similarities and their differences.[4] In turn, this presents an opportunity to do more with the information, as it may well be that a solution found to a particular family law problem in one society offers an approach that could be adopted, to good effect, in another.

1.3 The suggestion that child and family law is unsuited to compara-tive analysis arises out of conflating comparativism and the very different objective of harmonisation. Comparativism is a benign process. It sim-ply involves looking at how legal systems other than one's own address the issues at hand and considering whether any of the approaches taken might work better, in their original form or with adaptations, in one's own jurisdiction than what is currently available. Not only does it allow law reformers, lawyers and courts to learn from experiences elsewhere, it provides an opportunity to be critically selective, bearing in mind, of course, the need for internal consistency within a given legal system.[5] In short, comparativism asks no more than that one keeps an open mind

---

[3] H. D. Krause, 'Comparative Family Law – Past Traditions Battle Future Trends and Vice Versa', in M. Reiman and R. Zimmerman (eds.) *The Oxford Handbook of Comparative Law* (Oxford University Press, 2006), p. 1101 ('For all their very real differences, nations around the world find themselves facing fundamentally similar dilemmas in defining and regulating the modern family. Accordingly, it makes sense to take stock of what has been tried and what has – or has not – worked elsewhere. Comparative family law's days as an unlikely pioneer are over'). For an economic per-spective, see F. Nicola, 'Family Law Exceptionalism in Comparative Law' (2010) 58 *American Journal of Comparative Law* 777 at 810 ('To make sense of the market/family dichotomy, rather than overcoming, subverting or reproducing it, scholarly projects should show the interdependence between the law of the family and the market … scholars have highlighted that family law reforms should not be about only moral values and universal right, but just like reforms of the market, about their economic and distributive consequences as well').

[4] There is no shortage of advice on comparative methodology and pitfalls to be avoided. For a useful summary, see P. de Cruz, *Family Law, Sex and Society* (London: Routledge, 2010), pp. 33–7. See also K. Boele-Woelki, 'What Comparative Family Law Should Entail' (2008) 4(2) *Utrecht Law Review* 1.

[5] For competing views on whether family law is structured and how, see J. Dewar, 'The Normal Chaos of Family Law' (1998) 61 *Modern Law Review* 467 and the reply, M. Hennaghan, 'The Normal Order of Family Law' (2008) 28(1) *Oxford Journal of Legal Studies* 165, a review article of J. Eekelaar, *Family Law and Personal Life* (Oxford University Press, 2006).

and is willing to consider other ways of doing things.[6] Unsurprisingly, it has long been employed in reform of child and family law, undoubtedly aided by the many excellent scholarly works on the subject.[7]

1.4   Harmonisation of substantive law is not a benign process since its primary goal is standardisation. Inherent in achieving this end is compromise: of negotiating; of finding the middle ground; and of accepting less-favoured outcomes on some issues in return for more-favoured outcomes on others. That it can be done in respect of aspects of child and family law is demonstrated by the Nordic countries.[8] Whether that experience can be carried through on a larger scale is questionable. It was never the purpose of this book to engage in the debate over whether global harmonisation of substantive child and family law is a worthwhile exercise.[9] Nor is this the place to address the very local question of harmonisation within the European Union, discussed so extensively elsewhere.[10] Suffice it

---

[6] In the past, of course, legal transplants occurred, not only by choice in the host legal system, but as a result of colonisation, sometimes leading to the temporary or permanent obliteration of the indigenous legal system. See paras. 1.31–1.33 below for discussion of the increased recognition of customary law.

[7] See, in particular, A. Chloros, M. Rheinstein and M. A. Glendon (eds.), *International Encyclopedia of Comparative Law*, Volume IV, *Persons and Family* (Tübinger: Mohr Siebeck, 2004). See also, M. A. Glendon, *The Transformation of Family Law: State, Law and Family in the United States and Western Europe* (University of Chicago Press, 1989); S. N. Katz, J. Eekelaar and M. Maclean (eds.), *Cross Currents: Family Law and Policy in the United States and England* (Oxford University Press, 2000); de Cruz, *Family Law, Sex and Society*.

[8] As Sverdrup notes, at para. 10.12 below, that process started at the beginning of the twentieth century with no-fault divorce. See also P. Lødrup, 'The Reharmonisation of Nordic Family Law', in K. Boele-Woelki and T. Sverdrup (eds.), *European Challenges in Contemporary Family Law* (Antwerp: Intersentia, 2008), p. 20. For a comparison between EU and Nordic efforts at harmonisation from a gendered perspective, see A. Pylkkänen, 'Liberal Family Law in the Making: Nordic and European Harmonisation' (2007) 15(3) *Feminist Legal Studies* 289.

[9] In *Model Family Code from a Global Perspective* (Antwerp: Intersentia, 2006), Preface, p. v, Ingeborg Schwenzer (in collaboration with M. Dimsey) sets herself the somewhat ambitious goal of seeking to 'remove all discrepancies persisting in national family laws due to different historical levels of – somewhat patchwork – development, and to create a wholly autonomous and consistent system of family law based on modern solutions'.

[10] See M. Antokolskaia, 'Harmonisation of Substantive Family Law in Europe: Myths and Reality' (2010) 22(4) *Child and Family Law Quarterly* 397; D. Bradley, 'A Family Law for Europe? Sovereignty, Political Economy and Legitmation' 4(1) *Global Jurist Frontiers*, available at: www.bepress.com/gj/frontiers/vol4/iss1/art3/; M. R. Marella, 'The Non-subversive Function of European Private Law: The Case of Harmonization of Family Law' (2006) 12(1) *European Law Journal* 78. Some thirty volumes, many of them collections of essays, have been published to date by Intersentia, in collaboration with the Commission on European Family Law, in its *European Family Law* series. See

to note that when he described 'a hopeless quest', involving the work 'more of a Sisyphus than a Hercules',[11] Otto Kahn-Freud was referring to harmonisation of family law, rather than comparative analysis of it.

1.5   What emerges from the various jurisdictions considered in this volume is often subtle and nuanced but, then, the diversity of family relationships with which any legal system must deal is rich and varied. A number of common themes emerge from most or all of the country-specific contributions, with systems converging and diverging on particular issues. Aspects of these themes – organised under the broad headings of equality, increased respect for children's rights, protection, diversity in adult relationships and the impact of developments in assisted reproductive technology – are discussed below to give a flavour of the rich pickings to be found in the chapters that follow. It goes without saying, but will be said, nonetheless, that this introduction simply offers a taste of what follows and each of these chapters will reward reading in its entirety.

1.6   Given the hazardous nature of speculating about the future, the contributors are to be commended for their courage in gambling on what some academics see as the greatest of all risks – the risk of being wrong. What, then, do the contributors see as driving child and family law forward in their respective countries? Often the answers are issue-specific, but a fairly constant theme is that many of them believe that the same imperatives that have driven child and family law to date will be the operative drivers of its future development: that there will be a process of linear development.

1.7   That suggests that existing divergence between jurisdictions may be magnified. In this, there is something of an assertion that 'Western' ways of doing things are not the only, nor the best, approach. As the Constitutional Court in South Africa pointed out, in the context of the rights of non-marital fathers, a 'nuanced and balanced consideration of a society in which the factual demographic picture and parental relationships are

---

particularly, K. Boele Woelki (ed.), *Perspectives on the Unification and Harmonisation of Family Law in Europe* (Antwerp: Intersentia, 2003); M. Antokolskaia, *Harmonisation of Family Law in Europe: A Historical Perspective: A Tale of Two Millennia* (Antwerp: Intersentia, 2006); K. Boele-Woelki and T. Sverdrup (eds.), *European Challenges in Contemporary Family Law* (Antwerp: Intersentia, 2008).

[11]   O. Kahn-Freud, 'Common Law and Civil Law – Imaginary and Real Obstacles to Assimilation', in M. Cappelletti (ed.), *New Perspectives for a Common Law of Europe* (Leyden: European University Institute, 1978), pp. 141 and 142.

often quite different from those upon which "first-world" western societies are premised'[12] was required in assessing the matter there. Similarly, the Malhotras point out that 'India has its own deeply embedded moral and cultural values and emulation of Western principles in matrimonial matters should be approached with the greatest caution'.[13] Given international mobility and communication, an appreciation of racial, ethnic, religious and cultural diversity will become increasingly relevant to the 'first-world' nations, something understood by Atkin, speaking of New Zealand, when he notes 'The Western model can no longer be taken for granted … Flexibility rather than black and white rules may well have its merits in enabling diversity to be appropriately embraced'.[14]

1.8   Before we turn to the imperatives and challenges, it may be helpful to set the scene by giving the reader a brief overview of the law-making process and operation of the legal systems under discussion and by placing child and family law in its international context.

A The legal systems and the context

The domestic context

Law-making

1.9   While government itself may initiate law reform, proposals for innovation in child and family law often come from, or via, a standing law reform commission or a committee appointed to examine a specific topic.[15] Of course, the fact that the issue is being examined at all will often be the result

---

[12] *Fraser* v. *Children's Court, Pretoria North* 1997 (2) SA 261 (CC) para. 29, discussed by Heaton, at para. 13.27 below.

[13] Para. 5.58 below.   [14] Para. 9.3 below.

[15] New Zealand, Scotland and South Africa have standing law reform commissions, although their existence does not preclude the use of ad hoc committees. While Australia has a law reform commission, another body, the Family Law Council, is the driving force in family law reform. Some provincial law reform commissions remain in Canada, but others and the federal equivalent were disbanded and reliance is placed on specially appointed committees. In India the law commission is established for a fixed period of time, with the current commission serving for the period 2009–2012. In the United States the Commissioners on Uniform State Laws and the American Law Institute produce draft laws available for adoption, in whole or in part, by individual states. In Israel, the Netherlands, Norway and Russia use is made of committees appointed to deal with specific issues. The China Association of Marriage and Family Studies is the key agency in terms of reform of statute there.

of lobbying efforts by groups and individuals with an interest in the outcome. Those who are sufficiently motivated have another avenue in those parts of the United States where citizen-initiated legislation is built into their states' legal systems through the 'ballot initiative' process.[16] A rather more anodyne approach is found in Scotland through the possibility of lodging a petition in support of a desired reform with a committee of the Scottish parliament.[17]

1.10 The court structure is, of course, jurisdiction-specific. Where the applicable family law is governed by an individual's religion, most or all disputes will be addressed before the appropriate religious court, although the civil courts may also have a role.[18] While many of the secular jurisdictions have dedicated family courts, others do not, with family-related litigation being dealt with in the ordinary courts, whether adversarial or inquisitorial in nature. Increasingly, various forms of alternative dispute resolution are employed in child and family law cases.[19]

1.11 There is wide variation in the interaction between the courts and the legislature in developing child and family law in the various jurisdictions. At one end of the spectrum is India, where the Supreme Court has constitutional authority to declare law,[20] something the Malhotras note is particularly valuable in light of delays in the legislative process.[21] At the other end is the United States, where Melli points to accusations of 'judicial activism' being levelled at courts by critics of their decisions, particularly those supporting same-sex marriage and reproductive rights.[22] In South Africa[23] judicial reform is viewed more favourably, by Heaton, as a by-product of a constitution containing a bill of rights, while in Israel Schuz and Blecher-Prigat describe the judiciary as fulfilling a crucial role in bridging the gap between religious law and modern secular philosophy.[24] Vlaardingerbroek is equally positive about the role of the courts

---

[16] A typical model requires that the requisite number of voter signatures in support of a proposition be collected. The proposition is then put on the ballot at the next election. If the majority of those voting approve the proposition, the legislature is bound to introduce legislation implementing the proposition. See further, W. E. Adams, Jr, 'Is it Animus or a Difference of Opinion? The Problem Caused by the Invidious Intent of the Anti-Gay Ballot Measures' (1998) 34 *Willamette Law Review* 449.

[17] Whether the proposal goes forward is at the discretion of the committee and, even then, the Scottish parliament is not obliged to act upon it. See para. 12.10 below.

[18] See para. 1.27 below.   [19] Para. 1.17 below.

[20] Art. 141 of the Constitution of India provides: 'The law declared by the Supreme Court shall be binding on all courts within the territory of India.'

[21] Para. 5.80 below.   [22] Para. 14.2 below.   [23] Para. 13.9 below.

[24] Para. 6.74 below.

in the Netherlands, noting that 'legislators can barely keep up with modern social changes, leaving much to the judiciary'.[25] A less rosy picture is painted by Bates when he observes that tensions exist between policy-makers, legislators and the courts and notes 'a tendency for courts, particularly the Family Court of Australia, to undermine particular legislative goals'.[26] Even where courts might claim that they are simply applying the law, as enacted by the legislature, there is no denying the contribution that the former can make to development of the law. Rogerson demonstrates this process at work in Canada, where a series of lower court decisions led, ultimately, to the introduction of same-sex marriage.[27]

Access to legal advice

1.12   In almost all of the jurisdictions discussed, there is some provision for legal aid to enable those who cannot afford to pay for legal advice and representation to receive at least some legal services at state expense. However, there is an almost universal lament over the inadequacy of provision and the fear that matters are only likely to get worse. Norway stands out as the lone exception, with Sverdrup noting that less-stringent financial thresholds for access to legal aid have been proposed there.[28]

1.13   The problem of access to legal advice is exacerbated by another common concern – the complexity of the law itself. As Sutherland observes, in Scotland the absence of a single child and family code, combined with the proliferation of statutory provisions and court decisions, 'renders aspects of the law almost impenetrable to all but the most determined lay person'.[29] Discussing financial provision on divorce in Australia, Bates observes that 'The system resembles a patchwork quilt, with a rather confused chameleon lost on it'.[30]

Dispute resolution

1.14   Legal systems are, inevitably, a product of the culture and politics in which they are situated and nowhere is that illustrated better than in the approach to dispute resolution. All of the legal systems discussed in this volume envisage some role for the courts in family proceedings, but the precise scope and timing of that role varies, with courts being seen increasingly as the destination of last resort.

---

[25] Para. 8.1 below.   [26] Para. 2.1 below.
[27] Para. 3.48 below.   [28] Para. 10.14 below.
[29] Para. 12.8 below.   [30] Para. 2.53 below.

1.15   Occasionally, in the divorce context, there must be an attempt to repair the relationship before recourse to the courts is competent. In Malaysia, for example, Awal notes that divorce must be preceded by conciliation, designed not simply to resolve outstanding disputes on issues like property, but to effect reconciliation between the parties.[31] Similarly in India, attempting reconciliation is an inherent part of the divorce process.[32] In most of the other jurisdictions there is no legal requirement that a couple seeks to repair a damaged relationship before moving to terminate it.[33]

1.16   A particularly clear reminder of the importance of a legal system's cultural roots comes from China, where Palmer observes that 'Confucian values of compromise, reconciliation and community interests predomi-nated in traditional China's approach to dispute resolution',[34] explaining the long-standing use of community and judicial mediation. In addition, in countries with a Western legal system, if such a generalisation may be permitted, the indigenous population may have continued to employ its traditional methods of dispute resolution.[35] In New Zealand the Maori model of family group conferencing is now being embraced by the main-stream dispute resolution process.[36]

1.17   Alternative dispute resolution (ADR) is now employed in all the jurisdictions in our enquiry, either as a means of diverting the dispute from the court system or, where the dispute has reached the court, resolving it without resort to the traditional adversarial or other court process. The forms of ADR available vary with the coun-try, of course, but they include counselling, out-of-court mediation,[37] judicial mediation,[38] collaborative law[39] and comprehensive support

---

[31] Paras. 7.13ff. below.   [32] Para. 5.17 below.

[33] So, for example, in Russia, while a case can be continued for reconciliation to be attempted, Khasova describes the process as often being 'just a formality and only delays the final decision': para. 11.38 below.

[34] Para. 4.7 below.   [35] As occurred in South Africa; see para. 13.11 below.

[36] See para. 1.31 below.

[37] See the Netherlands (para. 8.9), Norway (para. 10.13), Scotland (para. 12.11) and the United States (para. 14.15).

[38] See New Zealand, where Atkin describes the process as 'not genuine mediation but more like a settlement or pre-trial conference': para. 9.20 below.

[39] Scotland (para. 12.11) and the United States (para. 14.16). Assistance is also provided in a number of state courts in the United States to help *pro se* litigants negotiate their way through the legal process (para. 14.17), something that may be particularly important since the recent US Supreme Court decision in *Turner* v. *Rogers*, 131 S.Ct. 2507 (2011),

services,[40] often wholly or party funded by the state. The growing popularity of ADR is motivated by a belief that it offers a kinder, more constructive way to address family conflict, avoiding the delay and acrimony often associated with litigation, something that becomes particularly important when the adult parties will continue to be involved with each other as parents. There is also the attraction of saving on the costs associated with protracted legal disputes.[41] Indeed, it is the fact that 'litigation in Russia is cheaper and faster than in the West', combined with the fact that mediation is not embedded in the culture, that leads Khasova to conclude that it may take some time there to raise public and lawyer awareness of the benefits of mediation.[42]

The international context

1.18   It is easier to move around the world than it used to be and the cost of international travel makes it an option for many who would not have been able to afford it in the past. In addition, international communication has become much more accessible. Individuals and families take advantage of these developments to relocate to another country, temporarily or permanently, while others use the opportunities presented for a particular purpose, like obtaining medical treatment not available in their home country or adopting a child from abroad. This mobility has presented challenges to child and family law, or at least challenges on a scale unknown hitherto. The international community has sought to address some of them through international instruments. However, problems remain and the contributors to this volume address issues faced in their legal systems as a result of increased international mobility.

holding that there was no right to counsel in civil cases even where resulting contempt proceedings could result in imprisonment.

[40] See Australia (para. 2.8), Canada (para. 3.11) and Israel (para. 6.8).

[41] Another way to reduce the cost associated with relationship breakdown is to use an administrative process for the divorce itself, leaving outstanding disputes over the care of children and property to be addressed by alternative dispute resolution mechanisms or the courts. What is actually or effectively administrative divorce is available, at least for certain kinds of cases, in Norway (paras. 10.16 and 10.66), Russia (para. 11.61) and Scotland (para. 12.53) and is being considered in a number of other countries, including the Netherlands (para. 8.64).

[42] Paras. 11.19–11.20 below.

International instruments

1.19 International instruments in the field of child and family law serve a variety of purposes. They may seek to promote common standards around the world, with the goal of ensuring equal respect for the human rights of all. The Universal Declaration of Human Rights[43] is a good example of an attempt to get broad, general consensus, in principle, while the International Covenant on Civil and Political Rights (ICCPR)[44] seeks to establish more specific and enforceable human rights standards, something elaborated upon in respect of specific groups in the United Nations Convention on the Elimination of Discrimination Against Women[45] and the United Nations Convention on the Rights of the Child.[46] It is worth noting, however, that these instruments do not seek harmonisation of the law itself. While the conventions require compliance with their principles and rules, they largely leave it to states parties to implement and enforce these standards.

1.20 Another function of international instruments is to establish a system for international cooperation on specific issues where the international dimension has given rise to problems in the past. Thus, for example, the Hague Convention on Civil Aspects of Child Abduction[47] established a system for international cooperation, designed to ensure the prompt return of an abducted child to his or her home jurisdiction, removing the incentive for an aggrieved parent to remove the child in the first place. The effectiveness of the system, combined with recent instances of parental child abduction, prompted Russia to ratify the convention in June 2011.[48] Similarly, the Hague Convention on the Protection of Children and Co-operation in Respect of Intercountry Adoption[49] sought to address a number of concerns that had arisen over inter-country

---

[43] UN Doc. A/RES/217/111.

[44] 999 UNTS 171, ratified by all of the countries examined here except China and Malaysia.

[45] 1249 UNTS 13, ratified by all of the countries examined here except the United States.

[46] 1577 UNTS 3; (1989) 28 ILM 1448, ratified by all of the countries examined here except the United States.

[47] 25 October 1980, HCCH 28. All the countries examined except China, India and Malaysia are parties to it and legislation before the Indian parliament would pave the way for ratification: paras. 5.36–5.37 below.

[48] Para. 11.40 below.

[49] 29 May 1993, HCCH No. 33. The earlier attempt to regulate international adoption, the Hague Convention on Jurisdiction, Applicable Law and Recognition of Decrees Relating to Adoption, 15 November 1965, HCCH 13, was not a success since only Austria, Switzerland and the United Kingdom ratified it.

adoption, allocating responsibilities between the child's 'state of origin' and the 'receiving state' in the attempt to ensure that the rights and welfare of the child are protected. The Hague Convention on Jurisdiction, Applicable Law, Recognition, Enforcement and Co-operation in Respect of Parental Responsibility and Measures for the Protection of Children[50] is slightly different, addressing, not only recognition and enforcement parental responsibilities and rights, but also jurisdiction and choice of law rules. Thus, it reaches further in the direction of harmonisation of substantive law than did the previous Hague Conventions dealing with issues involving children, something that may explain why only two of the countries discussed here, Australia and the Netherlands, have ratified it to date.[51]

1.21   In addition to instruments of substantially worldwide application, there are numerous regional instruments that have a direct impact on child and family law. Modelled to some extent on the Universal Declaration of Human Rights are the European Convention for the Protection of Human Rights and Fundamental Freedoms,[52] the American Convention on Human Rights (the Pact of San José)[53] and the African Charter on Human and Peoples' Rights (the Bajul Charter).[54] More recently implemented is the Charter of Fundamental Rights of the European Union.[55] The African Charter on the Rights and Welfare of the Child[56] and the European Convention on the Exercise of Children's Rights[57] draw on the United Nations Convention on the Rights of the Child for their inspiration, supplementing its provisions regionally.

---

[50] 19 October 1996, HCCH 34, abbreviated to 'the Hague Children's Convention' in ordinary usage.
[51] There are indications that others, including New Zealand, may do so within the next few years: see para. 9.58 below.
[52] ETS No. 5 (1950) and 155 (1994).
[53] 22 November 1969, 1144 UNTS 123, in force 18 July 1978.
[54] 17 June 1981, 1520 UNTS 217, in force 21 October 1986.
[55] 2000/C 364/01, in force, 1 December 2009. Sverdrup, at para. 10.9 below, clarifies the Norwegian position in respect of the European Union as follows: 'Even though Norway is not a member of the European Union (EU), Norway has taken on the obligation to implement all EU legislation relevant to the functioning of the internal market through the European Economic Area (EEA) agreement: OJ No L 1, 3.1.1994, p 3. However, it should be remembered that EU cooperation on civil law matters concerning, for example, private international law, is outside the competencies of the EEA.'
[56] 11 July 1990, OAU Doc. CAB/LEG/24.9/49, in force 29 November 1999.
[57] ETS No. 163 (1996).

The impact of international mobility: some illustrations

1.22   International mobility can present challenges for family law. For example, it is the desire to gain access to a particular country or, if there, to secure a right to remain, that drives many individuals to enter into sham marriages, concluded solely for immigration purposes. The contributors from Australia and the Netherlands discuss specific measures taken by their legal systems to combat the problem.[58] While Canada has no equivalent measures in place, there are increased calls for their introduction.[59] Forced marriage is very much a home-grown phenomenon in some countries,[60] but in others it has come to the fore as a result of international mobility, with various jurisdictions seeking to combat it through the use of public education,[61] civil protection order[62] and criminal penalties.[63]

1.23   Not all of the challenges posed by international mobility result from immigration and, as the Malhotras point out, there are some thirty million Indians living outside the country. This gives rise to wives being abandoned in India by husbands who then use foreign courts to secure divorce decrees[64] and to parents abducting children abroad, something exacerbated by India's failure to ratify the Hague Convention on Civil Aspects of International Child Abduction.[65] Parental relocation after separation or divorce can be problematic in the domestic setting and, often, the bigger the country, the greater the score for disputes, something illustrated by the United States with its highly mobile population.[66] International relocation adds another layer of difficulty due not only to

---

[58] See Australia (para. 2.39), the Netherlands (paras. 8.55 and 8.57), Scotland (para. 12.41).

[59] Para. 3.51 below.

[60] This is the case in parts of China (para. 4.34) and Russia (para. 11.23) and in some communities in India (para. 5.70) and South Africa (para. 13.49).

[61] See, for example, Canada (para. 3.51).

[62] See, for example, Scotland (para. 12.43), where breach of the civil order is a criminal offence. In addition, in the course of attempting to force a person into marriage, separate criminal offences may be committed and, where this occurs, prosecution may follow.

[63] See, for example, Norway (para. 10.57), where a multifaceted approach has been taken, including the creation of a specific criminal offence.

[64] Para. 5.60 below.   [65] Para. 5.35 below.

[66] See para. 14.51 below. Similar issues arise in Australia (paras. 2.23–2.24 and 2.55) and Canada (para. 3.39). The increase in both domestic and international relocation in Russia prompted ratification of the Hague Convention on International Child Abduction: see para. 11.40 below.

distance,[67] but to questions over the enforceability of court decrees from the country of origin.

1.24   Ratification of the relevant international instrument may go some way to minimising problems associated with international mobility, but difficulties remain. For example, while both India and the Netherlands have ratified the Hague Convention on Adoption, Vlaardingerbroek highlights cases of distraught Indian parents seeking the return of their children from the Netherlands after Dutch adopters were tricked in India into believing the children were free for adoption.[68]

1.25   While international mobility undoubtedly presents challenges, its positive effects, not just for the individuals involved, but in helping legal systems to develop, should not be underestimated. As Atkin observes, 'one of the most significant themes for the future of family law in New Zealand is the emergence of cultural pluralism' arising 'first and foremost in relation to the indigenous Maori, and then immigrant populations especially from the Pacific, India and China'.[69] Similarly, Sutherland notes that, 'increased international mobility has enriched Scotland, making it more ethnically and racially diverse. This, combined with existing religious diversity, requires sensitive responses from a secular legal system in order to accommodate the needs of the whole population.'[70]

B   Imperatives and challenges

Religion and custom

Religion

1.26   Given that religion is a driving force in some legal systems, while it is of minimal significance in others, it may seem curious to find it mentioned as the first of the imperatives and challenges explored here.[71] Its prime position might be justified on historical grounds. Even if religion is no longer influential in a particular country, there will be a time in that

---

[67] See Atkin's observations in respect of New Zealand, at para. 9.56 below.

[68] Paras. 8.26–8.27 below.

[69] Para. 9.3 below.   [70] Para. 12.3 below.

[71] See generally, P. Cane, C. Evans and Z. Robinson (eds.), *Law and Religion in Theoretical and Historical Context* (Cambridge University Press, 2011). In the context of children, see M. A. Fineman and K. Worthington (eds.), *What is Right for Children? The Competing Paradigms of Religion and Human Rights* (Farnham: Ashgate, 2009).

country's history when it shaped child and family law. However, in truth, that is not the reason. Rather, the explanation is that, where religion is crucial in a society, its impact on child and family law can be pervasive and, thus, it has an impact on all of the other operative imperatives. In addition, even in secular legal systems it would be a mistake to assume that religion is irrelevant.

1.27 In three of our jurisdictions – India,[72] Israel[73] and Malaysia[74] – family law is wholly or largely dependent on personal law, that personal law being determined by the individual's religion. Since the result of applying different religious personal laws to different groups is that two or more systems of family law operate within the country simultaneously, this approach undoubtedly brings its own challenges. Of course, family law systems based on religion are not homogeneous and the contributors discuss the subtle accommodations found and problems remaining within their own systems. Are there religious and secular courts and, if so, how is jurisdiction determined?[75] What, if any, provision is made for those professing no religion or those whose religion is not recognised in the country or for bi-religious couples?[76] Is any provision made for an individual who converts from one religion to another or seeks to abandon religion altogether?[77]

1.28 The future role of religion in these three jurisdictions, at least as predicted by the contributors to this volume, ranges across the spectrum. In India, creating a unified secular family code, applying to everyone in the country, is seen by the Malhotras as imperative 'for the sake of national unity and solidarity'.[78] In contrast, in Malaysia, while there have been calls for harmonisation, Awal predicts that 'change is very unlikely since Malaysia is becoming more religious as a reaction to modernity'.[79] Between these positions lies Israel, where Schuz and Blecher-Prigat argue that the courts have found 'creative solutions to the dissonance between religious law and modern secular philosophy'[80]

---

[72] Paras. 5.7–5.8 below.   [73] Paras. 6.1–6.3 below.   [74] Paras. 7.4–7.7 below.

[75] For the Israeli approach, see para. 6.46 below. On the matter of religious courts, the final decision of the Indian Supreme Court in *Vishwa Lochan Madan* v. *Union of India and others* on the continued existence of extra-judicial courts that operate outside the official legal system in parts of the country is keenly awaited: see paras. 5.12–5.15 below.

[76] See the Israeli solution, discussed at para. 6.58 below.

[77] See, particularly, the Malaysian solution when a married, non-Muslim man converts to Islam and becomes entitled to take a second wife, discussed at paras. 7.44–7.50 below.

[78] Para. 5.76 below.   [79] Para. 7.60 below.   [80] Para. 6.73 below.

that have served the country well and that this approach is likely to continue in the future.

1.29   For the remainder of the jurisdictions, family law itself may be secular law, but religion is rarely completely irrelevant. In many countries freedom of religion is guaranteed either expressly in a constitution or bill of rights or through some other mechanism such as the European Convention on Human Rights. Inevitably, conflicts arise between an individual claiming the right to pursue a particular course of action for religious reasons and secular legal provisions, something illustrated by the recent and ongoing cases in Canada and the United States, with the right to freedom of religion, as well as the right to privacy, being used to challenge criminal prosecutions relating to the practice of polygamy (polygyny).[81]

1.30   At a policy level, the voices of religious groups can reach a considerable volume and nowhere is this illustrated more graphically than in the debate over same-sex marriage. In chapter after chapter there are references to religious opposition.[82] The place of religion in a secular legal system presents a curious irony. Commenting on the position in the United States, Melli observes: 'For a country founded on principles of separation of church and state, organized religion plays an important role on issues that those religions care about.'[83]

Custom

1.31   In the countries with a colonial past where European settlers rapidly outnumbered and displaced the indigenous population – Australia, Canada, New Zealand, South Africa and the United States – indigenous custom yielded to the law brought and developed by the settlers. However, there are signs of these legal systems showing greater respect for indigenous culture and custom.[84] In New Zealand, for example, there has been something of a 'Maori renaissance' and it is particularly apparent in the development and expanding use of family group conferences, something firmly rooted in Maori tradition.[85]

---

[81] See further, para. 1.75 below.
[82] See, Canada (para. 3.48), Russia (para. 11.53), Scotland (para. 12.37) and the United States (para. 14.2).
[83] Para. 14.2 below.
[84] On increased awareness of the need for cultural sensitivity in the child protection context, see para. 1.67 below.
[85] Para. 9.9 below.

1.32 In South Africa, while customary law received little official attention in the past, it is now recognised on an equal footing with the Roman–Dutch common law. While 'harmonisation is being select-ively employed',[86] for example in respect of customary and civil mar-riages, Heaton predicts that 'unification of laws is unlikely to take place because it would probably unjustifiably limit the constitutional rights to freedom of culture and religion'.[87] Thus, like the legal systems based on religion discussed above, different systems of family law will often apply to different groups in the country.

1.33 Of course, a country's citizens being subject to different systems of family law need not be driven by either religion or the coexistence of customary and common law, as is amply demonstrated in the United States, where there is 'not one, but 50 sets of child and family laws – one for each of the 50 states'.[88] A less dramatic example is found in the United Kingdom, where one of the component parts, Scotland, has always had a system of family law distinct from the rest of the country and, since 1999, has had its own parliament, legislating on many areas of law including child and family law, and a separate court system.[89]

Equality

1.34 The most striking feature in the chapters that follow is the various legal systems' attempts to foster equality between the sexes. When one remembers that, as long ago as 1948, the United Nations declared that 'all human beings are born free and equal in dignity and rights',[90] perhaps this commitment is unsurprising. At the international level that principle was given substance, for women and girls, when the Convention on the Elimination of Discrimination Against Women[91] was adopted in 1979. For children the principle is embodied in Article 2 of the United Nations Convention on the Rights of the Child, adopted ten years later.[92] All of the countries discussed in this volume, except the United States, have ratified

---

[86] Para. 13.5 below.   [87] *Ibid.*   [88] Para. 14.6 below   [89] Paras. 12.6–12.7 below.
[90] Universal Declaration of Human Rights, Art. 1.
[91] L. C. McClain, *The Place of Families: Fostering Capacity, Equality, and Responsibility* (Cambridge, MA: Harvard University Press, 2006), p. 61 (ratification will 'preclude States from requiring or supporting a patriarchal form of family governance').
[92] Article 2 prohibits 'discrimination of any kind' and goes on to list examples, including the child's or the parents' 'birth or other status', as prohibited grounds of discrimination.

both conventions[93] and many of them, including the United States, were taking steps to promote equality well before they were drafted.

1.35   When the pursuit of equality came to the fore in the legal systems examined here varies, of course, between jurisdictions and depending on the particular topic at issue, with Russia and Norway leading the field.[94] The mechanism employed to secure equality also varies between jurisdictions. Some offer a guarantee of equality through a constitution, a bill of rights and the like; others rely on issue-specific legislation; and many do both.

1.36   In all of this, three points merit mention. First, while a broad, general commitment to equality is important in itself, since it can create a climate for other developments,[95] it is of limited impact on the day-to-day operation of child and family law if it is not given meaningful content. Secondly, even if equality is articulated on specific issues, whether in legislation or through judicial decisions, one must then examine how the law actually operates in practice before being satisfied that equality has been secured. In that, a strength of this volume is that each country-specific chapter has been written by a contributor with local knowledge of the legal system's operation and contributors have not shied away from pointing out examples of practice lagging behind the law.

1.37   Finally, applying the principle of equality requires treating people who are in the same situation in the same way. It does not require treating fundamentally different relationships as if they were the same – and, indeed, to do so can result in inequality.[96] This gives rise to a further challenge. How particular relationships are characterised and classified is inherent in the process of assessing whether they should benefit from equal treatment and there is no shortage of examples of proponents of a

---

[93] On international instruments, see further paras. 1.19–1.21 above.

[94] In Russia this resulted from the 1917 Revolution (paras. 11.4 and 11.9–11.10), while in Norway (para. 10.1) the process occurred more peacefully at the beginning of the twentieth century. Specific limited statutory provisions can be found earlier in some of the other jurisdictions. See, for example, the Married Women's Property Act 1881 in Scotland.

[95] P. McG. Crotty, 'Legislating Equality' (1996) 10 *International Journal of Law, Policy and the Family* 317, at 318 ('law can be a starting point and basic foundation for the attainment of equal rights … [n]o matter what type of law is involved or how closely it reflects a nation's culture, law can serve as a first step in transforming social realities and fostering equal rights').

[96] See, for example, financial provision on divorce, discussed at para. 1.51 below.

particular outcome using characterisation and classification, quite deliberately, in order to frame the equality question. Nowhere is that more apparent than in the debate over same-sex marriage.

Children

1.38 A notable similarity in most of the jurisdictions examined is that 'illegitimacy' has lost all or much of its significance. Whereas, at the beginning of the twentieth century, real legal distinctions were drawn between children born to married and unmarried parents, there has been a widespread rejection of this discrimination, at least as far as the rights of the child are concerned. In some countries this resulted from a simple commitment to the principle of equality for children, while in others and on the basis of timing one can discern the influence of the United Nations Convention on the Rights of the Child.[97]

1.39 That is not to say, however, that birth status has lost all importance. A range of social, political or religious influences create exceptions to, and anomalies within, this picture of equality. So, for example, there is the position of a *mamzer* under Jewish law[98] and the very British fixation with legitimacy in the aristocratic context.[99] More generally, where law reform has preceded changing social attitudes, rather than resulting from them, children born outside marriage may continue to face social stigmatisation and this problem is noted by numerous contributors, often in respect of parts of the country or amongst particular groups within it.[100]

---

[97] In particular, Article 2 thereof and note 92 above.

[98] A *mamzer* is a child born to a Jewish woman, but fathered by a Jewish man other than her husband, and such an individual may not marry a Jew except another *mamzer* or a convert: para. 6.17 below.

[99] While birth status is largely irrelevant to succession (inheritance), only children born in marriage may succeed to titles and honours: see para. 12.17 below. The much-publicised plan for legislation that would remove the rule of primogeniture from succession to the British Crown in two generations' time will not remove the requirement that the heir be legitimate, nor will it have any impact on succession to other titles and honours.

[100] See, for example, China (para. 4.11) where, despite the removal of the legitimacy–illegitimacy distinction, there is a strong social expectation that children will be born within marriage. This, combined with the system of household registration and the country's unique birth planning system, resulted in children who were classified as illegal and who were discriminated against.

Parenting

1.40   Alongside this general picture of equality in terms of a child's status is one of equal parental authority for married parents, albeit that equality has to be understood in its cultural context. For unmarried parents, while there is certainly something of a movement towards parental equality, closer examination of the treatment of the non-marital father reveals that he often faces obstacles in his quest for involvement in the life of his child, and subtle differences between jurisdictions emerge. Where the jurisdictions part company most clearly is how to approach parenting roles when separating and divorcing parents are in dispute.

1.41   Historically, the non-marital father has been both a demonised and a tragic figure and that may be, in part, because such fathers are so varied. Even today, they range from stereotypical 'deadbeat dads', whose irresponsibility is exceeded only by their fertility, to caring co-parents who may or may not live with their child's mother. While disputed cases may still end up in court, the path to establishing paternity has been eased in most of our jurisdictions, with many having a process whereby the non-marital father may simply acknowledge paternity, the mother's consent usually being required as well.[101] Some have a paternal presumption based on cohabitation, akin to that applying to married fathers, in the non-marital situation.[102]

1.42   Distinctions emerge where the child's mother is resisting a man's assertion of paternity and apparent similarities can mask real differences. So, for example, while in both Norway and Scotland a registered non-marital father has equal rights with the child's mother, a cohabiting Norwegian father does not need the mother's consent to register his paternity,[103] whereas the mother's consent is a prerequisite for all non-marital fathers seeking registration in Scotland.[104] In addition, Norwegian

[101]   See the interesting limitations on acknowledgement in the Netherlands (para. 8.16). The option, adopted in England and Wales, is to 'require' unmarried couples to register the child's birth jointly, subject to exceptions necessary to accommodate maternal ignorance or fear of harm from the child's father: Welfare Reform Act 2009, s. 56 and Sched. 6.

[102]   See, for example, Australia (para. 2.12) and Canada (para. 3.19) and 'permanent life partners' in South Africa (para. 13.27). A similar approach was recommended by the Law Commission in New Zealand (para. 9.27).

[103]   Para. 10.26 below. Difficulties in proving cohabitation have impeded the smooth operation of this provision and Sverdrup predicts it may be short-lived.

[104]   Para. 12.24 below.

courts can order DNA testing of the child,[105] while Scottish courts are restricted to 'drawing an inference' from the mother's refusal to consent to the child being tested.

1.43   Establishing paternity can often be just the first step for the father who seeks involvement in his child's life, beyond acquiring a child support obligation. Thus, in the United States parental equality is sometimes tied to a demonstration of commitment by the father.[106] In Russia, where parental equality, irrespective of marital status, has long been the norm, there is an interesting proposal to reform the law. While fathers who acknowledge paternity voluntarily would continue to benefit from this equal position, fathers whose paternity is established only after court proceedings have been raised against them would not, being liable only to support the child.[107]

1.44   Most separating and divorcing parents reach agreement on how they will care for their children in the future, sometimes employing alternative dispute resolution mechanisms to assist them in achieving that solution. Of course, the fact that they have been able to resolve the matter does not render the law irrelevant, since parental negotiations will often have taken place, to borrow the oft-quoted words of Mnookin and Kornhausert, 'in the shadow of the law'.[108] Where parents cannot agree, the courts will be called upon to decide the matter and then how the legal system approaches these disputes becomes central.

1.45   As we shall see, all of our jurisdictions have accepted that decisions should proceed on the basis of the primacy of the child's best interests[109] and many give the child involved an opportunity to have some input into the decision-making process.[110] The idea of fathers or mothers having a presumed 'right' to the child, on the basis of parental gender, has long

---

[105] Para 10.26. While courts in Israel may order DNA testing to establish the paternity of an unmarried woman's child, the relevant legislation was amended to prevent such an order applying to a married Jewish woman since the consequences of her child being found to be a *mamzer* were thought to be so detrimental to the child: paras. 6.18–6.19 below.

[106] Para. 14.29 below. This is the position as expressed by the US Supreme Court, most famously by Justice Stevens in *Lehr* v. *Robertson*, 463 U.S. 248, p. 262 (1983). Some states have statutory provisions creating substantial equality for all parents.

[107] Para. 11.27 below.

[108] R. H. Mnookin and L. Kornhausert, 'Bargaining in the Shadow of the Law: The Case of Divorce' (1979) 88 *Yale Law Journal* 950.

[109] Paras. 1.56–1.57 below.   [110] Para. 1.61 below.

since disappeared in most jurisdictions,[111] albeit in the debate over the criteria to be applied by courts, the competing arguments play out along profoundly gendered lines in many countries.[112]

1.46 In the past, legal systems often approached post-divorce parenting on the basis that one parent would have the primary position in decision-making and the child would live with him or her most of the time, often using the terms 'custody' to describe this right.[113] The other parent's involvement would be limited to 'access' or 'visitation', usually involving spending time with the child and sometimes overnight stays.[114] The not unreasonable premise that most children benefit from continued involvement of both parents is now the starting point for many of our jurisdictions, with shared parental decision-making and, sometimes, joint legal custody emerging.[115] Sometimes terminology has been modernised to replace 'custody' with 'residence' and 'access' with 'contact'.

1.47 The gendered nature of this debate has magnified in recent years with fathers' rights groups in various countries seeking a statutory presumption of equal rights in respect of, and equal time with, the child.[116] While they assert that this would benefit children, there is no escaping their emphasis on adult, rather than children's, rights. Women's groups have opposed this approach for a variety of reasons,[117] not least of which

---

[111] Israel has retained the 'tender years presumption', whereby maternal custody is the norm for children under the age of six: see para. 6.47 below.

[112] The assertion by Patrick Parkinson that 'The history of family law reform is not only, or even mainly, a history of a gender war' is singular indeed and, when applied to parenting after divorce and separation, confuses what is actually happening with what would be desirable in an ideal world. See P. Parkinson, *Family Law and the Indissolubility of Parenthood* (Cambridge University Press, 2011), p. 14.

[113] Particular care should be taken with terminology here, not only between jurisdictions but also within them, since a particular term like 'custody' may have a range of meanings. For example, 'legal custody', carrying with it decision-making power, should be distinguished from 'physical custody', being the right to control the child's place of residence. Interestingly, the concept of 'custody' is not part of the Russian legal system, although the increase in cases with a foreign element makes it more difficult to avoid use of the term: para. 11.33 below. The conceptual difference may explain why parents litigate over where the child will live and financial support, but rarely address visitation, at least at the time of divorce: para. 11.30 below.

[114] See, for example, Israel (para. 6.47).

[115] See, for example, Canada (para. 3.36), Scotland (para. 12.30) and South Africa (13.33).

[116] See, for example, Canada (para. 3.36), Norway (para. 10.38), Scotland (para. 12.30), United States (para. 14.48).

[117] See H. Rhoades and S. B. Boyle, 'Reforming Custody Laws: A Comparative Study' (2004) 18 *International Journal of Law, Policy and the Family* 119.

is the dangers it presents in exposing children to conflict and women to harm by enabling an abusive former partner to continue the abuse.[118] In addition, it fails to distinguish between quality and quantity of contact[119] and there is a suspicion, at least in the United States, that the objective of fathers was 'not to spend more time with their children but to reduce their child support obligation'.[120]

1.48   Australia led the way in the most recent round of 'shared parenting' legislation when, in 2006, the existing statute was amended to prioritise the child having a 'meaningful relationship' with both parents.[121] Following several reviews of how the amendments were working,[122] further legislation, aimed at protecting against domestic abuse, was introduced in the federal parliament.[123] It was, in part, this experience that led a recent review of the law in England and Wales to recommend: 'No legislation should be introduced that creates or risks creating the perception that there is a parental right to substantially shared or equal time for both parents.'[124]

---

[118] See P. R. Amato, 'Good Enough Marriages: Parental Discord, Divorce and Children's Long-Term Well-Being' (2001) 9 *Virginia Journal of Social Policy and Law* 71; J. McIntosh, 'Enduring Conflict in Parental Separation: Pathways of Impact on Child Development' (2003) 9(1) *Journal of Family Studies* 63; M. Shaffer, 'Joint Custody, Parental Conflict and Children's Adjustment to Divorce: What the Social Science Literature Does and Does Not Tell Us' (2007) 26 *Canadian Family Law Quarterly* 286.

[119] Para. 11.38 below.

[120] Para. 14.48 below. The American Law Institute proposed an 'approximation rule', providing that the amount of time allocated to separated parents should approximate the time they spent with the child when the parents were together: American Law Institute, *Principles of the Law of Family Dissolution: Analysis and Recommendations* (Newark: West Publishing, 2002), §2.08. The recommendation bears a resemblance to the 'primary caretaker standard' articulated by Justice Neely in *Garska* v. *McCoy*, 278 S.E.2d 357 (W.Va. 1981).

[121] Family Law Amendment (Shared Parental Responsibility) Act 2006.

[122] R. Kaspiew, M. Gray, R. Weston *et al.*, *Evaluation of the 2006 Family Law Reforms* (Melbourne: Australian Institute of Family Studies, 2009); R. Chisholm, *Family Courts Violence Review* (2009), available at: www.ag.gov.au/Documents/Chisholm_report (last accessed 20 March 2012); Family Law Council, *Improving Responses to Family Violence in the Family Law System: An Advice on the Intersection of Family Violence And Family Law Issues* (Barton: Family Law Council, 2009); and Social Policy Research Centre, *Shared Care Parenting Arrangements since the 2006 Family Law Reforms* (Sydney: University of New South Wales, 2010).

[123] Family Law Legislation Amendment (Family Violence and Other Measures) Bill 2011.

[124] *Family Justice Review: Final Report* (London: Ministry of Justice, 2011), p. 142. Reviewing the problems with the family justice system, the Report offered the troubling observation, at para. 2.22: 'Family justice does not operate as a coherent, managed system. In fact, in many ways, it is not a system at all.'

Adult relationships

1.49   Another striking feature in all of the chapters that follow is the movement from a patriarchal family structure to spousal equality, at least in strictly legal terms, something that is consistent with the findings of empirical studies examining aspects of family law across various jurisdictions[125] and the important part family law plays in the quest for equality.[126] The relationship here appears symbiotic: that is, while changes in family law can, indeed, create a climate of greater gender equality, those changes were often driven by the fact that women were acquiring more social, political and economic power.[127] These developments must be understood in their cultural context[128] and the harsh reality that, to a greater or lesser extent, equality between men and women remains a goal to be realised fully. Undoubtedly, this is tied to the ways in which families operate[129] and that uniquely female activity, child-bearing,[130] leading one

---

[125] See, for example, A. Gautier, 'Legal Regulation of Marital Relations: A Historical and Comparative Approach' (2005) 19 *International Journal of Law, Policy and the Family* 47 at 63 (referring to a study of 142 countries, she observes: 'In comparison to 1938, the legal implications of marriage for women changed completely in 2003. Some types of discrimination that were very widespread have completely disappeared, such as the loss of nationality, of name, of civil capacity, the management of a wife's own property, and salary by her husband or the right to work without the husband's authorisation.').

[126] Crotty, 'Legislating Equality', 331 (using various sources to construct indices of equal treatment for women and asking the question: 'Does the presence of statutory protections and the absence of statutory restrictions on the rights of women under family law lead to an improvement in the de facto position of women?' She concludes that: 'The evidence presented points to a moderate affirmative answer to that question').

[127] M. A. Glendon, 'Three Decades of Legal and Social Change', in A. Chloros, M. Rheinstein and M. A. Glendon (eds.), *International Encyclopedia of Comparative Law*, Volume IV, *Persons and Family* (Tübinger: Mohr Siebeck, 2004), p. 3 ('In affluent modern societies, the principal transformative forces affecting the law of persons, formation of marriage, interspousal relations, divorce, the creation of kinship relations and the relation of parents and children were ideas about individual freedom, equality and women's rights').

[128] See particularly, China (para. 4.22) and Malaysia (paras. 7.3 and 7.12).

[129] J. Scott and S. Dex, 'Paid and Unpaid Work: Can Policy Improve Gender Inequalities?', in J. Miles and R. Probert (eds.), *Sharing Lives, Diving Assets: An Inter-Disciplinary Study* (Oxford: Hart Publishing, 2009), p. 41 (increased gender equality in the workplace has not led to the great equality in domestic work that was anticipated). For why this need not be the case, see H. Reece, *Divorcing Responsibly* (Oxford: Hart Publishing, 2003).

[130] J. Miles and R. Probert, 'Sharing Lives, Dividing Assets: Legal Principles and Real Life', in J. Miles and R. Probert, *Sharing Lives, Diving Assets: An Inter-Disciplinary Study* (Oxford: Hart Publishing, 2009), p. 20 ('the extent of downward mobility for those who move out of the labour market even for a short period is greater for today's women than it was for previous generations').

commentator to question whether 'equal marriage' should be seen as a classic oxymoron.[131]

1.50 Confining the discussion to monogamous, different-sex marriage for the moment, the general rule is that it is open to single people of sufficient age who are not too closely related to each other, albeit there is variation on the age of marriage and the relationships that act as a bar to it. While the prohibitions on bi-racial marriage that once existed in South Africa[132] and parts of the United States[133] are, happily, relics of a bygone era, bi-religious and inter-caste marriages continue to present legal or social challenges in some countries.[134]

1.51 Divorce is increasingly, but not universally, a no-fault affair, with the norm being for spouses to have equal access to it. There are exceptions in the context of religious divorces, specifically, the *get*[135] and the *talaq*,[136] where the husband retains a dominant position. As we have seen, access to legal services is problematic in a number of our jurisdictions, with cost being a significant obstacle.[137] In terms of property division and post-divorce support, the general picture is one of legal equality,[138] but applying the principle of equality, without modification, can result in treating people in the same way when their circumstances are different, leading to inequality of outcomes. Thus, equal division of the property acquired during the marriage can penalise the homemaker spouse if pension entitlement is excluded from the definition of property.[139] If this is coupled with a reluctance to award spousal support, the problem is exacerbated.[140]

---

[131] S. Gavigan, 'Equal Families, Equal Parents, Equal Spouses, Equal Marriage: The Case of the Missing Patriarch' (2006) 33 *Supreme Court Law Review* (2d) 317, 320.

[132] Para. 13.50 below.

[133] *Loving* v. *Virginia*, 388 U.S. 1 (1967), discussed at para. 14.62 below.

[134] See Israel (para. 6.55) and India (paras. 5.15 and 5.47–5.48) below.

[135] A *get* (also *ghet*) is a document, given by the husband to the wife, releasing her from the marriage: see further, para. 6.67 below. In Canada (para. 3.54) and Scotland (para. 12.51) legislative efforts have been made to address this issue.

[136] See, further, in India (para. 5.72), Israel (para. 6.68) and Malaysia (paras. 7.15 and 7.54).

[137] Para. 1.12 above.

[138] For an exception, see South Africa (para. 13.62), where autonomy is prioritised over equality in respect of civil marriage, with the result that the courts must apply the system the parties chose prior to marriage in dividing assets on divorce. The courts have more extensive powers in respect of customary marriages.

[139] See Australia (paras. 2.46–2.52) and Norway (para. 10.71).

[140] See, the Netherlands (para. 8.66), Norway (para. 10.71) and Russia (para. 11.63).

1.52   Thus far, equality in adult relationships has been discussed in the context of monogamous, different-sex marriage – of wives obtaining parity with husbands. What of other adult relationships – same-sex relationships, same- and different-sex cohabitation and polygamy? Given the range of options available in many of the legal systems in our enquiry, these varied relationships and their consequences are examined separately below.[141]

Increased respect for the rights of the child

1.53   A commitment to increased respect for the rights of children is another of the themes that permeates all of the country-specific discussions in this volume. While this is most encouraging, it is, again, unsurprising since all but one of the countries discussed in our study have ratified the United Nations Convention on the Rights of the Child.[142]

1.54   The precise status of the Convention in the domestic legal hierarchy varies between countries. It was incorporated into Norwegian law in 2003.[143] A failure to incorporate the Convention expressly may not be crucial in countries, including the Netherlands[144] and Russia,[145] where international obligations take precedence over domestic law. In many of the other jurisdictions every effort is made to honour treaty obligations and, where domestic law is ambiguous, it will usually be interpreted in a way that will lead to compliance with international law. However, where domestic law is clear, it will take precedence, even if it is inconsistent with international obligations.

1.55   Ratification of the Convention is a welcome first step, since it implies a commitment to the rights of children embodied in it. However, as was the case in the context of equality, giving meaningful content to these rights requires that they are implemented in respect of specific issues that affect the lives of children and their families. The system of periodic reports to the United Nations Committee on the Rights of the

---

[141] See paras. 1.72–1.83 below.

[142] In world terms, only two countries have failed to ratify the Convention – Somalia and the United States – but both have signed it. As Melli reminds us, at para. 14.19, family law is determined in the United States on a state-by-state basis and 'the protections urged by the ... Convention ... are also valued by the individual American states and, indeed, the United States delegation was much involved in the drafting of the Convention.'

[143] Para. 10.8 below.   [144] Para. 8.1 below.   [145] Para. 11.15 below.

Child is designed to monitor compliance with the Convention and, in the chapters that follow, contributors have not been slow to highlight occasions where law or practice in their own countries has attracted criticism from the Committee.

1.56 Across our jurisdictions there is widespread acceptance of the primacy of the child's best interests (welfare) in the decision-making context, as required by Article 3, one of the pillars of the Convention.[146] It may be a reflection of this commitment to prioritising the child's welfare that the principle is so often co-opted by anyone with an agenda. If one wants to promote a particular reform, it has become routine to claim that it will serve the best interests of children. Conversely, if one wants to oppose the reform, the claim is that it will harm children's interests. Yet again, the same-sex marriage debate provides a good example of this phenomenon at work.

1.57 In many jurisdictions a 'best interests of the child test' is articulated in legislation. The test itself has long been criticised as vague or indeterminate,[147] being described as 'a highly contingent social construction'[148] that effectively leaves judges free to apply their own beliefs about what is good or bad for children. Some of our jurisdictions seek to rein in this tendency by prescribing the content of the test by means of a checklist of factors to be used in assessing welfare. Others do not, but this may not make all that much difference, since, in the absence of a statutory checklist, unofficial checklists are often found in the domestic literature and accepted, at least on some level, by lawyers and judges working in the field. In addition, many statutory checklists include a provision requiring 'all other relevant circumstances', or the like, to be taken into account,[149] adding subjectivity to the apparently objective.

---

[146] Only in China is this standard not articulated expressly, but even there, when one looks, for example, at parental obligations to children, elements of best interests are clearly present.

[147] See R. H. Mnookin, 'Child Custody Adjudication: Judicial Functions in the Face of Indeterminacy' (1975) 39 *Law and Contemporary Problems* 227. For an attempt to reformulate the welfare test, see J. Eekelaar, 'Beyond the Welfare Principle' (2002) 14 *Child and Family Law Quarterly* 237.

[148] K. Bartlett, 'Re-Expressing Parenthood', in M. D. Freeman (ed.), *Family, State and Law* (Aldershot: Ashgate, 1999), p. 173.

[149] In Australia, for example, this opened the door for one court to add 'the child's level of contentment and happiness' to the existing statutory checklist: see para. 2.19 below.

1.58   Beyond best interests, giving meaningful content to the obligations under the UN Convention implicates all aspects of child law and the
chapters that follow address the extent to which the rights of the child are
truly being implemented in a whole range of contexts. How two issues,
one general in nature, the other rather more specific – the child's voice
and physical punishment of children – play out are discussed here by way
of illustration.[150] As we shall see, while there is widespread compliance,
at least in terms of legislative provision, with the right of the child to participate in decision-making, there is substantial variation on the issue of
physical punishment of children. There is no escaping the conclusion that
legislators are most comfortable bestowing rights on children where their
exercise will remain subject to adult oversight. When it comes to prioritising children's rights over so-called parental rights, legislators are more
cautious.

The child's voice

1.59   Another pillar of the Convention, Article 12, gives the child who is
capable of forming views the right to express those views freely in all matters affecting the child, these views being given due weight in accordance
with the child's age and maturity. In addition, it requires that the child
be afforded the opportunity to be heard in any judicial or administrative
proceedings affecting him or her.[151]

1.60   Given the breadth of Article 12, there is scope for compliance at
a number of levels. As far as decision-making in the family setting is
concerned, in some of our jurisdictions parents are under a statutory
obligation to consult sufficiently mature children, at least on important
matters.[152] While the law may serve climate-setting and educational functions here, there is no escaping the fact that whether parents comply with
the obligation is probably driven more by the dynamics of the particular
family than it is by the law. A variety of mechanisms have been put in
place to give children a voice in the wider community with many countries having a designated government minister responsible for children's

---

[150]   Another such issue, the extent to which the child's right to identity, as manifested in the
right to know genetic parents, is discussed at para. 1.89 below, in the context of assisted
reproduction.

[151]   The UN Committee on the Rights of the Child has offered further guidance on the content of this right: Committee on the Rights of the Child, *General Comment No 12: The
Right of the Child to Be Heard*, July 2009, CRC/C/GC/12.

[152]   See, for example, China (para. 4.19), Russia (para. 11.21) and Scotland (para. 12.27).

issues, with discussion fora like youth parliaments being another feature. Norway led the world when it created the Ombudsman for Children in 1981, and numerous other countries have created similar positions.[153]

1.61   A broadly consistent picture emerges, in the chapters that follow, in respect of the child's right to be heard in judicial and administrative proceedings, with some degree of statutory recognition being widespread. However, many of the contributors see what has been achieved to date as very much a work in progress with more needing to be done to ensure comprehensive and meaningful respect for the participation rights of children.[154] In some cases, caution over children's participation is a manifestation of the wider 'rights v. welfare' debate: essentially, the fear that giving the child an active role in the decision-making process, particularly in the context of divorce, can put him or her in a burdensome and invidious position.[155] In addition, there is the issue of what is to be ascertained, with the terms 'wishes' rather that 'views' being used in a number of our jurisdictions.[156] Then there is what is meant by 'participation', since there is a world of difference between having one's preference conveyed to a court by a third party and being represented by a lawyer as a party to the proceedings. However the child's participation is effected, it is usually the case that, ultimately, the court will almost always prioritise its perception of the child's welfare over the child's wishes or views.[157]

---

[153] The term 'ombudsman' is used widely in Scandinavian countries, as well as in the Netherlands and Russia. The term 'commissioners' is used in New Zealand and there are commissioners for children in the constituent parts of the United Kingdom, with the Scottish Commissioner for Children and Young People being the designated person in Scotland. In the United States such an office has been created on a state or, sometimes, city or county, basis. At present, there appears to be no equivalent office in China, India, Malaysia or South Africa. In Australia, Canada and Israel there have been calls to create such an office. For information on the current position, see the European Network of Ombudspersons for Children (ENOC), hosted by the Children's Rights Information Network (CRIN): www.crin.org/enoc/network/index.asp. Together, ENOC and CRIN seek to share information and strategies on a global scale.

[154] See Canada (para. 3.37), Israel (para. 6.13), Malaysia (para. 7.28), New Zealand (para. 9.52), Norway (para. 10.41), Russia (para. 11.24) and Scotland (para. 12.30).

[155] See, for example, Canada (para. 3.37) and Norway (para. 10.40).

[156] See, for example, New Zealand, where the term 'wishes' was replaced with 'views', something Atkin explains as being 'regarded as wider because a child's views may not be as clearly articulated as wishes': para. 9.52 below.

[157] However, in Malaysia a Muslim child who has reached the age of *mumaiyiz* has the right to choose the parent with whom he or she will live. *Mumaiyiz* can occur between the ages of seven years and majority and is tied to the concept of *baligh*. See further, paras. 7.26 and 7.30 below.

Physical punishment

1.62   It will be remembered that the UN Convention is unequivocal in requiring states parties to 'protect the child from all forms of physical or mental violence'[158] and in requiring states parties to ensure that 'no child shall be subjected to torture, or other cruel, inhuman or degrading treatment or punishment'.[159] Again, the UN Committee on the Rights of the Child has elaborated further, confirming that it rejects 'any justification of violence and humiliation as forms of punishment for children'.[160] In 2006 the UN Secretary-General's Study on Violence against Children,[161] endorsed by the UN General Assembly,[162] set 2009 as the target date for a prohibition on all physical punishment of children in all countries. A follow-up study by non-governmental organisations (NGOs) in 2011 makes clear that this goal remains far from being realised.[163]

1.63   Sweden led the world in banning all physical punishment of children as long ago as 1979 and a number of our jurisdictions followed suit, either through legislation[164] or by judicial decision.[165] However, it is disappointing that in other countries, while a strong commitment to the principles of children's rights is often expressed, parental physical chastisement of children continues to be permitted.[166] Certainly, in some of these countries this so-called parental right has been curtailed by more refined definition,[167] but as Sutherland observes, 'the very act of defining the violence permitted sends a message to parents that it is acceptable for them to hit their children, provided they stick to the rules'.[168]

---

[158]   Article 19(1).   [159]   Article 37(a).

[160]   Committee on the Rights of the Child, *General Comment No 8: The Rights of the Child to Protection from Corporal Punishment and other Cruel or Degrading Forms of Punishment*, August 2006, CRC/C/GC/8, para. 13.

[161]   UN Doc. A/61/299 (2006).

[162]   UN Doc. A/RES/62/141 (2007).

[163]   *Five Years On: A Global Update on Violence Against Children* (NGO Advisory Council, 2011). For an ongoing assessment of progress, see the Global Initiative to End All Corporal Punishment of Children website, at: www.endcorporalpunishment.org/.

[164]   Norway (1987, with further clarification in 2010, para. 10.32), New Zealand (2007, paras. 9.43–9.44).

[165]   In Israel, see *State of Israel* v. *Plonit*, P.D. 44(1) 145, discussed at para. 6.50 below.

[166]   Some, but not all, of these countries prohibit the use of physical punishment in schools or in institutional care or in both.

[167]   This has occurred, for example, through legislation in Scotland (para. 12.28). In Canada (para. 3.31) curtailment resulted from the decision in *Canadian Foundation for Children, Youth and the Law* v. *Canada (Attorney-General)*, [2004] 1 S.C.R. 76.

[168]   Para. 12.28 below.

Valiant lobbying efforts to end physical punishment of children continues in many of our jurisdictions, sometimes with a degree of official
support.[169]

Protection from abuse

1.64   Abuse within the family, whether perpetrated against children
(child abuse) or adult partners (domestic abuse) has always been with
us,[170] but it was not until the latter half of the last century that it began
to receive concerted international attention. While each form of abuse is
distinct, there is overlap, not least because misuse of power is inherent in
both. Overlap is apparent in terms of both classification and effects. So,
for example, forced marriage may include child marriage and victimisa-
tion as a child may have effects that last well into adulthood and can have
an impact on future relationships. There is now heightened awareness of
both problems and practitioners and academics[171] across a range of disciplines are learning to work together on prediction, prevention, identification and appropriate responses to them.

1.65   It is therefore no surprise to find that efforts are being made to
tackle both child abuse and domestic abuse in all of the countries discussed in this volume. While that is encouraging, the message from most
contributors is that these efforts are of limited success and that more
needs to be done. Part of the problem here lies in general societal attitudes
to behaviour within the family, parental power, gender roles and family
privacy.[172] While the law can have an impact on societal attitudes,[173] its

---

[169] See, for example, the (unimplemented) recommendation of the South African Law
Reform Commission to end physical punishment of children: para. 13.30 below.

[170] The terminology used here is only one option. 'Domestic abuse' or 'family violence' can
be used to include abuse of both children and adults – and to include older family members and those with disabilities – in the domestic or family setting, but 'domestic abuse'
is also used widely to refer only to partner abuse.

[171] One of the earlier comprehensive international efforts was the International Society of
Family Law conference on Violence in the Family, held in Montreal in 1977. Papers from
the conference were published as J. Eekelaar and S. Katz (eds.), *Family Violence* (Toronto:
Butterworths Canada, 1978).

[172] J. Pahl (ed.), *Private Violence and Public Policy: The Needs of Battered Women and the
Response of the Public Services* (London: Routledge and Kegan Paul, 1985); M. A. Fineman
and R. Mykitiuk (eds.), *The Public Nature of Private Violence* (New York: Routledge,
1994); S. E. Boyd (ed.), *Challenging the Public/Private Divide: Feminism, Law, and Public
Policy* (University of Toronto Press, 1997).

[173]   A good example of the educational impact of law and its capacity to change attitudes is
found in Sweden. In 1965 an opinion poll found that over half of the Swedish population

effect is limited. That is not to suggest that the legal system should stop trying; it is simply an acknowledgement that a broader approach, involving multiple agencies and public education, is needed as well.

Child abuse

1.66   Child abuse is addressed squarely by the United Nations Convention on the Rights of the Child, which places states parties under an affirmative obligation to combat 'all forms of physical or mental violence, injury or abuse, neglect or negligent treatment, maltreatment or exploitation, including sexual abuse'.[174] The jurisdictions discussed in this volume have made efforts – often strenuous efforts – to address child abuse and neglect; practitioners[175] and academics in law and a host of other disciplines gather frequently to explore the problem; and it is discussed in the copious literature, some with an international or comparative focus.[176] Yet the problem remains.

1.67   Most of our jurisdictions use the familiar methods of the criminal law[177] and civil orders authorising the short- or long-term removal of children from the home, with parental rights being terminated as a measure of last resort. In a number of countries there is provision for the removal of the abuser from the home, enabling the child to remain in a

---

believed that corporal punishment was necessary to child-rearing. By 1994, some fifteen years after physical punishment of children was prohibited, that figure had fallen to 11 per cent: J. E. Durrant, *A Generation Without Smacking: The Impact of Sweden's Ban on Physical Punishment* (London: Save the Children, 2000), p. 9.

[174]   Article 19(1).

[175]   The paper on the 'Battered-Child Syndrome', presented by Dr C. Henry Kempe at the American Academy of Pediatrics conference in Chicago in 1961, and the article he co-authored the following year, are widely regarded as landmarks in the recognition of child abuse: see C. H. Kempe, F. N. Silverman, B. F. Steele, W. Droegemueller and H. K. Silver, 'The Battered-Child Syndrome' (1962) 181 *Journal of the American Medical Association* 17. This was followed by Kempe and Helfer's seminal work, C. H. Kempe and R. E. Helfer (eds.), *The Battered Child* (Chicago University Press, 1968). This book is now in its fifth edition: M. E. Helfer, R. S. Kempe and R. D. Krugman (eds.), *The Battered Child*, 5th edn (Chicago University Press, 1997).

[176]   See N. Freymond and G. Cameron (eds.), *Towards Positive Systems of Child and Family Welfare: International Comparisons of Child Protection, Family Service, and Community Caring Systems* (University of Toronto Press, 2006); L. Hoyano and C. Keenan, *Child Abuse: Law and Policy Across Boundaries* (Oxford University Press, 2007); N. Gilbert, N. Parton and M. Skivenes (eds.), *Child Protection Systems: International Trends and Orientations* (Oxford University Press, 2011).

[177]   In New Zealand the Law Commission has recommended strengthening of criminal penalties for abuse of children and vulnerable family members: para. 9.59.

familiar environment.[178] Mandating the reporting of child abuse, either by professionals who are likely to encounter children in their work or more generally, is not yet widespread.[179] Thereafter, there is the issue of how to care for children who have been removed from their home, with the adequacy of foster care being questioned by a number of the commentators.[180] Some of our jurisdictions face very specific problems and have found novel ways to address them.[181] While children from indigenous groups are over-represented in the child protection context, there is now far greater recognition of a need to respect their cultural rights.[182] Amid all these efforts to protect children who are being neglected and abused, there is the need to remember the rights of the children *and* their parents and the possibility of erroneous or false accusations. In rights-based legal systems, this can lead to the 'legalisation' of the child protection process.[183]

1.68   Despite these, very real, efforts to combat the problem, several contributors note that the child protection system continues to fail children and the adequacy of resources remains a challenge. The system in place has been reformed recently in a number of our jurisdictions,[184] is undergoing review in others[185] and the contributors believe that re-examination is needed in yet others.[186]

Domestic abuse

1.69   While domestic abuse clearly violates a number of human rights guarantees, including the right to physical and moral integrity, liberty

---

[178] See, for example, Israel: para. 6.52 below. This is also possible in Scotland, but in each country little use is made of these orders.

[179] Such reporting is mandated in all states in the United States: para. 14.55 below.

[180] See, for example, paras. 12.35 (Scotland) and 14.58 (United States).

[181] See, for example, South Africa where, in addition to the options found in many other countries, a 'cluster foster care scheme' has been introduced, 'child-headed households' are recognised and 'drop-in centres' are utilised: paras. 13.35–13.38 below.

[182] Australia (para. 2.28), Canada (para. 3.42), New Zealand (paras. 9.60–9.61) and the United States (para. 14.36).

[183] See, for example, paras. 3.41 (Canada), 10.45 (Norway), Scotland (12.33).

[184] See, for example, the Netherlands (para. 8.39) and Scotland (para. 12.34).

[185] See, for example, Malaysia (para. 7.32), New Zealand (in respect of the Law Commission recommendation to increase criminal penalties, para. 9.62) and Scotland (para. 12.34). In India, while legislation provides for the care of neglected and delinquent children, there is no dedicated child abuse legislation and a bill is currently before the parliament: para. 5.38 below.

[186] See, for example, Canada (para. 3.41) and Russia (para. 11.46).

and security of the person,[187] it is somewhat surprising to find no specific reference to it in the United Nations Convention on the Elimination of All Forms of Discrimination Against Women (CEDAW). However, the Committee established to monitor compliance with that Convention took the issue on board, and one of its most notable recommendations was that CEDAW should be interpreted as imposing an obligation on states to 'act to protect women against any kind of violence within the family'.[188] Since 1994 the United Nations Commission on Human Rights (now the Human Rights Council) has appointed successive Special Rapporteurs on violence against women, the mandate of whom is wider than domestic abuse and includes trafficking, women in armed conflict and reproductive rights.[189] The World Health Organization addresses violence against women as a public health issue.[190]

1.70   Early definitions of the problem tended to focus on physical violence, but it is now acknowledged that domestic abuse is multifaceted and has psychological, emotional, sexual and economic dimensions. While female victims of male violence remain the most numerous in recorded statistics, there is increased recognition of male victims of female abuse and of abuse in same-sex relationships. The phenomenon of abuse amongst dating partners,[191] including adolescents, has attracted attention

---

[187] Universal Declaration of Human Rights and Fundamental Freedoms, 1948, General Assembly Res. 217A (III), Art. 3; International Covenant on Civil and Political Rights, 1966, 993 UNTS 3, Art. 9.

[188] General Recommendation 19, 1992, UN Doc. A/47/38.

[189] UN Doc. E/CN.4/RES/1994/45. The Special Rapporteur receives information, makes recommendations, works with other agencies, transmits urgent communications to states in individual cases, undertakes fact-finding country visits and submits annual reports to the Commission on Human Rights. The relevant documents can be found on the site of the Office of the United Nations High Commission for Human Rights at: www.ohchr.org/EN/Issues/Women/SRWomen/Pages/SRWomenIndex.aspx. See *15 Years of the United Nations Special Rapporteur on Violence against Women: A Critical Appraisal* (2009), UN Doc. A/HRC/11/6/Add.5.

[190] See *WHO Multi-country Study on Women's Health and Domestic Violence against Women: Initial Results on Prevalence, Health Outcomes and Women's Responses* (2005), available at: www.who.int/gender/violence/who_multicountry_study/en/.

[191] Professor Murray A. Straus at the University of New Hampshire set up the International Dating Violence Study to conduct ongoing research into violence in 'dating relationships' involving university students. The research is being conducted through a consortium of members located at universities in twenty-three countries administering a standard questionnaire to undergraduate students. Full details of the study and articles based on the findings are available at: http://pubpages.unh.edu/~mas2/ID.htm.

more recently, particularly in the United States.[192] While, as is the case with child abuse, the suggestion that domestic abuse is confined to particular socio-economic or other groups has long since been laid to rest, women from indigenous groups are often over-represented in reported cases. Various contributors highlight aspects of domestic abuse that may be specific to particular countries or groups.[193]

1.71 The responses of the various legal systems to domestic abuse usually involves the criminal law. While this sends a clear message that domestic abuse is unacceptable, the prospect of a partner facing criminal penalties may reduce the willingness of the victim to seek help. Loyalty, family pressure and fear of reprisal play their part here, but there is also the very real problem that an incarcerated breadwinner cannot support the family. Another response acknowledges the importance of the victim (and often children) having a safe place to live by guaranteeing the woman's continuing right to live in the family home and, sometimes, providing for exclusion of the abuser from the home. In addition, court orders (injunctions, interdicts and restraining orders) are used in many of our jurisdictions in an attempt to keep the abuser away from the victim, but their effectiveness in providing real protection is questioned. In all of this, the attitudes of courts, social workers and the police are crucial in securing protection for the victim and a number of contributors note improvements, while others acknowledge that further efforts are required.

Diversity in adult relationships

1.72 When considering which adult relationships are recognised by the legal systems in our enquiry, diversity is very much the order of the day, both between jurisdictions and within many of them. Some permit polygamy, at least for sections of the population; others criminalise it. Same-sex marriage is available in some countries; others

---

[192] For research and focused responses, in the United States, see E. M. Hyman, W. Lucibello, and E. Meyer, 'In Love or In Trouble: Examining Ways Court Professionals Can Better Respond to Victims of Adolescent Partner Violence' (2010) 61(4) *Juvenile and Family Court Journal* 17.

[193] For example, in South Africa (para. 13.52) forced and child marriage connected to *ukuthwala* (the kidnapping of the future bride) and *lobolo* (bride wealth), and in India (paras. 5.49–5.50) dowries and related wife abuse and suicide. See also R. W. Summers and A. M. Hoffman (eds.) *Domestic Violence – A Global View* (Westport: Greenwood Press, 2002) (a comparative analysis of the ways in which domestic abuse is viewed and handled among thirteen different countries from around the world).

offer a marriage-equivalent to same-sex couples and, in one, same-sex relationships are not only unrecognised, but homosexuality remains criminal. In some jurisdictions the legal consequences attaching to non-marital cohabitation place it on a par with marriage; more limited legal consequences attach to cohabitation in others; and it remains largely unregulated in a few.

The (sometimes diminishing) centrality of marriage

1.73 Different-sex marriage once lay at the heart of family law, with other relationships being regarded as aberrant if not criminal, something reinforced by international recognition of the 'right to marry' as a basic human right.[194] While marriage remains important in all of our jurisdictions and the only acceptable option in two,[195] its centrality and, sometimes, its popularity, is diminishing in many of the Western countries.

1.74 Where the significance of marriage has waned – something lamented by some[196] and greeted with unbridled enthusiasm by others[197] – this decline is often attributed to the fact that the legal system has made marriage available to same-sex couples or has recognised non-marital cohabitation as having legal consequences, or has done both.[198] It is difficult to see how making marriage available to more couples can do anything

---

[194] As Mary Ann Glendon observed, some thirty years ago, 'Ironically, marriage has become a basic human right just when it is losing much of its former economic importance': M. A. Glendon, *The New Family and The New Property* (Toronto: Butterworths, 1981), p. 32. That the place of marriage was under scrutiny at this time is illustrated by the fact that, almost contemporaneously, Eric Clive was questioning the legal system's need for a concept of marriage. Written first as a conference paper, it was published in the collection of conference proceedings: E. M. Clive, 'Marriage – An Unnecessary Legal Concept?', in J. M. Eekelaar and S. N. Katz (eds.), *Marriage and Cohabitation in Contemporary Societies* (London: Butterworths, 1980), p. 71.

[195] This is particularly true of Malaysia, where the basic rights of a wife and children flow from a valid marriage for Muslims and non-Muslims alike (para. 7.33) and 'so long as Islam remains the religion of the Federation it is highly unlikely that any other form of union will be recognised' (para. 7.60). In India, while homosexual acts between adults in private are no longer criminal (para. 5.43, discussing *Naz Foundation* v. *Government of NCT of Delhi* (2009) 60 Delhi Law Times 277), non-marital relationships are not regarded as acceptable (para. 6.42).

[196] W. C. Duncan, 'The State Interest in Marriage' (2004) 2 *Ave Maria Law Review* 153; N. Glenn, 'Is the Current Concern About American Marriage Warranted?' (2001) 9 *Virginia Journal of Social Policy and the Law* 5.

[197] N. D. Polikoff, *Beyond (Straight and Gay) Marriage* (Boston: Beacon Press, 2008).

[198] Lynn Wardle has written on this theme extensively, often attributing a range of social ills to what he sees as the dilution of marriage. See, for example, L. D. Wardle, 'Is Marriage

but bolster its importance in so far as more people will be invested in it. Marriage is not like an antique or an expensive perfume, where its value derives from its rarity or the fact that price puts it beyond the reach of many. Nonetheless, as long as marriage had unique legal consequences, its special nature was being signalled and the singular nature of its consequences reinforced its importance. In many Western jurisdictions the consequences themselves have reduced significantly. If, in addition, all or some of the remaining effects of marriage apply to cohabitants, then the special status of marriage is eroded further.

1.75   Discussions of marriage being under threat tend to focus on a very Western notion of the institution. Legal recognition of customary marriage, practised by indigenous peoples, is a recent phenomenon where it has happened at all.[199] Then there is polygamous marriage, an ancient practice that is an established part of the legal system in several of our jurisdictions, at least, for sections of the population.[200] In the other countries discussed here, bigamy is usually an offence with the crime normally being understood to mean that an individual has sought to use the formal procedure for marriage to marry again while already married or in an equivalent relationship. However, in Canada and Utah the offence is framed much more broadly to include, in the former, entering 'any kind of conjugal union with more than one person at the same time'[201] and, in the latter, it is committed by anyone who 'purports to marry another person or *cohabits* with another person' while either party is married.[202] Legal challenges to the legislation, founded largely on

---

Obsolete?' (2003) 10 *Michigan Journal of Gender & Law* 189, 190 ('Several reasons for opposing the redefinition of marriage to include same-sex and co-habitating nonmarital couples are suggested, including the foundational importance of marriage, the need for a "critical mass" of citizens willing to maintain the family for the sake of society, the serious if not irreversible disintegration and decline of families that is associated with going down that road, and the inappropriate promotion of special private interests at the expense of the public good').

[199] In South Africa customary marriage is now recognised on an equal footing with civil marriage (para. 13.42), while in New Zealand it is not, but customary marriages will often qualify as a de facto relationship, with essentially the same consequences as marriage (para. 9.63).

[200] In India (para. 5.41), Israel (para. 6.57), Malaysia (para. 7.35) and South Africa (para. 13.55). In addition, 'polygamy de facto exists in Russia and bigamy is no longer considered as a crime' (para. 11.44). See also the re-emergence in China of wealthy men 'taking a concubine' (para. 4.32).

[201] Criminal Code of Canada, R.S.C. 1985, s. 293(1).

[202] Utah Code Ann. §76–7–101(1) (West, 2011) (emphasis added).

freedom of religion and on privacy grounds, have been brought recently in each jurisdiction.[203]

Same-sex relationships

1.76 The 'great debate' for family law in the late twentieth and early twenty-first centuries, at least in Western countries, has been over what, if any, legal recognition should be accorded to same-sex relationships. Given that homophobia was widespread in most of these countries for so long, acceptance of same-sex relationships has usually been a process that follows a familiar pattern, beginning with decriminalisation and ending with legal recognition of the relationships.[204] The mechanism for that recognition varies and in some countries it is incremental, with registered partnership or the like preceding same-sex marriage.[205]

1.77 In 2001 the Netherlands was the first country in the world to permit same-sex couples to marry and the list of others doing so grows by the year. At the time of writing, of the jurisdictions considered in this volume, that list includes Canada, Norway, South Africa and a small minority of states in the United States. Some of our jurisdictions that do not recognise same-sex marriage have created marriage-equivalent relationships – civil

---

[203] In each jurisdiction the cases have arisen out of the polygynous activities of the Fundamentalist Church of Jesus Christ of Latter Day Saints, a group that has broken away from the mainstream church, which prohibits polygyny. The Canadian case is *Reference re: Section 293 of the Criminal Code of Canada*, 2011 BCSC 1588, discussed at para. 3.50 below. The Utah case, *Brown* v. *Herbert*, is in the early stages and the complaint, filed 13 July 2011, can be found at: http://jonathanturley.files.wordpress.com/2011/07/brown-complaint.pdf.

[204] In 'Comparative Law and the Same-Sex Marriage Debate: A Step-By-Step Approach Toward State Recognition' (1999–2000) 31 *McGeorge Law Review* 641, 647, William N. Eskridge charts the pattern as follows: 'repealing laws criminalizing consensual sodomy, equalising the age for same-sex and different-sex intercourse, prohibiting discrimination on the basis of sexual orientation, affording same-sex cohabiting couples the same rights and obligations as different-sex couples, recognising same-sex unions as "registered partnerships" or the like, and expressly allowing same-sex partners to adopt children on the same terms as married couples'. Kees Waaldijk offers a similar analysis in 'Civil Developments: Patterns of Reform in the Legal Position of Same-Sex Partners in Europe' (2000) 17 *Canadian Journal of Family Law* 62.

[205] In Norway, for example, registered partnership became available to same-sex couples in 1993, with that option being removed when same-sex marriage was introduced in 2008: para. 10.51 below. In the Netherlands registered partnership was created for all couples in 1998, with same-sex marriage following in 2001 and both relationships remain available: paras. 8.50–8.51 below.

unions, registered partnerships, civil partnerships – either primarily or exclusively for same-sex couples.[206] In others the consequences of cohabitation (of a defined kind) are such that many same-sex couples will acquire all or most of the consequences of marriage simply by living together.[207]

1.78 Offering a separate status, even if it has identical consequences to marriage, however, is not the same thing as permitting a couple to marry and this continuing discrimination may prompt more countries to embrace same-sex marriage, either *proprio motu* or consequent upon a successful human rights challenge.[208] However, as some of the contributors make clear, that will not be the case worldwide.[209]

Cohabitation

1.79 Thus far we have focused on relationships that require the parties to comply with a procedure, whether secular or religious, in order to gain access to them.[210] Historically, legal systems have been reluctant to extend the consequences of these relationships to couples who do not take advantage of the official procedure.

1.80 What appears, at first sight, to be an exception is found in common law marriage. A number of the legal systems explored here have a tradition of recognising common law marriage, requiring cohabitation for a substantial, but usually unspecified period of time, accompanied by the parties being regarded in their community as husband and wife. Increasingly, common law marriage has been abolished by statute.[211] That this is not a true exception becomes apparent when one examines the public face of common law marriage and contrasts it with that of cohabitation. The traditional 'common law' couple was not challenging

---

[206] So, for example, civil partnership throughout the United Kingdom (including Scotland) is available only to same-sex couples (paras. 12.37–12.38), while registered partnership in the Netherlands is available to all couples (see n. 205 above).

[207] See, for example Australia (para. 2.34) and New Zealand (para. 9.64).

[208] In Scotland (para. 12.38), for example, there has been formal consultation on introducing same-sex marriage and there are indications that other parts of the United Kingdom will follow this lead.

[209] Awal sees 'no prospect of same-sex marriage', in Malaysia (para. 7.60), and Khasova predicts that such a development is 'highly unlikely' in Russia (para. 11.53).

[210] In India registration of marriage is not required, something criticised by the Supreme Court: paras. 5.44–5.45 below.

[211] For example, in Scotland, 'irregular marriage', as common law marriage was known there, was almost entirely abolished in 2006: para. 12.37 below. In the United States common law marriage remains in eleven states, far fewer than was the case at one time: para. 14.68, n. 104 below.

the accepted norms of the society in which they lived. They looked and behaved like married couples, often keeping their unmarried status to themselves. Modern cohabitants, at least in Western societies, make no secret of their not being married and, indeed, may express their rejection of the concept of marriage and its social and legal trappings. Others are 'testing the waters' to see if a more formal relationship might work for them, again suggesting that they are rejecting marital commitment, at least for the time being. Yet others are driven, or rather not driven, by simple inertia.

1.81   These varied motives for cohabiting, combined with an increase in the incidence of cohabitation,[212] presents legal systems with something of a dilemma.[213] From a functional perspective, cohabitants are often very similar to married couples, combining their efforts, making sacrifices for the relationship, developing the same levels of dependence and, sometimes, having or adopting children together. This has prompted some of our jurisdictions to attach all or most of the consequences of marriage to cohabitants who meet the criteria for 'de facto relationships',[214] 'common law partners',[215] 'reputed spouses'[216] or 'domestic partners'.[217]

---

[212] R. Probert and A. Barlow, 'Displacing Marriage – Diversification and Harmonisation Within Europe', [2000] *Child and Family Law Quarterly* 153, 153 ('Comparisons between countries are problematic, as data is not always collected in the same way or for the same period. The fact that cohabitation may be terminated either by marriage or by relationship breakdown further complicates the calculations'); D Bradley, 'Regulation of Unmarried Cohabitation in West-European Jurisdictions – Determinants of Legal Policy' (2001) 15 *International Journal of Law, Policy and the Family* 22, 24 ('The difficulty in linking legal initiatives to demographic trends is that responses in jurisdictions with a comparable incidence of cohabitation differ significantly').

[213] J. Lewis, 'Debates and Issues Regarding Marriage and Cohabitation in the British and American Literature' (2001) 15 *International Journal of Law, Policy and the Family* 159, 160 ('the political and policy debates show little sensitivity to the range of cohabiting behaviour, tending rather to be caught in the same central concern about the fate of the traditional family in the face of profound change, which is in turn linked to much greater caution regarding the legal recognition of new family forms').

[214] Australia (2.34) and New Zealand (paras. 9.66–9.67).

[215] The term used in federal legislation in Canada, with the provinces using a variety of terms: see paras. 3.44–3.47 below.

[216] Israel: paras. 6.60–6.61 below.

[217] This is the term used by the American Law Institute in its *Principles of the Law of Family Dissolution: Analysis and Recommendations* (Newark: West Publishing, 2002), discussed at para. 14.69. The recommendations have not been adopted by any state: see M. R. Clisham and R. F. Wilson, 'American Law Institute's Principles of the Law of Family Dissolution, Eight Years After Adoption: Guiding Principles or Obligatory Footnote?' (2008) 42 *Family Law Quarterly* 573.

1.82   Yet if the cohabitants have chosen not to marry because they reject the concept or its consequences, the legal system is undermining their autonomy by imposing those very consequences on them. Thus, some of our jurisdictions have taken a very deliberate decision to attach no or few consequences to cohabitation.[218] Others have taken something of a middle path, attaching only limited consequences;[219] the problem with this position is the scope for the list of consequences to expand without a clear policy decision being taken to create what amounts to marriage by ascription.

'Other' relationships

1.83   It is apparent from our discussion that precisely which relationships will be recognised and the legal consequences attaching to them varies enormously between jurisdictions and, even in the legal systems that embrace a board range of relationships, some are left out in the cold. They fall into three broad categories. First, there are the relationships of cohabitants that fail to meet the criteria set out in the specific statutory definition of 'de facto relationship' or 'life partner' or whatever term is used in the jurisdiction to define cohabitation with consequences – a problem inherent in legal definitions. Then there are relationships that the parties and, often, their (minority) ethnic or religious group, recognise as marriage, but the legal system does not.[220] The impetus for legal recognition is the offence caused to the partners and their wider community by suggesting that their rites are of a lesser value than those of the dominant population. In addition, it is easier to recognise these relationships because they fit the marriage mould. The final group of relationships is wide-ranging, but includes polyamorous relationships,[221] couples 'living

---

[218]   See, for example, the Netherlands (paras. 8.51) and Norway (para. 10.54).

[219]   See, for example, Scotland (paras. 12.39–12.40) and South Africa (para. 13.47).

[220]   See, for example, customary marriage in New Zealand (para. 9.64), and the religious marriages of Muslims and Hindus in South Africa (para. 13.46).

[221]   From the Greek ('poly' meaning 'many') and Latin ('amor' meaning 'love'), also known as 'ethical nonmanogamy'. Its precise scope is debated amongst scholars and practitioners. See further, M. Strassberg, 'The Crime of Polygamy' (2003) 12 *Temple Political and Civil Rights Law Review* 353, 355 (describing it as a 'post-modern form of multi-partner relationships unburdened by patriarchal gender roles, heterosexual constraints, or monogamous exclusivity'), and E. F. Emens, 'Monogamy's Law: Compulsory Monogamy and Polyamorous Existence' (2004) 29 *North Texas University Review of Law and Social Change* 277, 283, quoting Lana Tibbetts' unpublished manuscript (describing the main principles of polyamory as being 'self-knowledge, radical honesty, consent, self-possession and privileging love and sex over other emotions and activities such as jealousy').

apart together'[222] and casual liaisons. The challenge for legal systems is whether and how to address these relationships. Certainly, the parties to them may not be seeking legal consequences, but that is not the sole criterion, since cohabitants in a number of our jurisdictions may be in exactly the same position.

The impact of developments in assisted reproductive technology

1.84   Advances in assisted reproductive technology (ART) have expanded access to parenthood significantly. Couples can now have children when they could not have done so in the past; single women can become mothers without direct contact with the sperm donor; lesbian couples can have a child, genetically related to one, and borne by the other; single men and homosexual couples can use the services of a surrogate to bear their child; and parents can make choices about their child's gender and other characteristics. The possibilities seem endless, but with these opportunities come responsibilities, not least of which is prioritising the welfare of the resulting child.

1.85   For legal systems, there are hard choices to be made. Should some or all of the options offered under the broad umbrella of 'ART' be permitted? Should they be regulated and, if so, how should that be achieved? To whom should the options be accessible? Should donors be paid for their gametes and surrogates for their services? Who controls the fate of frozen embryos in disputed cases?[223] Who are a donor child's legal parents? Should a donor child have a 'right to know' that he or she is a donor child and, if so, the identity of the donor? The very varied answers to these questions, explored in the chapters that follow, are instructive.

---

[222]   See I. Levin, 'Living Apart Together: A New Family Form' (2004) 52(2) *Current Sociology* 223, 226–7 (giving the criteria as follows: 'Each of the two partners lives in his or her own home in which other people might live as well. They define themselves as a couple and they perceive that their close surrounding personal network does so as well. The definition requires three conditions: the couple has to agree they are a couple; others have to see them as such; and they must live in separate homes').

[223]   Contrast the approach of the European Court of Human Rights in *Evans* v. *United Kingdom* (2006) 43 EHRR 1025, with that of the Israeli Supreme Court in *Nachmani* v. *Nachmani* 50(4) P.D. 661. See para. 6.28 for discussion of the current Israeli statutory provision on surrogacy. For an international overview and analysis of the range of criteria adopted by various courts in the United States, see A. J. Walker, 'His, Hers or Ours? Who Has the Right to Determine the Disposition of Frozen Embryos After Separation or Divorce?' (2008) 16 *Buffalo Women's Law Journal* 39.

1.86 Regulation of ART takes very different forms in the countries in our enquiry. The United Kingdom (including Scotland) was an early proponent of comprehensive regulation,[224] and it is constitutional considerations, rather than a lack of the desire to regulate, that present obstacles to country-wide regulation in some of our jurisdictions.[225] In others, only certain aspects of ART are regulated, with commentators usually calling for more comprehensive legislation.[226] None of our legal systems prohibits the use of ART completely, but not every option is embraced by all of them. Surrogacy provides a good example since, across our jurisdictions, it is variously prohibited,[227] restricted to gestational (full) surrogacy[228] or broadly accommodated.[229] However a particular jurisdiction seeks to regulate ART, individuals and couples with sufficient resources may simply travel abroad to obtain services not available at home or to avoid domestic rules.[230]

1.87 Our jurisdictions demonstrate marked divisions over the place of commercialism in ART. Selling of gametes is strictly prohibited in China,[231] while in the United States paid gamete donation and surrogacy are not unusual.[232] Again, surrogacy brings the debate over payment into sharp focus, with the concern being that poor women will be exploited by

---

[224] ART is a 'reserved' matter, regulated by the Westminster parliament for the whole of the United Kingdom: see para. 12.7 below.

[225] See, for example, Canada (paras. 3.20–3.22). In the United States, George A. Annas laments the lack of national regulation and attributes it to historic, economic and political factors and argues for federal regulation of at least the interstate commercial aspects of ART: G. A. Annas, 'The Regulation of Human Reproduction in the US', in S. N. Katz, J. Eekelaar and M. Maclean (eds.), *Cross Currents: Family Law and Policy in the United States and England* (Oxford University Press, 2000), p. 145. In each, the answer seems to lie in uniform statutes being made available for the provinces and states, respectively, to adopt at their discretion.

[226] See, for example, Israel (para. 6.24) and Russia (para. 11.28).

[227] See, for example, Norway (para. 10.29).

[228] See, for example, Israel (para. 6.28) and Russia (para. 11.28).

[229] See, for example, the United Kingdom, where adoption by the intending parents is facilitated by an expedited adoption procedure: para. 12.19 below.

[230] See, for example, Norway (para. 10.29), where surrogacy is not permitted and some couples make use of surrogates in other countries, leading to problems over the nationality of the resulting child, and the Netherlands (para. 8.29), where intending parents may use services abroad in order to avoid the child having access to identifying information about their donor parents.

[231] Para. 4.15 below.

[232] J. L. Dolgin, *Defining the Family: Law, Technology, and Reproduction in an Uneasy Age* (New York University Press, 1997), p. 3 (referring to the United States, she observes:

the more prosperous, possibly accompanied by something of a distaste for paying for such an intimate activity.[233] While not wishing to minimise the very real potential for exploitation, this concern is often expressed by individuals living in comfortable circumstances in affluent countries and may not reflect the perspective of an impoverished woman who can make life a little more tolerable for herself and her family by acting as a surrogate.[234]

1.88   The advent of ART presents challenges to established notions of parenthood and there has been a tendency to craft rules that fit donor children into the traditional models.[235] Thus, early legislation often provided that the woman who gave birth is treated by the legal system as the mother of the child, regardless of genetic reality, and a separate fiction treated the husband of a woman who had a child as a result of donor insemination as

'In a society accustomed to individualism, at least in the marketplace, and practically obsessed with consumer choice, it was perhaps inevitable that the possibility of separating gametes and embryos from the bodies that produce them would lead to the sale and purchase of gamete and embryonic material, and that the possibilities of separating conception from sexual intercourse and of dividing biological maternity into genetic and gestational components would lead to surrogacy contracts and paid surrogate mothers').

[233]   It is sometimes suggested that 'feminist writers' equate commercial surrogacy with prostitution, although the same few writers are cited over and over again in support of this proposition: A. Dworkin, *Right-Wing Women* (New York: Perigee Books, 1983); G. Corea, *The Mother Machine: Reproductive Technologies from Artificial Insemination to Artificial Wombs* (New York: Harper and Row, 1985). For a thought-provoking discussion of why the two should not be equated, see J. M. Sera, 'Surrogacy and Prostitution: A Comparative Analysis' (1997) 5 *American University Journal of Gender and Law* 315.

[234]   The attraction for poor women, who can earn the equivalent of a year's wages by becoming a surrogate, was summed up by one intending Indian surrogate with the words: 'Any fool can have a baby, it takes a smart woman to get paid for it'; N. S. Roy, 'Protecting the Rights of Surrogate Mothers in India', *New York Times*, 4 November 2011. The prevalence of paid surrogacy in India has prompted the introduction in the Indian parliament of legislation designed to protect the surrogate and the commissioning parties: see paras. 5.26–5.27 below.

[235]   Editors' 'Introduction', in A. Bainham, S. D. Sclater and M. Richards (eds.), *What is a Parent? A Socio-Legal Analysis* (Oxford: Hart Publishing, 1999), p. 15 ('no sooner have ideas about parents begun to take on a biological hue, than developments in reproductive biotechnologies seem likely to disrupt the new certainties'); C. Smart, 'Making Kin: Relationality and Law', in A. Bottomly and S. Wong (eds.), *Changing Contours of Domestic Life, Family and Law: Caring and Sharing* (Oxford: Hart Publishing, 2009), p. 7 ('we should now resist a continued emphasis on how family law seeks to pin down and normalise kinship (in particular to mould new forms of kinship into pre-ordained patriarchal and heterosexual shapes), and instead focus on

the child's father. Some of our jurisdictions have extending second parent recognition to the mother's female partner and have made provision for male couples to be treated as the child's parents.[236] Hitherto, legal systems have proved reluctant to embrace the possibility of multiple parenthood: that is, to acknowledge that a child might have more than two parents by extending parental status to donors and intending parents simultaneously. Recently, however, courts in Canada and the United States did just that, suggesting that the challenge to established notions of parenthood is producing tangible results.[237]

1.89   For most children, the identity of their genetic parents coincides with that of their social parents (the people who are raising them), but that is not the case for donor children.[238] Given that the importance of identity to an individual's sense of well-being has long been recognised,[239] what right, if any, does a child have to know the truth? While the United Nations Convention on the Rights of the Child acknowledges the child's rights to an identity, including the 'right to know and be cared for by his or her parents',[240] and the right to 'preserve his or her identity',[241] it also anticipates adoption[242] and does not address assisted reproduction expressly. Nonetheless, since genetic origins form a part of identity, an argument can be made that sufficiently mature children should be informed that they *are* donor

---

how contemporary practices of kinship require law to keep up with rapid changes, thus requiring law itself to be more flexible and fluid').

[236] See Australia (para. 2.13), New Zealand (para. 9.29), Norway (para. 10.25) and the United Kingdom (para. 12.45). In the Netherlands legislation acknowledging the mother's female partner as a second parent has been drafted: para. 8.18 below.

[237] In Canada, see *A.(A.)* v. *B.(B.)* (2007), 278 D.L.R. (4th) 519 (Ont. C.A.), discussed at paras. 3.20–3.22 below. In the United States, see *Jacob* v. *Shultz-Jacob*, 923 A.2d 473 (Pa. Super. Ct. 2007). Both cases and a selection of the extensive US literature on 'multiple parenthood', 'less binary parenthood' and 'community parenting' are discussed in S. F. Appleton, 'Parents by the Numbers' (2008) 37 *Hofstra Law Review* 11.

[238] Adoption provides another example of a separation between genetic parents and social parents and our jurisdictions vary in their response to 'the child's right to know' in this context as well, both in terms of whether the child will know that he or she is adopted and, if so, what, if any, information about his or her birth parents is accessible thereafter. Contrast the different legal approaches taken in Russia (para. 11.31), Scotland (para. 12.21) and the Unites States (para. 14.41).

[239] J. Triseliotis, *In Search of Origins* (London: Routledge and Kegan Paul, 1973); J. Goldstein, A. J. Solnit and A. Freud, *Beyond the Best Interests of the Child* (New York: Free Press, 1st edn 1973, revised edn 1979).

[240] Article 7(1).   [241] Article 8(1).   [242] Article 21.

children.[243] Indeed, having that knowledge is a prerequisite to being aware that there is further information to be sought,[244] and research with donor children indicates that they favour disclosure.[245] Particular sensitivity to religious or cultural factors is often called for in this context.[246] None of our jurisdictions gives the child that first 'right to know' – that he or she is, indeed, a donor child. However, a number of them permit donor children who are aware of their status access to identifying information about the donor.[247] In each, the legislation applies only to children born after it came into effect and, for the time

---

[243] A. Bissett-Johnston, 'The Child's Identity', in A. Cleland and E. E. Sutherland (eds.), *Children's Rights in Scotland*, 2nd edn (Edinburgh: W. Green, 2001); J. M. Masson and C. Harrison, 'Identity: Mapping the Frontiers', in N. V. Lowe and G. Douglas (eds.), *Families Across Frontiers* (The Hague: Nijhoff Publishers, 1996); J. Fortin, *Children's Rights and the Developing Law*, 3rd edn (Cambridge University Press, 2009), pp. 468–80. See further, J. R. Spencer and A. Du Bois-Pedain, *Freedom and Responsibility in Reproductive Choice* (Oxford: Hart Publishing, 2006); R. J. Blauwhoff, *Foundational Facts, Relative Truths: A Comparative Law Study on Children's Right to Know Their Genetic Origins* (Antwerp: Intersentia, 2009).

[244] A. Bainham, 'What is the Point of Birth Registration?' (2008) 20(4) *Child and Family Law Quarterly* 449.

[245] A. McWhinnie, 'Should Offspring from Donated Gametes Continue to be Denied Knowledge of their Origins and Antecedents?' (2001) 16 *Human Reproduction* 807 (discussing the harm that can result from deceiving the child about such a fundamental matter). See also D. R. Beeson, P. K. Jennings and W. Kramer, 'Offspring Searching for their Sperm Donors: How Family Type Shapes the Process' (2011) 26(10) *Human Reproduction* 1093 (study of 741 donor insemination offspring recruited through the Donor Sibling Registry, collecting data on family composition, offspring's feelings regarding the method of their conception, communication within families, donor anonymity and their search for their donors. The sample indicated a desire for greater openness and contact with their donor). Working with a number of others, Susan Golombok has carried out empirical research on attitudes of parents of donor children to disclosure and the donor children's well-being and reported reactions where disclosure has taken place. The children appear to be socially and emotionally well adjusted and mothers of donor children expressed greater warmth towards their children than did mothers of naturally conceived children: S. Golombok *et al.*, 'Families with Children Conceived by Donor Insemination: A Follow-Up at Age Twelve' (2002) 73(3) *Child Development* 952. It appears that parents are still reluctant to disclose the fact of donor insemination to the child, with 39 per cent of parents in one study reporting that they were inclined to tell their children and the remainder not inclined to do so: E. Lycell *et al.*, 'School-aged Children of Donor Insemination: a Study of Parents' Disclosure Patterns' (2005) 20(3) *Human Reproduction* 810.

[246] For examples, see Israel (paras. 6.22–6.24) and New Zealand (para. 9.29).

[247] The Netherlands (8.26), New Zealand (para. 9.29), Norway (para. 10.28) and Scotland (para. 12.21). In Canada, see para. 3.25 below, discussing *Pratten* v. *British Columbia (A.G.)*, 2011 BCSC 656. For the varied position in the United States, see para. 14.42 below.

being, the rights of donors who were promised anonymity are trumping the child's right to know. The release of, sometimes very limited, non-identifying information is permitted in some countries,[248] while donor children have no right of access to this information in others.[249]

[248] See, for example, South Africa (para. 13.25) and Israel (paras. 6.23 and 6.27).
[249] See, for example, China (para. 4.12) and Russia (para. 11.31).

2

Australia

The certain uncertainty

FRANK BATES

A   Introduction

2.1   As will become apparent, the condition of Australian family law, in almost all of its central areas, is in a state of genuine uncertainty. By way of introduction, it should be said that this state of affairs has been brought about because the major family law statute, the Family Law Act 1975, has been subject to continual amendment that has often lacked a sound conceptual basis. The Family Law Act 1975 has been amended, sometimes significantly, no fewer than eighty times from its coming into force in 1976. In addition, there has been a tendency for courts, particularly the Family Court of Australia,[1] to undermine particular legislative goals. The tensions between the aims of the original framers of the Family Law Act and traditional legal processes were doubtless in part responsible for that state of affairs and, as will be seen, tensions continue to exist between legislators, policymakers and courts.[2] It would be struthious indeed for any commentator to attempt to gloss over these difficulties and the uncertainties to which these forces have given – and continue to give – rise. The thesis which this commentary seeks to pursue is that, since the 1975 Act came into force at least, the pressures to which the law and its administrators have been subjected have led to a state of uncertainty about both the present and the future. Put another way, neither the legislators nor the administrators seem to be aware of what the other wants or, indeed, is likely to do.

2.2   It may, though, be possible to detect some more general trends, though it must be said that, very often, there may be a reaction against those trends from time to time that makes them difficult to discern

---

[1]   The Court was created by the Family Law Act 1975, Part IV.
[2]   See para. 2.55 below.

accurately. However, the ensuing discussion seeks to point to legislative and curial attempts to emphasise equality of roles within the family structure, both formalised and unformalised. There has also been recognition of culture and the role of other extended family members, but at the same time, unlike many other common law jurisdictions, the federal government has hitherto firmly set its face against same-gender marriage. It may be that some of the tensions that have surfaced are the product of an ambivalent view of human rights. Thus, the debate over a federal Bill of Rights continues and Australia's attitude to the United Nations Convention on the Rights of the Child is more than a little uncertain.[3]

Historical roots, sources and law reform

Historical roots

2.3   Australian family law is, of course, rooted in the common law tradition and, at any rate until 1975, its origins in English law were quite apparent. The Commonwealth of Australia, created in 1901,[4] adopted a federal model, with the six separate former colonies (New South Wales, Victoria, Queensland, Western Australia, South Australia and Tasmania) becoming separate states in a federation. Originally, family law was a state matter with each separate state having their own systems, all of which were solidly based in a family law derived from England and its ecclesiastical courts.[5]

Sources

2.4   In terms of independent law-making, an important landmark was achieved in 1959 when the Commonwealth Matrimonial Causes Act was passed by the Parliament of the Commonwealth of Australia, even though it did not come into effect until two years later. It provided one law relating to matrimonial causes for the whole of Australia for the first time. Not perhaps altogether surprisingly, that Act gave rise to an outburst of self-adulation. In the words of a leading practitioner's text, the

---

[3]   See *B (Infants) and B (Interventions) and the Minister for Immigration Affairs* (2003) FLC 93–141. For comment, see M. Otlowski and M. Tsamenyi, 'Parental Authority and the United Nations Convention on the Right of the Child: Are the Fears Justified?' (1992) *G Aust J. Fam. L.* 137; J. N. Turner, 'Panic Over Children's Rights' (1996) 1(2) *Newcastle L R* 56; F. Bates, '"Out of Everywhere into Here" – The Disparate Bases of Children's Rights in Australia' (2007) 15 *Asia Pacific LR* 235.

[4]   Commonwealth of Australia Constitution Act 1900.

[5]   See A. Dickey, *Family Law*, 5th edn (Sydney: Law Book Co., 2007).

Act was 'widely acknowledged to reach a peak of legislative excellence unequalled in the countries which have inherited the English tradition as to marriage and divorce'.[6] The Act was largely concerned with divorce and its consequences. It created fourteen grounds for divorce,[7] all but one of which was based on the notion of matrimonial offence. Even within that dubious framework, the grounds were less than coherent. Thus, one act of adultery, without more, was grounds for divorce,[8] whereas cruelty was required to be *habitual* and to be persisted in for not less than one year.[9] Inevitably, given the common law tradition, the legislation soon attracted an encrustation of case law, which did little to detract from its original nature. However, by means of the grounds which permitted divorce after five years' separation, it did open the way for the Family Law Act 1975, which removed the fault basis for dissolution of marriage.[10] Contemporaneous with the Matrimonial Causes Act coming into force in 1961, the Commonwealth Parliament passed the Marriage Act 1961, which, with little amendment, has remained in force since then.[11] Both the Marriage Act and the Family Law Act apply to all Australia.

Law reform

2.5   The significant number of amendments to the Family Law Act suggests that there is a fairly sophisticated system of law reform. By far the most important law reform body is the Family Law Council, established by that statute.[12] One can confidently make that statement because of the successful implementation of many of its recommendations.[13]

Dispute resolution

2.6   Given the common law origins of Australian family law, it is not wholly surprising that the major method of dispute resolution is through the courts, especially the Family Court of Australia. However, it should

---

[6] P. Toose, R. Watson and D. J. Benjafield, *Australian Matrimonial Law and Practice* (Sydney: Law Book Co., 1998), p. vii.

[7] Matrimonial Causes Act 1959 s. 28.

[8] *Ibid.*, s. 28(a).

[9] *Ibid.* at s. 28(d). For comment, see F. Bates, 'Habitual Cruelty – The Right Approach?' (1973) 47 *ALJ* 178.

[10] See para. 2.42 below.

[11] That Act has only been amended nineteen times since coming into force.

[12] Family Law Act 1975, s. 115.

[13] See B. Hughes, *The Family Law Council 1976–1996: A Record of Achievement* (Canberra: AGPS, 1996).

be borne in mind that states may, should they choose, create their own Family Courts.[14] The only state so to do, largely for topographical reasons, is Western Australia, where the state court exercises both Commonwealth and state jurisdiction in family law matters in that state. In addition to those courts, the Federal Magistrates Court has jurisdiction in all matrimonial causes as well as matters of international family law.[15] That court was set up to provide a cheaper and speedier alternative in family law matters to the Family Court of Australia, though appeals lie to the Full Court of the Family Court of Australia.

2.7 As well as these formal means of dispute resolution, the Family Law Rules 2004[16] have introduced new procedures with the aim of attempting to ensure that litigation is regarded as a last resort. The Rules specify five procedures for the resolution of family disputes informally – arbitration, conciliation, counselling, mediation and negotiation.[17] The Rules also state that a party must have a good reason for instituting proceedings in the Family Court without first undertaking an appropriate alternative procedure.[18]

2.8 In the context of informal dispute resolution procedures, community-based Family Relationship Centres have been created, which provide many of the conciliation and counselling services that were previously provided through the Family Court of Australia. These centres were regarded by the then federal government as the 'cornerstone' of the new family law system that they were seeking to impose. They were to 'offer individual, group and joint sessions to help separating families make workable arrangements for their children without having to go to court'.[19] They also provided information, advice and referral to families in a much wider range of circumstances than separation. However, as they were operated generally by established groups outside the Family Court, they have been perceived as fragmenting the provision

---

[14] Family Law Act, s. 41.

[15] Federal Magistrates Act 1999. It also has jurisdiction in a wide variety of other federal matters including consumer protection law, trade practices law, human rights and immigration law. For further discussion of its jurisdiction, see Dickey, *Family Law*, pp. 106ff.

[16] Family Law Rules 2004.

[17] Schedule 1, Part 1, Part Z.

[18] Rule 1.05(2). 'Good reason' would include family violence, the need for urgent relief or an especially intractable dispute. A genuine effort to resolve the proceedings must have been made to utilise these procedures.

[19] Family Relationships Online, available at: www.familyrelationships.gov.au.

of services.[20] The Court continues to maintain such services. It may be that the emphasis in dispute resolution is moving away from litigation per se, but it may be some time before such change becomes clearly apparent.

B   Children in the family setting and state intervention

Defining and classifying children

2.9   The Family Law Act 1975 provides that, for the purposes of Part VII of the Act, the term 'child' includes an adopted or stillborn child.[21] However, it goes on to state that, for the purposes of Part VII, Division 6, Subdivision E, the word means a person who is under the age of 18, including an adopted child.[22] There is some dispute as to how far that view is to be taken. Thus, in *In the Marriage of Blair and Jenkins*[23] it was stated that the word 'child' in the Family Law Act was limited to children under the age of 18 years. However, that dictum seems at odds with the decision of the High Court of Australia in *Dougherty* v. *Dougherty*,[24] where a property order was made in favour of a child who was significantly older than that age. In more general terms, it is clear from *In the Marriage of F*[25] that the word 'child' does not include a child yet to be born.

2.10   In addition to the definition of 'child', the Act provides a definition of 'child of a marriage',[26] which includes a child of a husband and wife born before the marriage, a child adopted since a marriage either by the husband or the wife together or by either of them with the consent of the other, and a child born as a result of an artificial conception procedure who is deemed to be a child of the marriage by reason of section 60H(1) of the statute. A child will remain a child of a marriage for the purposes of the Act regardless of whether the marriage is terminated by dissolution or annulment, in Australia or elsewhere, or the marriage has been terminated by the death of a party to it.[27]

---

[20] Senate Legal and Constitutional Legislation Committee, Parliament of Australia, Provisions of the Family Law Amendment (Shared Parental Responsibilities) Bill 2005 (Canberra, AGPS, 2006).

[21] Section 4(1). Part VII deals with 'Children'.

[22] The part of the legislation that deals with 'Obligations under parenting orders relating to taking or sending children from Australia'.

[23] (1988) 90 FLR 182, at 187.   [24] (1987) 163 CLR 278.

[25] (1989) FLC 92–031.   [26] Family Law Act 1975, s. 60F.

[27] Family Law Act 1975 s. 60F(2).

2.11   For all practical purposes in modern Australian family law notions of legitimacy and illegitimacy are irrelevant, although it should be said that that process was sporadic and achieved through legislative action on a state-by-state basis in the 1970s as a response to perceived changes in social attitudes.

Recognising parentage and other family ties

2.12   It is clear that, in defining 'child' and 'child of the marriage' as outlined above, the Family Law Act 1975 provides a clear indication of who will be regarded as a child's parent in the marital context. In the case of an unmarried couple, the Family Law Act provides that if a child is born to a woman who cohabited with a man at any time between 20 and 44 weeks before the child's birth, the man will be presumed to be the father.[28] As regards parentage testing, the Act empowers the court to make an order, where the parentage of a child is in question, requiring any person to give such evidence as is material to the issue[29] and to make orders for the carrying out of parentage testing procedures if the parentage of a child is in issue in the relevant proceedings.[30] Should a party refuse to take part in such procedures, it is clear from the decision of the High Court of Australia in *G* v. *H*[31] that an adverse inference may be drawn from such a refusal, though any such inference will depend on the circumstances of the particular case and must be consistent with the evidence and findings.

2.13   Where a child is born as the result of artificial conception procedures,[32] and, at the time that procedure is carried out, the woman was married or was living in an unformalised (de facto) relationship with a man, the child will be regarded as the child of the woman and the man provided that the procedure was carried out with their consent.[33] Consent will be presumed unless the contrary is proved on the preponderance of probabilities.[34] In addition, it would appear, notably from the case of *Re Patrick*,[35] as well as from the legislative provisions themselves, that a

---

[28] Family Law Act 1975, s. 69.   [29] Family Law Act 1975, s. 69V.
[30] Family Law Act 1975, s. 69W.   [31] (1994) FLC 92–504.
[32] The Family Law Act 1975, s. 4(1), defines 'artificial conception procedure' as including artificial insemination and the implantation of an embryo into the body of a woman. That provision is clearly inclusive and hence includes procedures conducted privately. See *B* v. *J* (1996) FLC 92–716.
[33] Family Law Regulations 1984, Sch. 7.
[34] *In the Marriage of P* (1997) FLC 92–700.
[35] (2002) FLC 93–096.

person who donated products for a procedure will not be regarded as a parent for the purposes of the Family Law Act.

Delivering parenting

2.14 Parental responsibilities are governed by the Family Law Act 1975, which was amended extensively in 1995[36] and again in 2006.[37] The 1995 amendments derived from recommendations of the Family Law Council,[38] and their object was:

> to ensure that children receive adequate and proper parenting to help them achieve their full potential and to ensure that parents fulfil their duties and meet their responsibilities concerning the care, welfare and development of their children.[39]

The statute went on to state that the principles underlying those objects were, first, that children had the right to know and be cared for by both of their parents, regardless of whether those parents are married, separated, have never married or have never lived together.[40] Second, it was stated that children have a right of contact on a daily basis with both of their parents, as well as other people who are significant to their care, welfare and development.[41] In addition, the Act also required that parents shared duties and responsibilities regarding the care, welfare and development of their children[42] and that they should agree regarding the future parenting of the children.[43] All of those objectives and principles were subject to the overriding criterion of the child's best interests.[44]

2.15 'Parental responsibility' itself is defined as 'all the duties, powers, responsibility and authority which, by law, parents have in relation to children'.[45] It seems from the decision of the High Court of Australia in *Secretary, Department of Health and Community Services* v. *JWB and SMB*[46] that the expression 'by law' to be found in that definition refers to those powers which have traditionally been recognised as such at common law, although modified by legislation. What is instantly clear, though, is

---

[36] The Family Law Reform Act 1995 added a new Part VII into the 1975 Act.
[37] The reforms of 2006 are discussed in the context of intra-family disputes at paras. 2.25–2.31 below.
[38] Family Law Council, *Patterns of Parenting After Separation* (Canberra, AGPS, 1992).
[39] Family Law Act 1975, s. 60B(1). [40] *Ibid.*, s. 60B(2)(a).
[41] *Ibid.*, s. 60B(2)(b). [42] *Ibid.*, s. 60B(2)(c). [43] *Ibid.*, s. 60B(2)(d).
[44] *Ibid.*, s. 65E. [45] *Ibid.*, s. 61B. [46] (1992) 175 CLR 218 at 290.

the circular nature of the definition: that is, 'responsibility' defined in terms of 'responsibilities'.

2.16   Any starting point for a discussion of the notion of parental responsibility must, necessarily, be the decision of the House of Lords in *Gillick* v. *West Norfolk and Wisbech Area Health Authority*,[47] on which much has been written.[48] In that case, as is well known, Lord Scarman made the landmark comment that 'Parental rights yield to the child's right to make his own decisions when he reaches a sufficient understanding and intelligence to be capable of making up his own mind on the matter requiring decision'.[49] From an Australian standpoint, that dictum was important because it was adopted by the High Court of Australia in the *JWB* case.[50] There, the child's parents had sought to have a sterilisation procedure carried out on their intellectually disabled daughter, not because it was necessary for therapeutic purposes (that is, to alleviate an immediate medical condition), but because it was thought to be in the child's best interests. A majority of the High Court of Australia held that a parent or guardian could not authorise such a procedure and that the leave of the court, normally the Family Court of Australia, was required. The Court was at pains to emphasise that Lord Scarman's principle was as applicable to *JWB* as to any other child.[51] Both *Gillick* and *JWB* represent significant milestones on the road to increased limitations on parental rights, at any rate to the extent that it existed in earlier cases.[52] These decisions, notably *JWB*, mean that there is likely to be a de facto greater recognition of children's rights. However, it would be erroneous to draw too global a conclusion from it in the light of the factual situation and the specific approach adopted by the High Court.

Intra-family disputes

2.17   Allusion has already been made to the proliferation of amendments to legislation and the tension that has emerged between the results of that process and the courts' interpretation of the legislation.[53] Where divorcing or separating parents are in dispute over their children, these

---

[47]   [1986] AC 112.

[48]   See J. M. Eekelaar, 'The Emergence of Children's Rights' (1986) 6 *Oxf. J. Legal S.* 161.

[49]   *Gillick*, [1986] AC 112, p. 186.   [50]   (1992) 175 CLR 218, at 237ff.

[51]   *Ibid.* at 238ff.

[52]   For comment, see F. Bates, 'Redefining the Parent/Child Relationship: A Blueprint' (1977) 12 *UWALR* 518.

[53]   Para. 2.1 above.

difficulties become clearly apparent. The development of the Family Law Act 1975, Part VII,[54] has seen, between the Act's inception and the present day, a great deal more specificity as well as a doctrinal shift from balancing the competing interests of parents to a rather greater focus on children's rights and, more noticeably, towards cooperative parenting subsequent to separation. Whether that trend will continue remains to be seen. Thus, in 1987 the Act provided that, in proceedings with respect to the custody, guardianship or welfare of, or access to a child, 'the court shall regard the welfare of the child as the paramount consideration'.[55] In so doing, courts were required to consider the child's wishes and to give them such weight as was appropriate in the circumstances of the case,[56] and was required to make orders which would be least likely to lead to the institution of further proceedings.[57] Perhaps most importantly, courts were only required to take six particular matters into account.[58] Apart from one open-ended concluding factor, the six factors emphasised parental capacity overlaid by an apparent requirement of relationship stability. Yet the law, as it stood in 1987, was notable for its lack of tendentiousness, which sharply contrasts with the situation today.

2.18　Inevitably in a structure of that kind, there were some apparent omissions. Thus, for example, there was no provision that related to the conduct of the parents. Hence, in *In the Marriage of Smythe*[59] it was argued that the person who was responsible for the breakdown of the marriage should not, in general, be entitled to seek custody. That view was not accepted by the Full Court of the Family Court of Australia and Evatt CJ and Asche J were of the view that there was:

> no justification for saying that if all the factors relevant to the decision were evenly balanced some other factor must be decisive of the issue … Such factors should be treated as being of minor or no significance when set alongside the children's welfare.[60]

---

[54]　See para. 2.9 above.

[55]　Family Law Act 1975, s. 64(1).　[56]　*Ibid.*, s. 64(1)(b).　[57]　*Ibid.*, s. 64(1)(6a).

[58]　*Ibid.*, s. 64(1)(bb). These matters were: first, the nature of the relationship of the child with each of the parents and with other persons; second, the effect on the child of separation from either parent or other person; third, the desirability of, and the effect of, any change in the existing arrangements for the case of the child; fourth, the attitude to the child and the responsibilities of parenthood demonstrated by each parent; fifth, the capacity of either parent, or other person, to provide adequately for the needs of the child, including the child's emotional and intellectual needs and, finally, any other fact or circumstance, including the child's education and upbringing, which the court considers that the welfare of the child requires to be taken into account.

[59]　(1983) FLC 91–227.　[60]　*Ibid.* at 78, 286.

Thus, *Smythe* is illustrative of an approach to issues that were not specifically covered in the legislation.

2.19 But the issue of parental conduct is not the whole story by any means. In the context of the Act as a whole, which sought to remove fault as a basis for dissolution and, by analogy, from ancillary matters, *Smythe* represents a predictable response. With *Smythe* may be compared the later decision of the same Court in *K* v. *Z*,[61] where at issue was the relevance of the *happiness* of the children in question – a consideration of unquestionable relevance – but of which there was no mention in the legislation, even as amended. Paradoxically perhaps, the Court began by emphasising the necessity of the trial judge remaining wholly focused on the legislative provisions setting out the criteria that must be taken into account in deciding the course of action that was in accord with the children's welfare. At the same time, the Court noted that some 'most significant factors', which included children's contentment and happiness. The Court stated that:

> If both parents offer reasonable homes for a child with comparable standards of excellence in child care, the child's level of contentment and happiness in the one household as compared with that in the other must become a most significant, and almost determinant factor in deciding with which parent the child should live.[62]

Still more emphatically, it was stated that courts should avoid the spectre of placing or leaving a child in a situation of sadness and continued unhappiness where it was able to do so consistently with meeting the other, specified criteria.[63] Perhaps the best reading of *K* v. *Z* is that it does suggest a greater awareness of the rights of children then might have previously been the case. Whether that awareness was derived from the case's own facts or more globally is not easy to detect from the decision itself.

2.20 It is, of course, quite clear that there are some varieties of parental conduct which must be taken into account, regardless of the statutory provisions. Thus, for instance, in *M* v. *M*[64] Mullane J made the following comment regarding one such manifestation of parental conduct:

---

[61] (1997) FLC 92–337.
[62] *Ibid.* at 84, 657.
[63] In addition, the Court did not, as would ordinarily have been the case, order a new trial, but substituted its own discretion because there was clear evidence that the children were distressed by separation from their mother.
[64] (2000) FLC 93–006.

The father's abusive behaviour presents a multi-faceted danger for the children. There is a risk of violence to them and injury. There is a risk that violence poses when it involves living with fear, insecurity and vigilance.[65]

2.21 Surely, there can be no doubt that behaviour of the kind judicially described in *M* cannot be conducive to the welfare or the best interests of children, regardless of any other criteria which may or may not be specified by statute. The situation represented by *K* v. *Z* is less straightforward. A major problem may be that notions of contentment and happiness may be alien to the kind of criteria that are normally to be found in statutes for the guidance of courts in these matters. Further, there may be a perception[66] that the law is not well placed to deal with such emotional-sounding matters.

2.22 It may have been issues of the kind raised by these cases that caused the need for legislation to be more specific. The Family Law Reform Act 1995 amended the 1975 Act and, while the child's best interests remained the overriding criterion,[67] the 1995 Act enshrined the child's right to be cared for by both parents and to have daily contact with them, regardless of the parents' marital status. It also provided for the child to have contact with other people who are significant to their care, welfare and development and placed parents under an obligation to agree the arrangements for their children.

2.23 In one important case, *In the Marriage of B: Family Law Reform Act 1995*,[68] it was argued that the 1995 Act had sought to move the focus of Australian family law from being a balancing process between the parents to an emphasis on the basic rights found in section 60B. This meant that section 60B defined normative criteria and that the rights of children were superior to, and, in appropriate cases, extinguished any rights which parents might have had. The Full Court of the Family Court of Australia declined to accept that contention when they stated that:

> Where there are no countervailing factors the court may be expected to conclude that it is in the best interests of children to have as much contact with each parent as is practicable. However, to impose that approach in cases where the best interests of the children may not indicate that

---

[65] *Ibid.*, 87 and 159.
[66] See F. Bates, "'Which Comforts While It Mocks": Some Paradoxes in Modern Family Law' (2000) 4(2) *Newcastle L. Rev.* 17, at 18ff.
[67] Family Law Act 1975.   [68] (1997) FLC 92–755.

conclusion as appropriate is contrary to the legislation and contrary to the long established views of this and other courts which deal daily with the welfare or best interests of the child.[69]

2.24 There was an immediate, predictable and hostile reaction to *B*, but it was often based on an erroneous understanding of the case. First, it was suggested that the factual outcome of the case created a rule that permitted individual parents (usually mothers) to relocate with their children. No such rule was, in fact, created. Second, the decision did not focus on the interests of one parent to the detriment of the other or of the children. Third, the case did not mean that the objects and principles of the legislations were of no effect. Finally – and of most direct importance – *B* did not undermine the 1995 Act or, and this was a central objection to the decision, demonstrate a bias in favour of women. Nonetheless, those criticisms proved to be most influential and resulted in radical change in a short time.

2.25 The Family Law Amendment (Shared Parental Responsibility) Act 2006 was heralded by the, then, Commonwealth Government as representing the:

> most significant reforms to the family law system for 30 years. The initiatives represent a generational change in family law and aim to bring about a cultural shift in how family separation is managed – away from litigation and towards co-operative parenting solutions. The Government wants to change the way people think about family breakdowns and to improve outcomes for children.[70]

2.26 The philosophy of that latest legislation, which, once again, introduces a wholly new Part VII into the Family Law Act 1975, is to be found in a continuation of that governmental statement:

> The reforms also aim to ensure that as many children as possible grow up in a safe environment with the love and support of both of their parents … [T]he Government hopes that through these changes, more children will have a loving and healthy home environment, whether their parents are together or not, to help them achieve their full potential.[71]

2.27 These were, doubtless, laudable goals, but whether the 2006 legislation is achieving, or is capable of achieving, them is quite another matter.

---

[69] *Ibid.* at 84, 221.
[70] Quoted in Law Council of Australia, Family Law Section, *The New Family Law Parenting System* (Sydney: LCA, 2006).
[71] *Ibid.*

When the legislation is examined,[72] its true aims are readily apparent. As was the case with the 1995 amendments, section 60B(1) sets out the object of the Part, which is to ensure that the best interests of children are met by ensuring that, first, children have the benefit of both of their parents having a meaningful involvement in their lives, to the maximum extent that it comports with those best interests; second, by protecting children from physical and psychological harm, from being subjected to, or exposed to, abuse, neglect and family violence; third, by ensuring that children receive adequate and proper parenting to help them achieve their full potential and, last, by ensuring that parents fulfil their duties and meet their responsibilities concerning the care, welfare and development of their children.

2.28 Section 60B(2) then sets out the principles which underlie those objects, except where it would be contrary to the child's best interests, which still remain the paramount consideration.[73] There are five such principles. First, children have the right to know and be cared for by both parents regardless of whether the parents are married, separated, have never married or live together. Second, children have a right to spend time and communicate on a regular basis with both their parents, as well as with other people significant to their care, welfare and development, such as grandparents and other relatives. Third, parents should jointly share duties and responsibilities concerning the care, welfare and development of their children. Fourth, parents should agree about the future parenting of their children. Finally, aboriginal or Torres Strait Island children have a right to enjoy that culture, which includes[74] the right to maintain a connection with that culture and to have the support, opportunity and encouragement necessary to explore the full extent of that culture consistent with the child's age, developmental level and views to develop a positive appreciation of that culture, with other people who share the same culture. It may be possible to evaluate this provision in either or both of two ways to make it seem less obtuse; first, it may represent a respect for the cultural rights of children as represented in the United Nations Convention or, all being well, it may represent a greater cultural awareness in Australia at large.

---

[72] For more detailed commentary, see F. Bates, 'Blunting the Sword of Solomon – Australian Family Law in 2006', in B. Atkin (ed.), *International Survey of Family Law: 2008 Edition* (Bristol: Jordan, 2008), p. 21.

[73] Family Law Act 1975, s. 60CA.   [74] *Ibid.*, s. 60B(3).

2.29 The legislation, when taken as a whole, is extremely complex. However, there is no doubt that the leitmotiv of shared parenting permeates the new Part VII, which seems also to seek to further circumscribe judicial discretion. That latter aim is at clear odds with what the original Family Law Act 1975 was seeking to achieve. It was also likely to provoke a judicial reaction. That reaction, using other sections of the legislation as interpretive tools, was not slow in coming from the courts. Thus, in *Jacks and Sampson*[75] the Full Court of the Family Court of Australia used section 43(b) of the 1975 Act, which requires courts 'to give the widest possible protection and assistance to the family as the natural and fundamental group unit of society, particularly while it is responsible for the care and education of dependent children'. Whatever the questionable anthropological significance of that statutory provision may be, it does suggest that the judiciary have not wholly forgotten the aims of the original legislation.

2.30 An even stronger example can be seen in *MRR* v. *GR*,[76] where the High Court of Australia used other 2006 Act amendments to undermine the objects and principles therein enunciated. Section 65DAA(1)(b) of the Family Law Act 1975, as amended, requires courts, in the case of an order providing that parents are to have equal shared responsibility for the child, to consider whether the child spending equal time with each parent is 'reasonably practicable'. The High Court considered that the provision as a whole was 'concerned with the reality of the situation of parents and the child not whether it is desirable that there can be equal time spent by the child with each parent'.[77] The relevant paragraph, they thought, required a practical assessment of whether equal time with each parent was feasible. Hence, the Federal Magistrate, who had made the initial determination, was obliged to consider the circumstances of the parties, particularly the primary carer mother, in determining whether equal time parenting was reasonably practicable.

2.31 It may be possible simply to treat *MRR* v. *GR* as a decision based solely on the facts of the case itself. On that basis, no legitimate criticism of the decision is really possible. On the other hand, it is very likely that *MRR* v. *GR* has broader significance. By using a relatively minor provision in radical legislation so as to frustrate the stated aims of the 2006 legislation at large, the High Court may well have made an equally

---

[75] (2008) FLC 93–387.   [76] (2010) FLC 93–424.   [77] *Ibid.*, pp. 84 and 505.

radical statement about the legislation itself. Yet, undesirable in general terms as such a course may seem to be, the reality may be different. The 2006 amendments were very much the product of intensive political lobbying on the part of organisations representing male interests, which received sympathetic audience from within the government at the time. This is a doubly unfortunate situation. Supporters of these radical amendments might argue that one of their aims is to seek to prevent the disempowerment of male parties and, thus, to equalise the roles of parents. However, it may simply have had the effect of disempowering female parties.[78] An especially unfortunate instance, it has been suggested, is s. 11AB of the Act, which was included in 2006 amendments, though only principally concerned with the major thrust. This provided that, if the court is satisfied that a party to the proceedings has knowingly made a false allegation or statement in the proceedings, the court must order that party to pay some or all of the costs of another party, or parties, to the proceedings. This relatively little-known provision has been perceived as a deliberately aimed deterrent to women litigants to make untruthful allegations of violence and, it is claimed, assumes them to be innately dishonest. Given the status of the Court that decided *MMR* v. *GR*, the case may go some way towards undermining the ethic which underlies the 2006 amendments to the Family Law Act 1975. At the same time, emphasis on the practicality of their provisions ought not to be underestimated.

Child protection and state intervention

2.32 Jurisdiction in child protection matters is divided between the federal government and the states. Although the Family Law Act 1975 Part VII empowers Commonwealth courts to make a range of orders aimed at the protection of children, intervention by state courts and bodies is also necessary. In general, state legislation is based on the principal that intervention is justified if the child is in need of *care and protection*. A variety of orders are available under this legislation. Such legislation, in accordance with Art. 9 of the United Nations Convention on the Rights of the Child, is drafted so as to ensure that a child is not removed from his or her family without appropriate justification.

---

[78] For comment, see H. Rhoades and S. B. Boyle, 'Reforming Custody Laws: A Comparative Study' (2004) 18 *Int. J. Law Policy and the Family* 119.

C   Adult relationships

The relationships

2.33   The Family Law Act 1975 has been, and essentially continues to be, focused on marriage, its dissolution and the consequence of its dissolution, with courts exercising jurisdiction under the Act being directed to have regard to 'the need to protect the institution of marriage as the union of a man and a woman to the exclusion of all others voluntarily entered into for life'.[79] There are various matters that arise from that definition. First, it is not a description that is by any means novel, being originally devised in all but identical terms by Lord Penzance in 1866 in the case of *Hyde* v. *Hyde and Woodmansee*.[80] Second, it was not until 2004 that it was incorporated into the definition section of the Marriage Act 1961,[81] apparently at the behest of the then prime minister. Third, the use of the word 'union' implies an element of formalisation. Fourth, reference to 'a man' and 'a woman' implies that marriage is monogamous and heterosexual. The requirement that marriage be 'for life' suggests that marriage cannot be entered into for a limited period of time. As will become clear, inroads have been made into many aspects of the definition. So, for example, the formalities that are required by the Marriage Act are not very formal.[82]

2.34   As in many other jurisdictions, the issue of same-sex relationships has attracted the attention of policymakers and politicians and the debate continues in Australia. The amendment to the Marriage Act, importing the substance of Lord Penzance's definition discussed above, was undoubtedly one response. The Family Law (De Facto Financial Matters and Other Measures) Act 2008 is another. That legislation provides for the majority of both heterosexual and same-sex de facto couples to have matters relating to finance and property dealt with under the Family Law Act 1975.[83] A de facto relationship is defined as existing between two persons where they are neither married to each other[84] nor 'related by family' and 'having regard to all the circumstances of the relationship, they have

---

[79] Family Law Act 1975, s. 43.   [80] (1865–1869) LR 1 P & D 130.
[81] Marriage Act 1961, s. 5.   [82] *Ibid.*, s. 45(1).
[83] All Australian states, with the exception of South and West Australia, have referred power to the Commonwealth legislature.
[84] A de facto relationship can exist even if one of the persons is married to someone else or in another de facto relationship: Family Law Act 1975, s. 4AA(5)(b).

a relationship as a couple of living together on a genuine domestic basis'.[85] Given that formulation, it becomes necessary for courts and, perhaps more problematically, administrative agencies to determine whether the 'genuine domestic basis' exists. To assist in such a process, the Act sets out nine specific criteria,[86] which, according to a major commentary on the new regime,[87] derive from the decision of Powell J of the New South Wales Supreme Court in *Roy* v. *Sturgeon*.[88] This, it is submitted, is regrettable since the judicial formulation is highly redolent of social security legislation that was aimed at denying particular benefits, especially to women who were living in such relationships. Granted, the original has been modified in some respects and the original references to the procreation of children and the performance of household duties have been omitted, while reference to registration has been added.[89] No single factor will be determinative of the fact that a de facto relationship exists and the court may take other circumstances into account.[90] Taking the legislation as a whole, it would be fair to say that the Commonwealth legislation was not intending that registration of relationships, notably, same-sex relationships, approximate to marriage.[91]

Entering an adult relationship

2.35 There are relatively few restrictions on entry into marriage in Australia. As we have seen, same-sex marriage is not an option.[92] The extant substantive law related to the sexual identity of a party whose gender is less than determinative, either by reasons of the situation occurring naturally or as a result of surgical intervention. As regards the former

---

[85] Family Law Act 1975, s. 4AA(1).

[86] The criteria are the duration of the relationship, the nature and extent of their common residence; whether a sexual relationship exists; the degree of financial dependence or interdependence, and any arrangements for financial support, between them; the ownership, use and acquisition of their property; the degree of mutual commitment to a shared life; whether the relationship is or was registered under a prescribed law of a state or territory as a prescribed kind of relationship; the care and support of children; and the reputation and public aspects of the relationship: Family Law Act 1975, s. 4AA(2).

[87] Law Council of Australia, Family Law Section, *The New De Facto Regime: A Handbook* (Canberra: LCA, 2009), p. 52.

[88] [1986] 11 Fam LR 271, at 274.

[89] Family Law Act 1975, s. 4AA(2)(g).

[90] *Ibid.*, s. 4AA(3) and (4).

[91] Law Council of Australia, Family Law Section, *The New De Facto Regime: A Handbook*, p. 9.

[92] See para. 2.2 above.

situation, the leading decision is that of *In the Marriage of C and D (falsely called C)*,[93] where the respondent displayed characteristics that were both male and female, where it was held that the marriage was a nullity on the ground that the purported husband was neither male nor female but, rather, a combination of both. Today, that situation would, most probably, be resolved by surgical intervention.[94]

2.36 On the issue of the effect of surgical intervention, the leading authority is the decision of the Full Court of the Family Court of Australia in *Re Kevin*.[95] In that case the applicant had been born female, but had subsequently undergone hormone treatment and surgery, which had the effect of his being unable to function reproductively as a woman. He also lived and worked as a male and was regarded as such by his peers. He went through a ceremony of marriage with a woman and sought a declaration that the marriage was valid. The Full Court upheld the view of the trial judge that, as there was widespread acceptance of people who had undergone such procedures as being of their reassigned gender, the marriage was valid. The decision in *Re Kevin* is consistent with decisions from other areas of law.[96]

2.37 Another area where some restrictions do pertain to the freedom to enter into marriage relates to relationship. A marriage is void[97] where the parties are within a prohibited relationship,[98] such a relationship existing where the parties are ancestor or descendent or brother or sister of either the whole or half blood.[99] These provisions mean that marriages that were prohibited prior to 1975, such as those between uncle or aunt and niece or nephew and step-parent and stepchild, are now permitted.

2.38 As a general rule, the marriageable age for both genders is 18 years.[100] If either party is under that age, the marriage is void. However,

---

[93] (1979) 35 FLR 340. It was held that, in addition, the marriage was a nullity because the applicant wife had been mistaken as to the respondent's identity.

[94] See para. 2.36 below.   [95] (2003) FLC 93–127.

[96] In the area of criminal law, see *R* v. *Harris and McGuiness* (1988) A Crim R 146 and *R* v. *Cogley* [1989] VR 799. In the area of social security law, see *Secretary, Department of Social Security* v. *SRA* (1993) AAR 487. For comment on that case in context, see F. Bates, 'When Is a Wife …?' (1993) 7 *Aust J Fam L* 274.

[97] The concept of a voidable marriage was abolished by section 51 of the Family Law Act 1975.

[98] Marriage Act 1961, s. 23B(1)(b).

[99] *Ibid.*, s. 23B(2).

[100] Marriage Act 1961 s. 11, as amended in 1991.

it is possible for people under the age of 18 to marry. Persons of 16 years may apply to a judge[101] for an order authorising them to marry a particular person who is of marriageable age. An administrative inquiry follows and, if the judge finds that the circumstances of the case 'are so exceptional and unusual to justify the making of the order', she or he may make an order authorising the marriage.[102] The phrase 'exceptional and unusual' suggests that orders should only be made in extremely rare situations, though, in reality, the major criterion appears to be whether that judicial officer considers that the parties are likely to have a successful marriage. The clearest statement to that effect is to be found in *Re Z*,[103] where Joske J stated that:

> If a judge is likely to conclude on the evidence before him that it indicates that the marriage is likely to be a successful and happy marriage, in my opinion he is unable to say that this is 'out of the ordinary', and that it is 'exceptional and unusual' since so many marriages of people of the young age referred to in s. 12 have been absolute failures and doomed to failure from the start.[104]

That comment was implicitly adopted in *Re Willis*,[105] where it was held that the word 'so' in section 12(2)(b) meant 'sufficiently' rather that 'very' or 'extremely'. Once again, we have an illustration of the tensions between the aims of legislation and the approach of the courts towards the subject matter in question.

2.39   One issue that has caused difficulty in Australian law is that of lack of consent – or the 'voluntary' nature of marriage.[106] A marriage will be void due to the lack of real consent where apparent consent was obtained by duress or fraud; where the applicant was mistaken as to the identity of the other party or the nature of the ceremony performed; or where the applicant was incapable of understanding the nature and effect of the marriage ceremony.[107] It is the first of these grounds, and fraud, in particular, that has proved most problematic. The catalytic decision is that of Frederico J in *In the Marriage of Deniz*.[108] There, a young woman of Lebanese ancestry had been induced to go through a form of marriage by a Turkish visitor to Australia, whose real motive was gaining permanent residence in the

---

[101]   Applications are usually made to a judge of the Family Court of Australia, but may be made to a magistrate.

[102]   Marriage Act 1961, s. 12(1).

[103]   (1970) 15 FLR 420.   [104]   *Ibid*. at 422.

[105]   (1997) FLC 92–725.   [106]   Family Law Act 1975, s. 43(1)(a).

[107]   Marriage Act 1961, s. 23B(1)(d).   [108]   (1977) 31 FLR 114.

country. When the marriage collapsed, and on discovering the truth, the woman suffered a nervous breakdown and attempted suicide. Frederico J held that the marriage was void on the grounds of fraud as the consent had been obtained through a trick and the motives of the respondent were corrupt.[109] Whatever the merits of Frederico J's approach to the issue, the weight of authority in Australia is very much against him and the traditional view is represented by McCall J in *In the Marriage of Otway*,[110] who sought to emphasise that the statutory formulation had not intended to expand the meaning of the word 'fraud'. However, the structure of the legislation, as Frederico J suggested in *Deniz*,[111] does seem to imply that the meaning is more specific than in the older cases. At the same time, one must agree with Frederico J that the fraud must be one 'which goes to the root of the marriage contract'.[112] It is hard, it is submitted, not to see the fraud perpetrated in *Deniz* as doing precisely that.

Consequences of adult relationships

2.40   The consequences of marriage in Australian law have, as might have been expected, been a little confused by constitutional issues. First, the marriage power as found in section 51(xxi) of the Australian Constitution was given a wide interpretation by the High Court of Australia in *Attorney-General (Vic) v. The Commonwealth*,[113] where the suggestion that the jurisdiction related only to the circumstances of the ceremony itself was rejected and it was held that it covered all matters sufficiently connected with the marriage. Hence, it included the power to make laws relating to property and maintenance of parties to a marriage and regarding the custody, guardianship and maintenance of children of a marriage, although the divorce power, contained in section 51(xxii), created some other difficulties, notably in relation to terms such as 'matrimonial cause', 'parental right' and 'infants'. However, notably in the decision in *Russell v. Russell; Farrelly v. Farrelly*,[114] the High Court of Australia devised a workable solution in relation to jurisdiction under the Family Law Act 1975.

---

[109] In the judge's own words, *ibid.* at 117, he had used the unfortunate applicant as 'a tool of his own convenience'.

[110] (1987) FLC 91–807. See also, *In the Marriage of El Soukmani* (1989) 96 FLR 388; *In the Marriage of Osman and Moumali* (1989) 96 FLR 362; *Najjarin v. Houlayce* (1991) 104 FLR 403.

[111] (1977) 31 FLR 114.   [112] *Ibid.* at 117.

[113] (1962) 107 CLR 529.   [114] (1976) 134 CLR 495.

2.41 Jurisdiction under that Act is set out in section 4 in the definition of 'matrimonial cause' and refers to the following ten matters: divorce and nullity of marriage; declarations as to the validity of marriages, divorces or annulments; children; property; spousal maintenance; child support; injunctions; enforcement; overseas maintenance orders; and the Hague Convention on Civil Aspects of International Child Abduction. Apart from those issues strictly connected with the formal creation and dissolution of marriage, the final seven of the 2008 amendments to the Family Law Act apply as much to de facto couples as they do to de jure couples.[115]

Termination of relationships

2.42 A major focus of the Family Law Act 1975 is the termination of marriage, as well as the attendant consequences for children[116] and property.[117] The sole ground for divorce is 'that marriage has broken down irretrievably',[118] irretrievable breakdown being established:

> if, and only if, the court is satisfied that the parties separated and thereafter lived separately and apart for a continuous period of not less than 12 months immediately preceding the date of the application for the divorce order.[119]

2.43 The immediate question that arises from those provisions is the meaning of living 'separately'. The Full Court of the Family Court of Australia in *In the Marriage of Pavey*[120] opined:

> 'Separation' means more than physical separation – it involves the breakdown of the marital relationship (the *consortium vitae*). Separation can only occur where one or both of the spouses form the intention to sever or not to resume the marital relationship and act on that intention, or alternatively act as if the marital relationship has been severed.[121]

The Court went on to note that what comprises the *consortium vitae* will vary since marriage involves various elements, some or all of which may be present in a particular marriage. These elements included matters such as living under the same roof, sexual relations, mutual society and protection, recognition of the existence of the marriage by both spouses in

---

[115] See para. 2.34 above. [116] See para. 2.17 above.
[117] See para. 2.46 below. [118] Family Law Act 1975, s. 48(1).
[119] *Ibid.*, s. 48(2). Those subsections are modified by s. 48(3), which provides that 'A divorce order shall not be made if the court is satisfied that there is a reasonable likelihood of cohabitation being resumed'.
[120] (1976) 25 FLR 450. [121] *Ibid.* at 453.

public and private relationships and the nurture and support of any children of the marriage.

2.44   Although that description is helpful in various regards, of itself it does not remove the need for courts to have to make difficult decisions. Thus, in *In the Marriage of Tye*[122] the husband had left Australia in early 1975 to live and work overseas. He told his wife, who remained in Australia, that he would send for her when he had settled in his new home. Within a very short time after arriving there, the husband determined to leave his wife and told her by letter some two months later. The wife then filed an application for dissolution of marriage on 29 January 1976. It was clear that the requirements of section 48(2) would only be satisfied if the separation had occurred by 28 January 1975. Emery J held that the relationship could be brought to an end by a spouse's unilateral act, even if the intention had not been communicated to the other. The judge, rightly, in any view, was critical of the respondent husband's behaviour and suggested[123] that it was doubtful whether he had ever cared for his wife at all. However, given the husband's behaviour and the fact that the wife had instituted the proceeding, it was clear that there was no chance of the parties becoming reconciled.

2.45   Another, perhaps exceptional, situation is illustrated by the decision of Murray J in *In the Marriage of Lane.*[124] There, the husband, a wealthy medical practitioner, continued to live in the same home as his wife despite his intention to separate from her. He gradually withdrew from her company, slept in a separate bedroom and required less in the way of domestic services. Although she had come to realise that the marriage was unhappy, his wife did not realise that the husband regarded it as being at an end. The husband was unsuccessful in his application for a divorce. The judge's reasons for dismissing the application were that the applicant had not completely withdrawn from cohabitation, nor had he appropriately communicated that he intended to end the marriage to his wife. Murray J described the situation in a witty and appropriate way, when she said that:

> Dr Lane presents as a kindly man who, although he had made up his mind, by at least 1974, that his marriage was finished and that he wanted to cut himself off from his wife could not bring himself to cut the umbilical cord grown out of the nearly 30 years of married life. He flourished the scissors

---

[122] (1976) 25 FLC 90–028.   [123] *Ibid.* at 75, 122.   [124] (1976) FLC 90–055.

and scraped at the tissues, but did not take the ultimate step of severance either through unequivocal conduct towards, or direct communication with his wife carrying out his intention to separate.[125]

Consequences of termination

2.46　Decisions such as *Tye* and *Lane* notwithstanding, the ground for divorce is now relatively settled and there are few cases that concern it. That, however, is not the case with matters concerning property distribution on divorce. It is also in that area of curial activity that tensions between legislation and interpretation are apparent. The Family Law Act 1975 gives courts a general power to alter the property interests of spouses or, if one spouse has become bankrupt, to alter property interests in the property that has vested in the trustee in bankruptcy,[126] subject to the qualification that a court 'shall not make an order under this section unless it is satisfied that, in all the circumstances, it is just and equitable to make the order'.[127] The relevant provision goes on to set out seven considerations that courts are required to take into account when contemplating the order to make, these considerations being very largely concerned with the various contributions that have been made by the parties. There is further provision dealing with the assessment of maintenance and the court is provided with seventeen considerations to take into account, most of which are concerned with needs.[128]

2.47　In *In the Marriage of Hickey; Attorney-General (Cth) Intervener*[129] the Full Court of the Family Court of Australia stated that the court must take three initial steps when dealing with an application for an alteration in property interests. First, the court must ascertain the property owned by each party to the marriage at the time of the hearing. Second, it must value that property, taking into account the liabilities of the parties. Third, the court must exercise its discretion as to whether to make such an order and what order to make. As regards that final step, Nygh J stated, in *In the Marriage of Hirst and Rosen*,[130] that 'the reference in s. 79(40) to considerations of justice and equity is controlled by the factors set out in s. 79(4). It is, therefore, not an open sesame for the court to administer such justice as it thinks fit. That, indeed, would be a grievous error.'

[125] *Ibid.* at 75, 225.　　[126] Family Law Act 1975, s. 79(1).
[127] *Ibid.*, s. 79(2).　　[128] *Ibid.*, s. 75(2).　　[129] (2003) FLC 93–143.
[130] (1982) FLC 91–230 at 77, 251.

2.48 The question of 'contributions' has been especially productive of difficulty in recent Australian law. One especially graphic instance is provided by the decision of Thackray AJ in *Woollams* v. *Woollams*.[131] That complex case illustrates graphically that it is all but impossible to separate issues relating to contributions from other matters that go to making up the financial picture of the parties' marriage. It is also clear from *Woollams* that a major problem that has been experienced by Australian courts in dealing with cases involving distribution of property on dissolution of marriage is the multiplicity of variations of contribution, whether recognised by the considerations enumerated in statute or not, which may have to be taken into account. Thus, one matter that was raised in *Woollams* was the conduct of the husband. It may very well be that, in the light of section 79(2) and the process noted in *Hickey*,[132] conduct, especially of a financial nature, may not be wholly irrelevant, whatever may have been the aims of the original legislation. At the very least, the parties' conduct cannot be always kept out of the pattern that has been created by those factors. *Woollams* also suggests, rather strongly, that the issues that go to make up that pattern must be disentangled from one another. Thus, issues relating to contributions must be disentangled from those relating to needs, which must be disentangled from those relating to other substantive areas that may be a part of the pattern, such as, for example, superannuation. That must be done because different issues, whether derived from statute or case law, apply to each.

2.49 These difficulties are predictable because of the different ways in which couples organise their property and financial affairs and, in many cases, it may be extraneous factors that influence that organisation. Attempts to take those extraneous factors into account have led to amendments to the Family Law Act being concerned with particular issues, including financial agreements,[133] superannuation and the position of third parties.[134] As regards contributions, there are some specific issues, such as the relevance of 'special'[135] contributions or that the relative (and possibly different) contributions in their respective capacities

---

[131] (2004) FLC 93–195. For more detailed comment see F. Bates, 'Discretions, Contributions and Needs – Family Property in Australia' [2005] *Int. Fam. L.* 218.

[132] Discussed at para. 2.47 above.

[133] Family Law Act 1975, s. 90K.   [134] *Ibid.*, Part VIIIA.

[135] See, for example, the, admittedly exceptional, case of *Figgins* v. *Figgins* (2002) FLC 93–112. For comment, see F. Bates, '"Exceptional Contributions" by a Spouse in Australian Family Law – A Road Mistaken' [2003] *Int. Fam. L.* 176.

have not been fully worked out, perhaps because they lack a sufficiently clear doctrinal basis.

2.50   The issue of superannuation has caused Australian courts not inconsiderable difficulty in the years prior to 2001.[136] In that year the federal government sought to resolve the matter in a manner which, of itself, was not difficult conceptually, although the relevant legislative and regulatory package was.[137] Essentially, it sought to treat superannuation as property that was available for division between the parties.[138] Despite the difficulties, hitherto, one distinguished commentator[139] suggested that courts were able to find just and equitable outcomes in the majority of cases. That comment was important because of what was to occur after the changes of 2001 came into effect and a new Part VIIIB of the Family Law Act empowered the court to split parties' superannuation interests into whatever proportions are considered appropriate. It also permitted courts to make immediate orders in situations where, as not infrequently occurs, superannuation is the only financial interest of any real value. That power is important because, previously, courts were frequently required to order lengthy adjournments until interests became available for division.[140] It should also be noted that the courts are given wide powers to split superannuation interests,[141] though still subject to the 'just and equitable' requirements to be found in section 79(2) of the Family Law Act 1975.

2.51   Given all of that, the problems that attach to splitting of superannuation interests are not all that different from those attaching to division of assets generally. Thus, it is not wholly surprising that problems have arisen in connection with the relative weight to be given to the contributions made by the spouse before, during or even after the marriage.[142]

---

[136]   It is probably correct to say that no coherent approach was apparent; see the case of *Webber and Webber* (1985) FLC 91–648.

[137]   It comprises the Family Law Legislation (Superannuation) Act 2001, the Family Law Legislation (Superannuation) (Consequential Provisions) Act 2001; the Superannuation Industry Supervision Regulations and the Family Law (Superannuation) Regulations. Much of the detail is contained in that last set of regulations.

[138]   Hitherto, the courts had tended to treat it as a financial resource; see Family Law Act 1975, s. 79(4) and *In the Marriage of Crapp* (1979) FLC 90–615.

[139]   I. Kennedy, 'The Superannuation Reforms' (2001) 15(2) *Aust. Family Lawyer* 15, at 18.

[140]   See *In the Marriage of O'Shea* (1988) FLC 91–964.

[141]   Family Law Act 1975, s. 9MT.

[142]   The extent of the difficulty may be gauged from the fact that quite a number of the relevant cases were heard by the five-judge bench of the Full Court of the Family Court of Australia. This is, of itself, sufficiently rare that attention is drawn to the seriousness and difficulty of some of the issues involved.

In *Hickey* the Court had said that, as a superannuation interest was to be treated as property, it followed that it would be included in the list of property and valued at the first step of the procedure there outlined.[143] However, a wholly different approach was to be found in the decision of the Full Court of the Family Court of Australia in *Coghlan and Coghlan*,[144] where the majority of the five-judge bench were of the view that there was no mandate in Part VIIIB of the Act to treat superannuation interests in the way in which the Court in *Hickey* had done. The question then arose as to how a superannuation interest could be classified. In *Coghlan* the majority stated[145] that superannuation interests remained 'another species of asset', different from those contained in the definition section of the Family Law Act.[146] Still more strongly they sought to justify that view by reference to pre-2001 developments. It is clear that *Coghlan* is a most unhappy decision, a view that was accepted by O'Ryan J, who delivered a separate judgment, though he concurred in the eventual orders.[147] He did not accept that the *Hickey* decision was necessarily productive of unintended or irrational consequences, as had the majority. Conversely, he thought that the processes employed by the majority would not provide a clear guide for the way in which superannuation interests were to be treated and, hence, would provide undesirable uncertainty.

2.52   In addition to satisfying the courts that de facto relationships exist in particular circumstances, applicants must satisfy the courts that one of four supplementary requirements is satisfied. These are that the period, or total periods, of the relationship is at least two years; or that there is a child of the de facto relationship; or that the party to a relationship who is applying for the order or the declaration made 'substantial contributions' and a failure to make the order or declaration would result in a 'serious injustice' to the applicant; or that the relationship was registered under a prescribed law of a state or territory.[148] That last is important because the Act permits the Federal prescription of state and territory registration laws.[149] The effect of that provision is that, if a de facto relationship exists, the registration of relationships which are not marriages may lead to the creation of rights and obligations that are very similar to those arising

---

[143] (2003) FLC 93–143 at 78, 393.   [144] (2005) FLC 93–220.
[145] (2005) FLC 93–220 qt. 79, 642.   [146] Family Law Act 1975, s. 4(1).
[147] (2005) FLC 930229, at 79, 660.
[148] Family Law Act 1975, s. 90SB.   [149] Family Law Act 1975, s. 90SB(d).

from formal marriage.[150] Hence, same-sex couples who register their relationship under state or territory law will be in very much the same situation as married couples, in relation to orders involving finance and property, should their relationship break down. In this context, the prohibition on same-sex marriages begins, even if it does not already do so, to appear distinctly and foolishly discriminatory.

2.53 Australian family property law may well form something of a microcosm of the situation at large. Thus, it has been observed that Australian law has not coped especially well with matters such as contributions and superannuation, which are both issues that are of immediate importance. The basal premise of Australian family property dissolution law is a separate property system coupled with a significantly varying degree of judicial discretion. Some areas though, such as superannuation, are fairly highly regulated by statute. The system resembles a patchwork quilt, with a rather confused chameleon lost on it.

D   Conclusions

2.54 Drawing conclusions about the imperatives that have driven Australian family law to date and predicting its future direction has not been facilitated by recent, and relatively recent, changes to the statutory base of Australian family law. However, it is safe to say that at least some of the major changes to the philosophy, structure and content of the original Family Law Act 1975 cannot be regarded as having been massively successful. One common characteristic of change over the years in which the ever-changing Act has been in operation has been the erosion of judicial discretion by a continuing process of legislative specificity. This is a process that does not seem likely to be halted, given the controversy that the 2006 amendments to the Family Law Act have generated.

2.55 A good example of this process in provided by section 60CC of the Act, as amended in 2006, which sets out the 'additional considerations' that courts are required to take into account when deciding the best interests of the child. Thus, the subsection refers to 'the practical

---

[150] Law Council of Australia, Family Law Section, *The New De Facto Regime: A Handbook*, p. 12.

difficulty and expense of a child spending time with and communicating with a parent and whether that difficulty or expense will substantially affect the child's right to maintain personal relations and direct contact with both parents on a regular basis'.[151] The provision also speaks of 'the maturity, sex, lifestyle and background (including lifestyle, culture and traditions) of the child and of either of the child's parents, and any other characteristics of the child as the court thinks are relevant'.[152] These provisions are specific in their structure but, at the same time, are not specific in their possible application. Thus, the first-quoted provision might very well have been aimed at discouraging relocation by one parent with the child. Indeed, given the criticisms that were made of the decisions in *In the Marriage of B: Family Law Reform Act 1995*,[153] that very well may be so. However, it is not immediately clear. The second example is less readily explicable, because specific provision is made elsewhere in relation to Aboriginal and Torres Strait Islander children.[154] It may be that the provision might be appropriately used in respect of children with disabilities, but, if that is the case, it should have been more specifically stated. At the same time, judicial discretion has been restrained by the fact that section 60CC(3) of the Act contains no less than thirteen such considerations. It may be that this greater specificity stems from an attempt to make family law more legalistic than it actually is, or indeed should be. Dewar's description of the issue is surely all too correct when he writes that academics in other areas regard family law as inherently inferior because it represents 'a falling away from the rigorous discipline of common law reasoning into a discretionary gloop that is beneath serious intellectual endeavour'.[155]

2.56   Yet there is a different ambience when matters relating to finance and property are concerned. In Australia the Commonwealth legislature dealt specifically with areas where the generally dispositive provisions are perceived to have operated less than satisfactorily. In turn, this suggests that Australia's legislative policymakers are seeking to do justice

---

[151] Family Law Act 1975, s. 60CC(3)(e).
[152] R. Chisholm, 'Assessing the Impact of the Family Law Reform Act 1995' (1996) 10 *Aust. J. Fam. L.* 177.
[153] See para. 2.23 above.
[154] Family Law Act 1975, s. 60CC(3)(h).
[155] J. Dewar, 'The Concepts, Coherence and Contract of Family Law', in P. B. H. Birks (ed.), *Examining the Law Syllabus: Beyond the Core* (Oxford University Press, 1994), p. 83.

in particular cases, rather than to provide predictability or a coherent, policy-based framework. It should also be said that these provisions have largely remained unaltered, except insofar as other statutory amendments have affected them. This, again, may suggest how the process of change in Australian family law may continue to develop. Throughout this commentary, a consistent theme has been the tension between changes made by the legislature and the reaction of the courts towards those changes. In view of prior experience, it may very well be that further amendments which will eventuate, especially in the area of parent and child, are likely to be even more specific than has been hitherto the case. More specifically still, a groundswell of opinion has arisen that regards the protection of children from violence as being more important than cooperative parenting, which is the fulcrum of the 2006 amendments. It may also be that the protection of the physical integrity of women, and of their rights, may receive greater legislative priority than it has done in the recent past.

2.57 Much legislative response appears to have been reactive, rather than proactive – even though claims were made regarding the didactic and policy aims of the Family Law Reform Act 1995.[156] That, together with the other issues that have been canvassed in this chapter, makes the process of prediction rather difficult. That assertion seems to have been borne out in the area of parent and child. There was considerable criticism of the Family Law Reform Act 1975 when it was initially implemented, on the major ground that it was unnecessary.[157] Then, in response to the activities of pressure groups, the 2006 amendments came into being. It is not yet possible to make an accurate assessment of these amendments since, as early as September 2006, the Minister for Community Services in New South Wales, Australia's most populous jurisdiction, referred an inquiry into their operation to the Standing Committee on Law and Justice.[158] Yet, despite a change in federal government, change in relation to Part VII appears to have emanated from the courts.[159] It may be that the demands

---

[156] See R. Chisholm, 'Assessing the Impact of the Family Law Reform Act 1995' (1996) 10 *Aust. J. Fam. L* 177.

[157] See R. Ingleby, 'The Family Law Reform Act – A Practitioner's Perspective' (1996) 10 *Aust. J. Fam. L* 8.

[158] The impetus for that course appeared to have been a journalistic suggestion – see *The Age* (Melbourne) for 18 September 2006 – that abused women were being forced into mediation regardless of its suitability.

[159] See para. 2.24 above.

for equality that led to the amendments are now, and more accurately, perceived as delivering rather more than they promised and genuine priorities may now be asserting themselves.

2.58   Taken all in all, after what was perceived by many as the golden age heralded by the Family Law Act 1975, all one can fairly say is that the only future certainty is continuing uncertainty.

3

Canada

A bold and progressive past but an unclear future

CAROL ROGERSON

A   Introduction

3.1   Canadian family law has been the site of remarkable change and development over the past four decades as the law has responded to dramatic and ongoing shifts in family relationships and values. The current Canadian family law system is the result of periods of bold, sustained, systemic legislative reform combined with many piecemeal reforms as legislatures have responded to particular crises or been forced to act by courts. Since the coming into force of the Charter of Rights in 1982, human rights norms, in particular norms of equality, have significantly shaped the development of family law.

3.2   One of the distinguishing features of the modern Canadian family law system is the broad, functional approach that has been adopted in defining the family. There is widespread recognition of informal or de facto family relationships and Canada was among the first countries in the world to legalize same-sex marriage. In responding to the no-fault divorce revolution, Canadian law has placed a heavy emphasis on protecting vulnerable parties, and in particular has gone much further than many other jurisdictions in ameliorating the economic hardship experienced by women and children after marriage breakdown. Values of gender equality have had a significant role in shaping Canadian family law, understood substantively and not just formally.

3.3   While there is much that is very progressive and positive in the evolution of Canadian family law over the past four decades, one can also identify shortcomings and a number of difficult, unresolved issues that lie ahead. The Canadian federal structure complicates and inhibits systematic reform. While the best interests of children is firmly entrenched as a principle, the concept of children as rights holders has been slower to take hold and Canada has fallen short in its implementation of the United Nations Convention on the Rights of the Child (the 'UN Convention'). Aboriginal peoples are not well served by the existing family law system. Moreover, the period of active, sustained legislative engagement with family law issues ended, for the most part, in the mid 1990s as we entered an era of fiscal constraint, more ideological politics and growing legislative disinterest in family law issues.

3.4 Ongoing technological and social change has put new substantive issues on the table that require attention. One example is assisted reproduction. Another is an increasing number of issues raised by shifting patterns of immigration. Canada is a country of immigrants. However, the increasing number of immigrants coming from non-Western countries is raising difficult questions of how to balance Canada's constitutional commitments to multiculturalism and accommodation of cultural and religious minorities with the strongly secular values around which the Canadian modern family law system has been structured. Finally, the most challenging issues that lie ahead relate to the pressing need for systemic procedural and institutional reforms to provide more effective and efficient resolution of family law disputes and to remove the significant barriers that exist to accessing the family justice system.

Historical roots, sources and law reform

Historical roots and sources

3.5 Under Canada's federal system of government legislative power is divided between the federal government and ten provincial governments.[1] This complicates family law, which is an area of divided (or in some cases concurrent) jurisdiction. The federal government has power over marriage and divorce. The divorce power has been interpreted to include the power to legislate with respect to 'corollary relief' sought in the context of divorce – this includes custody and access, spousal support and child support, but not property division. The federal government also has jurisdiction over criminal law. The bulk of family law falls within the provincial jurisdiction over 'property and civil rights'. Provinces have exclusive jurisdiction over matrimonial property rights. In addition, each province has the power to enact its own laws governing custody, access, child support and spousal support that apply outside of

---

[1] Constitution Act 1867.

the divorce context (that is, in cases involving unmarried couples or married couples who have separated but are not seeking a divorce).

3.6 One result of the Canadian federal structure is significant diversity in family law across the country, although ameliorated to some degree by inter-jurisdictional copying and a largely unitary court system in which Supreme Court of Canada decisions provide some overarching guidance and uniformity. A further complicating factor is that Quebec, unlike the other nine provinces, is a civil law jurisdiction, the result of an earlier period of French colonization. Given space constraints, this chapter will focus on federal legislation where it exists and, in areas of exclusive provincial jurisdiction, examples will most often be drawn from Ontario, the largest common law province.

3.7 In 1982 Canada added the Charter of Rights – an entrenched bill of rights – to its constitutional framework. Since 1982 the Charter has been a significant factor shaping the development of family law. In some cases it has been successfully invoked to invalidate existing laws; in other cases it has operated indirectly by transforming the policy context within which legislation is developed. While the equality guarantees in s. 15 of the Charter have had the most dramatic impact, freedom of religion and the s. 7 rights of life, liberty and security are also implicated in the family law context. The 1982 constitutional amendments also included a guarantee of aboriginal rights.

3.8 Since the late 1960s family law has been an area of significant legislative reform. While pockets of common law and aboriginal customary law remain, the bulk of family law consists of fairly comprehensive modern statutes, each of which may have gone through one or more significant revisions. Modern Canadian family law has largely distanced itself from its religious origins, with a strong emphasis on the separation between religious and secular law. For example, a proposal in Ontario to allow for arbitration of family law disputes under sharia law was rejected, primarily because of concerns about gender equality, and in the course of resolving this issue explicit legislation was enacted precluding any faith-based arbitration of family law disputes.[2] However, as will be shown below, this is an area rife with tension and conflicting values, and in other cases

---

[2] The Ontario government appointed former Attorney General Marion Boyd to review the issue and make recommendations. Based on values of inclusion and respect for autonomy, her report recommended that faith-based arbitration, including sharia arbitration, be allowed with appropriate protections: see Marion Boyd, *Dispute Resolution in Family*

the separation between religious and secular law has not always been so neatly maintained.

Law reform

3.9 It is difficult to attribute the impetus for or direction of family law reform to a single central body or institution. Law reform commissions at the federal and provincial levels played a central role in creating the legal blueprint for the first wave of modernization of family law from the late 1960s through to the early 1990s. Over time their role has diminished and some commissions have been disbanded. The institutional locus of reform is now much more dispersed. In some cases reform is initiated by government departments that structure their own consultation processes. Faced with legislative inertia on many family law issues in recent years, courts have come to play a larger role in initiating change, either through reliance on the Charter or through the incorporation of shifting policy values into their interpretation of vaguely worded family law statutes. In addition, in some areas family law professionals have assumed primary responsibility for developing policy initiatives, including informal guidelines. Finally, the Uniform Law Conference of Canada, a volunteer organization, promotes the harmonization of provincial laws through the development of uniform acts.

Dispute resolution and access to justice

3.10 While courts remain the ultimate forum for the resolution of family law disputes, settlement is encouraged and the majority of cases are resolved short of a full trial. In many cases parties are able to reach agreement without resort to litigation, either on their own or with the assistance of lawyers or mediators. Interest in collaborative law is growing. Even if litigation is commenced, family court processes typically emphasize settlement through mechanisms such as judicially supervised case and settlement conferences.

Law: Protecting Choice; Promoting Inclusion (Report to the Attorney General of Ontario, December 2004) available online at www.attorneygeneral.jus.gov.on.ca/english/about/ pubs/boyd/fullreport.pdf. The Ontario government rejected these recommendations and in 2006 enacted legislation requiring that family law arbitrations be conducted entirely in accordance with the law of Ontario: see Family Law Act, R.S.O 1990, c. F.3, ss. 59.1 to 60.

3.11   No jurisdiction in Canada has yet made family mediation mandatory and the issue remains contentious, raising concerns about the adequacy of screening mechanisms for violence and other vulnerabilities and about who will pay for such services. The model of a specialized, unified family court with comprehensive and exclusive jurisdiction over family law matters and offering a range of support services and dispute resolution mechanisms is only partially implemented across the country. As a result there is significant variation in access to specialist judges and to a range of publicly funded (or at least subsidized) services.

3.12   Ensuring access to justice is one of the main challenges currently confronting the family law system. Access to civil legal aid funding for family law matters varies across the country, but even at best operates with very stringent income cut-offs. Large numbers of lower and middle income Canadians are left unable or unwilling to pay the high cost of lawyers to resolve their disputes. The result is an increasingly dysfunctional system characterized by clogged court dockets, increasing numbers of unrepresented litigants and growing frustration with a system that is both costly and increasingly perceived as ineffective.[3] Some blueprints for reconfiguring the family justice system have emerged,[4] and governments are taking steps to implement them. However, the appropriate direction of reform remains contentious and the extent to which the system can truly be fixed without a major commitment of public resources – an unlikely outcome in times of fiscal constraint – remains in doubt.

B   Children in the family setting and state intervention

3.13   The best interests of children is a well-entrenched principle in Canadian law, although there are debates about what it entails in any given context. Canada is a signatory to the UN Convention, but it has not been incorporated into domestic legislation and its impact has been somewhat

---

[3] R. Roy McMurtry *et al.*, *Listening to Ontarians: Report of the Ontario Civil Legal Needs Project* (Toronto: Ontario Civil Legal Needs Project Steering Committee, 2010); Law Commission of Ontario, *Voices from a Broken Family Justice System: Sharing Consultations Results* (Toronto: LCO, 2010).

[4] Two recent articulations of this blueprint are the *White Paper on Family Relations Act Reform: Proposals for a new Family Law Act* (Victoria, BC: Ministry of Attorney General, 2010) (hereinafter, the 'BC *White Paper*'), many of the provisions of which have been incorporated into B.C.'s new Family Law Act, S.B.C. 2011, c.25, and *Family Law Process Reform: Supporting Families To Support Their Children* (Toronto: 2009), a joint submission to the Ontario Attorney of Ontario by the OBA Family Law Section, ADR Institute of Ontario and Ontario Association of Family Mediators.

limited. While there is a strong protectionist strand in Canadian child and family law that is consistent with the Convention, the idea of children as rights holders is less well anchored. The legal regulation of the parent–child relationship has been very much shaped by the functional approach to defining both parent–child and spousal relationships. Ensuring adequate financial support for children after their parents separate has been a priority, while there is less certainty about the appropriate framework for allocating parental responsibilities for the post-separation care of children.

Defining and classifying children

Age

3.14 The age of majority is set by provincial law; formerly 21, it is now either 18 or 19. However, in many contexts Canadian law now recognizes the decision-making capacity of young persons below the age of majority. Viewed in its best light, the Canadian move away from a stark legal dividing line between childhood and adulthood can be seen as reflecting respect for the evolving capacities of children, one of the basic principles embodied in the UN Convention. Indeed, the recent decision of the Supreme Court of Canada, in *A.(C.)* v. *Manitoba (Director of Child and Family Services)*[5] underscored the significance of this principle in Canadian law, with the Court ruling that legislative failure to respect an adolescent's developing autonomy interest would constitute age-based discrimination in violation of the Charter. However, the lack of consistency and coherence in the current legal framework also suggests that the balancing of protection and autonomy concerns is often done on an ad hoc basis rather than in accordance with a principled approach to children's rights.

3.15 Under the current legal patchwork, the ages of 12, 14 and 16 are common markers for the allocation of legal rights and responsibilities. To offer a few examples, many provinces have chosen 12 as the age at which children's consent is required for adoption (although in Ontario it is seven) and at which they are allowed to participate in child protection proceedings.[6] The age of criminal responsibility is 12 and, while federal legislation creates a separate youth justice system for offenders

[5] [2009] 2 S.C.R. 181.
[6] Ontario Child and Family Services Act (CFSA), R.S.O. 1990, c. C.11, s. 39(4).

under the age of 18, young persons 14 years of age or older who are found to have committed more serious offences can be given adult sentences.[7] The age of sexual consent is 16, recently raised from 14 because of concerns (arguably unfounded) about Canada becoming a haven for sexual predators.[8] In many provinces children are allowed to withdraw from parental control at age 16[9]. The age of medical consent is subject to a variety of approaches ranging from assessment of capacity on an individualized basis, as in Ontario,[10] to the setting of pre-determined ages – either 14 or 16. Provincial legislation often allows a competent minor's decision to be overridden on the basis of best interests, a power typically invoked in cases involving refusal of life-saving treatment. In *A.(C).* the Supreme Court of Canada, while emphasizing respect for adolescents' developing autonomy interests, nonetheless found that some limits on adolescent decision-making in the medical context could be justified.[11]

3.16   In contrast to the general tendency to treat adolescents more like adults, in the context of the child support obligation Canadian law extends childhood, imposing a parental obligation to support children over the age of majority who are pursuing post-secondary education.[12] Under the federal Divorce Act[13] there is no specific age cut-off and entitlement is likely to be found for a first degree, and in some cases even for a second graduate or professional degree.[14]

Illegitimacy

3.17   Illegitimacy has been completely abolished as a legal concept in Canada, one of many examples of the functional approach to defining

---

[7]   Youth Criminal Justice Act, S.C. 2002, c. 1.
[8]   Criminal Code, R.S.C. 1985, s. 150.1, as amended in 2008.
[9]   CFSA, s. 43.
[10]   Health Care Consent Act, S.O. 1996, c. 2, Sched. A, ss. 4(1) and (2).
[11]   On the facts the Court upheld the application of provincial child protection legislation to force a blood transfusion on a competent 15-year-old Jehovah's Witness. It appeared sufficient that the legislation required consideration of the child's wishes as part of the best interests analysis.
[12]   For an overview see Nicholas Bala and Colleen Feehan, 'Child Support for Adult Children: When Does Economic Childhood End?' *Queen's Faculty of Law, Legal Studies Research Paper Series*, No. 08–01 (23 April 2008), available online at http://ssrn.com/abstract=1123979.
[13]   Divorce Act, R.S.C. 1985, c. 3 (2nd Supp.), s. 2(1), definition of 'child of the marriage'.
[14]   Some provinces impose fixed age cut-offs and include additional requirements.

the family that has characterized the evolution of Canadian family law.[15] Changing social attitudes and a growing sense of the unfairness of discriminating against children on the basis of circumstances over which they have no control resulted in some provinces, such as Ontario and Quebec, making the move to remove illegitimacy in the 1970s and early 1980s. The advent of the Charter spurred further reform efforts in this direction, bolstered by Canada's signing of the UN Convention. Any remaining legal differences between children based on birth status stem largely from the practical difficulties of establishing paternity in cases where the parents have not married or cohabited. Unmarried fathers have successfully used the Charter to achieve equal parental rights with mothers[16] and courts increasingly see it as in children's best interests to have a relationship with their biological fathers, even when they were born as result of a casual relationship.[17]

Recognizing parentage and family ties

3.18   Canadian law with respect to parentage is complicated. The focus in this section will be on the determination of legal parentage, the formal status – part of a child's identity – that is assigned at birth. However, as will be discussed in more detail below, in some contexts, such as child support and custody and access, Canadian law also offers broad recognition of de facto or social parents through an expansive application of the doctrine of *in loco parentis*. It is important to keep in mind that legal parentage alone does not determine the way in which Canadian law allocates responsibility for the care and support of children.

3.19   For the most part, Canadian law continues to base *legal* parentage on biological parentage, subject to adoption. Provincial legislation determines legal parentage.[18] Much of it dates from the period of active reform in the 1970s and 1980s that abolished illegitimacy and replaced

---

[15] Nicholas Bala, 'The Evolving Definition of the Family: Towards a Pluralistic and Functional Approach' (1994) 8 *Int. J. Law and the Family* 293; Nicholas Bala and Rebecca Jaremko, 'Context and Inclusivity in Canada's Evolving Definition of the Family' (2002) 16 *Int. J. Law, Policy and the Family* 145.

[16] *Trociuk* v. *British Columbia (Attorney General)*, [2003] 1 S.C.R. 835.

[17] *Aziz* v. *Dolomont*, [2006] N.S.J. No 250 (N.S.S.C. (Fam. Div.)).

[18] The focus here will be on child status legislation that sets out the basis for determining legal parentage. There are also provisions in vital statistics legislation governing birth registration that deal with documentation of parentage and often create de facto presumptions of parentage.

marital status with biology ('natural' parenthood) as the basis for the assignment of legal parentage.[19] Reflecting the then prevailing concepts of biological parenthood, most provincial schemes from this period rest on the assumption that a child will have two parents of the opposite sex and set out certain presumptions (rebuttable by blood tests or other evidence) for determining paternity. These presumptions are generally based upon a man being the mother's partner (either through marriage or cohabitation) at the time of conception or birth or alternatively upon acknowledgement of paternity under provincial vital statistics legislation.[20] Under all provincial schemes, initial allocations of legal parenthood at the time of birth may be modified by the formal legal process of adoption.[21] Same-sex couples are now allowed to adopt on the same terms as opposite-sex couples.

Parentage and assisted reproduction: can a child have more than two parents?

3.20   In recent years the advent of assisted reproduction and the legal recognition of same-sex relationships have complicated the issue of parentage. The idea that biological connection rather than intention to parent should be the basis for assigning legal parentage at birth has come under question. Surprisingly, Canadian law, which has been at the forefront of family law reform on many issues and in particular on same-sex issues, has for the most part failed to comprehensively address these issues. One explanation may be the availability of the doctrine of *in loco parentis* to provide some degree of legal protection to those who have acted as a child's parent. Another may be jurisdictional uncertainty, only recently clarified in favour of the provinces.[22] This is an area that is ripe for legislative reform and some recent developments suggest the potential for a radical reconceptualization of parentage.

3.21   Only three provinces – Quebec, Alberta and Prince Edward Island – have enacted legislation that deals with parentage in cases involving assisted reproduction in anything approaching a comprehensive manner. The result of the failure to legislate in the other provinces

---

[19] See Ontario's Children's Law Reform Act (CLRA), R.S.O. 1990, c. C.12, s. 1(1).

[20] CLRA, s. 8.   [21] In Ontario, see CFSA, s. 158.

[22] In 2004 the federal government enacted comprehensive legislation, the Assisted Human Reproduction Act, S.C. 2004, c. 2, the constitutional status of which was uncertain and only recently clarified by a SCC judgment invalidating significant parts of the legislation and confining federal jurisdiction to criminal prohibition of harmful activities; see Reference re Assisted Human Reproduction Act 2010 SCC 6.

has been uncertainty and ongoing litigation, with courts being requested to either update anachronistic legislation through creative judicial interpretation or invalidate it under the Charter.[23] Out of this context arose a groundbreaking decision of the Ontario Court of Appeal. In *A.(A.)* v. *B.(B.)*[24] the court, relying on the *parens patriae* power, found that on the facts of the particular case it was in the child's best interest to recognize a third *legal* parent – his mother's lesbian partner – in addition to the two parents recognized under the existing legislation, that is his birth mother and his genetic father (a known sperm donor who continued to play a parental role in the child's life). The broad use of *in loco parentis*, which has accustomed us to the idea that a child may de facto have more than two parents, clearly helped pave the way for this reconceptualization of legal parentage.

3.22 There is hope that law reform may be triggered by the new Uniform Child Status Act, 2010 recently adopted by the Uniform Law Conference.[25] Greatly simplified, the provisions dealing with assisted reproduction are: the birth mother is always the child's legal mother, subject to change through adoption or surrogacy; the birth mother's partner (whether married or unmarried, opposite-sex or same-sex) is presumed to be the other legal parent unless there was no consent to the assisted reproduction; and gamete donors are not parents merely by virtue of their donation of genetic reproductive material. The most novel aspect of this model legislation is the provision, drawing on the precedent set by *A.(A.)* v. *B.(B.)*, that would allow a child to have more than two legal parents in circumstances where the parties agree in writing, prior to the assisted conception, that they will all be the child's parents.

The child's right to know genetic origins

3.23 The right to know one's genetic origins, which the UN Convention has been read as supporting,[26] remains contentious and has not been fully endorsed by Canadian law. This right engages a set of complex issues

---

[23] See *Rutherford* v. *Ontario (Deputy Registrar General)* (2006), 270 D.L.R. (4th) 90 (Ont. S.C.J.) for a successful Charter challenge on the basis of sexual orientation discrimination.

[24] (2007), 278 D.L.R. (4th) 519 (Ont. C.A.).

[25] Available online at www.ulcc.ca/en/us/UNIFORM%20CHILD%20STATUS%20ACT. doc. The B.C. *White Paper* recommended adoption of these provisions, subject to some minor modifications and they have recently been incorporated into B.C.'s new Family Law Act, above, note 4.

[26] Articles 7 and 8.

about the significance and respective roles of biological and social parents in the child's life with which Canadian law continues to struggle. Reviews of Canada's compliance with the Convention have noted the failure of Canadian laws governing adoption and assisted reproduction to ensure that children have access to the identity of their biological parents.[27]

3.24 Although there is a growing, informal practice of 'open' adoptions, the legal framework governing adoption still has a large element of the secrecy that came to surround adoption in the early and middle part of the twentieth century. Adoption records continue to be sealed at the time of the adoption order. Since the 1980s provincial legislatures have grappled with the question of whether adopted children (and reciprocally birth parents) in traditional 'closed' adoptions should be allowed access to these records, and thus to identifying information, once the adopted child becomes an adult. There is wide variation amongst the provinces in how they have balanced the competing interests at stake.[28] The three provinces that have gone the furthest in the direction of openness – British Columbia, Alberta and Ontario – still allow birth parents and adult children to file disclosure vetoes with respect to adoptions that were completed before the rules for open records came into effect. As initially enacted, the Ontario legislation did not offer this disclosure veto. However, in *Cheskes* v. *Ontario (Attorney General)* the legislation, in the absence of such a veto, was found to violate the Charter-protected privacy rights of both birth parents and adult adoptees (the majority of the applicants challenging the legislation were adult adoptees who did not want their identifying information disclosed to their birth parents). In its reasoning, the court expressly refused to characterize the interest of adoptees in accessing information about their biological parents as a Charter-protected right.[29]

3.25 Children conceived as a result of gamete donation have even less access to identifying information about their genetic parents than adopted children. Most gamete donors remain anonymous. Since 2004 the governing provisions, although never actually implemented, were those found in the federal Assisted Human Reproduction Act, which allowed for disclosure of health information relating to the donor but expressly precluded

---

[27] UN Convention, concluding observations on Canada's second periodic report, 27 October 2003, CRC/C/15/add.215, paras. 30 and 31.

[28] Cindy L. Baldassi, 'The Quest to Access Closed Adoption Files in Canada' (2005), 21 *Can. J. Fam. L.* 211.

[29] *Cheskes* v. *Ontario (Attorney General)* (2007), 42 R.F.L. (6th) 53 (Ont. S.C.J.).

disclosure of identifying information. As a result of significant portions of the Act having recently been found constitutionally invalid, including the disclosure provisions, the issue has now been placed squarely in the provinces' ballpark.[30] A recent trial decision in British Columbia, *Pratten* v. *British Columbia (A.G.)*,[31] suggests that although Canadian courts remain reluctant to recognize a free-standing right to knowledge of one's genetic origins, the strong commitment to equal treatment of children may effectively lead to the same result. In *Pratten* a woman who was trying to discover the identity of the anonymous donor with whose sperm she was conceived brought a successful Charter challenge to a provincial law that allows fertility clinics to destroy donor records after six years. Although the court was unwilling to recognize a free-standing s. 7 Charter right to know to one's origins, it did find that the failure to provide donor offspring with the same access to information about biological origins given to adopted children constituted discrimination and a violation of equality rights under s. 15 of the Charter.

Delivering parenting

3.26   Apart from the divorce context, the regulation of parenting is a provincial matter. Provincial law presumptively assigns to those designated as parents the responsibility for the care and rearing of children. In some provinces this set of parental rights and responsibilities is called 'guardianship'; in most it is simply called 'custody'. Unlike the more modern parenting legislation that has been enacted in some jurisdictions, most of the Canadian legislation dates from the late 1970s or 1980s and does not elaborate in any detail upon the rights and responsibilities of parents entailed by the terms custody or guardianship beyond indicating that they entail 'care and control'.[32] The sub-category of parental responsibility that is more specifically defined is 'access', which typically goes beyond the right of visitation to include the right to make inquiries and receive information about the child's health, education and welfare (but not the right to make major decisions about the child).[33] Access is most often relevant in cases of parental separation, although claims can also arise in cases where third parties, such as grandparents, are seeking a legally protected

---

[30]   Above, note 21.
[31]   2011 BCSC 656. The decision has been appealed to the B.C. Court of Appeal.
[32]   Quebec and Alberta are exceptions.
[33]   Divorce Act, s. 16(5) and Ontario CLRA, s. 20(5).

relationship with a child. One parental obligation explicitly set out and subject to distinctive and detailed legal elaboration is the obligation of financial support, the legal enforcement of which typically becomes an issue when parents separate and which will be dealt with below.[34]

3.27 Whether through express wording or judicial interpretation, it is clearly established that the powers of care and control that are presumptively assigned to a child's parents are to be exercised in the child's best interests and that they remain subject to reallocation or limitation by the state if the best interests of the child so require.[35] Parental powers and obligations are not exclusively confined to a child's legal parents. As has been noted above, one of the distinctive features of Canadian law, outside of Quebec, is the broad recognition and protection extended to significant de facto relationships that develop between children and non-legal parents through doctrines such as *in loco parentis* and the 'psychological parent'. *In loco parentis* finds its most obvious anchorage in child support law, with support obligations being imposed on step-parents and others who have taken on the parental role.[36] However, *in loco parentis* is also applicable in other contexts, including custody and access, child protection and adoption, with the result that those who act as the child's parents are treated as parents.

3.28 In custody and access determinations, Canadian law generally allows applications by 'any person', with the issues being resolved through an application of the best interests test. One of the factors given the most weight in custody and access decisions is the strength of the emotional ties between the child and the person requesting custody or access: that is to say, courts place great importance on maintaining emotional continuity and stability in children's lives. The fact of biological parenthood now carries much less weight in a custody dispute than it did in the 1950s when there was a presumption that, barring unfitness, it was in the best interests of children to be raised by their biological parents.[37]

---

[34] See paras. 3.33–3.35 below.   [35] Ontario CLRA, s. 20(2).

[36] Divorce Act, s. 2(2); Ontario CLRA, s. 1(1) uses the language of 'a settled intention to treat a child as child of [one's] family'. The leading case for determining when a person has taken on the role of parent is *Chartier* v. *Chartier*, [1999] 1 S.C.R. 242. For overviews see Carol Rogerson, 'The Child Support Obligation of Step-Parents' (2001) 18 *Can. J. of Fam. Law* 9 and Nicholas Bala and Meaghan Thomas, 'Who is a "Parent"? "Standing in the Place of a Parent" & Canada's Child Support Guidelines s. 5', *Queen's Faculty of Law, Legal Studies Research Paper Series*, No. 07–11 (12 July 2007), available online at http://ssrn.com/abstract=1023895.

[37] *Hepton* v. *Maat*, [1957] S.C.R. 606.

This shift in the law was endorsed by the Supreme Court of Canada in two leading cases decided in the 1980s.[38] In both cases biological parents sought to regain custody of children who had been in the care of non-parents for a significant period of time. Placing a great deal of weight on expert evidence of 'bonding', the Court awarded custody to the child's 'psychological parents'. In giving primacy to the welfare of children and rejecting the idea that biological parents have ownership rights over their children, these decisions exemplify a child-centred approach to the allocation of parental responsibilities. However, as knowledge of biological origins has taken on greater significance in evolving conceptions of the best interests of the child, it is not surprising that these decisions have also been criticized for discounting the significance of biological parenthood, most specifically as it relates to a child's cultural, ethnic and racial identity of origin.

3.29 The issue of grandparent access to children is one of the shifting fault lines in current Canadian family law. Legislatures have thus far rejected demands from grandparent advocacy groups for a legislative presumption of grandparent access, taking the position that such a presumption would be inconsistent with the primacy of the best interest principle, which requires deciding each case on its merits.[39] Judicial decisions under the current best interests framework reveal conflicting approaches. The dominant strand in the case law sets a high threshold for ordering grandparent access in the face of parental opposition – only where there has been disruption of a significant relationship resulting in serious harm to the child, such that the benefits of ordering access outweigh the costs of increased conflict and tension.[40] However, in an increasing number of cases judges have shown themselves more willing to treat grandparents as non-custodial parents, that is, to assume the benefits of a relationship with grandparents and to question the reasonableness of parental refusals to allow access, particularly in cases of parental separation or death.

---

[38] *Racine* v. *Woods*, [1983] 2 S.C.R.173; *King* v. *Low*, [1985] 1 S.C.R. 87.

[39] In its report *For the Sake of the Children* (Ottawa: Parliament of Canada, 1998) the Special Joint Committee on Child Custody and Access recommended legislative reform to highlight the importance to children of maintaining relationships with grandparents and other extended family members. For a review of Canadian law see Law Reform Commission of Nova Scotia, *Grandparent–Grandchild: Access*, Final Report (Halifax: 2007).

[40] This cautious approach was endorsed by the only appeal court decision on the issue, *Chapman* v. *Chapman* (2001) 15 R.F.L. (5th) 46 (Ont. C.A.).

3.30 While parental powers are limited by the best interests of children, in practice the law gives those adults to whom parental authority is allocated a fair amount of autonomy in determining how to carry out their responsibilities. The standard for state intervention in parenting tends to be the prevention of harm, as reflected in the standards set by the criminal law and child protection legislation. Societal notions of harm clearly shift over time and a currently contentious issue is corporal punishment. Section 43 of the Criminal Code exempts from criminal sanction parents who use reasonable corrective force against their children. The UN Committee on the Rights of the Child has taken a strong stand against corporal punishment and an increasing number of countries have taken action to ban it. Much to the embarrassment and disappointment of children's rights advocates, Canada has not done so, a failing noted in reviews of Canada's compliance with the UN Convention.[41] On this issue, the judiciary has deferred to the government.

3.31 In *Canadian Foundation for Children, Youth and the Law* v. *Canada (Attorney-General)*[42] a Charter challenge to s. 43, on the basis that it discriminated against children on the basis of age and violated their security of the person, was unsuccessful. A majority of the Supreme Court of Canada did narrow the scope of s. 43 by ruling that, properly interpreted, it only exempted certain mild forms of corporal punishment from criminal sanction. However, the Court went on to conclude that far from harming children, s. 43 actually benefits them because it minimizes the disruptive effect of the criminal law on family relationships. Notwithstanding the Court's reliance on the best interests of children, the result in this case suggests that respect for parental rights was the overriding constitutional value.[43] The case stands as a stunning repudiation of children's rights, reflecting both the troubling failure of the Charter to protect children's rights and the limited impact of the Convention on Canadian law.

---

[41] Note 26 above, at para. 32.

[42] [2004] 1 S.C.R. 76.

[43] The Supreme Court of Canada has not yet clearly ruled on whether parental rights of *decision-making* are constitutionally protected, as they are under the American constitution, as an aspect of the right to liberty. Section 7 of the Charter has, however, been clearly found to protect the integrity of the psychological and emotional *relationship* between parents and children, such that state removal of a child violates both parents' and children's rights of security of the person: *New Brunswick (Minister of Health and Community Services)* v. *G.J.*, [1999] 3 S.C.R. 46.

Intra-family disputes: parental separation

3.32   The main point at which the law becomes involved in children's lives is when their parents are not together, either because they never lived together or because they have separated or divorced. Two main issues then arise: child support and custody and access. When raised in the context of divorce proceedings, these matters are dealt with under the federal Divorce Act, otherwise under provincial laws. A dominant policy goal has been to reduce conflict and encourage out-of-court settlement, both to protect the interests of children and to reduce the cost of resolving family law disputes. Major reforms of child support law have been successfully implemented. As for custody and access law, while procedural reforms are ongoing, substantive reforms have been stalled by ideological disagreements that speak more of adult interests than those of children.

Child support guidelines

3.33   In 1997 Canada underwent a major reform of its child support laws. Prior to that child support was determined through a highly discretionary, individualized assessment of children's needs and parents' ability to pay. The late 1980s and early 1990s saw increasing concern in Canada with the inadequacy of child support awards, a result of growing public awareness of the impoverishment of women and children after divorce. Following in the footsteps of other jurisdictions such as the United States, the United Kingdom and Australia, the federal government and the provinces began to work together to develop child support guidelines which would use percentage of income formulas to determine child support amounts. Child support guidelines came into force at the federal level in 1997 through amendments to the Divorce Act.[44] In relatively short order, all of the provinces (with the exception of Quebec) enacted virtually identical guidelines applicable to child support determinations in contexts not involving divorce.[45]

3.34   The child support guidelines have been very successful and are widely supported by family lawyers, judges, mediators and parents.[46] In a

---

[44]   The Divorce Act was amended to require that child support determinations be made in accordance with the guidelines; see s. 15.1(3). The guidelines themselves were introduced in the form of regulations under the Divorce Act in order to facilitate ongoing revision: Federal Child Support Guidelines, SOR/97–175 as amended.

[45]   Quebec enacted its own, quite different scheme based on an income shares formula.

[46]   *Children Come First: A Report to Parliament Reviewing the Provisions and Operation of the Federal Child Support Guidelines* (Ottawa: Minister of Justice and Attorney General for Canada, April 2002).

standard case the calculation of child support is relatively easy. Although there are additional discretionary considerations which may be relevant in particular cases, the basic amount of child support is determined by child support tables based on two factors: the payer's income and the number of children. The table amounts have, on the whole, come to be seen as an objectively fair measure of child support and they have facilitated settlement and reduced parental conflict over child support.[47] The two provisions that continue to generate the most uncertainty and to prompt calls for further reform are the discretionary provisions dealing with persons in the place of parents and shared custody. Provinces have also begun to put in place administrative mechanisms for recalculation of child support on an annual basis in order to simplify the procedure and reduce the burden on courts.

3.35   As well as reflecting the priority given to the best interests of children, the enactment of the child support guidelines also exemplifies the increasing emphasis in Canadian law on developing clearer rules and reducing discretion in order to facilitate efficient dispute resolution. Increasingly the systemic advantages of average justice are being seen to outweigh the benefits of finely tuned individual justice.

Custody and access disputes

3.36   The legal framework for determining parenting arrangements after parental separation or divorce continues to utilize the concepts of custody and access. Embodying notions of children as property, these concepts have been criticized for focusing on the rights of parents and also for creating a winner–loser mentality that exacerbates conflict. Divorce Act reforms which would replace this archaic terminology with the language of parental responsibilities have been under discussion since 1998,[48] but have been stalled by ideological disagreements, largely along gender lines, and few provinces have decided to undertake such reforms on their own.[49] Fathers' rights advocates want stronger presumptions of equal sharing of

---

[47]   Although the percentages of income transferred under the Canadian guidelines may not be as high as in some other jurisdictions, spousal support is more widely available to top up child support.

[48]   Reforms were recommended in 1998 by a joint parliamentary committee, above note 39. The federal government's response, Bill C-22, was introduced in 2002, but never enacted because of a change of government in 2004. The Bill was never reintroduced.

[49]   Alberta and British Columbia are the exceptions. The B.C. *White Paper* recommendation to adopt the terminology of parental responsibilities has been followed in the new Family Law Act, note 4, above.

parental responsibilities, including a presumption of shared time, while women's advocates fear that the new language will create a de facto presumption of shared custody, exposing children to excessive levels of conflict and providing inadequate protection against domestic violence. Clearly this will continue to be a contentious issue.

3.37 Meanwhile, parenting disputes continue to be resolved under the legal framework of custody and access, which allows for two basic types of custodial arrangements: sole custody/access or joint custody. These labels deal only with decision-making authority, and say nothing about the actual amount of time the child spends with each parent, which must also be decided. The majority of cases settle and many agreements, particularly those resulting from mediation or collaborative processes, take the form of parenting plans. Ongoing procedural reforms (such as mandatory 'parenting-after-separation' programmes, enhanced opportunities for mediation, and special protocols for high conflict cases) are aimed at reducing conflict and getting parents to focus on the interests of their children. Disregarding children's rights of participation under Article 12 of the UN Convention, both federal and provincial governments in Canada have been slower than many other jurisdictions to create opportunities for children to participate in custody and access determinations. Protecting children from being caught in the middle of parental conflict has been the prevailing policy concern and the preference has been for children's views to be conveyed, if at all, by third-party professionals. However, children's right to be heard is beginning to receive increased attention.[50]

3.38 Custody and access determinations are to be made only on the basis of the best interests of the child. The Divorce Act contains no legislated criteria other than the 'maximum contact' principle[51] while provincial statutes tend to contain lengthy checklists of best interests factors, but these differences in drafting seem to make little difference in practice. Canadian custody law has been strongly influenced by the assumption that children benefit from the continued involvement of both parents in their lives, and this has been reflected by increases both in joint custody arrangements and in the amount of time non-residential parents

---

[50] Suzanne Williams, 'Perspective of the Child in Custody and Access Decisions: Implementing a Best Interests and Rights of the Child Test' (2007) 86 *Can. Bar Rev.* 633. For a recent decision expressing strong support for children's right to be heard see *B.J.D. v. D.L.G.* (2010) 324 D.L.R. (4th) 367 (Y.S.C.).

[51] Section 16(10) provides that a parent's willingness to facilitate access with the other parent should be a consideration in awarding custody.

spend with their children. However, in litigated cases a countervailing consideration is the recognition that children can be damaged by a high degree of continuing conflict. There is a great deal of debate, for example, about whether joint custody should be awarded when one of the parents is opposed to it and about the wisdom of imposing 'parallel parenting' arrangements in high conflict cases.[52]

3.39   Canada is a large country with a mobile population, both internally and internationally. It is no surprise that one of the most litigated issues is parental relocation. The current legal framework, governed by the Supreme Court of Canada decision in *Gordon* v. *Goertz*,[53] involves a discretionary balancing of factors that leads to significant uncertainty and creates incentives to litigate. Some judges seem to begin from a presumption that, barring bad faith, a primary custodial parent should be allowed to move; others begin from a presumption against mobility. Some clearer starting points are required and this is an area where we will continue to see developments.[54]

Child protection and state intervention

3.40   The criminal justice system deals with the most serious cases of child abuse by parents or other adults, but the primary mechanisms for dealing with child abuse and neglect are the child protection systems in place in each province. These allow child welfare agencies to utilize a range of interventions to protect children including, in serious cases, removal of the child on a temporary or permanent basis. Child welfare schemes have been in place since the early part of the twentieth century, but their modern form dates from the 1980s and early 1990s. The values underlying these modern statutes are in tension. An increased concern for the well-being of children and greater awareness of the risks to which they may be exposed within the family is reflected in new grounds for state intervention. However, at the same time, the social work philosophy of least intrusive intervention, subsequently reinforced by the rights-based culture of the Charter, has generated more controls on state power

---

[52] See Martha Shaffer, 'Joint Custody, Parental Conflict and Children's Adjustment to Divorce' (2007) 26 *Can. Fam. L. Q.* 285.

[53] [1996] 2 S.C.R. 27.

[54] BC *White Paper* recommended a presumption in favour of relocation except in cases where the parents have substantially equal parenting time that has been incorporated into the new Family Law Act, note 4, above.

to intervene in the family,[55] reflected in a greater legalization of the process to provide more due process protections to parents.[56]

3.41   In the 1980s this tension was resolved by an emphasis on family preservation and the provision of support to enable parents to effectively parent their children. In the 1990s policy shifted in response both to some highly publicized cases of parental abuse and to a new era of fiscal constraint. The result has been more removals of children and a court system overburdened with the demands of dealing with all of these cases through a highly legalized, adversarial process. There is growing awareness that the child protection system is in need of major redesign.[57]

3.42   Aboriginal children are the most disadvantaged in Canada and are significantly over-represented in the child welfare system. Between 30% and 40% of the children in care across the country are aboriginal, and in some provinces it is as high as 80%. Aboriginal children and families have different and complex needs, shaped in part by a legacy of residential schools and the 1960s' 'sweep' when hundreds of children were removed through adoption. Child protection laws do recognize the importance of cultural continuity when seeking placements for aboriginal children and the desirability of aboriginal communities providing their own child protection services.[58] However, there is an urgent need to do more and to work with aboriginal communities to develop and implement better approaches that respond directly to the needs of their children.

C   Adult relationships

3.43   Historically, Canadian family law was centred on marriage, understood as a monogamous, opposite-sex relationship. The most striking development in Canadian family law is how far it has moved in a

---

[55] Removal of a child has been found to implicate parents' s. 7 rights of security of the person; see above note 41.

[56] For an overview of Canadian child protection law see Nicholas Bala, 'Child Welfare Law in Canada: An Introduction', in Nicholas Bala *et al.* (eds.), *Canadian Child Welfare Law: Children, Families and the State*, 2nd edn (Toronto: Thompson Educational Publishing, 2004).

[57] In Ontario, for example, a Commission to Promote Sustainable Child Welfare was appointed in 2009, with a three-year mandate to develop and implement solutions to promote the sustainability of child welfare in the province; see www.sustainingchild-welfare.ca/.

[58] Ontario CFSA, s. 1(2).

relatively short period of time to recognizing a broader range of significant adult relationships. A functional, pragmatic approach to defining the family, reinforced by equality norms in the Charter, has led to the situation where same-sex couples now receive the same legal recognition as opposite-sex couples, including, as of 2005, access to marriage; and where unmarried cohabitation, whether same-sex or opposite-sex, gives rise for the most part to the same legal consequences as marriage. As a result of the Canadian legal system's willingness to accord legal recognition to same-sex couples through the existing regulatory frameworks governing de facto relationships and marriage, there has been little need to create intermediate formal institutions such as registered partnerships or civil unions. The civilian legal tradition in Quebec, with its emphasis on formality, has resulted in somewhat different patterns of relationship recognition in that province, including a reluctance to attach legal consequences to de facto relationships and the introduction of civil unions.

The relationships

Cohabitation: opposite-sex and same-sex de facto spouses

3.44   Canada has moved very far along the path of attaching to unmarried cohabitation – both opposite-sex and same-sex – the same legal consequences as marriage. This is the case not only in the public sphere, where family status is used as a basis for distributing government benefits, but also with respect to the private rights and obligations that flow from spousal status under family law. The legal terminology used varies by jurisdiction. Federal laws refer to 'common law partners'. Some provinces use similar terminology, others simply extend the definition of spouse to include unmarried couples, and Alberta uses the category of 'adult interdependent partners'.[59] Whatever the terminology, the mode of recognition is by *ascription* of spousal status rather than registration, and is typically based upon a period of cohabitation. Many jurisdictions have rejected this approach because of concerns about the intrusion on individual freedom and the lack of respect for the choice not to marry. In Canada these concerns, although not absent, have carried less weight and

---

[59]   Adult Interdependent Relationships Act, S.A. 2002, c. A-4.5. Alberta is the only jurisdiction in Canada to extend legal recognition to non-conjugal relationships, despite the recommendations contained in Law Commission of Canada, *Beyond Conjugality: Recognizing and Supporting Close Personal Adult Relationships* (Ottawa: Law Commission of Canada, 2001).

instead a functional approach focusing on the structure of relationships and the de facto merger of economic and emotional lives has prevailed. What explains this?

3.45 After the abolition of illegitimacy, which rendered formal marriage irrelevant for parental status, the earliest moves in the direction of recognizing unmarried couples were provincial laws imposing a spousal support (i.e. maintenance) obligation on unmarried cohabitants. Here, the state's interest in minimizing welfare expenditures was clearly one of the operative policy objectives. However, with the advent of the Charter, human rights concerns were added to the policy mix. In its 1995 decision in *Miron* v. *Trudel*,[60] the Supreme Court of Canada ruled that the equality rights guaranteed by the Charter included protection against discrimination on the basis of marital status. The Court went on to invalidate a law that confined certain spousal benefits under an automobile insurance policy to married persons, finding that both married and unmarried couples were involved in the kind of economically interdependent relationships the legislation was intended to benefit. The functional approach to defining the family thus seemed to become constitutionally entrenched.

3.46 Legal recognition of unmarried couples was further expanded as the legal system grappled with claims for recognition of same-sex relationships in the period before the legalization of same-sex marriage. Same-sex couples, for whom at the time the 'choice not to marry' argument was irrelevant, began to use the Charter to seek access to the benefits that had been extended to unmarried opposite-sex couples. In the groundbreaking decision in *M.* v. *H.*[61] in 1999, the Supreme Court of Canada ruled that the exclusion of same-sex couples from a provincial spousal support regime that had been extended to include unmarried, opposite-sex couples constituted discrimination on the basis of sexual orientation, thus violating s. 15 of the Charter. At the heart of the Court's reasoning was the finding that same-sex couples, like unmarried, opposite-sex couples, formed committed conjugal relationships characterized by economic and emotional interdependency. *M.* v. *H.* prompted a flurry of legislative activity at both the federal and provincial levels as governments, seeking to comply with the Charter, engaged in systemic reform to ensure that those rights and responsibilities granted to unmarried opposite-sex cohabiting couples were extended to same-sex couples. In the course of these reforms

---

[60] [1995] 2 S.C.R. 418.   [61] [1999] 2 S.C.R. 3.

terminology and definitions were often standardized. In addition, most remaining instances of differences in treatment between married and unmarried couples were eliminated. The main exception was matrimonial property rights.

3.47 While all provinces except Quebec have legislated to impose obligations of spousal support on unmarried couples,[62] only two have chosen to go further and include unmarried couples within matrimonial property regimes, regimes that grant a presumptive right to an equal division of matrimonial property upon relationship breakdown.[63] The issue of the constitutionality of that remaining distinction was challenged in the courts, leading to a very surprising and questionable result in the Supreme Court of Canada's 2002 decision in *Nova Scotia (Attorney General)* v. *Walsh*.[64] Contrary to the expectations generated by its past decisions, the Court found that the exclusion of unmarried couples was not arbitrary or discriminatory as subjection to a regime of equal sharing of matrimonial property was based on a choice exercised by the parties at the beginning of the relationship. Here, very late in the day, the 'choice' argument, addressing the issue of autonomy, prevailed, adding a degree of incoherence and uncertainty to the law governing unmarried couples that will take some time to resolve.

Same-sex marriage

3.48 Despite the ongoing opposition of many religious groups within the country, in 2005 Canada became the fourth country in the world (after the Netherlands, Belgium and Spain) to legalize same-sex marriage. Here the judiciary and the equality rights under the Charter played a major role, but it should also be recognized that an incremental approach to recognition of same-sex relationships was made possible because of an existing legal framework that recognized de facto relationships. The Supreme Court of Canada decision in *M. v. H.*, discussed above, which found functional similarity between same-sex and opposite-sex committed conjugal relationships, clearly paved the way for successful Charter

---

[62] The issue of that exclusion has been challenged under s. 15 of the Charter: see *A. c. B.*, 2010 QCCA 1978, now on appeal to the S.C.C.

[63] Despite strong recommendations to do so from several provincial law reform commissions: see Law Reform Commission of Nova Scotia, *Final Report: Reform of the Law Dealing with Matrimonial Property in Nova Scotia* (Halifax: 1997); Ontario Law Reform Commission, *Report on the Rights and Responsibilities of Cohabitants under the Family Law Act* (Toronto: 1993).

[64] [2002] 2 S.C.R. 325.

challenges to the opposite-sex requirement for marriage. After a series
of provincial court of appeal rulings, beginning in 2003, that invalidated
the opposite-sex requirement for marriage, the federal government chose
to enact uniform legislation recognizing the capacity of same-sex couples to marry rather than appealing these rulings to the Supreme Court
of Canada.[65] The Civil Marriage Act came into force in July 2005.[66]
Consequential revisions to numerous other laws, both federal and provincial, followed so that all references to marriage reflected that it was
no longer exclusively a relationship between persons of the opposite sex,
including removal of all references to 'husband' and 'wife'. The legalization of same-sex marriage marked a clear separation between religious
and secular law, the Charter guarantee of freedom of religion having been
interpreted to require only that there be recognition of the right of religious officials to refuse to perform same-sex marriages contrary to their
religious beliefs.[67]

Entering relationships

Marriage

3.49 Marriage is an area of divided jurisdiction. Although marriage is
a federal power, giving the federal government jurisdiction over the law
governing the essential validity of marriage, the constitution gives the
provinces control over the 'solemnization of marriage'. Provinces thus
regulate the formal or ceremonial requirements for a valid marriage, and
each has done so by means of a comprehensive marriage act. There is,
however, no comprehensive legislation at the federal level. As a result,
the law governing the essential validity of marriage remains the common law rules governing capacity and consent, except as modified in a
few specific instances by statute. The federal government has legislated to
significantly narrow the list of relationships within which marriage was
prohibited, confining the prohibitions to lineal blood relationships and

---

[65] The federal government did refer several constitutional questions regarding its capacity to legislate with respect to same-sex marriage to the SCC: *Reference re Same-Sex
Marriage*, [2004] 3 S.C.R. 698.

[66] S.C. 2005, c. 33.

[67] See *Reference re Same-Sex Marriage* and Civil Marriage Act, s. 3. The unresolved issue is
whether such exemptions can be claimed by *civil* marriage commissioners; see the recent
decision of the Saskatchewan Court of Appeal in *Marriage Commissioners under the
Marriage Act (Re)*, 2011 SKCA 3.

sibling relationships,[68] and more recently to legalize same-sex marriage. Some of the remaining common law requirements for a valid marriage appear decidedly archaic. Marriages can still be nullified on the common law ground of incapacity to consummate, despite the heterosexual nature of this requirement and its inconsistency with same-sex marriage. The age requirements are still the incredibly low ages set by the common law, although provincial laws have filled some of the federal legislative void by refusing marriage licences to those under 18.[69]

3.50   Under Canadian law marriage is a monogamous relationship, but in recent years this requirement has come under intense scrutiny and debate. It is unlikely that marriage law will change to allow polygamous marriages to be performed in Canada. The more contentious issue is how far the state should be allowed to go in enforcing the norm of monogamy, in particular whether it should be allowed to impose *criminal* sanctions on parties to valid foreign polygamous marriages or to informal plural marriages such as practised by fundamentalist Mormon groups. In Canada the norm of monogamous marriage is bolstered by the Criminal Code prohibition on the practice of polygamy, defined very broadly as 'being in any kind of conjugal relationship with more than one person at the same time'.[70] The issue of the constitutionality of the polygamy prohibition was recently referred to the B.C. Supreme Court in a case referred to as the 'polygamy reference', bringing to the forefront some difficult tensions in Canadian family law. The evolution of Canadian family law has been characterized by a pluralistic approach that recognizes a diversity of family forms, but polygamy also poses a challenge to the Canadian commitment to gender equality, and, as practised in some communities, to the best interests of children forced into early marriage. In a decision that has divided opinion, the court upheld the prohibition on polygamy.[71]

---

[68] Marriage (Prohibited Degrees Act), S.C. 1990, c. 46.

[69] With an exception for 16- and 17-year-olds who have parental consent.

[70] Section 293. There has been a great deal of writing on polygamy in Canada; for two examples see Martha Bailey, 'Should Polygamy be Criminalised' (November 2009) posted on SSRN at http://papers.ssrn.com/sol3/papers.cfm?abstract_id=1509459 and Rebecca Cook and Lisa Kelly, *Polygyny and Canada's Commitments Under International Human Rights Law* (Ottawa: Justice Canada, September 2006).

[71] The trial ruling in the reference, released in November 2011, upheld the polygamy provisions, concluding that any violations of freedom of religion or liberty were justified because of the harms arising out of the practice of polygamy, including 'harm to women, to children, to society and *to the institution of monogamous marriage*'; see *Reference re: Section 293 of the Criminal Code of Canada*, 2011 BCSC 1588, para. 5, emphasis added. The trial judge did, however, interpret s. 293 narrowly, confining its application to

3.51   Other issues that relate to immigration and culturally diverse marriage practices are also beginning to arise with more frequency. Although the issue of forced marriage is becoming a matter of increasing concern within cultural communities, in particular South Asian communities, the issue has not gained the political salience it has in other countries such as the UK, where specific legislation has been enacted to deal with the issue.[72] Currently, community efforts are focused on increased education and the provision of resources and support for victims and potential victims of forced marriage.[73] While Canadian marriage law does not allow proxy marriages (which are allowed under Islamic law), proxy marriages celebrated in jurisdictions where the practice is allowed will be recognized as valid under Canadian conflict of laws rules.[74] Cases of marriage fraud (marriages entered into only to facilitate immigration) are receiving increasing attention, but thus far Canada has not followed the path of other countries that have enacted more restrictive immigration laws to target sham marriages, based in part on a recognition of the difficulty of determining whether marriages are genuine or a sham. Victims of marriage fraud (Canadian citizens who find that their spouses only married them for immigration purposes) are becoming more politically vocal. They are often dismayed to learn that Canadian law recognizes their marriages as valid and that divorce, rather than annulment, is the appropriate remedy. In some cases criminal charges or tort actions may also be available as remedies.[75]

Cohabitation

3.52   Unlike marriage, there is no uniform status associated with so-called common law or de facto spousal relationships. Legal recognition is based on statutory definitions in a host of different federal and provincial laws that refer to spousal status. The definitions tend to vary not just between jurisdictions but also between different legislative contexts, although recent

---

marriage-like relationships that had some form of communal authorization or sanction, thus excluding multiple partner conjugal relationships arising only by virtue of the individual choice of the participants. In a surprising move, a decision was made not to appeal the opinion rendered by the trial judge.

[72] See the Forced Marriage (Civil Protection) Act 2007 (England, Wales and Northern Ireland) and the Forced Marriage etc. (Protection and Jurisdiction) (Scotland) Act 2011 (discussed at para. 12.43, note 154).

[73] See the Forced Marriage Project of the South Asian Legal Clinic in Toronto: online at www.forcedmarriages.ca/.

[74] See *Hassan* v. *Hassan*, 2006 ABQB 544.

[75] See *Raju* v. *Kumar*, 2006 BCSC 439.

legislative reforms have brought a somewhat greater degree of definitional consistency. Legal recognition is typically based on cohabitation for a specified period of time, and in addition cohabitation in a relationship of some permanence in which a child has been born or adopted. The definition of 'common law partner' used under many federal statutes requires one year of cohabitation. Under provincial laws where spousal status entails the imposition of obligations, such as the duty of support, the requisite periods of cohabitation are longer. In the 1970s the requirement was often five years of cohabitation, but now it is typically two or three.[76] Cohabitation tends not to be statutorily defined beyond living together in a 'conjugal' relationship or in a 'marriage-like' relationship, and courts have thus been left with the task of elaborating the checklist of factors that will determine whether a relationship has reached the level of commitment and integration of lives that would make it spousal. Borderline cases do generate some litigation, but the majority of cohabitation cases are fairly straightforward.

Consequences of relationships

3.53 Many of the significant legal consequences of marriage (and cohabitation) are triggered only when the relationship terminates. During marriage spouses retain separate legal personalities. Provincial matrimonial property laws do not, for the most part, affect ownership during the marriage apart from imposing controls on unilateral disposition of the matrimonial home. The obligation of mutual support is rarely enforced during ongoing marriages, outside of the context of social assistance where spousal incomes will be pooled to determine eligibility for public support. Spousal status is of course relevant under a host of regulatory schemes distributing various benefits and burdens where it is used as a convenient marker for relationships of economic and emotional interdependency. In addition, acts of violence between spouses are often subject to special legal provisions.

Terminating relationships

3.54 In Canada, as in many other Western jurisdictions, the introduction of no-fault divorce was a transformative moment, marking the beginning of modern family law. In Canada it was 1968 when the federal

---

[76] Three years in Ontario: Family Law Act (FLA), s. 29, definition of 'spouse'.

government, exercising its constitutional power over divorce, enacted the first national divorce statute and introduced no-fault divorce. The Divorce Act 1968 was a relatively cautious piece of legislation,[77] combining an extensive list of fault-based grounds for divorce with a no-fault ground based on a three- or five-year period of living separate and apart. In 1985 it was replaced by a new divorce act intended to be more responsive to realities of marriage breakdown, with an emphasis on making divorce less adversarial and providing a fairer resolution of its consequences. The 1985 Divorce Act[78] significantly liberalized the no-fault ground for divorce by reducing the required period of living separate and apart to one year and allowing parties to begin proceedings as soon as they have separated. As the result of a conservative government coming into power near the end of the reform process, the fault-based grounds of adultery and mental and physical cruelty were also retained, contrary to the original reform proposal, but presented as alternate methods of demonstrating marriage breakdown. Although traditional notions of fault have been removed from the rest of the family law system, they continue to play this residual role in the grounds for divorce, offering grounds for an immediate divorce.[79] In a move that somewhat blurred the separation between secular and religious law, the Divorce Act was amended in 1990 to deal with the problem of spouses who withhold access to divorce under religious law, in particular husbands who refuse to grant their wives a *get* under Jewish law: spouses refusing to remove barriers to religious remarriage can have their application for divorce or corollary relief dismissed and any pleadings they have filed under the Act can be struck out.[80] Although the stated justification for the amendment was the state's concern about the use of the threat to withhold a religious divorce to coerce unfair agreements with regard to corollary relief, it is difficult not to see these provisions, more contentiously, as a state attempt to remedy problems of gender equality within religious law.[81]

---

[77] R.S.C. 1970, c. D-8.   [78] Above note 13.

[79] The fault grounds account for only approximately 5 per cent of divorces. After the legalization of same-sex marriage, courts were required to reshape the common law concept of adultery to cover same-sex infidelity: see *P.(S.E.)* v. *P.(D.D.)* (2005), 259 D.L.R. (4th) 358 (B.C.S.C.).

[80] Divorce Act, s. 21.1. Somewhat similar provisions had previously been adopted in Ontario; see Family Law Act, ss. 2(4) to (7) and 55(4) to (7).

[81] See *Bruker* v. *Marcovitz*, [2007] 3 S.C.R. 607.

3.55   Divorce rates in Canada rose significantly after the 1985 Act came into force, but declined in the 1990s and have remained relatively stable since 1997, with approximately 38 per cent of marriages ending in divorce.[82] Divorce itself is a relatively straightforward procedure. Although a divorce must still be pronounced by a judge, it can be done by way of affidavit without any court appearances if there are no other issues in dispute.[83] The main legal issues that need to be resolved are the financial and parenting consequences of marriage breakdown. Much of the focus of family law reform in Canada has been to develop an appropriate legal framework to resolve these issues. Two strong policy concerns have been to reduce the adversarial nature of the process and to ameliorate the financial hardship of marriage breakdown on women and children.

3.56   De facto spousal relationships based on cohabitation require no formal act to bring about their termination; they end when the parties cease to cohabit. Unmarried couples are not covered by the federal Divorce Act and must resort to provincial laws to resolve parenting and financial issues when their relationships end.

Consequences of termination

3.57   The two main issues that arise upon termination of adult relationships, apart from any issues relating to children, are division of matrimonial property and spousal support. Canadian law provides fairly generous economic relief to the spouse who is in the weaker economic position when the relationship ends. The evolution of both areas of law has been shaped by a strong commitment to gender equality and a concern to provide fair compensation for women's work in the home; both areas also reflect an evolution towards more rule-based schemes to facilitate efficient dispute resolution.

Division of property

3.58   While each province has its own matrimonial property scheme, most of which have been in place since the 1970s or 1980s, they all incorporate the basic concept of marriage as an equal partnership, which in turn justifies a presumptive equal division of marital assets when the

---

[82]   Vanier Institute of the Family, *Families Count – Profiling Canada's Families IV* (Ottawa: Vanier Institute of the Family, 2010).

[83]   Divorce Act, s. 25(2)(b).

partnership ends.[84] Why did provincial legislatures gravitate towards a presumptive rule of equal division rather than toward the more discretionary standard of equitable distribution? One answer is the strong influence of norms of gender equality; another is the influence of civil law conceptions of marriage and marital property coming from Quebec. In addition, legislators were aware that the presumption of equal division fosters settlement and reduces the need for costly litigation.

3.59 Except in two provinces, unmarried couples are not covered by matrimonial property laws. The 2002 *Walsh* decision,[85] which found that this exclusion did not violate the Charter, removed the immediate impetus for reform. Common law partners must resort to equitable doctrines of unjust enrichment and constructive trust in order to share property when their relationships end. Over the years the Supreme Court of Canada has articulated an increasingly generous basis for such claims,[86] but they entail uncertainty and costly litigation. Given the widespread legal recognition of unmarried couples and the public expectations of similarity to marriage that this generates, it is likely that over time provincial legislatures will extend property rights to unmarried couples, requiring those who do not wish to share their property to enter into cohabitation agreements.[87]

Spousal support

3.60 Historically, the main matrimonial obligation imposed by Canadian law after spousal separation or divorce was that of spousal maintenance or alimony – the life-long support obligation owed to an 'innocent' wife. Like other Western jurisdictions, Canada has struggled with the difficult question of the appropriate role, if any, for spousal support in the context of a modern family law system characterized by no-fault divorce, gender equality and division of matrimonial property. In many jurisdictions the principle of promoting spousal independence after relationship termination, often referred to as the clean break

---

[84] Where the schemes differ is with respect to the pool of marital assets to which this presumption applies. Most provinces have deferred community schemes; however, in some provinces business assets are not included and are shared on a more discretionary basis. A nice review of the history and conceptual underpinnings of matrimonial property law in Canada is found in Justice L'Heureux-Dubé's judgment in *Nova Scotia (Attorney General) v. Walsh*, [2002] 2 S.C.R. 325.

[85] Above note 64.

[86] The most recent decision is *Kerr v. Baranow*, 2011 SCC 10.

[87] This was recommended in the BC *White Paper* and has been adopted in the new Family Law Act, note 4, above.

principle, has been given priority and spousal support has become largely a minimal, transitional remedy. Canadian law, although not abandoning the goal of promoting spousal self-sufficiency, has charted a different course, retaining a much more expansive role for spousal support.[88]

3.61 Spousal support, when sought in the context of divorce, is governed by provisions in the federal Divorce Act, in other cases by provincial support legislation. It is now a gender-neutral remedy, able to be claimed by men as well as women, in the context of both same-sex and opposite-sex relationships. Fault is explicitly excluded as a relevant factor. Support legislation tends to take the form of fairly open-ended legislation that provides checklists of factors and objectives to be taken into account in determining whether spousal support should be awarded, and if so, in what amount and for what duration. As a result, the real work of determining spousal support outcomes has been left to the judiciary.

3.62 Through a series of important decisions the Supreme Court of Canada has articulated a very expansive basis for entitlement to spousal support on both 'compensatory' and 'non-compensatory' grounds. Initially a 1987 decision[89] favoured time-limited support obligations in the interests of promoting clean breaks and finality. However, in 1992, in the groundbreaking decision in *Moge* v. *Moge*,[90] Canadian law shifted direction. The Court clearly rejected the clean break model and recognized an expansive 'compensatory' basis for spousal support, primarily directed at redressing the economic disadvantage suffered by spouses who have sacrificed labour force participation to care for children. Then in 1999, in *Bracklow* v. *Bracklow*,[91] the Court expanded entitlement by recognizing a 'non-compensatory' basis for spousal support based on 'need'.

3.63 The actual application of these broad principles of entitlement to the facts of individual cases leaves much room for discretion. Over time the resulting uncertainty and unpredictability in the law of spousal support became a source of concern, and led to the development of a set of Spousal Support Advisory Guidelines, released in 2008, to bring more structure to this area of law.[92] Although many jurisdictions have child

---

[88] For an overview see Carol Rogerson, 'The Canadian Law of Spousal Support' (2004) 38 *Fam. L. Q.* 69.

[89] *Pelech* v. *Pelech*, [1987] 1 S.C.R. 801.

[90] [1992] 3 S.C.R. 813.   [91] [1999] 1 S.C.R. 420.

[92] Carol Rogerson and Rollie Thompson, *Spousal Support Advisory Guidelines* (Department of Justice Canada, July 2008). For an overview, see Carol Rogerson and Rollie Thomson, 'The Canadian Experiment with Spousal Support Guidelines' (2011) 45 *Fam. L. Q.* 241.

support guidelines, Canada is somewhat unusual in that it has gone on to develop a guidelines approach to the much more complex and controversial issue of spousal support. The method of bringing about this reform was also novel. Although the project was supported by the federal government, the spousal support guidelines, unlike the child support guidelines, are not legislated and their application is not mandatory. They are informal, advisory guidelines, developed through consultation with family lawyers and judges and intended to reflect current practice under the existing legislation. Although only advisory, they have received the endorsement of several appellate courts[93] and are now widely used across the country.

Self-regulation and custom-made relationships

3.64   Marking a strong break with the past, the general direction of Canadian family law since the 1970s has been to open up opportunities for contractual ordering previously precluded and to accord increased respect to the terms of such agreements. Spouses are given a great deal of freedom not only to resolve the legal rights and obligations arising at the termination of their relationship through separation agreements, but also to structure their relationships at the point of entry through marriage contracts (pre-nuptial agreements) or cohabitation agreements.

3.65   This embrace of freedom of contract is consistent both with Canada's recognition of diversity and pluralism in personal relationships and with goals of facilitating efficient dispute resolution. At the same time, Canadian law recognizes that domestic agreements are negotiated in a unique context that creates less than ideal conditions for contractual ordering. The values of autonomy and finality that support contractual enforcement have found themselves in tension with Canadian family law's equally strong emphasis on gender equality and protecting vulnerable family members. In determining the appropriate limits to place on contractual ordering, Canadian law has struggled with achieving the appropriate balance between freedom and fairness. This remains an area of law in flux, although it is fair to say that since the 1980s and early 1990s, when support for the value of contractual autonomy reached its high-water mark,[94] a more balanced approach

---

[93] *Yemchuk* v. *Yemchuk* 2005 BCCA 406 and *Fisher* v. *Fisher* 2008 ONCA 11.

[94] Under the influence of the 1987 SCC decision in *Pelech*, above note 89.

is taking hold, reflected by the leading Supreme Court of Canada decision in the 2002 *Miglin* case.[95] Although specifically a case about the test for overriding spousal support agreements under the Divorce Act, the Court's general pronouncements in *Miglin* about the need to balance the values of autonomy and certainty promoted by contractual ordering with concern for the risks of unfair agreements raised in spousal negotiations provide a broad framework that continues to shape the developing law of domestic contracts in a range of other contexts.

3.66 The law governing domestic contracts is complex, drawing on a mix of sources, common law and statute, federal and provincial.[96] All that can be provided here is a very broad-brush overview of the kinds of limits that have generally been placed on contractual ordering.[97] Some patterns are clear. Significant limits have been placed on upholding parental agreements relating to children, which may be set aside if they are not in the best interests of children.[98] In addition the child support guidelines severely restrict parents' ability to contract out.[99] There is more uncertainty with respect to agreements dealing with spousal rights and obligations such as spousal support and property division. It is clear that they can be set aside on grounds of procedural fairness, the standards for which are progressively being raised, well beyond what the common law would require. Typically provincial law requires that domestic contracts be in writing and witnessed. In addition, there is increasing emphasis on full financial disclosure and on ensuring full understanding of the legal consequences of the agreement, which will often be compromised when parties lack effective legal representation.[100]

3.67 The more contentious and uncertain issue is the extent to which spousal agreements may be set aside on grounds of substantive unfairness.

---

[95] *Miglin* v. *Miglin*, [2003] 1 S.C.R. 303; also *Rick* v. *Brandsema*, [2009] 1 S.C.R. 295. On the facts of *Miglin*, the court refused to override a spousal support agreement which provided for only three years of spousal support.

[96] Primary jurisdiction rests with the provinces; see part IV of the Ontario FLA.

[97] The reform proposals in the BC *White Paper*, adpotedin the new Family Law Act, reflect these main patterns.

[98] As well parties are precluded from contracting about future custody and access arrangements in pre-nuptial agreements.

[99] Divorce Act, ss. 15.1(5) to (8).

[100] Ontario FLA, s. 56(4); *Miglin* and *Rick*, above note 95.

Here there are some differences between property agreements and spousal support agreements. In general, Canadian law allows parties significant freedom to contract out of the default regimes of matrimonial property division, both in separation agreements and pre-nuptial agreements, if the requirements of procedural fairness and basic common law validity have been satisfied.[101]

3.68   Not surprisingly given the prospective nature of the obligation and the state's interest in protecting the public purse, there is more discretion to relieve parties of substantively unfair spousal support agreements, although the basis for intervention remains contentious and somewhat uncertain. Many provincial laws allow spousal support agreements to be overridden if the agreement 'results in unconscionable circumstances' or alternatively if the claimant is on public assistance. Under the Divorce Act, there is the complex balancing test put in place by *Miglin* that leaves much scope for judicial discretion and conflicting interpretations. This remains a confused and uncertain area where one can predict ongoing shifts as the appropriate balance between certainty and fairness continues to be worked out.[102]

D   Conclusion

3.69   The first major wave of family law reform in Canada, beginning in the late 1960s and early 1970s, was focused on bold, progressive reform of substantive law. Much of that substantive reform agenda has been successfully completed, although, as has been shown, a few pieces of unfinished business remain: reform of custody and access law, including greater concern for hearing the voices of children, extending property rights to unmarried couples and resolving the financial implications of serial family formation. In addition, ongoing technological and social change has put some new substantive issues on the table that will require ongoing attention, for example assisted reproduction and an increasing number of challenging issues around multicultural accommodation.

3.70   The second major wave of family reform, which is currently in progress, is procedural. Currently, the most pressing and challenging issues

---

[101]   A few provinces have replaced the common law standard of unconscionability with the statutory test of 'grossly unfair' or 'unduly harsh'.

[102]   See Carol Rogerson, 'The Legacy of *Miglin*', 2012 *Can. Fam. L. Q.* forthcoming.

of reform relate to the implementation of more effective and efficient methods of dispute resolution and ensuring access to justice. Without an increased commitment of political will and financial resources, it is not so clear that Canada will be as successful in rising to the challenges raised in this second wave of family law reform as it was in responding to the need for reform of substantive law in the first wave.

4

China

Bringing the law back in

MICHAEL PALMER

A   Introduction

4.1   The family occupied a central position in traditional Chinese law and society. Within the family, the law and society, patriarchal values dominated. Despite some six decades of socialism, many efforts from the late nineteenth century onwards at reforming family life, and the recent emergence in the People's Republic of China (PRC) of an increasingly open-minded urban population, the family remains critically important today. Continuing enforcement of the official *hukou* or household registration system,[1] persisting official policy of using the family for provision of important rural welfare services, reliance on the family for correct socialization of children, and the revived importance of the family as an agricultural production unit, all mean that the family continues to be a key socio-economic entity. To this importance should be added the need felt by the PRC's leadership to limit family size severely through 'robust' birth control policies. Although the PRC is a Leninist authoritarian party-state, with limited freedom of expression, family law is an area of legal reform that often generates robust public argument.

4.2   The development of family law since the 'liberation' of China by the Chinese Communist Party (CCP) in 1949 manifests three broad phases. In 1950 a revolutionary code, the Marriage Law, attempted to transform marriage and family life in a 'socialist' direction. In 1980 a new Marriage Law introduced provisions on such matters as family planning and succession in order to readjust marriage and the family to new governmental policies promoting economic reforms and greater international

---

[1]   A system for registering family membership which gives the individual an identity as a family member, and also a place of internal domicile which serves important administrative purposes.

engagement. In the third and current phase, the Marriage Law was further revised, in 2001, and then judicially interpreted in several important ways. The current legal framework governing marriage and family operates in a rapidly changing social context. This context includes a greater diversity of viewpoints about marriage and family, growing market forces, stronger private property holdings, growing international pressures and a slowly emerging civil society.

Historical roots, sources and reform

Historical roots

4.3 Traditional Chinese family law, in addition to emphasizing patriarchal values, also essentially served to meet administrative needs and specified sometimes very heavy punishment for transgression of Confucian moral norms. Confucian ideology stressed the virtues of filial piety, defined family roles subordinating women and the young, and supported ancestor worship. Successive efforts at reforming marriage and family law from the mid nineteenth century onwards culminated in the Marriage Law of the PRC 1950. This attempted to eliminate many traditional norms in marriage and family life, replacing them with principles of consent, equality and mutual support, and protection of women and children. Not all reforms were effective, however, and in particular divorce applications by women were 'contained' by mediation. Despite major revisions to the Marriage Law in 1980 and 2001, the law still struggles to shed its traditional values and processes.

Sources

4.4 The current PRC legal system is a syncretic product of socialism, the civilian tradition and traditional Chinese legal values, with influences also from the common law and international law. The highest legislative authorities are the National People's Congress (NPC) and its Standing Committee. The State Council – China's central government – enacts administrative regulations, and its constituent ministries also issue normative declarations and orders. Local people's congresses and local governments enact subsidiary legislation consistent with national laws. Decided cases are not a formal source of law, but the Supreme People's Court is authorized to issue Judicial Interpretations (*Sifa Jieshi*) of legislation. These are binding on the courts.

'Law' reform

4.5 Family 'law' reform over the past decade in China has proceeded through statutory change, judicial interpretation and administrative regulation modifications. In 2001, after rigorous open debate made possible in part by new provisions for public consultation in the 2000 Legislation Law, there was significant revision of the 1980 Marriage Law. Although not characterized as a fully revised law, as the changes it introduced were intended to be but a small step on the way to a fuller revision of the Law to be contained in a very broad and detailed Civil Code, the 2001 amendments to the Marriage Law (hereafter 2001 ML) in reality introduced wide-ranging reforms of marriage, divorce, matrimonial property, domestic violence and liability for matrimonial misconduct. These changes were followed by two important interpretations of issues raised by the 2001 ML by the Supreme People's Court.[2] In August 2011 the Supreme People's Court issued a Third Interpretation of the 2001 ML, again amid debate over contentious areas such as matrimonial property ownership, third-party rights, paternity testing and reproductive rights.[3] A consolidating national code of family planning was finally introduced in 2001,[4] and extended in 2002 by State Council Measures on the Administration

---

[2] Hereafter, 'First Interpretation 2001', and 'Second Interpretation 2003'. The two Interpretations were: 2001 Zuigao Renmin Fayuan Guanyu Shiyong 'Zonghua Renmin Gongheguo Hunyin Fa' Ruogan Wenti de Jieshi [1] (Interpretation of the Supreme People's Court on Several Problems Concerning the Application of the Marriage Law of the PRC [1]), promulgated 24 December 2001 and in force 24 December 2001, and the 2003 Zuigao Renmin Fayuan Guanyu Shiyong 'Zonghua Renmin Gongheguo Hunyin Fa' Ruogan Wenti de Jieshi [2] (Interpretation of the Supreme People's Court on Several Problems Concerning the Application of the Marriage Law of the PRC [2]) promulgated 25 December 2003 and in force 1 April 2004.

[3] 2011 Zuigao Renmin Fayuan Guanyu Shiyong 'Zonghua Renmin Gongheguo Hunyin Fa' Ruogan Wenti de Jieshi [3] (Interpretation of the Supreme People's Court on Several Problems Concerning the Application of the Marriage Law of the PRC [3]), promulgated 9 August 2011 and in force 13 August 2011. A full text of the Interpretation is available in Chinese at: www.legaldaily.com.cn/zt/content/2011–12/21/content_3223900.htm.

[4] Zonghua Renmin Gongheguo Renkou yu Jihua Shengyu Fa, promulgated 29 December 2001, and in force 1 September 2002. Until the introduction of the national statute, the corpus of family planning regulations, which had developed at the principal level, provided the principal source of substantive law for implementing China's rigorous policies of birth control. In addition, a controversial eugenics law had been introduced in 1994: the Mother and Child Health Care Law – see Michael Palmer, 'Protecting the Health of Mothers and their Children? Developments in the Family Law of the People's Republic of China', in A. Bainham (ed.), *Annual Survey of Family Law: 1995* (Dordrecht: Kluwer, 1997), pp. 107–16.

of Social Upbringing Charges.[5] These changes were followed in 2003 by a further revision of the rules governing marriage (and divorce) registration – the State Council's Marriage Registration Regulations.[6]

4.6 A key agency in reforming statutory law relating to the family since its establishment thirty years ago has been the China Association of Marriage and Family Studies[7] or Zhongguo Hunyin Jiating Yanjiuhui, created in 1981. This body is officially characterized as a 'national level social organization of the first rank' (*guojia yiji shetuan*), and is administratively subordinate to the All-China Women's Federation (Zhonghua Quanguo Funü Lianhe Hui), a 'mass organization' intended by the Chinese party-state to serve as a 'bridge' between the authorities and society on women's matters.[8] The Association is composed of members from a wide range of academic disciplines considered relevant for family law issues, and there is also a strong presence of members from law enforcement agencies, the Ministry of Civil Affairs, the All-China Women's Federation and trade unions. The Association's Chair is invariably also Chairperson of the Women's Federation and a Deputy Chair of the Standing Committee of the NPC,[9] reflecting the Association's intended role as promoter of women's rights and legislative advances in marriage and family matters.[10]

Dispute resolution and access to legal services

4.7 Confucian values of compromise, reconciliation and community interests predominated in traditional China's approach to dispute resolution, and China's socialist leaders drew on this spirit from the 1930s

---

[5] Shehui Fuyang Zhengshou Guanli Banfa.

[6] Marriage Registration Regulations (Hunyin Dengji Tiaoli), promulgated by the State Council, 8 August 2003 and in force 1 October 2003.

[7] For further details (in Chinese) see the Association website at: www.camf.org.cn/family/intro/index.htm.

[8] For an early but informative account of mass organizations in the PRC see, in particular, Chao Kuo-Chün, 'Mass Organizations in Mainland China' (September 1954) 48(3) *The American Political Science Review* 752–65.

[9] See, for example, 'Zhongguo Hunyin Jiating Yanjiuhui Zuzhi Jigou Jiben Qingquang (The Basic Situation regarding the Organizational Structure of the China Marriage and Family Law Research Association)', available at www.camf.org.cn/family/intro/zzjg/index.htm.

[10] The nature and significance of the 2005 reform of this Law are dealt with further in Michael Palmer, 'On China's Slow Boat to Women's Rights: Revisions to the Women's Protection Law, 2005' (2007) 11(1–2) Special Issue of *International Journal of Human Rights on Equality in the Asia Pacific*, ed. P. W. Chan, 151–77.

onwards to develop community and judicial mediation, injecting a robust, activist and politically evaluative ethos intended both to resolve disputes and to transform society. As part of its efforts to promote social-ist legality over the past three decades, the Chinese leadership has also established an extensive system of civil and administrative courts. Nevertheless, traditional antipathy towards litigation remains import-ant, especially in family matters.

4.8   Although in cases involving matrimonial property of substantial value the parties may well seek professional legal representation, and for certain kinds of family case legal aid may be available,[11] the general emphasis on mediation discourages recourse to lawyers. There is also a long-standing distrust in Chinese legal culture for lawyer intervention in family cases, and many lawyers are reluctant to engage in this area of legal practice because it is not lucrative. As a result, advice on relevant law and procedural protection of weaker parties, as well as provision of social service-type support, becomes the responsibility of local mediation com-mittees, notaries or local offices of the Ministry of Justice and Ministry of Civil Affairs. It is not required that parties use lawyers when presenting their case in court (2007 Civil Procedure Law, Article 12). The emphasis on 'informal justice' in handling family disputes does, however, mean that the parties' differences are often resolved in an institutional setting that lacks professional autonomy and in which the relevant agencies have important responsibilities for implementing state policies.

B   Children in the family setting and state intervention

4.9   In China today children are cherished, but this value competes with other social ideals, state policies and administrative needs, and the often negative social impact of economic reforms. And while children are revered, this is more for their value to the family than as individ-uals, especially in rural areas. Male children are preferred, as their con-tribution to the family is seen as being crucial. The state simultaneously imposes contradictory measures in which children are to provide old-age

---

[11] Thus, for example, the Elders' Protection Law at Article 39 provides legal aid for elders who seek assistance from the courts to enforce their rights. See Michael Palmer, 'Protecting the Rights and Interests of the Elderly: Developments in the Family Law of the People's Republic of China, 1996–8', in A. Bainham (ed.), *International Survey of Family Law: 1999* (Dordrecht: Kluwer, 1999), pp. 95–107.

care and the family is to be a unit of production, but at the same time families are ideally restricted to one child only. Economic reforms have created greater geographical mobility, but this leads to problems for children especially when families become dispersed. Problems have emerged in respect of 'migrant children' (*liudong ertong*) or 'children left behind' (*liushou ertong*) by migrating parents, as well as children affected by HIV/AIDS (*shou aizibing yingxiang ertong*).

Defining and classifying children

Age

4.10   In PRC law today the term 'child' has various meanings, depending on context. In the Minors' Protection Law, at Article 2, minors (*wei chengnian ren*) are characterized as persons under the age of 18, which equates to the definition of 'child' in the UN Convention of the Rights of the Child (Article 1). The age of majority is generally defined as 18 and this is the position taken in the 1986 General Principles of the Civil Law (Article 11) and the 1982 Constitution (Article 34). In the PRC Criminal Law, the term 'child' refers to a minor under the age of 14, and a child below this age does not bear criminal responsibility, though children up to the age of 16 bear such responsibility if the offence is serious.[12]

Birth status

4.11   Both the 2001 ML (Article 25) and the 1985 Succession Law (Article 10) emphasize that no legal distinction should be drawn between children born within, and those born outside, marriage. Adopted children and step-children enjoy the same rights as natural children born within marriage.[13] However, the birth status of children is more complicated than this. First, there remains a widespread social expectation that birth should occur within marriage, and so children born outside marriage – and even step-children – may experience social stigmatization. Secondly, there is the household registration system

---

[12] See Article 17. The same provision also declares that if a person who is under 16 is not given criminal punishment because of her or his youth, the family head guardian may be ordered to impose discipline, or the minor may 'be taken in by the government for rehabilitation'. This provision also provides for reduced punishment for those between the ages of 14 and 18.

[13] 2001 ML, Articles 26 and 27.

(*hukou zhidu*), which may well restrict access to social services, especially education, for children with a rural domicile who have migrated to the city. Thirdly, in the late 1980s and early 1990s, children born outside the state-imposed birth planning system – regardless of their legitimacy – were characterized as illegal and discriminated against because they lacked household registration.[14] These '*hei haizi*' or 'black children', as they are pejoratively referred to, were often unable to secure birth certificates, passports and access to important social services and state subsidies. Since the introduction of the Population and Birth Planning Law 2001, the focus of the penalty system has been on financial sanctions against the parents, and the State Council in preparations for the Sixth National Census recently stated that children born outside the state plan should be able to be entered into the household register, and that in this process financial or other penalties may not be imposed.[15]

Recognizing parentage and family ties

4.12   The legal definition of parentage stresses social rather than genetic dimensions of parent–child relations, for the authorities' primary concern is to ensure that children are provided for by whoever may be in the position of parent. The 2001 Marriage Law stipulates at Article 21 that:

> Parents are under the obligation of bringing up and educating their children ... Where the parents fail to perform their obligations, underage children and children without the ability to live an independent life are entitled to ask their parents to make support payments.
>
> It is forbidden to drown or desert infants or commit any kind of infanticide.

Reflecting traditional family values of filial piety (*xiao*) and reciprocity (*bao*), as well as the Constitutional principle that rights and duties are

---

[14] 'The People's Republic of China: Reacting to Rapid Social Change', in M. Freeman (ed.), *Annual Survey of Family Law: 1988*, vol. 12 (London: The International Society on Family Law, 1990), pp.438–57.

[15] Sixth National Census Leading Small Group and Ministry of Public Security, 'Guanyu zai Diliuci Renkou Puchaqian Jinxing Hukou Zhengdun Gongzuo Yijian de Tongji' (Notice on the Opinion of the Sixth National Census Leading Small Group and Ministry of Public Security on Carrying Out Rectification Work to Household Registration prior to the Sixth National Census), General Office of the State Council Announcement No. 30 for 2010, available at http://zwgk.gd.gov.cn/006939748/201006/t20100612_11968. html.

CHINA: BRINGING THE LAW BACK IN

reciprocal,[16] the same Article adds that adult children are under an obligation to furnish care for their parents. In serious cases of failure to support,
the Criminal Law (Article 261) provides a sentence for up to three years'
imprisonment. A natural parent who does not take principal responsibility for the upbringing of her or his child must in law continue to provide
for that child.[17] Divorce does not relieve a parent from providing support
for a child. In adoptions, the law emphasizes the legal completeness of the
adoptive parent and adopted child relationship:

> Article 26: The state safeguards lawful adoptions. The relevant provisions
> in this law concerning the relationship between parents and children are
> applicable to adoptive parents and adopted children.
>   The rights and obligations between the adopted children and natural
> parents are eliminated by the creation of the adoption.

4.13   The provision continues, however, by indicating that the moment
an adoptive relationship is dissolved, the natural parents resume responsibility for parenting the child unless the adopted child has become an
adult.[18] In addition, the relationship between step-parent and stepchild
is characterized as being no different in law from ordinary parent–child
ties.[19] The Chinese leadership's concern to ensure that the family members – rather than the state – provide care means that grandparents and
older siblings are also placed under this legal obligation if a young child's
parents have died or are incapacitated.[20] Parents, adopters, step-parents,
grandparents and older siblings who fail in their duty to care for a child
may well find the matter taken up with them by a mediation committee or a local government department, or may even be sued by the child
for better parental performance.[21] In more serious cases, the power of
guardianship over the child may be removed from a parent by a court
acting under Article 16 of the 1986 General Principles of the Civil Law
and Article 53 of the Minors Protection Law.

---

[16] Article 33.   [17] 2001 ML, Article 25.
[18] Article 29 also specifies: 'with respect to the rights and duties in the relationship between
an adult adopted child and his or her parents and their close relatives, it may be decided
through consultation as to whether to restore them.'
[19] 2001 ML, Article 27.   [20] 2001 ML, Articles 28 and 29.
[21] For example, the Supreme People's Court's 2011 Third Interpretation of the Marriage
Law provides at Article 3: 'Where, during the existence of a marital relationship, both
parents refuse or one parent refuses to perform the obligation of supporting [*fuyang*]
children, and a minor or dependent child claims the support expenses, the people's court
shall support such a claim.'

4.14   In PRC law, although surrogacy is not recognized, and 'trading in sperm or ova' is prohibited,[22] technologically assisted reproduction is permitted. In particular, artificial insemination is allowed, and a 1991 Supreme People's Court Judicial Interpretation confirmed that if both spouses have agreed to bear a child by artificial insemination, then that child will be characterized in law as legitimate.[23] Some commentators argue that the use of artificial insemination is the exercise of reproduction rights (*shengyu quan*) under Article 17 of the Population Law 2001.[24] Complications arise, however, especially when it is unclear that both spouses have agreed to the procedure, and some commentators have also suggested that a sperm donor, as the biological father, should bear some degree of responsibility for upbringing costs. It would therefore be useful to introduce into Chinese law a 'reproduction agreement' (*shengyu xieyi*) in which the parties' established understanding of the arrangement is clearly recorded.[25]

The child's right to know

4.15   The idea that a child has the right to know her or his genetic origins is not established in PRC Law, although some academic commentators suggest that such a right should be introduced.[26] Prior to the 2011 Third Interpretation, it seems that the only authority to initiate parentage testing rested with the courts. However, Article 2 of the Third Interpretation now provides:

> Where one spouse files a lawsuit in the People's Court for confirmation of non-existence of parentage and has provided necessary evidence, if the other spouse has no contrary evidence and refuses a parentage test, the People's Court may presume that the claim of the spouse requesting confirmation of non-existence of parentage is correct.

[22] By Article 3 of the Ministry of Public Health's 1991 Renlei Fuzhu Shengzhi Jishu Guanli Banfa (Measures for the Management of Human Assisted Reproduction Technology).

[23] Supreme People's Court, 'Guanyu fu-qi lihun hou rengong shoujing suo sheng zinü de falü diwei ruhe de fuhan' (Concerning how to determine the legal status post divorce of all children born to the [former] husband and wife by artificial insemination), issued 8 July 1991.

[24] That provision reads: 'citizens have the right to bear children, and are also under the obligation of practicing birth planning according to law, [and] husbands and wives bear joint responsibility in the implementation of birth planning.'

[25] See, for example, Cao Xinming, 'Xiandai Shengzhi Jishu de Minfaxue Sikao' (Civil Law Theoretical Reflections on Contemporary Reproductive Technology) (2003) 4 *Fa-shang Yanjiu* 16–25.

[26] See, for example, Wang Hanhua, 'Rengong Shengzhi Falü Wenti Yanjiu' (Legal Problems Arising from Artificial Insemination) (2011) 2 *Xue Shu Jie* 192–97 at 195.

> Where a party files a lawsuit in the People's Court for confirmation of parentage and has provided necessary evidence, if the other party has no contrary evidence and refuses a parentage test, the People's Court may presume that the claim of the party requesting confirmation of parentage is correct.

Thus, if one party makes an application for confirmation of parentage or non-parentage, and the other party has no contrary evidence and refuses a parentage test, the court will presume in favour of the applicant party. This stipulation would appear to give a child the right to seek confirmation of parentage, provided she or he is able to identify a specific person as likely to be a parent.

Non-marital births

4.16   As we have seen, the law of the PRC does not discriminate against a child on the basis of parental marital status. This has been a fundamental principle in PRC family law throughout the period of socialist rule.[27] However, the social expectation is that every adult marries, and that all births take place within marriage. The legal expectation is that every marriage is registered and that all births are registered – especially as this is also a requirement of the household registration system, and without a *hukou* registration a child may enjoy only limited rights. Moreover, while China has made robust efforts in recent years to correct problems of non-registration, significant numbers of children continue to slip through the net and remain unregistered.[28]

4.17   The close-knit and mutually supportive nature of Chinese family life, and the moral pressures placed on women's sexual conduct, have meant that determination of paternity has perhaps not been an issue

---

[27] 1950 Marriage Law, Article 15. The current Marriage Law states, at Article 25, 'a natural child shall have the equal rights of a legitimate child, and shall not be harmed or discriminated against by any person'.

[28] United Nations Committee on the Rights of the Child, *Consideration of Reports Submitted By States Parties, Under Article 44 of the Convention [on the Rights of the Child], Concluding Observations: China*, 24 November 2005, CRC/C/CHN/CO/2, at paragraph 42. Thus, for example, in September 1998 Ministry of Public Security provisions on the residence of newborn children, including those born out of wedlock, allowed for registration of that residence in the place of permanent residence of *either* the father or the mother. This meant, inter alia, that children born either in or out of wedlock enjoyed equal rights to registration of birth and household, and gave children a degree of choice in selecting the most advantageous environment to grow up in (*ibid.*, para. 58).

of quite the same importance that it has in some other jurisdictions. Nevertheless, since the introduction of the 1950 Marriage Law, ascertaining paternity and imposing parental responsibility has been provided for: 'where the paternity of a child born out of wedlock is legally established by the mother of the child or by other witnesses or material evidence, the identified father must bear the whole or part of the cost of maintenance and education of the child until the age of eighteen'.[29] And, as we have seen, the Third Interpretation now allows for paternity testing upon application to a court, with a presumption in favour of the applicant.

Delivering parenting

4.18   As noted above, the Marriage Law insists on performance of parental duties by parents, a divorced parent, a step-parent, a natural parent in most circumstances and even grandparents and brothers and sisters of a child in need. At the same time, the Law emphasizes the reciprocity inherent in parent–child relations: adult children are expected to perform their filial duties of providing care for elderly parents. The manner in which parenting is delivered reflects social values rather than legal norms, and this is one reason why the regulatory framework does not stress the ideal of 'best interests of the child'. Indeed, the domestic expression of China's obligations under the Convention of the Rights of the Child – the Minors' Protection Law 2006 – avoids mention of this principle.

4.19   Nevertheless, legal flesh is increasingly being placed on the parenting bones, and it has a strongly moralistic tint. The Marriage Law does not detail the role of the parent, although financial support of the child is always regarded as paramount. The General Principles of the Civil Law 1986 declare a parent to be the child's guardian, and an important Supreme People's Court interpretation of the General Principles characterizes guardian duties as including protection of the ward's physical health, caring for the ward's daily life, managing and safeguarding the ward's property, educating and exercising (parental) control (*guanli*), and representing the ward in a dispute or in cases of infringement of the ward's rights and duties.[30] The 2006 Minors Protection Law contains an

---

[29]   Article 15.
[30]   Zuigao Renmin Fayuan, 'Zuigao Renmin Fayuan Guanyu Guanche Shixing "Zhonghua Renmin Gongheguo Minfa Tongze" Ruogan Wenti de Yijian (Shixing)', 1988 (Supreme People's Court, Opinions of the Supreme People's Court on Certain Issues Concerning the Implementation of the 'General Principles of the Civil Law of the People's Republic of China' (Trial) 1988.

important section of family protection, and this places significant 'legal' duties on parents. Parents should create a 'good and harmonious family environment', fulfil their guardianship and (financial) support functions, refrain from perpetrating violence against their children, and neither maltreat nor discriminate against 'female or handicapped' children.[31] Parents have important socialization responsibilities, for they must give due regard to their children's:

> physiological and psychological conditions as well as their conduct and habits, cultivate and influence the minors in respect of healthy ideology, good morality and proper methods, guide minors to carry out activities that are conducive to their physical and mental health, prevent and stop minors from smoking, drinking excessively, living a vagrant life, being addicted to the Internet, gambling, taking drugs or [indulging in] prostitution.[32]

In addition, parents are under a duty to provide 'family education guidance' (*jiating jiaoyu zhidao*)[33] and to ensure that minors complete compulsory education.[34] Further, parents must consult with a minor on matters affecting the child 'on the basis of the minor's age and intellect development status',[35] and parents may not enter into a betrothal nor arrange a marriage for their children.[36] A migrant worker is expected to ask another to perform guardianship duties in her or his absence.[37] In addition, a divorced non-custodial parent with visitation rights to a child may find these rights withdrawn by a court if the visits are considered to be harmful to the child physically or mentally.[38]

Intra-family disputes

4.20   As we emphasized earlier, the legal culture of China today continues to stress the use of mediation as a decision-making process in intra-family disputes, and provides an institutional framework in which community mediation and local governmental agencies encourage reliance on extra-judicial processes for resolving differences. The new People's Mediation Law 2010, inter alia, allows parties to get court assistance to enforce their mediation agreement if implementation is a problem. Even if a dispute

---

[31]   Article 10.
[32]   Article 11.   [33]   Article 12.
[34]   Article 13.   [35]   Article 14.
[36]   Article 15.   [37]   Article 16.
[38]   Article 38, Marriage Law 2001.

goes to court, the emphasis will be on securing a mediated outcome. In China, at least until very recently, the judge who mediated a case would also be the judge who would adjudicate, should mediation fail. This is consistent with a robust, didactic style of mediation in which moral values as well as legal norms are emphasized. Many family cases that come before the courts involve custody at divorce or financial support (an adult parent's duties to support a child, and an adult child's duties to support an elderly parent), and succession and related family property issues.[39] Over the past decade, domestic violence has also become a matter in which the criminal chambers of the People's Courts are expected to intervene where local mediatory efforts and administrative intervention fail.

4.21   In custody cases the court does not explicitly apply the principle of the child's best interests. The provisions in the Chapter on divorce in the 2001 Marriage Law do, however, make protection of the child's rights and interests an important factor to be borne in mind in the decision-making process where a child is no longer breast-fed.[40] They also reaffirm that both 'father and mother, after divorce, have the right and the obligation of bringing up their children', and 'after the divorce of the parents, the children remain the children of both parties regardless of whether they are supported directly by either the father or mother'. Non-custody does not relieve a parent from the duty to continue to support and provide for the education of her or his offspring, the extent of such support being determined by negotiations between the divorcing couple, and if that fails, then by a court decision.[41] The non-custodial parent has visitation rights, the precise nature of which is again to be determined by negotiations between the divorcing couple, but then by a court decision if such negotiations fail.[42]

Child protection and state intervention

4.22   In the PRC the official ideology is socialism and there is a particular concern with 'correct socialization' of children, so that they become worthy successors to the revolutionary cause. Yet, at the same time, much room is left for self-regulation by families, which often means that in

---

[39] See, for example, the Work Report of the Supreme People's Court 2010 (Zuigao Renmin Fayuan Gongzuo Niandu Baogao, 2010), available at www.court.gov.cn/qwfb/sfsj/201105/ t20110525_100996.htm. This indicates that about 25 per cent of all civil cases handled by the People's Courts in 2010 concerned family and succession.
[40] Article 36.   [41] Article 37.   [42] Article 38.

practice traditional patriarchal values predominate in family life. A further complication is the party-state's direct intervention in family life through the birth control programme, and its ideal of the single-child family.[43] In addition, as we have suggested above, emerging social problems regarding children have necessitated increasing state intervention in recent years. Child labour remains an issue in a largely rural society in which children typically work as agricultural labourers even though the Labour Law[44] and the Minors Protection Law[45] prohibit employment under the age of 16.[46] Further, children who have been abandoned, or who have run away, are ultimately the responsibility of the local state.[47] In addition, the PRC in its Criminal Law contains robust provisions criminalizing the abduction and sale of women and children, and committing such offences may even lead to application of the death penalty.[48] Involvement in child prostitution is also a serious criminal offence.[49] Finally, while there are no specific prohibitions on child pornography in the Criminal Law, taking part in pornographic activities is itself a criminal offence, with enhanced punishment if a minor is involved.[50]

4.23 The People's Courts have juvenile benches (*shaonian fating*) within their criminal divisions, and the Minors Protection Law at Article 50 stipulates that it is a duty of the courts and other law enforcement agencies to safeguard minors' rights and interests in juvenile cases. If necessary, specialist personnel should be appointed to help a young person in trouble, and courts and other law enforcement agencies are required to take into account the vulnerability of young people and their emotional and physical states.[51] Minors suspected of having committed crimes should be extended special care, dealt with by application of the principles of

---

[43] The concern has been primarily with excessive rates of population growth, but the family planning policy also has a eugenics dimension (Article 11, 2001 Population and Birth Planning Law). See Carole J. Petersen, 'Population Policy and Eugenic Theory: Implications of China's Ratification of the United Nations Convention on the Rights of Persons with Disabilities' (2010) 8 *China: An International Journal* 85–109.

[44] Article 15.   [45] Article 68.

[46] Article 41 of the Minors Protection Law also declares that 'it is prohibited to coerce, entice or make use of minors to go begging, or to organize minors to carry out the activities such as performances which are harmful to their physical and mental health'. For analysis of the continuing problem of child labour, see Hu Deping and Liu Yuan, 'Lun Zhongguo tong-gong Wenti' (A discussion of the problem of child-labour in China) (2010) 9 *Zhongguo Qingnian Yanjiu* 148–53.

[47] Article 43.   [48] Article 240, 1997 Criminal Law.

[49] Criminal Law, Articles 301, 359, and 360.

[50] Articles 363, 364.   [51] Article 55.

'education, persuasion and redemption' and in a spirit of prioritizing education over punishment.[52] A minor who has been convicted and committed to prison is entitled to be kept in detention separate from the adult prison population.[53]

4.24 Courts are required to bring to trial promptly cases involving infringement of minors' rights and interests, and to extend legal aid to minors when required.[54] In cases of alleged sexual assault of a minor, law enforcement agencies must ensure that the victim's reputation is protected.[55] In addition, a special duty is placed on the courts to make sure that in succession cases minors receive their due share of the estate, and in divorce cases that minors 'capable of expressing a view' are listened to and the rights and interests of minors are fully protected.[56] As noted above, Article 53 of the Law allows for removal and replacement of a poorly performing guardian.

4.25 There is a problem, however, with the regime of 'judicial protection' offered by the Minors Protection Law. To a significant extent, in 'criminal matters' the regime is not relevant. This is because court proceedings are not the principal process for handling juvenile deviance. In all likelihood, such cases will be dealt with by the administrative punishments system, in which a local 'Re-education Through Labour Management Committee' will determine if misconduct (typically, drug-taking, prostitution, petty theft and so on) justifies detention for a period of up to three years (with a one-year extension for bad behaviour) in a 'Re-Education Through Labour' camp. This system is a major factor preventing the PRC from acceding to the International Covenant on Civil and Political Rights (ICCPR), which it signed in 1998 and which requires at Article 9 prompt judicial intervention rather than administrative decision-making in cases involving deprivation of liberty.

Population control

4.26 Until the introduction of the 2001 Population and Birth Planning Law, the birth control programme was located in provincial-level regulations, although some steps had been taken at the national level in the mid 1990s with the 1994 Mother and Child Health Care Law.[57] In 2002 the State Council introduced Measures on the Administration of the

[52] Article 54. [53] Article 57. [54] Article 51.
[55] Article 56. [56] Article 52.
[57] See Palmer, 'Protecting the Health of Mothers and their Children?', pp. 107–16.

Upbringing Charge, emphasizing and specifying financial penalties for breach of birth-planning rules. In very broad terms, the system of population control that has been put in place is officially regarded as an administrative response to a demographic problem and, especially in the 1980s and 1990s, gave rise to serious human rights concerns. The 1982 Constitution laid the legal foundation for the system, but expressed the problem in demographic and economic developmental terms: 'the state promotes family planning so that population growth may fit the plans for economic and social development'.[58] Population control formed the basis for China's single reservation – to respect for the inherent right to life, at Article 6 – which it entered when acceding to the Convention on the Rights of the Child. Another area of difficulty is the Convention on the Elimination of All Forms of Discrimination Against Women, which provides for gender equality in marriage and childbirth matters at Article 16, and declares at paragraph (e) that women and men must be given the same rights to decide freely and responsibly on the number and spacing of their children. In the case of China, this decision-making authority is, however, taken away from women (and their husbands) so that even if China does not breach the letter of this provision, it does not comply with the spirit. Couples must apply for permission to give birth, and only in special circumstances will permission be given for a further pregnancy. The birth-planning system is subject to increasing critiques within China, as fears of an ageing population set in.[59] Complaints are made that China increasingly suffers from the '4–2–1' family – four elderly grandparents, two parents, and one child, with the middle generation pressured, and vulnerable later in life. Nevertheless, birth planning remains a fundamental state policy, and manifests not only quantitative but also qualitative – eugenics – dimensions.[60] It also places a disproportionate responsibility on women, and has given rise to the serious imbalance in sex ratios among younger age groups, as son preference leads to female infanticide and abandonment of daughters. The 2001 Population Law[61] prohibits the use of ultrasound and related technologies to determine the sex of a fetus, but this remains a practice which in turn encourages sex-selective abortion. One of the controversies surrounding the Third Interpretation concerns Article 9,[62] which indicates that courts should defend the reproductive

[58] Article 25.
[59] See, for example, Yi Fuxian, 'Guo wei fu, ren yi liu' (Running out of labour before the country becomes wealthy) (2010) 12 *Shehui Kexue Luntan* 73–86.
[60] See also Note 4 above.
[61] Article 36[b].   [62] Article 10 in the draft.

rights of women by rejecting any claims for compensation made by a husband that their wife decided to terminate the pregnancy. It has been argued that it violates the rights of men under Article 17 of the 2001 Law on Population and Family Planning, which declares that citizens have the right to bear children. These opponents also argue that the provision in the Third Interpretation will encourage needless abortions, and even allow the threat of abortion to be used for improper purposes.[63]

C   Adult relationships

4.27   Although China has experienced more than six decades of Communist Party family policies, traditional patriarchal views of marriage and family often still predominate, especially in rural areas. As a result, there have been serious difficulties in defining and implementing women's rights within the family. One very problematic area has been women's access to divorce. Same-sex unions are not recognized, and even cohabitation is given only limited recognition. At the same time, rights in the matrimonial estate and other domestic assets have been seriously complicated by economic reforms and growing private ownership of property.

The relationships

Marriage

4.28   In imperial China marriage formalities were essentially a private matter, and especially in the countryside – where the great majority of Chinese people continue to live today – there remains a social preference for family celebration in traditional manner of marriage rather than fulfilment of the state's requirement of compulsory registration. This requirement is regarded officially as a mechanism for helping to implement 'socialist' principles of marriage and family such as monogamy as well as, more latterly, population control. China's system of mandatory marriage registration has been enforced more rigorously in the past two decades.[64] But, at the same time, there emerged a more nuanced view of

---

[63] 'Xinhunyinfa sanda jiaodian jiedu: chongji bangdakuan deng niuqu hunlianguan' (Explaining the three foci of the New Marriage Law: attacking twisted concepts of marriage such as finding a sugar daddy), *Banyue Tan*, available at http://gov.people.com.cn/GB/13604631.html.

[64] Michael Palmer, 'Marriage Reform and Population Control: Changing Family Law in Contemporary China', in A. Bainham (ed.), *International Survey of Family Law: 2005* (Bristol: Jordon, 2005), pp. 173–201, especially pp. 178–84.

the process of marriage formation in the 2001 revision to the Marriage Law, the Supreme People's Court's interpretations of that Law and the 2003 amendments to the rules on marriage registration, in which the party-state in effect acknowledged that there had hitherto been too much direct control of family life. The 2003 amendments also introduced more liberal procedures, in which the intending spouses are given responsibility, for example, for providing evidence that they possess the capacity to marry.[65] Prior to this, the intended couple's work units often played a key role. Also, earlier policies encouraging and sometimes even requiring pre-marital medical examination,[66] in a spirit of eugenics, were abandoned in part.[67] The 2003 reform also creates a marriage registration system that broadly applies not only to residents on the Chinese mainland, but also to residents of Hong Kong, Macau and Taiwan, as well as foreign parties intending to marry in China. In these ways, then, the 2003 revisions of the Marriage Registration Regulation reflected both a decline in the role of the work unit in regulating social life and greater Chinese engagement with the outside world.

4.29   Although the system gives only limited recognition to custom as a source of law, courts sometimes may deal with 'customary' family norms by recharacterizing such norms so that they fall within the ambit of the General Principles of the Civil Law 1986. For example, betrothal (*ding-hun*) is not recognized in PRC family law, and the 'extraction of gifts' in connection with marriage is forbidden,[68] but the People's Courts do deal with cases of broken betrothal. The recent Third Interpretation introduces a clarification of the important situation in which a fiancé(e) or spouse makes a gift (*zeng*) of a housing unit to her or his partner but then revokes the gift before registration of changed ownership is completed. According to Article 6 of the Third Interpretation, such a case will be handled under Article 186 of the 1999 Contract Law, and the gift may be retracted unless it has been made for some good public purpose or has been notarized.

Civil partnership

4.30   The public debate surrounding the 2001 revisions to the Marriage Law included some radical substantive proposals from experts on family

---

[65]   2003 Marriage Registration Regulations, Article 5.
[66]   1994 Marriage Registration Regulations, Articles 9 and 10.
[67]   The 2005 revised Women's Protection Law still encourages, at Article 51, intending spouses to submit to such examinations.
[68]   2001 Marriage Law, Article 3.

life. Li Yinhe, sociologist and director of the Marriage and Family Research Office of the Chinese Academy of Social Sciences, advocated legalization of same-sex marriages, admitting that while she did not expect the idea to be accepted, she wanted to argue the case in public because the homosexual community in China has such a weak voice. She continues to make such arguments, and suggests that there is a need in China to introduce a specific law covering same-sex marriages, and to revise further the Marriage Law so that the terms 'husband and wife' (*fu-qi*) are replaced by 'spouses' (*pei'ou*) and adding where relevant the phrase 'regardless of sex' (*xingbie buxian*) in order to render the Marriage Law less patriarchal and more 'gender neutral' in its language.[69] Nevertheless, neither same-sex marriage nor civil partnerships have been given legal recognition in the PRC, and many homosexuals enter into heterosexual marital unions in order to disguise their sexual orientation and to meet parental expectation of child-bearing.[70]

Cohabitation

4.31 As indicated above, a significant problem in the PRC's marriage registration system has been the prevalence in many areas, especially in the countryside, of customary or 'unregistered marriages'. The social practice of avoiding registration has persisted not only because of rural preference for celebration rather than registration, but also because of a felt need to marry at a young age so as to start a family and thereby ensure effective family care in later life – more children equates to greater old-age security. This avoidance of the strict requirement of marriage registration gave rise to difficulties in matrimonial cases, for the People's Courts were often faced with a petition for divorce involving a couple who had failed to comply with the registration requirement. Since the early 1980s the courts have been allowed less and less room to solve this problem in the way that they did in the first three decades of Communist Party rule, namely by characterizing the couple as de facto married (*shishi hunyin*) provided they met such criteria as being '*zhengpai ren*' (upright, decent

---

[69] See Li Yinhe, 'Tongxing Hunyin Ti'an' (A Proposal for Same-sex Marriage), available at http://blog.sina.com.cn/s/blog_473d5336010007t1.html. In addition see also the article in *Zhong Xin Wang*, 9 March 9 2006: 'Li Yinhe tan san ti tongxing hunyin ti an beijing – cheng liu cheng wangmin zhichi' (Li Yinhe discusses the background to three proposals on same-sex marriage – six adult web citizens give support) www.chinanews.com/news/2006/2006–03–09/8/700634.shtml.

[70] Xiong Jincai, 'The Dilemma of Homosexuals' Conventional Marriage in China' 5(2) *Journal of Comparative Law* (forthcoming).

people), having given birth to children, having performed a wedding ceremony, and were recognized in the local community as 'being married'.

4.32   One of the consequences of the social and economic changes taking
place in China in recent years has been the re-emergence of the traditional
practice of taking a 'concubine' (*bao'er nai*), in which a well-off man, who
felt the need for sons or younger female company (or both), in effect takes
a 'secondary wife'. At the time of the revision to the Marriage Law in 2001,
this growing phenomenon was the subject of considerable public debate.
Eventually, it was agreed that the taking of a 'concubine' could be grounds
for divorce, and possibly an entitlement of compensation by the wife thus
wronged,[71] but it would not be characterized as a crime of bigamy, however offensive to notions of monogamous marriage and gender equality.
In 2010 the published draft of the Third Interpretation aroused great controversy in this area of marital relations by trying to protect the wife's
interests in the matrimonial estate against claims made by or on behalf of
the concubine. Article 3 of the draft declared that the court should reject
claims if the third party – that is, the concubine – sought compensation.
Opposing this position were commentators who asserted that in all likelihood such a provision would encourage men to take secondary wives as
men would now have nothing to lose in entering into an arrangement with
a concubine, and concubines would be cast aside despite giving their partner the best years of their lives. In the final version of the Interpretation
the Supreme People's Court simply omitted this 'third party provision'
(*xiaosan tiaokuan*).[72]

Entering relationships

Marriage

4.33   As indicated above, marriage is created in Chinese law by the formality of registration, not by celebration. The 2001 ML declares that a
marriage has been established when marriage registration certificates are
issued.[73] Consent is required by Article 5, which adds that such consent
should not be coerced nor the marriage negotiated by a third party (such
as the bride's parents). The requirements on capacity are that minimum

---

[71] Article 46.
[72] 'Hunyinfa Xinjieshi Huishi "Xiaosan" Xianxiang Dada Jianshao?' (Will the New
     Marriage Law Interpretation Greatly Reduce 'the Third Party' Phenomenon?), available
     at www.legaldaily.com.cn/zmbm/content/2011–08/23/content_2896317.htm.
[73] Article 8.

legal ages of marriage must have been attained (22 years old or more for the groom, and 20 or more for the bride).[74] The couple may not be first cousins or closer kin, nor 'suffering from any disease that is regarded by medical science as rendering a person unfit for marriage'.[75] The distinctly high minimum legal ages of marriage reflects population control policies, and the Law also explicitly encourages late marriage and late childbirth:[76] delayed marriage and childbirth are thought to result in fewer births. Social practice is, however, somewhat different, especially in the countryside, where early 'marriage' and early and multiple births are socially encouraged. Such under-age unions are in a sense 'customary unions', and for many decades in the PRC the courts and other agencies regarded such unions as 'de facto' marriages. But as a result of a tightening in policy, for more than a decade it has been difficult in law for judicial and administrative organs to characterize these relationships as anything other than cohabitation. The current solution is to allow retrospective registration under Article 8 of the 2001 ML, and in the 2001 Interpretation it is specified that the union may be characterized as lawful marriage when the parties attain the legal age of marriage and complete the formalities of remedial registration. Only if the relationship was entered into before 1994 will it be characterized as de facto marriage.[77]

4.34   The 2001 Law introduced a clear distinction between void and voidable marriages, one that had not existed hitherto in PRC family law. This distinction is especially important with respect to the social problem in China of forced marriage (*xiepo hunyin*) – and therefore in enhancing women's rights – for although Article 5 of the Law prohibits coercion, there are many difficulties in the Chinese countryside ranging from parental pressure to kidnap and sale for purposes of marriage. A party forced into marriage may seek a declaration that the marriage was void *ab initio* for lack of consent if she brings an application within one year from either the date of the forced marriage or from the date at which she secured her freedom. The coerced woman may bring an application to the court or a marriage registration organ.[78] Issues of property are to be dealt with by negotiated agreement between the parties, or if such negotiations fail, then by an order of the court 'favouring the innocent party' – ordinarily, the wife. Children born to the union are dealt with under the ordinary provisions of the Marriage Law governing parent–child relations.[79]

---

[74] Article 6.   [75] Article 7.   [76] Article 6.
[77] Article 5.   [78] Marriage Law, Article 11.   [79] Article 11.

Cohabitation

4.35   Unmarried young people cohabiting in cities is a growing social trend in the PRC, although the legal consequences of such relationships have not yet been addressed in the law. In traditional China the taking of a 'secondary wife' was recognized in law, and local customary law often prescribed certain formalities, but concubinage has long been prohibited in PRC law.[80] As we have seen, in some circumstances the state will recognize customary unions as lawful marriage, equal in status to a registered union, once remedial steps have been taken. And even when the courts or other agencies are unable to make such a determination, there are rights that spring from cohabitation that a court handling a 'divorce' case involving cohabitants must take into account.[81] Many relationships that are characterized officially as cohabitation are in fact 'customary unions' in which the formalities of marriage registration have not been carried out. Customary ceremonies, which afford social recognition in the local community, are considered sufficient in the eyes of local people.

4.36   Another key dimension of the problem of cohabitation is, as we have seen, the re-emergence of the traditional practice of taking a 'concubine' or 'secondary wife'. Ever since the 1950 Marriage Law was introduced, monogamy has been a strict principle in PRC family law and a key issue in the promotion of women's rights. Not surprisingly, in the public debate on the draft revisions to the Marriage Law in 2000 and 2001, robust arguments were put forward to the effect that the conduct of a married man in taking a concubine should be characterized as a criminal offence – bigamy. As we have noted, this argument did not succeed, but concubinage is in effect a specific ground for divorce[82] and is explicitly prohibited by Article 3, paragraph 2. Developments over the past decade indicate that the authorities find it difficult to address this issue. The 2003 Interpretation stipulates that the courts no longer have the authority to deal with ordinary cases of dissolving cohabitation – rather, it is only cases involving cohabitation between a married man and a concubine that the court is allowed to handle.[83] As we have seen, the published draft of the Third Interpretation issued in 2010 attempted to address explicitly

---

[80]   Marriage Law 1950, Article 2.
[81]   See Michael Palmer, 'The People's Republic of China: More Rules but Less Law', in M. Freeman (ed.), *Annual Survey of Family Law: 1989*, vol. 13 (London: The International Society on Family Law, 1991), pp. 325–42.
[82]   Article 23[a].   [83]   Article 1.

the property consequences of dissolving a relationship of concubinage, but such was the controversy over this matter that in the final version this was omitted.

Consequences of relationships

Marriage

4.37 The idealized effect of creating a registered marriage is to put in place a harmonious family[84] that practises family planning[85] and voluntarily implements the single-child family ideal,[86] supporting not only children born to the marriage but also ageing parents of the spouses. Within the family, husband and wife are equal – although in characterizing this equality the legislation invariably places the term 'husband' (*fu*) before that of 'wife' (*qi*)[87] – and each is entitled to use her or his own surname,[88] enjoy equal rights to work and study and so on.[89] Family members are locked into a nexus of mutual rights and obligations of support and, ultimately, succession.

4.38 Following registration, a matrimonial estate (*fu-qi gongtong caichan*) is created, although each spouse will likely retain some personal property. Article 17 of the 2001 Marriage Law indicates that the scope of the matrimonial estate is legally intended to be substantial as it includes wages and bonuses, income from 'production or management', intellectual property rights and most property acquired by gift or inheritance. Otherwise, it is property independently owned by the spouses prior to marriage, together with disability and medical entitlements, and property used for specific purposes by each partner that remains individually owned. The spouses also have an option under Article 19 to reach their own written agreement on the precise scope of the matrimonial and personal estates, covering both property held prior to marriage and property acquired during marriage. In the absence of a written agreement, the statutory rules apply. In divorce cases, when applying the statutory rules, the courts should take into account the nature of the property and apply the principle of giving preferential treatment to the wife and children,[90] as well as awarding compensation to a spouse who has played a major role in

---

[84] ML 2001, Article 4.   [85]   Article 16.
[86] Population Law, 2001, Article 27.
[87] Article 14.   [88] Article 13.   [89] Article 15.
[90] Article 39.

running the family home, given support to children, assisted elderly family members, and so on.[91] The court should also ensure debts are properly dealt with,[92] and render special assistance to a divorcing spouse who has serious livelihood difficulties.[93]

4.39 In wealthier parts of China, parents are increasingly concerned to ensure that their child or children, especially sons, takes a bride from a family of equal status. There is a significant worry that marriage to a girl from a modest background financially will threaten family wealth. This anxiety was another of the controversial areas in the drafting of the Third Interpretation, with the Supreme People's Court throwing a protective ring around parental property gifts made subsequent to marriage. Under the 2001 Marriage Law, the gift of (say) an apartment made prior to marriage is unlikely to be characterized as part of the intending spouses' matrimonial estate. Now that rule is extended to such gifts even if made after marriage. Thus, the Interpretation declares that real estate purchased by one of the couple's parents after marriage, so long as it is registered under that child's name, may be regarded as the parents' grant to that offspring and the personal property of that particular party.[94] It would not fall within the scope of the matrimonial estate of the newly married couple, and therefore would not be subject to division in the event of a divorce. Those supporting this change in the law argued, inter alia, that its enactment frees many people from the worry of having their pre-marriage property transformed into matrimonial property after marriage, encourages both spouses to contribute financially to the family and deters people from using marriage 'to make money', as expressed in the common sayings that 'houses are more reliable than men' (*fangzi dou bi nanren kekao*), it is best to 'find a sugar daddy' (*bang dakuan*), and so on.[95] Opposed to this change are those who assert that it will trigger a rise in the divorce rate by easing the worries of financial loss by the parties. In addition, it will be disadvantageous to women, because a woman's household contributions may well be underestimated, and promoting an

---

[91] Article 40.

[92] Article 41.

[93] Article 42.

[94] Article 7.

[95] 'Xinhunyinfa sanda jiaodian jiedu: chongji bang dakuan deng niuqu hunlianguan' (Explaining the three foci of the New Marriage Law: attacking twisted concepts of marriage such as leaning on a moneybags), *Banyue Tan* (China Comment), available at http://gov.people.com.cn/GB/13604631.html.

'individualist approach' to personal property protection will undermine the 'harmony' in marriage.[96]

Cohabitation

4.40   Difficulties in enforcing the compulsory requirement of registration of marriage have been noted above, and in the late 1980s a tightening of official policy on the issue of non-registration was expressed in the form of Supreme People's Court rules for courts handling applications for 'divorce' in which the couple had lived together in an unregistered 'marriage'.[97] These rules appear to have marked the introduction of a judicial presumption that unregistered cohabitation is often best characterized as 'illegal' (*feifa tongju*) – especially when one or both spouses are under the minimum legal age of marriage – and that parties living together as husband and wife without registration should be subject to 'criticism' and 'education', and given civil penalties. As we have also seen, the Law as it now stands has adopted a somewhat more relaxed approach, encouraging remedial marriage registration once the minimum legal ages of marriage have been attained. Some commentators argue that the concept of 'illegal cohabitation' has in effect been withdrawn, as the term has not been used in judicial practice since the mid 1990s nor employed in the 2001 and 2003 Interpretations. Indeed, the 2003 Interpretation at Article 1 declares that ordinarily the court should not even accept an application for dissolution of a relationship of cohabitation.[98]

Termination of relationships

Divorce

4.41   In the post-Mao era, as China's more pragmatic leadership hesitantly embraced the principle of socialist legality, a serious attempt was

---

[96] Ma Yinan, 'HunyinFa Jieshi San de jiazhi kunjing' (The value dilemma of the Third Interpretation of the Marriage Law) (2011) 218 *Zhongguo Shehui Kexue Bao* 11.

[97] Zhonghua Renmin Gongheguo Zuigao Renmin Fayuan (Supreme People's Court of the PRC), Guanyu renmin fayuan shenli wei ban jiehun dengji er yi fu-qi mingyi tongju shenghuo anjian de ruogan yijian (Some specific opinions regarding cases tried by people's courts in which couples live together as man and wife without performing marriage registration), November 1989.

[98] See Wang Wei, *Feihun tongju falü zhidu bijiao yanjiu* (Comparative Study of the Legal System of Non-marital Cohabitation) (Beijing: Renmin Chubanshe, 2009), p. 37.

made to provide 'freedom of divorce', especially for women.[99] Divorce rates remain relatively low by international standards, with one in five marriages ending in divorce, but divorce is a socially controversial issue and something of a 'moral panic'. In recent times complications have arisen in the treatment of property and money on divorce, especially in contested cases where the petitioner is the wife.

4.42 Nevertheless, some two-fifths of all Chinese divorces are by mutual consent[100] and secured through routine administrative rather than judicial processes. Marriage registrars are expected to attempt mediation, and to ensure that the key issues of children, money and property are agreed satisfactorily between the parties, and if mediation fails and the arrangements between the parties on the key issues are reasonable, to grant divorce (Article 31, ML 2001).

4.43 The majority of divorces in China are, however, contested. The authorities have made significant efforts through statutory law reform and improvements in judicial practice to enhance access to divorce justice, especially for women. Thus, in the 1980 Marriage Law an especially important change was the recognition of freedom of divorce.[101] This provided more liberal provisions on divorce and, in particular, specified – unlike its 1950 predecessor – that a breakdown in mutual affection (*ganqing polie*) between a married couple was a sufficient ground for divorce if mediatory efforts failed to achieve reconciliation. In 1989 a Supreme People's Court Opinion introduced new rules, specifying more precisely the circumstances in which the breakdown may be presumed.[102] The Opinion was a significant step in the development of genuine freedom of divorce for women, but also manifested more clearly than had hitherto been the case in PRC family law a distinction between the 'innocent' party (*wu guocuo fang*) and the party 'guilty' (*guocuo fang*) of matrimonial wrongdoing. This distinction was retained in the 2001 revisions to the Marriage Law, where at Article 32 four main grounds for divorce are now specified: bigamy and concubinage, domestic

---

[99] Michael Palmer, 'Some General Observations on Family Law in the People's Republic of China', in M. Freeman (ed.), *Annual Survey of Family Law: 1985*, vol. 9 (London: The International Society on Family Law, 1986), pp. 41–68.

[100] See Michael Palmer, 'The Re-emergence of Family Law in Post-Mao China: Marriage, Divorce and Reproduction' (1995) 141 Special Issue of *China Quarterly* 'Law in China Under Reform', guest editor Stanley Lubman, 110–34.

[101] Article 25.

[102] See Palmer, 'The People's Republic of China: More Rules but Less Law', pp. 325–42.

violence or other forms of maltreatment or desertion, gambling or drug addiction, and a breakdown in mutual affection plus separation for two years.

4.44   The 2001 First Interpretation at Article 23 to some extent limits the moralistic ethos of these provisions by stipulating that a petition for divorce may not be rejected on the ground that the petitioner is partly to blame. On the other hand, Article 46 of the 2001 revised Marriage Law also emphasizes wrongdoing, and provides the possibility of compensation for the serious misconduct. Further, the 2003 Second Interpretation at Article 27 stipulates that when divorce by mutual consent applications are being made, one party may still seek compensation from the other for matrimonial fault.

Domestic violence

4.45   Another very significant transformation in recent years has been a growing awareness of the importance of the problem of domestic violence (*jiating baoli*). The social tensions associated with rapid economic change, international pressures and greater recognition within China that the traditional response of using mediatory intervention to contain domestic violence is not always appropriate, have resulted in a more interventionist approach.[103] This growing awareness of the problem eventually resulted in the introduction in Article 43 of the Marriage Law (and also subsequently, in the 2005 revised Women's Protection Law)[104] of special provisions on domestic violence. While these continue to encourage mediatory and administrative intervention, they also stipulate that recourse to police intervention and criminal prosecution are also possible. The firmer approach taken in both policy and law in recent years is a significant advance, especially in the sense that domestic violence is now seen as a matter of public – not just private – concern, and therefore also of criminal law sanctions. Indeed, the Standing Committee of the NPC has announced plans for a full 'Anti-Domestic Violence Law' to be introduced soon.[105]

---

[103]   See Michael Palmer: 'Patriarchy, Privacy and Protection: Slowly Conceptualizing Domestic Violence in Chinese Law', in Natalia Iu. Erpyleva, Jane Henderson and M. Butler (eds.), *Forging a Common Legal Destiny: Liber Amicorum in Honour of Professor W. E. Butler* (London and New York: Wildy, Simmonds and Hill, 2005), pp. 786–812.

[104]   See Palmer, 'On China's Slow Boat to Women's Rights'.

[105]   'Quanguo Renda Weiyuanhui zhuoshou kaizhan fan jiating baoli fa yanjiu he lunzheng' (The Standing Committee of the National People's Congress is developing research and

Cohabitation

4.46   As we have noted, cohabitation may now be recharacterized as marriage through remedial registration, and in such cases dissolution therefore takes the form of divorce. In the past, the court was itself able to recharacterize cohabitation as marriage, and then to deal with the matrimonial dispute accordingly. However, in 1989 the Supreme People's Court issued an Opinion on the manner in which courts should handle disputes in which the couple's relationship could not be defined as matrimonial even though they had regarded themselves as married. This created all sorts of difficulty, and the Second Interpretation 2003 now simply declares that it is not the responsibility of the People's Courts to handle cases of dissolution of cohabitation. In many cases community mediation will help the couple to decide these matters, and in reality since unregistered unions are mainly found in the countryside, such mediatory intervention may well favour the man, as it will often be the case that the local mediation committee is composed of members who are kinsfolk of the 'husband'.

Consequences of termination

Marriage

4.47   A distinctive feature of PRC family law is that remarriage of divorced couples to each other is encouraged, and given the special term in Chinese of 'restored marriage' (*fuhun*). The party-state would prefer couples not to divorce, but if they do, then they should consider correcting their 'mistake' subsequently and go through another marriage ceremony with each other.[106]

4.48   Typically, the matrimonial estate is divided at divorce through a process of negotiation between the parties. If a judicial determination is required, then the court should take into account the circumstances of the property and adhere to the principle of favouring the wife and children.[107]

---

debate on anti-domestic violence legislation), *Zhongguo Funü Bao*, available at http://acwf.people.com.cn/GB/99051/15717372.html.

[106] 2001 ML, Article 25.

[107] 2001 ML, Article 39. In addition, rules likely to favour women in these circumstances are provided in two other articles of the Law. Thus, Article 40 stipulates: 'in the case both husband and wife agree to separately own the property they respectively obtain during the existence of their marriage and either of them has spent considerably more effort on supporting children, taking care of the old or assisting the other party in work, etc., this party shall be entitled to demand the other party to make compensations at the time of

Failure by either of the parties to negotiate in good faith by concealing or alienating the property covertly, or by creating false debts, may be sanctioned by the court under the Civil Procedure Law, and by the award by the court of a smaller share or even no share at all of the matrimonial estate.[108] It is also open to the other party, if such misconduct is discovered subsequent to the divorce, to apply for a repartition of the matrimonial estate.[109] An extensive corpus of rules has emerged in recent years dealing with such issues as intellectual property rights, the scope of the matrimonial estate to be divided, the role of debts, ownership of equity, partnership rights and so on.[110] Important issues surfaced in the drafting of the 2011 Third Interpretation over the division of property when a marriage is dissolved.[111] As we have seen, a draft provision regarding possible compensation to discarded concubines was not included in the final version of the Interpretation, although another controversial provision was retained and is now to be found in Article 7, making it possible

---

divorce, and the requested party shall make compensations.' And Article 42 reads: 'if, at the time of divorce, either party has difficulties in life, the other party shall render appropriate assistance from his or her personal property such as a house, and so on'. It adds that the People's Court will impose a decision if the couple cannot reach a detailed agreement.

[108] Article 47. Moreover, under the 2011 Third Interpretation such misconduct constitutes a ground for division of the matrimonial estate even if divorce is not being sought: 'where, during the existence of a marital relationship, a spouse claims division of community property, the People's Court shall not support such a claim unless any of the following material reasons exists and the creditor's interests are not damaged: ... A spouse conceals, transfers, sells, destroys or squanders community property, fabricates joint debts, or commits any other conduct that seriously damages the community property'; Article 4.

[109] Article 47.

[110] See, for example Marriage Law as revised 2001, Articles 17, 18, 19, 31, 40, 41 and 42; the Marriage Law First Interpretation, 2001, Article 27, and the Marriage Law Second Interpretation, Article 11, 13, 19, 20, 22, and 23. The relevant 2001 Third Interpretation provisions are discussed in the main text below.

[111] Division at time of separation is not permitted except in special circumstances: Article 4 of the 2011 Third Interpretation of the Marriage Law provides that 'where, during the existence of a marital relationship, a spouse claims division of community property, the People's Court shall not support such a claim unless any of the following material reasons exists and the creditor's interests are not damaged: (1) A spouse conceals, transfers, sells, destroys or squanders community property, fabricates joint debts, or commits any other conduct that seriously damages the community property; or (2) A person to whom a spouse has a statutory obligation of support suffers from a serious illness and needs medical treatment, but the other spouse refuses to pay the relevant medical expenses'.

for parental gifts of property post-marriage to be kept separate from the matrimonial estate.

Cohabitation

4.49 The Second Interpretation 2003 declares that it is not the responsibility of the People's Courts any longer ordinarily to handle cases of dissolution of cohabitation. Before this change, in the judicial termination of a relationship of cohabitation the court was expected, broadly speaking, to follow the principles that apply in a divorce case. However, in several important respects the court could make rulings somewhat less favourable to the woman than might have been the case in terminating a marriage,[112] especially on the issue of custody, even though in theory protection is given to the status and the support of children born to relations of cohabitation by the requirement in Article 25 of the 2001 revised Marriage Law that legitimate and illegitimate children be treated equally in law.

Self-regulation and custom-made relationships

4.50 The rather monolithic framework of family law and regulation outlined above is subject to variation and extension in several ways. Thus, under Article 50 of the Marriage Law 2001, Article 18 of the Population and Birth Planning Law 2001 and similar provisions elsewhere in Chinese family law, local people's congresses and governments are empowered to enact subsidiary legislation on the family consistent with national legislation but adapted to local conditions. Secondly, the People's Courts have over the years often dealt with cases in which local people have made their marriage arrangements in accordance with local customary norms, rather than state law. Although they have done so reluctantly, the courts have sometimes felt the need to give legal recognition directly or indirectly to such customary norms. Thirdly, the trajectory of family law reform has slowly expanded the extent to which parties are allowed to make their own arrangements, including pre-nuptial contracts, in order to avoid possible future difficulties, and to negotiate their own arrangements when marital relations break down.

---

[112] Palmer, 'The People's Republic of China: More Rules but Less Law', pp. 326 and 328–33.

D   Conclusions

4.51   The corpus of family law that has emerged in the PRC over the past three decades has introduced numerous significant reforms that are important for enhancing the lives of ordinary Chinese people. The emerging framework moved away from a predominant concern with social control and administrative needs, with often limited substantive law provisions and an overwhelming concern with mediation for dispute resolution purposes, to a fuller, more nuanced and law-based system. China remains in political terms essentially a one-party, centralized state, with a Leninist apparatus of CCP control, and with a normative preference for policy rather than law, and this encourages a monolithic and moralistic approach to family regulation. But the Deng Xiaoping-inspired market-orientated economic reforms, much greater engagement with the global community and significant generational change have created greater heterogeneity within Chinese society, encouraged stronger concern with the individual and her or his human rights, prompted more public involvement in the law-making process, and necessitated a higher degree of technical sophistication in the law.

4.52   It is likely that in the years to come the trajectory of Chinese family law will continue to stress and bring greater and more nuanced concern in a range of areas. These will include women's and (to a lesser extent) children's rights, access to divorce, domestic violence, reproductive rights, cohabitation and the matrimonial estate. But law reform in these areas will also be complicated and difficult, as increasing social complexities and tensions now need to be taken into account. In the past thirty years the contrasts in rural–urban lifestyle have been magnified, differences in social values across the generations have become greater, enormous disparities in the pace of economic development between the eastern littoral and the poorer inland western regions of China have appeared, greater wealth and personal freedoms encourage conduct that reflects the values of traditional rather than socialist China, the population is ageing, biotechnical advances are increasingly significant, and there is an ever-increasing engagement with the outside world. These complicating factors will need to be taken into account in reforming family law, but at the same time, official CCP ideology and therefore fundamental state policies on the family in China remain infused with a largely patriarchal moral conservativism, and the leadership in China still thinks of legal reform as a top-down process. There has been only limited political development in

China in recent years, and an autonomous civil society is still struggling to establish itself away from the shadow cast by China's gerontocratic leadership. As a result, unless there is major political change, in addressing through law the key marriage and family issues as they emerge in the years to come, significant tensions will be created. In addition, substantive law reform outcomes will be produced that are sometimes inconsistent with each other and also with the changing values and practices of Chinese society.

5

India

A perspective

ANIL MALHOTRA AND RANJIT MALHOTRA

A Introduction

5.1   Indian child and family law has undergone a sea change over the last fifty years with most family laws being enacted by the Indian Parliament after Indian independence from British rule in 1947.[1] The family law system that developed from the Mitakshara school,[2] which essentially focused on the extended family, has been transformed into one based on the nuclear family. This metamorphosis was an inevitable result of the changing social conditions and attitudes that, in turn, led to various social revolutions in India.

Historical roots, sources and law reform

5.2   The Constitution of India, which forms the basis of family law, was enacted on 26 November 1949 and its preamble resolved to constitute India as a union of states and a sovereign, socialist, secular democratic republic.[3] Today, a population of over one billion Indians live in twenty-eight states and seven Union Territories within India while some thirty million 'Non-Resident Indians' live in 130 foreign jurisdictions. Within the territory of India spread over an area of 3.28 million square kilometres, the large Indian population comprising multi-cultural societies, professing and practising different religions and speaking different local languages, coexists in harmony in the largest democracy in the world.

---

[1]   Indian Independence Act 1947, c.30 (UK).
[2]   Law according to the ancient scriptures of The Hindus.
[3]   The Preamble to the Constitution of India enacted on 26 November 1949 solemnly resolved to constitute India into a Sovereign Socialist Secular Democratic Republic.

5.3   The Indian Constitution established a High Court for each state and the Supreme Court of India.[4] Under Article 141 of the Constitution, the law declared by the Supreme Court is binding on all courts within the territory of India. However, the Supreme Court is not bound by its own earlier decisions.

5.4   Part III of the Constitution of India secures to its citizens 'fundamental rights', which can be enforced directly in the respective High Courts of the states or directly in the Supreme Court of India by issue of prerogative writs under Articles 225 and 32, respectively, of the Constitution of India. Under the constitutional scheme, freedom of religion and the right to freely profess, practise and propagate religion is sacrosanct and is thus enforceable by a writ.

5.5   Simultaneously, Part IV of the Indian Constitution lays down 'Directive Principles of State Policy' that are not enforceable by any court but are, nevertheless, fundamental in the governance of the country, and it is the duty of the state to apply these principles when making law. Under Article 44 of the Constitution, the state shall endeavour to secure for the citizens a uniform civil code throughout the territory of India. However, realistically speaking, a uniform civil code remains an aspiration that India has yet to realise.

5.6   India has ratified both the UN Convention on the Elimination of Discrimination Against Women[5] and the UN Convention on the Rights of the Child[6] and, as we shall see, legislative changes, designed to ensure compliance with these conventions, have followed.[7]

Diverse laws for different religious groups

5.7   The Indian legal system follows the common law model, but India is a land of diversity with numerous religions being practised in the country. Thus, personal law is often governed by statutes specific to particular religious groups, with those to whom the statute applies and the appropriate court or body where remedies can be sought being defined in the statute. While Hindu personal law has undergone a continuous process

---

[4] Article 214.   [5] (1979) 1249 UNTS 13.   [6] (1989) 1577 UNTS 3.

[7] See, for example, the Juvenile Justice (Care and Protection of Children) Act 2000, the Commissions for Protection of Child Rights Act 2005, the Protection of Women from Domestic Violence Act 2005 and the Right of Children to Free and Compulsory Education Act 2009.

of codification, reflecting changing social conditions, Muslim personal law has been left comparatively untouched by legislators. The Hindu Marriage Act 1955, codifying marriage law, applies to any person who is a Hindu, Buddhist, Jaina or Sikh and to any other person who is not a Muslim, Christian, Parsi or Jew. The Act also applies to Hindus resident outside the territory of India.[8] There are specific statutes applying to Parsis,[9] Christians[10] and Muslims[11] living in India. The Hindu Minority and Guardianship Act 1956 applies to Hindus, while the Guardian and Wards Act 1890 applies to non-Hindus.

5.8   This system of different personal laws does not tell the whole story, however. The Special Marriage Act 1954 governs all matrimonial causes of persons who do not profess any particular religion or are foreigners. It provides for a special form of marriage and for the registration of marriage and divorces and is used by some Hindus, non-Hindus and foreigners marrying in India who opt out of ceremonial marriage under their respective personal laws. Divorce can also be obtained by non-Hindus under this Act. While the Hindu Succession Act 1956 codifies testate and intestate succession for Hindus, the Indian Succession Act 1925, consolidating testamentary and intestate succession, applies to all unless parties opt out and choose to be governed by the codified law. Interestingly, section 125 of the Code of Criminal Procedure 1973 provides that any person may approach a magistrate seeking maintenance, giving an independent remedy irrespective of religion.[12]

5.9   The appropriate judicial forum for the enforcement and adjudication of matrimonial and other related disputes is designated in the relevant legislations. Every state in India has civil and criminal courts that operate under the overall jurisdiction of the state High Court. In addition, the Indian Parliament has enacted The Family Courts Act 1984 to provide for the establishment of Family Courts with a view to promoting conciliation and securing the speedy settlement of disputes relating to marriage and family affairs.[13] Despite the existence of an organised, well-regulated and established hierarchy

---

[8] See further paras. 5.60–5.65 below.
[9] The Parsi Marriage and Divorce Act 1936, as amended in 1988.
[10] The Christian Marriage Act 1872 and the Divorce Act 1869 as amended in 2001.
[11] The Muslim Personal Law (Shariat) Application Act 1937, the Dissolution of Muslim Marriages Act 1939 and the Muslim Women (Protection of Rights on Divorce) Act 1986.
[12] On the section's application to Muslim women, see para. 5.72 below.
[13] See further paras. 5.66–5.69 below.

of judicial courts in India, unrecognised parallel community and religious courts continue to operate and their role has been criticised by the judicial courts, since such unauthorised bodies work without the authority of law and are not part of the judicial system.[14]

Access to legal services

India's legal system

5.10   The development of a country may be judged by the capacity of its legal system to render effective justice. The practice of amicable resolution of disputes in India can be traced back to historic times, when village disputes were resolved between members of particular families or occupations, or between residents of a particular locality. In rural India, the *panchayats* (assembly of elders and respected inhabitants of the village) decided almost all disputes between the residents of the village, while disputes between members of a clan continued to be decided by the elders of the clan. These methods of amicable dispute resolution were recognised methods of administration of justice and not just an 'alternative' to the formal justice system formed by the sovereigns, feudal lords or the *adalat* systems initiated by the British and the formal court system. The two systems continued to function alongside each other.

5.11   India has a massive legal system comprising nearly 15,000 courts across the country. It is the constitutional obligation of the judiciary to exercise jurisdiction to reaffirm the faith of the people in the judicial system. Therefore, evolution of new juristic principles for dispute resolution is not only important but also imperative. In India the need to develop alternative mechanisms simultaneous with the revival and strengthening of traditional systems of dispute resolution has been reiterated in reports of expert bodies.[15] Each of these reports saw the process of improving access to justice through legal aid mechanisms and alternative dispute resolution (ADR) as a part of the systemic reform of the judiciary coupled with substantive reforms of laws and processes.

---

[14] See further paras. 5.12–5.15 below.
[15] Committee on Legal Aid, *Report of the Expert Committee on Legal Aid: Processual Justice to the People* (New Delhi: Government of India, 1971); Government of India, Ministry of Law, Justice and Company Affairs, *Report on National Juridicare Equal Justice – Social Justice* (New Delhi: Government of India, 1978).

Extra-judicial courts

5.12 Community practices in certain states in India amongst certain religious denominations have led to the creation of community or religious courts which are not authorised by law and are not sanctioned by the official legal system. In the matter of inter-caste or inter-religious marriages and divorces these self-styled extra-constitutional authorities take upon themselves the power of courts to issue community mandates. Such religious edicts result from summary hearings, often in violation of fundamental rights guaranteed by the Constitution of India. In *Vishwa Lochan Madan* v. *Union of India and others*[16] the Supreme Court of India issued notices to the central government, state governments, the All India Muslim Personal Law Board (AIMPLB) and Darul Uloom (an Islamic seminary) in respect of the existence of these parallel unconstitutional courts which pose a challenge to the Indian judicial system. The petitioner was seeking immediate dissolution of all Islamic and shariat (also known as sharia) courts in India. He sought a ban on the establishment of such Islamic courts, along with a declaration that *fatwas* have no legal authority, and requested the Court to direct the central and the state governments to take effective steps to dissolve all Darul Qazas and shariat courts in India. The petitioner further sought a direction from the Court to the AIMPLB and Darul Uloom, Deoband, other seminaries and Muslim organisations asking them to refrain from establishing a parallel Muslim Judicial System (Nizam-e-Qaza).

5.13 Clearly, this raises the crucial issue of whether there could be two parallel legal systems in operation: one secular and the other religious. In particular, it should be remembered that the Constitution of India prohibits discrimination on grounds of caste or religion. Furthermore, questions should be asked as to whether the right to freedom of religion could be extended to the establishment of a parallel judicial system. The matter is still pending final adjudication in the Supreme Court of India and no final judgment has been handed down.

5.14 On similar lines, there are the *caste panchayats* (village councils), especially in the State of Haryana in India. These *caste panchayats* become involved in disputes, often by declaring marriages invalid, and invariably their victims belong to the weakest sections of society. Traditionally, *caste*

---

[16] On 27 March 2006 the Supreme Court of India issued notices in this matter, but the Supreme Court website does not give any citation as the matter is pending and still not concluded.

panchayats have also played a powerful role at village level in several other states in the country. However, *khap panchayats* (caste-based village councils) are not elected bodies and their decisions are not enforceable by law. As such, these extra-constitutional bodies have no authority or recognition in law, but rather derive support from community recognition. *Khap panchayats* are so powerful because of their ability to mobilise a large number of people. They appear to be democratic from the outside, but they are not since they exclude women and young people as well as the groups who are lower down in the caste hierarchy in the village.

5.15 The decisions of the courts are undoubtedly a setback to the *caste panchayats* of Haryana, which have a powerful influence. While a positive step has been taken by the court, there cannot be a positive outcome until society as a whole seeks to demolish this obsolete system. The authorities have done little to check the extra-judicial activities of these courts, which are a blatant interference with the fundamental rights of the citizens. The responsibility of the state cannot be abdicated. The judiciary seems best placed to provide relief in matters involving blatant violation of fundamental rights by community councils. Courts cannot legislate, but must vindicate human rights. Notwithstanding, the duty of the state to enforce the law of the land is the need of the day. The courts should strike down any mandates of any such extra-judicial bodies without hesitation, since they have no legal authority in a civilised society.

Alternative dispute resolution

5.16 Access to legal services is a major problem, rendering the use of ADR vital. Empowering individuals to resolve their own disputes and assisting them by promoting ADR can bring many benefits, not least in avoiding the acrimony, delay and cost often associated with litigation. The duty to enact or amend law lies with the legislature, but its development and interpretation in a manner designed to best serve the needs and circumstances of society lies firmly with the judiciary. Accordingly, until the beneficial provisions of the matrimonial legislation promoting and advocating reconciliation in matrimonial disputes in India is favourably interpreted and strictly implemented by the courts, the letter of law may be an illusion which remains on the statute book only. It is the solemn duty of the matrimonial courts in India to ensure that the mandatory settlement efforts are actually put into practice and parties are encouraged to utilise them for out-of-court settlements. Thus, there is a heavy burden on the courts in discharging this solemn duty, failing which it will neither be possible nor useful to enforce reconciliatory measures in matrimonial disputes.

5.17   It is clear that the duty cast upon the matrimonial courts to attempt mandatory reconciliation cannot be avoided or circumvented, even when divorce is sought on certain exceptional grounds where the Hindu Marriage Act 1955 and the Special Marriage Act 1954 do not provide for compulsory settlement of actions. Accordingly, the Supreme Court in *Balwinder Kaur* v. *Hardeep Singh*[17] laid down that:

> stress should always be on preserving the institution of marriage. That is the requirement of law. For the purpose of settlement of family disputes emphasis is laid on conciliation and achieving socially desirable results and eliminating adherence to rigid rules of procedure and evidence.[18]

5.18   In light of this, the purpose of section 23(2) of the Hindu Marriage Act 1955 was explained in *Love Kumar* v. *Sunita Puri*[19] as follows:

> It is fundamental that reconciliation of a ruptured marriage is the first duty of the Judge. The sanctity of marriage is the cornerstone of civilization. The state is interested in the security and preservation of the institution of marriage and for this the Court is required to attempt reconciliation between the parties. Such an attempt can be and should be made at any stage. The matrimonial Court is required to call parties and make a genuine effort for their reconciliation; there is not even a whisper in this provision that the matrimonial Court has the power to strike off the defence of that spouse, who after being given opportunities for reconciliation, fails to appear.[20]

5.19   It is clear that reconciliation is a mandatory process. However, the timing and stage at which it is to be implemented may vary, depending on the facts and circumstances of each case. At the same time, causing prejudice to the rights of one party by striking off the defence or dismissing the petition may actually prove an injustice to the rights of such a party. Therefore, the Matrimonial Court may fashion and design the reconciliation process, depending on the facts of each case, without causing prejudice to the substantive rights of the parties.

---

[17] [1998] All India Reporter (Supreme Court) 764.
[18] *Ibid.*, paragraph 9.
[19] [1997] All India Reporter (Punjab and Haryana) 189.
[20] *Ibid.*, at paragraph 19.

B   Children in the family setting and state intervention

Defining and classifying children

5.20   As a general rule, a 'minor' is a person under 18 years old,[21] with a 'child' or a 'juvenile' having the same meaning.[22] Under the Indian Contract Act 1872 every person is competent to contract who is of the age of majority according to the law to which he is subject.[23] The Hindu Marriage Act 1955 and the Special Marriage Act 1954 use the term 'minor children', but do not define it. The Hindu Marriage Act 1955 confers legitimacy to children born to both void and voidable marriages[24] and the Hindu Adoptions and Maintenance Act 1956 permits a minor child, whether legitimate or illegitimate, to claim maintenance from his or her father or mother.[25]

Recognising parentage and family ties

5.21   A 'guardian' is defined by the Hindu Minority and Guardianship Act 1956 (hereinafter, the 'HMGA') as a person having the care of the person of the minor or of his property or both and includes a natural guardian, a guardian appointed by will of his natural parents, a guardian appointed or declared by the court and a person empowered to act as such under any enactment.[26]

Adoption

5.22   There are some twelve million orphan children in India in need of parents, and the Juvenile Justice (Care and Protection of Children) Act 2000 (JJ) permits adoption of orphaned, abandoned, neglected and abused children through institutional and non-institutional methods. However, the Guardian and Wards Act 1890 (GWA) continues to prohibit Muslims, Christians, Jews and Parsis from adopting children, permitting them to become guardians only. The Hindu Adoption and Maintenance Act 1956 (HAMA) prohibits the adoption of a Hindu child by non-Hindus, again permitting them to become guardians only.

---

[21] Indian Majority Act 1875, s. 3; Hindu Minority and Guardianship Act 1956, s. 4(a), respectively.
[22] Juvenile Justice (Care and Protection of Children) Act 2000, s. 2.
[23] Section 11.   [24] Section 16.   [25] Section 20.
[26] Section 4(b).

5.23   In addition to its ratification of the UN Convention on the Rights of the Child, India has ratified the Hague Convention on Inter-Country Adoption[27] with a view to strengthening international cooperation and the protection of Indian children placed for inter-country adoption. The Central Adoption Resource Authority (CARA), an autonomous body under the newly created Central Ministry of Women and Child Development, is the central authority for the purpose of the Hague Convention. In order to facilitate the implementation of the norms, principles and procedures relating to adoption of children from India to foreign countries, the Supreme Court, in three successive decisions under the same name, *Laxmi Kant Pandey* v. *Union of India*,[28] had directed the Government of India to issue guidelines for the above purposes. Accordingly, CARA has issued guidelines on both in-country and inter-country adoption. The recent announcement that new guidelines by CARA will mandate 'final adoption of Indian children' to go abroad with prospective parents and that these fresh guidelines will mandate 'final adoption of Indian children' seems attractive, but it is illusory, since the guidelines cannot overrule the statutory prohibition on non-Hindus adopting Hindu children.

5.24   That issue aside, further problems remain in respect of inter-country adoption. HAMA provides that an adoption deed, recording an adoption in compliance with its provisions, is conclusive. However, all foreign embassies and High Commissions in India still insist that the adoption deed is not enough, requiring the adoptive parents to obtain a guardianship order under the HMGA for Hindus, and a similar order under the GWA for non-Hindus. While this requirement has no foundation in Indian law, that is the position of foreign authorities.

5.25   How these difficulties will be resolved is unknown, but one solution would be law reform enabling any (otherwise suitable) person, irrespective of religion, race or caste, to adopt a child in and from India.

Surrogacy: a new law in the making

5.26   Recognising the advances in assisted reproductive technology (ART) and the fact that surrogacy was already taking place in the country,

---

[27] Hague Convention on the Protection of Children and Co-operation in respect of Inter-Country Adoption 1993, HCCH No. 33.

[28] [1984] All India Reporter (Supreme Court) 469, [1986] All India Reporter (Supreme Court) 272 and [1988] (1) Hindu Law Reporter 699.

draft legislation, the Assisted Reproductive Technology (Regulation) Bill and Rules 2010, is awaiting debate in the Indian Parliament. The draft Bill would provide for the regulation and supervision of ART and would legalise commercial surrogacy. There are numerous lacunae in the Bill and how it will fare is unknown at the time of writing.

5.27   Under the Bill's provisions, the parties would enter into an enforceable surrogacy agreement and the surrogate would receive monetary compensation as well as health care treatment expenses during pregnancy. A surrogate mother is to be aged between 21 and 35 years old and should have no more than five children, including her own. Commissioning would be open to single people or couples, whether married or not, and the child would be regarded (in India, at least) as the legitimate child of the commissioning party or couple. Once the agreed payment has been made, the surrogate would relinquish all parental rights and these would vest in the commissioning party or couple whose names(s) would appear on the child's birth certificate. The child would not be an Indian citizen and foreigners seeking fertility treatment in India would be required to demonstrate that they had registered with their own embassy and that they would be able to take the child to their country of origin or residence. Foreigners would also be required to appoint a local guardian to take care of the surrogate during the pregnancy and of the child, should the commissioning party or couple be unable or unwilling to receive the child.

Delivering parenting

5.28   In 1973 the Supreme Court established that the controlling consideration governing the custody of children is the welfare of the child and not the rights of the parents.[29] This settled position continues to govern parental custody disputes and, again, consistent with the UN Convention on the Rights of the Child, the wishes of the child are used to assist the court in reaching a decision. Reflecting the principles laid down in that Convention and in the Convention on the Elimination of All Forms of Discrimination, the Supreme Court later accepted that mothers have guardianship rights equal to fathers.[30] Consequently, natural guardians enjoy equal rights in respect of their minor children. A court-appointed guardian has the same responsibilities and powers as a natural guardian, subject to the limitations

---

[29]   *Rosy Jacob* v. *Jacob Chakramakkal* (1973) (1) Supreme Court Cases 840.
[30]   *Gita Hariharan* v. *Reserve Bank of India* (1999) (2) Supreme Court Cases 228.

prescribed by statute requiring the court's permission in respect of decisions about the child's immovable property.[31]

Intra-family disputes

5.29   As a general rule, Indian courts decide inter-parental child custody disputes on the basis that the welfare of the child is the paramount consideration, a position consistent with the UN Convention.[32]

The international dimension

5.30   Significant numbers of Indian nationals live abroad[33] and the Indian courts can become involved in their custody disputes when one parent returns to India with the child amid allegations of international child abduction. A foreign court custody order is only one of the considerations in adjudicating any such child custody dispute between parents. Foreign court orders dealing with child custody are no longer mechanically enforced, not least because India is not a signatory to the Hague Convention of 1980 on the Civil Aspects of International Child Abduction.[34] Instead, questions regarding the custody of such children are considered by the Indian courts on the merits of each case.

5.31   The High Court and the Supreme Court entertain petitions for issuance of a writ of habeas corpus, which seek to secure the custody of the minor[35] where the parent is in violation of a foreign court custody order[36] or is attempting to return the child to the country of the parent's jurisdiction. Invoking this judicial remedy provides the quickest and most effective solution. Indian courts have often given considerable respect to foreign custody orders.[37] Different High Courts have from time to time

---

[31]   Guardian and Wards Act 1890 and the Hindu Minority and Guardianship Act 1956.

[32]   See, for example, *Mandy Jane Collins* v. *James Michael Collins* [2006] (2) Hindu Law Reporter (Bombay) 446.

[33]   See para. 5.2 above.

[34]   Hague Convention on Civil Aspects of International Child Abduction 1980, HCCH No. 25.

[35]   For practical application, see *Marilynn Anita Dhillon Gilmore* v. *Margaret Nijjar and Others* [1984] (1) Indian Law Reports (Punjab and Haryana) 1. This case concerned the custody of American children who were taken to India. The US order at issue was respected by the Indian court, and the custody of the children was returned to the mother.

[36]   See, for example, *Kala Aggarwal* v. *Suraj Prakash Aggarwal* [1993] (1) Hindu Law Reporter (Delhi) 145.

[37]   See, for example, *Sarvajeet Kaur Mehmi* v. *State of Rajasthan* [1987] (2) Hindu Law Reporter (Rajasthan) 607; *Jacqueline Kapoor* v. *Surinder Pal Kapoor* [1994] (2) Hindu Law

expressed different views in matters of inter-parental child custody petitions when their jurisdiction has been invoked by an aggrieved parent seeking to enforce a foreign court custody order or to implement their parental rights upon removal of the child to India without parental consent. The Supreme Court of India has also rendered different decisions with different viewpoints on the subject over the past four decades.[38]

5.32   A recent example of such a case is *Ruchi Majoo* v. *Sanjeev Majoo*,[39] where the wife left her husband in the United States and returned to India with her son and was granted custody by the Delhi Guardian Court. Her estranged husband claimed that his wife had abducted the child and a US court issued an order directing her return to the USA. The Delhi Guardian Judge's order was set aside by the Delhi High Court on the basis that, as all the parties were US nationals and ordinarily residing in USA, the matter should be resolved in the courts there, the Guardian Judge having no jurisdiction. That decision was, in turn, set aside by the Apex Court, which directed that the case go before the Delhi Guardian Judge to be disposed of as expeditiously as possible. In the meantime, the mother was given interim custody of the child, the father enjoying visitation rights only.

5.33   The case raised complex issues, including the meaning of 'ordinarily resident', the principle of comity and the appropriateness of visitation. Interpreting the phrase 'ordinarily resident', the Court held that the intention of the parties would determine this important question. The fact that the child had been studying and resident in Delhi for the past three years assisted it in concluding that there had been no coercion or duress, not least because the father was a party to this arrangement.

Reporter (Punjab & Haryana) 97 and *Kulwinder Dhaliwal* v. *State of Punjab and Others* [2008] (2) Indian Law Reports (Punjab and Haryana) 730. In *Shilpa Aggarwal* v. *Aviral Mittal* (2010) (1) Supreme Court Cases 591 (a three-and-a-half-year-old girl, who was a British citizen born in the UK to Indian parents, was removed to India from the UK by the mother in contravention of British court orders: the mother was directed by the Supreme Court of India to return with the child to the UK).

[38] *Marggarate* v. *Chacko* [1970] All India Reporter (Kerala) 1 (where the welfare of the child so demands, the court can permit the child to be taken out of the country by one of the parents, with proper safeguards laid down by the court); *Dhanwanti Joshi* v. *Madhav Unde* (1998) (1) Supreme Court Cases 112 (the order of the foreign court will only be *one* of the facts that must be taken into consideration while dealing with child custody matters); *Kuldeep Sidhu* v. *Chanan Singh* [1989] All India Reporter (Punjab and Haryana) 103 (the welfare of the children would override any consensual custody arrangement and the children had a right to be brought up in the culture and environment of the country of their birth, in this case Canada).

[39] (2011) (6) Supreme Court Cases 167.

Thus, the child was ordinarily resident in Delhi rather than the USA, and the Guardian Judge had jurisdiction to decide the matter. Addressing the issue of comity, the Court saw no reason for the Guardian Judge to decline jurisdiction. No foreign court order had been violated by the wife since there was no final decision by any US court, the minor was voluntarily in India and the mother and child had no intention of returning to the USA. Distinguishing earlier judgments, the Supreme Court held that the interest of the minor could be better served by remaining in the custody of the mother. On the issue of visitation, the Supreme Court modified the order of the Guardian Judge and granted visitation rights to the father during the pendency of the petition before the court in Delhi. Holding that the 'father's care and guidance' is necessary during the 'formative and impressionable stage' of a child's life, the Court took the view that, in order to facilitate the 'child's healthy growth and to stay in touch and share moments of joy, learning and happiness with each other', the father be granted visitation rights through telephonic contact, video conferencing and visits during vacations as determined by the Guardian Judge. In this, the Court took a humane and a benevolent view of the whole situation, since discussions with the child in an interactive session revealed that the child wanted to be left alone by the father.

5.34   In appropriate circumstances, Indian courts will order the return of a child to a foreign jurisdiction. So, for example, in *Vikramvir Vohra* v. *Shalini Bhalla*[40] the Supreme Court held that child custody orders are interlocutory in nature and can be altered if to do so would serve the child's welfare. Consequently, it permitted a mother to take her minor son, aged ten, to Australia in light of the child's wishes to stay with his mother. In *Shilpa Aggarwal* v. *Aviral Mittal*[41] a three-and-a-half-year-old girl, who was a British citizen born in the UK to Indian parents, was removed to India from the UK by her mother in contravention of English court orders. The mother was directed by the Supreme Court of India to return with the child to the UK. In *Dr V. Ravi Chandaran* v. *Union of India and Others*[42] a seven-year-old boy who was a US citizen, born in the USA to Indian parents who had become US citizens, was removed to India from the USA by the mother contrary to US court orders. Again, the mother was directed by the Supreme Court of India to return to the USA with the child, failing which, the father would be entitled to take

---

[40] [2010] (3) Judgments Today 213.
[41] (2010) (1) Supreme Court Cases 591.
[42] (2010) (1) Supreme Court Cases 174.

the child to the USA. As these cases demonstrate, the Indian Supreme Court will treat the welfare of the child as a paramount consideration in deciding custody issues.

5.35 The more general problem is the lack of comprehensive legislation in India dealing with the subject of international parental removal of children. With the increasing number of non-resident Indians (NRIs), the issue is no longer a local problem; the phenomenon is global. Parallel court proceedings in two jurisdictions by warring parents reduce the child to the status of a trophy to be fought over. Clearly, it is essential for India to ratify the Hague Convention on Civil Aspects of International Child Abduction. Before that can be done, a uniform domestic law, implementing the principles of the Hague Convention, must be passed.

The Civil Aspects of International Child Abduction Bill 2007

5.36 The Civil Aspects of International Child Abduction Bill 2007 is designed to serve that purpose. The salient features of this proposed law are as follows. It will create a Central Authority for performance of duties under the Hague Convention for securing the return of removed children by instituting judicial proceedings in the relevant High Court. The appropriate authority or a person of a contracting country will be able to apply to the Central Authority for return of a removed child to the country of habitual residence. The High Court will be empowered to order the return of a removed child to the country of habitual residence, although it may refuse to make such an order if there is grave risk of harm or if it would put the child in an intolerable situation. Consent or acquiescence may also lead to refusal for return of a child by the court. In addition, the High Court will be able to refuse to return a child if the child objects to being returned, provided the court is satisfied that the child has attained sufficient age and degree of understanding. Before making an order of return, the High Court will be able to request the Central Authority to obtain from the relevant authorities of the country of habitual residence, a decision or determination as to whether the removal or retention of the child in India is wrongful. Finally, upon making an order of return, the High Court will be able to direct that the person who has removed the child to India pay the expenses and costs incurred in returning the child to the country of habitual residence.

5.37 This proposed law will be a welcome relief to distraught children who have been removed from their parents. The temptation to wrongfully remove will also be deterred. Moreover, the cruel abduction of non-resident Indian children for the purposes of forced marriages will be checked.

Child protection and state intervention

5.38 Since the constitutional mandate in Part IV of the Constitution of India, containing the Directive Principles of State Policy, are non-justiciable, the obligation on the state to secure social order by promoting of the welfare of children remains unimplemented. The policy of the state, under Article 39 of the Constitution, in respect of real and meaningful protection of children, thus has no comprehensive legislative voice. To date, there is no specific Indian legislation on child abuse, although a Bill on the subject is under discussion. The Juvenile Justice (Care and Protection of Children) Act 2000 addresses the care, protection, treatment, development and rehabilitation of neglected and delinquent juveniles and machinery exists for its practical implementation.

5.39 As we have seen,[43] there are some twelve million orphan children in India who need adoptive parents and current legislation on adoption creates obstacles to meeting their needs whether by adoption within the country or by adopters abroad. It is to be hoped that a legislative solution to this problem can be found.

C   Adult relationships

The relationships

5.40 As we have seen, while Article 44 of the Constitution of India requires the state to secure for the citizens of India a uniform civil code throughout the territory of India, a range of different systems of personal law apply to individuals depending on their religion.[44] Thus, marriage is governed by the applicable system of personal law. It will be recalled that persons who do not profess any particular religion or who are foreigners can avail themselves of the Special Marriage Act 1954: that is, any foreigner not professing any personal law can marry another foreigner or an Indian under the Special Marriage Act.[45] The Foreign Marriage Act

---

[43] See para. 5.22–5.24 above.   [44] See para. 5.7 above.
[45] See para. 5.8 above.

1969 makes provisions relating to marriages of citizens of India who are resident outside the territorial limits of India.

5.41 Polygamous relationships are not recognised except under Muslim law. Marrying again during the lifetime of husband or wife constitutes the offence of bigamy and is punishable by fine and imprisonment.[46]

5.42 While extra-marital cohabitation is not regarded as morally acceptable in traditional Indian society, a degree of statutory protection is provided by the Protection of Women from Domestic Violence Act 2005, which recognises the relationship of two people living in a shared household[47] and gives every woman in such a relationship the right to reside in the home whether or not she has any right, title or beneficial interest in the property.[48]

5.43 Adultery committed by a man with the wife of another man without the consent or connivance of that man is punishable under section 497 of the Indian Penal Code with fine and imprisonment.[49] The woman is not liable to be punished even as an abettor. Offences 'against the order of nature' with any man, woman or animal also attract fines and imprisonment.[50] However, in *Naz Foundation* v. *Government of NCT of Delhi*[51] the Delhi High Court declared section 377 of the Indian Penal Code, in so far as it criminalises consensual sexual acts of persons of or above 18 years of age in private, unconstitutional, being in violation of Article 21 (Protection of Life and Personal Liberty), Article 14 (Equality before Law) and Article 15 (Prohibition of Discrimination). Nevertheless, the Court upheld section 377 in respect of non-consensual homosexual acts involving minors.

Entering an adult relationship

The changing nature of marriage

5.44 Each statute on marriage in India stipulates the requirement for a valid marriage. The main areas of contention relate to the legal age of marriage and the registration of marriages, and the issues are interconnected to some extent. While the principal family law statute in India, the Hindu Marriage Act 1955, sets the minimum age for marriage at 21 for

---

[46] Indian Penal Code, s. 494.
[47] Section 2(f).   [48] Section 17.
[49] Indian Penal Code, s. 497.   [50] Indian Penal Code, s. 377.
[51] (2009) 160 Delhi Law Times, 277.

men and 18 for women, it does not render a marriage void or voidable in the event that one or both of the parties has not attained the requisite age. Child marriages are performed even though the Child Marriage Restraint Act 1929 renders criminal the solemnising of child marriages of boys below 20 years of age and girls below 18 years of age. To add to the problem, Indian law to date does not require the registration of marriages. Child marriages are accepted in almost all religious communities in India, although, of course, they cannot be registered since there has been non-compliance with the minimum age requirement.

5.45   The lack of will on the part of the Indian legislature to require registration of marriage has not gone unnoticed by the courts, however. The Supreme Court of India in *Seema* v. *Ashwani Kumar*[52] has directed all states in India to promulgate rules for compulsory registration of marriages, irrespective of religion, in a time-bound period. This reform, which has been spearheaded by the National Commission for Women, has struck a progressive blow. It hinders child marriages, prevents marriages without the consent of the parties, checks bigamy/polygamy, enables women's rights of maintenance, inheritance and residence, and deters men from deserting their wives.

5.46   The orders of the Indian Apex Court may open a Pandora's box. Besides Hindus, there are problems amongst other minority religious communities, including Muslims, where mere non-registration of a marriage will not render the marriage invalid. Codification of some personal laws in India is a very contentious issue in some religious communities. As a result of the non-registration of marriages, there are a large number of abandoned spouses in India, deserted by non-resident Indians who habitually reside abroad. Times have changed but the law has not. Education, economic prosperity, agricultural improvements, cross-border migration and Western influences have changed practices and lifestyles in urban India, while rural arrangements are still struggling with adherence to customary practices in family law matters. In some respects, the law lags behind social change. In others, it reflects social practices. Will anything change? That remains to be seen. However, the fact remains that, until the rural masses in India are educated and motivated to change for the better, any changes to the law may not really help. People must learn that child marriage is unacceptable and more needs to be done to avoid the

---

[52] [2006] (2) Judgments Today (Supreme Court) 378.

exploitation of married women. Awareness must come from the people themselves and cannot be enforced by the law alone.

Cross-border and inter-caste marriages

5.47   Article 14 of the Indian Constitution guarantees the fundamental right to equality and Article 21 guarantees protection of life and personal liberty. Equality protection under the law is the touchstone of these rights. In addition, the Directive Principles of State Policy endeavour to ensure that the state strives to promote the welfare of the people in a system in which justice and social, economic and political equality informs all the institutions of national life. However, the fact remains that in India, when young men and women marry outside their caste or community, it some-times evokes strong sentiments and even honour killings, even though there is no bar to inter-caste marriages under any codified marriage law.

5.48   In *Lata Singh* v. *State of UP*[53] it was held that the caste system is a curse on the nation and needs to be eradicated. Acts of violence and threats against inter-caste couples are wholly illegal and those who commit them should be severely punished. The Indian police authorities were directed by the Supreme Court to ensure that no inter-caste couple is harassed by anyone or subjected to any threat or acts of violence. The message of the Court is clear: India of the twenty-first century cannot be built on the basis of a caste-oriented approach. To amalgamate as a nation, inter-caste and inter-religious marriages among communities in India must be accepted by society. The barbaric practice of honour kill-ings must be obliterated. But how far can court decisions achieve this? The government must enforce the law of the land and uphold the citi-zen's fundamental rights. A heavy hand is required to check this menace. Therefore, law and society must act in tandem to root out such prejudicial practices.

Consequences of relationships

Dowry and the law: a social menace

5.49   The evil of dowry – any property or valuable security given or agreed to be given by parties to the marriage or to their parents, and given before or at any time after the marriage in connection with or in consideration of the marriage – is rampant in India. The Dowry

---

[53] [2006] (6) Judgments Today (Supreme Court) 173.

Prohibition Act 1961 was enacted to prohibit the giving and taking of dowry, but this social menace is a deep-rooted community practice which continues despite stringent court verdicts. The practice by which dowry seekers attempt to justify it by quoting examples from Hindu scriptures has percolated to all religions in India, though it has no customary or religious sanctity attached to it. Both the Dowry Prohibition Act 1961 and section 498A of the Indian Penal Code (IPC) deal with dowry-related harassment of a married woman. Unfortunately, sometimes dowry leads to violence and murder. Dowry deaths by burning or suicide have become a ponderous point. Decisions of the Supreme Court of India show that dowry deaths by suicide have resulted in the conviction of only one person, whereas dowry deaths by burning have resulted in the conviction of all concerned.[54] This legal anomaly does not mitigate the crime. In societal terms, the menace of dowry cannot be uprooted until the public is educated about the ills of this malpractice and awareness comes from within. At the same time, the law must come down with a heavy hand on dowry seekers and provide punishment as a deterrent to others. Harsher and more stringent penalties in law must be further advocated.

5.50 This has been recognised by the courts and appropriate judgments have been handed down in recent years. For example, in *Re: Enforcement and Implementation of Dowry Prohibition Act 1961*[55] the Apex Court directed the Indian Government to implement all the interim directions already issued by the Supreme Court and to take effective measures to eradicate the social evil of dowry through the machinery of the Act. Moreover, in *Sushil Kumar Sharma* v. *Union of India and others*[56] the Apex Court, upholding the constitutional validity of Section 498A of the Indian Penal Code, held that the object of Section 498A is the prevention of the menace of dowry. It further pronounced that its overarching purpose is to prevent cruelty to, and harassment of, women. Accordingly, the provision did not offend the Constitution of India.

---

[54] See *Vidhya Devi* v. *State of Haryana* [2004] India Reporter (Supreme Court) 1757, *Surinder Kaur* v. *State of Haryana* [2004] All India Reporter (Supreme Court) 1747, and *Kunhiabdulla* v. *State of Kerala* [2004] All India Reporter (Supreme Court) 1731.

[55] [2005] (5) Judgments Today (Supreme Court) 71.

[56] [2005] (6) Judgments Today (Supreme Court) 266.

Termination of relationships

The law of divorce in India

5.51 The two principal family law statutes in India, the Hindu Marriage Act 1955 and the Special Marriage Act 1954, contain three grounds for divorce: the fault ground; the breakdown ground on non-compliance with judicial separation; and the ground of mutual consent. The Parsi Marriage and Divorce Act 1936 and the Divorce Act 1869 have similar provisions. The Dissolution of Muslim Marriages Act 1939 lays down the grounds for a decree for dissolution of the marriages of Muslims. Irretrievable breakdown of marriage *simplicitor* is not a ground of divorce under any Indian statute, but that is not the end of the matter as we shall see presently.[57]

Customary divorces

5.52 Section 29 of the Hindu Marriage Act 1955 gives statutory recognition to customary divorces. This means that parties relying on a custom need not go to court and obtain a decree of divorce. However, the onus on the party who relies on a custom is indeed weighty and the custom should be ancient, certain, reasonable and not opposed to public policy. Even though courts take judicial notice of customs, the validity of a deed of dissolution of marriage under a customary practice has to be established by leading cogent evidence by the person founding on such custom. In *Subramani* v. *M. Chandralekha*[58] the Apex Court, following well-settled principles of law, held that, since there was no custom prevalent in the community to which the parties belonged for dissolution of marriage by mutual consent, the alleged deed of dissolution marriage could not be executed.

5.53 It is common for parties in India to set up customary divorce practices as a short cut to the statutory procedures but, with a vigilant judiciary, such abuse of the process of law does not succeed. Regardless, marriages are often solemnised in contravention of codified law by taking advantage of non-existent customs. Neither the law nor the courts come to the rescue of such parties. However, section 16 of the Hindu Marriage Act clearly provides that, notwithstanding that such marriage is null and void, any child of such marriage who would have been legitimate if the marriage had been valid shall be legitimate. Consequently, even

---

[57] See paras. 5.54–5.58 below.
[58] [2005] (11) Judgments Today (Supreme Court) 562.

though spouses may not gain, the statute protects and provides property and other inheritance rights to children of these unions. Conferring such rights upon children has recently been reiterated by the Supreme Court of India in *Bhogadi* v. *Vuggina*.[59] Clearly, the policy of the law is to provide beneficial effects to the offspring without condoning the contravention and violation of marriage laws. Customs will not die but their misuse must be prevented and curtailed.

Divorce on irretrievable breakdown of marriage

5.54   Keeping in mind that the institution of marriage, in Indian society and especially under the Hindu Marriage Act 1955, is largely still a sacrament rather than a contract, any major overhaul, like the introduction of irretrievable breakdown as a ground for divorce, may be offensive to the very concept of Hindu marriage. For some time the Supreme Court has been active in the debate on the matter, on occasion urging the legislature to amend the Hindu Marriage Act, adding irretrievable breakdown of marriage as a ground for divorce.[60] While it has been consistent in its view that neither the High Courts nor the subordinate courts may grant divorces on this ground, its own conduct has varied. In a number of cases it has granted divorce on the basis of irretrievable breakdown[61] or has waived the six-month waiting period,[62] using its extraordinary powers under Article 142 of the Indian Constitution. However, in other cases it has declined to do so, sometimes indicating that this is a matter for the legislature to decide.[63]

5.55   In the opinion of the authors, a civilised parting of spouses where a marriage has irretrievably broken down must be incorporated into statute as an additional ground for divorce. However, this should only be in cases where both parties to the marriage jointly petition the court for such relief. This will have an immediate two-fold benefit. First, where parties have irreconcilable differences and want to part amicably, an option will be available to them to part legally and logically without resorting to a protracted time-consuming legal battle on

---

[59] (2006) (5) Supreme Court Cases 532.
[60] *Naveen Kohli* v. *Neelu Kohli* [2006] (3) Judgments Today (Supreme Court) 491.
[61] *Durga Prasanna* v. *Arundhati* [2005] (7) Judgments Today (Supreme Court) 596.
[62] *Anil Kumar Jain* v. *Maya Jain* (2009) (10) Supreme Court Cases 415 and *Neeti Malviya* v. *Rakesh Malviya* (2010) (6) Supreme Court Cases 413.
[63] *Vishnu Dutt Sharma* v. *Manju Dutt Sharma* (2009) (6) Supreme Court Cases 379; *Manish Goel* v. *Rohini Goel* (2010) (3) Supreme Court Cases 189.

trumped-up grounds. Secondly, recourse to *ex parte* divorce in foreign jurisdictions by non-resident Indians against hapless spouses on Indian soil may decline once a proper legal option of irretrievable breakdown is available to spouses in India. However, to prevent hasty divorces or misuse, sufficient statutory safeguards must be incorporated to arm the judiciary to prevent any abuse of the process of law. Retaining the ceremonial and sacramental concept of marriage, irretrievable breakdown hedged with safeguards can be introduced where both parties consent to it. To harmonise and blend modern family requirements in urban areas with traditional Indian concepts of family law, this middle path is the best solution.

5.56 The Law Commission of India, *suo motu*, joined the debate and in 2009 recommended strongly that the Hindu Marriage Act 1955 and the Special Marriage Act 1954 be amended to add irretrievable breakdown as a ground for divorce.[64] The Commission also recommended that, before granting a decree for divorce on this ground, the court should examine whether adequate financial arrangements have been made for the parties and their children.

5.57 On 10 June 2010 the Union Cabinet approved the introduction of a Bill, the Marriage Laws (Amendment) Bill 2010, to be tabled in the forthcoming winter session of Parliament. It seeks to amend the Hindu Marriage Act 1955 and Special Marriage Act 1954 to provide for irretrievable breakdown of marriage as a ground for divorce.

5.58 India has its own deeply embedded moral and cultural values and emulation of Western principles in matrimonial matters should be approached with the greatest caution. A balance needs to be maintained whereby the sanctity of the institution of marriage is protected at the same time as the interests of aggrieved spouses and their children are secured. At present, a broken marriage limps towards dissolution and the law cannot reunite parties if the matrimonial bond has been severed. Thus, a peaceful parting is desirable if the spouses cannot be reconciled. Adding irretrievable breakdown of marriage as a ground for divorce may be the best solution, but only as long as other legislative amendments, ensuring the protection of the spouses and the welfare of their children, form part of the legislative package.

---

[64] Law Commission of India, *Irretrievable Breakdown of Marriage – Another Ground for Divorce*, 217th Report (New Delhi: Law Commission of India, 2009).

Consequences of termination

5.59   In domestic matrimonial disputes, settlement of maintenance, alimony and matrimonial property, as well as issues relating to the custody of children, are dealt with as ancillary relief in a matrimonial cause under the respective personal laws of the various religious communities. Maintenance is decided on the basis of need, the earning capacities of the parties and the standard of living of the spouses. There is no 50:50 division rule regarding division of matrimonial property, which is normally settled on a lump sum basis. Custody of children is generally awarded on the basis of the welfare of the child as a paramount consideration. All these issues are determined by respective courts of competent jurisdiction designated to hear matrimonial matters under the respective codified personal laws of the various religious communities in India.

Enforcement of foreign matrimonial judgments and orders in India

5.60   As we have seen, some thirty million Indians live or settle abroad.[65] However, their link with their home country is not necessarily severed and many retain family ties and property in India, leading to cross-border litigation. On occasion, NRIs use foreign courts to obtain favourable orders that they then seek to implement in India. There is no separate provision for the recognition of foreign matrimonial judgments in Indian law[66] and Indian courts are not strictly bound by a foreign court order in family matters. In the 1990s the Supreme Court of India spelt out guidelines for recognition of foreign court matrimonial judgments purporting to dissolve Hindu marriages solemnised in India[67] and proposed exploring the feasibility of enacting legislation to ensure that no marriage between an NRI and an Indian that had taken place in India was annulled by a foreign court.[68]

5.61   No such legislation has been enacted and, in the meantime, the Indian courts render laudable service in interpreting foreign court orders in the best interests of personal relationships rather than executing them

---

[65] See para. 5.2 above.
[66] The Indian Code of Civil Procedure, s. 13, provides for the conclusiveness of judgments of foreign courts.
[67] *Y. Narasimha Rao* v. *Y. Venkata Lakshmi* (1991) (3) Supreme Court Cases 451.
[68] *Neerja Saraph* v. *Jayant Saraph* (1994) (6) Supreme Court Cases 641.

simplicitor. The humane Indian judiciary apply principles of good conscience, natural justice, equity and fair play in implementing foreign court orders in a practical way, rather than engaging in a mechanical execution of the orders of overseas courts. High Courts across India have refused to cede jurisdiction to foreign courts and, on occasion, have declined to enforce foreign decrees.[69] Often the judgments of the judiciary are the only protection for hapless Indian wives, abandoned in India, who protest against the uncontested foreign divorce decrees obtained, invariably by default, by their spouses in overseas jurisdictions. In this respect, the rules of private international law are of little help.

5.62 However, a new tool has been added in the matrimonial arena in the form of anti-injunction suits, designed to prevent the filing of actions in different jurisdictions in respect of the same cause of action. Anti-injunction suits may be founded on lack of jurisdiction, either regarding the corpus of the Hindu marriage or the physical presence of an Indian spouse in the foreign territory. An example of the impact of these suits overseas can be seen in *Singh* v. *Singh*.[70] The Federal Magistrates Court of Australia, at Canberra, restrained the wife from taking any action to pursue a complaint in India against the husband under The Dowry Prohibition Act 1961. Both parties were Australian citizens, married according to Sikh rites in India. Settlement of maintenance, property and child custody had been resolved using Australian consent orders. The Canberra Court found that, on evidence presented, Ms Singh had not established that a dowry was either requested or paid as alleged. Accordingly, the Court held 'that the injunction acts *in personam* only in relation to Ms Singh, and does not, either in terms or otherwise, purport

---

[69] See, for example, *Moina* v. *Amardeep* [1996] All India Reporter (Delhi) 399 (foreign domicile was no bar to a divorce petition being lodged in India to dissolve a Hindu marriage celebrated in India); *Veena Kalia* v. *Jatinder Kalia* [1996] All India Reporter (Delhi) 54 (the *ex parte* decree of divorce of a foreign court being a nullity, there was no bar to a subsequent petition for divorce in India even though maintenance had been accepted under the foreign judgment); *Harmeeta Singh* v. *Rajat Taneja* (2003) (2) Recent Civil Reports (Civil) 197 (even if the Hindu marriage had been dissolved in the USA, dissolution would have to be confirmed by an Indian Court); *Navin Chander* v. *Leena*, [2005] (2) Hindu Law Reporter 582 (dispute concerning a ceremonial Hindu marriage celebrated in the USA was amenable to adjudication by the Pune Family Court); *Sondur Rajini* v. *Sondur Gopal*, 2006 (2) Hindu Law Reporter, 475 (foreign domicile of parties did not remove the jurisdiction of the Indian courts to determine the annulment of a ceremonial Hindu marriage solemnised when they were domiciled in India).

[70] [2010] FMCAfam 949.

to affect the administration of justice in India'. The judgment was said to be based on considerations of equity and justice.

5.63   Difficulties continue to occur, as is amply demonstrated by the recent decision of the Bombay High Court at Pune in *Kashmira Kale* v. *Kishore Kumar Mohan Kale*.[71] The parties married in Mumbai in 2005 according to Hindu rites, lived in the USA and intermittently visited Mumbai and Pune. In September 2008 the wife filed divorce proceedings in the USA, whose jurisdiction was challenged by the husband in the USA. Simultaneously, in October 2008 the husband filed a divorce petition in the Pune Family Court, claiming it was the competent forum for adjudication of their dispute. The husband did not participate in the wife's divorce petition in the USA and, in January 2009, the US Court dissolved the marriage and divided the assets of the parties. However, in September 2009 the Family Court in Pune held that it still had the jurisdiction to try the husband's petition for divorce in India. On appeal, the Bombay High Court set aside the order of the Family Court and upheld the US divorce decree dissolving the Hindu marriage on the basis that the marriage had broken down.

5.64   The present authors respectfully differ with the conclusions drawn by the Bombay High Court, not least its finding that, since the parties were domiciled in the USA, the Hindu Marriage Act did not apply to them. While the High Court noted that section 1(2) of the Hindu Marriage Act applies to Hindus in the territories to which it applies, it did not take account of the fact that it also 'applies to Hindus domiciled in the territories to which this Act extends who are outside the said territories'. In addition, section 2 applies to Hindus, irrespective of their domicile, nationality or citizenship, and previous decisions of other High Courts[72] have found that the Act applies to all Hindus

---

[71] [2011] (1) Hindu Law Reporter 333.

[72] See, for example, the decision of the Bombay High Court in *Sondur Rajini* v. *Sondur Gopal* [2006] (2) Hindu Law Reporter 475 (holding that the provisions of the HMA do not cease to apply on change of domicile which, in any event, is determined when the parties tie the nuptial knot under the Hindu Marriage Act and not on the date when an application is made for matrimonial relief); the decision of the Bombay High Court in *Naveen Chander Advani* v. *Leena Advani* [2005] (2) Hindu Law Reporter 582 (holding that the Family Court in Pune wrongly declined to entertain a matrimonial petition relating to a marriage where parties last resided and married in the USA according to Hindu rites and ceremonies); and the decision of the Delhi High Court in *Harmita* v. *Rajat* (2003) (2) Recent Civil Reports 197 (holding that in accordance with the princi-

irrespective of domicile or residence if they were married in India according to Hindu rites, giving the statute extra-territorial application in such cases. Equally flawed is the view of the Bombay High Court that, since the parties last resided together in Michigan, the US Court had territorial jurisdiction to decide their divorce dispute. This conclusion falls foul of the settled law laid down by the Supreme Court[73] and its own prior case law.[74] Above all, the view of the Bombay High Court is inconsistent with the celebrated view of the Apex Court in *Y. Narasimha Rao v. Y. Venkata Lakshmi*.[75]

5.65 In these circumstances, the Indian legislature must review this issue as a matter of urgency and provide statutory remedies for non-resident Indians in family law matters. Until this is done, they will use foreign courts in domestic matters and Indian courts will continue with their salutary efforts in interpreting foreign judgments in harmony with Indian law and doing substantial justice to parties in the most fair and equitable way. Despite this, parallel adjudication of matrimonial disputes simultaneously in Indian and foreign courts simply adds to the discord. There is scope for jurisdictional clashes, with foreign courts sometimes imposing penalties, oblivious of directions of Indian courts of superior hierarchy. Spouses, children and extended families bear the brunt of multifaceted parallel directives of courts of different overseas territories.

Self-regulation and custom-made relationships

5.66 Provisions for settlement of disputes outside the court find a prominent place in the Civil Procedure Code, codified marriage laws and the Family Courts Act, and settlement, reconciliation and mediation are increasingly unutilised in family matters. In *Jagraj Singh v. Birpal Kaur*[76] the Supreme Court confirmed that the requirement on parties to

---

ples of private international law, a US divorce decree would have to be confirmed by a court in India).

[73] *Jagir Kaur v. Jaswant Singh* 1963 SC 1521 (holding that the 'last residence' of a person with his wife can only mean his last residence in the territories of India and cannot mean his residing with her in a foreign country since an Indian statute cannot confer jurisdiction on a foreign court).

[74] *Meera v. Anil Kumar* [1992] (2) Hindu Law Reporter 284 (holding that 'last resided' in section 19 of HMA means last residence in India).

[75] (1991) (3) Supreme Court Cases 451.

[76] (2007) (2) Supreme Court Cases 564.

attempt reconciliation in the first instance is not an empty one. Similarly, in *Gaurav Nagpal* v. *Sumedha Nagpal*[77] the Court emphasised that efforts should be made to bring about conciliation to bridge communication gaps and prevent people from rushing to court.

5.67   Litigation in respect of any matter concerning the family, whether divorce, maintenance, alimony, child custody or any other matrimonial cause, should not be viewed in terms of the failure or success of legal actions. Adjudication of family disputes is entirely different from conventional civil or criminal proceedings, not least because of the social impact of family disputes. The amicable settlement of family conflicts is a socially therapeutic approach and, ideally, disputes should be resolved within the family so as not to disrupt the family structure. Resolution by mediation or conciliation may provide lasting solutions for the good of all. Family matters ought not to be litigated in any court unless extraordinarily grave and, where litigation proves necessary, it should take place in dedicated family courts. Trained counsellors, mediators and advisors should be available to assist in resolving disputes. Superior courts must also inject the spirit of mediation in appellate jurisdictions. Mandatory reconciliation procedures should be affirmed by the courts. The creation of more family courts under the Family Courts Act would contribute to resolution of family law disputes by ADR. The current handling of matrimonial litigation by conventional courts is a poignant reminder of what prevails today.

5.68   The culture of settlement needs propagation. ADR cannot see the light of the day unless citizens participate in the movement to promote it. The conventional People's Courts can be a means to this end. Spouses, parents and families need to realise the advantages of ADR in the family structure. Matrimonial relief carved out by settlement will serve better than results obtained by adversarial litigation involving time, effort, finances and, above all, breaking up a family.

5.69   In all of this, the Mediation Cell of the Punjab and Haryana High Court, which attempts to mediate matrimonial disputes, is an extremely positive development. Laws to promote ADR exist, but the infrastructure, professional assistance and medium through which these beneficial procedures may be implemented are lacking; thus there is a pressing need to

---

[77]   [2008] 2 Hindu Law Reporter 584.

create that infrastructure so that alternative disputes resolution can be offered comprehensively.

D   Conclusions

5.70   Today the nuclear Indian family is plagued by a new generation of ills. Forced marriages, honour killings, non-marital cohabitation, parental international child abduction, inter-country adoptions and surrogacy are not addressed adequately by existing law. The framers of traditional family law did not anticipate these issues. While judicial decisions daily render yeoman service in resolving these vexed questions, statutory provisions have simply not kept pace.

The need for a uniform civil code in India

5.71   Article 44 of the Constitution of India requires the state to secure for the citizens of India a uniform civil code throughout the territory of India. As has been noted above, India has a unique blend of codified personal laws of Hindus, Christians, Parsis and, to some extent, of Muslims. However, there is no single, uniform family law statute applicable to all Indians.

5.72   For the first time, in *Mohammad Ahmed Khan* v. *Shah Bano Begum*[78] in 1985, the Supreme Court of India directed the Indian Parliament to frame a uniform civil code. There, a penurious Muslim woman claimed maintenance from her husband under section 125 of the Code of Criminal Procedure after her husband pronounced triple *talaq*, effecting divorce by announcing the word '*talaq*' three times. The Apex Court held that the Muslim woman had a right to maintenance under section 125 of the Code and also held that Article 44 of the Constitution, prescribing that the state shall endeavour to secure for its citizens a uniform civil code in India, had remained a dead letter. To undo the above decision, the Muslim Women (Right to Protection on Divorce) Act 1986, which clarified the right of a Muslim woman to maintenance under section 125 of the Code, was enacted by the Indian Parliament.

5.73   Ten years later, in the case of *Sarla Mudgal* v. *Union of India*,[79] the question that arose was whether a Hindu husband, married under Hindu

---

[78] [1985] All India Reporter (Supreme Court) 945.
[79] [1995] All India Reporter (Supreme Court) 1531.

law, could, by embracing the Islamic religion, solemnise a second marriage. The Supreme Court held that a Hindu marriage solemnised under Hindu Law can only be dissolved under the Hindu Marriage Act and conversion to Islam and marrying again would not, by itself, dissolve the Hindu marriage. Further, it was held that a second marriage solemnised after converting to Islam constituted the offence of bigamy under Section 494 of the Indian Penal Code.

5.74 The Supreme Court reiterated the need for Parliament to frame a Common Civil Code that will help the cause of national integration by removing contradictions based on ideologies. Thus, the Directive Principle of enacting a uniform civil code has been urged by the Apex Court repeatedly in a number of decisions as a matter of urgency. Unfortunately, in a subsequent decision[80] the Apex Court clarified that the Court had not issued any directions for the codification of a common civil code and that the judges constituting the different benches had only expressed their views on the facts and the circumstances of the cases before them. However, this ought not to deter the efforts of the Supreme Court in issuing mandatory directions to the Indian Government to draft a common civil code, applicable to all communities, irrespective of their religion and practices in a secular India. Hopefully, the Apex Court may review its findings in some other case and issue mandatory directions to the Central Government to create a common civil code applicable to all communities irrespective of their religion.

Secularism and a uniform civil code

5.75 The preamble of the Indian Constitution resolves to constitute a 'Secular' Democratic Republic. This means that there is no state religion and that the state shall not discriminate on the ground of religion. Articles 25 and 26 of the Constitution of India guarantee the fundamental rights of freedom of religion and freedom to manage one's religious affairs. At the same time, Article 44 (which is not enforceable in a court of law) provides that the state shall endeavour to secure a uniform civil code in India. How are these different provisions to be reconciled? What will be the ingredients of a uniform civil code? Since the personal laws of each religion contain separate ingredients, the uniform civil code will need to strike a balance between protection of fundamental rights and respect for

---

[80] *Lily Thomas v. Union of India* [2000] (6) Supreme Court Cases 224.

the religious principles of different communities. Marriage, divorce, succession, inheritance and maintenance can be matters of a secular nature and law can regulate them. India needs a codified law that will cover all religions in relation to the personal laws of different communities.

5.76   It is imperative in a multi-religious society that a unified code is promulgated for the sake of national unity and solidarity. Different streams of religion have to merge towards a common destination and some unified principles must emerge in the true spirit of secularism. India needs a unified code of family law providing for all its constituent religions. Whether it is the endeavour of the state, the mandate of the court or the will of the people, it is an issue that only time will decide for a true Indian Secular Democratic Republic.

5.77   The views of the Indian Apex Court on matters such as the registration of marriages, inter-caste marriages, child marriages, the Dowry Prohibition Act 1961, divorce, a uniform civil code and a secular approach have been referred to earlier. A legislature that is slow to respond to societal changes and a proactive judiciary that is keen to encourage reforms in law is therefore clearly visible in India. Even in matters affecting the environment, pollution and the health of the people, the role of the judiciary in India has been very constructive. The vibrant, dynamic and open jurisprudential system in India is flexible and well suited to meeting the changing needs of the people. There could therefore be reform in family law through decisions of the courts even if there is opposition, in respect of personal laws, from religious communities. If a uniform civil code does not come about as a result of legislation, judicial precedent will always supply reforms to improve the plight of children and women who are affected the most. Accordingly, the Indian judiciary deserves to be applauded in this context.

Concluding thoughts on child and family law in India

5.78   While child and family law in India is advancing at a great pace, much still remains to be done to improve it. With the changing international atmosphere and interactive diplomatic relations, many new treaties and understandings are being concluded in the area of private international law. India is a part of that process and is successful in understanding the needs of both its resident and non-resident citizens, there being a pressing need for India to resolve the family law problems of the some thirty million non-resident Indians.

5.79   Modern concepts and issues including commercial surrogacy, inter-country adoptions, inter-parental child removal, inter-continental matrimonial litigation and instances of global child abuse present new challenges. The law never anticipated this new generation of legal issues and, so, statutory law in India contains no provisions to address them.

5.80   Marriage, divorce, child custody, maintenance and ancillary relief are undergoing a sea change in terms of the concepts themselves and the goals they seek to achieve in India. One finds that laws passed decades ago are now in urgent need of reform. Times have changed, but the law has not kept pace. The judiciary renders an indispensible service in providing relief on a case-by-case basis. But that is not enough. Often viewed as an example of judicial activism, a court decision may provide relief in a particular case on the basis of a given set of facts and circumstances. However, no broader precedent is set. Thus, responsibility for finding the solution lies with the legislature, which must enact legislation. Family laws – particularly those meant to protect and serve the interests of children – must be amended to provide a better future for India. The discussion herein is by no means exhaustive. It is merely an overview of a number of examples of law that require change for a better future for children. The global effort in this direction prompts India to follow suit.

6

Israel

Dynamism and schizophrenia

RHONA SCHUZ AND AYELET BLECHER-PRIGAT

A Introduction

Historical roots, sources and law reform

The split in law and jurisdiction

6.1 Israeli family law is characterized by a split in law as well as a split in jurisdiction. In terms of law, some aspects of family law are governed by civil (and territorial) law,[1] while other aspects, defined as 'matters of personal status',[2] are governed by the 'personal law' of the pertinent individual.[3] The personal law of Israeli citizens and residents is their religious law, provided they belong to a recognized religious community.[4] Various religious communities are recognized in Israel: Jews, Muslims, Druze and ten Christian denominations. For Israeli citizens who do not belong to a recognized religious community, either because they are members of a religious community not recognized under Israeli law, or because they do not belong to any religion, no applicable personal law applies.[5] The personal law of foreign citizens is the law of their nationality ('unless that

---

[1] For example, adoption of children, guardianship of children and matrimonial property.

[2] Such as child support and maintenance.

[3] See Ariel Rosen-Zvi, 'Family and Inheritance Law', in Amos Shapira and Keren C. DeWitt-Arar (eds.), *Introduction to the Law of Israel* (The Hague: Kluwer Law International, 1995), p. 75. The Israeli application of personal laws to 'matters of personal status' was inherited from the Ottoman Empire's *millet* (religious community) system, which was preserved by the British Mandatory Rule and later adopted by the Israeli legislature with certain amendments. *Ibid.,* p. 75.

[4] See Menashe Shava, 'Matters of Personal Status of Israeli Citizens not Belonging to a Recognized Religious Community', in Yoram Dinstein (ed.), *Yearbook of Human Rights*, vol. 11 (The Hague: Kluwer Law International, 1989), p. 238.

[5] For the impact on marriage, see paras. 6.55–6.56, and on divorce see para. 6.68 below.

law imports the law of their domicile, in which case the latter shall be applied').[6]

6.2 The split between the civil and religious systems on family law matters is not only in law but in jurisdiction as well. Recognized religious communities under Israeli law operate religious courts.[7] Here again, some aspects of family law are under the exclusive jurisdiction of the relevant religious courts, while others are under a parallel jurisdiction of the civil system of family courts and the religious system.[8]

6.3 It should be noted that religious affiliation for purposes of law and jurisdiction in Israel is independent from personal beliefs and instead relies on the relevant religious laws.[9] Each recognized religious community determines whether an individual does or does not belong, based on its own religious law. Thus, even those who identify themselves as secular, atheist or agnostic as a matter of personal belief, may still be considered members of a religious community for purposes of law and jurisdiction. Conversely, individuals who see themselves as affiliated with a particular religion may not be considered as belonging to this religion for purposes of personal law if the relevant religious law does not recognize them as such.

Law reform

6.4 The Israeli legislator is relatively dormant in the field of family law and most of the laws in this area are quite old.[10] One reason for this inactivity is that, as a result of the political constellation in the Knesset (Israeli Parliament), it has rarely been possible to enact laws without the support of the Jewish religious parties.

6.5 Many of the few legislative reforms that have taken place in the field of family law were the result of proposals of committees set up by the

---

[6] Article 64(2) of the Palestinian Order in Council.

[7] Rosen-Zvi, 'Family and Inheritance Law', p. 76.

[8] Once proceedings are initiated in one of these two systems, however, it assumes jurisdiction and precludes the other's intervention. The result has been the notorious 'race for jurisdiction', when each party seeks to precede the other in initiating legal proceedings in order to determine what court will hear a particular case. Ariel Rosen-Zvi, 'Forum Shopping between Religious and Secular Courts (and its Impact on the Legal System)' (1989) 9 *Tel Aviv University Studies in Law* 347, 348.

[9] Rosen-Zvi, 'Family and Inheritance Law', p. 78.

[10] For example, Family Amendment (Maintenance) Law 1959, Youth (Supervision and Care) Law 1960 and the Legal Capacity and Guardianship Law 1965.

government to review the existing law and consider the need for reform.[11] Perhaps the most important committee, 'the Rotlevi Committee', was set up in 1997 to consider the implications of Israel's ratification of the UN Convention on the Rights of the Child (hereinafter 'the UN Convention'). In 2004–2005 this Committee published six reports considering various aspects of the law relating to children.[12] To date, only a few of the recommendations in these reports have been enacted. In the past few years, four further committees have been set up to consider various aspects of the law relating to children: Adoption of Children;[13] Parental Responsibility Following Divorce; Children at Risk; and Child Support. Similarly, the government has recently set up a committee to consider the question of extending surrogacy to same-sex couples.

6.6   Thus, it can be seen that although there is no central law reform body in Israel, there is currently considerable law reform activity in the field of family law, although it is not clear that all of it will result in legislation.

The Family Court system

6.7   Between 1995 and 1997 a Family Court system was established in Israel in an attempt to centralize the adjudication of all family matters that are under the jurisdiction of the civil system under one roof and to create 'caring courts' that also offer therapeutic services.[14] An appeal on a Family Court decision can be brought as a matter of right to the District Court. A subsequent appeal to the Supreme Court requires permission, which is rarely given.[15] This means that there are a limited number of Supreme Court precedents in family matters.

6.8   In 1997 Social Service Units were established adjunct to the Family Court. These units, which operate under the Ministry of Social Services, aim to assist families litigating in the Family Courts as well as to assist the

---

[11]   For example, the Adoption of Children Law 1981 was based on proposals of the Etzioni Committee (1979) and the Surrogacy Law 1996 enacted the recommendations of the Aloni Committee (1991).

[12]   For further details, see Rhona Schuz, 'Surrogacy and PAS in the Israeli Supreme Court and the Reports of the Committee on Children's Rights', in A. Bainham (ed.), *The International Survey of Family Law* (Bristol: Jordans, 2004), p. 247.

[13]   Some of the recommendations in the first interim report of this committee were enacted in Amendment No. 8 to the Adoption Law 2010.

[14]   Daphna Hacker, 'A Legal Field in Action: The Case of Divorce Arrangements in Israel' (2008) 4(1) *International Journal of Law in Context* 1, 8.

[15]   Prior to the establishment of the Family Court, civil family matters were under the jurisdiction of the District Court, so that an appeal to the Supreme Court was a matter of right.

judges, by integrating the therapeutic and emotional aspects into the legal process. The Social Service Units perform three unique functions: consensual resolution of conflicts; interventions in relation to parenting in divorce proceedings; and assistance to families characterized by violent relations.[16]

6.9　In 2001 the Israeli Knesset enacted the Law of Family Courts Amendment (No. 5) giving parallel jurisdiction to the civil family courts over matters, such as child custody, that were previously under the exclusive jurisdiction of the Muslim sharia courts or the ecclesiastical courts. The purpose of this legislation was to equalize the scope of jurisdiction of sharia and ecclesiastical courts to that of the Jewish rabbinical courts and to provide Muslim and Christian litigants with greater freedom of choice between the religious and the civil courts, in all matters of personal status except for marriage and divorce in the narrow sense.[17] In reality, however, this reform has not led to an increase in the use of the Family Court by Muslim and Christian litigants.

Alternative dispute resolution

6.10　In 2005 a draft bill, the Early Settlement of a Dispute Bill, was published, seeking to implement mandatory mediation in Israeli family and religious courts.[18] Since its publication, however, the bill has made no progress. There are no accurate data on the current extent of divorce mediation in Israeli family law cases in general, and divorce cases in particular,[19] but it is clear that mediation has not become common practice in the family arena[20] and it is unlikely that this situation will change in the near future. Dafna Hacker suggests that the poor integration of mediation in the Israeli family arena can be explained not only by the

---

[16] Anat Inbar, Chaya Nevo and Susan Lehman, 'Social Services Units Ancillary to the Family Courts – A Decade of Action' (2008) 2 *The Family in Law* 25 (Hebrew).

[17] For historical reasons, which correspond to the adoption of the Ottoman *millet* system by Israel, sharia courts enjoyed the broadest jurisdiction than other religious courts in matters of personal status. Moussa Abou Ramadan, 'Judicial Activism of the Shari'ah Appeals Court in Israel (1994–2001): Rise And Crisis' (2003) 27 *Fordham International Law Journal* 254, 263.

[18] See www.justice.gov.il/NR/rdonlyres/51D2B374-F75A-46B9-98D7-D7B4FC97D819/0/sichsocey_mishpacha.pdf (Hebrew). The proposed law constituted the recommendation of a committee headed by Judge Yitzhak Shenhav, Vice President of the Ramat-Gan Family Court.

[19] Hacker, 'A Legal Field in Action', 23.

[20] *Ibid.*; Susan Zaidel, 'Mediation in Israel' (2002) 5(2) *ADR Bulletin*, Article 3, available at: http://epublications.bond.edu.au/adr/vol5/iss2/3.

lack of public awareness of the possibility of mediation, but also by factors relating to the non-prestigious reputation of the profession of mediation and to the reluctance of lawyers to refer their clients to a neutral mediator.[21] However, it should be added that Hacker's study shows that judges often put pressure on the parties to come to a solution. Thus, it is hardly surprising that in her study only 2.2 per cent of the cases ended up with a court ruling on custody or visitation.[22]

B   Children in the family setting and state intervention

Defining and classifying children

6.11   Under the Legal Capacity and Guardianship Law 1962 (hereinafter 'the Guardianship Law'), a person who has not reached the age of 18 is defined as a minor. The starting point of Israeli law is that a minor does not have legal capacity unless there is a specific statutory provision granting him such capacity. Criminal responsibility attaches to minors from the age of 12. The age of marriage is 17, but the court may grant permission for minors below this age to get married where the bride is pregnant or has given birth, or in relation to minors over the age of 16 where there are special circumstances.[23]

6.12   Legal acts performed by a minor without the consent of his guardian may be cancelled by the guardian, unless the act is one that it is usual for minors of his age to perform.[24] However, there are a number of enactments that provide that the consent of a minor above a certain age is required in relation to various legal acts[25] and others that grant the child capacity to act independently without the need for consent of his guardians.[26]

---

[21] Hacker, 'A Legal Field in Action', 23–4.

[22] *Ibid.*, 9. An additional reason for this phenomenon is the necessity for both of the parties to consent to the granting of a divorce. Often, a least one of the parties will withhold their consent until all of the issues have been agreed. This provides an incentive for the parties to come to an agreement in relation to the children and property rather than to litigate.

[23] The Age of Marriage Law 1950. The Israeli Government recently decided to promote a law to raise the minimum age of marriage to 18.

[24] Legal Capacity and Guardianship Law 1962, ss. 4–6.

[25] The Adoption of Children Law 1981, s. 7, requires consent of a child above nine to adoption. The Guardianship Law 1962, s. 13A, requires consent of a child above ten to conversion to another religion.

[26] For example, Penal Law 1977, s. 316(a)(5) provides that a pregnant minor who wishes to undergo an abortion does not need the consent of her guardian; the Adoption of Children

6.13   In recent years there has been a growing movement to recognize the rights of minors to participate in legal proceedings concerning them. In 2008 Amendment No. 14 to the Youth (Adjudication and Punishment) Law added a section entitled 'the right of the minor to participate in decisions concerning him'. This section provides that the minor should have the opportunity to express his position and his wishes and that appropriate weight should be given thereto. For this purpose, the minor is to be provided with relevant information in a way that is suited to his age and degree of maturity. The minor may only be denied the right to participate where the decision-maker holds that, for special reasons, exercise of this right would cause him real damage. Similarly, in the field of family proceedings a successful pilot project in two Family Courts,[27] in which children over the age of 6 were given the right to be heard directly by the judge deciding a matter concerning them, is now being extended.[28]

6.14   Thus, there is no doubt that overall the Israeli legal system is making progress in recognizing the evolving legal capacities of minors in accordance with the UN Convention and in particular there is growing implementation of the child's right to participate. However, the process is far from complete. For example, in care proceedings in which the state requests the removal of a child from his or her home, the child is not even a party, is not usually given the opportunity to express his or her views, and is rarely granted independent legal representation. Furthermore, research shows that even where children are heard by judges, this does not guarantee that any real weight is given to these views.[29]

Law 1981, s. 8(c) allows a minor parent to hand his/her child over for adoption without the consent of his/her guardian.

[27]   For details of the project, see Rhona Schuz, 'The Voice of the Child in the Israeli Family Court', B. Atkin (ed.), *The International Survey of Family Law* (Bristol: Jordans, 2008), p. 185. For research accompanying the project, see Y. Sorek and D. Rivkin, *Evaluation of a Pilot Project of Child Participation in Family Court Proceedings* (Jerusalem: Myers-JDC-Brookdale, 2010).

[28]   See Chapter 20(2): Participation of Children, added in 2010 to the Civil Proceedings Regulations 1984.

[29]   See Rhona Schuz, 'The Right of the Child to Participate: Theory and Practice in the Israeli Family Court' (2008) 2 *The Family in Law Review*, 207 (Hebrew). In half of the cases reviewed in this research, little weight was given to the views of the children.

Recognizing parentage and family ties

Parentage in cases of natural procreation

6.15   Legal parenthood is not considered a matter of personal status[30] and thus should be governed by civil–secular law. Nevertheless, no Israeli statute addresses the definition and determination of legal parenthood. Though nowhere codified, the basic assumption of Israeli law is that legal parenthood is based on 'natural' parenthood.[31] In contrast to the traditional common law approach that linked paternity to marriage, Israeli law has never made paternity contingent on the marital status of the parents.[32]

6.16   Despite the recurring statements in Israeli case law to the effect that legal parenthood is 'natural' parenthood and suggestions that it is based solely on the biological connection, when we move into the realm of actually establishing parenthood, other social policy considerations come into play and religious laws enter the discussion through the back door. This is because paternity under Jewish law may affect the capacity of an individual to marry.

6.17   Under Jewish law, a child born to a married woman[33] and fathered by a Jewish man other than her husband is considered a *mamzer* (the offspring of a union that is forbidden as adulterous or incestuous).[34] Under Jewish law, a *mamzer* cannot marry any Jew other than another *mamzer* or a convert. This means that, since marriage and divorce in Israel are

---

[30]   Except for Muslims, who are subject to some limitations as will be discussed below.

[31]   Ruth Zafran, 'More than One Mother: Determining Maternity for the Biological Child of a Female Same-sex Couple – the Israeli View' (2008) 9 *Georgetown Journal of Gender and Sexuality Law* 115, 118.

[32]   In the case of CA 3077/90 *Anonymous* v. *Anonymous*, P.D. 49(2) 578, 588–589 (Isr), the Supreme Court held that civil paternity, based on biological fatherhood, coexisted with the religious concept of paternity and thus for civil purposes the Muslim father of a child born out of wedlock was to be treated as the father, even though he was not so recognized under sharia law.

[33]   A 'married woman' for this purpose refers to a Jewish woman who is married to a Jewish man, in accordance with Jewish law.

[34]   It is inaccurate to translate *mamzer* as 'bastard' because the concept is different from bastardy in Anglo-American law in two respects. First, under Jewish law children born outside of wedlock, where the mother is not married to another man, are not considered *mamzerim*. Secondly, under Jewish law the biological father of a *mamzer* owes him all the duties owed by a legal father to his child.

governed exclusively by religious laws, and Israeli law does not provide for civil marriage, *mamzerim* cannot marry in Israel.

6.18 The social stigma facing *mamzerim* and the legal implications of this status in terms of the capacity to marry in Israel affect the legal approach to establishing paternity. Thus, in cases concerning unmarried mothers, Family Courts would usually authorize genetic testing in order to prove paternity,[35] and today may even compel such testing.[36] However, where the (Jewish) mother was married (to a Jewish man) and a Jewish man other than the husband was alleged to be the father, the traditional approach was to refuse authorization of testing because the risk of being categorized as a *mamzer* was seen as contrary to the best interests of the child.

6.19 In 2004 two family court decisions ordered paternity tests against men who were alleged to be the biological fathers of children, even though the mothers had been married to other men at the time of conception,[37] on the basis that the child's right to know the identity of his father and the benefits arising therefrom outweighed the possible consequences of being categorized as a *mamzer*. Following these decisions, the Genetic Information Law was amended in 2008[38] so that if the rabbinical authorities determine that a paternity test may render a child a *mamzer*, then the court has no discretion to order the test, save in cases where conducting the test is required in order to save the life of the child or prevent a severe handicap.[39] Today the legal position is, therefore, that if a child is born to a Jewish woman who is married to a Jewish man, under Israeli law paternity cannot be established with another Jewish man. In this respect it should be noted that even when the mother is living apart from her husband, and even where she has established a new relationship with the child's biological father, as long as she is still legally married, the paternity

---

[35] Since the enactment of the Genetic Information Law 2000, paternity testing requires court authorization, even where all the relevant adults consent.

[36] Genetic Information Law (Amendment No. 3) 2008, s. 11(a). Until this amendment, case law held that an individual could not be required to undergo a genetic test, because this would violate his right to privacy, but inferences could be drawn from the individual's refusal to undergo testing.

[37] FC (Tel-Aviv) 87471/00 *Anonymous.* v. *Anonymous*, Nevo (8 January 2004); FC 76760/01 (Tel-Aviv) *S.N.* v. *C.S.A.* Nevo (5 September 2004).

[38] Genetic Information Law (Amendment 3).

[39] Sometimes establishing a genetic connection is required in the context of a bone marrow or organ transplant.

of a man other than the husband cannot be proved. The implications of this situation are exacerbated by the difficulty that women may encounter in obtaining a divorce from their husbands under religious law, which will be discussed below.[40]

Parentage in cases of artificial reproduction

6.20   Israeli society enjoys the highest rate of assisted reproductive technologies (ART) intervention in the world as well as the highest rate of infertility therapy per capita.[41] Public health policy hardly imposes any restrictions on the eligibility of Israeli citizens to infertility treatments fully subsidized by National Health Insurance coverage. Nonetheless, the Israeli legislature has not regulated all of the assisted reproduction technologies employed.

6.21   The use of sperm donation is regulated by Rules as to the Administration of a Sperm Bank and Guidelines for Performing Artificial Insemination issued by the Director-General of the Health Ministry (hereinafter 'the Rules'). With regard to the issue of paternity, since 1989 the Rules have required that if the woman who wishes to use sperm donation is married, then her husband must agree to the procedure and declare that he is assuming paternal status. Nonetheless, because the Rules are purely administrative, they cannot establish paternity.[42]

6.22   The question of legal paternity in cases of sperm donation has only arisen in a small number of cases and has only once come before the Supreme Court. Israeli courts have refused to tackle the broad question of parenthood, and have chosen instead to confine themselves to the specific question before them (usually, the obligation of the mother's husband to pay child support).[43] In *Salameh* v. *Salameh*[44] the Supreme Court held that mother's husband was obliged to pay child support on the basis of an 'implied agreement', based on his consent to the performance of artificial

---

[40] See para. 6.68 below.

[41] Carmel Shalev and Sigal Goldin, 'The Uses and Misuses of In Vitro Fertilization in Israel: Some Sociological and Ethical Considerations' (2006) 12 *Nashim: A Journal of Jewish Women's Studies* 151.

[42] Therefore, the presumption, under which the husband is assumed to be the father of the child will continue to apply. Nonetheless, it is conceivable that genetic testing might be allowed because the prevalent rabbinical opinion is that a child born as a result of sperm donation is not considered to be a *mamzer*.

[43] Issues affecting child custody, visitation and inheritance have not yet been addressed by the courts.

[44] CA 449/79 *Salameh* v. *Salameh*, 34(2) P.D. 779 (1980).

insemination. Implicit in the Court's reasoning is the perception that the husband was not the 'real' legal father of the child. Although it provides a seemingly workable solution,[45] the implied agreement basis for establishing child support is somewhat flawed, since the right to financial support theoretically belongs to the child, but its contractual basis in cases of sperm donation makes it conditional upon the behaviour of adults.[46]

6.23   The problematic legal situation of the sperm donor, in a system that defines fatherhood based on biological parenthood, does not arise in practice because the mechanism for ensuring the donor's anonymity negates any realistic possibility of the sperm donor being declared the legal father.[47] However, this anonymity may cause other problems. In particular, in a case of an unmarried woman, the child's status under Jewish law may be uncertain because his father is unknown and therefore it is not possible to prevent marriage with half-siblings or other blood relatives.[48]

6.24   In summary, the practical solutions offered by Israeli law are unsatisfactory and a comprehensive legal arrangement regulating the parenthood of children born through sperm donation as well as the legal status of the donor is required. As with many other family issues which the legislature has avoided regulating, the absence of primary legislation regulating sperm donation may be explained by its controversial nature in the eyes of the Jewish and other religious authorities in Israel. A draft Sperm Donation Law has now been placed before the Knesset,[49] but it is not yet clear whether it will receive the support of the religious parties.

---

[45]   However, rabbinical courts, which have concurrent jurisdiction on child support issues, have at times refused to compel the husband to pay child support in view of their hostile attitude toward the use of sperm donations. Pinhas Shifman, 'Family Law in Israel: The Struggle Between Religious and Secular Law' (1990) 24 *Israel Law Review* 537, 543, in note 31, citing the decision of the Great Rabbinical Court in App. 49/5745 of 4 Tevet, 5746 (1986).

[46]   Indeed, in one case involving unmarried partners, the mother's ex-partner was relieved of his child support obligation since the court held that the mother herself had breached any implied agreement by failing to cooperate with registering him as the father and by discouraging a parent–child relationship between him and the child. FC (Jerusalem) 10681/98 *Anonymous* v. *Anonymous* (2000). See also Ruth Zafran, 'The Family in the Genetic Era: Defining Parenthood in Families Created through Assisted Reproduction Technologies as a Test Case' (2005) 2 *Haifa Law Review* 223, 250–1 (Hebrew).

[47]   Where the donor is known, he may be liable to pay child support. See, for example, FamC (Fam Ramat-Gan) 1241/05 *T.R. and others* v. *K.P.*, Nevo (31 May 2010).

[48]   In practice, this danger can be avoided by pre-marital genetic testing.

[49]   On 15 March 2010 (Ref. P 3103/18). This draft law provides inter alia that where the mother has a male partner, that partner will be considered to be the father of the child for all purposes other than those relating to the prohibited degrees of marriage.

6.25   Until recently, egg donation in Israel was regulated in the same way as sperm donation by secondary legislation and Health Ministry guidelines.[50] However, in June 2010 the Israeli Knesset enacted the Egg Donation Law 2010. Previously, only women who were undergoing in vitro fertilization treatments themselves could donate eggs in Israel.[51] This stringent precondition caused great hardship for Israeli women who needed donated eggs and were forced to turn to foreign egg donors.

6.26   The new legislation enables women above the age of 21 and below 35 to donate eggs, even if they themselves are not undergoing fertility treatment. The Egg Donation Law imposes some conditions, such as that the donor and the recipient must belong to the same religion, the donor cannot be a relative of either the recipient or the recipient's husband (if she has one), and the donor must not be married. Egg donation under this law is anonymous in line with the practice prior to its enactment.[52] However, a special committee may permit exceptions to these conditions.

6.27   Prior to the enactment of the Egg Donation Law, the IVF Regulations were silent about the definition of motherhood. The accepted practice in Israel was that the woman who gave birth was the child's mother and there was no practical way of inquiring into the use of egg donation in any given case.[53] The new Egg Donation Law defines the recipient, who delivers the child, as the legal mother, and clarifies that the donor has no parental rights or obligations towards the child. It severs any legal connection between the donor, her family and the child. At the same time, the law provides that a confidential databank shall be set up – the Newborns Registry – to be managed by the Adoptions Registrar. At the age of 18, anyone wishing to know if he or she was born from an ovum donation will be able to inquire at the registry.[54] The registrar will provide

---

[50] Public Health (In Vitro Fertilization) Regulation, 1987, KT 5035, 978 (hereinafter 'IVF Regulations').

[51] IVF Regulations s. 4.

[52] Section 39. As to the legal situation prior to the enactment of the Egg Donation Law, see Ruth Landau, 'The Management of Genetic Origins: Secrecy and Openness in Donor Assisted Conception in Israel and Elsewhere' (1998) 13 *Human Reproduction* 3268, 3268.

[53] Zafran 'More than One Mother', 127.

[54] According to s. 36, the registrar will provide that information after verifying that the information will not pose a risk to the physical or mental health of that individual; that the individual's mental and intellectual capacity allow him to understand the informa-tion and its significance; and that the benefit gained from providing the information out-weighs any damage which may potentially be caused by not providing it.

only a positive or negative answer regarding the use of a gamete donation without divulging the identity of the donor. Couples wishing to marry, where one of the partners was born from a donated ovum, will be able to inquire from the registrar whether there is a genetic family connection between them.

6.28 In 1996 the Israeli Knesset passed the Surrogate Motherhood Agreements (Approval of Agreement and Status of Newborn) Law 1996, governing the practice of surrogacy. Prior to its enactment, the Public Health (In Vitro Fertilization) Regulation (IVF Regulations) mandated that fertilized eggs could only be implanted in a woman who was to raise the ensuing child. Hence, surrogacy was, in fact, prohibited in Israel.[55] The Surrogacy Law adopts a regulatory approach to surrogacy.[56] The statute legalizes only gestational (full) surrogacy meaning that the egg to be used cannot be that of the surrogate mother. The egg can be either the egg of the designated mother or the egg of a donor. The sperm to be used must, however, be the sperm of the designated father. Surrogacy in Israel is available only to heterosexual couples and cannot be used by single women or same-sex couples. An attempt to challenge the constitutionality of this limitation failed.[57]

6.29 All parties to the surrogacy agreement must be of full age and Israeli residents. The surrogate mother must be an unmarried woman, with provision for exceptions in circumstances where it is not possible to find an unmarried woman willing to act as a surrogate. The surrogate mother must not be related by family ties to either the designated mother or the designated father. The surrogate mother and the designated mother must belong to the same religion.[58]

6.30 In addition to these substantive requirements, the law establishes a procedure for approving the actual agreement by a statutory committee

---

[55] For details of the *Nachmani* case, which was the trigger for the Surrogacy Law, see Rhona Schuz, 'The Right to Parenthood: Surrogacy and Frozen Embryos', in Andrew Bainham (ed.), *International Survey of Family Law* (The Hague: Martinus Nijhoff, 1996), p. 237.

[56] See *ibid.*; Rhona Schuz, 'Surrogacy in Israel: An Analysis of the Law in Practice', in R. Cook and S-D. Sclater (eds.), *Surrogate Motherhood: International Perspectives* (Oxford: Hart, 2003), p. 35; Ruth Halperin-Kaddari, 'Redefining Parenthood' (1999) 29 *California Western International Law Journal* 313, 319.

[57] HCJ 2458/01, *New Family v. Approvals Comm. for Surrogate Motherhood Agreements, Ministry of Health*, 57(1) P.D. 419. For discussion of this case, see Schuz, 'Surrogacy And PAS'.

[58] On these restrictions see Schuz, 'Surrogacy in Israel'.

appointed by the Minister of Health and composed of seven members of relevant professions (medicine, welfare, law and religion). The committee must verify that the agreement meets the statutory requirements specified above and that the surrogacy arrangement is needed for medical reasons due to the inability of the designated mother to become pregnant or carry a fetus. The committee must also confirm that all parties have undergone psychological evaluation or counselling and that the agreement was entered into on the basis of informed consent. The committee has also added a number of requirements in addition to those provided for in the Surrogacy Law, such as in relation to the maximum age of the intended parents.[59] Similarly, only a surrogate mother who has already given birth will be approved and a woman may only be a surrogate twice. The committee must also approve the payment to the surrogate, which under the statutory standard is intended to reimburse her for out-of-pocket expenses and compensation for lost income or earning capacity, loss of time, pain and suffering.

6.31   The basic premise of the Surrogacy Law is that the designated parents are the legal parents of the ensuing child. To formalize this principle, the designated parents must apply for a 'parenthood order' within a week of the child's birth. The court will grant the order unless it is persuaded that such an order would be contrary to the best interests of the child. The parenthood order recognizes the intended parents as the child's parents 'in all respects', and the surrogate's connection to the child is severed.

6.32   The Surrogacy Law strictly limits the ability of the surrogate mother to renege on the agreement. The court will only allow a surrogate mother to assert her legal maternity in rare instances, where she can demonstrate that circumstances have changed, that the change justifies her retraction and that the child's welfare will not thereby be impaired. To date, there has been no case where the surrogate mother has reneged on the agreement and has asked to be recognized as the legal mother.[60]

---

[59] The maximum age was 48, but a change in the guidelines provides that the extent to which the age of the parents is greater than that of usual natural parenthood (48–50) is a factor to be taken into account. In FamC 26140/07 (Tel-Aviv District) *Ploni and Plonit* v. *State Attorney*, Nevo (15 February 2007) the refusal to approve surrogacy for a 53-year-old woman and her 58-year-old husband was upheld.

[60] The reason for this would seem to be careful vetting of surrogates by the agencies and the Approvals Committee and the support given to them during the pregnancy by the social services. See Schuz, 'Surrogacy in Israel'.

Adoption

6.33 Since the Adoption Law 1961, which was superseded by the Adoption Law 1981 (hereinafter 'the Adoption Law'), adoption has been governed solely by civil law.[61] Children can only be placed for adoption by the State Children's Service. A child can only be placed for adoption if his parents consent thereto[62] or if he is declared as adoptable in relation to each of his parents on the basis of one of the grounds set out in s. 13(1) of the Adoption Law.

6.34 The most commonly used ground for declaring a child adoptable is that the parent is not capable of taking proper care of the child because of his situation or conduct and that the situation is unlikely to change in the foreseeable future, notwithstanding reasonable assistance from the welfare authorities. In most cases this ground is invoked after a history of out-of-home placements. Criticism has been levelled against the limitation placed by the welfare authorities on contact between the biological parents and the child in such situations, which make it very difficult for the parents to maintain a normal relationship with the child and to show that they are now capable of raising the child.[63]

6.35 The second most commonly used ground is that there is no reasonable chance of identifying the child's parent or of ascertaining his opinion. This ground is routinely invoked where an unmarried mother refuses to reveal the identity of the father. Case law has held that the mother's right to privacy should be respected and that attempts should not be made to locate the father in such a case.[64] However, a recent statutory amendment

---

[61] Religious courts can obtain jurisdiction over matters of adoption, provided that the written consent of all the parties involved has been obtained, but they should apply the civil law in the form of the Adoption of Children Law 1981, s. 27.

[62] For detailed discussion of the procedure for giving consent and withdrawing consent, see Rhona Schuz, 'The Right of the Child to Be Raised by his Biological Parents – Lessons from the Israeli "Baby of Strife" Case' (2007) 27 *Children's Legal Rights Journal* 85. It should be noted that in Amendment No. 8 to the Adoption Law of 2010, changes similar to many of those recommended in that article have been made. In particular, consent can only be given seven days after birth and the Social Services are obliged to explain to the parents the assistance they will receive if they raise the child themselves and to verify that the consent is genuine. Furthermore, a parent may only submit a request to withdraw his consent within sixty days of the day on which the child was placed with the adoptive parents.

[63] Mili Mass, *The Best Interests of the Child: Suffering and Loss in the Adoption Proceedings* (Israel: Resling, 2010) (Hebrew).

[64] FamA 5082/05 *A-G* v. *Plonit* Task-al 05(4) 387 (2005). For analysis of this case, see Schuz 'The Right of the Child to Be Raised by his Biological Parents'.

provides that the welfare authorities should make limited enquiries in order to identify the father unless this would involve a risk to the life or health of the mother or the child.[65]

6.36   The effect of an adoption order is that the adoptive parents are treated as the legal parents of the child for all purposes and the connection between the child and his biological parents is severed,[66] unless the court provides otherwise. Whilst the Israeli courts have recognized that this exception can be used to provide for open adoption, the policy is to allow continued contact with the biological parents only in exceptional cases. This policy has been criticized on the basis that it does not give recognition to the need of a child to a connection to his biological roots and to the 'bereavement' involved in the loss of any connection to the biological parents.[67]

6.37   Section 30 of the Adoption Law provides that when a child reaches 18, he or she may submit a request to a welfare officer from the Children's Service to receive details about his or her biological parents from the Adoption Registry. If the welfare officer refuses, the child may appeal to a court. Research into the implementation of this provision shows that the Children's Service's practice is not to provide identifying details about the biological parent without first obtaining their consent.[68] This practice severely limits the child's right to know his genetic origins in accordance with Article 7 of the UN Convention and it is doubtful whether it accords with the statutory provision.[69]

---

[65] Other exceptions are where the child was born as a result of a sexual offence or a forbidden relationship or where the father knew of the existence of the child and did not make any contact with him without any justification. Adoption Law 1981 s. 13(a)(1) and s. 13(A1) (as amended by Amendment No. 8 to the Adoption Law of 2010).

[66] Other than for the purposes of prohibited marriages and for the purposes of the child inheriting the property of the biological parents (but there is currently a proposal to abolish this latter provision).

[67] Milli Mass, 'Acknowledging the Child as an Independent Entity – a Proposal to Amend the Adoption of Minors Law 1981' (2009–10) 3–4 *The Family in Law*, 199 (Hebrew).

[68] Ruth Zafran, 'The Adoptee's Right to Know his Biological Parents – A Comparative Perspective' (2007) 1 *The Family In Law*, 25 (Hebrew).

[69] Ironically, whilst the 1961 Adoption Law, which allowed unrestricted access of adoptees to adoption records, was far more advanced than the closer records policy still prevalent in other Western countries in those days, the current practice of the Israeli Children's Service can be seen as lagging behind the statutory schemes allowing adoptees access to identifying details, which can be found in many Western countries today. See Zafran, 'The Adoptee's Right to Know his Biological Parents'.

Parentage and same-sex couples

6.38 Addressing the capacity to adopt, the Israeli Adoption Law provides that 'An Adoption may only be made by a man and his wife jointly'.[70] Nonetheless, in 2005 the Supreme Court in the *Yaros-Hakak* case[71] interpreted the Israeli Adoption Law as enabling second parent adoption in a same-sex family. Following the Supreme Court decision to allow second-parent adoption in the *Yaros-Hakak* case, the Attorney General issued guidelines according to which the Adoption Law should be interpreted so as to allow unmarried cohabitees, including same-sex couples, to adopt children.[72] These guidelines refer merely to the capacity to adopt, and a decision regarding the placement of a particular child should be made in light of the child's best interests. This means that in practice, and especially given the scarcity of children being placed for adoption, same-sex couples cannot adopt children unrelated to either of them, as the Welfare Services give preference to heterosexual married couples as the best familial framework for children.

6.39 In principle, same-sex couples can adopt children from abroad. Unlike internal adoption, inter-country adoptions are organized by private adoption agencies licensed by the state. However, adoptions from abroad have to satisfy the conditions for adoption under the law of the child's country of origin. Thus, it will only be possible for same-sex couples to adopt children from countries which allow same-sex adoption and in practice most of the countries with which the adoption agencies work do not allow same-sex adoption. The Supreme Court has held that an adoption order given abroad to a same-sex couple will enable registration of both parties as parents in the population registry in Israel.[73] However, this decision does not have any bearing on questions of recognition of status.[74]

6.40 In *Vitz* v. *Minister of Health* the Supreme Court (with the state's consent) abolished provisions of secondary legislation, according to which unmarried women and lesbians were required to undergo a psychiatric test that was not required of married women as a precondition for receiving artificial insemination and in vitro fertilization

---

[70] Section 3.
[71] CA 10280/01, *Yaros-Hakak* v. *Atty. Gen.*, P.D. 59(5) 64.
[72] Guidelines of the Attorney General regarding Adoption by Same-Sex Couples (Hebrew): www.justice.gov.il/MOJHeb/News/2008/imuz.htm.
[73] HC 1779/99 *Brenner-Kadish* v. *The Interior Minister* P.D. 44(2) 2000.
[74] FDHCJ 4252/00 *Minister of the Interior* v. *Brenner-Kadish*, Nevo (31 August 2008).

services.[75] Today, lesbian couples have access to sperm donation and IVF treatments in the same way as married and single women. As noted above, however, surrogacy is limited to heterosexual couples.[76]

6.41   In 2006 the Health Ministry permitted a woman to be impregnated with an egg of her female partner fertilized in vitro by sperm from an anonymous donor.[77] The couple underwent this procedure in view of a medical reason that necessitated fertility treatments. However, recently the Health Ministry approved this procedure for lesbian couples wishing to share in the process of bringing their child into the world. Very recently, the Tel Aviv Family Court held that both of the women could be considered as mothers of the child without the need for adoption.[78]

Delivering parenting

6.42   The rights and responsibilities of parents in relation to their children are set out in section 15 of the Legal Capacity and Guardianship Law 1962, which provides that:

> the guardianship of the parents shall include the duty and the right to take care of the needs of the minor, including his education, studies, vocational and occupational training and work, and to preserve and manage and develop his property: it shall also include the right to the custody of the minor, to determine his place of residence and the authority to act on his behalf.

6.43   Parents' duty to support their children financially is regulated by the Family Amendment (Maintenance) Law 1958, which provides for application of the personal law of the parent. However, where under the parent's personal law there is no duty to support the child, a civil obligation is created by the Family Amendment (Maintenance) Law.

6.44   In general, Israeli law takes an exclusive approach to parenthood so that those who are not recognized as legal parents have no rights and obligations with respect to the child. This approach has several limited exceptions. Grandparents have standing to seek visitation,[79] in particular

---

[75] HCJ 2078/96 *Vitz* v. *Minister of Health* (not published).

[76] See para. 6.28 above.

[77] Zafran, 'More than One Mother', 115.

[78] FC (Tel-Aviv) 60320-07 *T.Tz and others v. Attorney General*, Nevo (4 March 2012).

[79] FA (Be'er-Sheva Dist.) 135/08 *Z.H.* v. *Z.H.*, Nevo (3 December 2009). Whether there will be visitation is determined in accordance with the best interests of the child.

where their child (the grandchild's parent) is deceased.[80] Furthermore, grandparents may be required to support their grandchildren, where they have the required means in situations where it is not possible to enforce the parent's support obligation.[81]

6.45   Except for grandparents, Israeli law contains scant reference to the rights and obligations of other non-parents. No case law exists regarding the ability of step-parents to seek custody or visitation under Israeli law. Under formal law, step-parents are under an obligation to support their stepchildren as long as they are formally married to the stepchild's legal parent. Nonetheless, to date this duty has not been enforced.

Intra-family disputes

6.46   Religious and Family Courts have parallel jurisdiction in matters of child custody or child support and the court first seized will hear the case. However, in relation to all matters concerning children the civil law will be applied, except for child support which is governed by the personal law, as explained below. Thus, for example, religious courts are obliged to determine custody and visitation disputes according to the principle of the best interests of the child, as enacted in the Guardianship Law. Needless to say, however, the indeterminacy of the best interests standard allows the judge to apply that standard in accordance with his own values and worldview. Accordingly, judges in religious courts will inevitably be influenced by the religious law in relation to custody, but so long as they pay lip-service to the best interests standard, it will be difficult to attack their decision in the High Court of Justice.[82]

6.47   It should also be noted that s. 25 of the Capacity and Guardianship Law still contains the rebuttable presumption that children under six should be in the custody of their mother. This presumption, known as the tender years presumption, has become very controversial in recent years and its abolition is likely.[83] Nonetheless, some defend the need for a presumption in the light of the discrimination against women under the Jewish divorce law.[84] This presumption is one of the underlying reasons

[80] Guardianship Law 1962, s. 28a.
[81] Family Amendment (Maintenance) Law 1959, s. 4(3).
[82] See Iyad Zahalka, *The Shari'a Courts: Between Adjudication and Identity* (Israel: Israel Bar Association, 2009), p. 66 (Hebrew).
[83] The interim report of the Schnit Committee, note 13 above, recommended abolition.
[84] See para. 6.68 below.

for the dominance of maternal custody in Israel both within the family court system and within the rabbinical courts.[85] However, in recent years joint physical custody has gradually become more accepted. Usually, a court will only award joint custody where the parties agree, but there are a few cases in which joint custody has been awarded even without agreement of one party, where the court takes the view that the relationship between the parents and the living arrangements of the parties makes this possible.[86]

6.48   Where one parent is granted sole physical custody, the other parent (invariably the father) is usually accorded expansive visitation rights. Traditionally, visitation has been considered as the father's right, and he can choose whether or not to exercise it. Claims for compensation filed by mothers or children against fathers who failed to maintain contact with their children have been dismissed.[87] Interestingly, courts have been more willing to recognize tort claims against custodial mothers who were interfering with the father's relationship with the children.[88] However, tort compensation was awarded to children in a case where their father refused to have contact with them in a way that amounted to psychological abuse.[89]

6.49   As noted above, in the vast majority of cases arrangements for children, including custody, visitation and child support, are decided by agreement of the parents. Such agreements are subject to approval of the court.[90] In practice, courts rarely enquire into the welfare of the particular child when approving such agreements.[91]

---

[85] It should be noted that the presumption also indirectly influences the custody of older children because of the reluctance to split siblings. Research conducted by Dafna Hacker, *Parenthood in the Law* (Israel: Hakibbutz Hameuchad, 2008) (Hebrew), which related to minor children of all ages, found that in 90 per cent of the cases the result was that of maternal custody (the result was either judicially determined or reached by the parties).

[86] See, for example, FamC (Krayot) 17120/07 *Plonit* v. *Plonit*, Nevo (22 August 2010).

[87] See, for example, FamC (Hadera) 3426/02 *S.Y.* v. *S.A.*, Nevo (22 August 2007).

[88] MCA (Jerusalem) 51183/09 *Ploni* v. *Almonit*, Nevo (25 Mat 2009); FamC (Jerusalem) 13993/02 *Plonit* v. *Plonit*, Nevo (15 February 2007).

[89] CA (SC) 2034/98 *Amin* v. *Amin*, PD 53 (5) 69. For discussion of the case, see Rhona Schuz, 'Child Protection in the Israeli Supreme Court: Tortious Parenting, Physical Punishment and Criminal Child Abuse', in A. Bainham (ed.), *The International Survey of Family Law* (Bristol: Jordans, 2001).

[90] See, for example, Guardianship Law 1962, s. 24.

[91] See Hacker, 'A Legal Field in Action'. Provision for courts to check that children have been consulted by their parents before coming to an agreement is included in the chapter on Child Participation in the Civil Procedure Regulations, regulation 258(33)11, but this provision has not been implemented, in practice.

Child protection and state intervention

6.50 The Penal Law and child protection legislation provide wide-ranging scope for state intervention in family life in order to safeguard children[92] from harm and neglect. In 1990 an amendment to the Penal Law introduced a number of specific offences against children.[93] Furthermore, this amendment introduced mandatory reporting of offences against children, accompanied by a criminal sanction.[94] There has been a steady increase in the number of cases in which parents have been prosecuted for offences against their children. In the seminal case of *State of Israel* v. *Plonit*,[95] the Supreme Court held that all corporal punishment of children was a criminal offence, but the practice of only prosecuting in serious cases has not changed.[96]

6.51 The main child protection enactment is the Youth (Care and Supervision) Law 1960. Under this law, a minor is declared as 'in need of protection' if one of a number of conditions is fulfilled, the most commonly used of which is 'that his physical or psychical well-being is impaired or likely to be impaired'. The court may then order one of a number of modes of dealing with the minor, which include appointing a social worker to supervise the child and removing the child from the custody of his parents. While the Youth (Care and Supervision) Law states that removal from custody should only be used as a last resort, in practice welfare officers frequently recommend this course of action and courts are reluctant to differ from the 'experts'.[97] Not infrequently, parents agree to their children being placed in foster homes or institutions in

---

[92] It should be noted that, at the end of 2009, minors constituted 32.8 per cent of the population (2,468,700 minors).

[93] Amendment No. 26 to the Penal Law 1977 added a new chapter to the Penal Law, entitled 'Harm to minors and helpless persons'. Among the offences introduced are assault of a minor or helpless person (s. 368B) and abuse of a child or helpless person (s. 368C). The maximum punishments for these offences are greater where the offender is a person in charge of the child (e.g. for abuse nine years' imprisonment instead of seven years).

[94] S. 368D. Six months' imprisonment for professionals or those responsible for the child and three months for all other persons.

[95] CA 4596 /98 *Plonit* v. *State of Israel*, P.D. 44(1) 145.

[96] See Rhona Schuz, '"Three Years On": An Analysis of the Delegalisation of Physical Punishment of Children by the Israeli Court' (2003) 11 *The International Journal of Children's Rights* 235.

[97] For criticism of courts as rubber-stamps, see Y. Gilat, 'On the Legal Defect Inherent in Determining "The Best Interests of the Child" by the Welfare Services System' (2006) 5 *Netanya Academic College Law Review* 403 (Hebrew).

order to avoid such an order being made. In other words, many children are removed from their homes 'in the shadow of the law'. Whilst the number of children placed outside their homes has been gradually decreasing over the last twenty years,[98] the numbers are still by far the highest in the Western world.[99] Furthermore, the proportion of such children who are placed in institutions rather than foster care is much higher than in other countries.[100] A number of reasons can be given for the current situation, one of which is that various parties have an interest in the continued running of state institutions for children, which were set up after the Second World War to provide homes for the thousands of children and youngsters who arrived in Israel without parents.[101] Another reason would seem to be that overworked social workers are aware that they cannot provide adequate supervision for children who remain in homes where they are at risk and, in order to cover themselves and reduce their workload, they recommend placement in institutions.

6.52   In an emergency, where a social worker considers that the child is in immediate danger, he or she is entitled to remove a child from his home unilaterally,[102] although court approval of this action must be obtained within seven days.[103] Courts are usually reluctant to interfere with the social worker's discretion and so this draconian power very often creates an irreversible situation. An alternative method of protecting children at risk of violence from one parent is by means of an order requiring the violent parent to leave the home under the Prevention of Domestic Violence Law 1991, but, in practice, relatively few such orders are made in cases of child abuse.

6.53   Much criticism has been levelled against the ease with which children are removed from their homes in Israel. This is based both on the claim that such removal does not serve the best interests of the child,

---

[98] From 5 per thousand children in 1990 to 3.4 per thousand children in 2010 (The National Council for the Welfare of the Child, *Children in Israel: Statistical Yearbook* (Israel: Research and Data Department, 2010) (Hebrew).

[99] Y. Aliya, *Distant Children* (Israel: Ofakim: 2006) (Hebrew), p. 15.

[100] Less than one third of the children placed outside their homes in 2010 were placed in foster care. The National Council for the Welfare of the Child, *Children in Israel: Statistical Yearbook*.

[101] See Schuz 'Surrogacy and PAS'.

[102] Youth (Care and Supervision) Law, s. 11.

[103] In 2009 this power was used in 546 cases and in 537 of them the removal was authorized by the court.

especially in light of the poor long-term prognosis for children who spend years in institutions, and of the right of the child to be raised by his biological parents, entrenched in Article 7 of the UN Convention.[104] In response to this criticism, in 2004 the Ministry of Welfare declared a policy of providing assistance for children in need within the community. Whilst this did lead to some reduction in the number of children sent to institutions and even to children being returned home, the policy was inadequately funded and thus some children had to be sent to institutions in the end and others did not have their needs properly met.

6.54   One of the most promising steps in ensuring closer review of the removal of children from their homes is a pilot project for providing independent representation of children in such cases. However, it seems that real progress will only be made if considerably more resources are devoted to reducing social workers' workloads and providing effective alternatives to institutional care within the community.

C   Adult relationships

The relationships

Marriage

6.55   Marriage and divorce are matters of 'personal status' and, thus, are governed solely by the personal law of the relevant parties. Israeli law provides no uniform territorial law that applies to marriage and no civil marriage exists in Israel. As a result, various individuals and couples cannot marry in Israel. For example, people who do not belong to a recognized religious community and therefore have no law of marriage applicable to them[105] and inter-faith couples cannot marry since most recognized religions in Israel do not recognize inter-faith marriages (with the exception of marriage between a Muslim man and a Jewish or Christian woman, which the sharia law recognizes).

6.56   In addition, various restrictions under the pertinent religious laws may also prevent parties from marrying, such as the limitation under

---

[104]   See, for example, *Report of the Rotlevi Committee on Out of Home Placement for Children* (1997).

[105]   However, under the new Spousal Registration Law 2010, couples who do not belong to an officially recognized religion may register their union.

Jewish law on the marriage between a Cohen (a descendant of the priestly clan) and a divorcee. As for same-sex marriage, theoretically, if a relevant religious law recognized same-sex marriage, then same-sex couples could get married in Israel. As a matter of fact, however, the religious communities in Israel do not recognize same-sex marriage.[106]

6.57   The complete governance of religious laws over marriage also means that the validity of marriage is determined by the relevant religious law. Thus, although Israeli Penal Law criminalizes bigamy,[107] the validity of bigamous or polygamous relationships is determined by the religious laws.[108] Similarly, the Marriage Age Law 1950 sets the minimum age for marriage as 17 for both girls and boys. Here again, however, the secular statute only imposes criminal sanctions and the validity of underage marriages is determined by the relevant religious law.[109] Regarding the prohibition of marriage between persons related by blood or marriage, no secular law addresses this issue and thus it is the relevant religious law that specifies the degrees of relationship included in the prohibition.

6.58   Due to the religious restrictions on access to marriage in Israel, couples who could not marry in Israel (or do not want a religious marriage) have looked for ways to bypass these restrictions. One such commonly practised way is to get married abroad. Regardless of their validity, which shall be addressed below, civil marriages conducted abroad may be registered in the Israeli population registry.[110] This applies to same-sex marriages conducted outside Israel as well.[111] The records of the

---

[106]   Menachem Elon (ed.), *The Principles Of Jewish Law* (Jerusalem: Encyclopedia Judaica, 1975), p. 361.

[107]   Penal Law 1977, s. 176.

[108]   Furthermore, s. 179 of the Penal Law states that the criminal prohibition does not apply to the second marriage of a Jewish man who has received permission to remarry from a rabbinical court.

[109]   Criminal sanctions are imposed on the man or woman who marries an underage girl or boy, on those persons who perform the ceremony, and on anyone who assists them. S. 5 of the Marriage Age Law specifies two possible grounds on which a court may permit an underage marriage. The first concerns pregnancy of or the birth of a child to an underage girl who wishes to marry or whose father is an underage boy. The second concerns girls or boys who reached the age of 16 and, in the court's opinion, there are special circumstances that justify granting such permission. The statute does not specify exactly what these 'special circumstances' are.

[110]   This is based on the landmark decision of the Supreme Court in HCJ 143/62 *Funk Shlezinger* v. *Minister of the Interior*, 17 P.D. 225 (1963) (Isr).

[111]   In 2006 the *Funk-Shlezinger* precedent was applied to same-sex couples who were married in a civil ceremony outside Israel: HCJ 3045/05. An official translation can be found

population registry do not have the force of evidence or proof as to the veracity of the data they contain, especially regarding marital status.[112] Nonetheless, in reality, registration has broad practical implications. As a result, civilly married couples enjoy practically all the same economic benefits as couples who were formally married in religious marriages in Israel.[113]

6.59   As to the validity of civil marriage performed abroad between two Israeli citizens and residents, in a decision handed down by the former Chief Justice Barak in 2006, the Supreme Court held that when the parties had the capacity to legally marry in Israel, then their marriage is valid for all purposes under Israeli law.[114] The Court left open for future decision the question of the validity of civil marriages conducted abroad between individuals who could not get married in Israel (such as inter-faith couples or same-sex couples).

Unmarried cohabitants

6.60   Israeli law does not provide for registration of civil unions.[115] Though no formal framework exists for recognizing domestic partnership outside the marital framework, unmarried cohabitants, known under Israeli law as 'reputed spouses',[116] enjoy most of the rights and benefits and are under most of the same obligations as married couples. Legal recognition of 'reputed spouses' dates back to enactments from the early 1950s focusing mainly on social rights.[117] Where Israeli legislation has been silent, the Israeli Supreme Court has continued this trend of equalization, expanding

---

on the Israeli Supreme Court's website: http://elyon1.court.gov.il/files_eng/05/450/030/a09/05030450.a09.html.

[112] Population Registry Law 1964, s. 3. This section provides that some details registered in the population registry constitute prima facie evidence as to their veracity; however, personal status of an individual is not one of them.

[113] Ruth Halperin-Kaddari, *Women in Israel: A State of their Own* (Philadelphia: University of Pennsylvania Press, 2004). This reality triggered criticism over the *Funk-Shlezinger* decision.

[114] HCJ 2232/03 *Plonit* v. *The Regional Rabbinical Court Tel Aviv*, Nevo (21 December 2003).

[115] Other than in the case of parties who do not belong to a recognized religion. See para. 6.55 above.

[116] The literal translation is 'known in the public as spouses'.

[117] Rosen-Zvi, 'Family and Inheritance Law', p. 98; Menashe Shava, 'The Property Rights of Spouses Cohabiting Without Marriage in Israel – A Comparative Commentary' (1983) 13 *Georgia Journal of International and Comparative Law* 465, 468.

the list of rights, benefits and obligations accorded to non-married cohabitants to match those of married couples.[118] The extensive legal recognition accorded to unmarried cohabitants under Israeli law is commonly explained as the civil system's reaction to the strict religiously based restrictions on marriage in Israel.[119]

6.61   The extensive recognition of the rights, benefits and obligations of reputed spouses has been accompanied by a very open definition of reputed spouses and flexible criteria, which make it easier for couples to be considered reputed spouses. The essential criteria required by Israeli law are joint cohabitation and the running of a common household. Nonetheless, there is no formal requirement that the couple share a common registered address, and in some cases couples have been recognized as reputed spouses while not living together in the same residential unit.[120] In addition, most of the laws applicable to reputed spouses do not stipulate a minimum period of time for them to be recognized as such, and when they do, a relatively short time period is required (usually one year).[121] When legislation does not stipulate a minimum period, courts have sometimes recognized couples as reputed spouses within a very short period of time. Lastly, monogamy is not necessarily required and in several cases couples were recognized as reputed spouses, despite additional intimate relations.

Same-sex couples

6.62   In recent years Israeli case law has applied many of the rights, benefits and obligations of reputed spouses to same-sex couples as well. However, the Israeli Supreme Court refused to declare that the definition

---

[118]   See, for example, C.A. 52/80 *Shachar* v. *Friedman*, P.D. 38(1) 443 (holding that the then existing presumption of community property applied to married couples should be applied to unmarried cohabitants as well); C.A. 2000/97 *Lindorn* v. *Karnit*, 5 5(1) P.D. 12.

[119]   It is argued, however, that by equating the legal status of unmarried cohabitants to that of married couples, the Israeli system ignores the fact that not all the unmarried cohabitants in Israel were barred from marrying under the religious laws of marriage in Israel, or deterred from marrying by the religious nature of marriage in Israel. Rather, Israeli law failed to realize that some of these couples chose not to get married, as they rejected the institution of marriage. See, for example, Shahar Lifshitz, 'The External Rights of Cohabiting Couples in Israel' (2003–2004) 37 *Israel Law Review* 346.

[120]   See, for example, FLA 3497/09 *Plonit* v. *Plonit*, Nevo (4 May 2009).

[121]   Lifshitz, 'Cohabiting Couples In Israel', 407–8.

of reputed spouses under Israeli law includes same-sex couples.[122] Instead, each legislative enactment that refers to reputed spouses, whether expressly or by way of interpretation, and each right, benefit and obligation that is accorded to reputed spouses is to be examined separately, on a case-by-case basis, to consider whether it should be applied to same-sex couples as well.

Consequences of relationships

6.63   Spousal maintenance is, again, governed by the parties' religious laws.[123] The Jewish law of spousal maintenance places a unilateral obligation on the husband to maintain his wife.[124] This duty of support is considered a marital duty and is terminated upon divorce (or when a rabbinical court determines that the wife should accept a *get* from her husband).

6.64   The Supreme Court has held that the Maintenance Law 1959[125] does not apply to couples who were married in a civil ceremony abroad, and to reputed spouses.[126] Instead the court created a secular obligation to pay rehabilitative alimony, which is governed by civil–contractual principles and the principle of good faith.

6.65   Property relations are governed by secular law. The Spouses (Property Relations) Law 1972–73,[127] which applies to spouses who were married after 1 January 1974, adopts a regime of deferred community of property, according to which a separation of property exists during marriage, and following separation (or death), a resource-balancing arrangement applies. This Law provides for enforcement of marital property agreements between the parties provided that such agreements are signed in the presence of the court registrar or a notary, who must confirm that the parties entered into the agreement voluntarily and with understanding. Property relations among

---

[122] HCJ 721/94 *El-Al Israel Airlines Ltd* v. *Danielowitz*, 48(5) P.D. 749 (1994). An official translation can be found on the Israeli Supreme Court's website: http://elyon1.court.gov. il/files_eng/94/210/007/Z01/94007210.z01.htm.

[123] Family Law Amendment (Maintenance), s. 13.

[124] See, for example, Rosen-Zvi, 'Forum Shopping', note 8 above; Judith Romney Wegner, 'The Status of Women in Jewish and Islamic Marriage and Divorce Law' (1982) 5 *Harvard Women's Law Journal* 1, 21–2.

[125] Family Law Amendment (Maintenance) Law, 1959, 13 L.S.I. 73, (1958–59) (hereinafter: the Maintenance Law).

[126] LCA 8256/99 *A* v. *B*, P.D. 58(2) 213 (2004).

[127] The Spouses (Property Relations) Law, 5733–1973, 27 L.S.I 313 (1972–73).

spouses who were married prior to 1974 and among reputed spouses are governed in Israel by the presumption of co-ownership, an immediate community of property regime created by case law. According to this presumption, property accumulated during the marriage is considered joint property regardless of formal registration of this property.

Termination of relationships

6.66 In matters of divorce a distinction is made regarding jurisdiction between same-faith marriages of couples who belong to a recognized legal community in Israel and marriages that do not fall under this category (inter-faith marriages, marriages of individuals who do not belong to a recognized legal community, and individuals who have no religion). Where both parties belong to the same recognized religion, then the relevant religious court has exclusive jurisdiction over dissolution of the marital bond, even if the couple was married in a civil ceremony abroad.[128]

6.67 The law applicable to divorce between same-faith couples is also religious law (provided the parties belong to a recognized religion).[129] The governance of religious laws over matters of divorce causes an abundance of difficulties, due to the patriarchal character of religious laws. The scope of this chapter does not allow a detailed account of these difficulties, but they have been addressed extensively in the literature. Two issues receive most of the scholarly attention. The first concerns the problematic Jewish law of divorce, which requires the consent of the parties, and especially that of the husband, to divorce. Jewish women may thus find themselves unable to obtain the *get* – the Jewish bill of divorce – and break free from the marriage, or be subject to the husband's extortionate demands in return for the *get*.[130] The second concerns the Muslim sharia law of divorce

---

[128] HCJ 2232/03 *Plonit* v. *The Regional Rabbinical Court Tel Aviv*, Nevo (21 December 2006). Whether this rule applies to marriage of a same-sex couple who belong to the same recognized religion is questionable.

[129] In relation to Jewish law, according to some views, the rules of divorce for those who got married in a civil ceremony are different from those who got married in a religious ceremony. See HCJ 2232/03 *Plonit* v. *The Regional Rabbinical Court Tel Aviv*, Nevo (21 December 2006).

[130] See, for example, Halperin-Kaddari, *Women in Israel*; A. Hacohen, *The Tears of the Oppressed – An Examination of the Agunah Problem: Background and Halakhic Sources* (New York: Ktav, 2004); A. Blecher-Prigat and B. Shmueli, 'The Interplay Between Tort Law and Religious Family Law: The Israeli Case' (2009) 26 *Arizona Journal of International and Comparative Law* 279.

that enables a man to unilaterally divorce his wife against her will. Though divorcing one's wife in such a manner is criminalized under Israeli law,[131] which also provides the wife with ground for a civil tort action,[132] the validity of the divorce itself is governed by the sharia law.

6.68   The family court has jurisdiction over dissolution of inter-faith marriage, of marriages of parties who do not belong to a recognized legal community or when the parties lack any religious affiliation. In these cases the law controlling the dissolution of the marriage is the Matters of Dissolution of Marriage (Jurisdiction in Special Cases) Law 1969. This law determines that in principle the (civil) family court has jurisdiction to dissolve the marriage in such cases.[133] It expressly provides only one ground for granting a divorce, which is the consent of both parties to the divorce.[134] In the absence of mutual consent, the Law does not provide grounds for divorce but instead provides choice-of-law rules listed according to priority. In most cases the only relevant option is the substantive law of the state where the marriage took place. The Law does not enable the application of a law if no divorce can be obtained under its provisions.[135]

D   Conclusions

6.69   Israeli family law is a paradoxical mixture of traditional, anachronistic legal norms on the one hand and progressive innovation on the other. This schizophrenic dichotomy accompanied by creative dynamism can be seen in all facets of family law.

6.70   Regarding relationships between adults, the formation and dissolution of marriages is governed entirely by religious law and, thus, civil marriage does not exist. Nonetheless, wide recognition is given in practice to

---

[131]   Section 181(A) of the Penal Law 1977.

[132]   See, for example, CA 245/81 *Sultan* v. *Sultan*, P.D. 38(3) 169 (1984).

[133]   In cases where one or both of the parties belong to a recognized religious community, the family court must inquire with the relevant court or courts whether under their religious laws a religious dissolution of the marital bond is required to enable the relevant party to remarry in Israel. Where a religious dissolution is required by the relevant religious law, then the matter will be referred to the religious court. The religious court will have jurisdiction over dissolving the marriage but not over ancillary matters (such as economic consequences of the marital bond).

[134]   Matters of Dissolution of Marriage (Jurisdiction in Special Cases) Law, s. 5(c).

[135]   *Ibid.*, section 5(a).

new families and, in particular, cohabitants enjoy almost the same rights as married couples. This includes to some extent same-sex couples who are, for example, also able to adopt children.

6.71 Similarly, in relation to recognition of parentage, on the one hand biological parenthood is ignored in favour of the marital bond so as to prevent children being considered as *mamzerim*, whilst on the other hand Israel was the first country in the world to enact a law recognizing and regulating surrogacy.

6.72 Finally, in relation to children the influence of traditional concepts of the family is still felt, for example in the retention of the tender years presumption and the father's sole obligation to support young children. In contrast, a modern progressive approach has been adopted in relation to some aspects of recognition of children's rights, as can be seen inter alia from the judicial outlawing of corporal punishment, the pilot scheme giving children the opportunity to be heard directly by judges in relation to matters concerning them, and the reports of the Rotlevi Committee in general.

6.73 We would suggest that there is, at least to some extent, a logical explanation for the coexistence of anachronism and progressivity. Ever since the founding of the State of Israel, it has been necessary to find creative solutions to the dissonance between religious law and modern secular philosophy. For example, in response to the religious law's non-recognition of civil marriages, the secular courts held that where such marriages were conducted abroad they could be registered in Israel. Whilst technically the registration did not provide proof of their validity, in practice registration enabled the couple to be treated in the same way as married couples. Similarly, the restrictions on various marriages by religious law resulted in the recognition of rights for cohabitants, years ahead of other Western countries.[136] Having developed these tools to cope with problems caused by religious law, the courts were able to make use of them to provide solutions for new issues and in particular to provide remedies for couples who do not fit into the traditional mould, such as same-sex couples. Thus, for example, it has been held that same-sex couples who married abroad could register their marriage in Israel

---

[136] For example, the Succession Law 1965, s. 55, allows cohabitants to inherit from each other in the same way as married spouses.

and that foreign adoptions by same-sex couples could be automatically registered in Israel.

6.74   As far as the future is concerned, we believe that Israeli family law will continue to use the tools it has developed and the experience it has amassed over the past sixty years in order to cope with new challenges. In particular, whilst the influence of the religious parties hampers the ability of the Knesset to update many aspects of family law, the courts have usually found creative methods of overcoming this obstacle and will continue to do so.

7

Malaysia

What lies ahead?

NOOR AZIAH MOHD AWAL

A   Introduction

7.1   The federation of Malaysia is made up of thirteen states and three federal territories. It has a federal parliament with two chambers, namely the Dewan Negara, comprising appointed members, and the Dewan Rakyat, comprising members who are elected every five years. In each of the thirteen states there is a single-chamber state legislature where members are elected every five years. The federal territories are governed by the Federal Parliament. In relation to family law, there is a split or dual system of family law. Islamic family law, passed by the state legislature of each state and administered through the Syariah courts, applies to Muslims, with a different set of laws, falling under the jurisdiction of the Federal Parliament and administered through civil common law courts, applying to non-Muslims.[1]

7.2   The Child Act 2001 governs all matters relating to children except those involving Islamic law. A particular problem arises where parents were non-Muslims at the time they married, where one party later converts to Islam and then applies for divorce and custody of children in the Syariah Court, while the non-Muslim party applies in the civil High Court for the same.[2] Malaysia ratified the United Nations Convention on the Rights of the Child in 1995, subject to twelve reservations, but has worked hard to withdraw seven of them,[3] and this chapter will discuss some of the obstacles faced by Malaysia in implementing the Convention.

---

[1]   Some 60 per cent of Malaysia's population are Muslim.

[2]   See Noor Aziah Mohd Awal, 'Pertukaran Agama: Hak Penjagaan Anak – Isu dan Masalah' (Conversion to Islam: Rights to Guardianship and Custody Issues and Problems) [2004] *Malayan Law Journal* xxxiv and paras. 7.49–7.52 below.

[3]   The Women, Family and Community Development Ministry announced, in its media release on 6 July 2010, that Malaysia has withdrawn its reservation to Articles 1, 13 and 15. The remaining reservations are to Articles 2, 7, 14, 28(1)(a) and 37.

7.3 Both Muslim and non-Muslim family law are very much influenced by custom and religious laws. Many daily practices in family matters are intertwined with customary rules and may be seen as biased and discriminatory against women. When Malaysia signed and ratified the Convention on Eliminations of Discrimination against Women (CEDAW) in 1995, it entered reservations to a number of articles that were viewed as being in conflict with Islamic laws and the Federal Constitution. After the Beijing Conference in 1997, Malaysia withdrew a number of its reservations to CEDAW,[4] but others remain.[5] This chapter will also highlight some of the changes made to family law following the ratification of CEDAW.

Historical roots, sources and law reform

Historical roots

7.4 Malaysia has a unique legal history. During the era of the Malacca Sultanate, Islamic law and Malay customary law were practised.[6] The Malay Peninsula was colonised by the Portuguese in 1511, and later by the Dutch in 1641. When the British came, English law replaced Islamic and customary law. English courts and judges took over the role played by the Muslim judges in the administration of the law in the Peninsula. Islamic law was only applicable in family matters where parties were Muslim. Since in England at that time the rights of the child were merely incidental to giving women rights equal to those held by men, the position was very similar in Malaya. Most of the English family law statutes were adopted in Malaya, with some modifications, and remained after independence.

7.5 On 31 August 1957 the Federation of the Malay State (Tanah Melayu) achieved its independence and, since then, has had a written constitution.[7] In 1963 Malaysia was formed, consisting of Malaya (including Singapore), Sabah and Sarawak. In 1965 Singapore left the Federation and became an independent nation.

7.6 Since Malaysian family law has its roots in English common law, many of these English principles were adopted and apply in Malaysia

---

[4] To Articles 2(f), 9(1), 16(b), (d), (e) and (h).

[5] To Articles 5(a), 7(b), 9(2), 16(a), (c), (f) and (g).

[6] Ahmad Ibrahim and Ahilemah Joned, *The Malaysia Legal System*, 2nd edn (Kuala Lumpur: Dewan Bahasa dan Pustaka, 1995); Liaw Yock Fang, *The Laws of Melaka* (The Hague: Nijhoff, 1976), p. 62.

[7] Federal Constitution 1957.

where there are no specific Malaysian statutes on the matter. However, not all English common law principles are applicable in Malaysia and there are regional variations resulting from section 3 of the Civil Law Act 1956, which provides:

> save in so far as other provision has been made or may hereafter be made by any written law in force in Malaysia, the court shall apply the English common law, rules of equity and statutes of general application in so far as the circumstances of the state of Malaysia and their respective inhabitants permit and subject to such qualifications as local circumstances render necessary.

The version of English law to be applied was fixed at different dates for different parts of the country, the relevant dates being 7 April 1956 for West Malaysia, 1 December 1951 for Sabah and 12 December 1949 for Sarawak.

7.7   As a result, if there is no statute passed by the Malaysian Parliament on a particular matter, as is the case in respect of surrogate births or children resulting from in vitro fertilisation (IVF) or gamete intrafallopian transfer (GIFT), for example, the principles of common law and rules of equity will be applicable, but only up to the dates indicated above. However, there is an exception to these general rules since section 47 of the Law Reform (Marriage and Divorce) Act 1976 provides that:

> in all suits and proceedings relating to divorce, judicial separation and nullity, the court shall apply current English common law and rules of equity in matters relating to divorce, judicial separation and nullity of marriage.

Sources

7.8   By the time Malaysia (or Malaya and the states of North Borneo as it was known) became independent, family law, including child law, derived from various sources. The locals were allowed to marry in accordance with their own customs and religions[8] and Western people[9] married in accordance with their laws brought from their own

---

[8] In the Malay Peninsula, the Malays were married in accordance to Islamic law and the Indians and Chinese were married in accordance to their own customary laws. Natives of Sabah and Sarawak (north Borne States at that time) were also married in accordance with their customary laws.

[9] Prior to 1976, a whole range of ordinances governed numerous aspects of child and family law. See Civil Marriage Ordinance 1952, Christian Marriage Ordinance 1956, Divorce Ordinance 1952, Registration of Marriage Ordinance 1952, Sarawak Chinese Marriage

countries. Customary marriages were not registered and gave rise to a number of problems, one such problem being polygamy. Under both Chinese[10] and Indian[11] customary law, men may marry more then one wife. In the *Six Widows' Case*[12] the Court had difficulty in recognising a marriage between a Chinese man and six women. Such a marriage was not only unknown to English law, but also contrary to public policy. However, the local circumstances forced the court to hold the marriage to be valid and all the children born within the marriages as legitimate. As Malaysia is a multiracial nation, biracial marriages were quite common.

7.9 In relation to Muslims, family matters were governed by *hokum syarak* (Islamic law) and all sources of Islamic laws come from the Quran and the hadiths or the practices of the Prophet Mohammad. Sources of Islamic law are books and words passed on from person to person and through actual practices. Islamic law remained an unwritten source of laws in Malaysia.

Law reform

7.10 For non-Muslims, the main changes that took place in Malaysia in relation to child and family law resulted from the passing of the Law Reform (Marriage and Divorce) Act 1976 (LRA). This Act was based on the work of the Royal Commission,[13] which recommended, amongst other things, that all non-Muslim marriages should be monogamous and registered. While the draft bill was passed in 1976, it did not come into force until 1 May 1982 and the delay was due to the objections from various communities. The LRA unified the law on marriage for non-Muslims. All customary marriages prior to the LRA are recognised as valid and deemed to be registered.[14] Non-Muslims may still marry in accordance with their

Ordinance 1948, Sarawak Church and Civil Marriage Ordinance (Cap 93 of the Laws of Sarawak) 1958, Sarawak Matrimonial Causes Ordinance (Cap 94 of the Laws of Sarawak) 1958, Sabah Christian Marriage Ordinance (Cap 24 of the Laws of North Borneo) 1953, Sabah Marriage Ordinance 1959 and the Sabah Divorce Ordinance 1963.

[10] See *Dorothy Yee Yang Nam* v. *Lee Fah Kooi* [1956] *Malayan Law Journal* 257; *Yeap Leong Huat* v. *Yeap Leong Soon & Another* [1952] *Malayan Law Journal* 184.

[11] *Parameswari* v. *Ayadurai* [1959] *Malayan Law Journal* 195.

[12] Reported as *In the Matter of Choo Eng Choon* (1908) 12 Strait Settlement Law Reports 120.

[13] *Report of the Royal Commission on Non-Muslim Marriage and Divorce Laws* (1971).

[14] Section 4.

customs or religious rites, but they are now bound by the procedure under the LRA where marriage must be solemnised under section 23 or 24.[15]

7.11   The position of Islamic law has gone through a number of changes since Malaysian independence. The Federal Constitution did not define the term 'Islamic law', although common law, custom and usage are defined.[16] The first major change that took place after independence was to place Islamic law, the Syariah courts and all matters relating to the religion of Islam, including Islamic family law, under the jurisdiction and control of the state government.[17] A second reform came in 1983, when the Islamic family laws of each state were drafted. This process of codification was the new beginning for Islamic law in Malaysia. Since then, all states in Malaysia have passed a variety of Islamic statutes dealing with child and family law.[18] The main aim of the drafters was to have a uniform Islamic law throughout Malaysia. While a model statute was used in accomplishing this aim, each of the statutes had to be passed by the state legislative bodies and they differ slightly from state to state. The Syariah Court in one state has no jurisdiction over a citizen of another state and, as we shall see, this can produce anomalous results.[19] In 1988 the Syariah Court and Islamic law were given solid recognition when the Federal Constitution was amended to provide that, where any matter is within the jurisdiction of the Syariah Courts, the High Court and all the courts below it shall have no jurisdiction.[20] The amendment was the beginning of almost total separation of jurisdiction between civil and Syariah laws in Malaysia.[21]

7.12   The signing and ratifying of CEDAW was another important event in Malaysia.[22] For a very long time, women held traditional roles

---

[15]   Section 23 provides that a licence may be granted to enable the parties to marry according to custom at the place named in the licence, whereas section 24 provides for parties who wish to marry in Temple or Church according to their religious rites to do so where the celebrant has been appointed as an Assistant Registrar of marriage.

[16]   Federal Constitution, Article 160, defining 'law'.

[17]   *Ibid.*, 9th Schedule, List 11(1).

[18]   Since 1983, the Family Law Enactment, the Administration of Islamic Law Enactment, the Islamic Evidence Enactment, The Islamic Civil Procedure Enactment, the Islamic Criminal Procedure Enactments and the Islamic Criminal Law Enactment were passed and enforced in all of the states in Malaysia.

[19]   See paras. 7.37–7.39 below.

[20]   Clause (1A) was inserted into Article 121.

[21]   *Faridah bte Dato Talib* v. *Mohamed Habibullah bin Mahmood* [1990] 1 *Malayan Law Journal* 174; [1992] 2 *Malayan Law Journal* 793 (Supreme Court).

[22]   See para. 7.3 and footnotes 3 and 4, respectively, for past and present reservations.

and were subservient towards their male partners, this feature being
common to all women irrespective of their racial or cultural background. Generally, all Malaysian women are looked upon as inferior
to their male counterparts. This cultural and customary ideology is so
fundamental that it makes change difficult, if not impossible. While
this stereotyping can be seen in many laws in Malaysia, the amendment
of the Federal Constitution by inserting the word 'gender' in Article
8(2)[23] showed a serious attempt by the government to improve the status and position of women post CEDAW.[24] In Malaysia a Malay is a
person who professes the religion of Islam, speaks the Malay language
and practises the Malay *adat*.[25] Therefore, it is likely that the practice
of a Malay *adat* will be confused with the principles of Islamic law. For
example, under Islamic law a man is responsible as the protector of his
wife and children and must ensure that his wife and children are provided with sufficient food and drink, accommodation and clothing. In
the Malay community the normal practice is that the husband will go
out and work and the wife will look after the house and their children.
He will be in charge of external matters and the wife will take care
of internal family matters. The husband is also treated with respect,
as he is the head of the family. However, as the head of the family, he
must always consult his wife on all matters concerning the family,
whether external or internal. The Chinese and Indian communities are
governed by their own customs, which are often biased in favour of
the male. For example, in Chinese custom the celebration of the birth
of a male child involves the distribution of red hard-boiled eggs and
roast pork, while the birth of a girl child is generally not celebrated
at all.[26] While ratifying CEDAW meant that all customary practices
that are contrary to it should be abolished, religious practices cannot
be compromised as the Constitution guarantees freedom of religion.[27]
However, the first reform to result from CEDAW occurred in 1999,
when the Guardianship of Infants Act 1961 was amended to give both
parents equal rights to the custody and upbringing of a child and the

---

[23] Article 8 prohibits discrimination, subject to exceptions for personal law, religion and
   certain other matters.
[24] Article 8 prohibits discrimination, subject to exceptions for personal law, religion and
   certain other matters.
[25] Federal Constitution, Art. 160.
[26] *A Baseline Report on Marriage and Divorce: Art. 16* (Women's Aid Organization, 2002),
   p. 54.
[27] Federal Constitution, Art. 11.

administration of any property belonging to the infant. The goal was not to enhance the rights of the child personally, but, rather, to improve the position of his or her mother. The infant's guardian is responsible for his or her support, health and education. Thus, the statute does not provide for the right of children per se, but is concerned with the right to be protected and maintained.

Dispute resolution and access to legal services

7.13   Family disputes are resolved differently for Muslims and non-Muslims. For non-Muslims, dispute resolution in relation to matrimonial matters is provided for by the Law Reform (Marriage and Divorce) Act 1976, which provides:

> No person shall petition for divorce, except under sections 51 and 52, unless he or she has first referred the matrimonial difficulty to a conciliatory body and that body has certified that it has failed to reconcile the parties.[28]

It is provided further that:

> a matrimonial difficulty may be referred to any conciliatory body acceptable to both parties but, where they are unable to agree on a conciliatory body, shall be referred to the marriage tribunal for the area in which they reside or, where they are living in different areas, to the marriage tribunal for the area in which they had last resided together.[29]

Hence non-Muslims must attempt to resolve the conflict through a conciliatory body or marriage tribunal, otherwise their divorce petition will be rejected.[30]

7.14   For Muslims, family disputes may be solved in the manner described in Figure 7.1.

7.15   The methods of conciliation are quite complicated and lengthy under Islamic law. This is because, although Islam permits divorce, it is an act that Allah hates most. Hence, there is a duty to save a marriage but, should all efforts turn out to be futile, divorce should take place in a peaceful manner. The Syariah courts have been the centre of criticism from women's groups and women in general since the divorce

---

[28] Section 106(1).
[29] Section 106(2).   [30]   C v. A [1998] 6 *Malayan Law Journal* 222.

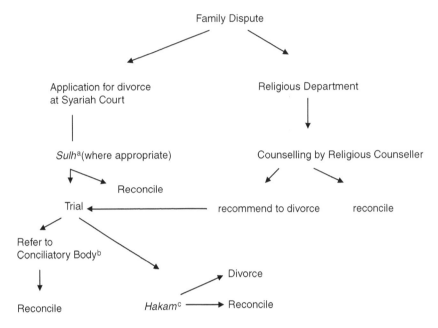

Figure 7.1   Muslim family dispute resolution

[a] *Sulh* simply means amicable settlement. *The Mejelle* (being an English translation of Majallah el-Ahkem-i-Adliya and a complete code of Islamic Law), trans. Tyser *et al.* (Lahore: Law Publishing Company, 1980, reprint of the 1901 edition), Article 1531, defines *sulh* as 'a contract removing a dispute by consent'. The *sulh* becomes a concluded contract by offer and acceptance.

[b] Islamic Family Law Enactment of Selangor, No. 4 of 2004, s. 47. A conciliatory body consists of a religious officer, who acts as the chairman, and two other people, one to act for the husband and the other for the wife. Preference is given to relatives of the parties.

[c] The appointment of *Hakam* is provided for under section 48 of the Islamic Family Law Enactments of each state (for example, Islamic Family Law Enactment of Selangor, No. 4 of 2004, section 48) and is made by a judge who appoints two people as arbitrators, one acting for the wife and the other for the husband. In making such an appointment, priority is given to close relatives of each of the parties concerned. The Court gives direction to *Hakam* as to how the case should be settled. If *Hakam* are unable to come to an agreement, the court may appoint a new *Hakam* with the power to pronounce *talaq* or divorce on behalf of the husband.

procedure is lengthy.[31] If a woman visits the Religious Department and consults a counsellor, by the time the counsellor made his or her report, six months will have elapsed. Once she files her divorce application, it will be another three months before the case is called and, should the husband refuse to pronounce *talaq* or divorce upon his wife, the Syariah Judge will send the case to a conciliatory body for another six months. Parties may divorce at the end of the six months if the husband agrees to pronounce divorce. If he refuses, the court may appoint a *Hakam* for another six months and the *Hakam* may have the power to divorce the parties. Hence, divorce by pronouncement of *talaq* may take up to a year and a half. However, if a wife applies for divorce by pronouncement of *talaq* and the husband agrees, the divorce is finalised in a day. Divorce by *fasakh*[32] takes almost two years as it relies heavily on evidence and witnesses. It is the only divorce pronounced by a court.

7.16   Due to much criticism of the delays outlined above, the Syariah Court introduced the *Sulh* procedure to reduce the backlog of cases. However, not all cases can be settled by *Sulh*. Cases which can be settled by *Sulh* are breach of promise to marry, certain applications related to divorce[33] and any other matters which the Registrar thinks reasonable and suitable. *Sulh* has certainly reduced the backlog of divorce cases as many couples reach an amicable agreement and the Syariah Court merely rubber-stamps the agreement. Such divorce agreements have made life a little more bearable for couples and children. Couples who cannot afford lawyers are able to resolve matters using the procedure since a *Sulh* session cannot be attended by lawyers.

7.17   *Sulh* procedure is set out in Figure 7.2.

7.18   Both Muslim and non-Muslims are eligible to apply for legal aid in the context of divorce as long as they qualify for a legal aid certificate,[34] requiring that the applicant's income is not more than RM25,000 per

---

[31]   Noor Aziah Mohd Awal, 'A Study of Delayed Divorce Cases in the Syariah Court of Negeri Sembilan, Selangor and Federal Territory of Kuala Lumpur: A Comparative Study with the Civil Court' [2004] 7(2) *Institut Kefahaman Islam Malaysia (IKIM) Law Journal* 95.

[32]   *Fasakh* literally means to annul a deed or to rescind a bargain. In the context of marriage, it means the annulment or abrogation of the marriage contract by the court after the wife has made an application for that.

[33]   These include *muta'ah* (consolation payment for divorce), maintenance of the wife and children, matrimonial property, custody of children and enforcement of maintenance orders.

[34]   Legal Aid Act 1971 (Act 26), s. 15.

Figure 7.2   *Sulh* procedure

annum. An applicant with an income between RM25,000 to RM30,000 per annum may also qualify, but may have to pay some contribution in order to get legal aid.[35] Apart from government-funded legal aid, the Bar Council of Malaysia has also run a Legal Aid Centre since 1982.[36] Each state has its own Legal Aid Centre. For Muslims in Selangor, the Islamic Religious Council provides assistance to petitioners who cannot afford to pay for a lawyer to represent them in the Syariah Court. The Department of the Syariah Judiciary has set up the Family Support Unit where the Family Support Officer may assist applicants in applying for and enforcing a maintenance order of the Syariah Court.[37]

---

[35] *Ibid.*, s. 16 and s. 16A.

[36] Ravi Nekoo, 'Legal Aid in Malaysia: The Need for Greater Government Commitment', 23 November 2009, available at: www.malaysianbar.org.my (last accessed 2 February 2011).

[37] The Family Support Unit or *Bahagian Sokongan Keluarga (BSK)* was set up on 1 October 2008. The author is currently a committee member of the Family Support Working Committee appointed by the Minister in Charge of Islamic Religious Matters. The committee meets monthly to assist the workings of the Unit and to ensure that the BSK is effective in enforcing maintenance orders. The BSK also provides temporary maintenance in cases where the person against whom the order was made refuses to pay or cannot be traced. The BSK pays maintenance for up to six months as a temporary procedure.

B   Children in the family setting and state intervention

Defining and classifying children

7.19   Historically, there is no written evidence of any form of legal recognition of children except their right to inherit under Islamic law. However, some of the Malay proverbs demonstrate that the Malay respect children and gave them a right to express their views. For example, *kecil jangan disangka anak, besar jangan disangka bapa*, translates literally as 'young does not mean that one is a child, and adult does not mean one is the father'. This proverb means that, even if one is a child, one may have the virtues and intelligence of an adult and must not be ignored. There is also a legendary story of a brave and intelligent boy in '*Singapura dilang-gar Todak*'. In this story, a boy, Hang Nadim, aged 10, saved Singapore from an attack by speared fish. He was rewarded by the king for his bravery and intelligence, but he was finally murdered because others (particularly adults) were envious of his ability. This story also highlights the difficulties faced by a child in expressing views and the fact that, in the Malay community, there is scepticism about listening to children's views. Thus, in the Malay community, a child is meant to be seen but not heard. Generally, it is considered rude for a child to listen to adult conversations or to try to participate in them. Obedience to parents is the most important element taught to children.

7.20   When Islam came to the Peninsula during the eleventh century, this was further enhanced because, according to the teachings of Islam, it is a very serious sin to disobey one's parents. The Quran says:

> And do well unto [thy] parents. Should one of them or both, attain too old age in thy care, never say 'Uhg' to them or scold them, but always speak unto them with reverent speech and spread over them humbly the wings of thy tenderness and say: 'O my sustainers! Bestow Thy grace upon them, as they cherished and reared me when I was a child.'[38]

7.21   During British rule, English laws relating to children were applied, particularly in relation to custody, guardianship and maintenance. The English Guardianship Act 1925 was the model for the Malaysian Guardianship of Infants Act 1961.[39]

[38]   Al Quran Surah Al Isra': 23–24.
[39]   Guardianship of Infants 1961 (Act 351).

7.22   Since the laws on children are scattered, there is no single definition of 'child'. The Age of Majority Act 1971 defines a child as a person
below the age of 18 years.[40] However, this definition only applies where
no other definition is given in the statute relevant to the particular topic[41]
and, indeed, there are many other definitions to be found in the federal
statutes. It was this variety of definitions of a child that led Malaysia to
enter a reservation when it ratified the United Nations Convention on
the Rights of the Child. So, for example, the Adoption Act 1952 defines a
child as 'an unmarried person under the age of 21 and includes a female
under that age who has been divorced'.[42] The Guardianship of Infants
Act 1961 (GIA) defines a 'Muslim child' as a person under the age of 18,
while a 'non-Muslim child' is a person under the age of 21.[43] However, in
Kanalingam v. *Kanagarajah*[44] a girl aged 18 left her father to live with the
respondent. The father applied to the court under the GIA for the return
of his daughter. The court of first instance held that the girl's marriage to
the respondent was invalid and ordered the girl to be sent to her aunt's
house. The respondent appealed. The federal court held that, despite her
age (being under 21), she should be allowed to choose her own life and
with whom to live.

7.23   The Law Reform (Marriage & Divorce) Act 1976 provides that 'child
of the marriage' means a child of both parties to the marriage in question
or a child of one party to the marriage accepted as one of the family by the
other party, and 'child' in this context includes an illegitimate child of,
and a child adopted by, either of the parties to the marriage in pursuance
of an adoption order made under any written law relating to adoption.[45]
Thus, under this Act a child is a person under 18 who is a child of the family and it does not matter whether he or she is adopted, or illegitimate or a
child of one of the parties to the marriage.

7.24   The Child Act 2001[46] defines a child as a person under the age of 18
years and, in relation to criminal proceedings, means a person who has
attained the age of criminal responsibility as prescribed in section 82 of

---

[40] Act 103 of 1971, s. 2.   [41] *Ibid.*, s. 4(c).
[42] Adoption Act 1952 (Act 257), s. 2.
[43] Act 13 of 1961, s. 2(3)(a)(i) and (ii).
[44] [1982] 1 *Malayan Law Journal* 264, discussed more fully at para. 7.29.
[45] Act 164 of 1976, s. 2.
[46] Act 611 of 2001, s. 2. The Child Act 2001 repeals the Juvenile Courts Act 1947 (Act 90), the
      Women and Girls Protection Act 1973 (Act 106) and the Child Protection Act 1991 (Act
      468).

the Penal Code. Section 82 of the Penal Code states that a child under the age of 10 cannot be held responsible for any criminal act or omission.

7.25 The Evidence Act 1950 used the term 'child of tender years' but gives no definition of it.[47] The Act makes reference to the child being 'possessed of sufficient intelligence to justify the reception of evidence and understands the duty of speaking the truth' but 'in the opinion of the court does not understand the nature of an oath'. The Domestic Violence Act 1994 defines 'child' as meaning a person under the age of 18 years who is living as a member of the offender's family or of the family of the offender's spouse or former spouse.[48] Hence, under the federal statutes a child is defined differently.

7.26 It is important to look at the definition of 'child' under Islamic law. According to Islamic law, a child is a person who has not attained *baligh*. For girls, *baligh* occurs as soon as she begins menstruation and this could be as early as 9 years old. If she does not begin menstruation or show any signs of maturity,[49] according to Abu Hanifah, the age of *baligh* for girls is 16 years. Boys become *baligh* as soon as they have had their adult dream. Imam Syafie agreed with the opinion of Imam Abu Yusuf and Muhammad Al-Shaybani that a boy becomes *baligh* if he had his adult dream and a girl does so if she had her menses or, in either case, if they have reached 12 years old.[50] Hence, under Islamic law a child may be someone below the age of 9 or 12 years. This may complicate matters, particularly in relation to eligibility to marry.

Recognising parentage and family ties

7.27 Despite the difficulties over the matter of defining a 'child' that led to the reservations to the United Nations Convention on the Rights of the Child, most of the principles of the Convention have been accepted and were implemented by the Child Act 2001. Basically, children have the right to be maintained, educated and protected from abuse and harm. However, cultural and customary influences are strong, particularly in respect of the deference shown to parental rights in the areas of education and consent to marry. The Federal Constitution gave absolute power

---

[47] Evidence Act 1950 (Act 56), s. 133A.
[48] Domestic Violence Act 1991 (Act 521), s. 2.
[49] Like growing of pubic hairs or being pregnant.
[50] Ahmad Ibrahim, 'Undang-undang Keluarga Islam di Malaysia', [1999] *Malayan Law Journal* 36, 37.

to either parent or guardian to determine the child's religious education until he or she is 18 years old.[51] In the case of *Teoh Eng Huat* v. *Khadi of Pasir Mas Kelantan*[52] the Supreme Court heard an appeal from the father of a girl who had converted to Islam when she was 17 years old. By the time of the appeal she was already 18 years of age. The trial judge referred to Article 11(1) and (4) of the Federal Constitution and held that the word 'every person' means all those who are of sound mind and are in the position to decide and cited Article 12 of the UN Convention in support of this conclusion. The Supreme Court, however, held that an infant (i.e. a person under the age of 18) does not have a right to choose his or her own religion, that being a matter for his or her guardian or parent until that infant achieves the age of majority. In *Tan Kong Meng* v. *Zainon bte Md Zain & Another*[53] a non-Muslim Chinese girl, Alvina, was purportedly adopted by a Muslim couple and the adoption was registered under the Registration of Adoption Act 1952. The High Court held that the registration of the adoption was void and the Muslim couple were no longer Alvina's adoptive parents. Instead of returning the child to her parents, the High Court appointed the 'adoptive' parents as her lawful guardians. However, the High Court specifically ordered that the lawful guardians could not determine Alvina's religion because Alvina was under 18. It was a very peculiar decision as the law specifically provides that a lawful guardian has the right to determine a child's religion.[54] The High Court could have avoided the difficulty by merely recognising the registration of adoption as valid and finding that it was in the best interests of the child that she should be brought up by the Muslim couple since they had raised her since she was a baby. Alternatively, even if the registration of adoption was void, the court could have found maintaining the status quo to be in the child's best interests.

Intra-family disputes

7.28   Intra-family disputes often arise in the context of divorce. In reaching decisions on the custody of a child in disputed cases, the paramount consideration is the welfare of the child[55] and is subject to the wishes of

---

[51] Federal Constitution, Article 12(4).
[52] [1990] 2 *Malayan Law Journal* 300.
[53] [1995] 3 *Malayan Law Journal* 408.
[54] According to the Federal Constitution, Article 12(4) the religion of a child under the age of 18 years shall be determined by the father, mother or guardian of the child.
[55] Guardianship of Infants Act 1961 (351), section 11.

the parents as well as the wishes of the child, where the latter is of an age to express an independent opinion.[56]

7.29   Whether the laws in Malaysia recognise that a child has any rights as against his or her parents is a matter that has been left open as a result of conflicting court decisions. As we saw in *Teoh Eng Huat*[57] and *Tan Kong Meng* v. *Zainon bte Md Zain*,[58] the issue was whether a child should be allowed to choose her own religion.[59] In both cases the dispute was between natural parents and foster parents or the religious authority. The court failed to consider the wishes of the child and gave priority to the wishes of parents or other considerations such as the constitutional provision. The only occasion when the court actually respected a child's wishes as to with whom she would like to live was in *Kanalingam* v. *Kanagarajah*.[60] There, a girl was below 21 years old when she eloped to marry despite the fact that her father did not consent to her marriage. Her father applied for a writ of habeas corpus but the High Court ordered her to be sent to her aunt's house. The husband appealed and the Federal Court held that the Judicial Commissioner should have considered the girl's wishes. The Federal Court released her from all restraint and held that she was at liberty to choose where she wished to go. For the first time in Malaysia, the court gave recognition to the wishes of a child and acknowledged her right to choose her partner. This marked a beginning for children's rights and the position was further enhanced when the LRA was passed[61] and by ratification of the UN Convention on the Rights of the Child.

7.30   Custody disputes involving Muslim children are governed by Islamic law and a child who has attained the age of *mumaiyiz* may be given a right to choose the parent with whom he or she wishes to live. *Mumaiyiz* occurs between the ages of seven and the age of majority (which is the age of *baligh* in Islam). As a general rule, a Muslim child may choose between his or her mother and father as early as 7 years old.

---

[56] Law Reform (Marriage and Divorce) 1976 (Act 611), s. 88.
[57] [1990] 2 *Malayan Law Journal* 300.
[58] [1995] 3 *Malayan Law Journal* 408.
[59] Discussed at para. 7.27 above.
[60] [1982] 1 *Malayan Law Journal* 264.
[61] Section 88 of the LRA provides that, in deciding in whose custody a child should be placed the paramount consideration shall be the welfare of the child and, subject to this, the court shall have regard to the wishes of the parents of the child, and to the wishes of the child where he or she is of an age to express an independent opinion.

Child protection and state intervention

7.31 Child protection has always been a concern in Malaysia. The Child Act 2001 was passed to deal with the growing number of child abuse cases and to implement the United Nations Convention on the Rights of the Child. The Act categorises children as follows: children in need of care and protection; children in need of protection and rehabilitation; children beyond control; children being abducted or trafficked; and children who commit crimes.

7.32 It established the Court for Children to replace the Juvenile Courts and repealed both the Juvenile Court Act 1947[62] and the Child Protection Act 1991[63]. The Child Act 2001 requires that a child must be brought before a Court for Children within twenty-four hours, excluding travelling time. The Act makes special provision for the setting up of places of safety[64] and places of refuge[65] and differentiates them from places of detention.[66] A female under the age of 18 who is involved in a domestic violence dispute between her parents or who is a victim of violence herself may be sent to a place of safety by an order of the Court. The 2001 Act makes abuse, neglect, abandoning, begging and trafficking of children offences punishable under the Act. Children who commit offences are also protected and they go before the Court for Children. Ten years after its implementation, the Child Act 2001 is being amended to make it more compliant with the UN Convention.

C   Adult relationships

The relationships

7.33 Marriage is still a very important institution in Malaysia for both Muslims and non-Muslims and the basic rights of a wife and children flow from a valid marriage. Malaysia does not recognise extra-marital relationships or cohabitation, and same-sex marriages and relationships are strictly prohibited. Hence, parties from such relationships do not have any rights whatsoever under family law and same-sex relationships are punishable under the Penal Code of Malaysia.[67] Even the Domestic Violence Act 1994 does not extend to cohabitants or same-sex partners.

---

[62] Act 90 of 1947.   [63] Act 468 of 1991.
[64] Act 611, s. 54.   [65] Act 611, s. 55.   [66] Act 611, s. 58.
[67] Penal Code of Malaysia (Act 574), s. 377C.

A purported marriage between a male and another male who had under-gone male-to-female sex-change reassignment surgery is considered void.[68]

7.34 For Muslims, extra-marital relationships are sinful and punish-able by the Islamic Criminal Law Enactments.[69] Same-sex relationships are strictly prohibited. Such acts are punishable under the Islamic Syariah enactments of each state as well as under the Penal Code of Malaysia.[70] Nor does Malaysia accept the possibility of a person changing sex. In 2011 the High Court in Terengganu rejected an application by Mohd Asraf Abd Aziz, who had undergone a sex-change operation in 2009 in Thailand, to change his name from Mohd Asraf to Aleesha Farhana. The Court held that, based on chromosomal factors and the fact that he was born a male, he remained male. For Muslims, sex-change operations are strictly prohibited and sinful. Mohd Asraf was very depressed with the High Court decision and was admitted to hospital soon after because of low blood pressure and extreme depression, dying the following day at the age of 26. Mohd Asraf's case was the first case of its kind to ever get to the High Court.[71]

Entering an adult relationship

7.35 Customarily, Chinese and Indian Malaysians had practised polygamy since they arrived in the Malay Peninsula. It was not easy to change customary practices which were so much part of their daily lives. The LRA gave the indigenous people of the Malay Peninsula and the natives of Sabah and Sarawak an option to marry under the LRA or in accordance with their customs. Since 1982 non-Muslims in Malaysia must marry in accordance with the LRA and, if they are indigenous or natives of Sabah and Sarawak, they may choose to marry under the LRA or their respective customs. All marriages must be registered except those under customary laws, which are deemed to be registered. Since the LRA came into force, all marriages of other non-Muslims must be monogamous.

---

[68] *Corbett* v. *Corbett* [1970] 2 All ER 33 is still a good law in Malaysia.
[69] Islamic Criminal Law, Selangor, No. 9 of 1995, s. 25.
[70] Islamic Criminal Law, Selangor, No. 9 of 1995, s. 28 makes same-sex relationships an offence.
[71] *New Strait Times*, 30 July 2011.

7.36 In order to marry, an application must be made in accordance with requirements of the LRA and the parties must be respectively male and female, single or divorced and not related within the prohibited degrees. The female must be at least 16 years old and the male must be at least 18 and, if either party is under 21, consent from the father of the person under 21 is required, if the person is legitimate, or the adoptive father, if he or she is adopted. If he or she is illegitimate, consent is required from his or her mother or person *in loco parentis*.

7.37 For Muslims, marriage must be solemnised in accordance to *hokum syarak* and marriage may be nullified if certain requirements are not fulfilled. One of the most important elements in the solemnisation of a Muslim marriage is that it is performed by or with the permission of a *wali*. Islamic law also requires that parties to the marriage be male and female, respectively, and not related within the prohibited degrees. Females must be at least 16 years old and males must be at least 18. However, parties who are under 18 years of age may still marry with the permission of the Shariah Court. Islam also permits men to take up to four wives and if a man wishes to take a second or subsequent wife, he must apply to the Shariah Court for permission to marry again. A marriage solemnised without such permission, whether it takes place in Malaysia or abroad, may still be recognised and registered upon payment of fines, provided it is valid under Islamic law.

7.38 This is illustrated in the case of *Aishah bt Abdul Rauf* v. *Wan Mohd Yusuf*.[72] There, the defendant applied to the Syariah High Court of Selangor to marry X as his second wife. The Syariah High Court allowed the application on the basis that the defendant was able to support his present and future wives. The plaintiff's first wife appealed to the Syariah Appeal Board of Selangor. The Appeal Board held that the High Court Judge had overemphasised the requirements of financial ability to support both present and future wives and had ignored or overlooked other requirements of the law. All these requirements needed to be proved and this had not been done. The Board of Appeal therefore allowed the appeal. That was not the end of the matter. Wan Mohd Yusuf was born and brought up in another state, Trengganu. He decided to go back to his home state and applied for permission to practise polygamy in his own

---

[72] (1991) Jurnal Hukum (1412) H, 152.

state. The Syariah High Court of Terengganu allowed his application and he finally married X.

7.39 In another case,[73] the husband, who lived in Selangor, applied to practise polygamy in the State of Negeri Sembilan while his wife applied for a divorce in her home State of Melaka. The couple had been married for more than ten years and had four children, the youngest of whom was only five months old. The petitioner wife could no longer tolerate the husband's behaviour. She was a full-time housewife and left the matrimonial home with the four children and returned to her parents' house. She filed for maintenance and a custody order in Melaka and her husband refused to negotiate. Later, he used his old address in Negeri Sembilan and applied to marry another woman in that state while his marriage to his first wife still subsisted.

Termination of relationships

7.40 Non-Muslim marriages may be terminated by annulment, divorce or judicial separation. Judicial separation is still available even though it is not used often.[74] The grounds for applying for judicial separation are the same as for nullity of marriage: that is, non-consummation of marriage; wilful refusal to consummate marriage; absence of valid consent due to duress, mistake, unsoundness of mind or otherwise; the mental incapacity of one of the parties under the Mental Disorders Ordinance 1952; that the respondent was suffering from venereal disease in a communicable form at the time of the marriage; or that the respondent was pregnant by some person other than the petitioner at the time of the marriage.[75]

7.41 Since many couples still insist on marrying in accordance with their religious rites, many of them register their marriage under the LRA, but decide not to live together because they have not had the requisite religious ceremony. One to two years after registration, they may apply to annul the marriage because it was never consummated or due to wilful refusal to consummate.[76]

---

[73] The petitioner wife was a client of the author. The author is the chairperson of the Free Legal Advice and Services Program, Women Association of UKM (SUKMANITA), UKM.
[74] LRA 1976 (Act 164), s. 54.
[75] LRA 1976 (Act 164), s. 70.
[76] *Tan Siew Choon* v. *Tan Kai Ho* [1973] *Malayan Law Journal* 9 and *Yong Fui Phin* v. *Lim Tow Siew* [1996] *Malayan Law Journal* 479.

7.42   Rules regulating divorce for non-Muslims are provided by the LRA under Part VI. In order to apply for divorce, marriage must be monogamous, registered or deemed to be registered and the parties must be domiciled in Malaysia.[77] The domicile rule proved to be unfair to women since Malaysia still applies the common law principles of domicile whereby, on marriage, a wife takes her husband's domicile. Hence section 49(1) of the LRA further provides that, notwithstanding anything to the contrary in section 48(1)(c), the court shall have jurisdiction to entertain proceedings by a wife even though her husband is not domiciled in Malaysia, if (a) the wife has been deserted by her husband or her husband has been deported from Malaysia and before such desertion or deportation he was domiciled in Malaysia, or (b) the wife is resident in Malaysia and has been ordinarily resident for a period of two years immediately preceding the commencement of the proceeding.[78]

7.43   Once the jurisdictional issues have been settled, parties to a marriage may apply for divorce on the following grounds: presumption of death;[79] divorce by conversion to Islam; divorce by mutual consent;[80] breakdown of marriage under section 54.[81]

7.44   Given the different treatment of Muslims and non-Muslims, problems can arise when a Muslim changes his or her religion or when a non-Muslim converts to Islam. It will be remembered that, as a result of the amendment to Article 121(1A) of the Federal Constitution, matters relating to Islamic law and Muslims are governed by the Shariah Court.[82] The strict application of Article 121(1A) has caused injustices to many as the civil courts have no jurisdiction to hear cases which involve Muslims and Islamic law, while the Syariah courts cannot hear and determine cases which involve non-Muslims and the civil law.

---

[77] LRA 1976 (Act 164), s. 48(1).

[78] Previously, under the Divorce Ordinance 1952, the length of residence was three years. See *Mahon* v. *Mahon* [1971] 2 *Malayan Law Journal* 266.

[79] Act 164 of 1976, s. 68(1).   [80] Act 164 of 1976, s. 52.

[81] Act 164 of 1976, s. 54 (a) respondent has committed adultery and the petitioner finds it intolerable to live with the respondent; (b) respondent has behaved in such a way that the petitioner cannot reasonably be expected to live with respondent; (c) respondent has deserted the petitioner for a continuous period of at least two years immediately preceding the presentation of the petition; or (d) parties have lived apart for a continuous period of two years immediately preceding the presentation of the petition.

[82] See para. 7.11 above.

7.45   Conversion to Islam is a special ground of divorce under section 51 of the Act, which provides:

> where one party to a marriage has converted to Islam, the other party who has not so converted may petition for divorce: Provided that no petition under this section shall be presented before the expiration of the period of three months from the date of the conversion.

7.46   The primary aim of section 51 was to safeguard the well-being of non-Muslim wives and children. However, its application and implementation has proved problematic, leaving many questions. After years of marriage, if one of the parties to the marriage converts to Islam and the non-converting party does not apply for divorce, does the non-Muslim marriage remain valid or has it been dissolved automatically by the conversion to Islam?[83] If the party who has converted to Islam and his non-Muslim wife does not apply for divorce and he later marries a Muslim woman, what is the status of the second marriage? What happens if, after many years living as a Muslim and married to a Muslim woman, the man decides to convert back to his old religion? Take A, for example, who was a non-Muslim and married to B under the LRA, who later converted to Islam and married M. Who is entitled to his estate when he dies? Did he commit bigamy? If A were a woman, would she be free to marry a Muslim man upon her conversion to Islam, just like a male non-Muslim who so converted?

7.47   All of these scenarios can be seen in the following cases. In *Letchumy* v. *Ramadason*,[84] the petitioner obtained a divorce from the respondent on the ground of desertion. After the decree was granted, she applied for maintenance and the matter came before the Judicial Commissioner after the decree became absolute. The Judicial Commissioner ordered the respondent to pay the petitioner $200 a month by way of maintenance. The respondent subsequently applied for the order to be set aside on the ground that he had become a Muslim and, under Islamic law, the petitioner had no right to claim maintenance because she had not converted to Islam with her husband during the *iddah*[85] period. The High Court

---

[83] *Esswari Viswalingam* v. *Government of Malaysia* [1990] 1 *Malayan Law Journal* 86. In this case, the non-Muslim wife was entitled to her deceased Muslim husband's pension as they were never divorced.

[84] [1984] 1 *Malayan Law Journal* 141.

[85] *Iddah* is the three-month waiting period after a husband has divorced a Muslim wife. It is like a 'cooling off' period where the couple may '*juju*' (get back together) without going through the solemnisation of marriage. After the three months has expired, should

held that, since section 3(1) of the LRA precludes the application of the Act to a Muslim, and as the respondent had become a Muslim, the Act could not apply to him.[86]

7.48   This certainly creates what conflict of law terms 'limping marriages'. Take, for example, a non-Muslim couple, married according to the civil law where the marriage is monogamous. Some years later, one of the parties converts to Islam. According to Islamic law, the marriage is terminated after the expiration of three months if the other party does not convert to Islam as well. Thus, the party who has converted is free to marry according to his or her personal law, that is Islamic law. This has happened in Malaysia. If the party who has converted is the husband, he may then marry another woman in accordance with Islamic law. Now there are two marriages in existence. According to the Penal Code,[87] he is guilty of bigamy because he is still married under the LRA. However, this law on bigamy is not applicable to Muslims. Thus, no action has been taken on the many occasions where non-Muslim men who have converted have married according to Islamic law, even though their first marriages under the LRA have not been terminated because the non-Muslim wife did not petition for divorce. The conflict continues when the husband dies, as happened in the case of *Eesawari Viswalingam* v. *Government of Malaysia*,[88] where the husband converted to Islam and the non-Muslim wife never petitioned for divorce. When the husband died, his non-Muslim wife sued the government for his pension and the court held that she was entitled to it. As far as the court was concerned, since there was no divorce, she was considered the widow of the deceased despite the fact that he had converted to Islam. Had he been married under Islamic law, his Muslim wife would have been entitled to his estate, including his pension. If they had any children, these children would also have been entitled to the estate of the deceased. What is their legal status? Who would be more entitled to his estate, his first wife and children from the civil marriage or his Muslim wife and children? These are common problems that have arisen out of the application of section 51 of the LRA.[89]

---

the couple wish to live together again, they have to go through a fresh solemnisation of marriage.

[86]   *Tan Sung Mooi* v. *Too Miew Kim* [1991] 3 *Malayan Law Journal* 117.

[87]   Penal Code, s. 494.

[88]   [1990] 1 *Malayan Law Journal* 86.

[89]   *Genga Devi a/p Chelliah* v. *Santanam a/l Damodaram* [2001] 2 All Malaysia Report 1485 and *Kung Lim Siew Wan* v. *Choong Chee Kuan* [2003] 6 *Malayan Law Journal* 260.

7.49 The saga finally came to a climax in the case of *Sharmala a/p Sathiyaseelan* v. *Dr Jeyaganesh a/l C Mogarajah*,[90] where the couple were married in 1998 in accordance with Hindu rites and had two children, aged 4 and 2 years old. On 19 November 2002 the husband (defendant) converted to Islam and later, on 25 November 2002, converted the two children. The plaintiff wife had left the defendant and gone back to Kedah. On 31 December 2002 she applied for custody of the children. The trial was fixed for 16 January 2003, but the defendant applied for postponement as he needed time to appoint a lawyer. The trial was then fixed for 25 February 2003. Meanwhile, on 7 January 2003 the defendant, through his lawyer, made an *ex parte* application to the Shah Alam Syariah Court for a custody order and this was not relayed to the High Court. On 12 April 2003 the High Court held that it had jurisdiction to hear the application and fixed the trial for 17 April 2003. Meanwhile, on the basis of the husband's *ex parte* application, the Shah Alam Syariah Court issued a warrant for the arrest of the plaintiff wife for her failure to attend the trial at the Syariah Court. On 14 April 2003 the High Court in Kuala Lumpur turned down the application of the plaintiff to revoke the conversion of the two children to Islam as the matter was within the jurisdiction of the Jabatan Agama Islam and the Syariah Courts.

7.50 On 17 April 2003 the High Court heard the custody application of the plaintiff wife and on 8 May 2003 the Shah Alam Syariah Court made an order giving custody to the defendant husband. The defendant did not observe the interim order made by the Kuala Lumpur High Court and took the children out of Alor Star. The plaintiff applied for a committal order. At the trial, Dato Faiza Thamby Chik J held that, under section 51, the defendant could not apply for divorce as he has converted to Islam and he could not apply for divorce in the Syariah Court as his wife was not a Muslim. Thus, the Syariah Court had no jurisdiction. He also held that the plaintiff was not bound by the Syariah Court order and, in fact, the order had no effect on the interim order given by the High Court in Kuala Lumpur. That was not the end of the case. Shamala, having obtained the interim custody order, took the children to Australia, an act that constituted a clear contempt of court. When the High Court convened to finally decide the issue of custody on 20 July 2004, its decision was academic since the children were no longer within the jurisdiction.

---

[90] [2004] 1 *Current Law Journal* 505. See also 'Shamala Gets Custody of Converted Children', *New Straits Times*, 21 July 2004.

The High Court held that the non-Muslim mother was entitled to the care and control of the two Muslim children and, as the plaintiff and defendant were the parents of the children, appointed them as joint custodians. The decision raised eyebrows and concern amongst Muslims and non-Muslims alike. The Federal Court recently decided that it would not adjudicate upon the issues as Shamala was in contempt of court.

7.51   In *Subashini Rajasingam* v. *Saravanan Thangathoray & Others*[91] the Hindu parties were married under the LRA. They had two children, born in 2003 and 2006. On 18 May 2006 the husband converted to Islam and converted his eldest son as well. The wife received a notice that her marriage had been dissolved by the Syariah Court. On 4 August 2006, which was two months and eighteen days after her husband's conversion, the wife applied for divorce under the LRA. The Federal Court held that, since the wife's application was less than three months after the husband's conversion, it had no jurisdiction to hear the case. However, it also held that, had her application been made in accordance with the LRA, the High Court would have had jurisdiction despite the husband's conversion and the husband could not hide behind the cloak of Article 11 of the Federal Constitution.[92] His conversion did not free him from all his responsibilities under his non-Muslim marriage. The Federal Court further held that it was the husband's right to seek a remedy in the Syariah Courts, but whatever decision the Syariah Court made was not binding upon the non-Muslim wife and the civil courts.

7.52   The above cases illustrated how freedom of religion is guaranteed and exercised but, to a certain extent, abused. Conversion to Islam does not mean that one can escape from one's obligations and responsibilities created before the conversion. It is also not a way to take away a child from his or her mother or father as, in Islam, difference of religion does not sever relationships and responsibilities. Amendment to the LRA has been suggested[93] and Parliament should listen to and act on these suggestions, as it has the power to resolve these problems.[94] However, merely

---

[91]   [2008] 2 *Current Law Journal* 1.
[92]   Article 11 of the Federal Constitution addresses freedom of religion.
[93]   Noor Aziah Mohd Awal, 'Section 51 of Law Reform (Marriage & Divorce) Act 1976: An Overview' [1999] 3(2) *Institut Kefahaman Islam Malaysia (IKIM) Law Journal* 127.
[94]   The Attorney General Department is believed to have drafted the amendments to be taken to Parliament in early 2010 but to date nothing has been done.

amending sections 3 and 51 of the LRA will not be a sufficient solution to this issue.

7.53   Muslims may dissolve their marriages in the following manner: by *talaq*,[95] *khul'*,[96] *ta'liq*,[97] *fasakh*,[98] *li'an*[99] or presumption of death.[100]

Consequences of termination

7.54   For non-Muslims, termination of a marriage means that the parties are free to marry once decree absolute is granted, three months from the date of the decree nisi. During the three months the husband and

---

[95] *Talaq* means repudiation is available only to the husband. It can be made by pronouncement as follows: 'I *talaq* you' or by implication where a husband sends his wife home to her parents and tells her never to come back to the matrimonial home. After each *talaq*, there will be period of three months' *iddah* or cooling off period. A husband may *rujuk* or return to his wife within the three-month period without new solemnisation of marriage. If the three months has expired, he may remarry his wife. However, *talaq* may only be used three times. If a man *talaq* his wife three times (he may pronounce it three times at once or he may pronounce *talaq* on three separate occasions), the third *talaq* is irrevocable. He is not permitted to remarry her after the *iddah* period unless she marries another man and is divorced by him. The Islamic Family Law Enactment of Selangor, No. 2 of 2003 provides for this in section 47 and similar provisions are found in all the thirteen states.

[96] *Khul'* is divorce by redemption or *tebus talaq* where a wife requests a divorce from her husband by offering him money or gifts. See section 49 of the Islamic Family Law Enactment of Selangor, No. 2 of 2003.

[97] *Ta'liq* means suspended or conditional divorce. This is where a husband puts a condition on the pronouncement of *talaq*. For example, he might say to his wife, 'if you tell your mother that I beat you up, I divorce you by one talaq'. Today, *ta'liq* is pronounced immediately after solemnisation of a marriage to safeguard a wife's right to divorce if she is deserted or abused. Immediately after solemnisation of a Muslim marriage, a husband will say the following: 'If I were to leave my wife for four months continuously without maintenance or if I were to injure or hurt my wife continuously and if she were to complain to the Syariah Court and her complaint is proven, she shall be divorce by one *talaq*.' See section 50 the Islamic Family Law Enactment of Selangor, No. 2 of 2003.

[98] *Fasakh* means to annul or rescind. This is the only method where a wife may seek divorce and it gives the Syariah Courts the power to annul the marriage on various grounds. See also section 53 of the Islamic Family Law Enactment of Selangor, No. 2 of 2003.

[99] *Lian* means divorce by imprecation where a man accuses his wife of adultery but he has no witnesses. He must testify by God four times that he truly believes his wife has committed adultery and the fifth time that, if he has lied, he will be cursed by God. His wife testifies, denying the allegation, four times and on the fifth time, she will be cursed if she has lied. As soon as she finishes her testimony, the parties are divorced permanently. See section 51 of the Islamic Family Law Enactment of Selangor, No. 2 of 2003.

[100] See section 54 of the Islamic Family Law Enactment of Selangor, No. 2 of 2003, where the party to be presumed dead must be missing for four years.

wife are not free to marry, and if one party dies, the surviving party may be able to inherit from the deceased. For Muslims, the *iddah* period is just like degree nisi where parties may get back together as husband and wife and withdraw the divorce. However, it must be differentiated from decree nisi because, under Islamic law, a husband need only pronounce *talaq* three times and, on the third time, the marriage is terminated permanently. Where the divorce is by imprecation or *li'an*, once the wife has completed her testimony, the marriage is dissolved irrevocably and permanently. Upon termination of marriages, under the LRA as well as under Islamic laws, the parties may apply for ancillary relief such as custody, maintenance and division of matrimonial property.

7.55   Prior to the LRA, wives had to rely on the Married Women Act 1957[101] in order to sue for matrimonial property. The LRA was drafted with the English Matrimonial Proceedings and Property Act 1970 in mind and later, when it was passed, some modifications were made to accommodate local circumstances and to avoid some of the problems of the English statute.[102] For non-Muslims, because it was based on the common law and later improved by statute, difficulties arose over providing evidence of direct contributions by wives and often wives were only given a small percentage of the property based on indirect contributions. In *Lee Yun Lan* v. *Lim Thain Chye*[103] the wife was given one-third of the price of the matrimonial home based on her indirect contributions. However, in *Re Heng Peng Hoo & Another*[104] the court could not find direct contributions by the wife and her application under section 76(1) failed. The court ordered the respondent to pay a lump sum of RM10,000 based on the wife's indirect contributions.

---

[101] (Act 450) and see also *Chin Shak Len* v. *Lin Fah* [1962] *Malayan Law Journal* 418.

[102] Act 164, s. 76, provides that (1) The court shall have power, when granting a decree of divorce or judicial separation, to order the division between the parties of any assets acquired by them during the marriage by their joint efforts or the sale of any such assets and the division between the parties of the proceeds of sale. (2) In exercising the power conferred by subsection (1) the court shall have regard to – (a) the extent of the contributions made by each party in money, property or work towards the acquiring of the assets; (b) any debts owing by either party which were contracted for their joint benefit; (c) the needs of the minor children, if any, of the marriage, and subject to those considerations, the court shall incline towards equality of division.

[103] [1984] 1 *Malayan Law Journal* 56.

[104] [1989] 3 *Malayan Law Journal* 103.

7.56   Muslim women are able to sue for matrimonial property in the following three circumstances: after divorce; upon her husband's application to take a second, third or fourth wife; or before the distribution of her husband's estate after his death. Under Islamic law, it is the husband's duty to provide and maintain his wife and, thus, upon the wife's application, the Syariah Court generally applies a one-third rule in recognition of the wife's indirect contributions. She is not required to show any evidence of contributions as her only duty towards her husband is to serve him dutifully. Other activities such as cooking, washing and looking after the children are defined as 'work' for which she must be paid if her husband cannot afford to provide a maid to help her around the house.[105]

D   Conclusions

7.57   Malaysian multicultural and religious society certainly poses challenges to family practitioners. It has been suggested that the English common law should be replaced by Malaysian common law based on customary laws and Islam.[106] This suggestion was opposed by the Bar Council of Malaysia.[107] Tun Hamid Muhammad, a Chief Justice of Malaysia, made proposals for the harmonisation of laws in Malaysia.[108] None of these suggestions has been implemented.

7.58   In fact, ever since the amendment to Article 121 of the Constitution, the gaps between the civil and Syariah laws have expanded. This is because Islam is spelled out as the religion of the Federation[109] and, as such, holds a stronger position than any other religion in Malaysia. Freedom of religion is guaranteed under Article

---

[105] *Haminahbe* v. *Shamsudin* [1979] 1 Jurnal Hukum 71; *dan dalam Yang Chik* v. *Abdul Jamal*, [1986] 6 Jurnal Hukum 146; and *Noor Bee* v. *Ahmad Sanusi* 1 Jurnal Hukum [1978] 63.

[106] Wan Azhar bin Wan Ahmad, *Malaysian Common Law II*, available at: www.ittaqullah. org/dr-wan-azhar-bin-wan-ahmad-malaysian-common-law/ (last accessed 20 March 2012). His article was based on remarks made by Tun Ahmad Fairuz, Chief Justice of Malaysia, on the matter on 22 August 2007 at Institut Kefahaman Islam Malaysia Conference.

[107] www.malaysianbar.org.my/press_statements/press_release_common_law.html.

[108] Ghani Patail, Attorney General of Malaysia, 'Harmonization of Civil Laws and Shariah: Effective Strategies For Implementation', Keynote Address on 4 December 2007. He noted that the idea was mooted by Ahmad Ibrahim and was supported by many Chief Justices of Malaysia including Tun Hamid Muhammad, a former Chief Justice of Malaysia.

[109] Article 3 of the Federal Constitution.

11 of the Federal Constitution, but Muslims are not free to convert to any other religion. A Muslim who converts out of Islam is liable to punishment under Islamic law. Conversion into and out of Islam is a very sensitive issue in Malaysia. In *Lina Joy* v. *Majlis Agama Islam Wilayah Persekutuan and Others*[110] the petitioner was born a Muslim. On 21 February 1997 she applied to the National Registration Department (NRD) to change her name. The reason she applied to change her name from Azlina binti Jailani to Lina Lelani was because she had converted to Christianity and wished to marry a Christian man. It is important to note that the LRA does not apply to Muslims and, as long as she had the word 'Islam' on her identity card, she would not be able to marry under the LRA. Her application was rejected without reason by the NRD on 11 August 1997. On 15 May 1999 she made a second application to change her name to Lina Joy and attached her statutory declaration of conversion. She was informed that her application was successful on 22 October 1999 and she asked to change her identification card. However, when she made the application on 25 October 1999, the NRD had retrospectively enforced regulation PU (A) 70/2000, requiring religion to be recorded on the identity card of a Muslim.[111] Her application was rejected. Finally, on 3 January 2000 she applied for the third time for the word 'Islam' to be deleted from her identity card. The clerk at the NRD refused to accept her documents as she did not have a Syariah court order stating that she has converted out of Islam. She made an application in the High Court where she sought the following declarations: (1) from the Religious Council of the Federal Territory and Government of Malaysia that she had freedom of religion as guaranteed under the constitution; (2) that section 2 of the Administration of Islamic Law of the Federal Territory conflicted with Article 11 of the Federal Constitution and was not applicable to her as she was no longer a Muslim; (3) that her name be registered in the Register as non-Muslim. The High Court dismissed her application and she appealed to Court of Appeal.[112] The question before the Court of Appeal was whether the Director General of NRD had correctly exercised his discretionary power in relation to Lina's application. The Court of Appeal answered in the affirmative[113]

[110] [2007] 4 *Malayan Law Journal* 585.
[111] It is important to have religion on identification cards as there are a number of criminal offences that relate only to Muslims.
[112] [2004] 2 *Malayan Law Journal* 199.
[113] [2005] 6 *Malayan Law Journal* 193.

and Lina appealed to the Federal Court. The Federal Court held, inter alia, that, since conversion to and out of Islam is within the Syariah Court's jurisdiction, under Article 121(1A) of the Federal Constitution, the civil court had no jurisdiction over Lina's case. As a Muslim, Lina is bound by the Islamic laws on apostasy and all the relevant procedures if she wished to convert out of Islam.

7.59 The *Lina Joy* case is the tip of the iceberg. How the two legal systems could be harmonised or unified is a challenge for Malaysia. Muslim women are not free to marry, as they need the consent of their *wali*,[114] and they cannot marry non-Muslims. Conversion to and out of Islam remains a controversial and sensitive issue in Malaysia.

7.60 Marriage is still an important institution in Malaysia and so long as Islam remains the religion of the Federation, it is highly unlikely that any other form of union will be recognised in Malaysia. The issue of transsexuals is not new in Malaysia,[115] but it remains taboo even to think of it. The *Mohd Asraf* case was an important legal event in Malaysia.[116] As a nation with a Muslim majority, sex-change may be unthinkable, but one must not forget that the multiracial background of Malaysia has a strong influence on the life of its inhabitants. If the marriage of a transsexual who had undergone a sex-change operation cannot be recognised as valid, there is no prospect of same-sex marriage in Malaysia. The laws on sodomy remain intact and persons guilty of such activities are prosecuted both under civil and Syariah laws. Change is very unlikely since Malaysia is becoming more religious as a reaction to modernity.

7.61 The only option left to Malaysia is to expand the jurisdiction of the High Court in relation to family matters that involve different races and religions. At present, the High Court has the power to refer such matters to a special referee[117] and this provision may be extended to family matters where complicated issues like the religion of children, conversion and declaration of apostasy are involved. The referee may be a civil court judge, a Syariah court judge, an academic or any other person who has wide knowledge, experience and research in the area. This could minimise racial conflict and safeguard the rights of children.

---

[114] See para. 7.37 above.
[115] Noor Aziah Mohd Awal, 'Status Transeksual Di Bawah Undang-undang di Malaysia' (Transsexual under the laws in Malaysia) [2005] 17(4) KANUN 1.
[116] Discussed at para. 7.34 above.
[117] Court of Judicature Act 1964 (Act 91), s. 24(A).

7.62 Malaysian multiple cultures and religious values are precious assets to the nation. These differences have come into conflict from time to time, but have been resolved amicably either through the courts or out of court. This is not the end but, rather, the beginning and it cannot be predicted how long this ad hoc and informal means of resolution will satisfy the masses.

8

The Netherlands

The growing role of the judge in child and family law

PAUL VLAARDINGERBROEK

A   Introduction

8.1   This chapter will address the stormy developments in juvenile law and in family law in the Netherlands in the last decades. Our legislators can barely keep up with modern social changes, leaving much to the judiciary and, fortunately, Dutch judges rank human rights and treaty obligations as superior to domestic law.

8.2   Since the 1970s Dutch juvenile law has undergone dramatic changes. Prior to these changes, children were seen as objects of care, education and protection, but now they are treated as subjects of law. A 2009 league table of young people's well-being in twenty-nine European states placed the Netherlands at the top, followed by Sweden and Norway.[1] The United Kingdom was ranked twenty-fourth and Malta was in last place. So, according to the media, 'the happiest children in Europe are in the Netherlands and Scandinavia'. We shall see whether this is really true. However, I will show that many children in the Netherlands still suffer from a lack of legal rights (e.g. young migrant children and young asylum seekers). The number of children who suffer from maltreatment is still too high and too many children do not attend school regularly.

8.3   As will be shown, in the last few decades adult relationships have undergone radical changes too. Looking at the trends in the last few decades

---

[1] Organisation for Economic Co-operation and Development, *Doing Better for Children* (Paris: OECD, 2009), available at: www.oecd.org/els/social/childwellbeing. The table, focusing on youngsters aged up to 19 was compiled by researchers at York University in northern England for the Child Poverty Action Group (CPAG) using data mainly from 2006. The researchers assessed the countries using forty-three separate criteria, ranging from infant mortality and obesity to factors such as poverty and housing.

in family life we can see a growing number of new living arrangements (e.g. the growing number of de facto relationships, same-sex marriages, adoption by same-sex couples) and the growing number of children born out of wedlock, leading to the modernisation of the law on affiliation. In addition, Dutch divorce law has also been modernised, although this has not marked the end of calls for change in the field of family law. Lesbians are demanding legal answers to their wish to become the legal co-parents of children, transsexuals seek recognition of their right to procreate, even after a change of gender, and others demand divorce without the need to involve the courts.

Historical roots, sources and law reform

Historical roots

8.4   Dutch law was originally based on a combination of old traditional, Roman and (from 1804) French law. The Dutch Civil Code dates from 1838. Since the Second World War all aspects of family law have undergone drastic changes. New international legal provisions have greatly influenced Dutch family law. In particular, the European Convention for the Protection of Human Rights and Fundamental Freedoms (ECHR) has, in addition to other important Conventions and treaties, been of great importance in the development of modern family law. The direct and extensive applicability of Article 8 (right to respect for private and family life) of the ECHR has been of paramount importance. We can also see the influence upon our law, especially case law, of the United Nations Convention on the Rights of the Child and European treaties as well as the Hague Conventions. Dutch law is mainly statutory law, but particularly since 1979 and the decision of the European Court of Human Rights in *Marckx* v. *Belgium*,[2] judge-made law has become more and more important. The impact of decisions from the European Court of Human Rights and the International Court of Justice is great although, in recent years, the Netherlands Supreme Court (Hoge Raad) has also reached many very modern and interesting decisions in the field of juvenile law and the law of affiliation, parental authority, child protection measures and child custody. Judges set aside domestic law if it is not in accordance with the ECHR or other international instruments.

---

[2] (1979–1980) 2 EHRR 330.

Sources

8.5   In the Netherlands there is no all-encompassing law on children or the family. The Civil Code governs general issues on parentage, parental authority, access rights, the name of the child and so forth. Juvenile law can also be found in the Penal Code and procedural law is contained in the Code on Civil Procedures and the Code on Penal Procedures. In addition, there are many different legal codes and regulations governing the legal position of children. The youth protection system functions within two legal contexts. First, there is the Dutch Civil Code, dealing with child protection measures. Secondly, there is the Dutch Youth Care Act, under which the implementation of guardianships and family supervision is arranged. Dutch provinces work within national frameworks when implementing child protection policies.

8.6   The main source for adult family law is the Civil Code, but other regulations in this field are spread across various statutes (e.g. with regard to change of name, family law procedures, inter-country adoption, the Registry, alimony, pension rights, artificial insemination).

Law reform

8.7   In the Netherlands there is no central law reform body, but the legislators receive advice from several advisory bodies, such as the Dutch Council of State (Raad van State; advisory body on legislation and administrative court), the Criminal Law Application and Juvenile Protection Council (RSJ), the Council for the Judiciary (Raad voor de Rechtspraak; RvdR), non-governmental organisations and 'think tanks', that put forward proposals for reform.

Dispute resolution and access to legal services

8.8   Reaching agreement through mediation is a vital component in making and maintaining cooperative relationships between parents, and also between parents and their children, because it reduces conflict and encourages continuing contact between children and both of their parents. Therefore, mediation is in the best interests of the children and will also greatly help the parties themselves to overcome any disputes.[3]

---

[3] Recommendation No. R (98) 1 of the Committee of Ministers to member states on family mediation (Adopted by the Committee of Ministers on 21 January 1998 at the 616th meeting of the Ministers' Deputies).

Although mediation is often connected with divorce cases, it may help to reduce conflict in many other situations. Because of the possible positive consequences for the parties involved, particular attention should be paid to the issue of providing equal access to mediation. Before trying to settle the family dispute before the court, family members can ask for help from social workers.

8.9   Mediation can take place out of court or in connection with judicial proceedings. In the case of out-of-court mediation, the parties may enter mediation in order to prevent judicial proceedings from arising from separation, divorce or other problems. This type of mediation is widespread in Europe and it can be used for all sorts of family conflicts. Usually, the judge will recommend to divorcing couples that they should make use of the mediation facilities and, while they suffer no sanction for failure to comply with the recommendation, the judge can weigh this non-co-operation in his or her final decision. Since 1 January 2011 parties must pay (at least part of) the cost of mediation themselves: €90 for the first two hours. If the parties need more contact with the mediator, they must pay the regular fee. Mediation for cases involving children is subsidised. Mediation is voluntary and will only take place if the parties give their consent. However, the judge may – at any stage of the proceedings – stay the proceedings and appoint an expert (usually a mediator). An important question is whether the judge should have a role as mediator or whether he or she should leave this to lawyers and/or others. Although the judge may mediate between the parties involved, he or she will usually try to prepare the parties for mediation by showing them the benefits of finding a solution for themselves and reaching agreement without the judge, for example, by using mediation or the collaborative divorce approach.

8.10   It is also important that children should be aware of their rights and have access to free legal advice and assistance through legal aid. Children's advocates, special curators or specialised lawyers trained to help children to secure their rights have much to offer. The Dutch government has taken steps in these respects but could do more.

8.11   Economic circumstances have meant that the Dutch government introduced new legislation to lower the subsidies for legal aid and to increase the registry costs for the courts, which will surely make it more difficult for individuals to resolve conflicts with their (former) partner or within the family. Doubtless, this will have negative consequences for many families and children. While family experts, lawyers and judges have highlighted these dangers, the government still has not changed its plans.

B   Children in the family setting and state intervention

Defining and classifying children

8.12   If a woman is pregnant, the unborn child is considered to be already born if that is in its interest. Stillborn children are, in principle, considered never to have existed, except in the case of property interests.[4] About thirty years ago, the 'best interest standard' for unborn children was used by pro-life groups in the abortion debate, though without much success in the Netherlands. More recently, it has been possible to protect the interests of the unborn child using child protection measures in the case of, for example, a drug-addicted mother.

8.13   The term 'children' is used for young children, but it is also used in the sense rendering everyone a child, because everyone has legal, or at least biological, parents. Thus, the term 'minor' is used for young persons who fall under the authority of their parents or guardians. In the Netherlands a person becomes an adult at the age of 18, or earlier if he or she marries.[5] However, there are exceptions to this rule. At 16 or 17, a minor who is pregnant or the mother of a child may ask the juvenile judge to declare her adult, with the result that she can perform all legal acts.[6] On request, a judge can pronounce a 16-year-old 'of age', in order to perform certain duties and fulfil certain obligations, as if he or she was an adult. If the child misuses the freedom, the court can withdraw this limited emancipation.[7] If the judge has given a minor person the right to perform certain duties, the order pronouncing (or withdrawing) the coming of age of a minor must be published in the *Official Gazette* and in some daily papers, indicating which restricted powers have been granted (for example, to buy and sell in relation to a bike shop). Minors have capacity to perform legal acts more generally, as long as they act with the consent of their legal representatives.[8]

---

[4] Civil Code: Art. 1:2.   [5] Civil Code: Art. 1:233.
[6] Civil Code: Art. 1:253ha.   [7] Civil Code: Art. 1:236.
[8] Civil Code: Art. 1:234.

Recognising parentage and family ties

8.14   Turning again to the term 'child', in the context of the law on affiliation, we mean the legal ties to a mother and to a father and, thus, to other family members. The legal mother is the woman who has given birth to the child or the woman who has adopted a child.[9]

8.15   The judicial father is the man who is married to the woman who gave birth to the child at the time of the birth; has died less than 306 days before the birth of the child (the presumed paternity of the husband of the child's mother); has recognised a child; whose fatherhood has been determined by the judge or who has adopted the child.[10] Where the child is born within marriage or within 306 days after the death of the husband, the husband automatically becomes the legal father. Fatherhood can be contested if he is not the biological father of the child or, in the context of assisted reproduction, he did not give his wife permission to the act that led to the pregnancy and birth of the child. This challenge may be brought by the mother, the father or the child. The court can order a DNA test. The periods of time during which fatherhood can be contested are different for the father, the mother and the child. The court will reject the claim of the father or mother if the father has consented to donor insemination or to another deed that could have led to a child being conceived, or if the father knew about the pregnancy before he married his wife, unless she deceived him about the begetter's identity.[11] If the claim is adjudicated, the child will lose his or her legal father. The child can then be recognised by another man or the biological father can be sued to establish paternity judicially. The biological father himself cannot contest another man's legal paternity. If the mother has given her consent for the recognition of her child by another man, he can ask the court to have this recognition be declared void, but he must prove that the recognition of the child was a tort by the mother.

8.16   Legal fatherhood between the child and a man who is not married to the child's mother at the time of its birth can also be established by recognition of the child. However, if the man who recognises the child is not the biological father, his paternity can later be contested by the child. Recognition of a child is not possible if the child already has two legal

---

[9]   Civil Code: Art. 1:198.
[10]   Civil Code: Art. 1:199.
[11]   Civil Code: Art. 1:200.

parents but, assuming the absence of two legal parents, any man, at least 16 years old and unmarried, may recognise the child. A married man may not recognise the child of a woman other than his wife, unless the court has established that he has, or has had, a marriage-like relationship with the child's mother (family life). Recognition is not valid if there is an absolute marriage impediment between the mother and the man, for example if they are brother and sister. The mother (as long as the child is under 16) and the child (when 12 years or older) must give written consent to the recognition. If they refuse to give consent, the consent can be substituted by the court, provided that the man is the begetter of the child and the recognition would not disturb the mother–child relationship and is not contrary to the child's best interests.

8.17   The paternity of the begetter or the partner of the mother who consented to a deed that could have led to a child being conceived (e.g. donor insemination) can also be established judicially.[12] The court is empowered to order a DNA test. The mother can bring a paternity suit before the court within five years after her child's birth, or within five years after she discovers the real identity or correct address of the begetter. However, she can only sue him before her child has reached the age of 16. The child can commence proceedings without any time limits. Judicially established paternity is not possible if the mother of the child and the man are related within the prohibited degrees of consanguinity, or against a man who is under the age of 16. Judicially established paternity has retrospective effect to the day of the child's birth (*ex tunc*), while recognition of the child takes effect from the day of recognition (*ex nunc*). Where the affiliation is disputed, the court will nominate a special curator, usually a lawyer, who will represent the child and his or her best interests before the court.[13]

8.18   In 2010 the Ministry of Justice published a so-called 'pre-bill' (a draft of legislation) dealing with the possibility of a child having two mothers, for example where the child is born in a lesbian partnership. In order to gather as wide a range of views as possible, in addition to traditional publication, the pre-bill was posted on the Internet. If the bill is enacted, the child will, by law, have two mothers when he or she is born within their marriage and they can prove that the child was conceived in a hospital with donor semen. If the female partners are not married, it will

[12] Civil Code: Art. 1:207.
[13] Civil Code: Art. 1:212.

also be possible for the birth mother's partner to recognise the child, or that her motherhood will be established by the court. If the birth mother became pregnant at the wish of her female partner and the couple separate, the mother can also sue her former partner for financial support for the child.

Delivering parenting

Parental authority and guardianship

8.19   Many new forms of adult relationships were recognised in the Netherlands over the last quarter of the twentieth century. The legislature has tried to cope with these new family forms and – in accordance with the positive obligation of Article 8 of the European Convention on Human Rights – has made new rules for the legal position of those people who have (created) family life with a child. The result of this is that there is now a rather complex scheme of possibilities for parents and others in respect of family life with the child.

Parental authority during marriage

8.20   When both legal parents of the child are married to each other, they exercise parental authority jointly. After divorce, they will continue their joint parental authority, but each of them can request sole custody, although the general rule is that joint parental authority must be continued.[14] Usually, just one of the parents will be entrusted with sole parental authority if the other parent has maltreated or abused the child. Parents who are not married can jointly exercise parental authority if they have registered their combined request in the custody register that is kept by the court.[15]

Cohabitants and other unmarried parent(s) and their parental authority

8.21   From the moment of her child's birth, an adult unmarried mother is entrusted with parental authority.[16] A minor who gives birth to a child can ask the court to be declared adult and, thus, acquire parental authority.[17] The father of her child can ask the court to change this situation where, for

---

[14] Civil Code: Art. 1:251.
[15] Civil Code: Arts. 1:244 and 252.
[16] Civil Code: Art. 1:253b.   [17] Civil Code: Art. 1:253ha.

example, he wishes to have joint parental authority or parental authority for himself.[18] The court may also give the other parent the requisite authority over the child after the death of the parent entrusted with authority.[19] If the parents place their child in a foster family and the foster care has lasted for one year or longer, the (biological) parents cannot change the residence of their child without the consent of the foster parents. This so-called 'blocking right' is meant as a protection for both the foster family and the child. Only the substituted consent of the court can overcome the blocking.[20]

Joint responsibility

8.22   Since 1 January 1998 one of the parents may exercise responsibility for the child together with a partner who is not the legal parent of the child. This may involve the mother and her girlfriend or boyfriend with whom she forms a family (or the father with his girlfriend or boyfriend). Joint responsibility gives the non-parent the same rights and duties of parental responsibility as it does the parent(s). In all respects, he or she is then responsible for the care and upbringing of the child together with the legal parent of the child. To obtain joint responsibility, the legal parent of the child must have parental authority himself or herself and, together with his or her partner, must jointly submit a request to the court.

8.23   Because children are only born into marriages and registered partnerships that include at least one woman, a male co-parent who wants to share the legal and financial responsibilities with the father of the child, will still need to go to court to ask for joint parental authority and maintenance duties. A gay or lesbian co-parent who wants to have full parental status, to complement these responsibilities, will have to go through the adoption procedure.

8.24   If a child is born in a heterosexual marriage, the child automatically has the husband of the mother as his or her legal father, and the father and mother both automatically share all legal and financial responsibilities for the child. Such joint parental authority and joint parental maintenance duties do not arise automatically where a child is born in a lesbian marriage (nor where a child is born in a lesbian or heterosexual registered partnership) and can only be obtained by petitioning the court.

---

[18] Civil Code: Art. 1:253c.
[19] Civil Code: Art. 1:253h.
[20] Civil Code: Art. 1:253s.

8.25   Since 1 January 2002 any child born into a lesbian marriage (or into a registered partnership of two women or of a man and a woman) will automatically, from the moment of his or her birth, have two fully responsible adults: his or her mother and her spouse or registered partner. That spouse or partner will still not be deemed to be the 'father' (nor 'parent' or 'second mother') of the child.[21] The parent and her partner (the legal parent of the child) will have an equal share in the authority over the child and in the maintenance duties towards the child. After the separation of the parent and her partner, this joint authority will automatically be continued. However, after the separation each of the former partners can ask for sole authority over the child.[22] Where this sole authority is entrusted to the legal parent, it is called 'parental authority'. Where the former partner, who is not the legal parent, is entitled to have this authority (for example, where he or she has had more family life with the child or where the parent maltreated the child), it is called 'guardianship' because, legally, he or she is a third party. Where joint responsibility has ended and parental authority has been entrusted to the parent, the former partner who has lost his or her parental authority is obliged to support the child financially for a period of time equivalent to the duration of the joint parental authority.[23] So, for example, where joint parental authority ends after five years, the (former) partner of the parent must support the child for another five years. This obligation always ends when the child reaches the age of 21. It will be apparent that this part of family law can be very difficult for laypersons to understand.

The child's right to know

8.26   Children have the right to know the identity of their parents, but if the mother refuses to identify the biological father, it can be very difficult to force her to do so. Recently, the issue of the child's identity has arisen in a very different context: that is, in cases involving social parents seeking to adopt a child whom they have brought to the Netherlands illegally. Often, the social parents will have raised the child for some time before they petition the court for adoption, producing adoption certificates from countries where it is difficult to get verification of these documents. Cases

---

[21]   If the man and woman live together in a registered partnership and the man has acknowledged the child before its birth, they will both have parental authority from the moment of the child's birth.

[22]   Civil Code: Art. 1:253v.

[23]   Civil Code: Art. 1:253t.

have emerged involving children, kidnapped in India, where an imposter pretended to be the child's mother and consented to the adoption.[24] Usually, the prospective adopters in the Netherlands are unaware of the kidnapping and other irregularities.

8.27   In a case currently before the courts, an Indian couple is trying to regain parental authority over their now 12-year-old son who was stolen from them at the age of 2 and sold to a children's home.[25] The boy himself wishes to stay with his adoptive parents. The claimant birth parents also asked the court to allow them access to their child. To date, the court has declined all requests from the claimant birth parents. Obviously, this is proving traumatic for everyone involved.

8.28   In vitro fertilisation, egg and/or sperm donation and surrogate motherhood offer new opportunities to infertile couples. However, from the outset participants are made aware that the child has the right to know his or her genetic origins. Similarly, sperm and egg donors are required to sign a form at the hospital at the time of donation, indicating that they have been informed fully of the child's (and their own) rights and duties in this respect.

8.29   Of course, couples who do not wish their child to know about the donation and the identity of the donor(s) sometimes try to get pregnant without the help of a hospital by using sperm from a person they know or by sexual intercourse with a third party. They often go abroad. A new phenomenon is the trip to foreign countries to 'buy' the baby of another woman or couple and to ask for a falsified birth certificate. Another possibility is to go to countries such as India and Ukraine to use a surrogate mother to give birth to a child and to bring this child to the Netherlands. Arguably, new (medical and legal) approaches are required in order to avoid illegal adoptions and falsified birth certificates, and to help infertile parents as much as possible in their quest for a child.

---

[24] 'Meiling en adoptie uit India. Onderzoek naar het handelen van vergunninghouder interlandelijke adoptie Meiling in de periode 1995 t/m 2002 naar aanleiding van signalen over mogelijke misstanden in India, Inspectie Jeugdzorg, Utrecht, oktober 2007', available at: www.inspectiejeugdzorg.nl/documenten/Meiling%20en%20adoptie%20uit%20India.pdf). See also: Aniket Alam, 'Adoption: probe reveals more shady deals', *The Hindu*, 26 December 2002.

[25] Rechtbank Zwolle 4 March 2011, LJN: BP6936 (for the English version of the court's decision, see: www.rechtspraak.nl/Organisatie/Rechtbanken/Zwolle-Lelystad/Nieuws/Pages/Request-Indian-parents-for-DNA-test-rejected.aspx).

Intra-family disputes

8.30   In the event of divorce, termination of registered partnership or legal separation, parents are obliged to record agreements about their children in a parenting plan.[26] If parents are not married or registered partners and have simply lived together, they are obliged to make a parenting plan if they have joint custody of their children. Parenting plans are provided for in the Promotion of Continued Parenting and Proper Divorce Act, which took effect on 1 March 2009. The legislation proceeds on the principle that, if both parents remain jointly responsible for the children after the divorce, both their children and the parties themselves will benefit. If they continue to have joint custody, it is essential that proper and verifiable agreements are made to avoid future problems. A solicitor and/or mediator may be of help in drawing up the parenting plan. This parenting plan forms part of the petition for a divorce.

8.31   The plan should, in any case, include agreements made by the parents on the following key subjects: division of care and parenting tasks; child maintenance; and exchange of information on important issues with regard to their children's personal development and assets. While clear agreements may prevent future conflicts, something essential to the children since divorce-related conflicts may be detrimental to a child's development, they may also help the parents and other family members, such as grandparents. Not all parents are capable of making agreements about their divorce or resolving conflicts arising after their divorce. In those cases, help from third parties is available. The court may refer these parents to a mediator. Results from research on divorce and access mediation show that mediation has a positive influence on both the settlement of the divorce and in resolving conflicts over access to the children. However, it is important that former partners should re-evaluate the parenting plan regularly and that this should be done in the event of important changes in the life of the parents or children (removal; new partner, illness, etc.).[27]

---

[26]   Code of Civil Procedures: Art. 815 Rv.

[27]   P. Vlaardingerbroek and M. de Hoon, 'Emotions in Court and the Role of the Judge. Results from Experimental Hearings in Divorce Proceedings' (2010) 4 *International Family Law* 319–32.

Child protection and state intervention

8.32 The majority of the Dutch youth are doing fine, but some youngsters are facing one or more serious problems. However, as several reports have noted, only a small portion of those children in need receive the necessary care and relief.[28] In 2005 the Youth Care Act entered into force, offering young people and parents help and support with problems associated with growing up and parenting. About 5 per cent of all Dutch children and young people receive some type of youth care (± 160,000) each year. A key priority of youth policy in the Netherlands is the support for children and young people at risk and their families.

8.33 The Netherlands has an extensive system of child protection in place, carried out by the Child Protection Board (CPB; Raad voor de Kinderbescherming) and responsibility for it lies with the Ministry of Security and Justice. The CPB is involved with families where upbringing has become a problem; is called in when divorcing parents are incapable of making arrangements concerning their children (e.g. visitation rights); plays a role in criminal cases involving under-age children; and is involved with cases concerning adoption and descent.

8.34 The CPB represents the interests of these children by making inquiries into their (home) situation, usually after complaints by third parties, and by recommending professional help or imposing measures. All the CPB's activities give priority to the interests of the child, but it does not provide assistance to families itself. The CPB is a so-called 'second-line organisation'. Only a limited number of organisations, including the Bureau Jeugdzorg/Advies- en Meldpunt Kindermishandeling (BJZ/AMK), the police and the courts are authorised to make direct contact with the CPB and other agencies call on its assistance only in extremely grave situations. To avoid two organisations working on the same case, the AMK is notified when the CPB accepts a crisis report as basis for an inquiry.

8.35 A child protection measure can only be taken if voluntary help and assistance has not worked or if a family refuses to accept any help. Youth

---

[28] L. Van Dorsselaer, E. Zeijl, S. Eeckhout, T. van der Bogt and W. Vollebergh, *Gezondheid en welzijn van jongeren in Nederland* (Utrecht: Trimbos-Instituut, 2007). Ministry of Health, Welfare and Sport, *National Youth Monitor 2010* (The Hague: December 2010), available at: http://jeugdmonitor.cbs.nl/en-GB/menu/home/default.htm.

and Family Centres act as the front line for municipal youth care services. Every parent and every child can ask for help and assistance, but a more proactive approach to families is needed. Since August 2009, every municipality works with a *Reference Index* for youth at risk. This is a national electronic system that brings together risk signals of youth (up to 23 years of age), as reported by social workers, teachers and those who work in health care.

8.36   After making its enquiries, the CPB may petition the court (juvenile judge) to order a child protection remedy. The ruling of the court will be based, in part, on the information provided by the CPB. A child protection remedy limits the authority of the parents, in whole or in part, until the situation of the child has improved. The family is obligated to accept this help.[29] The number of child protection orders has increased over recent years and is expected to continue to do so, mainly due to more public concern over child abuse and domestic violence. The previous government launched the so-called 'Better Protection' programme, which is aimed at improving the child protection system. It introduced the Delta method of family supervision, which decreased the caseload of family guardians. The programme will also speed up the decision-making process in respect of child protection orders. The CPB advises the juvenile courts, which can impose a child protection order, impose a supervision order or overrule the standard parental authority. A supervision order restricts the parents' authority, part of which is then assumed by a family guardian. When parental authority is removed outright, a guardian (usually the BJZ) is appointed.[30]

Family guardianship; supervision order

8.37   If the moral, mental or physical interests of a child are threatened and other non-compulsory measures to improve the situation have failed, the court can order a family guardianship.[31] An organisation for family guardianship (Bureau Jeugdzorg) will be appointed to advise and help

---

[29] For further information, see the brochure *When upbringing is a problem*, available at: www.rvdk.nl.

[30] T. van Yperen, Netherlands Youth Institute, NJI, 'Prevention of Child Abuse', available at: www.nji.nl.

[31] Civil Code: Art. 1:254. Also called custodial control. For statistics on Dutch youth, see *The National Youth Monitor*, available at: http://jeugdmonitor.cbs.nl/en-GB/menu/indicatoren/bevolking/default.htm. For figures on the domain 'Safety and justice' of the National Youth Monitor see: http://jeugdmonitor.cbs.nl/en-GB/menu/indicatoren/justitie/default.htm.

the family members for one year.[32] This term can be extended. The so-called 'family guardian' is charged with implementing custodial control. He or she supervises the process whereby the problems with upbringing that threaten the development of the child are resolved and will support the parents and their child(ren) and organise professional help for the family. The family guardian may give instructions with which parents and children are required to comply. The court can suspend, abrogate or withdraw these instructions. If necessary, the court may authorise the agency to place the child in foster or residential care for a maximum of one year, but an extension for another year is always possible.[33] It is even possible that the child will be placed in a closed institution. During the family guardianship, the Bureau Jeugdzorg can take all kinds of measures, for example, concerning access to or contact with the minor or concerning medical treatment.[34]

Parental authority: relief or dismissal

8.38   Dutch law recognises two ways of ending parental authority: relief and dismissal. If a parent is unfit or unable to fulfil his or her parental duties, the court can order the parent to be relieved of his or her parental authority. A third-party guardian, usually a guardianship agency (Bureau Jeugdzorg), will take care of the children for as long as the parents are relieved of, or dismissed from, their parental authority. The second way to lose parental authority is by a dismissal ordered by the court. The grounds for such an order are: maltreatment, serious neglect of the care for one or more of the children or sexual abuse, or misconduct and/or a conviction for committing a crime with the minor or against the minor. In principle, relief and dismissal continue until the child has reached majority or until the court is persuaded that the child can be returned to his or her parent(s). In the latter case, the court can pronounce a reinstatement of parental rights, usually after a trial reinstatement of, at most, six months.[35]

New regulations on child protection

8.39   In July 2009 the Dutch government introduced legislation designed to expand the grounds for placing a minor under supervision. The legislative proposal was accepted by the Lower Chamber of

---

[32]   Civil Code: Arts. 1:256 and 257.   [33]   Civil Code: Arts. 1:261 and 263.
[34]   Civil Code: Arts. 1:263a and 264.   [35]   Civil Code: Arts. 1:277 and 278.

the Parliament in March 2011 and is now open for discussion in the Senate. It is expected to enter into effect on 1 January 2013. In the future the courts will also be able to impose a new measure of family help/advice in the event of less serious problems. The legislation will also improve the implementation of family supervision orders. The juvenile court judge may, upon request, order that specific components of parental authority be exercised by the Youth Care Agency (Bureau Jeugdzorg; BJZ) if a juvenile is placed outside the home. The interests of the child will remain, of course, of primary importance.

8.40   In addition, in future there will be one measure (instead of the current two child protection measures) to terminate parental authority. The parents' consent is not required for the new 'authority-ending' measure. A family supervision order will often precede such a termination of authority. However, if it is clear from the start of the child protection process that the parents cannot meet their responsibilities for raising their child within an acceptable time-frame, an authority-ending measure may be imposed immediately (for example, where the parents are addicted to hard drugs). Other amendments include the improvement of the legal position of foster parents and simplifying the exchange of data between (youth care) agencies or institutions during ongoing family supervision orders. Even without the consent from the parents, the Youth Care Agency will be entitled to obtain information from third parties.

Custody

8.41   In his or her last will or by special notarial act, a parent can designate a third party (not an institution) to exercise custody over his or her minor children after the parent's death. When parents are dismissed or released from their authority over their children, the district court has the competence to appoint a guardian, usually a youth care agency (BJZ).

Rights of access, information and consultation during the child's outplacement

8.42   The child and the parents have a reciprocal right to see and meet each other, but not only can the court regulate access (for example, frequency of contact), it can also deny the parent contact altogether.[36] If the

---

[36]   Civil Code: Art. 1:377a.

parents have joint parental authority, both are entitled to have access to the child and to be informed and consulted by the other parent. The parent who is entrusted with the custody of the minor is obliged to consult and to inform the non-custodial parent about important circumstances concerning the person and the property of the child (for example, periodically providing a recent photograph or a school report).[37] If required, a third party who has professional knowledge about a child (for example, a school teacher or a social worker) can be obliged to give the non-custodial parent information about the child.[38] The rules about access and information can be amended if the circumstances change.[39]

8.43   In principle, the child will continue to live at home during the life of the family guardianship order. However, in some cases it is better for the child or for the parents that the child is placed somewhere else, in a home or with a foster family for instance. If the family guardian wants to place the child away from home, he or she is required to petition the (juvenile) judge for an authorisation, any authorisation being for a maximum of one year, subject to renewal. A placement order ends when the child reaches the age of 18 or when the guardianship order ends. The family guardian may also petition the court for a placement order in a secure youth care institution for non-criminal youngsters. In those cases, the judge must hear the child, and the child will be assisted by a solicitor. Bureau Jeugdzorg must also prove that an expert has declared that the placement in a secure institution is necessary. Placement in a closed youth care institute can be for no longer than one year in the first instance, subject to renewal for further periods of up to a year. In general, during a period of placement away from home parents will be allowed to maintain contact with their child, but the family guardian may also decide that, in the interests of the child, no contact should be permitted. The family guardian can intervene in the care and upbringing of the child, both when solicited and when not. He or she is authorised to give the parents an 'instruction in writing': an official order with which parents and/or children are legally required to comply. The parents and/or the child (when aged 12 or older) may lodge an objection with the Juvenile Care Bureau (BJZ) that assigned this family guardian. If the parents or the child are not in agreement with the final decision of the youth care agency, they may appeal to the court to have the instruction annulled. No further appeal from the judge's decision is permitted.

[37] Civil Code: Art. 1:377b.
[38] Civil Code: Art. 1:377c.   [39] Civil Code: Art. 1:377e.

8.44 Children aged 12 or older who have committed a crime can be sent to juvenile offenders institutions (JJIs). Since 1 August 2011 the regulations governing juvenile offenders institutions have changed to permit greater treatment of youngsters, because most of them have severe behavioural disorders. These problems are ten times more prevalent in this setting than in the general population of young persons in the Netherlands. Young persons in the JJIs are also more often from minority ethnic or cultural population groups. In its advice to the Ministry of Justice, the Criminal Law Application and Juvenile Protection Council (RSJ) advanced the view that mental health care should first and foremost devote attention to early identification, diagnosis and treatment in order to prevent young persons with psychological disorders ending up in JJIs. The Council supported the UN Convention on the Rights of the Child requirement that young persons who commit offences should be placed in JJIs less often, with non-custodial sanctions, like behaviour-influencing measures, being used instead. While the present author supports this advice, the present economic situation renders it unlikely that these proposals will be implemented in legislation.

Young migrant children

8.45 The UN Convention gives children the right to an adequate standard of living: that is, a standard of living 'adequate for the physical, mental, intellectual, moral and social development of the child'.[40] While the primary responsibility for meeting this requirement lies with the child's parents, States Parties are required to assist parents in this respect, so that children have food, clothing and a roof over their heads at a minimum.[41] The United Nations Committee on the Rights of the Child has often made it clear that the UN Convention applies regardless of the child's residence status. Article 2 of the Convention provides that no child should face discrimination on the basis of their parents' status. Thus, the Convention applies equally to all children in the Netherlands. The right to shelter has also been laid down in the European Social Charter.[42] Despite this, young asylum seekers and children of refugees from non-European countries are in a very weak position in the Netherlands. Aliens, including children, without residence status are excluded from general and special assistance on the basis of the Dutch Work and Social Assistance Act.[43] The

---

[40] Art. 27(1).   [41] Art. 27(1).   [42] Art. 31.
[43] Art. 11(2), in conjunction with Art. 16(2).

justification for this exclusion is that aliens who are in the Netherlands illegally should not be encouraged to stay by benefits being granted and that they themselves are responsible for the difficult situation in which they find themselves.[44] Fortunately, things have changed slightly in the Netherlands, but, in October 2010, a liberal–conservative government was elected, so the legal position of (young) asylum seekers and migrants is again under discussion.

8.46   The organisation Defence for Children International (DCI) is the main advocate for homeless children in the Netherlands. DCI considers that it is not in the best interests of children who have spent years in the Netherlands and who are rooted in Dutch society to be deported and, thus, that any deportation is a violation of the UN Convention on the Rights of the Child. According to DCI, three issues, in particular, merit highlighting. First, the state of the Netherlands violates children's rights by deporting children who are rooted in the Netherlands, since deportation will fracture the development of these vulnerable children and cause damage to them. Secondly, once a child is denied a residence permit, it is extremely difficult for that child to obtain certain basic facilities, such as health care, housing and education. Some children without a residence permit are in need of special care, because they have physical or psychological problems or because they are traumatised by war or by fleeing their country of origin. Such extra care is only sparsely available for children without a residence permit. Finally, these children run the risk of being put in detention because of their immigration status, which violates not only their right to freedom, but also their right to education and their right to recreation.

Outstanding children's issues

8.47   In 2009 teenagers in the 12–16 age group gave their psycho-social well-being a score of 7.9 (out of 10). They were asked to give a mark for how they feel in general. Boys gave a slightly higher mark than girls. The new figures were added to the domain Health and Welfare in May 2011 from the Ministry of Justice.[45] Nevertheless, there are still numerous families in need due to financial and or social problems.

---

[44] *A Home for Every Child. The Right to Shelter for 'Illegal' Children in the Netherlands* (The Hague: DCI, The Netherlands, 2009), p. 36.

[45] See also the *Dutch National Youth Monitor*, May 2011, available at: www.landelijkejeugdmonitor.nl. It provides a summary of information, available in print and on the Internet, about the situation of young people in the Netherlands. The purpose of the monitor is to inform policymakers, researchers and other interested parties about the situation of the youth in the Netherlands today. The monitor is compiled on the basis of

8.48   In their 2011 Annual Report, DCI International shows that the legal position of young children has not improved much, although the Netherlands is one of the richest countries in the world. This report shows that the waiting lists for youth care increased in 2010 and that the total number of sexually exploited children increased 'more than 100% and that it still takes too long before children receive the necessary care from child protection agencies and that the legal position of young migrant children who have been raised here, is still too weak'.[46]

C   Adult relationships

The relationships

8.49   Historically, in the Netherlands, as in other jurisdictions, different-sex marriage had long been the legal relationship recognised by the legal system. With the addition of the registered partnership model to the Dutch Civil Code on 1 January 1998, same-sex couples, too, could legalise their relationships. In the first three years after the introduction of registered partnerships, many couples took the opportunity to have their relationship officially registered. Later, the number of same-sex registrations dropped. Since the introduction of the registration of partnerships on 1 January 1998, the number of registered homosexual couples has varied between 200 and 300, with the number of registered lesbian couples falling within the same range.

8.50   Same-sex marriage became possible in 2001. In recent years more lesbian than homosexual couples got married: nearly 800 as against 600 in 2010. The number of homosexual and lesbian couples living together totalled 57,000 in 2010. One in three of these couples had their relationships officially registered, with nearly 11,000 homosexual couples being married and more than 6,000 in registered partnerships.[47] Over the last few years, the trend has been for more and more (hetero- and homosexual) partners not marrying (at least, not within 5–10 years) and not registering as partners. Most young couples and couples where one or both of the parties is widowed or divorced, live together outside marriage. In

---

existing reports and datasets and presents a picture of how the population, aged 0–24 years, is doing.

[46]   DCI Netherlands, *Annual Report 2011*, p. 30.

[47]   CBS, 2010: http://statline.cbs.nl/StatWeb/publication/?VW=T&DM=SLEN&PA=37772e ng&LA=EN.

2010 four in ten babies out of 185,000 first babies were born to mothers who were not married. The number of second children whose parents are not married is also rising dramatically. So, more and more parents retain their unmarried status after the birth of their first child. However, when the second or third child is born, more mothers are married. The average age of the mother at the time of the birth is 29.4 years.

8.51 Thus, the Dutch Civil Code recognises two types of formal relationship: marriage and registered partnership. However, the Civil Code also recognises relationships that have not been formalised at all, albeit to a more limited extent than the recognition accorded to formal relationships. Examples of recognition being extended to non-formal relationships include the right of a partner to ask for joint custody of a child; the right to petition the court for measures where a partner has become incapable; the right to continue to rent the home where a partner dies; the right to pensions; and the right to tax relief.

Entering an adult relationship

8.52 As we have seen, registration of partnership became possible for all couples, irrespective of gender, from 1 January 1998 and marriage was extended to same-sex couples from 1 April 2001. In each case the gender of the parties makes almost no difference to the consequences of the respective relationships. However, marriage between a same-sex couple will have no effect where a child is born during the marriage of a lesbian couple, nor does a registered partnership give the partner of the woman who gave birth to the child an automatic right to legal parenthood.[48]

8.53 The age of consent for marriage is 18 for both men and women.[49] However, an exception is made for a woman who has reached the age of 16 and wishes to marry, provided she can demonstrate that either she is pregnant or that she has already given birth to a child. Dispensation may be sought from the Minister of Justice in all other circumstances (for example, in the case of a younger person) although, in practice, it is seldom granted. In these cases the minor child also needs the consent of his or her parents but, if they refuse, consent can be given by the court at the request of the child. A mentally disabled person who is incapable of determining his or her free will or of understanding the meaning of

---

[48] See para. 8.25 above.   [49] Civil Code: Art. 1:31(1).

marriage cannot marry. A person under tutelage for reason of mental handicap is only allowed to marry with the consent of the cantonal judge (*kantonrechter*). If this person is put under tutelage for reasons of dissipation or alcoholism, he or she must obtain the consent of his or her guardian in order to marry and, if the guardian refuses, substitute consent may be requested from the *kantonrechter*. Two persons who are related within the prohibited degrees of consanguinity may not marry, being too closely related to each other. The same absolute prohibition applies to brothers and sisters. Polygamous marriage is not possible in the Netherlands, so a man or woman can only be married to one person at a time.

8.54   In the Netherlands a person can never be forced to marry or to register a partnership, even on the basis of having promised to do so. In cases of simple breach of promise, neither party may sue either for the solemnisation of the marriage or for damages. Only if the wedding has been announced formally may a party claim for the real costs and material damages (for example, the costs of the photographer or the restaurant that had to be cancelled). No claim may be made for immaterial damage (sorrow, the loss of a good party).

8.55   Where certain requirements for marriage have not been met, some family members, curators and trustees may seek to prevent the actual wedding going ahead by issuing a summons against the Registrar to 'suspend the marriage'. The Public Prosecutor is obliged to suspend a planned marriage if he or she knows of any legal impediment or is of the opinion that the marriage is a sham (for example, designed only to obtain residency status). Thereafter, the person who wants to go through with the wedding or registered partnership has to take legal action and address himself or herself to the court. In the meantime, the planned marriage or registered partnership will remain suspended.

8.56   Marriages are solemnised in public in the official municipal town hall in the presence of the Registrar and at least two, and at most four, adult witnesses. This is also the case for the registration of partnership. Religious confirmations of marriages can only take place after the solemnisation of the civil marriage by the Registrar.

8.57   A marriage may be declared void at the request of the Public Prosecutor if it is proved that it was a sham marriage and its sole purpose was to enable one of the parties to acquire a right of residence in the Netherlands. This is possible even after the dissolution of that marriage.

Each of the spouses has the right to file for annulment on the basis of intimidation or a mistake as to the identity of the other party or a misunderstanding about the real meaning of the solemn vow to take the other party as his or her spouse. The rules for annulment are also applicable in case of registered partnerships. Other family members may also request annulment on the same grounds.

8.58   With regard to other living arrangements, everyone is entitled to start living together in a relationship with one, two or more persons, as long this is not against the (penal) law. If parents do not agree to their daughter under the age of 16 participating in such a relationship, they can (try to) prevent it by applying for help from a youth care agency.

Consequences of relationships

8.59   Dutch law contains provisions concerning the more immaterial personal relations between the spouses as well as the very material regime governing property. The same regulations apply to registered partners. Spouses and registered partners owe each other fidelity, help and support, although they are not obliged to live together. They must supply each other with the necessities of life and they have a duty to bring up, educate and support the (minor) children of the family. Children engaged in education or who are in need may expect parental financial support until they are 21 years old. Couples have a mutual duty to bear the costs of the household and the liabilities evolving from this duty to third parties. Both parties must contribute to housekeeping money. Disputes over any of these matters may be taken to court for resolution.

8.60   Irrespective of the property regime applying to the couple, spouses need each other's consent for some legal acts.[50] The Dutch legal community of goods system, applying to spouses and civil partners, is somewhat unique. If the spouses did not make any arrangements before the wedding, they are married in *community of goods*, which compromises all present and future property, but also all debts acquired by either of them from the moment the marriage is solemnised. There are only a few exceptions to this complete community of property. First, it does not include property that the donor or testator excluded from the community expressly. Secondly, it does not cover goods and debts that attached specifically to one of the parties. Lastly, pensions are not part of the community of goods.

---

[50]   Civil Code: Art. 1:88.

At present, equalisation of pensions is proving to be a rather difficult issue to resolve. The administration of a property is in the hands of the spouse who brought it to the community. Spouses are obliged to inform each other about the state of the goods and the debts of the community. The community of property is dissolved by any of the following: the end of the marriage; a legal separation; a court decision dissolving the community; or a post-nuptial settlement to dissolve the community.[51] From 1 January 2012 the Dutch total community of goods system changed slightly, but the main aspects remain the same.[52] The main difference is that the administration of property (except gifts and inheritance) is now in the hands of both spouses.

8.61   While most Dutch people (some 72 per cent) do not do so, the parties may make different arrangements for their property by means of a marriage settlement, provided the terms are not in conflict with good morals or public order. A marriage settlement must be executed by a deed before a civil law notary before the wedding or registration of partnership. This can also be done during the marriage or registered partnership. The notarial deeds of marriage settlements must be filed in a public register, and held at the court in the district where the partners married or registered their partnership.[53] The law recognises the following major categories of marriage contracts (but variations are possible): a total exclusion of community of property; a limited community (for example a community of benefit and income or gains and losses); and other contracts, such as the most popular *verrekenbedingen*, which means that there is a total exclusion of community of property, but the partners' saved income will be shared between them at the end of each year or at the dissolution of marriage or registration of partnership or in specific other cases.[54] There is a growing tendency, especially amongst elderly couples who have been married for a long time, to change the marriage settlements they made when they married some thirty or forty years before, largely for tax reasons. Such a change requires permission from a court in order to ensure that creditors are not prejudiced by any change.

8.62   Domestic violence is a real issue in the Netherlands and the government has set up several campaigns to deal with this problem. A survey

---

[51] Civil Code: Art. 1:99.

[52] Act of 18 April 2011, State Gazette 2011, No. 205.

[53] Civil Code: Art. 1:116.

[54] Civil Code: Arts. 1:132–144, Act of 14 March 2002; *Stb.* 2002, 152; enacted 1 September 2002.

carried out in 1997 confirmed what social workers and police officers already suspected: domestic violence was extremely widespread.[55] In 2009 new legislation introduced temporary restraining orders for perpetrators of domestic violence in situations where there is an acute threat to victims and/or any children. Domestic violence is defined as 'an act of violence committed by a person from within the victim's domestic circle', which includes partners, ex-partners, family members and family friends. Under the new legislation, mayors were empowered to impose a ten-day restraining order although, in practice, they delegated this power to executive police officers. The court can review the order within three days of its commencement and, after the ten days have elapsed, a judge may decide to extend the order by another four weeks. Restraining orders also apply in child abuse cases. The people involved, both perpetrators and victims,[56] will receive professional help during the ten-day period. The number of ten-day restraining orders granted rose from 2,107 in 2009, to 2,935 in 2010.[57]

Termination of relationships

8.63   Marriage and registered partnerships, may be dissolved by death or by divorce. In 2009 a total of 85,697 marriages were dissolved, 54,918 by death and 30,779 by divorce. Dissolution is a straightforward matter since the Netherlands embraces no-fault divorce. The permanent disruption of marriage is the only ground for divorce,[58] which does not have

---

[55]   Annually, approximately 200,000 persons are believed to be victims of domestic violence (60% of them are women and 40% are men) and domestic violence results in fifty deaths, one third of the total homicides in the Netherland. Every ten minutes the police receive an urgent call as a result of of domestic violence. More than 25% of the Dutch population reported that they had experienced domestic violence on a daily or weekly basis over long periods of time. Nearly one third said it had changed their lives dramatically, leading to divorce, anxiety or problems in forming close relationships. Roughly as many males as females are victims of domestic violence. The main difference is that violence perpetrated against women is usually more serious and often takes the form of sexual abuse. Moreover, males are more likely to be abused at a relatively early age, girls and women throughout their lives and 80% of the offenders are men. See www.huiselijkgeweld.nl (partly in English).

[56]   In many cases, perpetrators have been or still are victims of domestic violence.

[57]   See H. C. J. van der Veen (Ministerie van Justitie, WODC), S. Bogaerts (Universiteit van Tilburg, Intervict), *Huiselijk geweld in Nederland WODC*, Boom Juridisch (2010). English summary p. 144, available at: www.government.nl/documents-and-publications/press-releases/2011/01/14/domestic-violence-more-than-200–000-victims-each-year.html (last accessed 20 March 2012).

[58]   Civil Code: Art. 1:151BW.

to be proved. The courts simply accept the allegations without evidence. Over the last decade, while divorce itself has been relatively uncontentious, attention has focused on ancillary matters, including alimony, joint parental authority, access rights and pension rights. Marriage is terminated by registering the divorce decision in the civil register within six months of the court decision. Either party may request this registration, but registration is essential since, after a period of six months without registration, the divorce is no longer valid.[59] There are a whole range of agencies and voluntary workers to help the couple and family during and after the divorce with, for example, legal, financial, social or pedagogic issues.

8.64   At present, it is not possible to divorce without a judge's decision. However, registered partners who wish to separate can ask the registrar of the local community to dissolve their partnership. This is not possible if they have minor children together. Recently, MPs indicated that they would favour dissolution of marriage by mutual consent if the spouses do not have minor children. It is likely that this reform will be effected in the future since it is consistent with the liberal views of the present government and will save on judicial costs.

Consequences of termination

8.65   On dissolution of marriage (or registered partnership) the community will be divided in two equal parts if the partners were living in a total community of goods system: one half going to one spouse (or registered partner) or his/her heirs and one half going to the other spouse or his/her heirs.[60] Parties may arrange the division of martial property themselves, but this is usually done by a solicitor, a notary or a judge. However, even after the dissolution each of the spouses remains liable for the total of the common debts for which he or she was liable previously and each spouse or registered partner is still liable for half of the other's debts.[61] After the dissolution of the community, each of the spouses has the right to buy the clothes and jewellery he or she used to wear, his or her professional tools and the papers and documents belonging to his or her family. The money paid for these items falls into the community of goods.[62]

---

[59] Civil Code: Art. 1:163BW.   [60] Civil Code: Art. 1:100.
[61] Civil Code: Art. 1:102.   [62] Civil Code: Art. 1:101.

8.66   If the ex-spouse does not have sufficient income to provide himself or herself with the necessities of life, or is not in a position to obtain enough income, the court can award alimony. In doing so, it must take into account the needs of the person claiming maintenance and the financial strength of the other party.[63] Usually, alimony is not payable for longer than twelve years after registration of the divorce. However, in cases of hardship, the court can lengthen this period at the request of the person in need. If the marriage lasted less than five years and there are no children born from this marriage, the maintenance obligation lasts exactly as long as the marriage itself lasted. Maintenance payments are indexed annually.

8.67   The entitlement to maintenance ceases when the person who has this right remarries, registers a partnership or starts living with another person in a relationship like a marriage or registered partnership. Whether the right to obtain alimony from the former spouse or registered partner should be limited to a shorter period is a matter of current debate, because more and more women continue to work (although often part-time) during their relationship and can more easily work for more hours a week after their divorce. Whether the period of support for the former spouse or registered partner should be limited to eight, five or even two years is also being discussed. The duty to support children will continue until they are 18 or 21 (in case of need or study) years old.

Self-regulation and custom-made relationships

8.68   With regard to other living arrangements, there are no legal provisions concerning de facto marriages although this form of informal living arrangement has been popular in the Netherlands for many years and is not regarded as contrary to good morals or public order. However, there are many models of living-together contracts that may be drawn up by a notary or solicitor. In addition, couples sometimes draw up these contracts for themselves, often copying a draft contract from the Internet. The property relations of unmarried cohabitants who have not concluded a cohabitation agreement are very similar to those of married couples who have chosen total separation of property by marital contract. Dutch law does not provide for maintenance obligations between cohabitants. Indeed, even in cases where the cohabitants have made a cohabitation

---

[63]   Civil Code: Art. 1:157.

agreement, their property often remains completely separate, since their cohabitation agreement goes no further than regulating contributions to household costs, division of pensions and distribution of property in case of death. Incorporation of provisions on sharing incomes or assets (netting covenants) is rare. Several authors have criticised this.[64]

8.69   If the parties fail to conclude a contract with regard to their property, there will be no community of goods. After the separation each party will take his or her own belongings and debts. Another problem with regard to partners in informal relationships is the lack of legal consequences with regard to the mutual financial support during or after the relationship. However, a number of statutes acknowledge these de facto marriages, including those on inheritance tax, pensions and property rental.

8.70   In a new report for the Dutch government, researchers concluded that 'there are sufficient grounds to consider a regulation providing for the mitigation of financial problems and unfair effects of the termination of informal relationships, especially when the interests of minor or dependant growing-up children [sic] of the couple are concerned'.[65] It is now up to the legislature to decide whether or not these grounds are weighty enough to justify legislation.

8.71   The researchers confined themselves to making an inventory of the legal provision that could be applied. One of the most obvious provisions is to extrapolate partner maintenance to all informal marriage-like relationships. This provision would allow the temporary mitigation of the reduction of the earning capacity of the child-caring partner, taking into consideration both the needs of the receiving partner and the financial capacity of the paying partner. When doing so, one should allow for the difference between spouses, who by entering into marriage have explicitly committed themselves to a certain legal status, and partners in informal relationships who did not make such commitment. Hence, unmarried partners should be given the opportunity to opt out

---

[64] W. Schrama, *De niet-huwelijkse samenleving in het Nederlandse en Duitse recht* (Amsterdam: Kluwer, 2004), pp. 394–5. See also C. Forder, *Het informele huwelijk: de verbondenheid tussen mens, goed en schuld* (Deventer: Kluwer, 2000), pp. 30–6.

[65] M. V. Antokolskaia *et al.*, *Koude Uitsluiting. Materiële problemen en onbillijkheden na scheiding van in koude uitsluiting gehuwde echtgenoten en na scheiding van ongehuwd samenlevende partners, alsmede instrumenten voor de overheid om deze tegen te gaan* (The Hague: Netherlands Institute for Law and Governance (WODC), 2010).

of maintenance obligations by a contract verified by a notary.[66] Several other provisions currently applying to spouses could, according to the researchers, be applied equally to partners in informal relationships. They would include the provisions dealing with the following: household expenses; compensation for the reallocation of property;[67] fair compensation for unpaid work in the business of the other partner; the discretionary power of the court to amend a cohabitation contract; and procedural rules regarding provisional orders and orders on ancillary matters in separation cases.

8.72   While it is very important that, at the very least, the most vulnerable people (especially children) in these living arrangements should be protected, the question arises whether the government or legislators should protect those persons who do not wish to adopt the legal regulations attaching to marriage or registered partnership and who do not make their own living arrangement, with or without the help of a legal advisor. On the other hand, the justification for legal intervention can be found in the aspiration to provide fair and equitable regulation for the property relations governed by a marital agreement. In contrast to an ordinary civil contract, a marital agreement is typified by such features as long duration and the possible effects of the affective relationships between its parties on their choices. Persons in affective relationships often appear not to be able to foresee and properly accommodate in the marital contract all possible future developments that can negatively affect their respective property situation. Clearly, this will be an important issue in the future.

D   Conclusions

8.73   Over the last thirty years the increased impact of human rights on the legal system, generally, and on family law in particular, has been noteworthy in the Netherlands. In particular, Article 8 (the right to respect for private and family life) of the European Convention on Human Rights has had a significant effect and has led to greater recognition of those who were often ignored by child and family law in the past. In essence, Article 8 contains a whole code of family law and continues to exercise a considerable degree of influence upon the national judges and the legislature.

---

[66] *Ibid.*

[67] Act of 18 April 2011, State Gazette 2011, No. 205. The Act came into force on 1 January 2012.

However, other international conventions and treaties have also had an impact in Dutch law.

8.74   There have been many changes to Dutch family and child law over this time. It is to be expected that in the near future there will be more and more judge-made law because the legislature cannot respond to social change quickly enough.

8.75   In addition, while the Dutch government has tried to address the concerns of the various political, cultural and religious interest groups in this field, it is not easy to find a solution that is acceptable to people who want more state interventions in family life on the one hand, and those who do not wish any intervention at all on the other. Ultimately, a judge will have to make the decision.

8.76   General trends apparent in the Netherlands are the growing individualism with respect to partnership and relatives, but also more homogeneity with respect to parenthood, deinstitutionalisation of separation, divorce and parenthood. There is little doubt that new developments in family and child law will come soon, because appropriate solutions still need to be found on such issues as surrogate motherhood, inter-country adoption, the legal position of children and especially young migrants or the children of these migrants who have lived in the Netherlands for some time. Child protection must also be improved, whether the child's need arises from maltreatment, abuse or neglect. How to address the parents of these children is also an issue requiring attention.

8.77   Thanks to the open-mindedness of the Supreme Court, the lower courts and a modern legislature, the Netherlands' Family Code has become a modern law that can serve in this new century, at least for the coming years. Of course, this law does not reflect everyone's opinion, because some people and some (small) political parties think it is too modern and oppose, for example, same-sex marriage or permitting the adoption of a child by a same-sex couple. In addition, even a modern law cannot realise everyone's wishes and cannot end all painful situations nor find solutions to bad family relationships. It is the task of legal scholars, experts and judges to find proper solutions to improve the legal position of children and families.

9

New Zealand

The emergence of cultural diversity

BILL ATKIN

A   Introduction

9.1   Family law and social change go hand-in-hand. In the Western world, including New Zealand, the ideology of indissoluble marriage as the cornerstone of the law has long been overtaken by events that have their source in circumstances that go back many decades. The rehabilitation of many men who served in the Second World War took its toll on relationships and families. Subsequently, divorce became a reality for many and the stigma attaching to it slowly disappeared. More recently, the fact that large numbers of couples have lived together without getting married or doing so only after a period of cohabitation has led to a similar shift in attitudes, now extended to same-sex couples. The greater presence of women in the workforce, increased international travel, longer life expectancy and smaller families are all part of the modern social scene.

9.2   Some legal changes in New Zealand have been procedural, such as the setting up of the Family Court and the use of family group conferences. Others have been substantive: for example, easier divorce, the no-fault philosophy (but, despite this, greater provision to deal with domestic violence and child abuse), equal division of property, laws relating to de facto relationships, the creation of civil unions, the centrality of the welfare of the child to issues dealing with children, abolition of illegitimacy and a simplified system for financial child support. Most law reform has been piecemeal. The result has not always been coherent.[1] Enshrining some consistency may be one of the challenges for the future, but where we are dealing with human nature and personal relations, this may be

---

Special thanks to my research assistant, David Neild, for his excellent work.

[1] See further, Bill Atkin, 'Harmonising Family Law' (2006) 37 *Victoria University of Wellington Law Review* 465.

too much to hope for. Governments are more likely to take action when a pressing need arises.

9.3   A further challenge is the change in society that creeps up on us. As will become apparent in this chapter, one of the most significant themes for the future of family law in New Zealand is the emergence of cultural pluralism. This arises first and foremost in relation to the indigenous Maori, and then immigrant populations especially from the Pacific, India and China. The Western model can no longer be taken for granted. Even the open-textured welfare of the child principle may clash with some cultures. Flexibility rather than black-and-white rules may well have its merits in enabling diversity to be appropriately embraced.

Historical roots, sources and law reform

Historical roots

9.4   New Zealand has been the home of the indigenous Maori for many centuries. Most notably in the nineteenth century it was colonised by the British, although French settlers were also trying to gain a foothold. The critical date in the development of New Zealand's colonised history is 1840 when the Treaty of Waitangi was signed. This was an agreement between the Crown and most but not all of the Maori chiefs, ensuring a degree of self-determination for the latter and governance for the British. The interpretation of the Treaty and its legal status have been in dispute, but it ensured that the new colony drew primarily on the English common law rather than any other legal system. Rightly or wrongly, customary Maori law remained in the background.

9.5   In contrast to Maori culture, colonial law for a long time took its inspiration from Britain. Indeed, it was only in 2004 that New Zealand abolished appeals to the Privy Council and set up its own Supreme Court for final appeals.[2] Despite this, New Zealand was very progressive in developing its own personal laws.[3] Following a depression in the latter part of the nineteenth century, the first signs of a generous welfare state were put in place. New Zealand was the first British colony to provide

[2] Supreme Court Act 2003, with the first hearings of the Supreme Court able to occur from 1 July 2004.
[3] See B. D. Inglis *Family Law*, 2nd edn (Wellington: Sweet and Maxwell (NZ) Ltd, 1968), Volume 1, 5ff, for a fuller discussion.

for legal adoption[4] and it also enacted testator's family maintenance legislation,[5] now found in the Family Protection Act 1955. Following the Great Depression of the late 1920s and early 1930s, the welfare state was cemented in place and, despite attacks on it from time to time, it remains a feature of New Zealand family and social policy.

9.6   New Zealand has also had no-fault divorce since 1920,[6] although fault-based grounds also existed until finally abolished in 1980. Legislation passed in 1980 also set up the Family Court, now an entrenched part of family law in New Zealand.[7] In 1976 the Matrimonial Property Act was passed, introducing a form of deferred community property. In 2001 this Act, now called the Property (Relationships) Act 1976,[8] was extended to de facto relationships and more recently, since their creation by the Civil Union Act 2004, to civil unions. Inheritance laws also now cover de facto relationships and civil unions. New Zealand abolished illegitimacy in 1969, one of the first Commonwealth countries to do so.[9] Although some of these reforms were once controversial[10] and divided Parliament, there is now no suggestion in government circles of back-tracking on them.

9.7   By and large, the above snapshot of the history of the law in New Zealand indicates the prevalence of a progressive mind. Without a wealthy class or significant private resources for charitable giving, the Victorian laissez-faire philosophy was not going to meet the needs of the community. The high involvement of the state was over time inevitable, and in many respects remains so.

9.8   The colonial dominance of the law is also apparent in the snapshot of the law's development. This reflects the massive settlement that occurred after 1840 and at one point the near extinction of the Maori because of imported diseases. The prevalence of Western values may not persist, however. In the latter part of the twentieth century, Maori values and *tikanga* (ways of doing things) resurfaced in public policy and law reform, and remain crucial today. Central is the concept of the *whanau*, the Maori word for family but extending beyond parents to other generations and

---

[4] Adoption of Children Act 1881.
[5] Testator's Family Maintenance Act 1900.
[6] Divorce and Matrimonial Causes Amendment Act 1920.
[7] Family Courts Act 1980, in force 1 October 1981.
[8] This terminology was copied from some of the Australian states.
[9] Status of Children Act 1969, in force 1970.
[10] One leading commentator saw recent changes as 'social engineering': B. D. Inglis *New Zealand Family Law in the 21st Century* (Wellington: Thomson Brookers, 2007), p. 32.

to people such as siblings. It contrasts with the Western 'nuclear family'. Also important are *hapu*, loosely translated as sub-tribe, and *iwi* or tribe, along with *whakapapa* (genealogy and blood links), which are vital to a person's sense of well-being and belonging.

9.9 The Maori renaissance has already brought about changes in approach. The most notable example is the Children, Young Persons, and Their Families Act 1989, which deals with child abuse and youth offending. In large measure because of Maori lobbying, supported by pacific nation views, the 'family group conference' was introduced. These conferences have become the core element in dealing with issues where Maori are sadly over-represented in the statistics. The reality is that, like many Western nations, New Zealand is becoming much more ethnically mixed. The four largest ethnicities in New Zealand are European 67.6%, Maori 14.6%, Asian 9.2% and Pacific 6.9%.[11] While the Moslem population is small, religious issues are already surfacing in litigation. The motif of cultural pluralism is one to which we shall return.[12]

Sources

9.10 Parliamentary sovereignty is the basis of New Zealand's unwritten constitution. So legislation is the primary source of law, and family law is almost wholly statute-based. It is not possible for the courts to declare legislation to be unconstitutional. This is despite the existence of the New Zealand Bill of Rights Act 1990, which is based on the International Covenant on Civil and Political Rights. This Act contains basic freedoms and human rights, although it does not include a right to form a family or to marry. It cannot be invoked to overturn legislation that is inconsistent with its provisions but can be used in interpreting legislation.

9.11 Unsurprisingly, the courts are a major source of family law as they have to implement and construe legislation that is sometimes vague or by its very nature discretionary. The High Court retains inherent powers with respect to children and people with incapacities.[13] These powers are taken from the inherent jurisdiction of the English courts but are used rarely and only in residual situations.

---

[11] *2006 Census Data QuickStats About Culture and Identity* (Wellington: Statistics New Zealand, 2006), available at: www.stats.govt.nz/Census/2006CensusHomePage/ QuickStats/quickstats-about-a-subject.aspx.

[12] See, for example, paras. 9.34–9.35 (adoption), 9.41 (guardianship) and 9.49 (intra-family disputes) below.

[13] Judicature Act 1908, ss. 16 and 17.

9.12 Some international instruments such as the Hague Conventions on inter-country adoption and child abduction are incorporated into domestic legislation. The Hague Convention on Child Protection is under active consideration by the government and is likely to be incorporated in the near future.[14] New Zealand ratified the United Nations Convention on the Rights of the Child, which is contained in a schedule to the Children's Commissioner Act 2003. The courts regularly cite this Convention.

Law reform

9.13 The major law reform body is the Law Commission. While it has produced reports on family topics, its track record in getting legislation passed based on its proposals is not that great. A notable example is a report on adoption,[15] which has lain dormant for ten years.[16] The experience with inheritance law is similar, although a new Wills Act was passed in 2007 along with legislation on homicidal heirs. The bigger question of what to do with the Family Protection Act 1955 has been put to one side.[17]

9.14 The truth is that much family law reform owes its existence to other factors. In some instances an ad hoc inquiry will produce a report. This happened, for instance, with respect to relationship property[18] and assisted human reproduction.[19] The relevant government ministry, often the Ministry of Justice, will promote legislation either on its own initiative or on instructions from the Minister. In other instances the route to reform may be a lobby group or similar movement. The civil union legislation is an example of this, originally proposed by backbench Members of Parliament. Legislation allowing adult adopted persons to access information about their birth parents was also based on a Bill introduced into Parliament by an ordinary Member.[20]

---

[14] See para. 9.58 below.

[15] *Adoption and its Alternatives: A Different Approach and a New Framework* (Wellington: Report 65, Law Commission, 2000).

[16] See para. 9.32 below. [17] See para. 9.5 above.

[18] *Report of the Working Group on Matrimonial Property and Family Protection* (Department of Justice, Wellington, 1988).

[19] Report of the Ministerial Committee on Assisted Reproductive Technologies, *Assisted Human Reproduction Navigating Our Future* (Wellington: Department of Justice, 1994).

[20] Adult Adoption Information Act 1985.

Dispute resolution and access to legal services

9.15 The Family Court is the primary judicial decision-making body for New Zealand family cases. Its judges are specially appointed and, although they are officially District Court judges and sometimes do ordinary District Court work, they are in practice a separate judiciary, with their own ethos and Principal Judge. The jurisdiction of the Family Court has expanded over the years. It began with divorce and ancillary matters such as maintenance and custody. It shared property issues with the High Court. However, it has since added, among others, child abuse, mental health, family protection, wardship of the court, adult guardianship and property management for those with incapacities, and is now the originating court for all relationship property applications.

9.16 One result of the expansion of the Family Court's jurisdiction is that various areas of the law are awkwardly split between the Family Court and the 'superior' High Court. While some inheritance matters are heard in the Family Court, others, ostensibly of no greater difficulty, remain with the High Court. For example, most issues to do with wills must go to the High Court, while the significant power to award an overlooked family member a share of a deceased's estate is now usually heard by the Family Court.[21] Although going against tradition, there is surely a sound argument for giving the Family Court overall jurisdiction in inheritance matters. There is a similar awkwardness in relation to trusts. The Family Court can in effect reconstruct a family trust following the dissolution of a marriage or civil union,[22] but it lacks other powers such as appointing new trustees. For this, the parties must go to the High Court. In general, the Family Court is more accessible, more informal and less costly than the High Court. While its judgments are subject to appeal, in some significant areas it has survived the rigours of appellate oversight as well as or better than the High Court.

9.17 The status of the Court is another issue. There is still the unfortunate distinction between 'inferior' courts and 'superior' ones. Could the Family Court be severed from the District Court and made a court in its own right? An example of the problem in being an 'inferior' court relates to the law of contempt. While a District Court can punish for contempt in the face of the court,[23] it took a High Court judgment to

---

[21] Family Protection Act 1955, s. 3A.
[22] Family Proceedings Act 1980, s. 182.   [23] District Courts Act 1947, s. 112.

rule that the Family Court can also do so for failure to comply with a court order.[24] Other forms of contempt, for example outside the court, must go to the High Court.

9.18   One difficulty with reform of the status of the Family Court is that the line of appeals would need to be considered. Currently, appeals can go to the High Court, Court of Appeal and finally the Supreme Court. This is likely to be maintained. Suggestions of a separate division of the High Court to hear family appeals have not been taken up, but the idea of an appellate body consisting of one High Court judge and two Family Court judges could one day prove attractive.

9.19   The nature of Family Court hearings is changing. Originally, the emphasis was on informality. Now, a degree of formality has been brought back, for example with judges wearing gowns.[25] On the other hand, the traditional adversarial process remains relaxed. Latterly, a more inquisitorial approach to judging has emerged and much closer management of cases by the court.[26] One of the genuine motivations for this is to reduce waiting times for hearings. While delay is endemic in the court system, it is especially problematic for couples and children going through the trauma of a break-up. On the other hand, lawyers are less convinced that recent procedural changes are entirely warranted or thought through. The right to cross-examination is fundamental to the common law system of justice and in the context of criminal justice is spelt out in section 25 of the New Zealand Bill of Rights Act 1990. To what extent, some may ask, should family law procedures be divorced from others in the trial process?

9.20   Nevertheless, a formal hearing tends to be a last resort step and applications need not necessarily lead to court orders. The Family Court endeavours to resolve as many cases as possible without adjudication. From the Court's creation, the first port of call for most applicants has been counselling, arranged by the Court staff and paid for out of government funds.[27] This is often successful in helping parties to reach solutions that suit their circumstances, but if they cannot, the second stage until

---

[24] *KLP* v. *RSF [Contempt of court]* [2009] NZFLR 833. The case concerned an order about which school a child should attend.

[25] Family Courts Act 1980, s. 10(2), as amended in 2008.

[26] E.g. see Peter Boshier, 'Getting it right in the Family Court' (2010) 150 *New Zealand Lawyer* 10. The author is the Principal Family Court Judge.

[27] Family Proceedings Act 1980, s. 9ff.

recently has been a mediation conference chaired by a Family Court judge. The name may be a little misleading as the procedure is not genuine mediation but more like a settlement or pre-trial conference. In many respects, these conferences have fallen into disuse and in the meantime mediation by qualified mediators has been trialled. The story now becomes a little bizarre. In 2008 Parliament passed legislation placing mediation on a proper statutory basis[28] but, somewhat curiously, kept the mediation conference provisions, now thought to be largely redundant. Since then, following a change of government and the global recession, the new provisions have not been implemented. Despite this, the Principal Judge has introduced a new system for cases involving parenting issues. This is called the National Early Intervention Process and one of its surprising hallmarks is the use of lawyers as mediators. These lawyers are officially appointed as 'lawyers to assist the court', which is provided for in section 139 of the Care of Children Act 2004. The conventional understanding is that such lawyers are appointed for the purposes of the trial, for example where there is a novel point of law that would not otherwise be properly tested. This view is supported by section 139, which refers to the lawyer's right to cross-examine, a concept not relevant to mediation. Furthermore, only lawyers can be appointed under this system, not non-lawyer mediators. So, there are question marks over the scheme.

9.21   All this indicates that the scope of the Family Court, its powers and its allied decision-making procedures are in a considerable state of flux and this will doubtless continue. Despite the load on the Court, there are periodic calls for cost-cutting. This is most apparent in relation to legal aid, which of course allows access to civil justice for many people who would not otherwise be able to afford it, and also pays for the appointment of a lawyer for the child, regarded as vital for ensuring that the child's perspective is presented to the judge. Expenditure, style and jurisdiction thus remain as ongoing questions.

9.22   Two other critical points need to be made about the future of the Family Court. First, the Court's ethos and mode of resolution are not congruent with Maori *tikanga*.[29] While in some instances the Court hears a

---

[28] Family Proceedings Act 1980, s. 12Cff. and Care of Children Act 2004, s. 46Fff. See generally J. Caldwell, 'Developments in Dispute Resolution and Achieving Fairness in Property Division', in B. Atkin (ed.), *International Survey of Family Law 2009 Edition* (Bristol: Jordans, 2009), p. 355.

[29] John Te Manihera Chadwick, 'Whanaungatanga and the Family Court' (2002) 4 *Butterworths Family Law Journal* 91.

case on a *marae* (Maori meeting place), there is no power in the Care of Children Act 2004 to arrange for a family group conference, the model referred to above that is used for child abuse and youth justice.

9.23 Secondly, the secrecy of the Family Court has been criticised, especially by men's groups. In response to this, Parliament has allowed media representatives to attend Court hearings but, unless the Court grants leave, reports of cases involving children and vulnerable persons must not use names or identifying details. While the debate on this question has died for now, it may well resurface.

B Children in the family setting and state intervention

Defining and classifying children

9.24 The age of majority in New Zealand is 20. However, this is no longer of great practical significance. Instead, different ages apply for different purposes. Under the Care of Children Act 2004 a child is defined as a person under 18, consistent with the United Nations Convention on the Rights of the Child. By 16, the child can consent to medical procedures and can decide with whom to live.[30] A person can vote at 18 and can buy alcohol at the same age, but both of these are the subject of debate in the community. It is not impossible that the age for voting may go down while the age for buying alcohol goes up. A 15-year-old can drive a car. Child support (that is, financial assistance) is payable until the child turns 19, which is inconsistent with ages for other matters, but there is an argument that the age should actually be extended to cover tertiary education and training.[31]

9.25 Under the Children, Young Persons, and Their Families Act 1989, a person is a 'child' up to the age of 14 and a 'young person', to whom the youth justice provisions apply, is aged 14, 15 or 16. A proposal to bring this in line with the United Nations Convention by adding 17-year-olds to the definition of young person has languished in Parliament for five years.[32] The importance of the young person's age is that all but serious matters will be kept out of the ordinary criminal courts. Instead, the family group

---

[30] Care of Children Act 2004, ss. 36 and 34(2).

[31] The government recently asked for submissions on the question of age: Inland Revenue Department, *Supporting Children. A Government Discussion Document on Updating the Child Support Scheme* (Wellington: Policy Advice Divisions of Inland Revenue, 2011).

[32] Children, Young Persons, and Their Families Amendment Bill (No. 6) 2009.

conference model and the use of diversion (that is, diverted from the usual criminal procedures) are favoured and, where necessary, the specialist Youth Court will be involved. The risk in failing to make this change is that 17-year-olds get more deeply caught up in criminal lifestyle and then face the populist cry of retribution.

9.26   There is a good deal of inconsistency with respect to ages. This may be justifiable in some instances. For example, there is no reason to require minors to wait until they turn 18 before they get married or have a civil union. Given the wide-ranging concern about the drinking culture among young people, it is understandable that politicians are considering raising the age for the purchase of alcohol. However, there may be a need to look overall, rather than ad hoc, at the question of age and its consequences.

Recognising parentage and family ties

9.27   The underlying principle of the law relating to parentage is that the birth mother is prima facie a child's legal mother and her partner is the other legal parent. Two rules relate to this. First, there is a presumption that the mother's husband is the father of the child so long as the birth took place within ten months of the ending of the marriage either by dissolution or death.[33] This presumption can be rebutted by evidence and proof on the balance of probabilities. The presumption shows its datedness. It does not apply to the many couples who have children outside of marriage or those heterosexual couples who are in a civil union. Further, the ten-month rule, reflecting the common duration of a pregnancy, is out of place with the requirement that divorcing parties be separated for two years before obtaining a dissolution of their marriage. The Law Commission has recommended that the presumption be extended to civil unions and de facto relationships and that the test be whether the child was conceived during cohabitation.[34] There is no sign of this being implemented.

9.28   Secondly, where the birth is the result of an assisted human reproductive procedure such as donor insemination, the birth mother's partner, if consenting and whether male or female, is deemed to be the child's

---

[33] Status of Children Act 1969, s. 5.
[34] *New Issues in Legal Parenthood* (Wellington: Report 88, New Zealand Law Commission, 2005).

legal parent irrespective of the genetic reality.[35] This rule will often make sense and bypasses the need for an adoption. Arguably it is in the interests of the child to be legally recognised as the child of the couple who from the start intended to raise the child. Given New Zealand's non-discrimination laws, which include sexual orientation,[36] it would be inconsistent not to apply this rule to lesbian couples.

9.29   Yet there are two concerns with the rule. It means that legal parentage does not always coincide with genetic truth; a fiction is involved in these situations. Perhaps this is legally appropriate where there has been donation as a child can have no more than two legal parents.[37] However, this is not to say that genetic origins are to be ignored, a point especially true for the Maori, with their emphasis on *whakapapa* (ancestry).[38] The Human Assisted Reproductive Technology Act 2004 therefore provides for the recording of information about donation of semen, ova and embryos, including the name of the donor,[39] with accompanying rules on access. This policy of open information is a hallmark of the legislation, but a drawback is that it applies only after the Act came into force, leaving donor children born before then without access to information.

9.30   The second concern relates to surrogacy. The law is arguably suited to genuine cases of donation but it also applies to surrogacy, where it is ill-suited. Surrogacy is not outlawed, although commercial arrangements are.[40] Cases of altruistic surrogacy, where the genetic parents use in vitro fertilisation with a relative or friend, occur but in practice only after approval has been given by the Ethics Committee on Assisted Reproductive Technology. The assumption is that parentage will be regularised by adoption. Where the birth occurs overseas, commonly in Australia, it has been held that it is not necessary to invoke the Hague Convention on inter-country adoption.[41] This makes the process in New Zealand more straightforward but a simple procedure that transfers

---

[35]   *Ibid.*, Part 2. This law was first introduced in 1987 and amended in 2004.

[36]   Human Rights Act 1993, s. 21 and the New Zealand Bill of Rights Act 1990, s. 19.

[37]   The Law Commission recommended that a child with a 'known' donor should be able to have three legal parents: *New Issues in Legal Parenthood* (Wellington: Report 88, New Zealand Law Commission, 2005).

[38]   Report of the Ministerial Committee on Assisted Reproductive Technologies *Assisted Human Reproduction: Navigating Our Future* (Wellington: Department of Justice, 1994).

[39]   Human Assisted Reproductive Technology Act 2004, s. 37.

[40]   *Ibid.*, s. 14.

[41]   *In re adoption by L* [2003] NZFLR 529. See also *Re KJB and LRB [Adoption]* [2010] NZFLR 97.

parentage to the genetic parents so long as the Ethics Committee has approved would much better.

9.31   However, this is far from the end of the matter. Some jurisdictions allow commercial surrogacy and some also treat the commissioning couple automatically as the legal parents. The common situation is where the commissioning parties are also the child's genetic parents, but they could also be (for example) two men. Problems have arisen when the couple have wished to secure entry into New Zealand for the child or to immigrate to New Zealand. There are some major policy issues here: as already noted, commercial surrogacy is against New Zealand law. Should the bottom line be the welfare and best interests of the child even where this compromises other principles or should a wider view be taken, which considers the welfare of children in general? Currently, citizenship is being granted to the child by the relevant Minster on the basis of 'exceptional circumstances',[42] but this ad hoc approach can create uncertainty and better solutions need to be found.

9.32   We now come to the law on adoption. The principal piece of legislation is the Adoption Act 1955 with important companion Acts dealing with inter-country adoption and access to birth information.[43] The year of the Act indicates that it is from a different era, when adoption was a means of covering up births outside of marriage and of providing infertile couples with babies whom they could treat as 'their own'. Adoption practices and values have changed considerably. Many adoptions are inter-family or step-parent ones, and the policy of 'open' rather than 'secret' adoption has been implemented for over thirty years despite the lack of statutory backing for it. While an adoption must promote the child's interests, the child's welfare is not stated to be paramount.

9.33   Two recent judgments raise other questions about the 1955 Act. The first is *AMM* v. *KJO*,[44] which involved a step-parent adoption by two people who were in a de facto relationship. The child was born as a result of donor insemination and the genetic father was unknown. The couple began their relationship eighteen months after the boy's birth and had

---

[42] Citizenship Act 1977, s. 9(1)(c).

[43] Adoption (Intercountry) Act 1997 and Adult Adoption Information Act 1985.

[44] *Re Application by AMM* v. *KJO* [2010] NZFLR 629. See Nathan Crombie and Bill Atkin 'New meaning for historic term: de factos as "spouses" in new High Court ruling' (2010) 6 *New Zealand Family Law Journal* 313.

been bringing him up together for ten years. The Act expressly mentions only 'spouses' when referring to couples who may adopt. Although some Family Court decisions had allowed unmarried couples to adopt (in one case involving a customary Maori adoption[45] and another also involving assisted human reproduction[46]), not everyone was confident that this stated the law correctly. Yet, when the issue was referred to two High Court judges, they accepted that the adoption by the de facto couple could proceed. They were no doubt assisted by the Crown's concession that the law was discriminatory. The judges were careful to restrict their decision to heterosexual de facto partners. While logically civil union partners, a fortiori heterosexual ones, ought to have an even stronger argument to be able to adopt, the judges raised some doubts about this because, when it had the opportunity, Parliament had expressly declined to extend adoption to civil unions. De facto same-sex partners are also left in a state of limbo, despite the ability of one of them to adopt on their own.[47]

9.34   The second case also typifies twenty-first century trends: internationalisation and cultural pluralism. In *IS* v. *Attorney-General*,[48] two New Zealand citizens born in Pakistan and of Muslim faith had trouble conceiving their own child. In accordance with practice, friends in Pakistan agreed to give up their new-born son to the New Zealand couple and they entered into a joint deed of adoption. This was backed up by a Pakistani court order, which however referred to 'guardianship'. The child's birth certificate named the New Zealand couple as the parents but the boy had no inheritance rights. The New Zealand immigration authorities refused to accept the Pakistani procedure as creating an adoption recognisable under New Zealand law. Certainly, despite being permanent and exclusive, it fell short of an adoption order that would be made in New Zealand. Allan J nevertheless held that there had been an adoption valid according to Pakistani customary law. It could be recognised under section 17 of the Adoption Act 1955, the relevant section for recognising overseas adoptions that do not fall under the Hague Convention,[49] because, inter alia, section 17 placed adoptions in British Commonwealth countries in a special position.

---

[45] *Re Adoption by Paul and Hauraki* [1993] NZFLR 266.
[46] *In the matter of C [Adoption]* [2008] NZFLR 141.
[47] As happened in *Adoption Application by T* [2008] NZFLR 185.
[48] *IS* v. *Attorney-General [Adoption: Shariah Law]* [2011] NZFLR 145.
[49] Pakistan is not a contracting state for the purposes of the Convention.

9.35 The case is interesting for a variety of reasons. It takes account of a wider concept of adoption than is usually associated with the Adoption Act. Does this foreshadow that a broader approach is possible when New Zealand's adoption laws are finally brought up to date? The Maori have a system of customary adoption not unlike that which was used by the parties in this case, called *whangai*, yet it is not recognised by the law expect for a few marginal purposes. If New Zealand can accept an adoption based on Pakistani custom, can it not do so with respect to *whangai*? The case also illustrates an anomaly: if the parties had been from a Muslim country that was not part of the Commonwealth, the judge's reasoning would not have prevailed. Does this not suggest that the whole question of the recognition of overseas adoptions needs to be carefully re-examined? Many instances of such recognition relate to people from Pacific nations. Whether *IS* applies may depend on the precise nature of the procedures followed and in some cases whether the country belongs to the Commonwealth. Adoption reform needs to occur but, when in power, politicians have not treated it as high priority.

Delivering parenting

9.36 The law relating to parenting was substantially reformed by the Care of Children Act 2004. This Act does not deal with all aspects of parenting: child abuse and neglect are dealt with in the Children, Young Persons, and Their Families Act 1989, where the underlying principles and procedures are very different.

Guardianship

9.37 The central concept in the 2004 Act is that of guardianship. Guardians have prime responsibility for the child's upbringing.[50] This will usually include day-to-day care unless by agreement or court order this has been determined otherwise.[51] While certain rights go with guardianship, the 2004 Act shifted the emphasis from rights to responsibilities. Thus, guardians should contribute 'to the child's intellectual, emotional, physical, social cultural and other personal development' and determine 'for or with the child, or [help] the child to determine,

---

[50] Care of Children Act 2004, ss. 16 and 17. Contrariwise, s. 13 of the Children, Young Persons, and Their Families Act 1989 vests this responsibility in the family, *whanau*, family group, etc.

[51] See para. 9.48 below.

questions about important matters affecting the child'. 'Important matters' include name, residence and travel, medical treatment, education, and 'the child's culture, language, and religious denomination and practice'.

9.38   While a child's legal parents are usually both guardians, this is not always so, and others may also become guardians. Except where there has been an adoption, the birth mother will always be a guardian.[52] The father will be a guardian if he was married to or in a civil union with the mother during the period of pregnancy. Likewise, a father will be a guardian if he was the mother's de facto partner during pregnancy. Fathers will also be guardians where their name is on the birth certificate or where they have been appointed by the court. In the latter situation, the court must make an appointment unless this would be against the child's welfare and best interests. The effect of these rules is that very few fathers will not be guardians.

9.39   The court can appoint another party as an additional guardian, and this is especially appropriate where that person is doing the primary parenting. This may occur where, for instance, grandparents are looking after their grandchild or, to use the Maori word, *mokopuna*. Foster parents may also obtain guardianship but, if the child has been abused, it is more likely that the appointment will be made under the Children, Young Persons, and Their Families Act 1989. A person can appoint someone a testamentary guardian in their will, but this does not give the appointee an automatic right to have the child on a day-to-day basis. An innovative procedure in the 2004 Act is the appointment of a step-parent as a guardian without having to obtain a court order.[53] This is a recognition of the phenomenon of family break-up and re-formation, but there are no statistics on how often the procedure has been used. It depends on everyone's agreement and the appointee must have shared responsibility for the child for at least a year. Finally, the Family Court or the High Court (which also has inherent powers in this respect) can take over guardianship of a child, usually for a specific purpose such as health decisions (for example, blood transfusions refused by the parents for religious reasons).[54] In a controversial decision, a High Court judge

---

[52] Care of Children Act 2004, ss. 17–29.
[53] Esther J. Watt, 'The DIY Procedure for Appointing Step-Parents as Additional Guardians' (2006) 5 *New Zealand Family Law Journal* 118.
[54] *Re J (An Infant): B and B* v. *Director-General of Social Welfare* [1996] 2 NZLR 134.

held that an unborn child who, it was thought, was to be filmed for the purposes of pornography could be the subject of a wardship order.[55]

9.40   Under section 16(5) of the Care of Children Act 2004, it is stated that a guardian must act jointly with any other guardians. This seems to rule out unilateral guardianship decisions but the full impact of the 'joint action' rule is muddied by some additional words that appear in brackets: 'in particular, by consulting, wherever practicable, with the aim of securing agreement'. Does this mean that consultation is enough? Does it mean that a guardian can act alone where consultation fails to reach agreement or where another guardian holds a different view? The point has not been tested in any case law but it is important for everyone concerned to know whether a unilateral decision is valid, all the more so where the parents of a child have separated.

9.41   As has been pointed out in one judgment,[56] the language used to describe guardianship reflects the landmark decision of the House of Lords in *Gillick* v. *West Norfolk and Wisbech Area Health Authority*,[57] where it was held that a child with the appropriate level of understanding and maturity can make certain decisions without parental consent (in that case, a decision about contraception but the principles are of much wider application). The New Zealand legislation does not go as far as *Gillick*, but does incorporate the idea that a guardian's role gradually transforms from one of heavy control to one that is more supportive than controlling. It would of course be helpful if the legislation were more specific in relation to decision-making. It is specific in relation to medical, dental and surgical procedures for children aged 16 and over: under section 36 they can consent or refuse to consent as if of full age. Also, a girl of any age can consent to an abortion under section 38 (irrespective of whether she has the necessary degree of competence required under *Gillick*). The lack of clear legislative guidance on other matters leaves some agencies in doubt about what to do. For example, when a school organises a trip away, can a 15-year-old provide the necessary consent or must the guardians also do so? May the guardians veto the child's wishes and vice versa? A school trip is less significant than major surgery but nevertheless is a matter where the school is expected to follow proper practice. To take another education example, how are schools to cope with pupils whose parents disagree

---

[55] *Re an Unborn Child* [2003] 1 NZLR 115.

[56] *Hawthorne* v. *Cox* [2008] 1 NZLR 409, per Heath J at para. [59].

[57] [1986] AC 112.

over religious practices such as what to wear? Tensions in this area are likely only to increase with cultural pluralism and a rights-based rhetoric becoming entrenched.

9.42   It is unlikely that there will be legislation to solve these problems. This may be inevitable. To an extent, we can only speculate what tensions will arise in the future and they may be better left for the courts to handle on a case-by-case basis.

Discipline

9.43   Another area that may be the subject of ongoing debate is child discipline. What powers do guardians have when their young child runs amok in the supermarket, or their older child is over-indulging in alcohol or drugs? The latter situation sits awkwardly to the notion that the guardianship role becomes supportive rather than controlling as the child gets older. The former is a little clearer. Section 59 of the Crimes Act 1961 used to allow caregivers a defence to a charge of assault if reasonable force was used for the purposes of correction. Despite massive hostility, Parliament abolished this right of corporal punishment in 2007 by 113 votes to 8.[58] At the same time, it inserted a new section 59 with the heading 'parental control':

(1)   Every parent of a child and every person in the place of a parent of the child is justified in using force if the force used is reasonable in the circumstances and is for the purpose of –
   (a)   preventing or minimising harm to the child or another person; or
   (b)   preventing the child from engaging or continuing to engage in conduct that amounts to a criminal offence; or
   (c)   preventing the child from engaging or continuing to engage in offensive or disruptive behaviour; or
   (d)   performing the normal daily tasks that are incidental to good care and parenting.
(2)   Nothing in subsection (1) or in any rule of common law justifies the use of force for the purpose of correction.

9.44   While the precise interpretation of some of these provisions may be open to question, the overall goal is clear: children should not be beaten

[58]   In general, see B. Wood, I. Hassall and G. Hook, *Unreasonable Force: New Zealand's Journey Towards Banning the Physical Punishment Of Children* (Wellington: Save the Children, 2008).

or spanked as a form of punishment. Instead, alternative methods of discipline must be learned and used. While certain parts of the community wish to bring back corporal punishment and will doubtless continue to be vociferous, it is predicted that there will be no retrenchment on this issue.[59]

Child support

9.45   One of the major consequences of legal parentage is financial support. The Child Support Act 1991 largely followed an Australian model, replacing agreements and court orders with a formulaic system administered through the tax department. The formula is based on taxable income, taking into account the number of children and the liable parent's dependants. Adjustments are made for shared and split custody of children. A modification of the formula, either to raise or lower the amount to be paid, can be obtained by means of a 'departure'.

9.46   When it came into force, the law caused an unprecedented amount of litigation as existing arrangements were upset. Only the Family Court could grant a departure, now changed so that review officers appointed by the tax department make the initial decision. Antagonism towards the scheme remains, and even at governmental level it is recognised that reform is needed. Various social changes have occurred that have led to the distribution of a discussion paper. Among the changes are the greater prevalence of shared parenting agreements and orders[60] and the greater participation of mothers in the workforce: the recipient parent's income is not taken into account in the formula.

9.47   Australia has substantially changed its scheme and it is this model that New Zealand is again looking to. In future, the formula is likely to be related to the costs of bringing up children, with an acknowledgment that teenagers cost more than younger children. The contribution that each parent makes directly to the care of the child will be factored into the

---

[59]   A Bill by a right-wing MP was rejected by 115 votes to 5 on its first appearance in Parliament on 8 September 2010: Crimes (Reasonable Parental Control and Correction) Amendment Bill.

[60]   Although they remain a clear minority of court orders: most day-to-day care orders favour the mother or the father alone. Shared orders (mother and father) are about 10 per cent. See, *Family Court Statistics: An Overview of Family Court Statistics in New Zealand 2004 to 2008* (Wellington: Ministry of Justice, 2010), available at: www.justice.govt. nz/publications/global-publications/f/family-court-statistics-an-overview-of-family-court-statistics-in-new-zealand-2004-to-2008/publication.

scheme in a much more comprehensive way, and the income of both parties will be used in the formula. At this stage there are no proposals to make the welfare of the child a core principle, the absence of which not only is contrary to the United Nations Convention on the Rights of the Child but also fails to integrate the child support scheme into the canon of family law. The Maori perspective on families is totally absent from the current scheme. Other issues that ought to be tackled properly are the ease with which agreements on financial support can be obviated by applying for child support, and the ability of the self-employed to get round the scheme by recording low taxable incomes.

Intra-family disputes

9.48   Disputes can arise over guardianship issues such as which school a child should attend. A child who has reached the age of 16 can challenge a guardianship decision in the Family Court, but this rarely happens.[61] Far more common are disputes about parenting orders where the parents have separated. These orders may determine who has 'day-to-day care', whether it is one person alone or with others, and who has 'contact'.[62] The Care of Children Act 2004 revised the terminology, eschewing the old terms 'custody' and 'access' but retaining 'guardianship'.[63] Contact can take various forms, including visitation and electronic means. Under section 49 an applicant must set out how other people are going to be involved. The subtext of this is that both parents should normally play a part in the child's ongoing life.

9.49   Parents, guardians and step-parents (whether married or not) have an automatic right to apply for an order.[64] A member of the child's 'family, whanau, or other culturally recognised family group' may also apply but must be granted leave by the court. 'Other culturally recognised family group' is unlimited but particularly has in mind Pacific populations: for example the Samoan *aiga*, which is similar to *whanau*. Non-Western cultures including Maori are therefore acknowledged but in a grudging way. Overall, the Care of Children Act assumes the Western 'nuclear family'

---

[61] Care of Children Act 2004, s. 44 (disputes between guardians) and s. 46 (review sought by child).

[62] Care of Children Act 2004, s. 47.

[63] The Child Support Act 1991 and the Children, Young Persons, and Their Families Act 1989 retain the old terms.

[64] Care of Children Act 2004, s. 48.

as the standard parenting arrangement. There is a final category of applicants: 'any other person granted leave to apply by the Court'. Again, there is the hurdle of obtaining leave, but it does enable others with an interest in the child's life to seek an order in appropriate cases.

9.50   As discussed above,[65] mechanisms exist to help parties resolve their differences. A hearing thus occurs only in a small minority of cases. In any event, the paramount consideration is the welfare and best interests of the child.[66] Misconduct is relevant only in so far as it affects welfare and best interests[67] and there is no principle that a parent should be favoured because of his or her sex. The Care of Children Act innovatively gives more guidance on how to understand welfare and best interests. It must be assessed in relation to the child's particular circumstances and take account of the child's 'sense of time'. Six further principles are listed, summarised as follows:

(a) primary responsibility for the child resting with parents and guardians, who are 'encouraged' to agree on arrangements;
(b) continuity, including stable relationships with family, family group, *whanau*, *hapu* and *iwi*;
(c) ongoing consultation and cooperation between the relevant parties;
(d) preservation and strengthening of relationships between child and family, *whanau*, and so on;
(e) the child's safety;
(f) the child's identity.

9.51   According to the Chief Justice, these principles 'are important legislative reminders to decision-makers (parents, guardians, and courts) of the context in which the paramount consideration of the welfare and best interests of the particular child must be considered'.[68] She points out that the principles 'are not entirely distinct' and overlap.

9.52   The paramountcy consideration needs to be put alongside another core concept: the views of the child as found in section 6. The 2004 Act replaced 'wishes' with 'views', regarded as wider because a child's views may not be as clearly articulated as wishes. Section 6 also makes no reference to the child's age and maturity, which appeared in the old law, and

---

[65] See para. 9.20 above.
[66] Care of Children Act 2004, ss. 4 and 5.
[67] For example, where there has been abuse: see para. 9.59 below.
[68] *Kacem* v. *Bashir* [2010] NZFLR 884, para. [5]; [2011] 2 NZLR 1.

thus the views of a young and immature child should be obtained and taken into account as well as that of an older more mature child. Needless to say, the court is not bound by what the child says. If the child's views clash with his or her welfare and best interests, the latter must prevail.

9.53 The application of the paramountcy principle is not always easy and often involves an inherent lack of predictability. Yet the Supreme Court does not necessarily lament this: '[t]he difficulties which are said to beset the field are not conceptual or legal difficulties, they are inherent in the nature of the assessments which the court must make.'[69] It is all part of judging. There are, however, some situations that can be especially problematic and will continue to be so.

9.54 First, what about the violent parent? Under the current law, a party who is proven to have used physical and sexual violence against a child or partner can be granted unsupervised contact only if it is shown that the child will be safe.[70] Legislation recently enacted extends this to the situation where there is a protection order made against the party. A protection order is made under the Domestic Violence Act 1995, and typically in favour of a victimised woman against her spouse or partner. The grounds for a protection order include 'psychological abuse', which was not included in the Care of Children Act provisions before. Psychological abuse is therefore now indirectly relevant to Care of Children Act cases under the legislation just passed. Domestic violence has been a contemporary theme of family law and this will doubtless continue.

9.55 Secondly, do the parents have any prior rights over non-parents? The short answer is 'no' because the paramountcy principle must not be compromised.[71] However, there are forces in the community that resist any constraints on parents and employ matching rhetoric. The tension between the roles of parents and the state, not to mention the Maori perspective, which gives centre stage to the *whanau* rather than to the parents, will remain.

9.56 Thirdly, what about the parent who wants to relocate, either to somewhere in New Zealand or to an overseas country? Increased mobility is a

---

[69] *Ibid.*, para. [35].
[70] Care of Children Act 2004, ss. 58–62.
[71] *K* v. *G* [2004] NZFLR 1105, where a 7-year-old child had been with the mother's cousin since he was 14 months old because of a violent early upbringing. The parents, claiming to have sorted out their difficulties, sought to get their son back, but the High Court upheld the Family Court decision that he should remain where he was.

feature of contemporary life. For New Zealanders, coming from a far-off island nation, travel usually involves distance, sometimes to the other side of the world. Where families are separated, these issues can be especially fraught. Relocation has been a constant theme in the courts and contrasting attitudes are taken, as pointed out by the Supreme Court: some people consider relocation should generally be approved, others that it should not.[72] On the one hand, returning to take advantage of wider family support may make life more accommodating for the primary caregiver. On the other hand, this would for the most part cut the other parent out of the child's life. As already noted, the Care of Children Act now contains the principle of continuity (principle (b) above),[73] joint guardianship and shared parenting orders. Nevertheless, the Supreme Court held that principle (b) does not give any priority to the maintenance of links with both parents and there is certainly no presumption one way or the other when determining relocation cases. The facts of the Supreme Court case are redolent of so many situations arising today. In *Kacem*[74] the father and his first wife fled from Algeria and were interned for several years in a detention centre in Australia. The father met another woman when she was visiting the centre and they underwent an Islamic marriage ceremony. Despite using false passports, they were granted refugee status in New Zealand, but this second 'marriage' ran into strife and was dissolved according to Islamic tradition. There had been two children and the second 'wife' wished to return to Australia where the rest of her family lived. Relocation was denied and a shared parenting arrangement upheld. Religion, ethnicity, cultural diversity, divorce, family conflict, the value of the wider families of both parties – these and other features of the case are likely to be replicated more and more.

9.57   Fourthly, there is the endemic problem of international child abduction, which again is more likely to be exacerbated than curtailed in the twenty-first century. Through its adoption of the Hague Convention, New Zealand is part of an international effort to address the problem. The Convention is a gloss on the paramountcy principle, but only in the sense that New Zealand forfeits jurisdiction in favour of the welfare decision being made by a more appropriate forum. Nevertheless, the welfare of the child still played a role in the leading New Zealand decision on the Convention, *Secretary for Justice* v. *HJ*.[75] The mother had abducted two

---

[72] *Kacem* v. *Bashir* [2010] NZFLR 884, para. [36]; [2011] 2 NZLR 1.
[73] See para. 9.50 above.
[74] *Kacem* v. *Bashir* [2010] NZFLR 884, paras. [13]–[15]; [2011] 2 NZLR 1.
[75] [2007] 2 NZLR 289.

children from Australia but they had been settled in New Zealand for over a year, meaning that return to Australia was not obligatory. The majority held that the outcome turned on a balancing of the welfare of the child and the purpose of the Convention. If the child's welfare did not favour return, then some other feature such as concealment of the whereabouts of the child would clearly have to outweigh the welfare assessment. On the facts, the children stayed in New Zealand.

9.58   A companion to the abduction convention is the Hague Convention on Child Protection.[76] The New Zealand government has already received positive feedback on the Convention and is likely to implement it in the next couple of years. This may well herald further efforts to resolve family issues on bilateral[77] and international bases.

Child protection and state intervention

9.59   As already mentioned, the Children, Young Persons, and Their Families Act 1989 deals with child protection issues. It contains powers for state officials such as social workers and the police to intervene to protect children at risk. Reporting of child abuse is not mandatory despite calls for this to occur from time to time. Many of the main agencies and professions, such as those in the education sector, have protocols that set out a process for suspected abuse and so many instances are notified without a legal obligation to do so. Where the environment is especially risky, there are urgent powers under which a child can be removed instantly.

9.60   In marked contrast to the rest of family law, the family group conference is the centrepiece of the law. The family group or *whanau* has the primary task of deciding what should happen to an abused child and the Family Court's role is residual. Unlike earlier days, priority is given to the placement of a child within the wider family and professionals assist rather than determine outcomes.

9.61   The system is widely regarded as an appropriate one, especially conducive to the Maori and Pacific communities who are over-represented in the statistics for child abuse. Maori represent roughly half of child abuse

[76] Hague Convention on Jurisdiction, Applicable Law, Recognition, Enforcement and Co-operation in Respect of Parental Responsibility and Measures of Child Protection.

[77] For example, the Trans-Tasman Proceedings Act 2010 streamlines proceedings in general that have New Zealand and Australian elements.

reports.[78] The basic structure of the scheme is unlikely to be changed and, in due course, may well find its way into other areas of decision-making such as child care on separation, care of citizens lacking capacity and alcohol and drug abusers.[79] There may, however, be refinements, in particular greater control by tribal and similar bodies. Already, a programme called *Whanau Ora* has been instituted by which funding and responsibility for various social services have been delegated to Maori organisations.

9.62   There have long been provisions in the general criminal law that can be applied to home violence. However, until fairly recently such situations were low priority for the police and the value of family privacy ranked more highly. This was especially true of partner abuse. Today, the tables have turned and these cases are treated very seriously. In a review of crimes against the person, the Law Commission has recommended that the criminal law relating to ill-treatment and neglect of children and vulnerable victims be strengthened.[80] The main offence would be changed to raise the upper age of children from under 16 to under 18, and the maximum penalty from five to ten years' imprisonment. The current test of wilfulness will be expanded to cover situations where the caregiver has been grossly negligent. In other words an objective test is proposed. The Commission advocates the test of '[a person] living in the same household [who] knows that there is a risk to a child (or vulnerable adult) but fails to take reasonable steps to prevent it'. Unlike the 1989 Act, the criminal law requires proof of guilt. This is not always possible, especially where family members refuse to cooperate with investigators.[81]

---

[78] In a speech Paula Bennett, Minister of Social Development, claimed: 'Of the nearly 21,000 of substantiated cases of neglect and abuse 11,003 were Maori and four died.' See www.beehive.govt.nz/speech/iwi-leaders-meeting; also see the following Child Youth and Family report: www.beehive.govt.nz/sites/all/files/CYF_Why_you_should_care.pdf.

[79] Nevertheless, a very recent Law Commission report entitled *Compulsory Treatment for Substance Dependence* (Wellington: Report 118, New Zealand Law Commission, 2010) makes no recommendations about family or *whanau* involvement. Instead it follows a heavily medical model with the Family Court fulfilling a secondary role.

[80] *Review of Part 8 of the Crimes Act 1961: Crimes against the Person* (Wellington: Report 111, New Zealand Law Commission, 2009), Chapter 5. See now ss. 195 and 195A Crimes Act 1961, added in 2011.

[81] This happened in a high-profile case where two twin babies died. The father, Chris Kahui, was acquitted and nobody else was charged. The inquest into the death was held in the middle of 2011, but at the time of writing no coroner's report had been released and there was talk of a legal challenge to the investigation: www.stuff.co.nz/national/6139931/ Legal-challenge-looms-in-Kahui-case (last accessed 20 March 2012). The coroner has called for legal duties on health professionals to report child abuse: www.stuff.co.nz/ national/4298426/Backing-for-child-abuse-reporting-call (last accessed 20 March 2012).

C   Adult relationships

The relationships

9.63   New Zealand law recognises marriage, civil unions and 'de facto relationships' (the legal term used). Customary Maori marriages are not recognised as legal marriages and are thus treated as de facto relationships.

Entering an adult relationship

9.64   The minimum age of marriage or civil union is 16, but parental consent is required up to the age of 18.[82] An underage marriage or one without consent is nevertheless valid but a civil union, somewhat incongruously, is not. Children aged 16 and 17 years old can also obtain parental consent to enter a de facto relationship, required for some purposes such as making a will.[83] Marriage is restricted to opposite-sex couples,[84] but civil unions are open to both opposite-sex and same-sex couples. There was considerable debate about homosexuality when the Civil Union Act 2004 was before Parliament, but that has since largely died away. While same-sex marriage is likely one day, there is no strong call for it in the immediate future. One of the reasons is that gay and lesbian couples can avail themselves of virtually all the benefits of marriage anyway.

9.65   Bigamy is still a serious offence and renders a marriage (or civil union) void. However, there is no such restriction on de facto relationships, and nothing to stop a married person contemporaneously having one or more de facto partners.

Consequences of relationships

9.66   New Zealand prohibits discrimination on the grounds of marital status and sexual orientation,[85] so for most purposes the different kinds of relationships are treated the same. Thus, the rules on inheritance and *inter vivos* property transactions are largely identical for all forms of relationship.

---

[82] The Family Court has a residual power to consent.
[83] Care of Children Act 2004, s. 46A. On wills, see the Wills Act 2007, ss. 6 and 9 and the Interpretation Act 1999, s. 29A.
[84] *Quilter* v. *Attorney-General* [1998] 1 NZLR 523.
[85] Human Rights Act 1993, s. 21 and the New Zealand Bill of Rights Act 1990, s. 19.

9.67   There are occasional exceptions. For example, the presumption of parenthood applies only to marriage.[86] However, with the reliability of DNA evidence, the practical effect of the presumption may be minimal. A marriage or civil union causes the automatic revocation of a prior will unless it was made in contemplation of the marriage or union.[87] This does not apply to de facto partners.

9.68   The coalescence of the law raises the question of why marriage is still retained as a legal institution. It retains important social and religious functions and some people may like the official seal of approval that comes with legal registration. However, for most practical purposes it is no longer of legal significance domestically.

Termination of relationships

9.69   Under New Zealand law, a marriage or civil union can be dissolved after the parties have lived apart for two years.[88] In general, divorce is a formality and will often be the result of a joint application. While there is no move at the moment to shorten the period, by the end of the 2010s it may well be either one year or six months. De facto relationships end at the will of the parties and there is no process for recording this. As the date of cessation may be important for property division purposes – usually a relationship has to have lasted three years to come within the statutory division scheme – the recording of the date of separation could be wise and one can envisage an official system for this to happen. However, it is probably expecting too much of most people to be aware of such a system and take advantage of this.

Consequences of termination

9.70   Divorce is no longer the significant event it once was. The two-year waiting period means that most of the ancillary issues will have been sorted out already. While there are some legal consequences, such as the freedom to enter a subsequent marriage or civil union and the voiding of testamentary gifts to the former partner,[89] most laws operate from the date of separation. Those laws that call for comment relate to financial issues.

---

[86] See para. 9.27 above.   [87] Wills Act 2007, s. 18.
[88] Family Proceedings Act 1980, s. 39.   [89] Wills Act 2007, s. 19.

Property

9.71   New Zealand has a form of property division that is loosely described as a regime of 'deferred community'. This means that the property of the relationship (or community) is divided equally but this is 'deferred' until the parties separate. The regime has been in place for three-and-a-half decades but was revised in 2001 when de facto partners and widowed parties were incorporated.[90] Also included as part of that revision is a new power for the court to grant compensation for 'economic disparity', where it is likely that one party's future income and living standards will be significantly less than the other party's as a result of the relationship.

9.72   The equal division rule applies only to 'relationship property' and not to 'separate property'. The former includes the home and chattels, along with other items that have been acquired during the relationship, including pension rights. The latter includes property owned before the relationship and other acquisitions such as gifts and bequests that are personal. The division rule is subject to two exceptions but they are narrow: where the parties lived together for less than three years and where there are 'extraordinary circumstances that make equal sharing … repugnant to justice'.[91]

Economic disparity

9.73   While for many couples the property system works well, there are inevitably matters that present problems. First, economic disparity compensation in effect creates an unequal split, although its aim is to ensure equality in a much wider sense. The person, usually the woman, who has given up a career to assist the other party and care for the children may be left considerably disadvantaged as far as earning capacity is concerned. Yet will it always be clear that this is because of the relationship? And how exactly is the level of compensation to be calculated? The leading Court of Appeal decision has given some guidance on quantum, but it uses a reasonably complex formula that, at least in big money cases, necessitates the advice of actuarial experts.[92]

---

[90]   Property (Relationships) Act 1976. See B. Atkin and W. Parker, *Relationship Property in New Zealand*, 2nd edn (Wellington: LexisNexis, 2009).

[91]   Property (Relationships) Act 1976, ss. 13–14A.

[92]   *X* v. *X [Economic disparity]* [2010] 1 NZLR 601.

9.74   The issue of ongoing financial support is one that may become
more acute in times of recession, unemployment and welfare cutbacks.
While New Zealand's welfare state is still reasonably extensive, payments
inevitably leave recipients and their children hovering around the poverty
line. The division of relationship property and even a generous award of
economic disparity provide only a partial solution. The laws on maintenance found in the Family Proceedings Act 1980 are based on the claimant's reasonable needs and are designed to be transitional. Only in a few
situations will they provide a solution to the demand for ongoing support,
all the more so where the payer has begun a new family and acquired
fresh financial obligations. This is doubtless an area that will continue to
be fraught.

Trusts

9.75   Secondly, in many instances family property has been diverted to
family trusts, and for most this means that it is outside the scope of the
property that can be divided equally. One estimate is that there could be
as many as 600,000 family trusts, an enormous number given the size of
the country. It was noted above that the respective jurisdictions of the
Family Court and the High Court need to be rationalised with respect
to trusts. The deeper and much more troubling issue is the substantive
one: should the trust law principles be thwarted in the interests of justice under the property division regime? Should family law trump trust
law or vice versa? Already, the court has power to award compensation
where the disposition of relationship property to a trust effectively defeats
a party's claim under the 1976 Act.[93] The anomalous and anachronistic
section 182 of the Family Proceedings Act 1980 allows the court to make
orders with respect to ante-nuptial and post-nuptial settlements. The
Supreme Court[94] has confirmed that this can be used in relation to family
trusts, even allowing the court to restructure the trust itself (in the case,
a trust was divided into two 'mirror trusts', basically one for each party).
However, section 182 can be invoked only where a marriage or civil union
has been dissolved and thus has no application on separation or at the end
of a de facto relationship. It is foreshadowed that the interaction of relationship property laws and trusts will be a battleground in future.[95]

---

[93]   Property (Relationships) Act 1976, s. 44C.
[94]   *Ward* v. *Ward* [2010] 2 NZLR 31.
[95]   The Law Commission has a project on trusts: see in particular *Some Issues with the Use of
Trusts in New Zealand* (Wellington: Issues Paper 20, Law Commission, 2010).

Negative equity

9.76   Thirdly, how does the law deal with indebtedness? The 1976 Act contains provisions in relation to debts, classifying them as either 'relationship' or 'personal' ones. However, in an age of recession the novel problem of negative equity has arisen: that is, where the parties' debts outweigh their positive property. There is no explicit jurisdiction for the court to decide these cases, although some imaginative judges have pragmatically assumed jurisdiction. It is predicted that similar issues will arise in the future.

Interests of children

9.77   Finally, brief reference should be made to a wider tension in the financial area, that of the potential clash between the interests of partners and those of children. Where a child is still dependent, the interests of the child and the caregiver will often coincide. Questions about income maintenance and child support have already been discussed.[96] Security of accommodation may also be relevant, but where there is shared parenting, this usually means two homes, not one, that have to be paid for. Where the child is no longer dependent, a different set of tensions arises especially where one of the parties has died. Here the relationship property laws can run into conflict with inheritance laws, and the situation is exacerbated where the children are from an earlier relationship. Who should get priority in this situation and how should the balance between the competing claims be determined? The Western tradition tends to favour the surviving partner, while, as we have seen, the Maori perspective is much more communal. There are issues here that may become keener as the population ages.

Self-regulation and custom-made relationships

9.78   In an age of individual self-determination, family law tends to be fairly prescriptive. While parties are encouraged to reach their own solutions to disputed matters, this must be done with the legal framework in mind. The main exception to this is contracting out of the relationship property scheme.[97] This can occur at any stage. Pre-nuptial agreements are accepted, as are agreements during the course of cohabitation. The

---

[96] See paras. 9.73 (income disparity) and 9.45–9.47 (child support) above.
[97] Property (Relationships) Act 1976, Part 6.

latter may be motivated by tax advantages. Agreements at the end of a relationship are more by way of settlement.

9.79   An agreement is subject to the ordinary law of contract, but more commonly parties will invoke a special power enabling the court to set aside an agreement on the grounds of serious injustice. The word 'serious' was added in 2001 to emphasise the binding nature of agreements. The leading case on this relates to an agreement entered when the parties were reconciling after a separation.[98] The husband made the agreement a condition of the reconciliation but the parties again separated for a final time. Despite the pressure on the wife, the Court of Appeal upheld the agreement. Further changes to the law in this are unlikely.

D   Conclusions

9.80   New Zealand has often been in the vanguard of family law reform. The reform process continues unabated and more can be expected in the future. Some changes have already been foreshadowed in various quarters. Others are speculative but social trends help to point the way.

9.81   The Family Court has been in existence for thirty years and remains the rock on which family disputes are resolved. A full mediation system will be implemented when public finances permit and the search for effective procedures to streamline court hearings will continue. The recession will make legal aid less available and less lucrative for lawyers, but representation for children will not be diminished. The jurisdiction of the Family Court may be extended, with new powers over substance abusers, and quite possibly over wills and trusts. The interplay of family relations and trust law will be a matter for considerable debate, and wider inheritance law reforms may occur.

9.82   Child support law will be reformed and there will be legislation to enact the Hague Convention on Child Protection.[99] Calls for adoption reform will eventually be heeded and the advances of medical science in areas such as reproduction will throw up fresh challenges. Same-sex marriage is likely but not immediately foreseen, and the two-year waiting period for divorce may be shortened. Child and partner abuse are volatile subjects, but they capture the imagination of politicians. We can

---

[98]   *Harrison* v. *Harrison* [2005] 2 NZLR 349.
[99]   See para. 9.58 above.

predict further advances in both the civil and the criminal law to tackle the endemic problems of home violence.

9.83   These are some of the specific changes that may happen. At a deeper level, permutations in society, some of them demographic and some moral, will potentially have profound impacts on family law. The ageing population means that issues relating to the care and financial support of senior citizens will be increasingly apparent. The fledgling area of elder law is really a cousin of family law, and at the other end of the spectrum, the same is true of education law.

9.84   Internationalisation is already having a considerable influence on family law. The courts have grappled with relocation and abduction for some time, and with increasing mobility these issues will not go away. More cases on forum conveniens, recognition of overseas orders and private international law more generally will exercise lawyers and judges. Harmonisation of laws between nations, especially Australia, may be ahead.

9.85   Arguably, the most significant aspect of social change is cultural pluralism. This is patent with respect to the indigenous Maori. Family group conferences are emblematic of the importance of the Maori perspective. It is predicted that their use may be extended, and that questions relating to custom will have to be confronted. There are also sizeable minorities of Pacific and Asian people in New Zealand. Topics such as inter-family relations, religion and traditional practices are bound to surface more and more. Parts of family law are still monocultural and will come under the microscope. Possibly the biggest challenge facing New Zealand family law in the next period is how to provide satisfactorily for the diversity of values and conduct.

10

Norway

Equal rights at any cost?

TONE SVERDRUP

A Introduction

10.1 At the beginning of the twentieth century the idea of equality between family members received strong support in Norway and this caused significant legal differences to disappear – both between children born in and out of wedlock, and between husband and wife. Since then, equality principles have included new groups, culminating in 2008 when same-sex couples were permitted to marry. Children went from being treated as objects in the legal system to being the holders of rights. In 2003 children's rights were further secured through the incorporation of the United Nations Convention on the Rights of the Child (the 'UN Convention') into Norwegian law. Although the rights of the child may look impressive on paper, they have proven difficult to realise in practice. Eventually the interests of adults often prevail.

10.2 Changing social conceptions, new psychological knowledge and biotechnological achievements have made child law a labile field of law with frequent legislative amendments. Child law has also become an arena for political disputes, often pitting mothers' rights against the rights of fathers and biological parenthood against social parenthood. Concepts and ideas finding favour vary with the passage of time.

10.3 Legal developments in family law have occurred partly as a result of changes in society – the equal division rule upon divorce was, for example, limited to certain assets in 1991 due to the increasing number of divorces; child support provisions were amended as a result of women's growing participation in the labour force. But these developments have also been the result of an active and guiding family policy adopted by government. Women's entry into the labour market was to some extent promoted by depriving them of the legal safety net both regarding spousal support and certain social benefits. Meanwhile, fathers' participation in child care was promoted by granting them more rights in child law under the label of 'equal parenthood'. This policy raises several dilemmas for the legislator. How much account should be taken of existing inequalities between various groups in society and should legislation be based on the ideal objective or on reality as it is today? Who shall be sacrificed on the altar of equality?

Historical roots, sources and law reform

Historical roots

10.4   In the early Middle Ages no distinct legal demarcation lines existed between children born in and out of wedlock and, according to the first unified code of laws applying to the whole of Norway, Magnus Lagabøte's (Lawmender) Landslov 1274, children born out of wedlock could claim inheritance from their fathers. Especially after the Protestant Reformation, the legal position of children born outside marriage worsened as extramarital relations became illegal. Children lost their right to inheritance from their fathers in 1604.[1] In comparison to other Western European countries, however, the differences between children born in and out of wedlock with regard to their legal status were eliminated at an early stage. As early as 1915 the so-called Castberg Acts were enacted, under which the father of an illegitimate child was compelled to assume the full obligation as for a lawful child, for example, with regard to name, maintenance and inheritance.[2]

10.5   The direct roots of Norwegian indigenous law and Roman law are more visible in family law (marriage, divorce, marital property, etc.) than in child law. In 1687 Christian V's Norwegian Law introduced a marital property regime that contained elements from both legal systems,[3] with equal division of assets taking place upon termination of marriage. The

---

[1]   Christian IV's Norwegian Law 1604.

[2]   Enacted 10 April 1915, see L. Smith and P. Lødrup, *Barn og foreldre*, 7th edn (Oslo: Gyldendal Akademisk, 2006), pp. 27–9.

[3]   S. Iuul, *Fællig og hovedlod: studier over formueforholdet mellem ægtefæller i tiden før Christian V's danske lov* (Copenhagen: Busck, 1940), pp. 303–16. This double influence gave rise to several legal disputes regarding its interpretation; see T. Sverdrup, *Stiftelse av sameie i ekteskap og ugift samliv* (Oslo: Universitetsforlaget, 1997), pp. 49–52.

present marital property regime is the result of Nordic legal cooperation, which led to almost identical regulations in the Nordic countries
at the beginning of the twentieth century. As earlier, assets were divided
equally upon the dissolution of marriage. However, whereas previously
a husband had controlled the property of both spouses, under the new
Marriage Act of 1927 women were given the right to dispose of their
own property.

Sources

10.6   For child law, the most significant legislation is the Children Act
1981,[4] which concerns the relationship between children and parents
regarding paternity, parental responsibility, residence, contact, maintenance and so on. Another important statute is the Child Welfare Act 1992
concerning children living in conditions that may be detrimental to their
health, and state intervention in this respect. A number of other laws and
individual provisions govern matters relating to children. Case law plays
an important part as a source of the current law, especially regarding disputes over parental responsibilities, questions over the residence of the
child, and state intervention guided by the welfare principle.

10.7   In the field of family law, the Marriage Act 1991 is the most
important piece of legislation. In 2008 an amendment to the Act gave
same-sex couples the right to enter into marriage on the same basis as
heterosexuals. The financial consequences upon termination of unmarried cohabitation remain largely unregulated by statute and, in this field,
non-statutory rules developed through Supreme Court practice are an
important source of law.[5] In 2008, however, Parliament enacted a law that
gives unmarried cohabitants with common children a right to inherit
from each other.[6]

10.8   The European Convention on Human Rights was incorporated into
Norwegian law by the Human Rights Act 1999, giving it precedence over
other Norwegian legislation, and the Convention has increasingly gained
domestic significance in the field of child and family law. In 2003 the UN
Convention and its optional protocols were incorporated into Norwegian
law through an amendment of the Human Rights Act.[7] Thus, the UN

---

[4] English version available at: www.regjeringen.no/en/dep/bld/Documents/Laws-and-
rules.html?id=276069 (last accessed 1 December 2010).
[5] See para. 10.74 below.   [6] Inheritance Act 1972, Chapter III A.
[7] The incorporation of the UN Convention through the Human Rights Act 1999, which
entered into force on 1 October 2003.

Convention applies as Norwegian law and takes precedence if any conflict should arise between the Convention and other Norwegian legislation.[8]

10.9   Even though Norway is not a member of the European Union (EU), it has taken on the obligation to implement all EU legislation relevant to the functioning of the internal market through the European Economic Area (EEA) agreement.[9] However, it should be remembered that EU cooperation on civil law matters concerning, for example, private international law is outside the competencies of the EEA.

Law reform

10.10   There is no central law reform body that deals with child law or family law, and reforms in this field of law follow the usual legal procedure in Norway. If the matter is of importance, an expert commission is appointed by the government to consider law reform, and the commission's report is published in the Norwegian Official Reports.[10] After the report has been circulated among various bodies for their opinion, the government submits a Proposition to the Parliament (Storting) for the enactment of the bill.[11]

10.11   In the past, child law reforms were often the result of the efforts of energetic policy advocates and fiery enthusiasts.[12] Since the enactment of the Children Act in 1981, child law has become a key policy area for political parties and interest groups. The eras during which individuals took initiatives seem long past.

10.12   Family law was an important policy area at the beginning of the twentieth century. The main objective of the Nordic legal collaboration at the time was no-fault divorce (introduced in Norway in 1909) and equality between husband and wife with regard to the disposal of marital property (introduced in 1927). Since then, developments in the Nordic countries have been characterised by unilateral law reforms where national politicians have set the agenda.[13] However, with the exception of equal rights

---

[8]   Human Rights Act 1999, §3.

[9]   OJ No L 1, 3.1.1994, p. 3.

[10]   NOU: Norges offentlige utredninger (green paper).

[11]   English version available at: www.stortinget.no/en/In-English/About-the-Storting/ Parliamentary-procedure/ (last accessed 28 December 2010).

[12]   For example Castberg Acts 1915 and the abolition of the right of parents to punish children physically (1972).

[13]   P. Lødrup, 'The Reharmonisation of Nordic Family Law', in K. Boele-Woelki and T. Sverdrup (eds.), *European Challenges in Contemporary Family Law* (Antwerp: Intersentia, 2008), p. 20.

for same-sex couples, family law has seldom been at the centre of political
debate.

Dispute resolution and access to legal services

10.13 Norwegian child law is based on the assumption that it is in the
child's interests that an agreement is reached between the parents regarding parental responsibilities, residence and contact rights, and that such
an agreement will provide a better basis for future cooperation between
the parents.[14] In 1991 mandatory mediation was introduced in order
to help parents reach agreement in custody cases. Today, married and
cohabiting parents with children under 16 years of age who separate or
are considering legal proceedings can be provided with up to seven hours
of free mediation, including one compulsory hour.[15] The parents' agreement is not subject to any public scrutiny.

10.14 If an agreement is not reached, the dispute will be settled by the
courts. A minority of child custody cases are brought before the court,
but the numbers are increasing. In 2007 around 2,200 child custody cases
were brought before the district courts (first instance in Norway), which
accounted for 17 per cent of all the incoming civil cases to the district
courts.[16] Access to the court is fairly good in child custody cases. The state
covers the costs of mediators and of certain experts. In addition, the free
legal aid scheme helps many parents with low incomes and little capital.
People with low incomes receive free legal advice and have their lawyer's
expenses and court costs covered. The upper income threshold is 30,750
euros per year for a single person to qualify for free legal aid.[17] However,
there are still financial risks involved in litigation, since the court is

---

[14] In 2010 1.1 million children were living with their parents in Norway. About 75% of them
lived with both parents (57% with married parents and 18% with cohabiting parents),
while about 21% lived with their mother and 4% with their father; see www.ssb.no/eng-
lish/subjects/02/01/20/barn_en/ (last accessed 12 March 2012).

[15] Marriage Act 1991, §26 and Children Act 1981, §51; see Mediation Regulation §§8 and
13. For 2007, 1.7 million euros were allocated for payments to mediators; see Norway's
Fourth Report to the UN Child Committee on the Rights of the Child 2008, para. 195,
English version available at: www.regjeringen.no/en/dep/bld/tema/barn_og_ungdom/
fns_barnekonvensjon/norges-rapporter-til-fns-komite-for-barn.html?id=415461 (last
accessed 4 February 2011).

[16] St.meld. nr. 26 (2008–2009) Om offentleg rettshjelp (Report to the Storting on public
legal assistance), ch. 11.1 (estimated number).

[17] Legal Aid Act 1980; see Legal Aid Regulation, FOR-2005–12–12–1443 §1–1.

empowered to order the losing party to pay the other's legal costs, and these expenses are normally not covered by the legal aid scheme. In three-quarters of the child custody cases at least one of the parties received free legal aid, and more than 60 per cent of government expenditure on legal aid was spent on child custody cases.[18] The question has been raised as to whether it is in the child's best interest that the government covers the costs when the parents present the case for a second hearing, often resulting in negligible modification of the original decision. Moreover, the current regulations might seem unfair to the parents who fall outside the scheme. New regulations with less harsh threshold effects have therefore been proposed.[19]

10.15 The legal procedure in custody cases was reformed in 2003. The aim was to bring more professional expertise into the court in order to achieve a more targeted process and more durable agreements focusing on the child's welfare.[20] The costs of these initiatives are covered to a certain extent by the state.[21] One basic idea behind the reform is that the combination of the solemnity of the court and the assistance of professionals – judges, lawyers and experts – would facilitate the process of finding a solution. The reform has proven successful in several respects. However, between 2001 and 2006 the number of custody cases increased by about 50 per cent, and a substantial part of this increase could be related to the introduction of the procedural law reform.[22] Many disputes are settled in court, but these settlements have not proven to be more durable than the previous settlements. Time-consuming court cases and parents returning to the court to have their cases heard a second or a third time are commonplace. Furthermore, the mixing of roles is problematic – for example, the role of mediator prior to the case and then the role of expert witness in the legal proceedings are difficult to reconcile. Therefore, there is reason to expect further legal reforms in this area in the years to come.

---

[18] Numbers are for 2007; see St.meld. nr. 26 (2008–2009) Om offentleg rettshjelp, ch. 11.4.1 and ch. 11.1.

[19] St.meld. nr. 26 (2008–2009) ch. 11.4.2.

[20] Ot.prp. nr. 29 (2002–2003) ch. 1.

[21] Children Act 1981, §61, second paragraph.

[22] K. Koch, 'Evaluering av saksbehandlingsreglene for domstolene i barneloven – saker om foreldreansvar, fast bosted og samvær' (Assessment of the legal procedure reform) Report (2008), summary in English available at: www.regjeringen.no/en/dep/bld/dok/rapporter_planer/rapporter/2008/evaluering-av-saksbehandlingsreglene-for.html?id=503721 (last accessed 4 February 2011).

10.16   Because each spouse may unilaterally demand divorce after a period of separation, very few disputes occur on the issue of divorce, and the vast majority of divorce cases are settled administratively. Conflicts arise when assets are to be divided between spouses and between cohabitants, and a significant number of cases end up in court. Disputes may be traced back partly to the unfortunate design of the provisions.[23]

B   Children in the family setting and state intervention

10.17   Compared with other countries, Norway has been at the forefront in terms of prioritising children's rights. Norway was the first country, in 1981, to establish an Ombudsman for Children with statutory authority to protect children and their rights, and Norway is among the few countries to incorporate the UN Convention into domestic law with precedence over other domestic legislation.[24]

10.18   The factual legal position of children is quite another issue. In child custody cases the child runs the risk of being the 'losing party' and it has proven extremely difficult for the legislator to change this pattern through reform of legal procedures.[25] To what extent are parents' rights and interests masked as the rights and interests of the child? When children are granted status as parties, do they actually become the front-line soldiers for the adults? Furthermore, Norway has a long way to go in safeguarding the rights of children and young people at risk including children who are victims of domestic abuse, child refugees and unaccompanied asylum seekers.[26]

Defining and classifying children

10.19   The age of majority in Norway is 18 years.[27] However, children and young people gain rights and responsibilities from an earlier age in many

---

[23] See para. 10.70 below.   [24] See para. 10.1 above.

[25] See paras. 10.34–10.40 below.

[26] See 'Supplementary Report to the UN Committee on the Rights of the Child 2009' from the Ombudsman for Children in Norway, English version available at: www.barneom-budet.no/sfiles/48/24/1/file/suplementary-report-to-the-un_english.pdf (last accessed 2 February 2011). Difficult questions arise when children are used by their parents as a bond to the new country (anchor child); see Rt. 2009 p. 1261 (Norwegian Supreme Court Reports). Other urgent issues to be addressed are bullying at school, internet-related abuse of children and several issues related to minorities and immigrants.

[27] Guardianship Act 1927, §1.

fields of law with frequently used age limits in the legislation being 7, 12, 15 and 16 years. The guiding legislative principle is to provide children with legal capacities when they have the ability to acknowledge and foresee the consequences of their choices.

10.20 Young people are criminally liable when they reach 15 years of age.[28] As regards responsibility for damages, no specific age threshold exists. Compulsory schooling is of ten years' duration, which means that children normally are above compulsory school age at 16.

10.21 In connection with the incorporation of the UN Convention Article 12 (the right of the child to be heard), domestic legislation was reviewed in order to eliminate discrepancies in relation to the Convention. This has led to the amendment of several Acts, among them the Adoption Act 1986, the Child Welfare Act 1992 and the Children Act 1991, whereby both children of 7 years old and younger children who are capable of forming their own views must be given an opportunity to express their views before decisions are made in cases that affect them.[29] The two first-mentioned Acts expressly state that the child must also be informed. However, a number of Acts have specific age thresholds with no measure to ensure that the views of younger children are considered. This includes the right to be heard in schools, religious communities and regarding health issues.[30] The UN Child Committee has been concerned that the child's right to be heard in Norway is in practice not effectively implemented and practised in all phases of decisions about children's lives, in particular in child-care and immigration cases. The UN Committee also points out that children in Norway only have the right to be heard regarding health issues after the age of 12.[31] The project of implementing the Convention through specification and visualisation of the requirements is an ongoing project where new legislation is expected.

10.22 As regards the child's right to self-determination, the holders of parental responsibility are committed to continually extend the child's

---

[28] Penal Code 1902, §46. The age threshold was raised from 14 to 15 years of age in 1987.
[29] Adoption Act 1986, §6, Child Welfare Act 1992, §6–3, Children Act 1981, §31.
[30] See K. H. Søvig, 'Barnets rettigheter på barnets premisser – utfordringer i møtet mellom FNs barnekonvensjon og norsk rett' (expert review of the relation between the UN Convention and Norwegian law), Report (2009), pp. 55–8. Norwegian version available at: www.regjeringen.no/nb/dep/bld/pressesenter/pressemeldinger/2009/forholdet-mellom-fns-barnekonvensjon-og-.html?id=578215 (last accessed 1 March 2012).
[31] UN Child Committee's Concluding Observations on the Fourth Report of Norway (2010), paras. 9 and 24.

right to make his/her own decisions in personal matters until majority is reached.[32] Specific age thresholds exist in many respects. For example, consent to one's own adoption and consent to change one's name and nationality is required from the age of 12. A young person has the right to engage in full-time employment from the age of 15 (or when the child is above compulsory school age). At the same age, he or she can make all decisions in educational and religious matters. The legal age of sexual consent is 16, and the same age permits the young person to consent to medical treatment. On the other hand, in order to make a will or to marry, a person normally must have reached the age of majority (18 years). In order to vote, a person must turn 18 years of age in the course of the election year. However, the government conducted a pilot project that allowed children from age 16 to vote in about twenty municipalities in the 2011 local elections.

10.23   The trend has been to lower the age limits and this development will probably continue. An exception must be made for provisions with an explicit protective purpose. The sale of tobacco products and alcohol to persons under 18 years of age is prohibited (20 years for liquor) and the age limit for driving a car is 18 years. There is no indication that these or similar age limits will be lowered in the future. On the contrary, new protective age thresholds have been proposed, among other things for the use of solariums (18 years).

Recognising parentage and family ties

10.24   The principle of paternal affiliation by presumption is fundamental to the establishment of paternity in Norway, but these presumptions are rebuttable. Through law reforms in 1997 and 2002, legislation went a long way in respect of allowing legal action on paternity in cases where the child already had a father. The basic philosophy behind the current rules on parentage is that it is in the best interest of the child that the man who is the biological father should also be considered the legal father. However, there are indications that the pendulum is starting to swing back, and that more account will be taken of social parentage. In turn, more weight is being given to the child's right to know the truth about his/her genetic origins.

---

[32] Children Act 1981, §33.

10.25 The husband of the mother is automatically established as a child's father and the child is thus ensured a social and legal framework from the start of his or her life.[33] Likewise, the woman to whom the mother is married is established as a child's co-mother when the child is conceived by means of assisted fertilisation.[34]

10.26 When the mother is unmarried, paternity is determined either by the father's acknowledgement or by judgment.[35] Acknowledgement by a non-cohabiting father is only valid with the consent of the child's mother. However, the authorities are responsible for establishing paternity in these cases, and the mother cannot refuse to permit a sample to be taken from the child for DNA analysis.[36] The cohabiting father is allowed to register his paternity without the consent of the child's mother.[37] This provision, introduced in 2005, may prove to be of short duration. Mainly due to practical problems associated with the provision of documentary evidence that the cohabitation actually exists, the Law Commission on Paternity 2009 has recommended repeal of this rule.[38] The Commission also proposed to amend the terminology altogether: the fathers should no longer 'acknowledge', but rather 'declare' paternity. The intention of this proposal is to raise the standing of the current voluntary recognition and emphasise the emotional aspect of childbirth and parenthood. The mother's female cohabitant may acknowledge co-maternity pursuant to the same provisions when the child is born following assisted fertilisation.[39]

10.27 The child, either of the parents and a third party who believes he is truly the father of a child that already has a legal father are all entitled to institute legal proceedings concerning change of paternity.[40] This means

---

[33] Children Act 1981, §3.

[34] This presumption only applies if the fertilisation is provided by an approved health service with the woman's consent to the fertilisation; see the Children Act 1981, §3.

[35] The Children Act 1981, §§4 and 5; see also §9.

[36] The Children Act 1981, §§5, 9 and 24.

[37] Consent is not needed when the cohabitants are registered in the National Population Register at the same address or if they declare in a notification to the Register that they are cohabiting. The mother shall be notified of the acknowledgement; see the Children Act 1981, §4, third paragraph.

[38] Commission on Paternity NOU 2009: 5, Farskap og annen morskap, ch. 10.4. Summary in English available at: www.regjeringen.no/en/dep/bld/Documents/Reports-and-plans/Reports/2009-2/commission-on-paternity-nou-2009-5.html?id=576775 (last accessed 6 February 2011).

[39] Children Act 1981, §4, sixth paragraph.

[40] Children Act 1981, §6.

that a man who claims to be the biological father of a child born in marriage may bring an action before the courts relating to paternity at any time: that is, there is no time limit on when such legal proceedings may be initiated.[41] Neither the mother, the child nor the husband may impede such legal proceedings. The court may require that blood tests be taken and permission from the mother of the child is not required.[42] If a man is identified as the father on the basis of the DNA analysis, he must be adjudged to be the father.[43] The fact that a third party can intrude in this way on an existing family unit and disturb the harmony of an established family relationship has been criticised. It is maintained that the child's right to know the identity of his or her biological father could be satisfied without entailing a change of paternity. It was in this context that the Commission on Paternity 2009 proposed reintroduction of time limits for the parties' entitlement to institute legal proceedings.[44] The Commission also proposed that a putative father who is deprived of paternity by a court judgment should be given an opportunity to institute legal proceedings to claim right of access.[45] The proposals of the Commission are expected to lead to new legislation in the foreseeable future.

10.28   A sperm donor cannot be adjudged to be the father, but in 2003 children were given the right to know the identity of their biological father when they reached the age of majority.[46] However, not all children will learn about their origins, as it is up to the parents whether they want to tell the child that donor gametes have been used.[47] The Ministry wanted to gain experience from the new regulations before it considered imposing a duty of disclosure in this respect.[48]

---

[41] These rules were the result of law reforms in 1997 and 2002; see P. Lødrup, 'Challenges to an Established Paternity – Radical Changes in Norwegian Law', in A. Bainham (ed.), *The International Survey of Family Law. 2003 Edition* (Bristol: Jordan Publishing, 2003), pp. 353–62.

[42] Children Act 1981, §24.

[43] Children Act 1981, §9 (with the exception of sperm donors).

[44] NOU 2009: 5, ch. 14.

[45] NOU 2009: 5, ch. 14.7. The Commission further proposed a new provision giving the child a right to know the identity of his or her biological father without this entailing a change of paternity; see chs. 14.2 and 14.3, pp. 139 and 146.

[46] Biotechnology Act 2003, §2–7.

[47] The legal situation is different as regards adoption. Adoptive parents shall 'as soon as is advisable' tell the adopted child that he or she is adopted, and when the child has reached 18 years of age, he or she is entitled to be informed by the Ministry of the identity of his or her biological parents; see Adoption Act 1986, §12.

[48] Ot.prp. nr. 64 (2002–2003) p. ch. 2.9.6.2.

Furthermore, children conceived before 1 January 2004 do not have the right to know, as the donors prior to this date had been promised anonymity. There is reason to believe that these questions will be considered and the provisions may possibly be changed, depending on the future developments in the interpretations of the European Convention on Human Rights, Article 8, and the UN Convention, Article 7.

10.29 As regards maternity, the law expressly states that the woman who gives birth to a child is the child's legal mother. Surrogacy is not permitted in Norway, and an agreement to give birth to a child for another woman is not binding.[49] If a couple residing in Norway enters into an agreement with a surrogate mother in a foreign country, there is a chance that the parenthood will not be recognised and the child will become stateless. In any case, the transfer of maternity to the non-biological mother is only possible by means of adoption. The Commission on Paternity 2009 recommended that the main features of the current law in this area be upheld, and maintains that it 'does *not* find it correct to adapt Norwegian statutory provisions concerning parenthood in order to enable residents of Norway more easily to make use of facilities available abroad that are not permitted in Norway'.[50] Surrogacy cases involve difficult and delicate moral and legal issues, and there are no easy answers. However, as the Swedish professor Anna Singer points out, for the time being surrogate children find themselves in a situation similar to that of illegitimate children in the last century. Because society has disdain for the way they are conceived, they must bear the burden of society's lack of legal recognition of their family ties.[51] In the longer term new solutions to these problems will probably emerge.

[49] Children Act 1981, §2.
[50] NOU 2009: 5, ch. 1.2, pp. 101–2 (emphasis in original). As a result, the child runs the risk of losing the opportunity to live with its social (and genetic) mother if she did not apply for adoption when returning to Norway, but instead pretended to be the mother. If the couple later divorce and the legal father then refuses to consent to the mother's adoption, he will remain the only legal parent. In March 2012, the Ministry presented a draft of a 'temporary act' to address some of these problems, cf. www.regjeringen.no/nb/dep/bld/pressesenter/pressemeldinger/2012/lovforslag-skal-sikre-rettigheter-for-ba.html?id=677750 (last accessed 20 April 2012).
[51] See A. Singer, 'Den moderna reproduktionstekniken – en utmaning för familjerätten' (2008) 6 *Tidsskrift for familierett, arverett og barnevernrettslige spørsmål* 95–106 at 106.

Delivering parenting

10.30   Parental responsibilities consist of a duty to take care of the child as well as a right to decide on behalf of the child in personal matters.[52] In order to avoid any misunderstanding as to whether parental authority has been given to the parents for their own sake, the law expressly states that the parental responsibilities 'shall be exercised on the basis of the child's interests and needs'.[53] The parents may share parental responsibilities or one of them may have the responsibilities alone.[54] The duty to provide financial support is not part of parental responsibility, but follows directly from being a parent.[55] No person other than the parents can obtain parental responsibilities pursuant to the Children Act except after the death of a parent.[56] However, if the child is neglected, the parents can be deprived of all or some of their parental responsibilities pursuant to the Child Welfare Act.[57]

10.31   Bio-scientific developments have made current the thought of a more differentiated concept of parenthood and parental responsibility, where different people have the status of biological/genetic, social and legal parents, and where various legal consequences are attached to the different roles. Even though the idea was rejected by the Commission on Paternity 2009,[58] one can see the germ of such a development in the establishment of visitation contact for biological parents after their child has been adopted in child welfare cases,[59] the proposed contact rights for people who lose paternity in legal proceedings[60] and for intended parents in surrogacy cases who are denied adoption.[61]

---

[52]   The rights and duties related to the property of a child (guardianship) are laid down in the Guardianship Act.

[53]   Children Act 1981 §30 first paragraph and NOU 1977: 35 p. 123. Furthermore, according to §30, the child is entitled to care and consideration from those who have parental responsibilities. They are under an obligation to bring up and maintain the child properly. They shall ensure that the child receives an education according to his or her abilities and aptitudes and that the child not be subjected to violence. The holders of parental responsibilities have a right and a duty to make decisions for the child in personal matters, within the limits set by §31 (the child's right of codetermination) and §33 (the child's right of self-determination).

[54]   Children Act 1981, §§34, 35 and 48.

[55]   Children Act 1981, §66.   [56]   Children Act 1981, §§38 and 63.

[57]   See paras. 10.42ff. below.   [58]   NOU 2009: 5, ch. 3.9.

[59]   Child Welfare Act 1992, §4–20a.

[60]   NOU 2009: 5, ch. 14.7.3.   [61]   NOU 2009: 5, ch. 14.7.4.

10.32 The Children Act states that parental responsibility 'shall be exercised on the basis of the child's interests and needs'.[62] But the law has little to offer when it comes to ensuring children optimal parenting in the family. Only when the child is neglected will the state take action, pursuant to the Child Welfare Act. However, on the issue of physical and psychological punishment of children, both legislators and judges have been active. After much political debate, the right of parents to punish children physically was rescinded in 1972. In 1987 punishment of children was expressly prohibited in the Children Act, section 30, which states: 'The child must not be subjected to violence or in any other way be treated so as to harm or endanger his or her mental or physical health.' Violation of this provision was punishable under penal law, which was illustrated by a Supreme Court decision in 1990 where a father was convicted after having reprimanded his son once by pinching his lip.[63] However, a Supreme Court decision in 2005 created uncertainty in the interpretation of the provisions. In that case the stepfather was convicted, but the presiding Justice observed *obiter* that a 'light smack' in the course of child-rearing should not be punishable.[64] The government, however, wanted to make it clear that the right of parents to use physical and psychological punishment had been fully eliminated in Norway and the Children Act was therefore amended in 2010. In order to remove all discussion about the interpretation of its provisions, Parliament voted for an addition to the original wording in section 30: 'This shall also apply when violence is carried out in connection with the upbringing of the child. Use of violence and frightening or annoying behaviour or other inconsiderate conduct towards the child is prohibited.' Violation is punishable under penal law.[65]

Intra-family disputes

10.33 The majority of intra-family disputes concern the child's residence and access rights after relationship breakdown, as parental responsibilities are normally shared even if the parents move apart. As we have

---

[62] Children Act 1981, §30.

[63] Rt. 1990 s. 1155. The father was irritated that his son of one-and-three-quarter years had bitten his hand and the pinch resulted in cuts in the boy's lip. The Supreme Court held that such behaviour was not acceptable and the incident was viewed as a regular violation of the Penal Code 1902, §228 (assault).

[64] Rt. 2005 s. 1567.

[65] For example the Penal Code 1902, §§223, 228, 246, 247 and 390a.

seen, the number of custody cases brought before the court has risen sharply in recent years.[66]

10.34   Decisions in all custody cases 'shall first and foremost' have regard to the best interests of the child pursuant to the Children Act, section 48. In 2006 this provision was amended to add a requirement that regard should be had to ensuring that the child was not subjected to violence or in any other way treated in such a manner as to impair or endanger his or her physical or mental health. However, child abuse has been difficult to prove, partly due to lack of resources and police priorities. In some child custody cases the judges seem to set a high burden of proof that would be more appropriate in a criminal case.

10.35   When deciding the child's permanent residence, there are no further statutory guidelines. Case law assigns particular importance to certain factors, such as the child's emotional attachment and the parents' personal qualities, the regard for stability, the risk associated with a change of environment and the regard for the best possible overall parental contact.[67] As in other countries, a long-standing disagreement has taken place in Norway as to whether the court ought to rule that residence should be divided between the parents. A compromise was adopted in 2010. As a general rule, the court must decide that the child shall live permanently with one of the parents, but when special reasons so indicate, the court may decide that the child shall live with both of them.[68]

10.36   In deciding access rights, the statute provides a checklist. Importance shall be attached, among other things, to ensuring the best possible overall parental contact, to the age of the child, the degree to which the child is attached to the local neighbourhood, the distance that must be travelled between the parents and the child's interests in all other respects.[69] The decision on the parents' right to access can be enforced by means of a coercive fine.[70] The child has a right of access to both parents as well. The child's right cannot be sanctioned at present, but this situation might well change in the future.

---

[66] See para. 10.14 above.

[67] See I. L. Backer, *Barneloven. Kommentarutgave*, 2nd edn (Oslo: Universitetsforlaget, 2008), pp. 337–49.

[68] Children Act 1981, §36, second paragraph.

[69] Children Act 1981, §43, second paragraph.

[70] Children Act 1981, §65.

10.37 A recurrent dilemma is the extent to which the concern for the individual child's well-being can be set aside so that children as a group will achieve a better legal position. The question is relevant in cases where one of the parents obstructs access. When a parent prevents the right of access from being exercised, the other parent can demand a new decision on the child's permanent residence. A rule to this effect was adopted in 1989.[71] A few years later, the Supreme Court decided in favour of transferring the residence of a 7-year-old boy from the mother to the father in a case where the mother had obstructed access.[72] As the boy barely knew his father, the decision created much debate.[73] The court justified its decision by stating that it would lead to the best overall parental contact in that particular case, but simultaneously the judgment sent a powerful message to custodial parents who might consider denying access.

10.38 'Equal parenthood' has become the keyword denoting an important political objective of recent child law reforms.[74] But confusion reigns as to what it entails. The Child Law Commission 2008 stated that the concern for the 'greatest possible overall parental contact' will frequently be in the child's best interest.[75] The Commission has been accused of not seeing the difference between quantity and quality – it is not the 'largest' but the 'best' overall parental contact that is in line with the child's best interest and with legal doctrine. It is maintained that the question of how parent cooperation functions after relationship breakdown is of much greater importance to the child than the exact residential or access solutions that are decided upon.[76] The Commission, on the other hand, found that equal parenthood – in quantitative terms – will often be in the best interest of the child.[77] The debate is symptomatic of the difficulties that arise when the interests of the child and gender equality come together over a single issue.

---

[71] Children Act 1981, §43, fifth paragraph.

[72] Rt. 1991 p. 1148.

[73] See Backer, *Barneloven. Kommentarutgave*, p. 345 with further references.

[74] Child Law Commission 2008, NOU 2008: 9 Med barnet i fokus, p. 15. Norwegian version available at: www.regjeringen.no/pages/2067864/PDFS/ NOU200820080009000DDDPDFS.pdf (last accessed 1 March 2012).

[75] NOU 2008: 9, pp. 29, 40, 62 and 63.

[76] See T. Haugli, 'Er barnet i fokus?' (2008) 6 *Tidsskrift for familierett, arverett og barnevernrettslige spørsmål* 156–72 at 157–8. See also Smith and Lødrup, *Barn og foreldre*, pp. 164–5.

[77] NOU 2008: 9, p. 29.

10.39 At present, disputes related to specific issues concerning the upbringing of the child, cannot be resolved by the legal system. The legislators have sought to reduce the number of such conflicts after relationship breakdown by allowing the parent with whom the child lives to make decisions concerning important aspects of the child's care.[78] One of these aspects is the place in the country where the child shall live and this provision is perceived as discriminatory by many, especially fathers' groups. The reason is that the right of access can be made illusory when a child is moved across great distances inside Norway. After a heated debate, however, the provision was upheld in 2010. An obligation to notify change of residence was adopted instead.[79]

10.40 Child law has become a battlefield for gender policy. Equality has a strong footing in Norwegian legal heritage, and the objective of 'equal parenthood' has a favourable wind behind it. In the years to come we will probably experience more legal reforms that in practice will strengthen the legal position of fathers concerning, among other things, the child's residence. However, there is also significant awareness of the fact that children are harmed by having to experience conflict between the parents, as well as the dangers of the 'juridification' of private life. A stronger emphasis on equality between parents may bring the judicial system deeper into the private sphere of people's lives. If both parents must decide upon issues like relocation, overseas holidays, choice of school and so on, mechanisms for conflict resolution must be available as well. Admittedly, the primary goal of the authorities is to facilitate agreements between parents, but this policy could be experienced like an infringement in itself by those parents who are not able to agree. The Danish scholar Anette Kronborg points out that vulnerable parents find themselves trapped in an ideology of cooperation where mediation, counselling, revised agreements and court cases supersede each other in what would seem like an ever-lasting process.[80] Another example of juridification of private life is the child's right to be heard. Such rights may have unfortunate side effects when children are made accountable and drawn into the adults' conflict. Efforts to develop procedural and substantive provisions that could prevent and ease conflict will most certainly continue.

---

[78] Children Act 1981, §37.
[79] Children Act 1981, §42, first paragraph.
[80] A. Kronborg, *Forældremyndighed & menneskelig integritet* (Copenhagen: Jurist- og Økonomforbundets forlag, 2007).

10.41 Child maintenance payment is determined in such a way that expected costs for the support of the child are shared between the parents according to their income. The authorities provided a 'maintenance calculator' on the website[81] and, as a result, few maintenance disputes end up in court. However, as the non-custodial parent's share of the maintenance cost is reduced as a result of agreed or fixed time spent with the child, the regulation tends to promote conflicts between parents about contact rights. There is, however, little to suggest that the link between money and rights to access will be changed in this respect.

10.41 It has been suggested that the Children Act should undergo a thorough revision – more than thirty legislative changes over the years have led to inconsistencies. It is expected that a revision will take place in the foreseeable future.

Child protection and state intervention

10.42 In addition to practical and financial help to families, the authorities are obliged to institute assistive measures for children and families when they are in particular need of help pursuant to the Child Welfare Act 1992.[82] If measures in the home are not sufficient, the child welfare service can intervene, even against the will of the parents. The age threshold for assuming criminal responsibility is 15 years old. However, a child, regardless of age, who has shown serious behavioural problems may be placed in a treatment or training institution against the child's will.[83] When applying these provisions, 'decisive importance' shall be attached to implementing measures which are in the child's best interests.[84]

10.43 The number of children receiving assistance has seen a large increase since 2000.[85] At the end of 2009 about 35,650 children were under protective care from the child welfare service in Norway and, of these, 6,600 were in alternative care, most of them – 5,870 – in foster homes.[86]

---

[81] http://tjenester.nav.no/bidragsveileder/steg1.action (last accessed 7 February 2011).
[82] English version of the Child Welfare Act 1992 available at: www.regjeringen.no/en/doc/Laws/Acts/The-Child-Welfare-Act.html?id=448398 (last accessed 6 January 2011).
[83] Child Welfare Act 1992, §4–24.
[84] Child Welfare Act 1992, §4–1.
[85] From 21.8 per 1,000 children at the end of 2000 to 29.5 per 1,000 children in 2009; see www.ssb.no/english/subjects/03/03/barneverng_en/ (last accessed 6 January 2011).
[86] As at 31 December 2009; see www.ssb.no/english/subjects/03/03/barneverng_en/ (last accessed 6 January 2011).

Surveys show that many children in alternative care have poor future prospects, particularly children who have been in institutions.[87] A recurring problem is the unstable living conditions when children are moved between foster homes with poor supervision.[88]

10.44 These problems are partly due to understaffing and lack of resources in the municipalities. Critics have regularly called into question the capability of the child welfare service to take action when a child is neglected. The UN Committee on the Rights of the Child has expressed concern that unaccompanied asylum-seeker children are not being adequately followed up by child welfare services in Norway.[89] Criticism has also focused on the propensity to act without sufficient reason. The European Court of Human Rights has criticised Norway for failure to respect privacy and family life in an adoption case.[90]

10.45 The Child Welfare Act will undergo evaluation, among other things with a view to balancing the biological parents' rights to respect for private and family life with the child's right to protection and respect.[91] Some measures have already been taken. In order to facilitate decisions on adoption of children placed in foster care at an early stage, an opportunity to establish visitation contact between the child and its biological parents, after the child has been adopted, has been introduced.[92] In public policy debates some critics have called into question the role of expert witnesses in child welfare cases, citing factors such as their qualifications, methods, judgment and power. This is part of the reason why a permanent commission was established in 2009 designed to provide quality assurance of all expert reports in child welfare cases.[93]

10.46 Today, the child welfare authorities have legal obligations that do not correspond with similar rights for the children. Several critics have

---

[87] T. Haugli, 'Barnerett – utviklingstrekk og utfordringer' (2010) 8 *Tidsskrift for familierett, arverett og barnevernrettslige spørsmål* 5–24 at 20.

[88] UN Child Committee's Concluding Observations on the Fourth Report of Norway (2010), paras. 34–5.

[89] UN Child Committee's Concluding Observations on the Fourth Report of Norway (2010), para. 50.

[90] *Johansen* v. *Norway* (1996) 23 EHRR 33 (decision that deprived the mother of her access and parental rights in respect of her daughter violated Article 8).

[91] Press release, www.regjeringen.no/nb/dep/bld/pressesenter/pressemeldinger/2010/et-bedre-barnevern -for-barna.html?id=624648 (last accessed 7 February 2011).

[92] Child Welfare Act 1992, §4–20a.

[93] Child Welfare Act 1992, §2–5.

advocated that the Child Welfare Act should provide children with individual statutory rights.[94] A codification of rights will have the greatest practical significance with respect to measures in the home. Except in cases of severe neglect and abuse, parental consent is normally needed before the authorities can provide assistance and, because of this, a child in need may not receive help.[95] A rights-based approach would indicate more clearly the conflict of interest between parents and children in these matters. Statutory rights could also help reduce the disparity of services between the various municipalities and improve the ability to follow up on children in alternative care. Due to the principle of local self-government, welfare services vary according to where in Norway the child lives. So far, the authorities have resisted a more rights-based approach.[96] However, there is reason to believe that statutory rights will be introduced under the Child Welfare Act in the future.

C   Adult relationships

10.47   Since the Second World War remarkable changes in family life have taken place in Norway as in many other Western countries. The changes include a dramatic increase in divorce rates and extramarital cohabitation and the accompanying increase in children born out of wedlock and women joining the paid work force to a great extent influencing, among other things, parental roles and property relations among partners. The rise in the standard of living has led to conflicts often involving substantial assets.

10.48   In many Western countries these changes led to important reforms in family law in the 1970s and 1980s.[97] In Norway the most comprehensive legal reform took place within the field of child law, as described above. The law affecting family economics, however, remained

---

[94] NOU 2000:12 Barnevernet i Norge, p. 299 and K. H. Søvig, 'Barnets rettigheter på barnets premisser – utfordringer i møtet mellom FNs barnekonvensjon og norsk rett', Report (2009), p. 99, with further references.

[95] UN Child Committee's Concluding Observations on the Fourth Report of Norway (2010), para. 32, and E. Gording Stang, *Det er barnets sak* (Oslo: Universitetsforlaget, 2007), pp. 397–8.

[96] St.meld. nr. 40 (2001–2002) Om barne- og ungdomsvernet, ch. 9.10 (Recommendation to the Storting).

[97] M. A. Glendon, *The Transformation of Family Law: State, Law and Family in the United States and Western Europe* (Chicago and London: University of Chicago Press, 1989), pp. 233–8.

largely unchanged. The reason why reforms in Norway in the 1970s and 1980s have been more limited than in many other European countries is partly due to the fact that the legislation was already modernised by the Nordic reform efforts in the beginning of the twentieth century.[98] Nevertheless, social development over the last thirty years or so has not been reflected in the law to any appreciable extent. Most striking in this respect is the fact that the financial consequences upon termination of cohabitation remain mostly unregulated by statute in Norway, except for the limited possibility to inherit introduced in 2008.

10.49 Even though the laws regarding financial settlements have maintained their basic features, one can nonetheless discern a development towards greater focus on the parties' contributions in marriage and cohabitation law. While the main rationale behind the earlier Marriage Act's equal division rule lay in community and support ideas, the 'unequal division rule' in the current Marriage Act 1991 is explicitly justified by the parties' contributions. And when the ownership of assets is disputed among spouses or cohabitants (and no explicit agreement exists), the court will emphasise and measure the individual's direct and indirect contributions in each case.

10.50 More recent social changes include the growing acceptance of same-sex relationships and new techniques for medically assisted reproduction. Within these fields the legislators have been more active, and equality of rights for different-sex and same-sex couples through the Marriage Act and other regulations constitute recent milestones. While these transformations took place, Norway has experienced a new and large cross-border migration of people from other continents and cultures. To date, however, this has not led to any significant changes in family law legislation.

The relationships

10.51 At present, the legal system in Norway recognises two main types of relationships: marriage and cohabitation. After 1993 two persons of the same sex were allowed to register their partnership and thus obtain the same rights as married couples throughout the legal system with very few exceptions. This opportunity to register partnerships is no longer

---

[98] See para. 10.5 above and Lødrup, 'The Reharmonisation of Nordic Family Law'.

available, as the Act was repealed when the Marriage Act was opened for inclusion of same-sex couples in 2008.[99] Registered partners can have their partnerships converted into marriage, if they agree, and existing partnerships will still remain in force.[100]

Marriage

10.52   For a long time marriage was the only socially acceptable form of family union, and the only one that was recognised by the legal system. The fact that spouses had to be of different sexes was so self-evident that it was unnecessary to state this explicitly in the law. When Norway passed the Registered Partnership Act in 1993, it was therefore a milestone in social acceptance of homosexual and lesbian cohabitation – the Act legitimised relationships that had been labelled as criminal only twenty years earlier. However, complete equality was not attained, as the institution of marriage was still reserved for different-sex couples and registered partners were not allowed to adopt children jointly. After another seventeen years, the institution of marriage was finally opened up to couples of the same sex in 2008. The bill was enacted into law after long and hard discussion in Parliament. Even though several political parties have announced that they want to revise the law, there is every reason to believe that this comprehensive Marriage Act is here to stay.

Cohabitation

10.53   There is no statute that specifically regulates cohabitation in Norway. The Household Community Act 1991 applies to two or more unmarried adult persons who have lived together in a household, and includes cohabitants, siblings, students and others who live together. This Act, however, is of minor importance, as the law provides only a limited opportunity for a member to purchase the previously common residence at market value upon termination.

10.54   Since the early 1980s the regulation of unmarried cohabitation has been the subject of political discussions.[101] Key opponents to legal regulation have been religious-oriented groups as well as radical forces that want to keep cohabitation an unregulated alternative to marriage. As the number of cohabiting couples has increased, the opposition to legal

---

[99]   The Registered Partnership Act 1993 was repealed as of 1 January 2009.
[100]   Marriage Act 1991, §95.
[101]   NOU 1980: 50 Samliv uten vigsel and P. Lødrup and T. Sverdrup, *Familieretten*, 7th edn (Oslo) pp. 334–7.

regulation has diminished. This change in the political climate resulted in the enactment of inheritance rules for cohabiting couples in 2008,[102] and will probably lead to other statutory regulations as well.

Entering an adult relationship

Marriage

10.55   Marriage cannot be contracted between relatives in direct line of ascent or descent or between brothers and sisters, and is also forbidden if a previous marriage (or registered partnership) subsists. No person under 18 years of age may contract a marriage without the consent of the people having parental responsibility as well as the permission of the county governor. According to the statute, the governor can only give permission when there are 'strong reasons for contracting a marriage', and not at all if the applicant is under 16 years of age.[103] The 16-years age limit was introduced in 2007 as one of many measures to prevent forced marriages. However, even before 2007 permission was hardly ever given in cases where the applicant was below 16 years of age. The applicant's age and maturity and the fact that they already live with a partner are factors in favour of granting permission. If the bride is pregnant, as a general rule permission is given.[104]

10.56   The Marriage Act expressly states that two 'persons of opposite sex or of the same sex' may contract marriage.[105] A marriage may be solemnised by means of a civil or a religious ceremony,[106] but, presently, same-sex marriages will for the most part have to occur through civil ceremonies. The Church of Norway[107] and other faith communities have the right, but not the obligation, to solemnise marriages, and according to the present liturgy, the clergy of the Church of Norway are not permitted

---

[102]   Inheritance Act 1972, Chapter III A; see para. 10.59 below.

[103]   Marriage Act 1991, §1 a, first paragraph.

[104]   Circular from the Ministry of Children, Equality and Social Inclusion Q-20/09, pp. 7–8.

[105]   Marriage Act 1991, §1.   [106]   Marriage Act 1991, §12.

[107]   The Church of Norway is a protestant (Evangelical Lutheran) state church, headed by the King, with the Parliament (Storting) as the supreme legislative body. A state church reform will take place in the near future and entail looser ties between church and state, but the church will still be established. Most importantly, bishops and deans will be appointed by the Church of Norway instead of by the Government and there will be more democracy in the Church; see Innst.O.nr.57 (2008–2009).

to perform marriages for same-sex couples. Religion plays a subordinate role in Norwegian society, even though 82 per cent of the population are members of the Church of Norway.[108] To prevent individual progressive clergymen from solemnising marriages in conflict with the liturgy, Parliament enacted a clarifying amendment to the Act, specifying that a marriage is invalid if a clergyman of the Church of Norway has not complied with the liturgy laid down by the Church of Norway General Synod.[109] At present, it is the prerogative of the General Synod to change its consecration liturgy. While this will probably not happen very soon, it is expected that the Church will allow its clergy to solemnise same-sex marriage in the foreseeable future.[110]

10.57   A marriage is invalid if the spouse has been forced by unlawful conduct to contract the marriage, and this applies regardless of who has exercised such force.[111] Since 2000 the government has put much effort into combating forced marriages. Despite the fact that several action plans, containing numerous initiatives and measures, have been launched, it has proven difficult to prevent this practice. This is partly due to the fact that forced marriages among some minority groups involve the extended family in the country of origin. In 2003 it was made an offence to force a person to enter into marriage.[112] The Supreme Court tried the first case under this provision in 2006 and a father who had attempted to coerce his daughter into marriage was sentenced to two-and-a-half years in prison, with her brother being sentenced to two years for the same offence.[113] Other statutory regulations include transference of the authority to verify fulfilment of the conditions of marriage from the solemnisers of marriage

---

[108] Numbers are from 2008; see www.ssb.no/samfunnsspeilet/utg/200903/03/index.html (last accessed 28 June 2011).

[109] Marriage Act 1991, §16, first paragraph.

[110] The Church of Sweden has declared its willingness to marry same-sex couples; see C. Sørgjerd, 'Reconstructing Marriage in a Changing Legal and Societal Landscape. Challenges of New Cohabitation Models in Sweden', Dissertation, Uppsala Universitet (2011), p. 196.

[111] Marriage Act 1991, §16, third paragraph.

[112] The Penal Code 1902, §222, second paragraph, reads as follows: 'Any person who by force, deprivation of liberty, improper pressure or any other unlawful conduct or by threats of such conduct forces anyone to enter into a marriage shall be guilty of causing forced marriage. The penalty for causing forced marriage is imprisonment for a term not exceeding six years. Any person who aids and abets such an offence shall be liable to the same penalty.'

[113] Rt. 2006 p. 140.

to the National Population Register.[114] Presently, each of the parties to the
marriage shall individually solemnly declare that they are contracting the
marriage of their own free will and that they recognise each other's equal
right to divorce.[115] Because many forced marriages are contracted outside
the country, the Marriage Act was amended in 2007 to make it clear that
marriages involving Norwegian nationals will not be recognised in the
realm if the marriage was contracted without the presence of both parties
at the ceremony, or if one of the parties was under 18 years of age, or if one
of the parties is already married.[116] Statutory amendments in family law
have, however, played a minor role in preventing forced marriages, and no
further, significant amendments are expected in this respect.[117]

Cohabitation

10.58   As mentioned, no act specifically regulates cohabitation in
Norway. However, non-statutory rules have developed in case law concerning co-ownership based on indirect contributions.[118] These cases
are restricted to relationships between two persons living together as a
couple (in a marriage-like relationship), and this is also the core of the
definitions used in various statutory regulations, including tax laws
and social security laws.

10.59   When cohabitants with common[119] children were given inheritance rights in 2008, 'cohabitation' was defined as two people above the age
of 18 living together in a marriage-like relationship as long as they were
not married, registered partners or cohabiting with others.[120] Same-sex
couples are included in this definition. The two people must permanently
reside together, but it is expressly stated that shorter periods of separation
due to education, work, illness and the like are no disqualification. Two

---

[114] Marriage Act 1991, Chapter 2.
[115] Marriage Act 1991, §7, 1.   [116] Marriage Act 1991, §18a.
[117] Combating forced marriage requires initiatives from various governmental agencies
     and public services such as schools, health services and emergency houses, as well as
     private initiatives such as the crisis centres and the Red Cross; see Action Plan against
     Forced Marriage 2008–2011. English version available at: www.regjeringen.no/upload/
     BLD/Planer/2007/Tvangsekteskap_engelsk2007.pdf (last accessed 25 January 2011).
[118] See para. 10.64 below.
[119] This implies that they have, have had or expect a child together.
[120] Inheritance Act 1972, Chapter III A and J. Asland and P. Hambro, 'New Developments
     and Expansion of Relationships Covered by Norwegian Law', in B. Atkin (ed.), *The
     International Survey of Family Law. 2009 Edition* (Bristol: Jordan Publishing, 2009),
     pp. 378–84.

people who are so closely related that they cannot marry are excluded from the definition of 'cohabitation'.[121]

Consequences of relationships

Marriage

10.60   Polygamy is forbidden in Norway as it is in the rest of Europe – spouses cannot marry again while still married.[122] Another personal consequence associated only with marriage is the possibility of adopting children jointly. This opportunity is not available for cohabitants (or registered partners).[123] The 2008 amendments to the law allowed married couples of the same sex to be evaluated as prospective adoptive parents.[124] Furthermore, female spouses (and cohabitants) were given the same access to medically assisted reproduction as different-sex couples and they were also given the status of co-mothers.[125]

10.61   As a general rule, marriage itself entails no limitation of the right of a spouse to dispose of his or her property (deferred community property), the only exception being the limited right to dispose of the common residence and household goods during marriage.[126] Even though each spouse owns his or her property separately during the currency of a marriage, specific items of property are frequently co-owned. This is partly due to the fact that co-ownership is established on the basis of the spouses' – and cohabitants' – indirect contribution in the form of domestic work[127] and the covering of the family's current

---

[121] Inheritance Act 1972, §28a.   [122] Marriage Act 1991, §4.

[123] Adoption Act 1986, §5.

[124] A spouse may also adopt the other spouse's child, unless the spouses are of the same sex and the child is an adopted child whose origin is a foreign state that does not permit such adoption; see Adoption Act 1986, §5a.

[125] Biotechnology Act 2003, §§2–2 and 2–3, Children Act 1981, §§3 and 4.

[126] Marriage Act 1991, §31, first paragraph, §§32 and 33.

[127] A homemaker's indirect contributions in the form of care for small children are sufficient in the majority of cases to make her an equal co-owner of an item bought by the breadwinner with income earned during the same period of time. If the children are of compulsory school age and the homemaker still works full-time at home, her work will normally constitute a lesser contribution. This rule is codified in the Marriage Act 1991, §31, third paragraph, and covers items of property for common personal use. The rule applies regardless of which marital property regime the spouses have chosen; see T. Sverdrup, 'Compensating Gain and Loss in Marriage: A Scandinavian Comment on the ALI Principles', in R. F. Wilson (ed.), *Reconceiving the Family. Critique*

expenditures.[128] This method of acquisition, developed in case law in the 1970s and 1980s, departs sharply from the traditional methods of acquiring co-ownership as the justification is not linked to a 'common intention' requirement. In practice, co-ownership limits the exclusive right of the spouses to dispose of an item, and creditors must respect this co-ownership as well.

10.62   Spouses have a mutual duty to provide support during the marriage. They are also obliged to provide each other with the information necessary to assess their financial position.[129]

Cohabitation

10.63   As cohabitation is an informal relationship, cohabitants are, in principle, free to marry another person while cohabiting. Cohabiting couples are not eligible to adopt a child jointly, but the cohabitants may apply individually.[130] Medically assisted reproduction is available to different-sex cohabitants as well as to female cohabitants.[131]

10.64   Cohabitants own their property separately. However, specific items of property are frequently owned jointly, because the method for acquiring co-ownership on the basis of indirect contributions mentioned above applies to cohabitants as well.[132] The advantage is that the party who has not paid for an item of property is not left too vulnerable in bankruptcy cases. The greatest overall financial significance of such co-ownership occurs when the cohabitants separate.[133]

10.65   In contrast to spouses, cohabitants are not legally obliged to support one another. Therefore, when granting means-tested financial social assistance, the authorities cannot take the other cohabitant's income into account as a starting point. However, such income might still be considered if the partner is actually supporting the applicant.[134]

---

on the American Law Institute's Principles of the Law of Family Dissolution (New York: Cambridge University Press, 2006), pp. 476–8.
[128] Rt. 1977 p. 533 and Rt. 1979 p. 1436.
[129] Marriage Act 1991, §§38 and 39.   [130] Adoption Act 1986, §5.
[131] Biotechnology Act 2003, §§2–2 and 2–3; see Children Act 1981, §4.
[132] Rt. 1978, p. 1352 and Rt. 1984, p. 497.
[133] See para. 10.74 below.
[134] Social Services Act 2009, §18; see Circular from the Ministry of Labour (I-34/2001, chapter 5.1.2.4). Another matter is the Ministry's guidelines for calculating support for subsistence – these rates are somewhat lower for people living together in households.

Termination of relationships

Marriage

10.66 Christian V Norwegian Law of 1687 allowed three grounds for divorce (adultery, impotency and desertion) but, from 1790, divorce was granted in administrative practice after a period of legal separation (three years) or factual separation (six to seven years). Divorce by consent was introduced in 1909 after a period of legal separation of one year. In cases where the spouses did not agree upon divorce, several fault grounds existed, in addition to divorce due to irretrievable breakdown. After a Supreme Court judgment in 1952, legal separation, and subsequently divorce, was usually granted on the grounds of irretrievable breakdown without any requirements of proof.[135] The present Marriage Act 1991 introduced a new divorce regime whereby each spouse could demand legal separation and subsequently demand divorce after one year of legal separation or two years of factual separation.[136] This, however, did not represent an essential change in practice due to the 1952 judgment mentioned above. In addition, abuse and forced marriage give the right to immediate divorce.[137] Agreements on children or financial matters are not a prerequisite for separation or divorce, but spouses who have children younger than 16 years of age must attend mediation proceedings.[138] As the consequences of termination occur from the date on which the legal separation is granted,[139] the only real difference between legal separation and divorce is the right to remarry.

10.67 The present divorce regime enjoys substantial support across political dividing lines, and therefore no significant amendments are expected.[140] The lack of real access to divorce among women from minority groups, however, raises concern. Each of the parties to the marriage must now individually declare that they recognise each other's equal right to divorce,[141] but this requirement will hardly improve matters to any appreciable extent.

---

[135] Rt. 1952 p. 812.   [136] Marriage Act 1991, §§21 and 22.

[137] Marriage Act 1991, §23.

[138] Marriage Act 1991, §26; see Children Act 1981, §51.

[139] See for example Marriage Act 1991, §57 and the Inheritance Act 1972, §8.

[140] St. meld. nr. 29 (2002–2003) Om familien – forpliktende samliv og foreldreskap, ch. 2.2.2.

[141] Marriage Act 1991, §7 litra l.

Cohabitation

10.68 Cohabitations are dissolved informally concurrent with the termination of the living relationship. Cohabitants who have children under 16 years of age must, however, attend mediation proceedings.[142] Disputes concerning children and financial matters occur frequently.[143]

Consequences of termination

Marriage

10.69 The personal consequences of divorce include the right to remarry and the right to retain or change one's surname. As regards financial consequences, the Marriage Act 1991 perpetuated the earlier deferred community system, but limited the scope of equal division to apply only to property acquired during the marriage. The essence of this default system is separation of property during the marriage and the division of assets upon dissolution. The assets are divided according to fixed rules, regardless of whether or not maintenance is granted to the ex-spouse. Upon divorce, the net value of assets of the spouses are divided equally after each spouse has withheld from the division the value of assets that can clearly be traced back to premarital assets, gifts and inheritance.[144] This settlement may be adjusted by the courts if the result is obviously unfair, but such adjustments only take place in exceptional cases.[145]

10.70 Experience indicates that this regime constitutes grounds for dispute in many divorce cases. The issue of whether current assets can be traced back to pre-marital assets, inheritance or gifts will be crucial to the financial outcome. Fact-finding becomes paramount and the rules invite disputes and conflicts on a large scale. Furthermore, since only assets acquired during the marriage are subject to division, the rule does not take into account the situation where the favourable financial position of one spouse at the beginning of the marriage – ownership of the house, for example – is an impediment to capital accumulation in a family home during the currency of a marriage. Because many marriages dissolve after a relatively short period of time, it seems natural to limit the divisible assets to those created during the marriage. But the concrete design of

---

[142] Children Act 1981, §51, third paragraph.
[143] See para. 10.74 below.
[144] Marriage Act 1991, §§58 and 59.
[145] Marriage Act 1991, §59; see also §§61 and 63

the rules has been criticised by lawyers and a minor revision might be expected in the future.

10.71 A spouse may also withhold pension rights from division[146] and spousal maintenance is granted only in exceptional cases in Norway. Because 40 per cent of all women are engaged in part-time work, wives earn small pensions, and are thus disadvantaged by these provisions. The sharing of pensions has been the subject of political and legal dispute for many years. However, proposals for reform have gained little support from the political establishment.[147] The self-sufficiency principle has prevailed in Norway for more than thirty years. The idea is that part-time work should not be favoured indirectly through pension-sharing as this could cement gender roles. However, the number of women working part-time has remained fairly constant for the last few decades. Nevertheless, it is highly uncertain whether any amendments to the law will occur with regard to pension-sharing.

10.72 Neither the marital law nor the law of succession is well suited for the present situation where numerous families have children from previous relationships. The Inheritance Act 1972 has to a very small degree taken into consideration the possibility of remarriage and separate children and this Act will now be revised.

Cohabitation

10.73 Upon dissolution, each cohabitant retains his or her property and his or her debts. There is no statutory intervention, apart from a very limited possibility to buy the previously common residence at market value if strong reasons so indicate.[148]

10.74 In many countries the general law of property and trusts has a tendency to produce unfair and arbitrary outcomes for cohabitants upon termination of their relationship. The most obvious reason for this is that cohabitants tend to live as interdependent entities in terms of work, investment and consumption and, unlike market relationships, the exchange of services is not dependent on any closure of contracts.[149] In Norway the

---

[146] Marriage Act 1991, §61.
[147] St. meld. nr. 29 (2002–2003) Om familien – forpliktende samliv og foreldreskap, ch. 2.2.3.
[148] Household Community Act 1991.
[149] See T. Sverdrup, 'An Ill-Fitting Garment: Why the Logic of Private Law Falls Short between Cohabitants', in B. Verschraegen (ed.), *Family Finances* (Vienna: Jan Sramek Verlag, 2009), pp. 353–7.

situation is somewhat better, as co-ownership can be established on the basis of the cohabitants' indirect contribution in the form of domestic work and payment of the family's current expenses.[150] Compensation to avert unjust enrichment may also be granted along the same lines. These are non-statutory rules developed through Supreme Court practice.[151] These case law rules, however, have proven to be poorly suited for settlements after relationship breakdown since, in contrast to the precisely phrased laws with predictable outcomes found in other areas of family law, they contain a degree of ambiguity, leading to an increased level of litigation. The weaker party will often find it too costly to enforce her rights through the legal system. Furthermore, general impressions seem to suggest that a whole range of details are given legal relevance in practice. An unlimited number of facts and incidents are subject to dispute and the rules seem to create conflicts that could harm the future relationship between the cohabitants. Primarily out of consideration for the children of the relationship, this, of course, should be avoided.

10.75   As mentioned above, the opposition to legal regulation of cohabiting relationships has diminished.[152] Moreover, it has become evident that the reason why people live in cohabitating relationships is not necessarily a conscious, mutual desire to avoid legal regulation. As it takes two to make a contract, the reluctant party always has the right of veto. The expression 'freedom for the couple' conceals the fact that the whole issue is about contracting within the couple; that is, it is not about couple autonomy, but about individual autonomy.

10.76   Based on experience gained from the newly enacted inheritance rules for cohabitants, the question of statutory regulation of cohabitation relationships will most certainly be raised again. There is reason to believe that some form of default statutory regulation will be introduced in the course of the next decade.

Self-regulation and custom-made relationships

Marriage

10.77   Spouses may opt out of the default property regime by nuptial or pre-nuptial agreements.[153] Such nuptial agreements may be annulled or

---

[150] See para. 10.64 above.   [151] Rt. 1948 p. 479, Rt. 2000 p. 1089 and Rt. 2011 p. 1168.
[152] See para. 10.54 above.   [153] Marriage Act 1991, §§42–44.

adjusted if they 'affect one of the spouses unfairly', but this provision is interpreted restrictively in practice and is rarely used.[154] One can question whether there is any legitimate reason for the spouses to decide that all assets acquired during a relationship shall be one spouse's separate property with the consequence that the other party is left empty-handed after a long-term relationship. However, the existing regulation allows such agreements to a large extent, and the freedom of contract in this regard is not expected to be restricted any time soon.

Cohabitation

10.78 Cohabitants are free to enter into an agreement aimed at regulating financial consequences upon termination of the relationship, although the contracts may be fully or partially annulled if they affect one of the cohabitants unfairly.[155] However, such annulments only happen in exceptional cases.

10.79 Not many cohabitants regulate financial consequences by an agreement, and outreach to provide the public with information about the importance of making such arrangements do not seem to have helped, even though unmarried cohabitation has been common for more than three decades.[156] This should come as no surprise. Any closure of such a contract is a zero-sum game in which one will lose and one will win, and an agreement does not always provide reliability and predictability for the relationship.

D Conclusions

Children

10.80 Children have become the holder of rights in the course of the last three or four decades, and there have been major steps forward at the legislative level. More statutory measures can be expected in the future, for example regarding the right of the child to be heard, the child's right of access to both parents and individual statutory rights for children in the Child Welfare Act.

---

[154] Marriage Act 1991, §46; see Rt. 1999 p. 718 and Rt. 2006 p. 833.
[155] Act Relating to Conclusion of Agreements 1918, §36.
[156] In 1997 about 20 per cent of Norwegian cohabiting couples had contracted an agreement; see NOU 1999: 25 Samboerne og samfunnnet, p. 71.

10.81 'Equal parenting' has become the key phrase, denoting important political objectives underpinning recent child law reforms in Norway. The debate is symptomatic of the difficulties that arise when the interests of the child and gender equality coalesce over a single issue. In the years to come we will probably experience more legal reforms that in practice will strengthen the legal position of fathers. Efforts to develop procedural and substantive provisions that could prevent and ease conflict will continue, as well. The numbers of custody cases have increased dramatically in recent years and it has proven difficult for the legislator to find suitable legal procedures. Further reforms are therefore expected.

10.82 A recurrent dilemma in child law is the extent to which concern for the individual child's well-being can be set aside so that children as a group will achieve a better position. This question is relevant to numerous issues, including surrogacy and cases where one of the parents obstructs access. There are no easy answers to these questions and we may expect new legal solutions in the future.

10.83 In some respects developments in recent decades can be described as 'two steps forward and one back'. Ten years ago biological parenthood was given high priority at the expense of social parenthood, in terms of paternity, child custody and adoption. This tendency to prioritise the biological parent seems to have been reversed and we are now seeing an increasing emphasis on the child's right to a stable legal framework around the social parenthood.[157] Bio-scientific developments have made current the thought of a more differentiated concept of parenthood and parental responsibility, and one can see the germ of such a development in some of the recent enactments and proposals.[158] Future legal measures will also be determined by what is happening internationally on the human rights front.

---

[157] See para. 10.24 above (proposals to introduce time limits for instituting paternity proceedings) and case law concerning adoption in child welfare cases; see also Rt. 2007 p. 561.

[158] For example, visitation contact for biological parents after their child has been adopted in child welfare cases, proposed contact rights both for people who lose paternity in legal proceedings and pretended parents in surrogacy cases who are denied adoption, discussed above at paras. 10.29 and 10.31.

Adult relationships

10.84   When same-sex couples were allowed to marry in 2008, legal equality between different-sex and same-sex couples was to a large extent achieved, although the debate continues in certain areas such as church marriage and the right to surrogacy for male couples. Church marriage for same-sex couples is to be expected in the foreseeable future, but surrogacy is not.

10.85   Equality is one of the most highly esteemed goals in political circles in Norway and it is not too daring to predict that the differences in financial consequences between marriage and cohabitation will diminish in the years to come, thus entailing a certain amount of default statutory regulation of cohabiting relationships. Introducing limitations on the almost universal contractual freedom that exists both between spouses and between cohabitants is probably further into the future.

10.86   We have seen that other, more specific, ideals and principles underlie the legislation as well. Benefits, for example, are increasingly justified by the parties' contributions rather than their needs. Moreover, the self-sufficiency principle has prevailed for a long time and the ideal is that all females should be engaged in full-time work. These ideals and principles have been subject to criticism in recent years, but it is difficult to predict whether they will be as prevalent in future legal policy as they are today. However, there is a possibility that pensions will be at least partly split in the future. What is certain, however, is that future legislation will take more account of diverse family patterns with regard to stepchildren and remarriage and maybe also with regard to minority groups. Furthermore, there is reason to believe that the best interests of the child will be a more important consideration when future legislation on financial matters is drawn up.

11

Russia

Looking back, evaluating the present and glancing into the future

OLGA A. KHAZOVA

A   Introduction

11.1   Russia is still a country in transition from the totalitarian Soviet regime to a democratic state and, to a certain extent, family law reflects this transitional stage of development. The family law revision in 1994–95 was part of comprehensive reform of the Russian legal system and the Family Code 1995 was adopted on a wave of democratic transformation. Its adoption took place one year before Russia became a member of the Council of Europe and three years before it ratified the European Convention for the Protection of Human Rights and Fundamental Freedoms.

11.2   On the one hand, the family law revision aimed to bring family law into line with the new social and economic realities that resulted from tremendous political change. The Family Code introduced significant changes to a wide spectrum of family law issues, and this undoubtedly explains its strong reception. Amongst the main 'achievements' of the Family Code are an enlargement of citizens' rights in family relations, an increase in the number of dispositive rules and a decrease in the number of imperative rules.[1] Specific changes affected different aspects of family relations, including property relations between the spouses during the marriage and after its dissolution, divorce procedure, children's rights, the types of family placement of neglected children and matters of private international law.

---

[1] For a more detailed analysis of the Russian Family Code, see: M. V. Antokolskaia, 'The 1995 Russian Family Code: A New Approach to the Regulation of Family Relations' (1996) 22 *Review of Central and East European Law* 635; O. Khazova, 'The New Codification of Russian Law', in John Eekelaar and Thandabantu Nhlapo (eds.), *The Changing Family* (Oxford: Hart Publishing, 1998); and O. Khazova, 'Five Years of the Russian Family Code: The First Results', in Andrew Bainham (ed.), *The International Survey of Family Law: 2002 Edition* (Bristol: Jordans Publishing, 2002), p. 347.

11.3   On the other hand, the Family Code was not planned to be as radical as might have been expected taking into account the period of its promulgation. It was a revision but not a reform. The initial 'directive' was to preserve those positive family law provisions that had accumulated during the Soviet era and to adjust them to the new realities without changing family law completely. In this respect, the Family Code 1995 was a more conservative document when compared with the Civil Code 1994–95, which aimed to be the legal basis for 'the economic revolution in Russia'.[2] In the opinion of one commentator, the legislator took account of the complexity and delicacy of family relations and 'treated building up of new legal constructions with care' and the Family Code 'cannot be, luckily, called a revolutionary document'.[3]

11.4   There is an objective explanation for this, namely that family law in the Soviet Union was relatively liberal and, at one stage, even outstripped that in the West. In the Soviet Union there were very liberal divorce regulations; there was no discrimination between children born within and out of lawful wedlock; biological fathers not married to their children's mothers, if their paternity was officially recognised, had the same rights towards their children as those whose children were born within marriage, and so forth. All these provisions have been preserved in the Russian post-Soviet family legislation. Therefore, at least by the time Russia ratified the European Convention on Human Rights, most of the sound reasons that served as the grounds for complaints to the European Court of Human Rights from other countries were absent in Russia. The first case against Russia where the applicant claimed violation of the right to respect for family life was *Nikishina* v. *Russia*.[4] This case originated from a dispute over a child between the applicant, the child's mother, who was a member of the Jehovah's Witnesses, and her former partner, the child's father. *Nikishina* was followed by other cases against Russia, some of which were called 'casus cases'[5] because, although they

---

[2] A. L. Makovsky, 'Preface to the English Translation of the Civil Code', in P. B. Maggs and A. N. Zhiltsov (eds. and trans.), *The Civil Code of the Russian Federation* (Moscow: International Centre for Financial and Economic Development, 1997).

[3] P. V. Krasheninnikov, 'Introduction', in *The Family Code of the Russian Federation with the Clause-By-Clause Comments* (in Russian) (Moscow: Spark, 1996), p. 5.

[4] *Nikishina* v. *Russia*, Application No. 45665/99. At the stage when the application was communicated to the government the parents reached an amicable agreement and the applicant lost the status of victim.

[5] M. R. Voskobitova, 'Strategies for the Conducting of cases in the European Court of Human Rights' (2009) 11 *Zakon* 85.

indicated certain gaps in Russian legislation, they did not reveal any systemic problems.[6]

11.5   Now, sixteen years since enactment of the Family Code, many of its provisions attract a good deal of criticism, which is partly explained by the Code's initial conservatism and, partly, by the haste with which the Code was drafted. Recent years, however, brought new changes and challenges to the country, and to those difficulties that the country faced at the end of the twentieth century, numerous others should be added. A lot of them directly affected many families and include the following, to name just a few. Disparity in wealth and privilege is growing, and the income gap between rich and poor is widening.[7] There has been a dramatic and rapid increase in migration to Russia from the former Soviet Union territories and this has heightened social tensions in the country and posed the problems the true dimension of which it was impossible to anticipate in advance. Aggression and violence, in general, and domestic violence, in particular, have increased tremendously in society.[8] The number of state institutions for neglected children has not decreased despite all the efforts undertaken by the state, and the number of neglected children exceeds that found in the Soviet Union after the Second World War. At the same time, globalisation and its effects, such as increased international migration and transnational marriages, have led to numerous cross-border disputes between divorcing spouses over property and children. There is simply no domestic regulation in place to resolve these disputes. Finally, the Russian Orthodox Church seeks to play an active role in the development of social institutions, particularly the institution of the family, and tries to influence legal regulation in this area.[9] However, the people of Russia profess different

---

[6] Therefore, I will not dwell on them specifically. See for instance: *Shoffman* v. *Russia*, Application No. 74826/01, Judgment 24 November 2005; *Znamenskaya* v. *Russia*, Application No. 77785/01, Judgment 2 June 2005; *Kalacheva* v. *Russia*, Application No. 3451/05, Judgment 7 May 2009.

[7] Sixty per cent of Russians do not make enough money to meet their economic potential. See: 'Optimum Inequality: The Gap between Rich and Poor', available at: http://rbth.ru/articles/2008/01/30/optimum_inequality.html (last accessed 1 March 2012).

[8] In the opinion of E. Mizulina, Chair of the Parliamentary Committee on Matters of Family, Women, and Children, the number of incidences of family violence towards children increased three times for the last five years in Russia. See: www.familycommittee.ru/obratnaya_svyaz/ (in Russian) (last accessed 22 January 2011). See also: 'Domestic Abuse Is Up', *The Moscow Times*, 26 November 2010.

[9] To a significant extent, this is a reaction to the suppression of the Church under the Soviet regime.

religions and, under the Constitution, Russia is a secular state.[10] Another dimension was added to the issue of religion by the expansion of sharia law in the Russian regions where there is a strong Islamic influence.

11.6 It would be a mistake to expect that it would be possible to create a 'perfect' family code that would correspond to reality in full and endure for a long period of time when a country is in transition. Indeed, the Family Code 1995 is, to a certain extent, already outdated. At the same time, many of those challenges that Russia has faced are new to the country and it is not quite clear yet how the law should react to them and, indeed, whether it is the law or other social instruments that should seek to resolve these problems.

Historical roots, sources and law reform

Historical roots

11.7 Although the historical roots of Russian family law go back to the Middle Ages, the more appropriate starting point for discussion is the Bolshevik October Revolution 1917.[11] This was the date when the new family law was created – family law that, to a significant extent, was the basis for contemporary regulation. In this regard, evolution of Russian family law is very different from that in the majority of Western countries. The disrupting event of 1917 led to a 180-degree turn in the life of the country, its political and legal systems, economy, social institutions and social relations. In the process of building a new socialist society, family law was designated a very special role.

11.8 From 1917 and until the breakdown of the Soviet Union in 1991, there were three main reforms of family law in the country: in 1918, 1926 and 1969. All of them took the form of codification of family law. All three codifications, despite all their shortcomings, were very progressive for their time, although their 'fates' were different and reflected the ups and downs in the history of the country during the relevant period.

11.9 The Bolsheviks understood that, to establish a new social order in the most efficient way, it was necessary, as quickly as possible, to break down the old stereotypes within the family and the old family law

---

[10] 'And no religion may be established as the State religion; religious associations shall be separate from the State': Russian Federation Constitution, Art. 14.
[11] In Soviet times this was called 'The Great October Socialist Revolution' and is now more often called 'The October *coup d'état*'.

rules.[12] To do so, to reorganise the family completely, it was necessary to withdraw marriage from the jurisdiction of the ecclesiastical courts and introduce civil (secular) marriage; to make women equal to men and, to use Lenin's expression, to release women from their husbands' 'tyranny'; to make abortion available; to abolish fault-based divorce; to introduce divorce by consent; and, finally, to equalise the status of children born within and outside marriage, eliminating the very concept of illegitimacy from the law. All this was achieved in 1917–18 through the Bolshevik's new legislation on marriage and the family. Later, in 1926, the validity of de facto marriage, or what we now call extramarital cohabitation, was recognised. Thus, during the first post-revolutionary years, the family law that was created was entirely different from Western family law of the same period. It could be seen, to quote M. Antokolskaia, 'as an early herald of the pan-European "family law revolution" '.[13] It would take the West fifty to sixty years to pass similar reforms.

11.10   The Bolsheviks declared marriage to be free from mercantile considerations and to be based on love. Marriage was not considered any longer as an economic necessity for a woman and, accordingly, it ceased to be a way of getting spousal maintenance as well. Under the new social order, everybody, irrespective of sex and family status, was supposed to work, and the right of a woman to claim maintenance from her husband solely because of her status as a wife was abolished as 'a bourgeois survival of the past'. The state, being in economic collapse after the revolution and the civil war, badly needed the female workforce and pushing women out of their homes into the labour market became its family policy. As to children, the state itself was supposed to take care of them, and a programme for the communal upbringing of children was elaborated during the first years of Soviet power. Simultaneously, such a policy was also supposed to ensure that the children would be raised ideologically loyal to the Soviet regime and protected against the possible 'negative' influence of their parents. Fortunately, however, at that stage the family could not be put aside completely since the state was not yet in a position to take full responsibility for children's maintenance and upbringing; it was too weak and too poor.[14]

---

[12] Before October 1917 family law in the Russian Empire did not differ significantly from Western family law of those times.

[13] M. Antokolskaia, *Harmonisation of Family Law in Europe: A Historical Perspective* (Antwerp and Oxford: Intersentia, 2006), p. 238.

[14] The policy of communal upbringing of children did not prove successful. The large number of neglected children produced an enormous rise in juvenile crime. It turned out that

11.11   As the result of a policy aimed at 'strengthening the family', during the subsequent Stalinist period most of the liberal provisions of the first post-revolutionary legislation were rescinded by the infamous Act of 8 July 1944.[15] In particular, Stalin's Act abolished de facto marriages, made divorce very difficult and expensive and put it under strict control of the courts. It also abolished the institution of establishing paternity outside legal marriage and went to the opposite extreme, since it became impossible for a man to legally recognise his child born out of wedlock at all and for an unmarried mother to institute paternity proceedings. The Act abolished abortion,[16] but enabled a woman who gave birth to a child outside marriage to place the child into a state children's institution to be supported and brought up at the expense of the state, irrespective of the reasons for her decision to leave the child. Thus, unmarried mothers were entitled to deliver their parental duties in full to the state and the fathers were completely released from any obligations towards their 'illegitimate' children. Such a 'pro-family' policy, taken together with the post-revolutionary policy of separating the children from their parents, fostered irresponsibility by parents for the fates of their children and legalised 'fatherlessness', or rather 'parentlessness', when a father or parents were clearly available, the consequence of which is still felt today.

11.12   Most of the liberal family law provisions of the post-revolutionary period were restored in the Russian Soviet Federal Socialist Republic (RSFSR) Code on Marriage and the Family of 1969. The exception was de facto marriage, which has not been recognised since its abolition in 1944. In particular, the Code of 1969 made divorce easier and abolished all the rules preventing a person from establishing paternity. Nevertheless, the majority of the rules in the 1969 Code remained strictly imperative in

---

children 'needed' the family and parental care and that there was a strong connection between juvenile delinquency and the absence of family upbringing. On the fate of the 'orphans of the Revolution' during the early years of the new order, see: O. Figes, *The People's Tragedy. The Russian Revolution. 1891–1924* (London: Pimlico, 1997), pp. 780–2.

[15] On Abolition of Abortions, Increase of Financial Aid to Women in Childbirth, Establishing the State Aid to Large Families, Expanding the Network of Maternity Homes, Kindergardens, Strengthening of Punishment for Non-Payment of Alimony, and on Some Changes in the Legislation on Marriage and the Family.

On Increase of State Help to Pregnant Women, Women with Numerous Children, and to Lonely Mothers, Strengthening of Protection of Motherhood and Childhood, on Establishing of the Honorary Title of 'Mother the Hero', Order of 'Mother's Glory' and the Medal known as the 'Medal of Motherhood'.

[16] Termination of pregnancy by abortion was first abolished and made a punishable offence by the Resolution of the Central Executive Committee and Council of People's Commissars of the USSR in 1936.

character and one can find few, if any, dispositive provisions. The 1969 Code was designed to meet the demands of Soviet society and has been described as 'a synthesis of Bolshevik and Stalinist approaches'.[17] By the end of the twentieth century, after the breakdown of the Soviet Union and the subsequent radical changes, the 1969 Code became obsolete and it became evident that a new revision of family law was needed.

Sources

11.13   The Russian Constitution 1993 is the basic law of the country and other legal acts (federal laws, presidential edicts, governmental decrees and so forth) must be in conformity with the constitutional provisions. The Family Code 1995[18] that is currently in force is the main federal law, operating all over the country. There are other federal laws that regulate some aspects of marriage and family: for instance, the Law on the Acts of Legal Status 1997 and the Federal Law on the Basics of Citizens' Health 2011.

11.14   Russia is a federal state. It consists of eighty-three subjects of Federation, often conventionally called 'regions'.[19] Russian Federation subjects are vested with the right to enact family laws within their competence, so long as they are in conformity with the provisions of Family Code ('regional laws'). However, the Family Code covers the overwhelming majority of family law issues, leaving little space for legislative activity by the regions.

11.15   The commonly recognised principles and norms of international law and international treaties of the Russian Federation are declared by the Constitution to be a constituent part of the Russian legal system. The Constitution states that if an international treaty of the Russian Federation stipulates other rules than those provided by Russian law, the rules of the international treaty take precedence.[20] Amongst numerous international agreements and treaties to which Russia is a party, and which consequently have full force in Russian territory, two Conventions should be mentioned especially with regard to the issues under discussion here: the European Convention for the Protection of Human Rights

---

[17]   P. H. Juviler, 'Foreword', in Y. I. Luryi, *Soviet Family Law* (Buffalo: William S. Hein & Co., 1980), p. vi.

[18]   Entered into force on the 1 March 1996.

[19]   Republics, provinces, regions, areas, two cities with federal status (Moscow and Saint Petersburg) and other autonomous units.

[20]   Art. 15(4).

and Fundamental Freedoms 1950 ('European Convention') and the UN Convention on the Rights of the Child 1989 ('UN Convention').[21]

11.16   The Russian legal system is a civil law system, belonging to the legal family of continental law. Although it is not based on judge-made law, the highly authoritative view of the Supreme Court and its guiding instructions are, in fact, mandatory for the courts and are always taken into consideration. Whether the judgments of the Russian superior courts are mandatory for other courts considering similar cases or, in other words, whether Russia recognises precedent as a source of law, has been the subject of one of the most heated debates of recent years and, as yet, there is no clear answer to this question. The issue became particularly topical after creation in 1993 of the Constitutional Court, which can issue judgments on the unconstitutionality of laws (or specific provisions) that are mandatory for all the state bodies that apply the law, including the courts.

Law reform

11.17   There is no particular state law reform body akin to the law commissions found in some other countries. Laws are adopted by the State Duma (Lower Chamber of Russian Parliament – the Federal Assembly) and approved by the Council of Federation (the Upper Chamber of the Russian Federation Parliament). Draft-laws are often worked out in committees of the Parliament, which create special working groups of experts, including lawyers and non-lawyers, in a respective area. However, under the Constitution the right of legislative initiative belongs, in addition to the Council of Federation, to members of the Council of Federation and deputies of the State Duma, the President of the Russian Federation, the Government of the Russian Federation, the legislative (representative) bodies of constituent units of the Russian Federation (Russian Federation 'subjects'), the Russian Federation Constitutional Court, the Russian Federation Supreme Court, and the Russian Federation High *Arbitrazh* (Economic) Court on issues within their competence. Accordingly, each of these bodies can create its own working group to elaborate a bill to be submitted to Parliament.

Dispute resolution and access to legal services

11.18   If the parties fail to solve family disputes themselves, the overwhelming majority are handled by the courts. To date, the courts have not

[21] Ratified by the USSR; entered into force in the territory of the Russian Federation on 15 September 1990.

used mediation techniques in family cases as, until recently, there was no mention of family mediation in legislative or other instruments. The rules on civil procedure for family matters contain provisions on amicable agreements only and entitle the court to adjourn divorce proceedings in order to let the divorcing spouses reconcile. In the majority of cases, however, adjournment for reconciliation is just a formality and only delays the final decision.

11.19 A new law – the Law on Alternative Dispute Resolution with Participation of an Intermediary (Mediation Procedure) – came into force on 1 January 2011. This law governs the application of mediation to commercial disputes, as well as to labour and family disputes.[22] Although several centres and dispute resolution groups had been providing mediation services, including family mediation, before the enactment of this law, general awareness of this form of dispute resolution amongst the conflicting parties, their lawyers and society as a whole was and remains low. Most of the initiative in developing mediation in general comes from the business community and particularly judges, practising lawyers and legal scholars involved in dealing with commercial disputes. Therefore, the prospects for family mediation in Russia are, to a certain extent, connected to the prospects for mediation itself. Hopefully, the new law on mediation will act as a catalyst of development of mediation in general, and family mediation in particular, in the country.

11.20 Apart from a general lack of awareness of the advantages of family mediation, there are other factors that make the promotion of family mediation in Russia problematic. In particular, there is the lack of certainty about its effectiveness and concerns about the enforceability of agreements reached as a result of this procedure. In addition, specialists recognise that litigation in Russia is cheaper and faster than in the West, so the incentive of mediation being a more economic alternative to litigation is lacking in Russia. The main challenges, however, seem to be on a different plane. Mediation is part of the culture of a given country. In Russia it has many different, though interconnected, implications. One of the most important is that mediation assumes a certain level of development of civil society and certain levels of personal autonomy and personal freedom, and, accordingly, personal responsibility. It also assumes, on the one hand, personal self-esteem and, on the other hand, respect for other people and their opinion, as well as tolerance in the society in general.

---

[22] Section 1(2).

The ability to negotiate and not to fight is a mandatory prerequisite for successful mediation. These are characteristics that will require further development in Russia.

B   Children in the family setting and state intervention

11.21   For the first time in the Family Code of 1995, an attempt was made 'to take children's rights seriously' and to treat them as individuals and as subjects of law, and not just as objects of 'parental authority'.[23] For a long time a 'one-sided view' of the protection of children that dominated the law of the former USSR prevailed, with the child being viewed through the prism of the parents and the child's interests being protected in an indirect way, primarily by means of protection of the interests of the child's mother. Such an exclusively paternalistic approach left practically no place for the child's own rights and interests. The Code of 1995 contains a chapter, based on the UN Convention, dedicated to the rights of children, where it aims to place the child in the centre of family relations, to guarantee an independent position for the child and to secure respect for his or her opinion.[24] Although in practice, to a significant extent, it is still a goal to be achieved, the very fact that children's rights were articulated in the main national family law act was itself important. All the provisions of the chapter are based on the UN Convention on the Rights of the Child.

Defining and classifying children

11.22   The Family Code defines a child as a person who has not reached 18 years of age.[25] This is the age of majority and also the age at which a person is allowed to marry without the consent of an appropriate authority, and this definition is fully consistent with the UN Convention. The bodies that are authorised to permit underage marriage, provided the individual has reached 16 years of age, are local governments. The Family Code does not stipulate even a model list of situations when such dispensation is possible. In practice, these are usually pregnancy of a bride, birth of a child or stable extramarital cohabitation.[26] In addition, the Family Code grants

---

[23]   M. G. Masevich, I. M. Kuznetsova, N. I. Marysheva, 'The New Family Code of the Russian Federation (Brief Commentary)', in *Semeinyi Kodeks RF s Kratkim Kommentariem (Family Code with Brief Commentary)* (Moscow: BEK, 1996), p. XXVI.

[24]   Chapter 11.   [25]   Family Code, s. 54(1).

[26]   O. N. Nizamieva (ed.), *Commentary to the Family Code of the Russian Federation* (Moscow: Prospekt, 2011), p. 51.

the Russian Federation regions the right, 'in exceptional cases taking into account special circumstances', to enact laws which allow marriage of those who have not reached 16 years of age.[27] Not that many regions adopted such laws, but those that did stipulated pregnancy of a bride and birth of a child as conditions when it is possible to lower the marriage age. Most important differences concern the lower age limit. For instance, the Family Code of the Tatarstan Republic does not establish any lower age limit, which was rightly criticised by commentators.[28] If an underage child receives permission to marry from an appropriate body before he or she reaches the age of majority, the child acquires active dispositive legal capacity in full upon entry into marriage.[29] In addition, a child who has attained 16 years of age and works under a labour contract or engages in business activity may be declared an 'emancipated minor' and given full active dispositive legal capacity.[30] This, however, does not give the emancipated minor the right to get married without the consent of an appropriate body discussed above. Administrative and criminal legal responsibility attaches from the age of 16,[31] although a minor child is criminally liable from the age of 14 for especially grave crimes.[32]

11.23 There is not much discussion of a problem connected with what is now known as forced or coerced marriage, although this does not mean that such a problem does not exist. It is known that the number of incidences of forced marriages of young women and teenage girls is common in the southern areas of Russia. Usually it takes the form of bride kidnapping with subsequent release of a bride on condition that her parents will promise to consent to her marriage with the abductor. Despite regional governments making attempts to eradicate bride kidnapping, it is on the increase and is becoming a growing problem.[33]

---

[27] Family Code, s. 13(2).

[28] Nizamieva (ed.), *Commentary to the Family Code of the Russian Federation*, p. 53.

[29] Russian Federation Civil Code, s. 21.   [30] *Ibid.*, s. 27.

[31] Russian Federation Administrative Offences Code s. 2.3 and Russian Federation Criminal Code s. 20.

[32] Homicide, intentional infliction of grave bodily injury causing an impairment of health, kidnapping, rape, theft, robbery, and some others: Russian Federation Criminal Code, s. 20.

[33] On this matter see, for instance: www.rferl.org/content/Despite_Official_Measures_Bride_Kidnapping_Endemic_In_Chechnya/2197575.html (last accessed 10 September 2011), www.allvoices.com/contributed-news/7892261-muslim-chechnya-struggles-to-end-bride-kidnapping (last accessed 20 March 2012), http://en.rian.ru/society/20071016/84145392.html (last accessed 10 September 2011) and http://en.rian.ru/russia/20101006/160855432.html (last accessed 10 September 2011).

11.24   In conformity with the UN Convention, the Family Code provides that the child has 'the right to express his opinion when any matter affecting his interests is being decided in the family, as well as [to] be heard in any judicial and administrative proceedings'.[34] In family matters it is mandatory for the court to take account of the opinion of a child who has attained 10 years of age, provided that it 'does not contradict the child's interests'.[35] In addition, there are cases, including changing a child's name or placing a child for adoption, when the court may not dispense with the consent of a child who has reached the age of 10. Much still needs to be done, however, to ensure that children have an effective way to exercise their rights to participate in proceedings and to meet the requirements of the Council of Europe Guidelines on Child-Friendly Justice.[36] A child may bring a suit in court from the age of 14, although this provision is more theoretical than real.[37]

11.25   As we have seen, Russian law does not discriminate between children born in lawful wedlock and outside it. All children, irrespective of their birth status, have the same rights in respect of their fathers, as well as mothers, provided their filiation was established in a proper way.

Recognising parentage and family ties

11.26   Properly registered blood parentage is the ground for creation of legal relations between parents and children. This has been a fundamental principle since October 1917, repeated in all subsequent family laws and provided for now in the Family Code 1995. Thus, to have parental rights and responsibilities, a person must establish his or her parental status. In order to do so the mother and father of a child must be registered as the child's parents in the birth registration book and on their child's birth certificate.

11.27   Russian family law strongly adheres to the presumption that a husband is the father of his wife's child. The presumption can be rebutted in court by the child's parents or by a person who considers himself to be the child's father or by the child himself or herself upon reaching the age of majority. If a child has been born out of wedlock, paternity can be

---

[34] Family Code, s. 27.   [35] *Ibid.*, s. 57.

[36] www.coe.int/t/DGHL/STANDARDSETTING/FAMILY/default_en.asp (last accessed 1 March 2012).

[37] *Ibid.*, s. 56(1).

established voluntarily by the body for registration of civil status under a joint application of the father and the mother. If a biological father refuses to establish his paternity voluntarily, it may be established in court proceedings. Where a petition to establish paternity is granted, despite the father's reluctance to recognise his paternity voluntarily, he acquires not only a duty to maintain the child, but also all the parental rights of a father who established paternity voluntarily. This 'all or nothing approach' of Russian family law has been justly criticised, although the suggestion that a father who did not establish his paternity voluntarily should be denied full parental authority remains a proposal *de lege ferenda*.[38]

11.28 Ideally, social and biological parentage coincide. Until recently, the only exception to this was adoption where, in accordance with Russian law, adoptive parents replace natural parents both legally and socially. Biomedical advances in assisted reproduction (ART) have brought a new dimension to the regulation of parentage. However, despite widespread use of ART in Russian medical practice, Russian law is still not well developed and there are a lot of serious gaps in this regard. Nevertheless, there are a few important provisions. One of them concerns surrogate motherhood. First, only full, or gestational, surrogacy is permitted by law. Secondly, the surrogate mother has the right to keep the child. Spouses who have agreed to the implantation of an embryo into another woman can be registered as the child's parents, but only if the surrogate mother gives her consent to such a registration.[39] This legal rule followed the European principles on surrogate motherhood and is based on a concept that 'the woman who gave birth to the child is considered in law as the mother'.[40] If the surrogate mother gave her consent to the spouses being registered as the child's parents and the child's birth was registered in a proper way, she is considered at law as a stranger to that child and may not claim to have contact with him or her.

11.29 Applying a literal interpretation to the current wording of the Family Code provisions on assisted reproduction, only married couples can be registered as a child's legal parents, while cohabiting couples and unmarried women are excluded.[41] This provision was designed to serve as a response to the highly controversial question of the right of unmarried

---

[38] Meaning literally, 'with a view to the future': Antokolskaia, 'The 1995 Russian Family Code', 657.

[39] Family Code, s. 51(4).

[40] Council of Europe, *Ad Hoc Committee of Experts on Bioethics, Report on Human Artificial Procreation* (Strasbourg: 1989), Principle 14.

[41] Family Code, s. 51.

couples to have access to ART. However, it led to numerous violations of human rights because the bodies responsible for registration of civil status based their actions on this provision of the Family Code and refused to register unmarried couples and single women in the birth registry book and on the birth certificate as the parents or mother of a child born to a surrogate mother. Many 'commissioning couples', single women and, recently, even men ('intended single fathers') were successful in challenging this refusal in the courts.[42] The new Law on Citizens' Health to a certain extent solved this problem too, as it opened the way to assisted reproduction for non-married couples. This Law states that "a man and a woman, married as well as not married, have the right to have access to assisted reproduction, provided they gave their mutual informed consent to medical interference".[43] Following the previous regulation, this Law also gave single women lawful access to assisted reproduction. However, the Law is silent on whether men have a similar right and, from the wording of the provision, it follows that they do not. Therefore, in the future, we can expect applications claiming this provision is unconstitutional, due to a violation of the equality principle, will be filed with the Constitution Court.

11.30   In the case of artificial insemination or in vitro fertilisation where no surrogate is involved, the general rule is that a married couple who consented to ART shall be registered as the child's parents, with all the legal consequences thereof. For birth registration purposes, whether a couple are genetically related to a child or not makes no difference. Donors of genetic material remain anonymous and acquire no rights or responsibilities towards a child conceived through ART. Non-biological paternity or maternity, once recognised cannot be revoked later on the ground that ART was used.

11.31   Although Russian family law recognises the child's right, as far as possible, to know his or her origins, this legal rule is ahead of social reality and other rules reflecting the latter. For instance, it is still common to keep the adoption of a newborn child secret and there are special provisions in Family Code that allow the court, upon receiving a request

---

[42] One of such cases reached the Russian Federation Supreme Court: Ruling of the Russian Federation Supreme Court No. 78-Ф08–1314 of 8 September 2008. See also: http://rus.ruvr.ru/_print/20505223.html (in Russian) (last accessed 10 September 2011).

[43] Section 55(3). This will require amending the above-mentioned provision of the Family Code. However, until such amendments are made, there will be a contradiction between these two federal laws.

from the adoptive parents, to indicate in the adoption order that the adoptive parents should be registered as the child's biological parents and even to change the date and the place of birth of an adopted child in order to keep adoption secret.[44] There is also a provision in the Criminal Code supporting secrecy in adoption that makes disclosure of adoption a crime.[45] Although there is no clear reference to donor anonymity in the new Law on Citizens' Health, we can assume that, in the context of ART, it upholds donor anonymity in the same way as did the previous Law. This conclusion follows from the provision of the new Law stating that persons undergoing IVF and AI treatment with the use of donor gametes and embryos have the right to information about the results of medical and genetic tests on a donor, the donor's ethnicity and nationality, as well as his or her outward appearance.[46] Therefore, both theoretically and technically, upon reaching the age of majority a child might claim to have access to general information about his or her origins, or at least to as much information about the donor as was given to the child's mother before the child's conception.[47] There are, however, no specific provisions in law in this regard except the very broad provision in the Family Code mentioned above and there are no reported cases. There is no public discussion of the matter either.

11.32   The majority of Russian children are born within marriage. Nevertheless, the number of non-marital births is significant. It has increased threefold since 1980 and constituted 30% of all births in 2002,[48] although recent studies showed a slight decrease in this number.[49] Nearly 50% of children born outside marriage were registered on the joint application of both parents.[50]

---

[44] Family Code, ss. 135–136. It is possible to change the date of the child's birth as long as the child is under one year old.

[45] Section 155 of the Criminal Code provides: 'Disclosure of the secret of adoption contrary to the will of the adopter, committed by a person who is duty-bound to keep the fact of adoption as an official or professional secret, or by any other person out of mercenary or other ignoble motives.'

[46] The Federal Law on the Basics of Protection of Citizens' Health 2011, s. 55(8).

[47] Under the Fundamentals, s. 35, the woman undergoing IVF treatment has the right to information about, inter alia, the donor's outward appearance and ethnicity.

[48] According to the results of the 2002 population census, available at: www.gks.ru/PEREPIS/report.htm (in Russian) (last accessed 1 March 2012).

[49] In 2008 the number of children born to unmarried mothers constituted 26.9% of total births, and in 2009 it constituted 26.1%. See: *The Demographic Yearbook of Russia 2010*. Statistical handbook (Moscow: Rosstat, 2010), pp. 165–6, available at: www.gks.ru/doc_2010/demo.pdf (last accessed 20 March 2012).

[50] See: www.gks.ru/PEREPIS/report.htm (last accessed 1 March 2012).

Delivering parenting

11.33   Under Russian law both parents have equal rights and duties with regard to their children regardless of their marital status.[51] The extent of their parental rights is not affected by parental divorce, nor dependent on which parent the child resides with. Technically, the concept of custody, as it is used in Western family law, is unknown in Russian legal doctrine and legislation and a parent with whom a child resides is not considered at law as a 'custodial parent'.[52] At the same time, the more Russian courts face parental disputes over children with a so-called 'foreign element' (i.e. between the parents, one of whom is either a foreigner or resides abroad or both), the more difficult it becomes to avoid using the Western term 'custody'.

11.34   Both parents have the right and, at the same time, the duty to take care of their children and to raise them. They both bear responsibility for the maintenance of their children, their nurture and development, and they are both obliged to take care of the children's health and their physical, mental, spiritual and moral development.[53] Parental rights may not be exercised contrary to the interests of their children and, as the law provides, the parents' main concern shall be ensuring the interests of their children.[54] When exercising parental rights, parents must not cause harm to their children's physical and mental health nor their moral development. Methods of upbringing shall exclude contemptuous, cruel, coarse or humiliating treatment, as well as insult to, or exploitation of, children.[55] Parents who exercise their parental rights to the prejudice of the rights and interests of their children bear responsibility under the law: in particular, such parents may, by a court order, be limited in or deprived of their parental rights.[56]

---

[51] Russian Federation Constitution 1993, Art. 38; Family Code, s. 61.

[52] The notion of 'custody' exists in Russian law, but it is applicable to different kinds of cases. In particular, custody or guardianship over minor children may be established if they lack parents or adoptive parents, if the court has deprived the parents of parental rights or in other cases where the children have been left without parental care. Custody may be established over minor children who have not yet attained 14 years of age, and guardianship over children between 14 and 18 years of age: Civil Code, ss. 31–33. Custody may also be established over adults for protection of their rights and interests, if they have been declared by a court order to be lacking dispositive capacity due to a mental disorder: CC, s. 33.

[53] Family Code, s. 63.   [54] Family Code, s. 65(1).

[55] Family Code, s. 65(1).

[56] See further, para. 11.45 below.

11.35   Parents have a preferential right, superior to that of all other persons, to nurture their children.[57] They also have the right to demand the return of their child from any person withholding the child without lawful authority.[58] In cases of a dispute, the parents can apply to a court to protect parental rights. All other things being equal, such a child-related dispute should be resolved in favour of the parents.[59] Depending on the facts and taking into account the opinion of the child, the court may, however, refuse to satisfy the parents' claim if it comes to the conclusion that the return of the child to the parents does not correspond to the child's best interests.[60] Such an intrusion into parental rights is considered as an extreme measure, justified by extraordinary circumstances, the best interests of the child being paramount. From a legal point of view, this will lead to parents being deprived of their parental rights or having them restricted.

11.36   The grandparents, brothers and sisters of a child, as well as other relatives, have the right to communicate with the child.[61] However, the law provides a remedy only for close relatives of the child and not just any relative. There is no precise definition of 'close relatives' in the Family Code, but the term usually includes grandparents, brothers and sisters. The Code expressly states that if the parents (or one of them) refuse to grant to 'close relatives' the possibility of communicating with the child, the custody and guardianship body[62] may oblige the parents (or one of them) not to obstruct this communication. If the parents do not obey, a relative whose right to communicate with the child has been violated or the custody and guardianship body itself may bring a suit to remove the obstacles to communication with the child.

Intra-family disputes

11.37   Parents are encouraged by law to decide all questions that concern the upbringing and education of their children by mutual consent, bearing in mind the children's interests and taking into account their opinion.[63] The same is true with regard to the place of child's residence when the parents reside separately.[64] Too often, however, the parents fail

---

[57] Family Code, s. 63(1).   [58] Family Code, s. 68(1).
[59] Nizamieva (ed.), *Commentary to the Family Code of the Russian Federation*, pp. 238–9.
[60] Family Code, s. 68(1).   [61] Family Code, s. 67(1).
[62] For more detail on custody and guardianship bodies, see para. 11.38 below.
[63] Family Code, s. 65(2).   [64] Family Code, s. 65(3).

to reach agreement regarding their common children and have to go to court.

11.38   In all court proceedings where a dispute over children is under consideration, participation of a custody and guardianship body is mandatory.[65] These are the state bodies at the regional level.[66] One of their main tasks is the protection of the rights and interests of underage children when there is a dispute over a child between the parents or when the parents, for whatever reason, are unable to fulfil their parental duties. The custody and guardianship body performs a home-study and submits the results of the study to the court, along with its opinion on the preferred solution. However, the custody and guardianship bodies are Soviet-style bodies; they do not have enough personnel, and the child protection inspectors are unable to monitor all problem families within their respective districts and to participate in all the parental disputes that go to court. Often, they are not specially trained and do not have the skills necessary to deal with difficult cases. Thus, the home-studies performed by custody and guardianship bodies, as well as their involvement in divorce proceedings, is often just a formality and practising lawyers consider these bodies easy to manipulate.

11.39   As is the case in other jurisdictions, disputes over children usually occur when the parents divorce or if they live separately and are not able to come to an agreement regarding the child's place of residence, child maintenance and/or the visitation rights of the non-resident parent. Interestingly, in Russia in divorce proceedings parents usually address the child's residence and maintenance, but not the visitation rights of the non-resident parent. As the result of such short-sightedness, the non-resident parent often has to bring another suit dealing with visitation, typically one or two years later,[67] because the resident parent is violating the other parent's right of access to the child. By that time, the child has already been seriously traumatised by the parents' divorce, by the parents' conflicts over the child and by the fact that he or she has lost contact with one of the parents, a common occurrence in conflict situations. In addition, it is not yet common practice to provide a detailed visitation schedule for a non-resident parent, either in the parental agreement or in

---

[65] Family Code, s. 78.

[66] Federal Law On Custody and Guardianship of 24 April 2008.

[67] F. S. Safuanov, N. K. Kharitonova, O. A. Rusakovskaia, *Psychological and Psychiatric Expert Examination in Litigation between the Parents on the Child's Upbringing and Place of Residence* (Moscow: Genesis, 2011), pp. 60, 67.

the court order. Failure to do so often significantly complicates relations between separately residing parents over their children and enforcement of the court's access orders.[68]

11.40   There are no special provisions in Russian family legislation and case law governing one of the parents relocating within the country along with the child. This omission is explained by the fact that, at least until recently, there was no tradition in Russia of moving from one place to another frequently (to the extent that is typical, for instance, in the USA or within the European Union). However, the number of disputes between parents over the child's place of residence and access, where unauthorised relocation of the child is the key issue, has increased considerably.[69] If one of the parents relocates a child abroad without the other parent's consent, the problem becomes insoluble due to the absence of any effective national legal mechanism aimed at prevention of child abduction or the return of an abducted child. Some of the recent abduction cases became truly scandalous. Russia only acceded to the Hague Convention on the Civil Aspects of International Child Abduction 1980[70] in June 2011; therefore, the process of implementing the new regulation has just begun. The legal rules on child's relocation that have been applied in Russia so far produced a great deal of confusion, in practice. For instance, the law does not require the notarially certified consent of another parent to the child being taken abroad.[71] At the same time, it allows a parent who opposes his or her child's exit from Russia to submit an application to the immigration authorities to put the child on a 'stop list' at the Russian state border without any explanation of the reasons for such a request.[72] It is very difficult to lift the ban on a child's exit from the country later, even if the only motivation of a parent who submitted the application was to vex his or her former spouse. Regulation of these

---

[68] *Annual 2004 Report of Moscow Ombudsman for Children's Rights*, available at: http://ombudsman.mos.ru/index.php?id=yearreports&tx_ptreports_pi1[showUid]=10&cHash=8b6a09e190 (in Russian), p. 41 (last accessed 1 March 2012).

[69] According to E. B. Mizulina, Chair of the Parliamentary Committee on Matters of Family, Women, and Children, the number of such disputes in the country currently exceeds 100,000: see: http://echo.msk.ru/programs/razvorot-morning/756182-echo.phtml (in Russian) (last accessed 1 March 2012). See also: http://kp.ru/print/article/25649.4/813017 (in Russian) (last accessed 1 March 2012).

[70] HCCH No. 25.

[71] Consular departments of foreign embassies usually require such consent for visa purposes.

[72] Federal Law on the Order of Exit from the Russian Federation and Entry to the Russian Federation 1996, ss. 20–21.

issues, in particular, will have to be changed and adapted to meet the requirements of the Hague Convention on Abduction. As mediation is an integral part of international settlement of cross-border family disputes, it will, hopefully, also expand opportunities for the development of international family mediation in Russia.

11.41   When the court resolves issues related to a child's place of residence or visitation rights, it is required to take all the facts of the particular case into account, the main guiding principle for the court being the interests of the child.[73] The court must give preference to the parent who ensures or can ensure the most favourable conditions for the child's upbringing.[74] This is what the law provides. The reality is often different.

11.42   Indeed, it is often a hard task for the court to determine what decision is in the best interests of a particular child. To assist it in reaching the correct decision, the court can order a psychologist and/or psychiatrist to render an expert opinion,[75] something that was rarely done until recently, and there has been a steady increase in the involvement of psychologists and psychiatrists in disputes over children.[76] Apart from the objective difficulties that the judge resolving a child-related dispute faces, there are also other factors that, although contextual, influence the way a particular dispute is resolved. Too often the courts fail to investigate all the facts of a case under consideration. They are often reluctant to go deeply into all the details, often relying on unreliable or meagre evidence, and give inadequate reasoning in support of their judgments. There are numerous cases that demonstrate that the parent who is more powerful and has more money usually wins.[77]

---

[73] Family Code, s. 65(3).

[74] The Family Code contains an exemplary list of circumstances that the court shall consider. These are the age of a child; attachment of a child to a particular parent, brother, or sister; moral and other personal characteristics of the parents; relations that exist between a child and each of the parents; potential to create the proper conditions for the child's upbringing and development; the parents' occupation and work regime; and their financial circumstances and family status: Family Code, s. 65(3).

[75] See: T. B. Dmitrieva and F. C. Safuanova (eds.), *Meditsinskaya i sudebnaya psykhologiya: kurs lektsyi (Medical and Judicial Psychology: Lectures)* (in Russian) (Moscow: Genesis, 2004), pp. 179–81.

[76] Safuanov *et al.*, *Psychological and Psychiatric Expert Examination in Litigation between the Parents*, p. 7.

[77] See, for instance: A. Malpas 'In the Spotlight: Slutsker vs. Slutsker', *The St Petersburg Times*, 25 September 2009, available at www.sptimesrussia.com/index.php?action_id=100&story_id=29897 (last accessed 1 March 2012).

Child protection and state intervention

11.43   Broadly speaking, there are two sets of situations when the state, whether through the courts or other state bodies, intervenes in the family in order to provide protection to a particular child or children. These are, first, disputes between the parents when the parents fail to come to an agreement over their child,[78] and secondly, cases when parents fail to fulfil their parental rights and duties (including abuse of parental rights) and/ or when children are left without parental care (due to the parents' failure to fulfil their parental rights or due to the absence of parents at all).

11.44   The parents, being the primary caregivers, should maintain their children and provide them with everything the children need for their proper upbringing and development. If the parents fail to fulfil their duties, the state steps in. In this regard, the Family Code stipulates three types of remedy: deprivation of parental rights,[79] restriction of parental rights[80] and taking the child away in case of direct threat to the child's life or health.[81]

11.45   Deprivation of parental rights, being designed as a measure of last resort, is a very serious interference with family relations since it terminates parental rights in respect of a particular child completely. It is supposed to be used in extreme situations only, in case of a serious parental misconduct, when it is dangerous for the child to remain with the parents and when there is virtually no chance of the family situation improving. Restriction of parental rights, in contrast, is seen and used as a preventive measure, when it is still possible to work with the family, to help parents to overcome the difficulties and to return the children to the parents. However, court statistics show that the state usually intervenes when it is too late to help the family and the only thing that the court can do is to deprive the parents of their rights and take the children away from the family as soon as possible. Moreover, the number of children whose parents have been deprived of parental rights remains very high.[82] This number exceeds, by several times, the

---

[78] See paras. 11.37–11.41 above.
[79] Family Code, s. 69.   [80] Family Code, s. 73.   [81] Family Code, s. 77.
[82] See: www.rfdeti.ru/files/1294742625_deti_v_possii.pdf, p. 111 (last accessed 20 March 2012). See also: *Children in a Difficult Life Situation: New Approaches to Solution of the Problems* (Moscow: Foundation for the Support of Children in a Difficult Life Situation, 2010), pp. 18–19.

number of children whose parents' rights have been restricted.[83] The picture is worsened by the fact that the number of cases where parental rights are restored is miserably low.[84]

11.46 This sad situation results from a number of factors, some undoubtedly connected to the economic and social difficulties that many Russian families have faced since the breakdown of the Soviet Union and the increased aggression and violence in society. At the same time, the origins of this situation, to a significant extent, go back to Soviet times. The point is that one of the fundamental principles of Soviet policy with regard to the family, originating straight after October 1917 and continuing through the whole Soviet period, was a paternalistic approach towards the family and preference for the so-called 'public upbringing of children'. The state deemed itself, rather than the parents, to be better able to raise children and to be responsible for their fate. To reiterate, the parents were supposed to work. Therefore, in the Soviet Union there was a well-developed network of kindergartens, day nurseries, schools with extended day classes, boarding schools and different kinds of institutions for neglected children. This system aimed to help mothers to get involved in full-time work and also – what is of equal importance – to guarantee that a child would be properly raised as 'a true soviet man' (or 'soviet woman'). This ideological function of public upbringing was prioritised up to the very end of the Soviet era. It is not surprising, therefore, that the state focused mostly on institutions for children and not on working with families in trouble. Accordingly, there were neither specialists trained to work with families (such as social workers, for instance), nor a system of organisations or bodies specialised in helping families to cope with problems at the earliest possible stage. At present, the negative results of this policy are still being felt as there is no system of early intervention for problem families that could, instead of taking the child away from the family and placing the child in a state institution, provide families with professional advice and help to keep the child with his or her biological family. Without such a system, it is difficult to identify the families that may need help. Usually, it becomes obvious that a particular family is in trouble when

---

[83] Just to compare, in 2008 the number of children whose parents were restricted in parental rights was equal to 6,865. See: *Children in Russia*, 2009.

[84] In the opinion of federal experts, the number of decisions on restoration of parental rights is so small that there are no statistics on this matter. See, T. A. Gurko, *Marriage and Parenthood in Russia* (Moscow: Institute of Sociology RAS, 2008), p. 254.

it is too late and no 'remedial treatment' can help at that late stage. As a rule, a child in such a family is aged 7 and older, and it is almost impossible for such a child to be adopted and, thus, to find a new family.[85]

C   Adult relationships

The relationships

11.47   Under Russian law, the spousal relationship arises only from a lawful marriage: that is, a marriage registered with a state body for the registration of civil status. As a result, extramarital cohabitation has no legal consequences under family law. In this respect, Russian law is in obvious dissonance with the recent trends in Western family law and jurisprudence of the European Court of Human Rights.

11.48   Non-recognition of extramarital cohabitation by the legal system does not mean, however, that such cohabitation does not exist. It does and its number is constantly increasing.[86] The Russian population census undertaken in 2002 showed that about 10% of those interviewed said that they lived in de facto marriages.[87] In comparison, in 1989 extramarital cohabitation constituted approximately 5–6% of relationships.[88] Other data and assessments of indirect factors demonstrate that unregistered cohabitation is more widespread in Russia than the official statistics reflect.[89] In addition, the results of one recent survey conducted in 2009 showed that the number of couples who did not register their 'marriage' was higher than that recorded in the population census

[85] E. B. Mizulina, 'In a Healthy Society There Can Be No Children who Do Not Belong to Anyone', 6 March 2008 *Parliamentary Gazette*, pp. 15–16. (In Russian: V zdorovom obshchestve ne mozhet byt' nicheinykh detei // Parlamentsakaya Gazeta).

[86] This is called the 'quiet revolution' in attitudes towards marriage that has occurred over the last two decades in Russia. See: S. Zakharov, 'The Most Recent Trends of Formation of the Family in Russia' (in Russian: Noveishie tendentsii formirovaniya semyi v Rosii), *Demoskop Weekly*, 16 March 2006, available at: www.polit.ru/research/2006/03/16/demoscope237.html (last accessed 1 March 2012).

[87] Available at: www.perepis2002.ru/content.html?id=7&docid=10715289081450 (www.gks.ru/PEREPIS/report.htm) (last accessed 1 March 2012).

[88] Newspaper '*Trud*', 25 December 2007, p. 5, available at: www.trud.ru/issue/article.php?id=200712252370101 (last accessed 1 March 2012).

[89] See, for example, A. A. Avdeev, 'Marriages and Divorces in Russia', in E. V. Izotova, E. V. Kochkina and E. V. M. Mashkova (eds.), *Gender Expertise and Legislative Policy* (in Russian: *Gendernaia expertisa i zakonodatelnaia politika*), 2 vols. (Moscow: Avanti-plus, 2004), Vol. 1, pp. 219–20.

in 2002.[90] According to the Russian population census of 2010, the number of unregistered marriages constituted 13%.[91]

11.49   In 2004 the European Court of Human Rights issued an 'epoch-making' judgment[92] in the case of *Prokopovich* v. *Russia*,[93] where it unanimously found a violation of applicant's right to respect for his home protected under Article 8 of the European Convention, because after her partner's death Russian state officials evicted the applicant from her home in a flat, in which she had been living with her late partner without marriage for ten years. The first case against Russia, where non-recognition of extramarital cohabitation with regard to respect for family life was an issue, was considered by the European Court of Human Rights in 2007.[94] In this case the applicant claimed violation of her rights under Article 8 of the European Convention based on the domestic courts' denial of compensation for non-pecuniary damage in connection with the death, in a plane crash, of her non-marital partner. After the European Court declared the application admissible, the Russian Federation Supreme Court heard an application for supervisory review lodged by the applicant and referred it for examination on the merits to the Presidium of the relevant regional court. In a new trial, the regional court reversed the initial judgment and satisfied the applicant's claim. It pointed out that 'the law does not make the right to receive compensation for non-pecuniary damage conditional on the existence of a marital relationship. Family ties may arise not only from marriage or cognation, and the death of a breadwinner may cause damage not only to the spouse or blood relatives, but also to other family members.'[95] Not surprisingly, as a result the European Court of Human Rights, when it considered the application, found no violation of Article 8. Thus, if we can expect any change with regard to legal recognition of non-marital cohabitation, it will no doubt be the result not only of the requirements of social reality, but also of European Court of Human Rights case law.

---

[90] See, 'Brief Results of a Sampling Survey: Family and Birthrate 2009' (in Russian), available at: www.gks.ru/wps/wcm/connect/rosstat/rosstatsite/main/population/demography/ (last accessed 1 March 2012).

[91] 'That Is What We Are – the Russians. About the Results of the 2010 Population Census', *Russian Newspaper*, 16 December 2011, available at: www.rg.ru/2011/12/16/stat.html.

[92] A. T. Bonner and O. Y. Kotov, 'The Principle of Legal Certainty in Case Law of the European Court on Human Rights' (2008) 4 *Zakon* 202 (in Russian).

[93] *Prokopovich* v. *Russia*, Application No. 58255/00, Judgment 18 November 2004.

[94] *Gavrikova* v. *Russia*, Application No. 42180/02, Judgement 15 March 2007.

[95] *Gavrikova* v. *Russia*, para. 14.

11.50 Russian law recognises only civil (secular) marriage: that is, marriage concluded and registered by the state bodies for registration of civil status.[96] Since their abolition in 1917, religious forms of marriage never entailed any legal consequences in the Soviet Union.[97] In this regard, the post-soviet Russian family law followed Soviet tradition and, unlike Estonian, Latvian and Lithuanian family law, did not restore religious marriage.[98] A religious ceremony in church is permitted and, as opposed to Soviet times, is widely used nowadays,[99] although it produces no legal effect. There are no legal rules that require a religious marriage ceremony to be conducted only after the registration of the marriage by the state body. These issues are regulated by the rules of the particular religion. Most of the Christian Orthodox churches, however, at least in Moscow, try to perform weddings only after the couple have married officially and can present the marriage certificate to the priest.

11.51 While the Family Code 1995, like its predecessor, does not contain a definition of marriage, the requirements under it make clear that marriage is a monogamous voluntary union that is concluded in accordance with the rules stipulated by law between a man and a woman, enjoying equal rights, that creates mutual (property and personal) rights and duties between the spouses.

Entering an adult relationship

11.52 To conclude a valid marriage, certain conditions must be met. The law requires that the parties are of different sexes, give their mutual consent to become husband and wife and are of marriageable age. Neither party may be married to another person, the parties must not be closely related[100] and the parties must have legal capacity.[101] Without going into a

---

[96] Family Code, s. 10.

[97] The only exception was made later for marriages concluded in religious form during the Second World War in the occupied Soviet territories until the Soviet state bodies for registration of civil status were restored there.

[98] For more detail see: O. Khazova, 'Family Law on Post-Soviet European Territory: A Comparative Overview of Some Recent Trends' (2010) 14(1) *Electronic Journal of Comparative Law*, available at: www.ejcl.org.

[99] With the growth of the role of the Church in society and the growth of the number of believers since the breakdown of the Soviet Union, religious wedding ceremonies have become more and more widespread in Russia.

[100] Marriage between parents and children, grandparents and grandchildren, brothers and sisters, and adoptive parents and adopted children is prohibited: Family Code, s. 14.

[101] The court can declare a person legally incapable due to mental disorder or illness.

detailed analysis of these conditions, some comment in respect of them is, nevertheless, necessary.

11.53   First, Russian family law has always been based on the idea that marriage is a union of a man and a woman and this has always been an implied condition of a valid marriage, being regarded as inherent in the natural requirements of the formation and functioning of a family. Before the adoption of the Family Code 1995, this approach was fixed in legislation as one of the general principles of family law.[102] The Family Code strengthened the importance of this principle, having stipulated it not only as a general rule,[103] but also as a specific requirement for marriage.[104] This was undoubtedly the legislators' response to the demands from same-sex couples to legalise their unions. There were unsuccessful attempts by same-sex couples to be married by the Russian bodies for registration of civil status in recent years and refusal was based on reference to the Family Code.[105] Despite certain activity on behalf of the gay and lesbian community, it is highly unlikely that same-sex marriage will be allowed in the foreseeable future due to a political situation extremely unfavourable to same-sex marriage in Russia and the strong opposition of the Orthodox Church.

11.54   Secondly, the principle of monogamy means that it is impossible to get married to somebody else if a person is already lawfully married. Before October 1917, the principle of monogamy was considered as mandatory for Christian marriage. At the same time, because there was no unified marriage law in the Russian Empire and regulation of marriage was determined by the rules of the relevant religion, polygamous marriages between Muslims were considered to be valid if concluded in accordance with the rules of their denomination. In particular, polygamy was permitted by Mohammedans.[106] As we have seen, after the revolution of 1917 all the religious marriage laws were abolished, and

---

[102] RSFSR Code on Marriage and the Family 1969, s. 1.

[103] Family Code, s. 1(3).

[104] Family Code, s. 12(2).

[105] See, for example, M. Schwirtz, 'In Moscow, an Attempt to Wed Pushes Gay Rights', *New York Times*, 12 May 2009, available at: www.nytimes.com/2009/05/13/world/europe/13moscow.html?_r=3 (last accessed 1 March 2012).

[106] See: D. I. Meier, *Russian Civil Law (in 2 Parts)* (in Russian) (Moscow: Statut, 1902/2003), p. 724. Under the draft of the Civil Code 1910, it was stipulated that polygamy was also permitted for Lamaists and pagans as far as it was permitted by their creeds. See: I. M. Tyutryumov (ed.), *Civil Code. Book 2. Family Law: Draft*, reprint version of 1910 edition (Moscow: Wolters Kluwer, 2008), p. 13.

it was declared that marriage, as a purely secular institution, should be concluded by the state bodies. Interestingly, monogamous marriage was preserved as a basic institution, though it completely lost its religious flavour, as was the case in many other countries with the secularisation of marriage. Polygamy, which had been practised in some areas with significant Muslim populations, was abolished in the Soviet Union, and bigamy and plural marriages (polygamy) became a crime under the Soviet criminal law provided they took place in the territories within the Russian Federation where this was 'a local custom carried over from the old days'.[107]

11.55   At present, though not recognised by law, polygamy de facto exists in Russia and bigamy is no longer considered as a crime under criminal legislation.[108] It is especially widespread in the regions with a significant number of Muslims and it seems to become more and more common there.[109] There was an attempt to legalise polygamous marriage in 1999, when the President of Ingushetia, a Muslim region in the south of Russia, enacted a decree allowing men in this region to have up to four wives. One of the goals of this decree, according to Ingushetia's leader, was to legalise 'the *de facto* situation'.[110] The decree was dismissed as unconstitutional by the Minister of Justice because it contradicted federal laws, particularly the Family Code. However, this abolished Ingushetia's decree but not polygamy itself.[111] Muslims do not view the legal ban on entering a second marriage while already married as an obstacle to entering into a polygamous marriage because a marriage registered by the state bodies, by itself, is not considered automatically as a sharia marriage, and vice versa. In order to conclude a valid sharia marriage, there is no need, in principle, to go

---

[107]   RSFSR Criminal Code 1960, ss. 235–236.

[108]   Russian Federation Criminal Code 1996.

[109]   Particularly in Dagestan, Ingushetia, Chechnya and Tatarstan. See, for example, 'Chechen Women Face Strict Rule of Islam', *The Washington Times*, 2 March 2009.

[110]   See, 'Russia says no to polygamy', BBC news, 21 July 1999, available at: http://news.bbc. co.uk/2/hi/europe/400351.stm (last accessed 1 March 2012) (for a version in Russian, see: http://gazeta.lenta.ru/daynews/22–07–1999/40polygam.htm) (last accessed 20 March 2012).

[111]   Ten years later, in 2009, the President of Chechnya, another Muslim region, also stated that polygamy was allowed by Chechen customs and religion and encouraged Chechen men, who could afford it, 'to take the second wife': see: I. Svinarenko, 'The President of Chechnya Ramzan Kadyrov: About the Military Past, Its History and Lessons', available at: www.rg.ru/2009/04/07/kadirov.html (in Russian) (last accessed 1 March 2012). See also: www.interfax-religion.com/?act=news&div=8227.

through the official registration procedure.[112] It goes without saying that the rights of women in such marriages are unprotected under the law.

Consequences of relationships

Non-property relations

11.56   As a result of marriage, mutual rights and duties arise between spouses. They are based on the constitutional principle of sex equality or, in the context of family relations, equality between the spouses. Each of the spouses retains freedom of choice in his or her activities, occupation and place of temporary or permanent residence. All family matters are resolved by the spouses jointly, based on their equality.[113]

11.57   Spouses are autonomous individuals under the law and are not considered as legal representatives of each other. If one of them needs to delegate his or her rights (for instance, to make a contract or represent the spouse in court), this spouse should give the other spouse a notarised power of attorney to perform certain actions. At the same time, following the Russian Federation Constitution, the Russian Federation Criminal Code releases a spouse from criminal liability for refusing to give testimony against the other spouse.[114] Having been introduced into Russian law relatively recently, this important provision did not exist in Soviet law and being a husband or a wife in Soviet times did not serve as an excuse for not testifying against one's spouse. There is hardly any reference in Russian commentaries on the Constitution or criminal legislation to the biblical origin of this provision, where husband and wife were regarded as 'one flesh'.[115] Rather, it is explained as 'an expanded interpretation'[116] of Article 14(3) of the International Covenant on Civil and Political Rights 1966, which states that 'in the determination of any criminal charge

---

[112] See: A. F. Yezhova, 'Is it Necessary to Legalize Polygamy in Russia?', *Women in Islam*, available at: http://tatarmoscow.ru/index.php?option=com_content&view=article&id =114&catid=22&Itemid=48 (in Russian) (last accessed 20 March 2012).

[113] Family Code, s. 31.

[114] Russian Federation Constitution 1993, Article 51; Russian Federation Criminal Code, s. 308. Russian Federation Criminal Code, s. 316 also releases a spouse from criminal liability for concealment of especially grave crimes committed by another spouse, if such concealment was not promised in advance.

[115] Genesis 2:24; Mark 10:8.

[116] V. A. Chetvernin (ed.), *Constitution of the Russian Federation: Problem-Specific Commentaries* (Moscow: Centre for Constitutional Studies of the Moscow Public Scientific Foundation, 1997), p. 292.

against him, everyone shall be entitled … not to be compelled to testify against himself'. There is no doubt, however, that this provision also aims to protect family privacy and family harmony, although the time when Russian family law was based on the concept of marital unity, embodied in the phrase 'the husband and wife are one body', is long past.[117]

Property relations

11.58   In Russia property relations between the spouses are based on the legal regime of community of property, or, more precisely, common joint ownership. It operates by default and is effective immediately after registration of marriage, provided the spouses did not make a marriage contract. In essence, the legal regime of common joint property, stipulated by the Family Code 1995, is substantially the same as the system that existed in the Soviet Union since 1926. In accordance with this regime, all the property acquired by the spouses during the marriage is considered as their joint property which they manage jointly. Apart from articles for personal use, the separate property of each of the spouses consists of the property that belonged to each of them before marriage, as well as property acquired during the marriage as a gift, by inheritance or through other uncompensated transactions. The main changes introduced by Family Code in this regard consist in expanding the list of items of property either or both of the spouses may own.

11.59   One may question why the common joint property regime was accepted without any particular amendment in post-Soviet Russia. The explanation is twofold. First, partly as a result of a degree of inertia, it may have been decided not to change what seemed to have been working smoothly during the Soviet era. The regime of common joint property, being a variation of the community regime, has often been considered as the most compatible with the well-functioning family. That is true, however, only if we either have in mind an idealistic picture of the family or consider that the law provides for detailed regulation of management of common property while the marriage lasts and of its division when it breaks down. In the absence of either of these, even a slight disagreement between the spouses, not to mention a serious conflict, may significantly complicate or even block the use of common property. Secondly, the Family Code 1995 was drafted only three years after the breakdown of the Soviet Union. At

---

[117] And the husband was considered as 'the head of the wife'. See, for instance, K. P. Pobedonostsev, *The Course of Civil Law* (*Kurs grazhdanskogo prava*), 2 vols. (Moscow: Garant, 2003, reprint version of 1896 edition), vol. 2, p. 110.

that time, market mechanisms were at the very early stages of their development in the country, and the complexity and variety of spousal property issues under the new economic conditions had not manifested themselves in full. This factor was probably underestimated by the Family Code drafters. This is not surprising as, in the USSR, the situation was different. The overwhelming majority of the Soviet population earned low salaries; there was no private business in the country; and families owned no significant assets. Items of private property were confined to articles of daily necessity. Disputes over the division of property between divorcing couples usually came down to division of 'spoons and pans'. Accordingly, there was no legal regulation of how to deal with the types of assets that the spouses might own in a market economy, whether in a functioning marriage or on divorce. The legal rules that did exist were very primitive and, in a sense, underdeveloped. Now we have a different picture and the courts have already faced 'big money' cases.[118]

11.60   The introduction of marriage contracts in post-soviet Russian law was probably thought to be a solution to all cases where spouses had significant assets and were not satisfied with the scheme suggested by the legal regime. In reality, however, they cannot be a panacea for all difficulties. A marriage contract does solve the problems of property settlement, but only works in cases when the spouses or would-be spouses feel like finding a solution and coming to an agreement. For all other cases there must be a legal mechanism that can be used by the courts when disagreements between spouses arise. Such a mechanism should be provided by a legal regime of matrimonial property with detailed rules and differentiated regulation of different types of property and income that the spouses acquire during the marriage.

Termination of relationships

11.61   Marriage can be terminated by divorce on the application of either spouse or on their joint application. There are two types of divorce proceedings under Russian family law: administrative (in a state body for registration for a civil status) and judicial. A marriage can be dissolved by the state bodies upon the application of both spouses only if there are

---

[118]   It is enough to mention the divorce case of Roman Abramovich, the owner of Chelsea Football Club, where, according to *Forbes Magazine*, assets worth $18.7 billion were at stake.

no under-age children and both spouses agree to divorce. Accordingly, a marriage is dissolved in court if there are minor common or adopted children in the family and/or one of the spouses does not consent to the divorce. When designing the legal rules on divorce procedure, the drafters of the Family Code aimed at making divorce easier for those spouses who mutually agree to divorce, while providing more protection for the minor children of a divorcing couple and putting child-related issues under strict control of the court. The initial idea was that a divorce decree should not be granted unless matters concerning the children's place of residence and maintenance had been resolved. However, in practice the court frequently does not resolve these questions if the parents simply declare orally in the courtroom that there is no dispute over the children even if the parents do not present a written agreement on child-related matters. In such a case, the question often remains whether the parents' oral statement is true and there are, indeed, no conflicts between them regarding the child's place of residence, maintenance and visitation rights. Experience shows that it is often not the case and children in divorce proceedings often remain totally unprotected, as no court order dealing with the child's place of residence and maintenance accompanies a divorce decree. In addition, despite the general requirement of the Family Code that the child has 'the right to express his opinion when any matter affecting his interests is being decided in the family, as well as [to] be heard in any judicial and administrative proceedings', in divorce proceedings involving a dispute over the child's place of residence, the child's opinion is often overlooked and fails to be assessed objectively.[119] Hopefully, certain changes in this regard will be inevitable in the course of implementation of the Hague Convention of the Civil Aspects of Child Abduction 1980 in Russia.

Consequences of termination

11.62   Divorce means the end of a marriage. Spouses become ex-spouses, becoming strangers towards each other, and are free to enter into another marriage. They can divide their property, finalise their financial relations – and the sooner they do this the better off they are. Russian family law, however, does not contain any rule similar to the 'clean break' principle. This means that the spouses can be divorced, but have left their property and financial matters unsettled. Apart from the personal discomfort

---

[119] Nizamieva (ed.), *Commentary to the Family Code of Russian Federation*, pp. 248–9.

that such uncertainty may cause, there are some legal consequences that could significantly complicate the ex-spouses' life in the future. In particular, a three-year statutory limitation period for ex-spouses' property division claims was established.[120] This period begins to run not, as one could expect, from the date when the divorce became final, but from the moment when one of the ex-spouses knew or should have known about the violation of his or her rights.[121] This means that if there is a piece of property that the spouses acquired while married as their common joint property and that they did not divide at the time of the divorce or later, this property will remain in their joint ownership as long as such property exists. One can imagine how difficult it may be to resolve property dispute years later.

11.63 Although, in principle under Russian family law, each spouse owes the other a duty of support, in reality it is limited to very exceptional cases. It will be remembered that the origin of this rule lies in the postrevolutionary period, when the 1917 law declared women equal to men and, in order to push women out of their homes and into the labour market, minimised any possibility of claiming spousal maintenance, whether within marriage or after divorce. Spousal alimony is an area where, again surprisingly, the law remained unchanged despite the visible revival of traditional marriage, with a homemaker spouse – a phenomenon that acquired the name of the 'patriarchal renaissance'.[122] The result is that, under the current law, if a spouse decides to dedicate himself or, usually, herself, to the family, in the overwhelming majority of cases such a spouse will not be entitled to any support unless she is disabled, too old, pregnant or has a common child under three years old or a common disabled child, even if there are five children in the family. In the event of divorce, the position of such a homemaker spouse may turn out to be very difficult or even desperate, as her chances of finding any decent job may be low. Under Russian law such a spouse is not entitled to any payments, even on a temporary basis, that would allow her to adjust to the post-divorce financial situation.

---

[120] Family Code, s. 38(7).

[121] The Plenum of the Russian Federation Supreme Court Ruling No. 15 on 5 November 1998, 'On Courts' Application of Legislation when Considering Divorce Matters' (Postanovlenie Plenuma Verkhovnogo Suda RF, 'O primenenii sudami zakonodatelstva pri rassmotrenii del o rastorzhenii braka'), para. 19.

[122] See: L. V. Babaeva, *Women of Russia in a Situation of Social Fracture: Work, Politics, Everyday Life* (Moscow: Russian Public Scientific Fund, 1996), p. 82 (in Russian).

D   Conclusions

11.64   At the end of the twentieth century Russian (and earlier, Russian Soviet) family law was at the forefront of liberal regulation in this area. Two decades later, it has lost its leading position when viewed through the prism of recent trends in Western and, specifically, European family law. The present-day social and economic realities make the revision of Russian family law necessary, both at the national and international levels. Extramarital cohabitation; polygamous marriages; underage marriages often compounded by coercion; ART (assisted reproduction) matters; divorce proceedings where children are involved; children's rights, especially the child's right 'to have a say' in all matters that affect him or her; regulation of spousal property and maintenance – this is not nearly a complete list of issues that need to be revised. Among the numerous problems that remain unsolved in Russian family law and many challenges that it faces, there are two, in particular, which seem to be especially topical in the international context.

11.65   First, legal recognition of extramarital cohabitation or de facto marriages constitutes one of the most direct and serious challenges in this regard. The increase in cohabitation in the country and the clear position of the European Court of Human Rights on this matter will probably force the Russian legislator to reconsider its negative attitude towards 'unregistered relations'. Until it happens we may expect more Strasbourg cases to come, where applicants will successfully claim their right to respect for family life has been violated.

11.66   Secondly, one of the inevitable consequences of globalisation and increased migration is an increase in international family disputes. Spouses may divorce or separate and struggle over division of property or alimony awards and the arrangements for their children. However, if they fail to come to an agreement on child-related matters, the children become victims of their inability to cooperate. Cross-border disputes over child custody are often compounded by incidents of child abduction, and due to the vulnerability of children, these disputes are amongst the most difficult to resolve. Russia's accession to the Hague Convention on Abduction should help to create a national legal framework for civilised settlement of cross-border child custody disputes. Hopefully it will also affect the whole national system of family dispute resolution, at least to the extent it concerns child-related issues.

12

Scotland

The marriage of principle and pragmatism

ELAINE E. SUTHERLAND

A   Introduction

12.1   Modern Scots child and family law is a great deal more inclusive and functionalist than the patriarchal, marriage-based system that prevailed in the past. This metamorphosis is a product of the promotion of fundamental human rights principles and pragmatic responses to changing social conditions and attitudes. Inevitably, law and public opinion interact, with the relationship between the two being one of symbiosis, rather than unidirectional cause and effect.

12.2   What, then, are the principles at work? The advent of the welfare state in the early twentieth century marked acceptance of government as the safety net for the most vulnerable families. The women's movement demanded and got a substantial degree of gender equality, at least in strictly legal terms. As human rights became more developed generally, the principles of equality, privacy and due process had increased impact. With the passing of the Human Rights Act 1998, which incorporated the European Convention on Human Rights ('ECHR')[1] into domestic law, these convention rights became more readily enforceable. The children's rights movement made its mark and children became the holders of rights, rather than objects of protection, a feature that gained focus with the ratification of the United Nations Convention on the Rights of the Child ('UN Convention').[2]

12.3   Alongside these developments – and sometimes resulting from them – the way people live their lives has changed.[3] The population is

---

[1] ETS No. 155 (1950).

[2] 1577 UNTS 3; (1989) 28 ILM 1448. See para. 12.9 below, for the distinction between incorporation and ratification of treaties.

[3] For recent demographic information, see *Scotland's Population 2010: The Registrar General's Annual Review of Demographic Trends* (Edinburgh: Scottish Government,

ageing. Women are delaying having children and are having fewer of them. The proportion of extra-marital births increased and they now out-number marital births. Bio-scientific developments enable individuals and couples to have children when that would have been impossible in the past. Non-marital cohabitation and same-sex relationships became more visible and, thus, more acceptable. Divorce became more commonplace, rendering it, too, unremarkable. Increased international mobility has enriched Scotland, making it more ethnically and racially diverse.[4] This, combined with existing religious diversity, requires sensitive responses from a secular legal system in order to accommodate the needs of the whole population.

12.4 The result is a system of child and family law that often reflects respect for the driving principles. Equality is the hallmark within adult relationships and a broader range of relationships, both different-sex and same-sex, is recognised by the legal system. There is increased recognition of the variety of settings in which parenting occurs, and while parental equality predominates, it is not yet universal. Emphasis has shifted from the extended family to the nuclear family, although the latter continues to have a role, particularly in the context of child protection.

12.5 The interaction of the principles has led to compromises: some of them comfortable, others unsatisfactory and, thus, predicted here to be nothing more than temporary. Inevitably, the legal system must some-times prioritise the rights of one group over those of another and where it does so, it must justify the decision. Of course, shortcomings and gaps remain and it is predicted here that law reform will address them in so far as it can. The fact that many legal developments have been incremental, often following a linear path, is helpful in predicting their likely future direction.

2011) (hereinafter '*Scotland's Population 2010*'), available at: www.gro-scotland.gov.uk/files2/stats/annual-review-2010/rgar2010.pdf.

[4] In 2010 immigration exceeded emigration by just under 25,000, with about 3,300 of these people coming from the rest of the United Kingdom and the remainder coming from overseas: *Scotland's Population 2010*, p. 15. The number of people living in Scotland who were born abroad grew to 326,000, in 2010, an increase of 122,000 on 2004: see www.gro-scotland.gov.uk/files2/stats/annual-review-2010/rgar2010.pdf.

Historical roots, sources and law reform

Historical roots

12.6 Constraints of space preclude exploring the rich history of Scots child and family law.[5] Suffice to say that little remains of its Celtic heritage or Roman law roots, those being replaced by modern statutory provision. From the eighteenth century, when the Treaty of Union was concluded, these statutes were passed by the Westminster Parliament, albeit the distinct nature of Scots private law was guaranteed[6] and Scots law developed drawing on influences from other jurisdictions around the world.

12.7 As the twentieth century drew to a close, federalism came to the United Kingdom, with the (re)creation of the Scottish Parliament, sitting in Edinburgh, and legislating on 'devolved matters'.[7] The United Kingdom Parliament continues to sit at Westminster and retains jurisdiction for Scotland on 'reserved matters'. While most of child and family law is devolved and, thus, the province of the Scottish Parliament, numerous matters that impact upon it are reserved to Westminster,[8] a familiar pattern in federal systems. In addition, even where an issue is devolved to the Scottish Parliament, it may, by its own motion, authorise the United Kingdom Parliament to legislate for Scotland.[9] As we shall see, on occasion it has availed itself of this option.[10]

---

[5] For an historical perspective, see Lord Fraser, *Treatise on Husband and Wife According to the Law of Scotland*, 2nd edn (Edinburgh: T. & T. Clark, 1876–78) and Lord Fraser, *A Treatise on the Law of Scotland Relating to Parent and Child*, ed. J. Clark, 3rd edn (Edinburgh: W. Green, 1906). See also E. M. Clive, *The Law of Husband and Wife in Scotland*, 4th edn (Edinburgh: W. Green, 1997), Chapter 1 and K. M. Marshall, 'The History and Philosophy of Children's Rights in Scotland', in A. Cleland and E. E. Sutherland (eds.), *Children's Rights in Scotland*, 3rd edn (Edinburgh: W. Green, 2009), Chapter 2.

[6] Treaty of Union, Article 18, given effect to by the Union with Scotland Act 1706 and the Union with England Act 1707.

[7] Scotland Act 1998, ss. 29 and 30 and Sched. 5 and the Scotland Act 2012. See E. E. Sutherland, K. E. Goodall, G. F. M. Little and F. P. Davidson (eds.), *Law Making and the Scottish Parliament: The Early Years* (Edinburgh University Press, 2011). Separate arrangements are in place for Wales and Northern Ireland.

[8] Reserved matters include child support (but not aliment), welfare benefits, (most of) taxation and, perhaps most controversially, abortion and assisted reproduction.

[9] This is done by means of a Legislative Consent Motion (formerly known as a 'Sewel Motion'): *Scottish Parliament Standing Orders* (Edinburgh: The Scottish Government, 3rd edn (1st revision), 2007), Chapter 9B.

[10] This legislative mechanism was used in respect of gender recognition and the creation of civil partnerships, the marriage-equivalent for same-sex couples.

Sources

12.8 The modern sources of domestic Scottish child and family law can best be described as 'manifold' and include the statutes of the Westminster and Scottish Parliaments, as amended, secondary legislation and the abundant case law thereunder. This embarrassment of riches is the source of frustration to lawyers and renders aspects of the law almost impenetrable to all but the most determined layperson. Thus, the first prediction for development is that Scots child and family law will be codified in the future and, indeed, the Scottish Law Commission provided a blueprint for a Child and Family Code in 1992.[11]

12.9 Scots law makes every effort to honour United Kingdom treaty obligations and, where domestic law is ambiguous, it will be interpreted in a way that will lead to compliance with international law.[12] However, where Scots law is clear, the fact that it is unambiguously inconsistent with international obligations will not diminish the domestic provision's validity within Scotland.[13] Hitherto, while the ECHR was accorded respect, Scotland generated its share of cases reaching the European Court of Human Rights.[14] The Human Rights Act 1998, incorporating the ECHR into the law of the various parts of the United Kingdom, rendered convention rights directly enforceable in the Scottish courts. In contrast, the UN Convention remains no more than a treaty and, while recent proposals for legislation would require Scottish Ministers to have 'due regard' (whatever that means) to its terms, its status would not change.[15] European Union law is increasingly turning its attention to the family sphere and is having an undeniable impact through EU directives and regulations and decisions of the European Court of Justice. Within Europe, there is some support, not simply for mutual recognition and enforcement of rights and court decisions, but for harmonisation of substantive family law.[16] Given

---

[11] Scottish Law Commission, *Report on Family Law*, Scot. Law Com. No. 135 (Edinburgh: HMSO, 1992).

[12] *Mortensen* v. *Peters* (1906) 8F(J) 93.

[13] *Kaur* v. *Lord Advocate* 1980 SC 319.

[14] See, for example, *Campbell and Cosans* v. *United Kingdom* (1984) 4 EHRR 293 (corporal punishment in schools), *McMichael* v. *United Kingdom* (1995) 20 EHRR 205 (child protection procedures) and *E* v. *United* Kingdom (2003) 36 EHRR 31 (failure of the child protection system).

[15] Consultation on the Rights of Children and Young People Bill (Edinburgh: Scottish Government, 2011, web only), available at: www.scotland.gov.uk/Publications/2011/09/07110058/0.

[16] The Commission on European Family Law (CEFL) is particularly active in this respect: see further www.ceflonline.net/.

that Scotland has only so recently regained control over its own destiny, enthusiasm for harmonisation is minimal.

Law reform

12.10   It is no exaggeration to say that the Scottish Law Commission[17] has been the driving force behind much of modern Scots child and family law[18] and, in this, credit goes to Professor Eric M. Clive, who served as a commissioner for nineteen years and to whom this volume is dedicated.[19] On occasion, the government appoints a committee of experts to explore possible reform.[20] While consultation on law reform proposals has long been the norm, there was a heightened expectation that the Scottish Parliament would be accessible and responsive to the views of the people, something reinforced by the creation of the Public Petitions Procedure, which provides for grass-roots law reform proposals to be considered by a committee of the Scottish Parliament.[21]

Dispute resolution and access to legal services

12.11   While negotiation, whether within families or with the assistance of a lawyer or other third party, has always played a significant part in resolving family conflicts, the courts remain the ultimate forum for dispute resolution. The most pressing problem facing the Scottish legal system is access to legal services. Many people simply cannot afford to pay for legal advice or representation, effectively denying their ECHR right to an effective remedy.[22] Certainly, state-funded legal aid has long been available to pay for lawyers for those who meet the financial (and other) criteria.[23] However, both the financial thresholds and the rate of remuneration reflect a level of parsimony that means many potential clients do not qualify and lawyers are unwilling to take on legal

---

[17] Law Commissions Act 1965, s. 2. The Commission's website is: www.scotlawcom.gov. uk/.

[18] See, for example, Scottish Law Commission, *Report on Family Law*.

[19] See Preface.

[20] See, for example, Adoption Policy Review Group, *Report of Phase II: Adoption: Better Choices for Our Children* (Edinburgh: Scottish Executive, 2005).

[21] For further details of the procedure and full details of those lodged and their progress, see www.scottish.parliament.uk/s3/committees/petitions/index.htm.

[22] Article 13.

[23] The Legal Aid (Scotland) Act 1949 introduced the first comprehensive scheme. See further, E. E. Sutherland, *Child and Family Law*, 2nd edn (Edinburgh: W. Green, 2008), paras. 1–044–1–047.

aid work.[24] This has led, in turn, to legislation that leaves people to sort out their own problems[25] and to greater reliance in alternative dispute resolution (ADR) and mediation, in particular, with collaborative law emerging more recently.[26]

12.12   Empowering individuals to resolve their own disputes can bring many benefits, not least in avoiding the acrimony, delay and cost often associated with litigation. However, people cannot negotiate meaningfully without understanding their rights and responsibilities, so ADR is not an alternative to legal advice. In addition, there will always be disputes that can only be brought to closure using the powers available to courts. Recent, far-reaching proposals for reform of the court system, designed to render it more efficient, may reduce costs.[27] While these proposals include support for ADR, the much-feared proposal for mandatory mediation in family law disputes did not materialise. Nonetheless, unless far more resources are devoted to legal aid (realistically, an unlikely prospect), resort will be had to the services of lay advisers, free legal advice clinics and greater use of public legal education. Again, each brings benefits, but there is no escaping the conclusion that the poor will simply be served less well by the legal system than will the affluent.

B   Children in the family setting and state intervention

12.13   Modern Scots child law is, by and large, characterised by respect for children's human and social rights, with the child's welfare being the paramount consideration. Patriarchy has given way to substantial parental equality and recognition of the diverse family types in which

---

[24] 'Legal Aid Troubles Hit Family Law Cases: Solicitors Quitting Publicly-Funded Work that No Longer Pays', 13 June 2006, *Journal of the Law Society of Scotland* (online), available at: www.journalonline.co.uk/News/1003157.aspx (over half of firms responding to a survey by the Family Law Association had reduced the amount of publicly funded family law work they undertake by at least 50 per cent).

[25] This can be seen clearly in the latest attempt to salvage the ill-starred child support system. It has all but taken pursuit of child support out of the courts altogether, with enforcement being the province of the Child Maintenance Enforcement Commission (C-MEC). Parents are to be encouraged to reach agreement and if they want the help of C-MEC, they will have to pay for it.

[26] In the family context, mediation is offered by individual solicitors accredited to do the job, and through Family Mediation Scotland. The Scottish Collaborative Family Law Group was launched in 2006.

[27] *Report of the Scottish Civil Courts Review* (Edinburgh: Scottish Government, 2009), available at: www.scotcourts.gov.uk/civilcourtsreview/.

children find themselves, albeit non-marital fathers continue to face discrimination.[28] Children now have a voice in the decision-making process and greater access to information about their ancestry. The state accepts, although does not always fulfil, its obligation to protect children from abuse and neglect. Successive Scottish governments have expressed support for the UN Convention and have sought to demonstrate their commitment to implementing its principles,[29] with the most recent example being the proposal for a Rights of Children and Young People (Scotland) Bill.[30] Government progress is keenly monitored by non-governmental organisations,[31] academics and practitioners.

12.14   Like their counterparts elsewhere, most Scottish parents try to do their best for their children. However, there is no escaping the fact whole sections of the adult population are ambivalent about young people: something to which the United Nations Committee on the Rights of the Child (the 'UN Committee') was alert when it urged government to take 'urgent measures to address the intolerance and inappropriate characterisation of children, especially adolescents, within the society, including the media'.[32]

Defining and classifying children

Age

12.15   While full adulthood is attained on reaching the age of 18,[33] modern Scots law has adopted a system of graduated empowerment of young people, with 12 and 16 years old being the significant legal landmarks.[34] Children and young people gain rights and powers on

---

[28] See further, paras. 12.22–12.24 below.

[29] *Report on the Implementation of the UN Convention on the Rights of the Child in Scotland 1999–2007* (Edinburgh: Scottish Executive, 2007), available at: www.scotland. gov.uk/Publications/2007/07/30114126/0; and *Do the Right Thing* (Edinburgh: Scottish Government, 2009), available at: www.scotland.gov.uk/Publications/2009/08/27133115 /0.

[30] See para. 12.9 above.

[31] *State of Children's Rights in Scotland 2011* (Edinburgh: Scottish Alliance for Children's Rights, 2011), available at: www.togetherscotland.org.uk/pdfs/Together_Report_2011_ PDF.pdf.

[32] *Concluding Observations of the Committee on the Rights of the Child on the United Kingdom of Great Britain and Northern Ireland* (2008), CCR/C/GBR/CO/4, para. 25(a).

[33] Age of Majority (Scotland) Act 1969, s. 1.

[34] Age of Legal Capacity (Scotland) Act 1991, implementing the *Report on Responsibilities and Rights of Minors and Pupil* (Scot. Law Com. No. 110, 1987).

reaching each age[35] and a child of 12 is presumed to be capable of understanding information and participating in decision-making,[36] while a younger child may demonstrate this capacity.[37] This UN Convention-compliant model is marred by the fact that criminal responsibility attaches to a child from the age of 8.[38] However, as a result of criticism from the UN Committee,[39] emerging European Court of Human Rights jurisprudence[40] and valiant lobbying efforts within the country, the Scottish Parliament made a limited attempt to address the issue and it is no longer competent to prosecute anyone below the age of 12.[41]

12.16 Thus far, the direction of law reform has been consistent. However, this picture of consistency begins to crack when we turn to efforts to protect children. Much of the legislation that seeks to protect children from perceived dangers was passed on a specific-issue basis in response to a burning concern of the day and it is littered with inconsistencies:[42] something that can be remedied by a simple statute law reform exercise. The recent trend has been to regulate more and to set higher age limits for children and young people being able to access

---

[35] For example, on reaching 12 years old, a young person may make a will, consent to post-mortem organ donation and his or her consent is usually required before he or she can be adopted. On attaining the age of 16, a young person acquires the legal capacity to consent to sexual activity, marriage or civil partnership registration and inter vivos organ donation. He or she may leave school and home, engage in full-time employment and transact as an adult.

[36] This presumption applies specifically to consent to medical treatment and to instructing a solicitor in a civil matter: Age of Legal Capacity (Scotland) Act 1991, ss. 2(2) and 2(4A), respectively. Younger children may instruct a solicitor in a criminal matter: Age of Legal Capacity (Scotland) Act 1991, s. 2(4)(c).

[37] So, for example, the court is required to give younger children the opportunity to express their views when a dispute over their future care arises: *Shields* v. *Shields* 2002 SLT 579.

[38] Criminal Procedure (Scotland) Act 1995, s. 41.

[39] See, most recently, *Concluding Observations of the Committee on the Rights of the Child on the United Kingdom of Great Britain and Northern Ireland* (2008), CCR/C/GBR/CO/4, para. 78.

[40] The key issue for the European Court is whether the young person can participate effectively in the proceedings: *V* v. *United Kingdom* (2000) 30 EHRR 121, para. 108 and *SC* v. *United Kingdom* (2005) EHRR 10, para. 27.

[41] Criminal Procedure (Scotland) Act 1995, s. 41A, added by the Criminal Justice and Licensing (Scotland) Act 2010, s. 52. Offenders aged between 8 and 11 may be referred to the children's hearings system, where their welfare is central to the disposal of the case: Children's Hearings (Scotland) Act 2011.

[42] So, for example, driving particular classes of vehicle or owning or possessing various kinds of weapons are subject to age limits of 14, 16, 17, 18 or 21, depending upon the vehicle or weapon at issue.

perceived dangers.[43] Undoubtedly, this infantilises young people and disempowers them, but, it might be argued, such is the nature of protection. However, closer examination reveals that young people are empowered, either where it does not matter much to the adult world (as with the right to make a will or engage in small transactions), or where any input is subject to adult oversight or supervision (giving of views to a court or consenting to medical treatment). It is only in the criminal arena that there is clear commitment to full responsibility from the age of 12. Criminal responsibility aside, the rest of the law reflects the UN Convention's concept of 'evolving capacity' and the marrying together of participation and protection. Criminal law included, the law mirrors the Scottish adult ambivalence to children and, thus, no significant change in the law is predicted.

Birth status

12.17   Like many other legal systems, Scots law sought to discourage pre- and extra-marital sex and procreation, and to express disapproval of it, by classifying children as 'legitimate' or 'illegitimate' and discriminating against the latter.[44] While earlier legislation had chipped away at some of the disadvantages suffered by people born outside of marriage, it was not until the twentieth century that increased respect for human rights and children's rights resulted in a concerted effort to end the discrimination.[45] The European Court of Human Rights[46] and the UN Convention[47] added their voices. In addition, the exercise in social control was failing abysmally, with non-marital births increasing steadily and, since 2008, accounting for over half of all births in Scotland.[48] Legislation continued down the path of equalising the rights of children, irrespective of birth circumstances, and, finally, in 2006 purported to abolish the

---

[43] Recent initiatives here have included raising the age for access to tobacco products and tanning salons to 18. See Smoking, Health and Social Care (Scotland) Act 2005 (Variation of age limit for the sale of tobacco purchase and consequential modifications) Order 2007, SSI 2007/437 and Public Health, etc. (Scotland) Act 2008, ss. 95–96, respectively.

[44] Classification was based on the parents' marital status at the time of the child's birth, with 'legitimation' being possible if the parents married later: Lord Fraser, *A Treatise on the Law of Scotland Relating to Parent and Child*, p. 37.

[45] See Sutherland, *Child and Family Law*, 2nd edn, paras. 6–052–6–060.

[46] *Marckx* v. *Belgium* (1979) 2 EHRR 330.

[47] Article 2(1).

[48] In 2010 50.2% of births were to unmarried parents, a rise from 42.6% in 2000, and 27.1% in 1990: *Scotland's Population 2010*, p. 25.

status of 'illegitimacy' altogether.[49] Two exceptions remain – the treatment of the non-martial father and its impact on the child, to which we will return presently,[50] and an anomaly that continues to affect a small number of members of the aristocracy.[51] While there is no groundswell of concern over the latter aristocratic problem, a child denied succession to a title on the basis of 'illegitimacy' could make a persuasive case under the ECHR and it may take such a challenge before that particular anomaly is removed.[52] While having an aristocracy at all in a modern democracy is, in itself, anachronistic, its abolition is not predicted here.

Recognising parentage and family ties

12.18   Recognising a child's 'parentage' has two distinct meanings in Scots law, each serving a different purpose and each having human and children's rights implications.[53] First, it denotes the recording of factual information about the people who contributed the child's genetic components. Secondly, it is the means of identifying the adults who owe responsibilities to a child and may be given the opportunity to engage in parenting (the social parents). Frequently, the two coincide: that is, the genetic and the social parents are the same people. Where they are not, most notably in the context of adoption and the use of assisted reproductive technology (ART), the legal system faces a challenge, not least in respect of 'the child's right to know' the truth about his or her genetic origins.

12.19   Scots law addresses the issue of access to social parenting through a number of presumptions, intended to reflect genetic reality, and legal fictions which, by definition, do not. The woman who gives birth to a child is presumed to be the child's mother,[54] an approach that was extended, by statute, to cover cases of ART involving donated gametes.[55] In terms of attributing paternity, statute begins with a number of rebuttable (disputable) presumptions. The husband of the woman who gives birth to a

[49] Law Reform (Parent and Child) (Scotland) Act 1986, s. 1(1), as substituted by the Family Law (Scotland) Act 2006, s. 21(2)(a).

[50] See paras. 12.22–12.24 below.

[51] The transmission of, or succession to, any title, coat of arms, honour or dignity is a specific exception to the recent reform: Law Reform (Parent and Child) (Scotland) Act 1986, s. 9.

[52] Articles 8 (right to respect for private and family life) and 14 (prohibition of discrimination) would be particularly helpful.

[53] ECHR, Art. 8; UN Convention, Arts. 2, 7, 8 and 18.

[54] *Douglas* v. *Duke of Hamilton* (1769) 2 Pat 143, a rare, pre-ART, example of the matter being disputed.

[55] Human Fertilisation and Embryology Act 2008, s. 33. Egg donation is expressly stated not to be a means of being treated as the child's mother: 2008 Act, s. 47.

child is presumed to be the child's father, failing whom, the honour falls to the man registered as the father or so indicated by court decree.[56] A legal fiction treats the adopters as the child's parents for most purposes.[57] The challenges posed by ART were, again, accommodated by the use of legal fictions and the mother's husband or civil partner is treated as the child's second parent, failing whom, the mother's male or female partner is so treated, provided that certain conditions are satisfied.[58] Where at least one of the adopters is the child's genetic parent and the surrogate consents to the adoption, an expedited adoption procedure is available in surrogacy cases.[59] This approach works well in most cases and no change in the general law is predicted. However, further refinements can be anticipated to address two specific problems: the child's right to know and non-marital births.

The child's right to know

12.20   Both the ECHR[60] and UN[61] Conventions recognise that information about one's origins forms an essential part of one's identity. Doubtless, countless Scots have lived and died in blissful ignorance of the fact that their father was someone other than their mother's husband and, short of DNA testing all babies at birth, no system can avoid this sort of deception. Considerations of privacy and cost preclude the introduction of any such system in Scotland.

12.21   Where the legal system creates the fictions that accommodate social parenting, however, arguably it acquires an obligation to ensure that the genetic information is available to the child at a later stage. Scots law has always acknowledged its obligation to adopted children, both in terms of alerting them to the fact that they are adopted,[62] and by giving them a right to access their birth records upon reaching the appropriate

---

[56]   Law Reform (Parent and Child) (Scotland) Act 1986, s. 5.

[57]   Adoption and Children (Scotland) Act 2007, s. 28(2).

[58]   Human Fertilisation and Embryology Act 2008, ss. 35, 36, 42 and 44. Reflecting state oversight of ART, these provisions apply only to cases where treatment was provided by a state-licensed facility: *X* v. *Y (Parental rights: insemination)* 2002 SLT (Sh Ct) 161.

[59]   Human Fertilisation and Embryology Act 2008, s. 54. Certain other conditions must also be satisfied.

[60]   Article 8. While the European Court upheld the French practice of *accouchement sous X* in *Odièvre* v. *France* (2004) 38 EHRR 43, its more recent decisions are more sympathetic to the child's right to know: *Mikulic* v. *Croatia*, Application No. 53176/99, February 7, 2002; *Jäggi* v. *Switzerland* (2008) 47 EHRR 30.

[61]   Articles 7 and 8.

[62]   The full birth certificate refers to adoption, with an abbreviated birth certificate being available for use in more public settings.

age.[63] The current provision for donor children is rather different. Their birth certificates do not reveal that donor gametes have been used, so whether they know of their status depends, in part, on disclosure by their parents. Obviously, deception is rather easier in some circumstances than in others. Assuming the child does know that he or she is a donor child, the information available to him or her depends upon when donation occurred. Many early sperm donors were promised anonymity and the original legislation permitted donor children access to a certain amount of non-identifying information only.[64] As a result of litigation that found withholding identifying information implicated the donor child's right to private life,[65] new regulations were put in place, requiring the disclosure of identifying information to the adult child upon request.[66] However, these regulations are of prospective effect and apply only to donors who provided information after 31 March 2005. Children of donors who did so before that date are no better off. Permitting them access to information identifying their donor-parents would reflect respect for their right to private life, but at the price of breaking the promise of anonymity made to donors.[67] In the light of developing European human rights jurisprudence, it is likely that the rights of the children will prevail.

Non-marital births

12.22   As we have seen, increased respect for children's rights means that Scots law no longer discriminates against children on the basis of their parents' marital status.[68] Provided a non-marital father is named on the child's birth certificate, he now acquires access to parenting (parental responsibilities and parental rights) automatically, in the same way as do mothers, civil partners and married fathers.[69] The problem arises if the father is not registered as such, since it may prevent him from engaging in parenting. In turn, the child is deprived of a second parent and, sometimes, to information about his or her ancestry.

12.23   While non-registration of fathers affects only a small proportion of children,[70] addressing it requires examining why it occurs. Where the

---

[63] Adoption and Children (Scotland) Act 2007, s. 55(4)(b). The current age is 16.
[64] Human Fertilisation and Embryology Act 1990, s. 31.
[65] *Rose* v. *Secretary of State for Health* [2002] 2 FLR 962.
[66] The Human Fertilisation and Embryology Authority (Disclosure of Information) Regulations 2004, S.I. 2004/1511.
[67] See para. 12.20 for further discussion.
[68] See para. 12.17 above.   [69] Children (Scotland) Act 1995, s. 3.
[70] Some 94 per cent of non-marital fathers do register: *Scotland's Population 2010*, p. 25.

mother truly does not know who the father is, there is nothing the legal system can do. More frequently, non-registration results from the choice of one or both of the parents. Scots law has long experience of making feckless men face their financial responsibilities and the child's mother or the state may do so through court proceedings to establish paternity.[71] Of course, the unwilling father may fail to offer social parenting in any meaningful sense, but at least his identity will be known to the child.

12.24   Law reform may have a little more to offer when we turn to mother-resistance to the child's father being registered. At present, the non-marital father may only register his paternity with the consent of the child's mother[72] and, should this consent not be forthcoming, his only option is to seek to establish paternity in court.[73] Assuming he has the personal and economic resources to pursue this course, the child's mother can, yet again, impede his progress by refusing to permit a sample to be taken from the child for DNA analysis.[74] While the court may draw an inference from the mother's refusal to consent to testing,[75] it cannot substitute its own consent for hers. Hitherto, the mother's privileged position has been justified on the basis that it protects women and their children from unworthy or dangerous men,[76] but the law has other means to achieve that end. Then there is the mother's right to privacy, but respecting her right comes at the price of the rights of the child and the father. Certainly, the European Court of Human Rights is showing increasing impatience with discrimination against non-marital fathers.[77] Empowering the court to compel the taking of samples for the purpose of DNA testing, something possible in the criminal context, would enable fathers to establish their paternity and, thus, secure registration.[78] In addition, the issue would be

---

[71] Law Reform (Parent and Child) (Scotland) Act 1986, s. 7.

[72] Registration of Births, Deaths and Marriages (Scotland) Act 1965, s. 18. Conversely, where the parties are not married, the mother cannot register a man as the child's father without his consent.

[73] Law Reform (Parent and Child) (Scotland) Act 1986, s. 7.

[74] Law Reform (Parent and Child) (Scotland) Act 1986, s. 6.

[75] Law Reform (Miscellaneous Provisions) (Scotland) Act 1990, s. 70. There is no guarantee the court will draw a contrary inference, particularly if the child's mother is married: *Smith* v. *Greenhill* 1993 S.C.L.R. 776 (refusing declarator of paternity to a married woman's former lover).

[76] The children resulting from rape or incest are the paradigm example cited here but such births make up a tiny fraction of the total.

[77] *Söderbäck* v. *Sweden* (1998) 29 EHRR 95; *Sahin* v. *Germany* (2003) 36 EHRR 43; *Zaunegger* v. *Germany* (2010) 50 EHRR 38.

[78] The option, adopted in England and Wales, of 'requiring' unmarried couples to register the child's birth jointly, subject to exceptions necessary to accommodate ignorance or

in the court's arena, so any collateral consequences of establishing paternity, most notably the right to participate in parenting, could be regulated in the child's best interests. It is predicted here that future Scottish law reform will take this path.

Delivering parenting

12.25   Initially, being registered or treated as a child's parent is the key that opens the door to parenting, with the responsibilities and rights of parents being spelt out clearly in legislation.[79] This is only the starting point, since the court retains the power to intervene and remove or regulate all or some of the parental responsibilities and parental rights.[80] All parents are obliged to support their children financially,[81] albeit the state makes significant contributions in terms of services, universal (for the time being) child benefit and means-tested benefits.

12.26   Anyone with an interest may apply to the court to be given parental responsibilities or rights or to have them regulated.[82] However, two groups have lobbied hard for greater legal recognition. Step-parents sought to acquire parental responsibilities and rights simply by agreement with the child's parents,[83] while grandparents wanted an automatic right of contact with grandchildren.[84] Neither proposal succeeded, largely because neither group is homogenous, with individual step-parents and grandparents varying enormously in terms of their involvement with the

---

danger (Welfare Reform Act 2009, s. 56 and Sched. 6) is rejected here on the basis that it promises more than it delivers.

[79] Parental responsibilities include safeguarding and promoting the child's health, development and welfare; directing and guiding the child; maintaining personal relations and direct contact with the child regularly; and acting as the child's legal representative: Children (Scotland) Act 1995, s. 1(1). Parental rights mirror the responsibilities: Children (Scotland) Act 1995, s. 2(1). Other statutory provisions detail the rights and responsibilities of parents or persons caring for a child in respect of specific matters such as safety, medical treatment and education. See further, Sutherland, *Child and Family Law*, 2nd edn, Chapter 6.

[80] See para. 12.30 below.

[81] Family Law (Scotland) Act 1985, s. 1 and Child Support Act 1991, as amended. See further, Sutherland, *Child and Family Law*, 2nd edn, Chapter 8.

[82] Children (Scotland) Act 1995, s. 11, discussed at para. 12.30 below.

[83] *Parents and Children* (Edinburgh: Scottish Executive, 2000), paras. 2.25–2.45 and proposal 2.

[84] In what was seen by many as a sop to grandparents, the government of the day published the *Charter for Grandchildren* (Edinburgh: Scottish Executive, 2006), a 'feel-good' statement of rather obvious sentiments having no legal effect.

child and what they have to offer. To allow a parent to hand over important powers to his or her chosen partner smacks of the commodification of children and there was concern that, unlike the situation where a court makes that decision, there is no guarantee that the child concerned would be consulted. In short, children's rights prevailed over adult interests. Each group continues its lobbying efforts, but it is unlikely that either will prevail given the cogent reasons to reject their proposals.

12.27   How well parents actually deliver parenting probably has little to do with the law and much to do with the parents' own experiences as children and the circumstances faced by a particular family. While some parents undoubtedly seek guidance on how to provide optimum parenting, parenting education is mandated by the state only after serious signs that something has gone wrong.[85] Nonetheless – and in so far as the law can influence behaviour – statute makes it quite clear that the child's best interests are central to the whole process of parenting and the only reason that parents have rights is to enable them to fulfil their responsibilities.[86] A person, whether a parent or not, taking a major decision (not defined) in the course of fulfilling these responsibilities or exercising these rights is obliged to take account of any views the child concerned wishes to express.[87]

12.28   There is a significant exception to this picture of child-centricity in so far as Scots law permits parents to mete out a certain amount of physical punishment to their children. As a result of the developing case law from the European Court of Human Rights,[88] the limited recommendation for reform from the Scottish Law Commission[89] and unrelenting lobbying efforts by children's rights activists, children may no longer be beaten at school[90] and parental power is now confined to 'justifiable assault' (the oxymoron that replaced 'reasonable chastisement').[91] Of

---

[85] Antisocial Behaviour etc. (Scotland) Act 2004, Part 9. See further, E. E. Sutherland, 'Parenting Orders: A Culturally-Alien Response of Questionable Efficacy' (2004) 49 *Juridical Review* 105.

[86] Children (Scotland) Act 1995, ss. 1(1) and 2(1).

[87] Children (Scotland) 1995 Act, s. 6. A child of 12 is presumed to be capable of expressing such a view, but that does not preclude a younger child from doing so. The decision maker must also take account of any views another person with responsibilities and rights wishes to express.

[88] *Campbell and Cosans* v. *United Kingdom* (1982) 4 EHRR 293; *A* v. *United Kingdom* (1999) 27 EHRR 611.

[89] Scottish Law Commission, *Report on Family Law*, paras. 2.67–2.105.

[90] Standards in Scotland's Schools etc. (Scotland) Act 2000, s. 16.

[91] Criminal Justice (Scotland) Act 2003. An assault will never be 'justifiable' if it involved a blow to the head, shaking or the use of an implement: Criminal Justice (Scotland) Act

course, the very act of defining the violence permitted sends a message to parents that it is acceptable for them to hit their children, provided they stick to the rules. As the United Nations Committee on the Rights of the Child has made clear in successive reports on the United Kingdom, this is wholly unacceptable.[92] The limited progress to date is encouraging, not least because it appears to be having an effect on public opinion. Certainly, those seeking further reform continue to campaign and it is predicted that, one day, Scotland will join the civilised nations of the world in banning all violence against children in all circumstances.

Intra-family disputes

12.29   As in most jurisdictions, disputes over where a child will live or with whom a child will spend time arise most often in Scotland between never-cohabiting or separating parents. However, they may involve other relatives, such as grandparents or step-parents, and some disputes relate to a specific issue, like the child's education or medical treatment.[93] Driven by the twin considerations that adversarial litigation is not usually the best way to resolve family disputes and the cost of litigation, the modern approach is to encourage the resolution of such disputes without resort to the courts.[94] Parents (and others) are armed with the tools to resolve their own disputes, with government guidance on 'parenting plans' being made available on the Internet,[95] and ADR is used extensively.[96]

12.30   For the cases that do reach the courts,[97] statute provides the mechanism for their resolution, using the tripartite test of giving paramountcy to the child's welfare, taking account of any views the child wishes to

---

[92] See, most recently, *Concluding Observations of the Committee on the Rights of the Child on the United Kingdom of Great Britain and Northern Ireland*, 2008, CCR/C/GBR/CO/4, paras. 40–43, repeating the unequivocal criticisms expressed in previous reports.

2003, s. 51(3). In other cases, the court is directed to a checklist of factors in assessing justifiability: Criminal Justice (Scotland) Act 2003, s. 51(1).

[93] See, for example, *M* v. *C* 2002 SLT (Sh Ct) 82 (child's name and religious education).

[94] Few parents use the courts: *2007 Scottish Child Contact Survey* (Edinburgh: Scottish Government, 2008), available at: www.scotland.gov.uk/Publications/2008/03/12145638/0.

[95] *Parenting Agreements for Scotland – Guide*, available at: www.scotland.gov.uk/Resource/Doc/112209/0027303.pdf.

[96] See para. 12.11 above.

[97] *Understanding Child Contact Cases in Scottish Sheriff Courts* (Edinburgh: Scottish Government Social Research, 2010), available at: www.scotland.gov.uk/Publications/2010/12/08145916/15.

express[98] and avoiding unnecessary orders.[99] All things being equal, the thrust of the law supports the continued involvement of both parents in a child's life. In assessing welfare, the statute initially avoided any statutory 'welfare checklist', quite deliberately, for fear of encouraging a mechanistic approach.[100] While there is a substantial body of case law on factors considered relevant to welfare, much of it analysed in the literature,[101] the lack of statutory guidance left the test open to the criticism that it was vague and arbitrary. Two issues emerged as particularly problematic: children being exposed to domestic abuse and uncooperative parents who obstruct contact (access or visitation) with the other parent. In an attempt to address them, the statute was amended in 2006. Welfare remains the paramount consideration, but the court is directed to consider these matters as part of it.[102] Arguably, the amendments were unnecessary, since judges were well aware of both issues. The result is a partial welfare checklist that not only renders the law untidy, but may divert attention from other, equally relevant, considerations.[103] Thus, it is predicted here that a comprehensive checklist will emerge in future legislation.

12.31   The precise content of that checklist will be the battleground in what is already a very gendered debate. When the 2006 amendments were being discussed, women's groups sought greater protection for women and their children from male abusers who use contact with a child as a means of continuing to abuse their victims, harming the children in the process.[104] They argued for a statutory provision of the type found in other jurisdictions, creating a presumption against permitting the abuser any contact (or, at least, unsupervised contact) with the child. Thus, it is likely that the provision sought will form part of the new welfare checklist since it would prioritise the rights of victims, both women and children, over those of abusers and would be wholly consistent with the direction of law reform efforts to date.

---

[98] *Shields* v. *Shields* 2002 SLT 579; *Treasure* v. *McGrath* 2006 Fam LR 100.

[99] Children (Scotland) Act 1995, s. 11(7).

[100] Scottish Law Commission, *Report on Family Law*, paras. 5.20–5.23.

[101] See Sutherland, *Child and Family Law*, 2nd edn, paras. 6.169–6.218.

[102] The court must now 'have regard in particular' to the need to protect the child from abuse and, when making an order that will require cooperation between two or more persons, to consider whether the order would be appropriate: Children (Scotland) Act 1995, s. 11(7A)–(7D), added by the Family Law (Scotland) Act 2006, s. 24.

[103] Parental mental illness or substance abuse present equally pressing problems.

[104] See paras. 12.49–12.50 below for legislative and other attempts to protect against domestic abuse.

12.32   Groups representing aggrieved men protested that the child's mother could obstruct paternal contact for no valid reason and with impunity and sought a more punitive legal response. That there are such obstructive mothers is not disputed, but the court already has ample powers to deal with them. Provided it is consistent with the child's welfare, it can transfer the child's residence to the wronged parent or to a third party.[105] It can penalise the uncooperative parent for contempt of court, through a fine or imprisonment, albeit imprisonment is rightly used as a remedy of last resort.[106] There is no need for further sanctions. However, since continued contact with both parents usually benefits the child, it would be perfectly reasonable to include parental willingness to cooperate in the new statutory checklist, provided an exception is made to address abuse cases.

Child protection and state intervention

12.33   The state, in its many guises, plays a pivotal role in protecting children from abuse and neglect, taking a multifaceted approach that involves state support for families;[107] statutory age limits (designed to keep children away from harmful substances and activities);[108] powers to remove children from the home (temporarily or permanently); restrictions on those who might pose a danger to children[109] and the criminal law.[110] Where abuse or neglect is suspected, it seeks to ensure prompt, appropriate and effective investigation of the allegations, coupled with a proportionate response

---

[105]   Usually, the courts content themselves with threatening this course of action: *Reid* v. *Cardno* 2000 GWD 27–1026 and *Ellis* v. *Ellis* 2003 Fam LR. 77.

[106]   *M* v. *S* 2009 Fam LR 129 (mother sentenced to three months' imprisonment for contempt of court for persistent obstruction of contact).

[107]   This takes the form of both practical assistance, delivered through local authority health, education and social work departments, and financial help: Children (Scotland) Act 1995, ss. 19–30.

[108]   See para. 12.16 above.

[109]   See, generally, the Sexual Offences (Scotland) Act 2009. Anyone seeking to work with children must be vetted and others are barred from such work automatically: Protection of Vulnerable Groups (Scotland) Act 2007. Certain sex offenders are required to register with the police upon their release from prison: Sexual Offences Act 2003, ss. 80 *et seq*. The courts may restrict the activities of potential sex offenders: Sexual Offences Act 2003, s. 105; Protection of Children and Prevention of Sexual Offences (Scotland) Act 2005, ss. 2 and 17(4). Specific legislation targets 'grooming' of potential child victims, particularly via the Internet: Protection of Children and Prevention of Sexual Offences (Scotland) Act 2005, s. 1.

[110]   See further, Sutherland, *Child and Family Law*, 2nd edn, Chapter 9.

when abuse is found to exist. In carrying out this task, the state must bear in mind not only the child's right to protection, but also his or her right to participate in decision-making and the child's and the parents' rights to respect for private and family life and to due process. Marrying respect for all of these rights, sometimes in a climate of urgency and when the stakes are so very high, is no easy task and the European Court has not been slow to criticise the system for failure to respect one or other of them.[111]

12.34 The starting point is that children should live with their own families where that is both possible and safe. Intervention, by means of court orders, enables local state agencies to investigate allegations of abuse and neglect and remove children from the home where necessary.[112] Where the child cannot live with his or her parents, other relatives, such as grandparents, often provide in-family care and 'kinship care' is receiving increasing attention and support.[113] In response to allegations of both overzealous intervention and cases of failure to act or, at least, to act appropriately, the late twentieth century brought reform of the law[114] and of child protection procedures.[115]

12.35 Despite these efforts, examples of the state failing to protect abused and neglected children continue to occur[116] and another round of legislative reform is underway.[117] But the law alone cannot provide the solution here. Child protection involves multiple agencies – social workers, health care professionals, educators, the police and, of course, lawyers – and ensuring

---

[111] See *McMichael* v. *United Kingdom* (1995) 20 EHRR 205 (failure to respect parental rights) and *E* v. *United* Kingdom (2003) 36 EHRR 31 (failure to protect the child).

[112] Children (Scotland) Act 1995, Adoption and Children (Scotland) Act 2007 and Children's Hearings (Scotland) Act 2011.

[113] See further: *Moving Forward in Kinship and Foster Care* (Edinburgh: Scottish Government, 2008), available at www.scotland.gov.uk/Resource/Doc/262356/0078450. pdf (last accessed 20 March 2012) and the The Looked After Children (Scotland) Regulations 2009, SSI 2009/210.

[114] Children (Scotland) Act 1995, Part II, a response to alleged overzealous intervention in *Sloan* v. *B* 1991 SLT 530, the infamous 'Orkney Case'.

[115] A new framework was launched with the title, *Getting It Right For Every Child* (GIRFEC); see www.scotland.gov.uk/Topics/People/Young-People/gettingitright.

[116] For cases involving children who died at the hands of family members, despite being known to the local social work department, see Sutherland, *Child and Family Law*, 2nd edn, paras. 9.035–9.041.

[117] The most recent effort is the Children's Hearings (Scotland) Act 2011, with a Rights of Children and Young People Bill being discussed and a Children's Services Bill in prospect. For further information, see Consultation on the Rights of Children and Young People Bill (www.scotland.gov.uk/Publications/2011/09/07110058/0).

that they work together seamlessly is not an easy task. While improved procedures can go some way towards addressing that problem, implementing the procedures will be obstructed as long as social workers remain overworked, carrying excessive caseloads. Then there is the matter of finding the optimum environment for children who cannot remain in their own families. The sad truth is that the state makes a lousy parent and children in long-term foster care consistently do worse on all measures of well-being.[118] In addition, the poverty–abuse/neglect nexus is widely acknowledged and there is significant child poverty in Scotland.[119] Given that these are largely resource problems, their speedy resolution is not anticipated.

C   Adult relationships

12.36   At one time, the only form of adult relationship recognised by Scots law was different-sex marriage and anything that did not fit that mould was treated by the legal system as aberrant, if not criminal. The current approach embraces two formal relationships – different-sex marriage and same-sex civil partnerships – and cohabitation, demonstrating far greater respect for diversity, if not complete equality. Proposals under discussion may herald Scots law taking a further step towards equality by introducing same-sex marriage.[120]

The relationships
Marriage and civil partnership

12.37   Marriage has a long history as the monogamous, formal,[121] legal relationship between one man and one woman recognised by Scots law.

---

[118]   *Getting it Right for Children in Residential Care* (Edinburgh: Audit Scotland, 2010), available at: www.audit-scotland.gov.uk/docs/local/2010/nr_100902_children_residential.pdf.

[119]   S. Sinclair and J. McKendrick, *Child Poverty in Scotland: Taking the Next Steps* (London: Rowntree Foundation, 2009) and E. Barham, *Differences in Decline – Relative Child Poverty in Scotland and England: 1998/99 to 2008/09* (Edinburgh: Scottish Government Communities Analytical Services, 2011), available at: www.scotland.gov.uk/Topics/Statistics/Browse/Social-Welfare/IncomePoverty/diffdecline/Q/forceupdate/on.

[120]   *The Registration of Civil Partnerships, Same Sex Marriage: A Consultation* (Edinburgh: Scottish Government, 2011), available at: www.scotland.gov.uk/Publications/2011/09/05153328/0.

[121]   The only remaining form of common law marriage, more correctly styled 'irregular marriage', in Scotland was prospectively abolished in 2006, save for the limited exception of curing a defective foreign marriage after the death of one of the parties: Family Law (Scotland) Act 2006, s. 3.

As in so many other jurisdictions in the later twentieth century, attention began to focus on same-sex relationships. Hitherto, the treatment of same-sex relationships in Scotland had followed the familiar pattern of decriminalisation and the gradual extension of specific rights to same-sex couples.[122] In part, these developments were a response to changing social attitudes, but decisions of the European Court of Human Rights[123] and developments in the European Union[124] played their part. When attention turned to according full legal recognition to same-sex relationships, sections of the population supported the introduction of same-sex marriage, other (almost exclusively religious) groups opposed any recognition at all,[125] and yet others supported the compromise solution of creating a new marriage-equivalent for same-sex couples that did not use the magic word 'marriage'. In the event, the compromise solution prevailed. In the attempt to distance itself from the controversy,[126] the Scottish (Labour) government of the day handed legislative competency over to Westminster, which passed the Civil Partnership Act 2004, creating civil partnerships, a new kind of formal, legal relationship exclusively for same-sex couples, but substantially modelled on marriage.

12.38 Like many compromises, this solution failed to satisfy whole sections of the population with any commitment to the issue. With the introduction of civil partnership, same-sex couples have became more visible as stable family units, something reinforced by later legislation acknowledging same-sex couples as co-parents.[127] Whether prompted by that heightened visibility or a greater appreciation of human rights,

---

[122] See para.1.76 above.

[123] *Da Silva Mouta* v. *Portugal* (2001) 31 EHRR 47; *Karner* v. *Austria* (2004) 38 EHRR 21.

[124] Employment Directive 2000/78/EC (prohibiting discrimination on the basis of sexual orientation in employment and training) and, more generally, Charter of Fundamental Rights of the European Union, O.J. (C 364) 2000.

[125] These groups tended to adopt the thoroughly familiar arguments, ranging from the homophobic, to appeals to circular definitions, history and tradition, idealised notions of the traditional nuclear family, their own notion of morality and, ultimately, religion.

[126] This was done by means of a Legislative Consent Motion (see para. 12.7 above) and the political motive lay in the fact that the Labour Party derives significant support from the Roman Catholic population. There is an interesting parallel with similar treatment of recognising gender reassignment and the resulting UK statute, the Gender Recognition Act 2004. In each case, the plausible, but not wholly convincing, argument was advanced that it was more efficient to take a UK-wide approach due to the number of statutes on reserved matters (for example taxation, social security, immigration) that would require amendment.

[127] See the Adoption and Children (Scotland) Act 2007 and the Human Fertilisation and Embryology Act 2008, discussed at para. 12.19 above.

some 61 per cent of the Scottish population now supports the introduction of same-sex marriage.[128] It will be remembered that the Scottish Parliament has the power to pass the necessary legislation and, at the time of writing, the Scottish Nationalist Party government is consulting on whether it should do so.[129] In truth, there is a certain inevitability here since same-sex marriage is the logical conclusion of the incremental, linear progression of the law to date. While the European Court of Human Rights has indicated that it is not yet in a position to view Article 12 (right to marry) of the ECHR, when read with Article 14 (prohibition on discrimination), as requiring states to take this step, it is moving in that direction.[130] As more European countries introduce same-sex marriage, the same result may prove inevitable Europe-wide.

Cohabitation

12.39   Less politically controversial, but challenging for the legal system nonetheless, was what, if any, legal consequences should flow from simple cohabitation. The difficulty stems from the reasons why couples cohabit, rather than taking the more formal step of marrying or registering a civil partnership. On the one hand, some couples cohabit with the express intention of avoiding the legal consequences of the formal options. Respect for their freedom of choice militates against imposing these very consequences on them. On the other hand, cohabitation is often the product of simple inertia and, even where it results from conscious choice, substantial sections of the population have little or no accurate understanding of the legal consequences of the decision.[131] In addition, many cohabitants make sacrifices, incur economic and other disadvantages and develop levels of economic dependence that parallel those of their counterparts in the more formal relationships. If the law has a role in protecting adults from ignorance and inequality, then there is a case for attaching at least some consequences to cohabitation.

---

[128] *Scottish Social Attitudes Survey 2010: Attitudes to Discrimination and Positive Action* (Edinburgh: Scottish Government, 2011, web only), para. 3.18, available at: www.scotland.gov.uk/Publications/2011/08/11112523/0.

[129] *The Registration of Civil Partnerships, Same Sex Marriage: A Consultation* (www.scotland.gov.uk/Publications/2011/09/05153328/0). See para. 12.36 above.

[130] *Schalk* v. *Austria* (2011) 53 EHRR 20, discussed in E. E. Sutherland, 'A Step Closer To Same-Sex Marriage Throughout Europe' (2011) 15 *Edinburgh Law Review* 97.

[131] *Scottish Social Attitudes Survey 2004: Family Module Report* (Edinburgh, Scottish Government, 2005), Chapter 2.

12.40   Scots law had long accepted some protective responsibility and thus, even prior to the most recent round of reform, legislation addressed matters such as domestic abuse in the context of cohabitants.[132] With the increased incidence of cohabitation,[133] the case for attaching additional, but limited, legal consequences to it became more pressing – a position supported by the Scottish Law Commission,[134] government[135] and whole sections of the public, not least because many people thought that some of these consequences already flowed from cohabitation.[136] As we shall see, these manifold voices prevailed[137] and, this time, resolution was a wholly Scottish affair, with the relevant legislation being passed by the Scottish Parliament.

Entering relationships

Marriage and civil partnership

12.41   As we have seen, marriage is currently available only to different-sex couples, with civil partnership being the formal option for same-sex couples.[138] Entry into each is subject to compliance with the familiar triumvirate of requirements: capacity, consent and observing the requisite formalities.[139] While these are virtually identical, the main difference in terms of entry into the relationship relates to choice over the method of celebration.[140] Most of the current requirements

---

[132]   Matrimonial Homes (Family Protection) (Scotland) Act 1981, s. 18.

[133]   Cohabiting couples make up some 10 per cent of households: *Scotland's People* (Edinburgh, Scottish Government, 2009), p. 10, available at: www.scotland.gov.uk/Resource/Doc/282618/0085510.pdf.

[134]   Scottish Law Commission, R*eport on Family Law*, Chapter 16.

[135]   *Parents and Children* (Edinburgh: Scottish Executive, 2000), p. 29, and *Family Matters: Improving Family Law in Scotland* (Edinburgh: Scottish Executive, 2004), pp. 21–2.

[136]   L. Nicholson, *Improving Family Law in Scotland: Analysis of Written Consultation Responses* (Edinburgh: Scottish Executive Social Research, 2004).

[137]   See paras. 12.47–12.48 below.

[138]   Marriage (Scotland) Act 1977, s. 5(4)(e) and Civil Partnership Act 2004, s. 86(1)(a). The passage of the Gender Recognition Act 2004 makes it possible to have a change of gender recognised for legal purposes.

[139]   See Sutherland, *Child and Family Law*, 2nd edn, Chapter 12. As part of a package of measures designed to stem 'sham' marriages, entered into for the purpose of subverting immigration rules, anyone coming from outside the European Economic Area to marry or register a civil partnership in the United Kingdom must obtain a special visa.

[140]   See para. 12.42 below. While the incurable impotency of one of the parties is the only ground on which a marriage is voidable (as opposed to void) in Scotland, there is no equivalent for civil partners.

operate satisfactorily and the only predictions for change relate to two outstanding problems, one amenable to simple resolution, the other more challenging.

12.42 While marriage may be solemnised by means of either a civil or a religious ceremony,[141] a civil partnership may be registered by means only of a civil process, there being no religious option.[142] The distinction stems from the legislature's desire to placate religious opponents of recognising same-sex relationships by demonstrating that civil partnership differs from marriage.[143] Arguably, the distinction violates the Articles 8 (respect for private and family life), 9 (freedom of thought, conscience and religion) and 14 (prohibition of discrimination) rights of same-sex couples who wish to become civilly enpartnered in a religious ceremony, subject to the couple finding a celebrant who is willing to perform the ceremony.[144] The Scottish Government is currently consulting on whether the legislation should be amended to provide for religious celebration of civil partnership and, if introduced, same-sex marriage.[145]

12.43 The second, more challenging, difficulty has arisen in the context of forced (coerced) marriage,[146] something relatively unknown to modern Scots law until recently.[147] Evidence began to emerge of a numbers of Scots, particularly young women of Indian or Pakistani ancestry, being coerced into marriage in Scotland or abroad.[148] A purported marriage secured by

---

[141] Marriage (Scotland) Act 1977, ss. 8 and 17.

[142] Civil Partnership Act 2004, s. 93. In addition, while civil marriage ceremonies may be performed in places that have a religious association, civil partnership registration cannot take place on 'religious premises'. Civil Partnership Act 2004, s. 93(3).

[143] That permitting same-sex marriage does not violate the religious freedom of those who oppose it on religious grounds has been demonstrated by courts in other jurisdictions. See *Re Same-Sex Marriage* 246 D.L.R. (4th) 193 (Sup. Ct. 2004), para. 46, and *Fourie* v. *Minister of Home Affairs* 2005 (3) SA 429, para. 81.

[144] There is no suggestion that any religious celebrant should be forced to participate in a ceremony to which he or she objects on conscientious (or any other) grounds, not least because such coercion would violate the celebrant's right to freedom of religion under Article 9 of the European Convention on Human Rights.

[145] *The Registration of Civil Partnerships, Same Sex Marriage: A Consultation* (www.scotland.gov.uk/Publications/2011/09/05153328/0).

[146] While forced civil partnership appears not to be a problem, the legislation applies to both marriage and civil partnership in order to address the possibility of it arising.

[147] In *Mahmood* v. *Mahmood* 1993 SLT 589, referring to duress, the Lord Ordinary noted: 'There appears to be no Scottish case within the last two centuries of a decree [of nullity] being pronounced on this ground.'

[148] Precise numbers are, necessarily, difficult to obtain.

duress is void if the ceremony took place in Scotland[149] or, where it took place abroad, if one of the parties was a domiciled Scot.[150] In addition, and depending on the circumstances, those exerting the pressure may be guilty of a number of offences under the criminal law.[151] The fact that the problem has arisen in the context of minority groups in the community adds a layer of sensitivity to the issue since it is crucial to avoid perpetuating racial stereotypes[152] or alienating the very groups where protection is needed most. Thus, the option of using the criminal law to create an offence of forcing (or attempting to force) a person to enter a marriage was explored and rejected, not least because many victims would be reluctant to report offenders (usually their relatives) if prosecution would result.[153] In 2011 the forced marriage protection order was introduced, enabling the victim or a person acting on his or her behalf, to seek a civil order from a court requiring a third party to refrain from certain conduct, such as attempting to force the protected person to enter a marriage, or take positive action, such as surrendering a passport.[154] Breach of such an order is an offence rendering the offender liable to up to two years' imprisonment.

Cohabitation

12.44 Having accepted that some automatic legal consequences should attach to cohabitation, the next issue for the legal system was one of definition. Hitherto, the pattern had been to recognise relationships that replicated familiar models, being couples 'living together as if they were' husband and wife or civil partners.[155] When the legal consequences flowing from cohabitation increased, further statutory guidance was provided

---

[149] Marriage (Scotland) Act 1977, s. 20A(2). For examples of marriages declared void due to family pressure amounting to duress, see *Mahmood* v. *Mahmood* 1993 SLT 589 (21-year-old woman), *Mahmud* v. *Mahmud* 1994 SLT 599 (31-year-old man) and *Sohrab* v. *Khan* 2002 SLT 1255 (16-year-old woman).

[150] *Singh* v. *Singh* 2005 SLT 749 (18-year-old woman, who was tricked by her mother into believing her trip to India was for a holiday, then was forced to participate in a marriage ceremony).

[151] Depending on the circumstances, offences might include abduction, assault, child cruelty, rape or other sexual offences and a variety of statutory offences relating to harassment or protective orders.

[152] This is exemplified in the occasional confusion between arranged, but consensual, marriage and forced marriage.

[153] *Forced Marriage: A Civil Remedy?* (Edinburgh: Scottish Government, 2008), p. 2.

[154] Forced Marriage etc (Protection and Jurisdiction) (Scotland) Act 2011.

[155] Matrimonial Homes (Family Protection) (Scotland) Act 1981, s. 18, as amended.

in the form of a non-exclusive list of relevant factors indicating who quali-fied as a 'cohabitant'.[156] Reflecting the Scottish preference for flexibility over bright line rules, the list makes no mention of children, nor of a min-imum length of time that will raise a presumption of cohabitation. While the statutory guidance has been operating for only a comparatively short time, the courts are having no difficulty in applying the criteria.[157] What this means, of course, is that there is legally significant cohabitation and other kinds of (non-marital, non-civil partnership) relationships – casual, intermittent, polyamorous, and so forth – that are largely ignored by the legal system.[158]

Consequences of relationships

Marriage and civil partnership

12.45   The personal consequences that attach to marriage and civil partnership automatically are premised on the equality of the parties and are almost identical.[159] Monogamy is the order of the day, so one can-not enter a marriage or civil partnership while in another of the formal relationships.[160] Civil partners and spouses are eligible to apply to adopt children[161] and are recognised as second parents of donor children.[162] However, while the legal system acknowledges the sexual dimension of the spousal relationship, it persists in ignoring that aspect of civil partner-ship.[163] Whether that is prompted by the desire to demonstrate that civil

---

[156]   Family Law (Scotland) Act 2006, s. 25. The factors are the length of time the parties lived together, the nature of the relationship and the nature and extent of any financial arrangements subsisting.

[157]   Cases to date have taken an inclusive approach to finding cohabitation established: *Chebotareva* v. *King's Executrix* 2008 Fam LR 66; *Savage* v. *Purches* 2009 SLT (Sh Ct) 36. On the operation of the cohabitation provisions of the Family Law (Scotland) Act 2006, see E. E. Sutherland, '"The easing of certain legal difficulties": Limited Legal Recognition of Cohabitation Under Scots Law', in B. Atkin (ed.), *International Survey of Family Law: 2011 Edition* (Bristol: Family Law, 2011), p. 335.

[158]   This is subject to the caveat that a personal relationship may trigger liability in contract or delict (tort) (e.g. *Shilliday* v. *Smith* 1998 SLT 976; *McKenzie* v. *Nutter* 2007 SLT (Sh Ct) 17) or under the criminal law (e.g. where one of the parties to a sexual relationship is under the age of 16).

[159]   Occasional, largely accidental statutory anomalies persist and will be addressed by legis-lation in due course.

[160]   Marriage (Scotland) Act 1977, s. 5(4)(b); Civil Partnership Act 2004, s. 86(1)(d).

[161]   Adoption and Children (Scotland) Act 2007, s. 29(3).

[162]   Human Fertilisation and Embryology Act 2008, ss. 35 and 42.

[163]   In respect of voidable unions, see note 140 above, and adultery, see para. 12.52 below.

partnership and marriage are different or by lingering homophobia is a matter for speculation.

12.46 During the currency of a marriage or civil partnership, the system of separate property is encroached upon only a little by the obligation to aliment a spouse or civil partner,[164] certain rebuttable presumptions that household goods and housekeeping allowances are shared equally[165] and the special treatment of the family home, designed to protect against domestic abuse and bankruptcy.[166] These exceptions aside and bearing in mind that some of them can be avoided by the couple contracting out of them,[167] it would be fair to say that marriage and civil partnership become important, in terms of legal consequences, upon termination of the relationship, whether by dissolution or the death of one of the parties.[168] The existing provisions operate well and no significant change in them is predicted.

Cohabitation

12.47 In strictly legal terms, cohabitants face fewer personal restrictions than do spouses or civil partners in so far as they are free to enter a formal relationship with one person while cohabiting with another. While cohabitants may be eligible to apply to adopt a child[169] and qualifying partners are recognised as second parents of donor children,[170] as we have seen, non-marital fathers are discriminated against by the legal system.[171]

12.48 In 2006 the limited rebuttable presumptions that household goods and housekeeping allowances are shared equally, already applying to spouses and civil partners, were extended to qualifying cohabitants.[172] Unlike spouses and civil partners, cohabitants do not owe each

---

[164] Family Law (Scotland) Act 1985, s. 1(1).

[165] Family Law (Scotland) Act 1985, ss. 25 and 26.

[166] Matrimonial Homes (Family Protection) (Scotland) Act 1981 and Bankruptcy and Diligence (Scotland) Act 2007.

[167] See para. 12.60 below.   [168] See paras. 12.55–12.57 below.

[169] The couple must be living together as husband and wife or civil partners, but must also be 'in an enduring family relationship': Adoption and Children (Scotland) Act 2007, s. 29(3).

[170] Human Fertilisation and Embryology Act 2008, s. 36 and 43. The status derives from agreement and cohabitation is not a prerequisite.

[171] See paras. 12.22–12.24 above.

[172] Family Law (Scotland) Act 2006, s. 26 and 27. 'Qualifying cohabitant' is as defined in section 25, discussed at para. 12.44 above.

other any alimentary (financial support) obligation during the relationship – a distinction that resulted from a, quite deliberate, policy
decision and was supported by public opinion.[173] Certainly, it signals a
difference between cohabitation and the formal relationships, but at a
price. Access to certain means-tested state benefits is calculated on the
basis that cohabitants are supporting each other, so a cohabitant may
be denied state benefits at the same time as having no remedy, in private law, against his or her partner. This, coupled with the increased
incidence of cohabitation, makes it likely that an alimentary obligation will be imposed on cohabitants in the future. Again, it is simply
another example of a linear progression continuing, with cohabitation
increasingly resembling marriage and civil partnership. As is the case
for spouses and civil partners, the most significant consequences apply
when the relationship terminates, whether by death or by choice.[174]
Again, legally savvy cohabitants can contract out of many of these
consequences.

Domestic abuse

12.49   Since the 1980s there have been concerted legislative and other
efforts aimed at tackling domestic abuse in Scotland.[175] These efforts
continued, after devolution, with successive Scottish governments developing a national strategy, establishing a national domestic abuse help-
line, funding an advertising campaign designed to highlight the issues,
funding projects aimed at tackling abuse and commissioning research on
various aspects of the problem.[176] A highly successful, dedicated domestic
abuse court was established in Glasgow, Scotland's most populous city, as
a pilot project.[177]

---

[173] Nicholson, *Improving Family Law in Scotland*, para. 5.2 and table 4.

[174] See paras. 12.58–12.59 below.

[175] The Matrimonial Homes (Family Protection) (Scotland) Act 1981 gave a spouse the
right to occupy the family home and to have the abusive partner excluded, with more
restricted rights being available to different-sex cohabitants. The spousal provisions
were extended to civil partners: Civil Partnership Act 2004, ss. 101–116. Eventually, the
Matrimonial Homes (Family Protection) (Scotland) Act 1981 was extended to same-
sex cohabitants: Family Law (Scotland) Act 2006, s. 34. See also the Protection from
Harassment Act 1997 and the Protection from Abuse (Scotland) Act 2001.

[176] See further, Sutherland, *Child and Family Law*, 2nd edn, paras. 13.135–13.163 and
Chapter 14.

[177] Reid Howie Associates, *Evaluation of The Pilot Domestic Abuse Court* (Edinburgh:
Scottish Government, 2007, web only), available at: www.scotland.gov.uk/
Publications/2007/03/28153424/15.

12.50   Yet domestic abuse remains a significant problem.[178] While female victims of male partner violence are still the most numerous in official statistics, there is increasing recognition of female-on-male abuse and abuse within same-sex relationships and, of course, the law is designed to protect all victims equally. Whether that plays out in practice is a matter of debate.[179] The draft of the latest legislation,[180] which sought to improve the remedies available to victims, contained a provision that would have provided every (alleged) victim of domestic abuse with free legal representation. Economic considerations resulted in that provision being dropped from the final statute. While plans to create dedicated domestic abuse courts across the country are being implemented slowly, financial reasons have been cited for delays.[181] Respect for dignity and equality may have driven law reform thus far, but resource constraints continue to impede progress.

Termination of relationships

Divorce and civil partnership dissolution

12.51   While Scots law permitted divorce from the time of the Reformation in the sixteenth century,[182] it was not until the latter half of the twentieth century that it became the widespread, socially acceptable phenomenon it is today. Escaping from marriage is now a fairly straightforward process,[183] at least in strictly legal terms, with some

---

[178] *2009/10 Scottish Crime and Justice Survey: Partner Abuse* (Edinburgh: Scottish Government, 2010), available at: www.scotland.gov.uk/Publications/2010/12/03094109/13. In 2009–2010, 51,926 separate incidents were recorded by the police, a slight decrease on the previous year. Of course, many incidents are not reported. See *Domestic Abuse Recorded by the Police in Scotland 2009–2010* (Edinburgh: Scottish Government, 2011, web only), available at: www.scotland.gov.uk/Resource/Doc/330575/0107237.pdf.

[179] B. Dempsey, 'Gender Neutral Laws and Heterocentric Policies: "Domestic Abuse as Gender-Based Abuse" and Same-Sex Couples' (2011) 15(3) *Edinburgh Law Review* 381.

[180] Domestic Abuse (Scotland) Act 2011 (asp 13).

[181] D. Leask, 'Abuse Court Roll-Out in Jeopardy', *Scotland on Sunday*, 20 December 2009. Only a few more domestic abuse courts have been established.

[182] See Divorce for Desertion Act 1573. There is some evidence of Kirk Sessions granting divorces before then.

[183] A new provision, s. 3A, was added to the Divorce (Scotland) Act 1976 in 2006, in the attempt to address the problem of Jewish wives trapped in marriages, at least in their own eyes and those of their religious community, by their husbands' refusal to grant a *get* (a release from the marriage) despite divorces being obtained from the secular courts. See, Sutherland, *Child and Family Law*, 2nd edn, paras. 15.086–15.091.

10,000 divorces being granted each year. Divorce is available on fault and no-fault grounds,[184] a continuation of the compromise reached in 1976, when no-fault divorce was introduced, albeit over 80 per cent of divorces proceed on a no-fault basis.[185] While a minority of the population bemoans the ease with which marriage can be terminated, there is no real movement to make divorce more difficult and, indeed, the justification for retaining fault grounds has largely disappeared.[186] Thus, it is predicted that, in the future, divorce will be a thoroughly no-fault affair, at least in strictly legal terms.

12.52   When civil partnership was introduced, a parallel system for dissolution was put in place, subject to one exception.[187] While adultery is one of the fault grounds of divorce, there is no express equivalent for civil partners. The absence of 'adultery' may be justified on the basis of the specific legal definition of the term in Scots law.[188] However, it is no justification for the failure to provide an 'infidelity' equivalent. Again, the explanation is the legislature's unwillingness to acknowledge the sexual component of same-sex relationships. This irritating inconsistency is probably of no great moment, since sexual infidelity (of whatever kind) will almost certainly entitle the innocent civil partner to a decree of dissolution on the 'behaviour' ground. The abolition of fault divorce would remove the anomaly.

12.53   Access to the process of divorce and civil partnership dissolution raises the issue of access to legal services more generally. For couples with

---

[184] Divorce (Scotland) Act 1976, s. 1. While the statute claims that divorce is available upon the issuing of a gender recognition certificate to either spouse or proof of irretrievable breakdown, the latter can only be established by the pursuer (plaintiff) proving one of the following: adultery by the other spouse; behaviour by the other spouse making it unreasonable to expect continued cohabitation; one year of non-cohabitation, accompanied by the consent of the other spouse; or two years' non-cohabitation.

[185] *Statistical Bulletin: Divorces and Dissolutions in Scotland, 2009–10* (Edinburgh: Scottish Government, 2011), available at: www.scotland.gov.uk/Resource/Doc/335819/0109833. pdf.

[186] Aside from the thoroughly unhealthy desire to record blame, the behaviour ground was once justified on the basis that it provided a 'quick exit route' for victims of domestic abuse. Arguably, with the shortening of the non-cohabitation periods, that justification falls.

[187] Civil Partnership Act 2004, s. 117. Given the novelty of civil partnership, the dissolution rate is low, with twenty-seven being dissolved in 2009–2010.

[188] Adultery is voluntary sexual intercourse with a person of the opposite sex who is not one's spouse and requires 'the introduction of the male organ into the female': *MacLennan* v. *MacLennan* 1958 S.C. 105, per Lord Wheatley, at p. 112.

no children under the age of 16 who can agree on property division (or have no property to divide) and financial matters, there is a relatively inexpensive do-it-yourself procedure. For all other couples, the cost will escalate with any dispute, rendering divorce or dissolution inaccessible to some. Were a wholly no-fault system for divorce and civil partnership dissolution to be adopted in the future, the case would become stronger for rendering all proceedings wholly administrative and leaving the courts as the venue for the resolution of ancillary disputes over children and property.

Cohabitation

12.54 It is in the nature of cohabitation and, indeed, probably one of its attractions, that terminating the relationship requires no legal process. However, formerly cohabiting couples who find themselves in dispute over children, money and property should be under no illusion that they will necessarily avoid litigation. Like spouses and civil partners, cohabitants may face problems over access to affordable legal services.

Consequences of termination

Marriage and civil partnership

12.55 On a personal level, the single most significant consequence of divorce or civil partnership dissolution is that it frees the parties to enter a new formal relationship, albeit being married or civilly enpartnered is no bar to entering a new de facto relationship.

12.56 The legal system had long refereed disputes between divorcing spouses over future financial support and property division. As we have seen, during the relationship a system of separate property prevails. Divorce and dissolution occasion the application of what amounts to a deferred community property system. The present system[189] resulted from a desire to have a clear, flexible and principled approach to disputes,[190] designed to encourage couples to reach agreement, rather than dissipate resources on litigation. The court is provided with guiding principles to apply in making a wide range of orders dealing with the

---

[189] Family Law (Scotland) Act 1985, based on the recommendations of the Scottish Law Commission: *Report on Aliment and Financial Provision* (Edinburgh: Scot Law Com No. 67, 1981).

[190] Previous systems relied either on the notional death of the guilty spouse or on 'rules of thumb' and judicial discretion in which fault sometimes played a part.

ongoing support and division of movable and heritable property, with the family home and pensions often being the focus.[191] The principles seek to reflect the combined efforts (both economic and non-economic) of the parties during the marriage and subject any resulting property to fair (prima facie, equal) division. The goal is to enable each party to move on with his or her life, unencumbered by the other, but the principles accommodate circumstances where instalment payments or continuing support, or both, are justified. Fault in causing the breakdown of the relationship is irrelevant to the calculation. With the advent of civil partnership, it simply slotted into the system for financial provision available to divorcing spouses. Spouses and civil partners may contract out of this system, subject to the possibility of any agreement being challenged later in court.

12.57   While it would be inaccurate to suggest that all spouses or civil partners now leave their relationships satisfied with the financial arrangements, their discontent is often a product of the sad reality that the available resources are inadequate to enable each of them to maintain their former standard of living in separate households. There is no real movement to alter a system that, on the whole, makes the best of a difficult situation.

Cohabitation

12.58   The challenge of respecting the autonomy of the parties while protecting the vulnerable, posed by simple cohabitation,[192] crystallises when relationships break down. Consistent with distinguishing cohabitation from marriage and civil partnership, Scots law provides separating cohabitants with remedies that are very much more limited than the comprehensive package available in the context of the formal relationships.[193] There is no attempt to effect 'fair sharing' of accrued assets, nor is there any power to transfer property or to share pensions, as is the case with spouses and civil partners. Rather, a 'qualifying cohabitant'[194] must raise the action within a year of the cohabitation

---

[191]   See Sutherland, *Child and Family Law*, 2nd edn, paras. 16.017–16.186.

[192]   See para. 12.39 above.

[193]   Family Law (Scotland) Act 2006, s. 28. Section 29 permits the surviving cohabitant to apply to the court for an award from the deceased partner's estate. For a detailed discussion of the provisions and the case law, see Sutherland, 'The Easing of Certain Legal Difficulties'.

[194]   See para. 12.44 above.

ending and, in addition to interim orders, the court may make an award under either or both of two heads. The first is for the payment of a capital sum, designed to balance economic advantages and disadvantages sustained by one party in the interests of the other or a 'relevant child' (including a child accepted into the family). The second type of award is not limited to a capital sum and relates to the future economic burden of caring for the couple's child. Cohabitants may contract out of these provisions.

12.59   While awards have been made since the legislation came into force in 2006, arguably there are problems both with its scope and the courts' application of it. The one-year time limit on claims does little to encourage amicable resolution of disputes. The courts have been somewhat ungenerous in giving credit for home-making contributions, particularly in child-free relationships, and in taking account of the true cost, in terms of lost career opportunities, of caring for a child. The legislation is based, in part, on recommendations made by the Scottish Law Commission some twenty years ago and cohabitation is now more common and more socially acceptable. This has led to calls for the issue to be revisited and, in time, it is likely that the courts will be given wider powers to effect end-of-relationship reckonings for cohabitants. Again, this would be no more than continuing the linear progression of law reform to date.

Self-regulation and custom-made relationships

12.60   Legal consequences flow automatically from marriage and civil partnership and, to a lesser extent, from cohabitation. Some are avoidable, in so far as the parties may contract out of them, putting the onus on the parties to exercise this option. Arguably, freedom of choice is supported by putting this onus on the informed since, in truth, they are the only ones who can exercise meaningful choice. Contracts may be challenged in court.[195] Other consequences, such as those designed to protect against domestic abuse, are not open to contracting out. But it is no denial of choice to attach consequences to behaviour that is legally impermissible and morally intolerable. While anecdotal evidence suggests that self-regulation is becoming increasingly popular, pre-relationship contracts remain rare.

---

[195]   Family Law (Scotland) Act 1985, ss. 8 and 16.

D   Conclusions

12.61   To date, much of the development of child and family law has followed a linear progression: from patriarchy to equality; from the extended family to the nuclear; from a narrow construction of relationships deemed worthy of recognition to greater diversity. The modern law has been driven by both principled respect for children's rights and human rights, more generally, and pragmatic responses to the changing face of Scottish society. There is every reason to believe that developments will continue along the path taken thus far.

12.62   As a result, many future developments will simply be logical progressions from the current law. The position of non-marital fathers will be improved by the introduction of court-ordered DNA testing in civil cases. All donor children will have access to identifying information about their donor parents. Disputes involving children will be resolved with the assistance of a comprehensive welfare checklist. Physical punishment of children will become a thing of the past. In all probability, marriage will become available to all adults, irrespective of sexual orientation, and the differences between the formal and informal relationships may narrow further. If this encourages more cohabitants to contract about the consequences of their relationships, then the truly informal nature of cohabitation will be eroded. Fault will disappear altogether from divorce and dissolution.

12.63   While respect for human rights will continue as a driving force, apparent or actual conflict between these rights themselves, or their co-option by specific groups or individuals, will continue to present challenges. Ultimately, the rights of one must prevail over those of the other. Sometimes the blow can be softened by subtle legal accommodations. How the legal system will reconcile the right of a donor child to identifying information about a donor parent with that parent's guarantee of anonymity is a case in point. It is predicted that the rights of donor children will prevail, albeit donors will be accommodated somewhat by a lack of parental obligation attaching to disclosure. Similarly, while attaching increased consequences to cohabitation denies those who have elected to avoid these consequences respect for their chosen form of family life, it is predicted that these consequences will only increase. The softening of the blow will come, this time, with the option to conclude a formal contract in order to avoid some, but not all, of the consequences, an option also available to spouses and civil partners.

12.64   Not all of the outstanding problems are capable of resolution through legal developments alone. Eradicating abuse within the family, whether of children or inter-adult, will take more than fine legal drafting and sound court decisions. Public education, better inter-agency cooperation and greater public ownership of the problem are all essential components of the solution.

12.65   Increased respect for diversity means that the legal system must encompass the flexibility necessary to enable it to address the varied circumstances that present themselves. In this, the Scottish preference for general definitions and guiding principles, rather than bright line rules, may serve well. So it has been in the non-definition of the 'best interests of the child', or the very fluid definition of 'cohabitant'. But flexibility comes at the price of uncertainty and reliance on judicial discretion, leaving the law open to the objection that its application is vague and arbitrary. Often, such a challenge can be met by pointing to an established body of case law that guides the courts in applying flexible definitions and principles.

12.66   Any such defence loses force, however, when individuals choose, or are forced, to rely on self-regulation. On the one hand, the increased availability of mediation can help family members to find constructive and workable solutions to problems and to avoid the cost, delay and toxicity associated with litigation. On the other hand, the lack of affordable legal services and the paucity of legal aid provision drives individuals to attempt to deal with legal problems without adequate legal advice. Sometimes, indeed, legislation, such as that most recently enacted in respect of child support, co-opts the mantle of empowering individuals in driving them to resolve disputes by themselves.

12.67   Perhaps the biggest challenge to modern child and family law in Scotland is accessibility – to the content of law itself, to legal services and to the courts. No matter how good the substantive law, justice cannot be served fully unless all, children and adults alike, have meaningful access to the tools that will enable them to benefit from it.

13

South Africa

Changing the contours of child and family law

JACQUELINE HEATON

A Introduction

13.1   South African child and family law has changed from a system of law geared towards protecting only heterosexual, monogamous marriage and the offspring born from this type of union to a much more inclusive system. Today, officially solemnised same-sex unions and polygynous customary marriages enjoy full recognition alongside heterosexual, monogamous civil marriage, and the absence of a marriage between a child's parents no longer entails limitation of the legal relationship between the child and his or her unmarried father to the duty to pay maintenance. As will become clear below, these changes are mainly the result of social change and the recognition of human rights.

Historical roots, sources and law reform

Historical roots

13.2   The first legal system that operated in South Africa was customary or indigenous law. Due to white settlement and subsequent Dutch and British occupation, the common law, which is Roman-Dutch law with some English influences, also applies in South Africa. With the coming into operation of the Constitution of the Republic of South Africa 200 of 1993, South Africa acquired its first Bill of Rights.[1] Now, the Constitution of the Republic of South Africa, 1996[2] (hereafter 'Constitution'), which also contains a Bill of Rights,[3] applies.

---

[1] Constitution of the Republic of South Africa 200 of 1993, Chapter 3.
[2] Constitutional Law Act 5 of 2005.   [3] Constitution, Chapter 2.

Sources

13.3   In the past, only one legal system was fully recognised in South Africa, namely, Roman-Dutch common law as influenced by English law, interpreted in case law and modified by statutory rules. Customary law, which used to be relegated to a traditional system deserving little recognition, now enjoys recognition alongside the common law.[4] Discovering the content of customary law is problematic, for this body of law is largely unwritten and is subject to tribal differences.[5] Case law provides some guidance on the content of customary law, as do publications by authors, but these sources are frequently criticised as conveying an official, stultified version of customary law that has been influenced by apartheid policies and perspectives. Thus, expert witnesses are sometimes used to establish current, living customary law.[6]

13.4   Religious law is not officially recognised as a source of law, although individuals and religious groups constitutionally enjoy the right to freedom of religion and belief, and to practise their religion and/or belief in association with others.[7]

13.5   In a multicultural and multi-religious society such as South Africa pluralism of laws is inevitable. Unification of laws is unlikely to take place because it would probably unjustifiably limit the constitutional rights to freedom of culture and religion.[8] However, harmonisation is being selectively employed. Thus, for example, the legislator and courts have attempted to harmonise the law relating to customary and civil marriages,[9] but these

---

[4] Constitution, s. 211(3).

[5] In KwaZulu-Natal customary law is partly codified: KwaZulu Act on the Code of Zulu Law 16 of 1985; Natal Code of Zulu Law Proclamation R151, *Government Gazette* 10966, 9 October 1987.

[6] On the differences between official and current, living customary law, and the difficulties in ascertaining the true content of customary law, see, for example, *Bhe v. Magistrate, Khayalitsa (Commission for Gender Equality as Amicus Curiae)*; *Shibi v. Sithole*; *South African Human Rights Commission v. President of the Republic of South Africa* 2005 (1) SA 580 (CC); *Gumede v. President of the Republic of South Africa* 2009 (3) SA 152 (CC).

[7] Constitution, ss. 15(1) and 18.

[8] Constitution, ss. 15(1), 30 and 31. A limitation of a right enshrined in the Bill of Rights is justifiable only if it occurs in terms of law of general application and is reasonable and justifiable in an open and democratic society based on human dignity, equality and freedom. Whether the limitation is justifiable is determined by taking all relevant factors into account, including those stipulated in s. 36.

[9] See, for example, the Recognition of Customary Marriages Act 120 of 1998 and *Gumede v. President of the Republic of South Africa* 2009 (3) SA 152 (CC).

attempts have been criticised as denuding customary marriage law and supplanting it with the law relating to civil marriages.[10]

13.6   The main written sources of South African law are the Constitution, legislation, case law, old texts and writings on Roman-Dutch law, and the writings of modern authors. The Constitution is the supreme law against which all other legal provisions must be tested.[11] Insofar as case law is concerned, the binding force of each decision is determined in accordance with the precedent system. Briefly, the decisions of the Constitutional Court bind all courts, and those of the Supreme Court of Appeal bind all the divisions of the High Court and the Magistrates' Court, while decisions by a particular division of the High Court bind that court and the Magistrates' Courts that fall within the geographical area of that division of the High Court. The decisions of the Magistrates' Courts do not serve as precedents.

13.7   Finally, courts, tribunals and forums that are confronted with interpreting the Bill of Rights must consider international law, and when interpreting any legislation, the courts must prefer any reasonable interpretation that is consistent with international law over an interpretation that is inconsistent with it.[12]

Law reform

13.8   The South African Law Reform Commission (or South African Law Commission, as it was known until 2003)[13] plays a major role in the development and reform of the law. The draft Bills the Commission prepares after doing research and publishing a report on a particular topic are frequently at the core of subsequent legislation tabled in Parliament.

13.9   A second, very important, avenue for law reform is the courts. The enactment of a Constitution containing a Bill of Rights in particular provided an impetus for judicial reform. Several of the judgments that reformed child and family law are mentioned in this chapter. Public

---

[10]   C. Himonga, 'The Advancement of African Women's Rights in the First Decade of Democracy in South Africa: The Reform of The Customary Law of Marriage and Succession' 2005 *Acta Juridica* 84; J. Bekker and G. van Niekerk, '*Gumede* v. *President of the Republic of South Africa*: Harmonisation, or the Creation of New Marriage Laws in South Africa?' (2009) 24 *SA Public Law* 214.

[11]   Constitution, s. 8(1) and (2).

[12]   Constitution, ss. 39(1)(b) and 233.

[13]   South African Law Reform Commission Act 19 of 1973, s. 2(2).

interest groups such as the Women's Legal Centre Trust, the Centre for Child Law and the National Coalition for Gay and Lesbian Equality (and its successor the Lesbian and Gay Equality Project) played a major role in enabling judicial reform to take place in the post-Bill of Rights era, for they have funded and initiated several of the cases leading to reform and have also acted as friends of the court in some cases.

13.10 An inevitable problem with judicial law reform is its piecemeal nature. The legislator remains the most suitable agent for major law reform.[14]

Dispute resolution and access to legal services

13.11 Dispute resolution ultimately takes place in court. Although the adversarial procedure remains the main procedural system, there is growing support from legislative and judicial quarters for alternative dispute resolution, especially mediation.[15] It is predicted that mediation will continue to grow in child and family law matters. The Department of Justice and Constitutional Development plans to extend mediation to maintenance matters and has already undertaken pilot projects in the Maintenance Courts.[16] Furthermore, mediation enjoys widespread support in indigenous communities as it is part of their tradition.[17] However, the mediation these communities practise is usually performed by untrained individuals.

13.12 Access to justice is a serious problem in the context of dispute resolution. The majority of the population cannot afford to pay lawyers' fees. Some people are able to obtain cheap or free legal advice and legal representation through Legal Aid South Africa (which is state-funded), legal aid clinics, non-governmental organisations and public/private partnerships such

---

[14] *Carmichele v. Minister of Safety and Security (Centre for Applied Legal Studies intervening)* 2001 (4) SA 938 (CC), para. 36.

[15] Mediation in Certain Divorce Matters Act 24 of 1987; Maintenance Act 99 of 1998, s. 10(1A); Domestic Violence Act 116 of 1998, s. 5(1A); Recognition of Customary Marriages Act 1998, s. 8(3); Children's Act 38 of 2005, ss. 6(4), 21, 22, 33–34, 49, 69–71; *Van den Berg v. Le Roux* [2003] 3 All SA 599 (NC); *Townsend-Turner v. Morrow* 2004 (2) SA 32 (C); *MB v. NB* 2010 (3) SA 220 (GSJ).

[16] M. de Jong, 'The Newly Introduced Public Mediation Service in the Maintenance Court Environment: Does it Make a Difference in the Short Term?' (2009) 72 *Journal for Contemporary Roman-Dutch Law* 274.

[17] M. de Jong, 'A Pragmatic Look at Mediation as an Alternative to Divorce Litigation' 2010 *Journal of South African Law* 528.

as the People's Family Law Centre.[18] Individual lawyers sometimes conduct the cases of deserving, impecunious clients on a pro bono basis. Some firms of lawyers are even devoted solely to public interest legal services. However, most of these organisations and individuals employ a means test, which excludes the middle class from legal assistance and representation. Furthermore, the venues where cheap or free legal advice can be obtained are limited. In general, therefore, the poor and the middle class have less access to justice than the wealthy have.

13.13   Insofar as children are concerned, the picture is less bleak. Section 28(2)(h) of the Constitution affords every child the right to legal representation by the state, and at state expense, in civil proceedings affecting the child, if substantial injustice would otherwise result. Under this section a 15-year-old boy has obtained representation in an application he brought for variation of a care order that had been made upon divorce,[19] and a 12-year-old girl has obtained representation in very acrimonious litigation between her parents about her care.[20] The Divorce Act 70 of 1979 also empowers the court to appoint a legal representative for the child of divorcing parents and to order the parents, or either of them, to pay the costs of such representation.[21] As this legal representation is not state-funded, it is reserved for the children of wealthy parents.

13.14   A third problem is that the adjudication of child and family law matters is fragmented as South Africa does not have specialised Family Courts with jurisdiction in all child and family law matters. Several years ago the creation of such courts was recommended,[22] but because of financial and other constraints they were never established. It is unlikely that they will be established in the future as the constraints are ever-present.

13.15   Finally, other problems with the South African court system that also affect the adjudication of child and family law matters are that the infrastructure of some courts has fallen into disrepair, the court administration is dysfunctional, it often takes years for matters to come to trial, judicial officers do not have equipment or resources such as laptops,

---

[18]   S. Burman and N. Glasser, 'Giving Effect to the Constitution: Helping Families to help Themselves' (2003) 19 *South African Journal on Human Rights* 490.

[19]   *Soller* v. *G* 2003 (5) SA 430 (W).

[20]   *Legal Aid Board* v. *R.* 2009 (2) SA 262 (D).   [21]   Section 6(4).

[22]   Hoexter Commission, *Fifth and Final Report RP 78/1983 Commission of Inquiry into the Structure and Functioning of the Courts* (Pretoria: Government Printer, 1983), paras. 9.4.1–9.4.2.

electronic reference material and properly updated libraries, and large numbers of judgments are delivered long after conclusion of the trial.[23]

B   Children in the family setting and state intervention

13.16   The legal position of children in South Africa has improved dramatically in recent years. In keeping with international trends, the focus of South African child law, and particularly of the private law rules regarding the parent–child relationship, has shifted from the rights and powers of parents to the rights and entitlements of children. South Africa's ratification of the United Nations Convention on the Rights of the Child and the African Charter on the Rights and Welfare of the Child, and the inclusion of a children's rights clause in the Constitution,[24] have resulted in specific additional rights being conferred on children.

13.17   The coming into operation of the Children's Act 2005 improved the legal position of children even further, inter alia by requiring that the standard that the child's best interests are of paramount importance be applied in all matters concerning a child's care, protection and well-being, and recognising the right to child participation.[25] The Act also provides that children below the minimum legal age for marriage may not marry or get engaged, and that once they reach the minimum marriageable age, they may not be given out in marriage or engagement without their consent.[26] Female circumcision and genital mutilation are prohibited, as is virginity testing of children below the age of 16 years.[27] Circumcision of a male child below the age of 16 years is permitted only for medical or religious reasons.[28]

---

[23]   M. Isaacson, 'Is Government Closing the Book on Court Library?', *Sunday Independent*, 24 October 2010, p. 5; Anon, 'Pretoria Court Ablaze', 27 October 2010, available at: www.timeslive.co.za/local/article730999.ece/Pretoria-court-ablaze? (last accessed 20 December 2010); F. Rabkin, 'State of Johannesburg court "shows lack of respect for rule of law"', *Business Day*, 12 November 2010, available at: www.businessday.co.za/articles/Content.aspx?id=126588 (last accessed 20 December 2010); Anon, 'Ngcobo: SA courts need reform', 13 November 2010, available at: www.news24.com/SouthAfrica/News/Ngobo-SA-courts-need-reform-20101113 (last accessed 20 December 2010); Anon, 'Magistrates Lack Basic Tools, Claims Joasa', *Legalbrief*, 25 November 2010, available at: www.legalbrief.co.za/article.php?story=201011250824374 (last accessed 20 December 2010); S. du Toit, 'Court Administration in Shambles', December 2010 *De Rebus* 5.

[24]   Section 28.

[25]   Sections 6(5), 9 and 10.   [26]   Section 12(2).

[27]   Section 12(3) and (4).   [28]   Section 12(8).

Defining and classifying children

Age

13.18   Until 2007 the age of majority was 21 years.[29] Now, full adulthood is reached at the age of 18 years,[30] although earlier ages are of legal importance for child and family law.[31] Within the category of minors, a distinction is made between emancipated and unemancipated minors. A minor is emancipated if his or her guardian grants him or her freedom independently to enter into contracts. Whether the rules regarding emancipation will remain relevant remains to be seen, for the lowering of the age of majority will probably result in a reduction in the number of cases where emancipation is at issue.

13.19   In respect of some legal matters a fixed age does not apply. Instead, an individual maturity assessment is employed. Thus, for example, the child's right to be informed of any action or decision in a matter that significantly affects him or her and his or her right to participate are determined in the light of his or her age, maturity and stage of development.[32] Another example is that a pregnant girl of any age can consent to termination of her pregnancy provided that she is able to give informed consent.[33] However, a child below the age of 12 requires parental consent to obtain contraceptives.[34] The illogicality of the different requirements in respect of terminating a pregnancy and obtaining contraceptives illustrates the law's inconsistent approach towards recognising children's evolving capacity.

Birth status

13.20   Until fairly recently, South African law categorised children as either legitimate or illegitimate and limited the legal obligations of an unmarried father towards his child to the duty to provide maintenance. As a result of growing dissatisfaction with the legal position, especially from gender equality and children's rights perspectives, the South African Law Reform Commission was tasked with investigating various aspects of child law. After completing a lengthy and thorough investigation, the

---

[29] Age of Majority Act 57 of 1992, s. 1.   [30] Children's Act 2005, s. 17.

[31] See, for example, Marriage Act 25 of 1961, s. 26(1); Child Justice Act 75 of 2008, ch. 2; Children's Act 2005, ss. 129(2)–(5), 133(2), 134.

[32] Children's Act 2005, ss. 6(5) and 10.

[33] Choice on Termination of Pregnancy Act 92 of 1996, s. 5(1)–(3); *Christian Lawyers Association of South Africa* v. *The Minister of Health (Reproductive Health Alliance as Amicus Curiae)* 2005 (1) SA 509 (T).

[34] Children's Act 2005, s. 134(1) and (2).

commission made extensive recommendations for the reform of several aspects of child law, including the law relating to parental responsibilities and rights.[35] With the coming into operation of the first batch of sections of the Children's Act on 1 July 2007,[36] the rules regarding the acquisition of parental responsibilities and rights in respect of children born of unmarried parents changed radically. Although the Act does not completely eliminate the relevance of the marital status of a child's parents insofar as parental responsibilities and rights are concerned, many unmarried fathers can now acquire parental responsibilities and rights without having to approach the court, as is explained below.[37] For purposes of the Act, a child is considered to be born of unmarried parents if his or her parents were not the parties to a civil union or a civil, customary or religious marriage with each other at the time of the child's birth or conception or at any intervening time.[38]

13.21 In customary law, discrimination against children born of unmarried parents is also being eliminated: the rule of male primogeniture as it applied in terms of the customary law of succession has been declared invalid to the extent that it precluded or hindered inheritance of property by children born of unmarried parents.[39]

Recognising parentage and family ties

13.22 In South African law parentage mainly refers to genetic/biological parentage and parentage that is acquired as a result of adoption and assisted reproduction. Step-parenthood could conceivably also be treated as a form of parentage even though the law does not yet attach automatic consequences to it.[40]

13.23 Although biological parentage is a factual issue, the law uses presumptions as a starting point. In the case of a child born of a woman who

---

[35] South African Law Commission, *Report on the Review of the Child Care Act Project 110* (Pretoria: Government Printer, 2002).

[36] Proclamation 13, *Government Gazette* 30030, 29 June 2007. The remaining sections came into operation on 1 April 2010: Proclamation R12, *Government Gazette* 33076, 1 April 2010.

[37] Para. 13.27.

[38] Children's Act 2005, ss. 1 and 20 read with Civil Union Act 17 of 2006, s. 13.

[39] *Bhe* v. *Magistrate, Khayelitsha (Commission for Gender Equality Intervening); Shibi* v. *Sithole; South African Human Rights Commission* v. *President of the Republic of South Africa* 2005 (1) SA 580 (CC).

[40] See further para. 13.29 below.

is a party to a marriage or civil union, it is presumed that the woman's husband or civil union partner is the child's father.[41] If a child is born of a woman who is not a party to a marriage or a civil union, the man who is proved to have had sex with the mother at any time when the child could have been conceived is presumed to be the child's father.[42] Both presumptions are rebuttable.[43] In the past the courts have been hesitant to declare a child who was born of a married woman to be 'illegitimate'.[44] Now that the difference between the legal position of children born of married parents and those born of unmarried parents has been reduced by the Children's Act, this hesitancy ought to grow weaker.

13.24 If a children's court grants an adoption order in terms of the Children's Act, the adoptive parents become the adopted child's parents for all purposes.[45] Customary adoption does not take place under the Act. It occurs by way of a private, family arrangement.[46] It is increasingly argued that a child who has been adopted in terms of customary law should enjoy the same rights as a child who has been adopted in terms of the Children's Act. On two occasions the courts have recognised customary adoption for purposes of children's claims for compensation for loss of maintenance resulting from the death of the parents who had adopted them in terms of customary law.[47] Recently, it has also been held that a child's right to claim maintenance from the person who adopted him or her in terms of customary law can be enforced in terms of the Maintenance Act.[48] It is predicted that parentage that arises as a result of customary adoption will continue to receive judicial recognition and that the purposes for which it is recognised will increase.

The child's right to know

13.25 South Africa lags behind many other jurisdictions insofar as the child's right to know his or her biological origin is concerned. A child who was born as a result of artificial fertilisation or surrogacy has the right to have access only to non-identifying information concerning his or her

---

[41] See, for example, *Van Lutterveld* v. *Engels* 1959 (2) SA 699 (A).

[42] Children's Act 2005, s. 36.

[43] Civil Proceedings Evidence Act 25 of 1965, s. 3; Children's Act 2005, s. 36.

[44] See, for example, *F* v. *L* 1987 (4) SA 525 (W); *B* v. *E* 1992 (3) SA 438 (T).

[45] Section 242(3).

[46] *Metiso* v. *Padongelukfonds* 2001 (3) SA 1142 (T).

[47] *Kewana* v. *Santam Insurance Co. Ltd* 1993 (4) SA 771 (TkA); *Metiso* v. *Padongelukfonds* 2001 (3) SA 1142 (T).

[48] *Maneli* v. *Maneli* 2010 (7) BCLR 703 (GSJ).

genetic parents.[49] An adopted child does have the right to know the identity of his or her biological parents, but only once he or she is an adult or if a court orders disclosure in his or her best interests while he or she is still a minor.[50] Even in paternity disputes the child's right to know his or her biological origin is not recognised. Even though the courts increasingly order scientific tests to establish paternity, the Supreme Court of Appeal recently held that the truth regarding parentage need not always prevail in a paternity dispute and that it may sometimes be in the child's best interests not to establish the truth regarding his or her biological parentage.[51] This is an area where law reform is sorely needed.

13.26   Another, altogether different, problem that affects the acquisition of parental responsibilities and rights and the child's right to know is the practice of 'Rent-a-Child'. This practice involves parents registering their child's birth under one father's surname and subsequently falsely changing the father's details to those of another man in order to enable the 'new' father to obtain an immigration permit.[52] This dishonest practice should become a thing of the past when the Births and Deaths Amendment Act 18 of 2010 comes into operation. The Act stipulates that if a man has acknowledged paternity, his particulars may be amended only if the amendment is supported by the prescribed conclusive proof that the man whose particulars are being provided is the child's father.[53]

Non-marital births

13.27   Parents who are married to each other or are civil union partners at the time of the child's birth or conception or at any intervening time automatically acquire joint parental responsibilities and rights upon the child's birth.[54] Unmarried parents[55] acquire joint parental responsibilities and rights only if they are permanent life partners when the child is born, or if the father consents or successfully applies to be identified as the child's father or pays damages in terms of customary law and

---

[49]   Children's Act 2005, s. 41(1).

[50]   Children's Act 2005, ss. 248(1)(a), 248(1)(e) and 248(3).

[51]   *YM* v. *LB* 2010 (6) SA 338 (SCA).

[52]   'Department of Home Affairs on the South African Citizenship Amendment Bill, Births & Deaths Registration Amendment Bill presentation', Slide 18, available as a link at: www.pmg.org.za/report/20100803-department-home-affairs-south-african-citizenship-amendment-bill-b17- (last accessed 20 December 2010).

[53]   Section 5(c).   [54]   Children's Act 2005, ss. 19(1) and 20.

[55]   See para. 13.20 above, on the circumstances in which a child is considered to be born of unmarried parents.

contributes or attempts in good faith to contribute to the child's upbring-ing and maintenance for a reasonable period.[56] In all other circumstances the unmarried mother has parental responsibilities and rights, while the unmarried father's only parental responsibility and right is to pay main-tenance for the child.[57] Thus, mere identification of an unmarried father or his acknowledgement of paternity does not confer parental responsibil-ities and rights on him. It is not envisaged that this position will change, for the Constitutional Court has indicated, albeit in an aside remark, that formal equality between all unmarried fathers is too blunt a rule and that a 'nuanced and balanced consideration of a society in which the factual demographic picture and parental relationships are often quite differ-ent from those upon which "first-world" western societies are premised' is required.[58] The current legislation meets this requirement, especially since an unmarried father who does not have automatic parental respon-sibilities and rights can acquire them by entering into a parental respon-sibilities and rights agreement with the child's mother or another person who has parental responsibilities and rights, by obtaining a court order, or by adopting the child.[59]

13.28   Identifying an unmarried father is not always a simple matter. A child's mother is not obliged to identify the father when the child's birth is registered; nor is she obliged to inform the father of the child's birth. A man who discovers that he is a father and who wants to acknowledge paternity and enter his particulars in the birth register after the child's birth has been registered needs the consent of the child's mother to do so, unless the court dispenses with her consent.[60] A man who suspects that he is a child's father cannot compel the mother or the child to submit to scientific tests to determine paternity. He may approach the court for an order compelling the mother to submit herself and her child to such tests, but it is by no means certain that the court will grant the order. Although the Supreme Court of Appeal recently held that the High Court as upper guardian of all minors has the power to dispense with the mother's consent to tests on the child, it also held that it may sometimes

---

[56] Children's Act 2005, s. 21(1).
[57] Maintenance Act 1998, s. 15(3)(a)(iii); Children's Act 2005, ss. 19, 21(1) and 21(2).
[58] *Fraser* v. *Children's Court, Pretoria North* 1997 (2) SA 261 (CC), para. 29.
[59] Children's Act 2005, ss. 22–24, 231(1)(d) and 242. Acting in its common-law capacity as upper guardian of all minors, the High Court also has the power to make any order that is in the child's best interests.
[60] Births and Deaths Registration Act 51 of 1992, s. 11(4) and (5); Children's Act 2005, s. 26.

be in the child's best interests not to establish the truth regarding his or her biological parentage.[61] Furthermore, it is still unclear whether the court has the power to order tests on the unwilling mother.[62] Whether the latter position will change is uncertain. Ordering a scientific test on an unwilling adult brings several constitutional rights into conflict – the paramountcy of the best interests of the child and the unwilling parent's rights to privacy, bodily integrity and dignity being among them.[63] I will not be so bold as to make a prediction regarding the eventual outcome of this tricky constitutional issue, but my hope is that the child's best interests in knowing his or her biological parentage will prevail.

Delivering parenting

13.29   Having parents and knowing who they are do not necessarily mean that the child will be provided with proper and adequate care or that parents are the only persons who should be endowed with parental responsibilities and rights. If parents exercise their parental responsibilities and rights improperly or inadequately, the court has various powers to intervene.[64] The law further affords any person who has an interest in the child's care, well-being and development the opportunity to acquire parental responsibilities and rights by entering into a parental responsibilities and rights agreement with a person who has parental responsibilities and rights[65] or by being awarded parental responsibilities and rights by the court.[66] People who have an interest in the child's care, well-being and development include step-parents who, at present, do not automatically have any parental responsibilities and rights in respect of their step-children. It is likely that step-parents will in future automatically acquire at least some parental responsibilities and rights. A first step in that direction has been a High Court decision that the child's constitutional right to parental care[67] extends to step-parents and encompasses the child's

---

[61] *YM* v. *LB* 2010 (6) SA 338 (SCA).

[62] On the conflicting case law, see T. Boezaart, *Law of Persons*, 5th edn (Wetton: Juta & Co Ltd, 2010), pp. 102–6; J. Heaton, *The South African Law of Persons*, 3rd edn (Durban: LexisNexis Butterworths, 2008), pp. 62–3.

[63] Constitution, ss. 10, 12(2), 14 and 28(2).

[64] See, for example, Marriage Act 1961, s. 25(4); Divorce Act 1970, s. 6(3); Children's Act 2005, ss. 28, 129(9), 130(1)(b)(ii), 130(2)(f), 135 and 155(7).

[65] Children's Act 2005, s. 22(1).

[66] The order can be made in terms of either the High Court's power as upper guardian or ss. 23 or 24 of the Children's Act 2005.

[67] Constitution, s. 28(1)(b).

maintenance needs, with the result that a step-parent must maintain his or her stepchild.[68] Although this decision is not binding on all court divisions, the court's broad interpretation of parental care may well find favour with other judges.

13.30   Some of the components of parental responsibilities and rights present problems and will continue to do so. Probably the most contentious component is the right to impose corporal punishment. The South African Law Reform Commission attempted to rid South African law of this right,[69] but the recommended prohibition on corporal punishment by parents never became law.[70] As public opinion has not yet shifted in favour of a ban on corporal punishment by parents and a complete ban on corporal punishment would be meaningless without such a shift,[71] it is not predicted that the position will change soon.

13.31   Another problematic issue is enforcement of maintenance. Despite many attempts at improving the efficiency of the Maintenance Courts and the enforcement of maintenance orders, compliance with maintenance orders remains poor. As indicated above,[72] mediation is being used in a pilot attempt to improve compliance rates. Despite the law's best efforts, many children will unfortunately continue to suffer financial deprivation because many parents quite simply cannot afford to pay child maintenance and South Africa's underdeveloped welfare system provides but a flimsy safety net for children whose parents are unable to support them.

13.32   Another maintenance issue that should be mentioned is an anticipated increase in the number of parents who will claim maintenance from their children, or even from their grandchildren. In terms of South African law, the duty of support between parent and child is reciprocal.[73] On the one hand, it is predicted that the HIV/AIDS pandemic will contribute to a rise in maintenance claims by parents. Many parents who have HIV/AIDS

---

[68] *Heystek* v. *Heystek* [2002] 2 All SA 401 (T).

[69] South African Law Commission *Report of the Review of the Child Care Act*, para. 9.7.2 and cl. 142 of the draft Children's Bill attached to the report.

[70] The original draft of the Children's Bill 70 of 2003, which was based on the Law Reform Commission's draft bill, contained a prohibition on corporal punishment by parents, as did the initial versions of the Children's Amendment Bill 19 of 2006. The prohibition was deleted when the latter Bill reached its fourth version (Bill 19D).

[71] South African Law Commission, *Report on the Review of the Child Care Act*, para. 9.7.2.

[72] Para. 13.11 above.

[73] See, for example, *Oosthuizen* v. *Stanley* 1938 AD 322.

are unable to work and to support themselves, and look to their children for maintenance.[74] On the other hand, the increased lifespan of the healthier, more privileged members of society will probably result in a growing number of retired adults outliving their sources of income and capital.[75] Their children (or even their grandchildren) will become liable for their maintenance. The result will be that a growing number of people will be liable, not only for their own maintenance and that of their children, but also for the maintenance of their parents and/or grandparents.

Intra-family disputes

13.33   In all disputes regarding the child, the child's best interests are paramount and he or she has the right to be informed and to participate.[76] The Children's Act contains a list of fourteen factors which must be taken into consideration in determining the child's best interests.[77] Although a checklist is of some assistance in applying the concept of 'the best interests of the child', giving content to those interests remains a difficult matter. No list of factors can ever remove the risk of the concept being manipulated to reflect subjective views or prevailing, and often stereotypical, social values. Thus, for example, in care disputes upon divorce, mothers used to be preferred on the stereotypical assumption that they make better caregivers than fathers do. Inter alia because of the constitutional gender equality provisions and an increased emphasis on the child's right to have a continuing relationship with both parents,[78] joint legal care has become the norm and joint physical care/joint residency is sometimes awarded.[79]

---

[74] In 2010 an estimated 43 per cent of deaths were attributable to AIDS: Statistics South Africa, *Mid-year Population Estimates, Statistical Release P0302*, 2010, Table 8, available at: www.statssa.gov.za/publications/P0302/P03022010.pdf (last accessed 20 December 2010).

[75] The estimated life expectancy for a male born in 2010 is 53.3 years and 55.2 years for a female: *ibid.*, Table 5. Despite the low life expectancy, the proportion of persons aged 60 and over is estimated to increase from 7% of the total population in 2006 to 11% in 2025 and 13% in 2050: K. Kinsella and M. Ferreira 'Aging Trends: South Africa', August 1997, available at: www.census.gov/ipc/prod/ib-9702.pdf (last accessed 20 December 2010); S. Z. Kalula, M. Ferreira, K. G. F. Thomas, L. de Villiers, J. A. Joska and L. Geffen, 'Profile and Management of Patients at a Memory Clinic' (2010) 100 *South African Medical Journal* 449.

[76] See para. 13.17 above.   [77] Section 7(1).

[78] See, for example, *Krugel* v. *Krugel* 2003 (6) SA 220 (T).

[79] Joint legal care is limited to joint decision-making about important issues, while joint physical care/joint residency entails that the child spends substantial amounts of time, such as part of each week, or alternate weeks, with each parent.

Because joint legal care does not involve sharing day-to-day care of the child, it usually 'puts the care-taking parent in a position of responsibility without power whilst giving the non-care-taker parent ... power without responsibility'.[80] It is predicted that joint care will remain the de facto default position for some time to come and that, unfortunately, it will be ordered without due consideration being given to the actual exercise of the day-to-day responsibilities entailed in care-giving. Thus, power without responsibility and responsibility without power is likely to continue.

Child protection and state intervention

13.34   In the past the child protection system responded only after problems such as abuse and neglect had occurred. Now, early intervention and family preservation programmes and services are used as preventive measures.[81] These programmes and services require greater skill and input from child welfare practitioners and also increase the financial demands on the state.

13.35   The range of orders the court may make if a child is found to be in need of care and protection has also been increased, with institutionalisation of the child being only one of a number of options. Some of the options, such as placing the child in a cluster foster care scheme, are novel in South African terms. Under such a scheme, children are not placed with individual foster parents, but rather with a group of people or an organisation.[82]

13.36   An area that reflects child law's catching up with social change is child-headed households. The Children's Act is the first statute to give official recognition to these households. A child-headed household is one in which the parent, guardian or caregiver is terminally ill, has died or has abandoned the children, no adult family member is available to provide care, and a child over the age of 16 years has assumed the role of caregiver in respect of the children.[83] Once the provincial head of the Department of Social Development has recognised a household as a child-headed household, the child who is the head of the household may take all day-to-day decisions relating to the household and the children in it and may collect

---

[80]   B. Clark and B. van Heerden, 'Joint Custody: Perspectives and Permutations' (1995) 112 *South African Law Journal* 323.

[81]   Children's Act 2005, ch. 8.

[82]   Children's Act 2005, s. 183 read with s. 1.   [83]   Section 137(1).

and administer any grant or assistance to which the children are entitled.[84] The household functions under the general supervision of an adult designated by a Children's Court, an organ of state or a non-governmental organisation, but the adult may not take any decision regarding the household or the children without consulting the child who is the head and (taking into account their age, maturity and stage of development) the other children.[85]

13.37 The recognition of child-headed households has been criticised as amounting to abandonment of children through the premature award of adult responsibility to them while they are entitled to the protection afforded by the status of childhood. It has also been argued that the recognition entails an irreversible loss of faith in the ability of the community and children's extended families to take care of them, and amounts to enabling the state to withdraw from its constitutional duty to provide alternative care to children who are removed from the family environment.[86] Although there is merit in these criticisms, the recognition of child-headed households is welcomed, for it officially enables siblings to remain together, recognises the evolving capacity of children, enables children to escape exploitation at the hands of family members and the community who dispossess them of their parents' land and of their inherited property, and discourages the practice of fostering children purely to enable the foster parents to obtain the foster care grant.[87] It must, nevertheless, be borne in mind that the problems experienced by child-headed households are largely of a socio-economic nature[88] and do not easily lend themselves to resolution by the law.

13.38 Another example of the law catching up with social change is the regulation of drop-in centres. These centres have existed for some time.

---

[84] Section 137(1), (5)(a) and (7).

[85] Section 137(2) and (6).

[86] J. Sloth-Nielsen, 'Protection of Children', in A. M. Skelton and C. J. Davel (eds.), *Commentary on the Children's Act* (Claremont: Juta, 2007), pp. 7–46. The right to alternative care is contained in s. 28(1)(b) of the Constitution.

[87] Sloth-Nielsen, 'Protection of children', pp. 7–46–7–47; E. Bonthuys, 'Legal Capacity and Family Status in Child-Headed Households: Challenges to Legal Paradigms and Concepts' (2010) 6 *International Journal of Law in Context* 55.

[88] For example, children living in child-headed households have substantially lower levels of access to basic municipal services such as piped water, electricity and adequate sanitation than those living in adult-headed households: H. Meintjies, K. Hall, D.-H. Marera and A. Boulle, 'Orphans of the AIDS Epidemic? The Extent, Nature and Circumstances of Child-Headed Households in South Africa' (2010) 22 *AIDS Care* 44, 45.

They offer inter alia food and basic health care services during the day to AIDS orphans, children living on the street and children living in households where the adult caregivers are ill. Some centres also have educational and recreational facilities. The Children's Act requires these centres to register and it sets national norms and standards for them.[89]

13.39   Juvenile justice has also been reformed. The Child Justice Act 75 of 2008 establishes a criminal justice system for children and provides for the possibility of diverting children who have committed offences away from the formal criminal justice system.

13.40   In view of the recent comprehensive law reform in the area of child protection, large-scale revision of this area of the law is not predicted. The socio-economic deprivation suffered by children needs urgent attention, but this is an issue that falls outside the purview of child and family law.[90]

C   Adult relationships

The relationships

13.41   Traditionally, South African law defined 'marriage' as the legally recognised voluntary union for life of one man and one woman to the exclusion of all others.[91] This definition clearly related only to the heterosexual, monogamous civil marriage that is concluded in terms of the common law and the Marriage Act. South African family law has since become more inclusive – chiefly as a result of the enactment of a Bill of Rights which, inter alia, entrenches the rights to equality and dignity, freedom of conscience, religion, thought, belief and opinion and the right to participate in the cultural life of one's choice.[92] Civil marriage has nevertheless retained its primacy, as many of the requirements for and consequences of the other relationships that are now recognised have been modelled on those of the civil marriage.

13.42   Today, two more types of marriages are recognised alongside civil marriage, namely customary marriages and marriages under

---

[89]   Sections 216 and 217.

[90]   For statistics on various issues affecting children's socio-economic welfare, see the figures provided by the Children Count Abantwana Babalulekile Project, available at: www.childrencount.ci.org.za (last accessed 2 March 2012).

[91]   See, for example, *Seedat's Executors* v. *The Master (Natal)* 1917 AD 302.

[92]   Constitution, ss. 9, 10, 15(1) and 30.

the Civil Union Act. Customary marriages are concluded in terms of 'the customs and usages traditionally observed among the indigenous African peoples of South Africa and which form part of the culture of those peoples'.[93] These customs and usages permit polygyny; in other words, the husband is allowed to take more than one wife. Customary marriages are mainly heterosexual, although woman-to-woman marriages do sometimes occur.[94] Marriages under the Civil Union Act 2006 are open to heterosexual and same-sex couples and are monogamous.

13.43   Civil partnerships are the other type of adult intimate relationship that is fully recognised. These partnerships are concluded in terms of the Civil Union Act, and are exactly the same type of relationship as a marriage under the Civil Union Act. The relationship simply bears a different name to accommodate those couples who, for personal reasons, do not wish their union to be known as a marriage and do not wish to be called 'spouses'.[95]

13.44   Cohabitation, or life or domestic partnerships as they are called in South Africa, enjoy only limited recognition, as do marriages by Muslim or Hindu rites. However, as is indicated below,[96] this state of affairs is set to change.

Marriages and civil unions

13.45   Given South Africa's conservative and oppressive history, the recognition of civil unions, and in particular, same-sex civil unions, is perhaps the most striking recent achievement of South African family law. The movement that led to the recognition of same-sex civil unions started with limited statutory and judicial recognition being afforded to same-sex life partnerships. Then, at the end of 2005, the Constitutional Court held that the restriction of marriage to heterosexuals was unconstitutional. It

---

[93] Recognition of Customary Marriages Act 1998, s. 1.

[94] Woman-to-woman customary marriages are concluded by childless women who want another woman to bear children for them with a male relative, and by powerful and wealthy women (such as traditional healers or leaders). These women are viewed as female husbands while the women they marry are considered to be wives: F. van Heerden, 'Lobola van Een Vrou deur 'n Ander (Vroue-huwelike)' (1991) 54 *Journal for Contemporary Roman-Dutch Law* 636; B. Oomen, 'Traditional Woman-to-Woman Marriages and the Recognition of Customary Marriages Act' (2000) 63 *Journal for Contemporary Roman-Dutch Law* 274.

[95] For statistics on the number of marriages and civil unions concluded and the number of divorces granted, see the annual P0307 statistics available at www.statssa.gov.za.

[96] Para. 13.47 below.

gave Parliament a year to correct the unconstitutionality.[97] Parliament's
first legislative response was an attempt at appeasing religious groups,
traditional leaders and the majority of the population who were bitterly
opposed to same-sex marriage. It created the civil partnership as a separate mechanism for conferring full legal recognition on same-sex relationships.[98] As a result of vehement criticism, inter alia from a constitutional
perspective, the Bill was amended to include both heterosexual and same-
sex couples within its ambit and to permit couples of any sexual orientation to call their union a marriage or a civil partnership for all purposes.[99]
The amended Bill became the Civil Union Act, which came into operation in 2006. The Act confers the consequences of a civil marriage on a
civil union regardless of whether the civil union is called a marriage or a
civil partnership.[100]

13.46 The coming into operation of the Act has by no means put an end
to the controversy about the recognition of same-sex relationships. While
some groups continue to bemoan the recognition of these relationships,
others argue that the Act does not go far enough because it reinforces the
superiority of heterosexual civil marriage and extends protection only to
those who are prepared to adopt a relationship model that deviates little
from the civil marriage.[101] Furthermore, because the Act is the only means
available to same-sex couples who want to obtain full legal recognition for
their relationship, while heterosexual couples can acquire such recognition by way of either a civil union or a civil marriage, some critics suggest
that the Marriage Act should be repealed, leaving the Civil Union Act
and the Recognition of Customary Marriages Act as the only vehicles for
entering into marriage.[102] Another view is that the Civil Union Act should
be repealed and the Marriage Act amended to apply to heterosexual and

---

[97] *Minister of Home Affairs* v. *Fourie (Doctors for Life International and Others, Amici
Curiae), Lesbian and Gay Equality Project* v. *Minister of Home Affairs* 2006 (1) SA 524
(CC).
[98] Civil Union Bill 26 of 2006, ch. 2.
[99] Civil Union Bill 26B of 2006, cll. 1 and 11.
[100] Section 13.
[101] E. Bonthuys, 'Race and Gender in the Civil Union Act' (2007) 23 *South African Journal
on Human Rights* 526; P. de Vos and J. Barnard, 'Same-sex Marriage, Civil Unions and
Domestic Partnerships in South Africa: Critical Reflections on an Ongoing Saga' (2007)
124 *South African Law Journal* 821.
[102] D. Bilchitz, and M. Judge, 'For whom Does the Bell Toll? The Challenges and Possibilities
of the Civil Union Act for Family Law in South Africa' (2007) 23 *South African Journal
on Human Rights* 488, 489; de Vos and Barnard, 'Same-sex Marriage, Civil Unions and
Domestic Partnerships in South Africa', 821, 822.

same-sex couples alike.[103] Despite these calls, it is not anticipated that fundamental change will be effected to the recognition of civil unions.

13.47   Marriages that are concluded purely in terms of religious rites are not yet fully recognised. However, the courts and legislature have extended limited recognition to Muslim and Hindu marriages for specific purposes.[104] It is predicted that these marriages will receive full recognition in the not too distant future, probably by way of separate legislation rather than a uniform Act on religious marriages. In 2003 the South African Law Reform Commission published a report on Muslim marriages, accompanied by the draft Muslim Marriages Bill, which recognises some Muslim marriages.[105] The Commission for Gender Equality has also compiled a draft Bill. This draft Bill, which is called the Recognition of Religious Marriages Bill, in a generic way deals with all religious marriages.[106] An amended version of the draft Bill prepared by the Law Reform Commission was published for public comment on 21 January 2011.[107]

Cohabitation

13.48   As a general rule, a life partnership does not confer automatic consequences on the life partners. Some Acts confer specific spousal benefits on life partners,[108] and court decisions have extended

---

[103] H. de Ru, 'The Civil Union Act 17 of 2006: A Transformative Act or a Substandard Product of a Failed Conciliation between Social, Legal and Political Issues?' (2010) 73 *Journal for Contemporary Roman-Dutch Law* 567.

[104] See, for example, Civil Proceedings Evidence Act 25 of 1965, s. 10A; Children's Act 2005, s. 1(1); *Amod (Born Peer)* v. *Multilateral Motor Vehicle Accidents Fund (Commission for Gender Equality Intervening)* 1999 (4) SA 1319 (SCA); *Khan* v. *Khan* 2005 (2) SA 272 (T); *Hassam* v. *Jacobs* 2009 (5) SA 572 (CC); *Hoosein* v. *Dangor* 2010 (4) BCLR 362 (WCC).

[105] *Report on Project 106 Islamic Marriages and Related Matters* (Pretoria: Government Printer, 2003). The commission has initiated a project on Hindu marriages, but has not yet published any research: see www.justice.gov.za/salrc/projects.htm (last accessed 20 December 2010).

[106] R. Manjoo, 'Making Rights Real: Facing the Challenges of Recognising Muslim Marriages in South Africa', in J. Sloth-Nielsen and Z. du Toit (eds.), *Trials and Tribulations, Trends and Triumphs* (Cape Town: Juta, 2008), p. 127; H. Abrahams-Fayker, 'Polygamous Muslim Marriages' October 2008 *De Rebus* 42.

[107] Draft Muslim Marriages Bill, 2011, published in General Notice 37 in *Government Gazette* 33946 of 21 January 2011.

[108] See, for example, s. 21(13) of the Insolvency Act 24 of 1936 and s. 22(1) read with s. 1 of the Compensation for Occupational Injuries and Diseases Act 130 of 1993, which treat heterosexual life partners as spouses, and s. 1 of the Pension Funds Act 24 of 1956 and s. 56(1)(b) read with s. 1 of the Income Tax Act 58 of 1962, which treat all life partners as spouses.

additional spousal benefits to same-sex life partners,[109] but not to heterosexual ones.[110] Life partners can also acquire a degree of protection for their life partnership by making use of contracts, wills and so forth. As it has been recognised that self-regulation and piecemeal extension of rights and duties to life partners are unsatisfactory, a draft Domestic Partnerships Bill has been compiled. Although the draft Bill was published for comment early in 2008,[111] the legislative process has not yet gone any further. It is anticipated that several amendments will be made before the proposed legislation is eventually tabled in Parliament. However, there is no doubt that life partnerships will eventually be regulated by statute; it is simply the terms of the regulation that are still unclear.

Entering relationships

Civil marriage and civil union

13.49   In South Africa an engagement or undertaking to enter into a civil marriage is still recognised as a contract. Although the contract can no longer be enforced by compelling an unwilling party to proceed with the marriage, breach of the promise to marry can give rise to a claim for damages.[112] In many jurisdictions breach of promise actions have been abolished. It is predicted that South Africa will follow suit. The Supreme Court of Appeal recently signalled its dissatisfaction with the present state of the law and gave non-binding guidelines on how the law should be developed.[113] It indicated that, as in the case of divorce, termination of an engagement should no longer be linked to one party's fault. Therefore, breaking off an engagement because of a lack of desire to continue with the marriage should constitute a just cause for terminating the engagement, with the result that the party who breaks off the engagement should not incur liability for contractual damages. It is predicted that this sensible approach will become law in the near future.

---

[109] See, for example, *National Coalition for Gay and Lesbian Equality* v. *Minister of Home Affairs* 2000 (2) SA 1 (CC); *J* v. *Director General, Department of Home Affairs* 2003 (5) BCLR 463 (CC); *Gory* v. *Kolver NO* 2007 (4) SA 97 (CC).

[110] *Volks* v. *Robinson* 2005 (5) BCLR 446 (CC).

[111] General Notice 36, *Government Gazette* 30663, 14 January 2008.

[112] See, for example, *Guggenheim* v. *Rosenbaum* 1961 (4) SA 21 (W); *Sepheri* v. *Scanlan* 2008 (1) SA 322 (C).

[113] *Van Jaarsveld* v. *Bridges* 2010 (4) SA 558 (SCA).

13.50   As indicated above,[114] South African law allows same-sex couples to enter into a fully recognised legal relationship by means of a civil union, while heterosexual couples can acquire full legal recognition for their relationship by way of either a civil union or a civil marriage. Law reform is not envisaged to remove the preservation of civil marriage for heterosexual couples, since, broadly speaking, the Civil Union Act confers the same right on all couples to enter into a fully recognised relationship and thus complies with the Constitution.

13.51   Under apartheid, inter-racial marriages were prohibited.[115] Now, the ethnic origin of the parties plays no role in determining their capacity to enter into a civil marriage or civil union.

Customary marriage

13.52   Customary marriage is sometimes preceded by *ukuthwala*, which is the practice of kidnapping the future bride. The practice is used inter alia to compel the bride's family to endorse marriage negotiations, to avoid the expense of a wedding, or to avoid paying *lobolo* (that is, bride wealth).[116] Sometimes the bride is a willing participant in the kidnapping, but frequently she is not. In the latter event, the subsequent customary marriage is a forced marriage. Particularly disconcerting is that a disproportionate number of the unwilling victims of *ukuthwala* are minors,[117] some of them as young as 12 years old.[118] Thus, a large number of the customary marriages that follow *ukuthwala* are not only forced, but are also child marriages. The Law Reform Commission is currently investigating *ukuthwala* and is due to publish a discussion paper containing preliminary law reform proposals designed to eliminate forced and child marriages

---

[114] See para. 13.45 above.

[115] Prohibition of Mixed Marriages Act 55 of 1949, repealed by s 7(1) of the Immorality and Prohibition of Mixed Marriages Amendment Act 72 of 1985.

[116] See, for example, T. W. Bennett, *Customary Law in South Africa* (Wetton: Juta, 2004) p. 212; D. McQuoid-Mason, 'The Practice of "Ukuthwala", the Constitution and the Criminal Law (Sexual Offences and Related Matters) Amendment Act' (2009) 30 *Obiter* 716.

[117] 'Law Reform Commission to Probe Forced Marriages', *Legalbrief*, 8 December 2010, available at: www.legalbrief.co.za/article.php?story=20101208084114878 (last accessed 20 December 2010).

[118] McQuoid-Mason, 'The Practice of "Ukuthwala"', 716; J. Maluleke, 'Ukuthwala', available at: www.justice.gov.za/docs/articles/2009_ukuthwala-kidnapping-girls.html (last accessed 20 December 2010).

under the pretext of *ukuthwala* in the near future.[119] Law reform in this area cannot occur soon enough.

Consequences of relationships

Civil marriage and civil union

13.53 South African matrimonial property law is complicated, first, because a multitude of matrimonial property systems are available to intending spouses or civil union partners and, secondly, because the patrimonial consequences of civil marriages black people concluded before 2 December 1988 differ from those concluded by white, coloured or Asian people.

13.54 The three main matrimonial property systems are community of property, complete separation of property and the accrual system. Civil marriages and civil unions of white, coloured and Asian people have always been, and still are, in community of property unless the parties enter into an antenuptial contract in which they select another matrimonial property system.[120] However, if the parties are black people who entered into a civil marriage before 2 December 1988, their marriage is subject to complete separation of property unless they made a joint declaration before a magistrate, commissioner or marriage officer within one month before the marriage that they wished to marry in community of property.[121] Fortunately, the Marriage and Matrimonial Property Law Amendment Act 3 of 1988 abolished this distinction for marriages entered into after 2 December 1988 (the date on which the Act came into operation). Thus, the proprietary consequences of civil marriages and civil unions entered into after that date are determined by the same rules, regardless of the parties' ethnic origin.

13.55 If community of property operates in a marriage or civil union, the parties jointly own everything they had at the time of entering into the marriage or civil union and everything they acquire during the subsistence of the marriage or civil union. In contrast, complete separation of property entails that each party retains the estate he or she had before

---

[119] 'Law Reform Commission to Probe Forced Marriages', www.legalbrief.co.za/article. php?story=20101208084114878.
[120] *Edelstein* v. *Edelstein NO* 1952 (3) SA 1 (A).
[121] Black Administration Act 38 of 1927, s. 22(6).

the marriage or civil union as well as everything he or she acquires during the marriage or civil union. In terms of the accrual system, the marriage or civil union is out of community of property but upon dissolution the parties share the growth their separate estates have shown during the course of the marriage or civil union.[122] This system applies to all marriages and civil unions out of community of property white, coloured and Asian people have concluded since 1 November 1984 unless the parties have excluded the system in their antenuptial contract.[123] As a result of the provisions of the Marriage and Matrimonial Property Law Amendment Act the same rule applies to marriages and civil unions out of community of property concluded by black people since 2 December 1988.

13.56 Regardless of their matrimonial property system, both parties have equal powers of administration in respect of the matrimonial property. If community of property applies, either spouse or civil union partner may perform any juristic act with regard to the joint estate, subject to the requirement of obtaining the consent of the other spouse or civil union partner for certain juristic acts.[124] If complete separation of property or the accrual system applies, either spouse or civil union partner may administer his or her own estate as he or she sees fit, and he or she has no powers of administration in respect of the other party's estate.

13.57 As the various types of matrimonial property systems each serve a distinct purpose, it is unlikely that the need for the different systems will disappear.

Customary marriage

13.58 One of the fundamental differences between the consequences of a civil marriage or civil union and a customary marriage is that, while the first group of relationships is monogamous, a husband in a customary marriage may enter into as many customary marriages as he likes. Furthermore, the patrimonial consequences of some customary marriages differ from those of civil marriages and civil unions. Like civil marriages and civil unions, monogamous customary marriages are in community of property unless the spouses enter into an antenuptial

---

[122] Matrimonial Property Act 88 of 1984, s. 3. This Act came into operation on 1 November 1984.

[123] Matrimonial Property Act 1984, s. 2.

[124] Matrimonial Property Act 1984, ss. 15(1)–(4) and 17(1).

contract.[125] The patrimonial consequences of a polygynous customary marriage depend on whether the marriage was concluded before or after the coming into operation of the Recognition of Customary Marriages Act 1998. If the marriage was concluded before the coming into operation of the Act, the patrimonial consequences are regulated by customary law, the content of which can be extremely difficult to determine.[126] If the marriage was concluded after the coming into operation of the Act, the patrimonial consequences are determined by the content of the contract the husband is supposed to submit to the court for its approval prior to celebrating another customary marriage.[127] The figures on the number of such contracts that have been registered are conflicting. They indicate that either none or three contracts have been registered in the decade since the Act came into operation,[128] while many more polygynous customary marriages have been concluded during that time. South Africa's president, Jacob Zuma, alone has married two more wives since the coming into operation of the Act. Unfortunately, the Act does not stipulate the consequences of failure to obtain a court-approved contract. Authors have adopted conflicting views on the issue, ranging from nullity of the subsequent customary marriage to the failure's having no bearing on the validity of the subsequent marriage at all.[129] In the only reported decision on the matter the High Court held that the subsequent marriage was void.[130] The issue is sure to arise again – especially in view of the ignorance of many people regarding the need to obtain a court-approved contract. Even President Zuma seems to have failed to comply with the

[125] Recognition of Customary Marriages Act 1998, s. 7(2) read with *Gumede* v. *President of the Republic of South Africa* 2009 (3) SA 152 (CC).

[126] See para. 13.3 above.

[127] Section 7(6).

[128] J. C. Bekker and G. J. van Niekerk, 'Broadening the Divide between Official and Living Customary Law. Mayelane v. Ngwenyama 2010 4 SA 286 (GNP); [2010] JOL 25422 (GNP)' (2010) 73 *Journal for Contemporary Roman-Dutch Law* 683, 684; F. Rabkin, 'Judgment Puts the Validity of Zuma's Marriages in Doubt', *Business Day*, 7 July 2010, available at: http://allafrica.com/stories/201007070003.html (last accessed 20 December 2010). Registration is required by the Recognition of Customary Marriages Act 1998, s. 7(9).

[129] See, for example, J. Heaton, *South African Family Law*, 3rd edn (Durban: LexisNexis, 2010), p. 212; L. L. Mofokeng, *Legal Pluralism in South Africa: Aspects of African Customary, Muslim and Hindu Family Law* (Pretoria: Van Schaik Publishers, 2009), p. 73; P. Bakker, 'The New Unofficial Customary Marriage: Application of Section 7(6) of the Recognition of Customary Marriages Act 120 of 1998' (2007) 70 *Journal for Contemporary Roman-Dutch* Law 487–9.

[130] *MM* v. *MN* 2010 (4) SA 286 (GNP).

requirement.[131] The deplorable lacuna in the Act needs to be addressed urgently.

Termination of relationships

Civil marriage and civil union

13.59   Civil marriages and civil unions are terminated by the death of either party or by divorce. Divorce is granted on one of three no-fault grounds: irretrievable breakdown, incurable mental illness of one of the parties or continuous unconsciousness of one of the parties.[132] It is likely that only one ground of divorce will eventually be recognised, namely irretrievable breakdown. This is already the position in respect of customary marriages.[133]

Customary marriage

13.60   The only ground for divorce in a customary marriage is the irretrievable breakdown of the marriage relationship. A change in this position is not anticipated.

13.61   As the Recognition of Customary Marriages Act is silent on the matter, it is unclear whether death terminates a customary marriage. In terms of traditional customary law, the sororate custom permits a husband to take a 'seed raiser' after his wife's death, while the levirate custom permits replacement of a deceased husband by one of his paternal male relatives. The extent to which these customs are practised nowadays is unknown.[134] If they are indeed still practised, law reform is needed to outlaw continuation of a customary marriage after the death of either of the spouses. Fortunately the ball is already rolling in that direction, for a suitable amendment to the Act has been drafted although it has not yet been tabled in Parliament.[135]

---

[131]   W. Jason da Costa and T. Broughton, 'Only One Wife Legally Wed to Zuma?', 2 August 2010, available at: www.iol.co.za/news/south-africa/only-one-wife-legally-wed-to-zuma-1.671604? (last accessed 20 December 2010); Rabkin, 'Judgment Puts the Validity of Zuma's Marriages in Doubt'.

[132]   Divorce Act 1970, s. 3.

[133]   Recognition of Customary Marriages Act 1998, s. 8(1).

[134]   Committee on the Elimination of Discrimination Against Women, *Combined Second, Third and Fourth Periodic Report of States Parties: South Africa*, CEDAW/C/ZAF/2–4, para. V.4.17, available at: www2.ohchr.org/english/bodies/cedaw/docs/CEDAW.C.ZAF.2–4.E.pdf (last accessed 20 December 2010).

[135]   Draft Recognition of Customary Marriages Amendment Bill, 2009, cl. 7.

Consequences of termination

Civil marriage and civil union

13.62   The consequences of the termination of a civil marriage or civil union are governed by the same rules.[136] The financial consequences depend, first, on the matrimonial property system that operated in the marriage or civil union.

13.63   A major problem with the patrimonial consequences of divorce is that, unless the parties are able to agree on a different division, the court is compelled to divide the matrimonial property strictly in accordance with the system the parties chose before they married or entered into a civil union. Only in certain 'old' civil marriages out of community of property does the court have the power to order redistribution of the parties' assets. This power is restricted to civil marriages that are subject to complete separation of property and were concluded prior to 1 November 1984 in the case of white, coloured or Asian people or prior to 2 December 1988 in the case of black people. It is further required that the spouse who seeks redistribution must have contributed to the maintenance or increase of the other spouse's estate during the subsistence of the marriage and that the contribution renders redistribution equitable and just.[137] The limited availability of the power has been justified on the ground that people who marry after the two cut-off dates can apply the accrual system to their marriage and that the legislature must respect the contractual choice of those who select complete separation of property instead of the accrual system.[138] This justification has lost much of its force, since the power to redistribute assets has subsequently been made available in all customary marriages that are dissolved by divorce, regardless of when the marriage was concluded and regardless of the matrimonial property system that operates in it.[139] Affording all spouses in customary marriages the remedy of seeking redistribution while limiting it to only a few spouses in civil marriages and completely denying it to civil union partners unjustifiably limits the constitutional rights to equality and dignity.[140] Therefore, it is

---

[136] Civil Union Act 2006, s. 13.   [137] Divorce Act 1970, s. 7(3) and (4).

[138] South African Law Commission, *Report on the Review of the Law of Divorce: Amendment of Section 7(3) of the Divorce Act, 1979 Project 12* (Pretoria: Government Printer, 1990) ch. 3 para. 1.3.10.

[139] Recognition of Customary Marriages Act 1998, s. 8(4)(a) and (b) read with *Gumede* v. *President of the Republic of South Africa* 2009 (3) SA 152 (CC).

[140] See further Heaton, *South African Family Law*, pp. 136–7.

predicted that the power will eventually be available in all marriages and civil unions. Thus, as in many foreign jurisdictions, the judicial power to redistribute assets will become the new method for division of matrimonial property upon divorce if the parties are unable to reach a settlement. This change will, hopefully, contribute to substantive financial gender equality between divorcing spouses and civil union partners.

13.64   The rules regarding maintenance upon divorce will probably not be changed in such a radical fashion. In keeping with international trends, South African courts have moved away from making permanent maintenance awards towards applying the clean-break principle. Unfortunately, this principle is all too frequently applied in a way that ignores or underplays the long-term consequences of the domestic and child-care responsibilities women bear both during the subsistence of the marriage or civil union and after its dissolution and the career sacrifices many of them make. As legislative reform is not envisaged in this regard, it is hoped that the judiciary will adapt its approach to the clean-break principle in order to give proper recognition to women's true financial position.

Customary marriage

13.65   Broadly speaking, the consequences of the dissolution of a customary marriage by divorce correspond to those that apply in civil marriages. However, as indicated above, the court has the power to make a redistribution order in any customary marriage.

Self-regulation and custom-made relationships

13.66   Apart from parental responsibilities and rights agreements,[141] self-regulation arises in three main contexts. First, at present life partnerships fall chiefly within the realm of self-regulation.[142]

13.67   The proprietary consequences of a marriage or civil union are the second context in which self-regulation features strongly. Insofar as polygynous customary marriages are concerned, the pervasive failure of husbands to obtain court-approved contracts and the lack of clarity on the consequences of this failure[143] illustrate the danger of compelling people to engage in self-regulation without expressly providing for the

---

[141] See paras. 13.27 and 13.29 above.
[142] See para. 13.48 above.   [143] See para. 13.58 above.

consequences of their failure to do so. In other marriages and in civil unions the position in respect of antenuptial contracts is different, for there a default matrimonial property system applies, namely community of property, and the parties are not compelled to enter into an antenuptial contract.

13.68   The purpose of an antenuptial contract is to enable the parties to select a different system that, in their view, better suits their circumstances. Such self-regulation can be very advantageous. However, the antenuptial contract may contain unfair clauses as a result of the parties' unequal bargaining power, differing expectations and cognitive distortion.[144] Furthermore, unless the parties enter into a settlement agreement that deviates from the provisions of their antenuptial contract, the antenuptial contract governs the division of their assets upon divorce regardless of any foreseen or unforeseen change in circumstances that might have occurred since the inception of the marriage or civil union. This inflexible rule gives rise to much injustice. If the judicial power to redistribute assets upon divorce were to be extended to all marriages and civil unions,[145] the court would be able to address the injustice arising from the inflexible application of the terms of the antenuptial contract.

13.69   The third context in which private ordering with all its advantages and disadvantages occurs regularly is divorce settlement agreements. Most divorcing parties regulate post-divorce maintenance, the division of their property, and parental responsibilities and rights in a settlement agreement, which the court may include in the divorce order.[146] These agreements sometimes contain unfair provisions due to unfair negotiating tactics and the parties' unequal bargaining power.[147] Due to crowded divorce rolls, presiding officers seldom give settlement agreements more than a cursory glance and incorporate the agreements without removing and/or replacing unfair provisions. The court ought to be compelled to investigate settlement agreements much more carefully and to take the circumstances in which each agreement was concluded into account, but it is doubted whether any such amendment will be forthcoming.

---

[144]   J. Heaton, 'Striving for Substantive Gender Equality in Family Law: Selected Issues' (2005) 21 *South African Journal on Human Rights* 554.

[145]   Para. 13.63 above.

[146]   Divorce Act 1970, s. 7(1).

[147]   Heaton, 'Striving for Substantive Gender Equality', 566–9.

D   Conclusions

13.70   Two major forces have driven, and will continue to drive, the development of South African child and family law. The first is social change, including modifications in the way adults arrange their intimate relationships, a growing number of births to unmarried parents, the availability of assisted reproduction, greater visibility of same-sex relationships and the HIV/AIDS pandemic. The enactment of the Bill of Rights has been, and will continue to be, the second powerful force for law reform.

13.71   Four trends can be discerned in developments in South African child and family law. The first is the movement from exclusivity to inclusivity. For example, customary marriages as well as heterosexual and same-sex civil unions have received full legal recognition alongside civil marriages. This movement is set to continue with the future recognition of Muslim and Hindu marriages and life partnerships. An obstacle in the path of the movement is that the marriage (or marriage-like) model remains at the heart of recognition of adult relationships. Thus, for example, recognition of non-intimate life partnerships between siblings or friends is not planned. A notable exception to the focus on the marriage model is the recognition of child-headed households. Another factor that has constrained the trend towards inclusivity is the courts' inconsistent approach towards the types of marriage-like adult relationships that are worthy of protection. By protecting same-sex life partners but not heterosexual ones, the Constitutional Court has shown that it is not ready to embrace a contextual, progressive approach towards adult, intimate relationships.

13.72   The second trend, which is linked to the first, is the increased focus on children's rights, accompanied by a reduction in the distinction between children on the ground of their parents' marital status. This trend is evident in customary law too, and is set to continue. Some components of parental responsibilities and rights, such as the right to impose corporal punishment and payment of maintenance, will remain problematic. Furthermore, although the enactment of the Children's Act has resulted in greater acknowledgement of children's evolving capacity and their right to participate, the law's ambivalent approach to individual maturity assessments will continue for the time being. Further, it is not envisaged that the marital status of parents will be completely eliminated as a ground for affording or withholding parental responsibilities and rights.

13.73 The third trend, which is partly related to the second, is the endeavour to achieve gender equality. Unfortunately, South Africa is far from achieving the goal of substantive gender equality. Although unmarried parents are in a position of substantive gender equality insofar as the acquisition of parental responsibilities and rights is concerned, gender equality between parents (whether married or not) is largely formal insofar as discharging childcare responsibilities is concerned. Substantive gender equality has also not yet been achieved in respect of the economic consequences of divorce. Extending the judicial power to redistribute assets to all marriages and civil unions and rethinking the application of the clean-break principle may assist in the latter regard.

13.74 The last trend is the increased use of alternative dispute resolution mechanisms. It is predicted that this trend will continue and that, especially, mediation will become compulsory in more circumstances. However, the growth in mediation will not solve all problems regarding dispute resolution. Access to justice, the fragmented child and family law jurisdiction and general problems with the court system will remain obstacles.

13.75 South African child and family law has taken huge strides forward. However, the expectations of fast, comprehensive transformation of the law that arose as a result of the coming into operation of the Bill of Rights have not been met. Fundamental revision of the law based on socially sound and constitutionally acceptable principles has not taken place. The process of change has been piecemeal and gradual, and is incomplete. Thus, although the contours of child and family law have shifted, and will continue to do so, a comprehensive transformation of this branch of the law – especially family law – has not yet occurred.

The United States of America

Changing laws for changing families

MARYGOLD (MARGO) SHIRE MELLI

A   Introduction

14.1   At the end of the first decade of the twenty-first century, American families and American family law have changed dramatically from what they were for most of the previous century. No-fault divorce is available in all fifty states – something unthinkable in 1950; but the divorce rate, which had been rising steadily since the Civil War, has been going down; at the same time the marriage rate has also decreased. Abortion and contraceptives – reproductive rights – are legal and available. There is a marked increase in different lifestyles – non-marital births, non-marital cohabitation, same-sex relationships. Beginning in the 1960s the status of women and their opportunities have changed dramatically and that has had a major impact on families and the issues in family law.[1]

14.2   These changes in the law have been made both by legislation and court decision. The change from fault to no-fault divorce was by legislative action with little public reaction.[2] The recognition of rights for same-sex partners and the availability of abortion and contraceptives are principally the result of court decisions, based on constitutional rights. Unlike no-fault divorce, abortion and rights for same-sex partners have been very controversial. There has been much criticism of these decisions. In particular, critics have denounced the decisions as 'judicial activism'. Although the term 'judicial activism' has a range

---

[1] For a review of the changes in the lives of women in the last half century, see Gail Collins, *When Everything Changed: The Amazing Journey of American Women From 1960 to the Present* (New York: Little, Brown & Co., 2009).

[2] The relatively quiet legislative change to no-fault divorce is described in Herbert Jacob, *The Silent Revolution: The Transformation of Divorce Law in the United States* (University of Chicago Press, 1988). Jacob is reviewed by Martha Fineman, 'Neither Silent, Nor Revolutionary' (1989) 23 *L. & Soc. Rev.* 945.

of meanings,[3] the critics of the reproductive rights and same-sex decisions undoubtedly mean that the judges shape the law in favour of their
personal preferred outcome. The conservative groups who criticize the
courts as activists include some mainline religious groups – Catholics
and Mormons, for example – as well as smaller conservative religions.
They carry tremendous political power. For a country founded on principles of separation of church and state, organized religion plays an
important role on issues that those religions care about.

14.3   The following brief survey attempts to give an overview of the
current state and future direction of family law in the fifty states that
comprise the United States.

Historical roots, sources and law reform

Historical roots

14.4   As we shall see, the family law systems in the United States differ
somewhat from state to state.[4] Historically, the background for most
states is the English common law system. Eight states, originally settled
by Spain (Arizona, California, Idaho, New Mexico, Nevada, Texas and
Washington) or France (Louisiana), base their family law on the European
civil law system.

14.5   The difference between the common law and civil law systems that
had a major effect on American family law was the way in which property
brought to and acquired during a marriage was held by the parties and
how it was divided at divorce. The common law rule was a 'title rule' – the
person who earned the money to purchase the property was the owner.
This rule usually resulted in the husband being awarded the bulk of the
property because often the wife, who had the major responsibility for the
care of the family, did not work at an income-producing job or, if she did,
she earned less than her husband. The civil law rule was that property
acquired during the marriage was community property and was divided
at divorce equally between the spouses. By the 1980s the distinction
between community property and common law property states became

---

[3] See Keenan D. Kmiec, 'Comment, The Origin and Correct Meaning of "Judicial Activism"'
    (2004) 92 *Calif. L. Rev.* 1441. Also, Edward McWhinney, 'The Supreme Court and the
    Dilemma of Judicial Policy Making' (1955) 39 *Minn. L. Rev.* 837.
[4] See paras. 14.6–14.11 below, for a discussion of the power of each state to legislate on
    family matters and why centralizing influences exist, nonetheless.

blurred at divorce. The common law property states adopted statutes – often referred to as equitable division statutes – authorizing the division of property on divorce. This includes either all the property owned by either spouse or property found to be marital property.[5]

Sources

14.6   Any review of the status of child and family law in the United States must begin with the recognition of its distinctive nature. There is not one, but fifty sets of child and family laws – one for each of the fifty states. Although under the United States Constitution the individual states have delegated authority to the federal government for many purposes, most areas of the law, including that affecting children and families, remain within the jurisdiction of the individual states. Therefore, to use an example of a current controversial issue, whether same-sex couples may marry depends on the law of each of the fifty states.

14.7   In spite of the diversity that results from fifty separate legal jurisdictions, there are at least three reasons why there are many similarities among the states in their child and family laws. These are: (1) the supremacy of the United States Constitution; (2) the role of the United States federal government and the use of the power of the purse; and (3) the influence of the National Conference of Commissioners on Uniform State Laws.

14.8   The text of the United States Constitution, the supreme law of the land, does not mention the family, but that document has played a vital role in shaping the law of the family in the United States.[6]

If, in the example given above of same-sex marriage, the United States Supreme Court rules that the United States Constitution requires that same-sex couples be allowed to marry, that will be the law of all American jurisdictions.

14.9   Although the federal government has no authority to legislate on the family law of the states, it plays a major role in the development of

---

[5] Homer H. Clark, Jr, *The Law of Domestic Relations in the United States*, 2nd edn, Hornbook Series (St Paul: West Publishing Co., 1988), p. 590.

[6] For example, the United States Supreme Court has held that the right to marry is a fundamental right that cannot be denied because a person has not supported children born of an earlier marriage (*Zablocki* v. *Redhail*, 434 U.S. 374 (1978)) or that a person cannot be prohibited from marrying someone of a different race (*Loving* v. *Virginia*, 388 U.S. 1 (1967)).

that law in the United States. As far back as 1912, when President Howard Taft signed legislation establishing the United States Children's Bureau to investigate and report upon all matters pertaining to the welfare of children,[7] the federal government has been interested and active in setting standards for the states and their jurisdiction over families. The main mechanism for accomplishing this has been the requirement that the states adopt certain legislation in return for federal funds. Two examples of this type of impact on state family law are offered by way of illustration. First, the Child Abuse Prevention and Treatment Act (CAPTA) required the states to adopt mandatory child abuse reporting laws in order to qualify for certain categories of federal funds.[8] Second, in 1988 the federal government required the states, in return for federal funds, to replace their discretionary child support rules with ones based on formulas related to the number of children and the incomes of the parents.[9] The American Academy of Matrimonial Lawyers has observed that these laws are part of the 'federalization of family law'.[10]

14.10   In the last decades of the nineteenth century, state officials and leaders of the American Bar Association recognized the problems that were being created by variations in state laws. In 1889 the American Bar Association voted to work for uniformity of the laws in the states. Then, in 1892, the first meeting of the National Conference of Commissioners on Uniform State Laws was held. Since its organization, the Conference has been influential in setting patterns of uniformity across the United States in a number of fields including family law. It has produced Uniform Acts related to a wide variety of Family Law issues: Child Abduction Prevention (2004); Child Custody Jurisdiction (1968); Child Custody Jurisdiction and Enforcement (1997); Interstate Enforcement of Domestic Violence Protection Orders (2000); Marital Property, Marriage and Divorce (1970 and 1973); Parentage (1973 and 2000); Premarital Agreements (1983); Status of Children of Assisted Conception (1988).

---

[7] The United States Children's Bureau is said to be the first government office in the world established to focus on the well-being of children and their mothers.

[8] 42 U.S.C. §§5101–5119 (2010).

[9] Personal Responsibility and Work Opportunity Reconciliation Act of 1996 (PRWORA), Pub. L. No. 104–193, 110 Stat. 2105 (1996).

[10] See the *Journal of the American Academy of Matrimonial Lawyers*, Vols. 16 (1999) and 20 (2007). The Academy also notes the number of federal laws that impact family law.

Law reform

14.11   In the United States family law reform is a state-by-state process. All state legislatures have research arms whose role is to research subjects on which the legislature seeks revision. The states have also cooperated to establish a National Conference of State Legislatures that provides assistance and information on law reform to the states.[11]

14.12   At a national level, the work of the Commissioners on Uniform State Laws, discussed earlier, plays a significant role in researching, drafting and proposing reform legislation for the states. That body has proposed widely adopted and influential uniform family laws.[12]

14.13   The American Law Institute, one of the most prestigious groups of practising lawyers, judges and legal scholars in the United States, sponsors influential studies of the law. It has recently published the results of several years' work on a proposal for future directions in family law, entitled *Principles of the Law of Family Dissolution.*[13] The Principles contain a number of controversial proposals and have generated considerable discussion and criticism.[14]

Dispute resolution and access to legal services

14.14   Family law in the United States is, to an important extent, court-oriented: that is, the parties must have adjudication or approval by a court for a number of important family matters. For example, although the parties may solve their differences through mediation or another form of alternate dispute resolution (ADR), the law requires a formal court decision or approval to grant a divorce or to complete an adoption, to give two examples. In the case of divorce, the United States Supreme Court has recognized the role of the court process and ruled that a state may not deny indigents access to divorce by requiring them to pay a filing fee.[15]

---

[11] See the website for The National Conference of State Legislators: www.NCSL.org.

[12] See www.nccusl.org/Acts.aspx?category=ULC_Family.

[13] American Law Institute, *Principles of the Law of Family Dissolution: Analysis and Recommendations* (Newark: West Publishing, 2002) (hereafter ALI Principles).

[14] See Robin Wilson (ed.), *Reconceiving the Family: Critique on the ALI's Principles of Family Dissolution* (Cambridge University Press, 2006); see also Council on Family Law, *The Future of Family Law* (New York: Institute for American Values, 2005).

[15] *Boddie* v. *Connecticut*, 407 U.S. 371 (1971).

14.15   In the United States in 2011, there are two trends in family law related to the role of legal services to obtain a divorce. The first relates to the use of alternatives to a court trial. Divorcing parties have learned that a traditional court trial with an up or down ruling by a judge may not be the best way to handle the complex issues of family finances and child custody. Parties – and the courts – have sought more flexible ways to gather and assess the facts and turned to alternative dispute resolution. Mediation, a resolution process using a neutral professional to help the parties reach an agreement, is the most prevalent form of ADR.

14.16   The newest type of alternative dispute resolution to gain support as a means of deciding the issues in divorce is Collaborative Law.[16] In collaborative divorce the parties are each represented by a lawyer, a requirement that recognizes the important role of the law in protecting the rights of divorcing parties and their children as they negotiate a resolution of the issues. Collaborative divorce requires the execution of a 'participation agreement' by both parties and their counsel in which they pledge to exchange all relevant information voluntarily and the lawyers must agree that they will not represent their clients if the negotiation process fails and the issues must be resolved by a court.[17] Proponents of collaborative divorce contend that the pledge not to litigate and to find resolution through negotiation has a major effect on the attitudes of the parties – and their lawyers. They argue that this is the best opportunity for creative problem-solving on which the parties can build a healthy post-divorce relationship, something that is very important if children are involved. The latest development in the collaborative law field is the approval of a Uniform Collaborative Divorce Law by the Commissioners on Uniform State Laws.[18] It will undoubtedly have a great influence on the collaborative divorce law process.

14.17   The second trend in legal services for family law is the explosion of pro se divorce litigants: that is, persons who represent themselves in seeking a divorce. The National Center for State Courts[19] reports that state

---

[16] For more information, see www.collaborativedivorce.net/what-is-collaborative-divorce/.

[17] 'Prefatory Note, Uniform Collaborative Law Act' (2009) 38 *Hofstra L. Rev.* 425.

[18] See the text of the Uniform Collaborative Law Act, at p. 467.

[19] National Center for State Courts, Madelynn Herman, *Self-Representation: Pro Se Statistics* (2006), available at: www.ncsconline.org/wc/publications/memos/prosestats-memo.htm. See also ABA Standing Committee on the Delivery of Legal Services: Pro Se/ Unbundling Resource Center: www.abanet.org/legalservices/delivery.

courts are seeing a large increase in self-represented litigants in divorce and other family litigation. There are no national statistics, but state court reports indicate that in a large number of divorces – sometimes in a majority – the parties are not represented by counsel. In response to these numbers state court systems have been creating informational services to help the litigants with the legal process, giving forms to be used and other necessary information.[20]

14.18   The trend to pro se divorce is partially a response to the lack of publicly funded legal services in the area of divorce. It is also part of a trend to self-representation in divorce[21] which has been facilitated by the no-fault revolution in divorce that has eliminated the need to prove fault on the part of one spouse. But a divorce usually involves more than the dissolution of the marriage bond. First, if there are children, arrangements for their custody and support must be made. Second, even couples of limited means often have some property – or debts – which must be evaluated and divided. Consequently, some judges feel that a pro se divorce may place them in a difficult position: the parties may not have a sufficient grasp of the applicable law to explain their problems – or one party may be more knowledgeable than the other. Some judges are concerned about unequal knowledge or position, and it may be that pro se divorces are more likely to require more time than cases involving lawyers.[22]

B   Children in the family setting and state intervention

14.19   The status of childhood, the rules for criminal responsibility and the grounds for government intervention in the family to protect a child are, as pointed out earlier, all matters determined by the individual states. The laws of the individual states, however, reflect in many ways the fact

---

[20] Maryland Legal Assistance Network, Ayn H. Crawley, *Helping Pro Se Litigants to Help Themselves*, available at: www.courts.ca.gov/partners/documents/HelpThemselves. pdf.

[21] Paula L. Hannaford-Agor, 'Helping the Pro Se Litigant: A Changing Landscape' (Winter 2003) *Court Review* 8. See also Judith G. McMullen and Debra Oswald, 'Why Do We Need a Lawyer? An Empirical Study of Divorce Cases' (2010) 12 *J. of Law and Family Studies* 57 (study of 567 divorce cases in a county with a higher than average median income suggests that inability to hire a lawyer is not the sole cause for self-representation).

[22] For an in-depth discussion of the problem of pro se divorce, see Carolyn D. Schwarz, 'Pro Se Divorce Litigants: Frustrating the Traditional Role of the Trial Court Judge and Court Personnel' (2004) 42 *Fam. Ct. Rev.* 655.

that the protections urged by the United Nations Convention on the Rights of the Child are also valued by the individual American states and, indeed, the United States delegation was much involved in the drafting of the Convention. The United States signed it in 1995 but it has, however, failed to ratify it.[23]

Defining and classifying children

Age

14.20   In a democracy such as the United States, the age at which a person has the right to vote is of high significance. The Twenty-sixth Amendment to the United States Constitution, adopted on 1 July 1971, provides that 'the right of citizens of the United States, who are eighteen years of age or older, to vote shall not be denied or abridged by the United States or by any State on account of age'. This change was the result of agitation and lobbying by those subject to the draft in the Vietnam War who were drafted at age 18 but not entitled to vote until they reached the age of 21. When the Twenty-sixth Amendment lowered the voting age to 18, most states also lowered the age of majority to 18.

14.21   One very important age for young people in the United States is the age of juvenile court delinquency jurisdiction, which covers criminal conduct by persons under certain ages and substitutes the procedures and dispositions of the juvenile court statute for that of the criminal law. There are significant differences between the states as to the type of criminal conduct and the ages covered by the juvenile court jurisdiction.

14.22   The role of the juvenile court in the United States goes back to 1899 when the first juvenile court was established in Cook County (Chicago), Illinois. Its model was a social service one, premised on the theory that the role of the court was to help and – if necessary – to discipline the child so that he/she would grow up to be a responsible citizen. In the following years juvenile courts were established throughout the United States based

---

[23] For insight into the reasons the United States has failed to ratify the Convention, see John J. Garman, 'International Law and Children's Human Rights: International, Constitutional, and Political Conflicts Blocking Passage of the Convention on the Rights of the Child' (2006–2007) 41 *Valparaiso University Law Review* 659; Lainie Rutkow and Joshua T. Lozman, 'Suffer the Children? A Call for United States Ratification of the United Nations Convention on the Rights of the Child' (2006) 19 *Harvard Human Rights Journal* 161.

on this philosophy. In 1967, in *In re Gault*,[24] the United States Supreme Court examined the juvenile court and found it lacking constitutional protections for juveniles alleged to be delinquent and committed to an institution. The Court held that juveniles alleged to be delinquent with the possibility of commitment to an institution were entitled to the same constitutional protections as an adult, including the right to a lawyer.

14.23   In the decades after *Gault*, beginning in the 1990s, public attitudes in the United States toward juveniles changed from concern that the juvenile become a law-abiding adult to punitive views reducing the age for juvenile court jurisdiction and, therefore, treating the juveniles as criminals.[25]

14.24   The United States has had an international reputation for the harsh treatment by some states of young people who commit crimes, including the imposition of the death penalty. The United States Supreme Court has found some of these penalties violate the US Constitution. In 2005, in *Roper* v. *Simmons*,[26] the Court by a vote of 5–4 ruled that imposition of the death penalty for a crime committed by a person under the age of 18 violated the Eighth[27] and Fourteenth[28] Amendments to the US Constitution. In 2010 the Court found that a sentence of life without parole for a non-homicide crime by a child under 14 also violated the Eighth and Fourteenth Amendments.[29] These changes in US law reflect international standards in Article 37 of the United Nations Convention on the Rights of the Child.

---

[24] 287 U.S. 1 (1967). The case involved 15-year-old Gerald Gault who was committed – after some remarkably informal court proceedings – to the State Industrial School until the age of 21 for making lewd remarks over the phone to a woman neighbour who never appeared in court. The Supreme Court noted that had Gerald been over 18 at the time, he would have been subject to a fine of $25 to $50 and imprisonment in jail for no more than two months.

[25] See discussion in Barbara Bennett Woodhouse, 'Constitutional Rights of Parents and Children in Child Protective and Juvenile Delinquency Investigations', in Bill Arkin (ed.), *The International Survey of Family Law* (Bristol: Jordans, 2011), p. 409.

[26] 543 U.S. 551 (2005).

[27] The Eighth Amendment to the United States Constitution is in the Bill of Rights, and prohibits cruel and unusual punishments.

[28] The Fourteenth Amendment provides in part: 'nor shall any State deprive any person of life, liberty or property, without due process of law; nor deny to any person within its jurisdiction the equal protection of the laws'.

[29] *Graham* v. *Florida*, 130 S.Ct. 2011 (2010). A child under 14 may still face life imprisonment without parole for homicide.

Birth status

14.25 The historic discrimination against a child born to an unwed mother, an 'illegitimate child', has largely disappeared from twenty-first-century American family law as a result of United States Supreme Court rulings[30] and changes in societal attitudes and practices. In 2006, for example, over 38 per cent of all births in the United States were extra-marital.[31] The impact this has had on the parent–child relationship is discussed more fully below.[32]

Recognizing parentage and family ties

Marital births

14.26 A child born to a married woman is presumed to be the child of the mother's husband and legitimate. This is the rule adopted by the National Conference of Uniform State Laws in the proposed Uniform Parentage Act. This presumption is strong in United States law, as illustrated by the United States Supreme Court decision in *Michael H.* v. *Gerald D.*[33] That case involved a child born to a married woman but whose father was a man with whom the mother had an affair – a fact found by blood tests of the mother and the boyfriend. The mother and child lived with the boyfriend for a time and he sought visitation with the child after the mother and child returned to live with the husband. A plurality of the Supreme Court denied that request, noting that to do so would 'award substantive parental rights to the natural father of a child conceived within and born into an extant marital union that wishes to embrace the child'.

---

[30] See, for example, *Levy* v. *Louisiana*, 391 U.S. 68 (1968) (illegitimate children entitled to bring a wrongful death action to recover for mother's death); *Glona* v. *American Guar. & Liab. Ins. Co.*, 391 U.S. 73 (1968) (mother may bring a wrongful death action for death of an illegitimate child). However, the Court has not been consistent on fathers and intestate succession: see, for example, *Trimble* v. *Gordon*, 430 U.S. 762 (1977), striking down an Illinois statute that denied a non-marital child the right to intestate succession unless the child's parents had married; and *Lalli* v. *Lalli*, 439 U.S. 259 (1978), upholding a New York statute that conditioned a non-marital child's right to intestate succession on the establishment of paternity during the father's lifetime.

[31] Statistical Abstract of the United States: 2009.

[32] See para. 14.29 below, for a discussion of the changing position of the non-marital father.

[33] 491 U.S. 110 (1989).

14.27   Parents are the primary providers of care for their children. They have a right to direct the education[34] and religious upbringing[35] of their children; to make medical decisions for them[36] and to discipline them. In the United States, unlike in some European countries, the parental right to discipline a child has not been a source of concern except in cases of child abuse where the right to discipline may be a defence.[37]

Non-marital births

14.28   Non-marital births skyrocketed from 1940 to 1990; and although the trends stabilized in the 1990s, the non-marital birth rate has been increasing.[38]

14.29   Until over halfway through the twentieth century, non-marital fathers had no rights. Then, in 1972, the United States Supreme Court ruled that a non-marital father, who had lived with his children and their mother, was entitled to a hearing on his fitness before his children could be removed from his care when their mother died.[39] Non-marital fathers then sought equal treatment at adoption with marital fathers who had the right to object to the adoption of the child. In *Quilloin* v. *Walcott*[40] the non-marital father had not supported or lived with the child and the Supreme Court found no basis to grant him the right to be heard on the issue of the adoption. In *Caban* v. *Mohammad*[41] the non-marital father had lived with the mother and the two children for seven years and then sought to maintain the relationship with the children when the parents separated. A majority of the court held that he was entitled to a hearing when the mother's husband sought to adopt the children. In *Lehr* v. *Robertson*[42] the non-marital father objected to the adoption of his two-year-old child by the mother's husband with whom the child had lived since she was eight months old. The father had not filed with the putative

---

[34] See, for example, *Meyer* v. *Nebraska*, 262 U.S. 390 (1923); *Farrington* v. *Tokushige*, 273 U.S. 284 (1927).

[35] *Pierce* v. *Society of Sisters*, 26 U.S. 510 (1925).

[36] *Parham* v. *J.R.*, 422 U.S. 584 (1979).

[37] See, for example, *Lovan C.* v. *Dept. of Children and Families*, 860 A.2d 1283 (2004).

[38] *Statement on Reducing Nonmarital Births* by Stephanie Ventura, National Center for Health Statistics, Centers for Disease Control and Prevention, US Department of Health and Human Services Before the House Committee on Ways and Means, Subcommittee on Human Resources, 29 June 1999.

[39] *Stanley* v. *Illinois*, 405 U.S. 645 (1972).

[40] 434 U.S. 246 (1978).   [41] 441 U.S. 380 (1978).   [42] 463 U.S. 249 (1983).

father registry[43] and had not supported the child. The father claimed that he had not done more because the mother had objected to him having contact with the child. The Supreme Court, with three justices dissenting, held the father had no right to object to the adoption. These cases suggest that the rights of a non-marital father are limited but evolving and are dependent on the father's assumption of the responsibilities of fatherhood, particularly support of his child. These cases may also mean that the right of a non-marital father to deny the adoption of the child by the mother's husband is limited.

Adoption

14.30 Adoption, the legal process by which a parent–child relationship is established between persons who are not biologically related, plays an important role in family law in the United States. It is the legal procedure by which a couple who wish to obtain custody of an infant or very young child to raise as if that child were their own biological child may fulfil their wishes. It also provides an opportunity for a family home for older children who have been removed from parental care for abuse and neglect and live in foster care because their family situation makes it unsafe to return them home. In addition, adoption of stepchildren may provide a legal status for a husband or wife who has a parental role in the family of his or her spouse.

14.31 The adoption process in the United States varies from state to state, but in all states that process requires that the biological parents of the child either consent to the adoption, have their consent waived or have their parental rights terminated either voluntarily or for cause.

14.32 In the case of the mother, the law has long been clear that her consent is required or her parental rights must be terminated. The role of the father is not as clear. If the parents are married, his status is the same as the mother and his consent is required. But if – as is often the case in an adoption – the parents are not married, the father's role is more complicated, as discussed in the previous section on non-marital births.[44]

---

[43] When the United States Supreme Court began to find that non-marital fathers had rights to some role relating to their children, states established ways in which the non-marital father could give notice that he was interested in receiving information on his child. These usually took the form of a Registry of non-marital fathers that could be checked in case of a proposed adoption.

[44] See para. 14.29 above.

14.33   Adoption of infants and young children to be raised in families as the child of that family is a twentieth-century development in the United States. By the middle of the twentieth century there were well-established organizations, usually child welfare agencies, involved in the process. Typically, the adoptive child was born to a single mother in an unfriendly society that stigmatized non-marital births and the agencies provided care for the single mother in that unfriendly society, screened adoptive parents and placed the child. Adoption was seen as a way of creating a family similar to the one the adoptive parents would have had naturally. There was emphasis on matching the backgrounds of the prospective adoptive parents and the children; the documents giving the identity of the natural parents were sealed.

14.34   Today, the goal of matching adoptive parents and the child has disappeared and the attitudes toward adoption have evolved. There is less attempt to conceal the identity of the birth parents of the adoptive child. For example, open adoption, that is one where the birth parents meet the adoptive parents and the parties agree to maintain contact as the child matures, has become one type of adoption. These adoptions typically involve post-adoption contact agreements between the adoptive and birth parents.[45]

14.35   As public attitudes have changed, the stigma of unmarried motherhood has generally disappeared and abortion is legal, the number of white infants available for adoption in the United States has dropped dramatically. As a result, prospective white adoptive parents have turned to other American children who need homes, primarily black and native American children in the foster care system, for adoption. But trans-racial adoption, that is, the adoption of black and native American children by white adopters, has had a difficult time. Native Americans and blacks have been concerned about transracial adoptions because they argued that those adoptions were changing the ties of the children with their native American or black societies. In 1978 the enactment of the Indian Child Welfare Act[46] drastically reduced the adoption of native American children by white parents. In 1972 the Association of Black Social Workers adopted a resolution opposing transracial

---

[45] See Children's Bureau publication, *Postadoptive Contact Agreements Between Birth and Adoptive Families: Summary of State Laws*, available at: www.childwelfare.gov.

[46] 25 U.S.C. §1901 et seq.; see also, *Mississippi Band of Choctaw Indians* v. *Holyfield*, 490 U.S. 30 (1989).

adoption and reducing the number of black children placed for adoption in white homes. Foster home placement agencies began a practice of placing black children only in the homes of black parents. In 1994 Congress enacted the Multiethnic Placement Act,[47] and in 1996 the Interethnic Adoption Provisions, which prohibited the use of the race, colour or national origin of a child or prospective parent to delay or deny the child's placement in a foster or adoptive home. These changes have increased the availability of transracial adoptive homes, particularly for black children. But increasing the availability of black children for adoption by white parents has not brought a major increase in the number of black children adopted by white parents,[48] partly because of lack of interest by white couples and partly as a result of opposition from the black community.[49]

14.36   In recent decades couples in the United States seeking to adopt have turned to adopting internationally.[50] Inter-country adoptions in the United States peaked in 2004 at just under 23,000, but they have been decreasing since then. One reason might be the cost, because the steps taken to protect against abuse of the system[51] have made inter-country adoptions expensive. However, there is also an international debate about the role of inter-country adoption that may be affecting the process. This debate involves the effect of the United Nations Convention on the Rights of the Child (CRC) and the Hague Convention on Protection of Children and Co-operation in Respect of Inter-country Adoption (the Hague Convention) that currently may be affecting the prospects of the process.[52]

---

[47]   42 U.S.C. §5115a (1994). In 1996 Congress adopted the Interethnic Adoption Provisions amending this Act in an effort to encourage placement of black children for adoption regardless of the race of the adoptive family.

[48]   A number of proposals have been made to increase adoption of black children by white couples in the United States. See S. Maldonado, 'Discouraging Racial Preferences in Adoption' (April 2006) 39 *U.C. Davis L. Rev.* 1415.

[49]   See, for example, Twila L. Perry, 'The Transracial Adoption Controversy: An Analysis of Discourse and Subordination' (1993–94) 21 *N.Y.U. Rev. of Law and Social Change* 33.

[50]   For a warm novel involving international adoption, see Anne Tyler, *Digging to America* (New York: Alfred A. Knopf, 2006).

[51]   For a discussion of problems with international adoption, see K. Herrmann, 'Establishing the Humanitarian Approach to Adoption: The Legal and Social Changes Necessary to End the Commodification of Children' (Fall, 2010) 44 *Fam. L. Q.* 409.

[52]   Richard Carlson, 'Seeking the Better Interests of Children with a New International Law of Adoption' (2010/11) 55 *N.Y.U. Law School Law Review* 735.

14.37   As we shall see,[53] there are a large number of children in foster care who cannot be reunited with their original family because that family is too dysfunctional to return the child. These children may live many years, sometimes reaching adulthood, in foster care.[54] In the last quarter century there has been increased interest in placing children in adoptive homes when they are in foster care and cannot be reunited with their original family. In 2009 there were 423,773 children in foster care.[55] The goal for 25 per cent of these children who could not be reunited with their original family was adoption.

14.38   Step-parent adoption of a child who resides with the step-parent is recognized by many state statutes. The adoption process usually does not require any investigation of the home. However, the non-custodial natural parent must consent or have his/her parental rights terminated.

14.39   One other adoption issue is the adoption of children by same-sex partners. Historically, adoption statutes have been premised on the assumption that the adopting couple is heterosexual, and the language of the statute presumes that. The most frequent occasion in which a same-sex couple wishes to adopt involves a woman who gives birth to a child and her same-sex partner seeks to adopt that child. Reactions to same-sex adoptions have been varied. Some courts have found that the adoption is not in the best interest of the child, but the number of courts granting approval is slowly increasing.[56]

The child's 'right to know'

14.40   In the United States, as elsewhere, the relationship between parents and child is based on genetic ties. There are two major exceptions to this relationship: first, the child who is adopted and, second, the child who is conceived with assisted reproductive technology, usually the sperm of a donor. Both of these groups of children have sought information on their genetic origins.[57]

---

[53] See paras. 14.53–14.60 below, for a discussion of the child protection system.

[54] In some cases the parent is imprisoned for a lengthy period. See situations discussed in *Matter of Gregory B.*, 542 N.E.2d 1052 (N.Y. 1989).

[55] Adoption and Foster Care Analysis and Reporting System (AFCARS) FY 2009 data (1 October 2008 to 30 September 2009).

[56] See cases collected in ALI Principles s. 2.12, Comment f, p. 313.

[57] See Richard J. Blauwhoff, *Foundational Facts, Relative Truths: A Comparative Study in Children's Right to Know Their Genetic Origins* (Mortsel: Intersentia, 2009).

14.41   For adopted children seeking information about their birth parents, the law in the United States has changed in the last half century. Beginning in the 1930s and 1940s, most identifying information was treated as confidential by the placing agency and the courts. Adoption was seen as ending a child's relationship with the birth family and replacing it with an adoptive family. The child's birth records, giving the names of the genetic parents, were sealed and public policy was against releasing that information to adopted people. Today, most, if not all, American jurisdictions allow adult adoptees to obtain 'non-identifying' information about their birth parents.[58] Many states also have made provision for adult adoptees and their parents to locate each other.

14.42   Children born as the result of artificial insemination with donated sperm (AID) have similar problems locating the identity of the sperm donor. The medical facilities that collect the sperm from donors promise anonymity to them. However, as the use of artificial insemination becomes more common and more women are involved, there is increased interest in sperm from donors who agree to the release of their identity when the child becomes 18.[59] In cases where the donor has been promised anonymity, some courts have ordered identity disclosure when there is a problem of an inherited disease.[60]

Delivering parenting

Child support

14.43   In the last forty years the payment of child support in the United States has been revolutionized. Historically, the amount of child support had been set at the discretion of the trial court with little guidance – statutes often told the court to set a 'reasonable amount' of support. It was collected, if at all, by a slow and uncertain court process.

---

[58]   Elizabeth J. Samuels, 'The Idea of Adoption: An Inquiry into the History of Adult Adoptee Access to Birth Records' (2001) 53 *Rutgers Law Review* 367.

[59]   Amy Harmon, 'First Comes The Baby Carriage', *New York Times*, E1, 13 October 2005. See also: www.pacrepro.com.

[60]   Jenna H. Bauman, 'Discovering Donors: Legal Rights to Access Information about Anonymous Sperm Donors Given to Children of Artificial Insemination in *Johnson* v. *Superior Court of Los Angeles County*' (2001) 31 *Golden Gate U.L. Rev.* 192; Gaionton Basu, 'Genetic Privacy: Resolving the Conflict between the Donor and the Child' (2004) 85 *Current Science* 1363.

14.44   Historically, non-marital fathers as well as divorced fathers have failed to support their children. The mothers of these children seek help from governmental programmes partially financed by the federal government. The cost of these programmes and the numbers of children supported under them escalated in the last quarter of the twentieth century. Therefore, one of the major public policy concerns became the issue of collecting child support from these 'absent fathers'.

14.45   Congress adopted an aggressive policy on child support and in the Family Support Act of 1988,[61] mandated the use of mathematical formulas or guidelines based on the number of children and the parent's income to set the amount of child support an 'absent father' was required to pay.[62] Congress also provided funding and required states to establish child support enforcement agencies and networks, both within the states and across state borders – an important problem in the United States.[63]

Intra-family disputes

14.46   Intra-family disputes between parents about the custody of children and visitation rights arise in three types of cases: first, when parents divorce; second, if they are not married and the cohabitation is ending; or third, the unmarried parents never lived together. In all cases, the guiding rule is the best interest of the child, a much criticized rule,[64] but one that continues to be the underlying focus for rules on child custody.

14.47   Over the last half century, the rules on child custody when parents live apart have evolved. In the 1970s most state statutes authorized the award of custody to only one parent, the custodial parent, usually the mother. The non-custodial parent was awarded time described as 'visitation'.

---

[61] 42 U.S.C. §667.

[62] This type of formula is now used in setting child support in all support actions whether or not public support is sought.

[63] See Comment, 'Uncle Sam's Cure for Deadbeat Dads' (2007) 20 *J. Am. A. M. L.* 311.

[64] See, for example, ALI Principles, §2.02, Comment c: 'While the best-interests-of-the-child test expresses the appropriate priority in favor of the interests of the child, and while it provides the flexibility that permits a court to reach what it believes is the best result in an individual case, it has long been criticized for its indeterminacy ... when the only guidance for the court is what best serves the child's interests, the court must rely on its own value judgements, or upon experts who have their own theories of what is good for children and what is effective parenting.'

14.48   Beginning in the 1980s, fathers' rights groups began to seek changes in the divorce custody rules with the objective of requiring shared time between mothers and fathers. The issue became controversial as fathers' rights groups promoted legislation providing for a presumption of equal custodial time on divorce even in contested cases. They pursued this objective in the face of overwhelming evidence that fathers in intact families do not share child care equally with mothers.[65] Feminists – and mothers – have opposed the shared custody initiative, concerned that the objective of fathers was not to spend more time with their children but to reduce their child support obligation.[66] The American Law Institute (ALI) has proposed an approach that not only is helpful at the point of setting the amount of time but also giving fathers a predictable role. The ALI proposed[67] what it called 'the Approximation Rule',[68] providing that the amount of time allocated to separated parents should approximate what they had when the parents were together.[69] Today, although mothers are still the primary custodians post-divorce, shared-time custody is increasingly a fact of post-divorce life.[70] One positive development in post-divorce custody is the requirement that divorcing parents submit 'parenting plans' to the court, detailing the arrangements to which the parents have agreed about how much time the children will spend with

---

[65] Although the evidence is clear that within an intact marriage mothers usually provide the majority of child care, many fathers, who may not provide a large amount of child care, regard themselves as very involved with their children – they do not want to be 'weekend' dads. Eleanor E. Maccoby and Robert H. Mnookin, *Dividing the Child: Social and Legal Dilemmas of Custody* (Cambridge, MA: Harvard University Press, 1992), pp. 92 and 279. Mothers have long sought to reconfigure family relationships in the intact family to promote more emotional and time commitment to children by fathers and shared responsibility for their care. Elizabeth S. Scott, 'Pluralism, Parental Preference and Child Custody' (1992) 80 *California Law Review* 615. The fathers' rights groups have fought for such involvement post-divorce. Carol Smart, 'Preface', in Richard Collier and Sally Sheldon (eds.), *Fathers' Rights Activism and Law Reform in Comparative Perspective* (Oxford: Hart Publishing, 2006).

[66] See, for example, Helen Rhoades and Susan B. Boyd, 'Reforming Custody Laws: A Comparative Study' (2004) 18 *Inter'l J of Law, Policy and Fam* 119.

[67] ALI Principles, §2.08.

[68] ALI Principles, §2.08, Comment b: 'While the best-interests-of-the-child test may appear well suited to this objective, the test is too subjective to produce predictable results. Its unpredictability encourages strategic bargaining and prolonged litigation.'

[69] The ALI Approximation Rule has been criticized. See Patrick Parkinson, 'The Past Caretaking Standard in Comparative Perspective', in Robin F. Wilson (ed.), *Reconceiving The Family* (Cambridge University Press: 2006).

[70] See, for example, the study discussed in Marygold S. Melli and Particia R. Brown, 'Exploring a New Family Form – The Shared Time Family' (2008) 22 *Intl. J. of Law, Policy and Fam.* 231.

each parent, who will be responsible for taking them to activities and school functions, and so on.[71]

14.49   Another type of intra-family dispute may arise about the issue of visitation. One prominent example of this type of dispute is between parents and grandparents when the parent objects to or limits grandparent visitation. In the latter part of the twentieth century as families began to change through divorce and cohabitation, grandparents – living longer and in better health than in the past – sought legislation protecting their rights to visit their grandchildren. As a result most, if not all states have statutes providing for grandparent visitation – sometimes in very broad terms. In 2000, in *Troxel* v. *Granville*,[72] a plurality of the United States Supreme Court held that a broadly worded grandparent visitation statute allowing visitation over the objection of a parent was unconstitutional.

14.50   Post *Troxel* there has been litigation and legislation limiting grandparents' rights to visitation and concern about the effect of intra-family litigation.[73] But, in a changing world in which grandparents often play a crucial role in raising grandchildren because of parental absence or dysfunction or who may provide essential daycare while a parent works, the rule of *Granville* may be modified.

Relocation

14.51   In a mobile society such as the United States, it is a common occurrence that one of the parents in the divorce will seek to move from the current home area sometime after the divorce.[74] If the parent who wishes to move is the custodial parent, there will be a need to have court approval to move the child's residence. These moves are problematic because it is very likely they will have an impact on the relationship of the non-custodial parent and the child.[75] Unfortunately, the problem is one for which there seems to be no universally acceptable rule to guide

---

[71] The American Law Institute's Principles of the Law of Family Dissolution requires parents to submit parenting plans, noting that a parenting plan encourages parents to cooperate. ALI Principles, §2.05.

[72] 530 U.S. 57 (2000).

[73] Annie Hsia, 'About Grandma's Visits' (14 October 2002) *The National Law Journal* A1.

[74] Census Bureau figures note that in a five-year period from 1990 to 1995, 54.9 per cent of divorced families relocated.

[75] If the parent who wishes to move is the non-custodial parent, there is no need for court approval – even though that parent's move may result in fracturing a close relationship with the children.

decision-making.[76] Some states have adopted presumptions – for or against – allowing relocation.

14.52   In 1997 the American Academy of Matrimonial Lawyers proposed a Model Act on Relocation, which included several possible presumptions to guide the court.[77] The American Law Institute has proposed that 'the court allow a parent who has been exercising the clear majority of custodial responsibility to relocate with the child if that parent shows that the relocation is for a valid purpose, in good faith, to a location that is reasonable in light of the purpose'.[78] But the issue continues to be contentious and some judges and scholars have concluded that using the traditional standard of 'best interest of the child' may be the most workable standard.[79]

Child protection and state intervention

14.53   In the United States protection for neglected and abused children is provided through the jurisdiction of the juvenile courts and government agencies at the local level, usually with countywide jurisdiction. They are governed by state statutes that, although they are all similar, differ somewhat among the fifty states. In addition, the United States Congress through federal legislation and monetary support plays an important role in the framework and services for child protection.

14.54   Juvenile court statutes typically provide for jurisdiction by the juvenile court over a child who is the victim of abuse or 'whose parent, guardian or legal custodian[80] neglects, refuses or is unable for reasons

---

[76]   It is also one that is complicated because it has become part of the 'gender wars': on one side are the fathers who are often the non-custodial parent and are supported by fathers' rights groups to oppose the relocation; on the other side are the custodial mothers, and the feminists supporting her desire to move.

[77]   15 *J. A. A. M. L.* 1 (1998).

[78]   ALI Principles, §2.17 (4)(a).

[79]   David Kowalski, 'Rush to Relocate: Are Presumptions In Favor of Relocating Parents Really in the Children's Best Interests?' (2008) 22 *Am. J. Fam. L.* 28. For an excellent review of the problems faced in relocation decisions and proposed solutions, see Linda Elrod, 'National and International Momentum Builds for More Child Focus in Relocation Disputes' (Fall 2010) 44 *Fam. L.Q.* 341.

[80]   Maxine Eichner in her book *The Supportive State* (Oxford University Press, 2010) notes that the United States child welfare system assumes that families are responsible for safeguarding children's welfare, and only after that support fails should the state intervene. She proposes a 'supportive state' in which the state has a concurrent rather than residual responsibility for children's welfare. She outlines a supportive state approach

other than poverty to provide necessary care, food, clothing, medical or dental care or shelter so as to endanger seriously the physical health of the child'.[81]

14.55   Out of concern that cases of child abuse and neglect may not be reported to the authorities, in 1974 Congress enacted the Child Abuse Prevention and Treatment Act and Adoption Reform Act (CAPTA)[82] that required states to adopt mandatory reporting statutes in order to be eligible for certain federal funds. As a result of this federal legislation mandatory reporting has become an integral part of child welfare services.

14.56   The limitations of the protection offered to defenceless children by the child welfare system were highlighted in the US Supreme Court case of *Deshaney* v. *Winnebago County Department of Social Services*.[83] There, the child Joshua was in the custody of his divorced father. Over a period from January 1982 to March 1984 the social services agency received several reports from credible sources, including a physician who treated Joshua and the hospital emergency room where he was taken for treatment, that Joshua's father was abusing him. Those reports were made under the state statute providing that persons who suspect child abuse must inform the social services department.[84] After investigating each report, the social worker assigned to Joshua's case apparently concluded that the situation did not require removal of Joshua from his father's custody. In March 1984 Joshua was beaten so severely by his father that he fell into a life-threatening coma and, although he did not die, he was so badly injured that the prediction was that for the rest of his life he would be confined to an institution for the profoundly retarded. His father was tried and convicted of child abuse.

14.57   Joshua and his mother sued the county social services department,[85] but the United States Supreme Court held, by five votes to four,

---

with programmes to alleviate child poverty and provide developmentally enriching child care programmes both pre-school and after school and suggests that some of the funding could come from the money spent on the present foster care system. Eichner, *The Supportive State*, pp. 123–6.

[81] See, for example, Wis. Stat. §48.13 (2009–2010).

[82] 42 U.S.C. §§5101–5119 (2010).

[83] 489 U.S. 189 (1989).

[84] This statute was adopted under the requirements of the Child Abuse Prevention and Treatment Act, noted above.

[85] The action was brought under 42 U.S.C. §1983 alleging a deprivation of Joshua's liberty interest in bodily integrity.

that the agency was not liable for the injuries inflicted on Joshua by his father when he was in his father's custody. The court majority said:

> nothing in the language of the Due Process Clause itself requires the State to protect the life, liberty and property of its citizens against invasion by private actors. The clause is phrased as a limitation on the State's power to act, not as a guarantee of certain minimal levels of safety and security. It forbids the State itself to deprive individuals of life, liberty or property without 'due process of law' but its language cannot fairly be extended to impose an affirmative obligation on the State to ensure that those interests do not come to harm through other means.[86]

14.58   When the juvenile court determines that a child is abused or neglected, it is faced with limited options: leaving the child in the home under supervision as in the use of *Joshua*, or ordering the child removed from the home and placed in foster care under the supervision of the local social services agency. Foster care usually means that the child is placed in a licensed foster home, which may be the home of a relative, and supervised by a licensed social worker. The objective of the court and the agency is to improve the situation at home so the child may be reunited with his parent or parents as soon as possible: that is to say, foster care should be a temporary short-term placement. But, as critics point out, that is not what always happens. In some cases the problems of the child's natural parent or parents are so great that they cannot be easily resolved to a point where the child can be safely returned. In addition, often the social workers who are charged with the task of rehabilitating the parents are overworked, with caseloads too large for such a difficult task.

14.59   As a result, children removed from their homes for neglect or abuse often become long-term foster children. Concerned about this situation, in 1980 Congress adopted the federal Adoption Assistance and Child Welfare Act, which required the states, as a condition of receiving federal foster care funds, to make 'reasonable efforts' to enable the foster child to return home. The legislation required the states to institute case planning and periodic case reviews as part of the 'reasonable efforts' to return the child home. By 1997 Congress concluded that the effort to return children to their home was failing and, in the Adoption and Safe Families Act of 1997,[87] required the states to terminate the parental rights of, and make available for adoption, any child

---

[86]   489 U.S. 189, 194 (1989).   [87]   42 U.S.C. §671.

who had been in foster care for fifteen of the last twenty-two months. This legislation has resulted in a large increase in the number of children in foster care who are available for adoption.

14.60   Termination of parental rights is the most drastic remedy in child protection because it severs the legal ties of the child and parents. All American states have statutory provisions setting forth the grounds for this procedure. Recognizing the importance of those rights, the United States Supreme Court has ruled that the burden of proof in a termination proceeding is the elevated standard of 'clear and convincing evidence'.[88] Unfortunately, the Supreme Court has held that the value of the parent–child relationship does not require the appointment of counsel to represent the interests of parents.[89]

C   Adult relationships

14.61   In less than half a century American attitudes and laws concerning adult relationships – marriage, divorce and beyond – have changed dramatically as the following discussion illustrates.

The relationships

Marriage and divorce

14.62   Historically marriage was the institution that governed the relationship of adult couples.[90] The right of a man and woman to marry has been held by the Supreme Court to be a fundamental right that cannot be denied because the couple is of different races (*Loving* v. *Virginia*[91]) or one of the parties has failed to support a child of another relationship (*Zablocki* v. *Redhail*[92]).

14.63   Marriage is an institution in decline, however. A report by the Pew Research Center in 2010 analysing the results of a nationwide survey[93] found that the number of adults who were married had declined from

---

[88]   *Santosky* v. *Kramer*, 455 U.S. 745 (1982).

[89]   *Lassiter* v. *Department of Social Services of Durham County*, 452 U.S. 18 (1981).

[90]   Although the statute might not have been explicit, the assumption was that the couple was heterosexual.

[91]   388 U.S. 1 (1967).   [92]   434 U.S. 374 (1978).

[93]   The survey was conducted in association with *Time* magazine and complemented by an analysis of demographic and economic data from the US Census Bureau http://pewresearch.org/pubs/1802/decline-marriage-rise-new-families.

72% in 1960 to 52% in 2008.[94] It also reported a striking difference by generation. In 1960 68% of people in their twenties were married; in 2008 the
number was reduced to 26%. The Pew Research Center study also found
a class difference in marriage rates. Marriage, although declining, is still
the norm for adults with a college degree and a good income. This finding
suggests that economic security is good for marriage.

14.64   Not only are Americans not entering into marriage, they are also
leaving it in very high numbers. Over 150 years ago, in the 1860s, the
divorce rate in the United States began to climb, peaking in 1979,[95] and
became an issue of national concern.[96] The rise in the number of divorces
had the salutary effect of encouraging public policymakers to re-examine
the operation of the divorce laws. Although the law of divorce was based
on proof of fault, study after study showed that the proof of fault was
fabricated or ignored and everyone – including the judge – knew that.[97]
Finally, there was a movement to adopt 'no-fault' grounds. Between 1970,
when California adopted the first no-fault divorce statute,[98] and 1985, all

---

[94] Earlier studies reported the same trend. In October 2006 the *New York Times* reported
that the American Community Survey, released by the Census Bureau that month, found
that in 2005 49.7 per cent of the nation's 111.1 million households were made up of married couples, down from the 52 per cent five years earlier. 'To Be Married Means To Be
Outnumbered', *New York Times*, 15 October 2006.

[95] US Bureau of Labor Statistics. After peaking in 1979, the divorce rate has been dropping
steadily; see: www.census.gov/compendia/statab/2010/tables/10s1300.pdf.

[96] Although the law of all the states required proof of fault on the part of one party as the
basis for granting a divorce, the requirements of the states on the issue of fault differed
considerably. For example, state A might grant a divorce based on fault grounds that state
B did not recognize. Although these differences in grounds were available only to the
residents of each state, some states required very short periods of residence. In a mobile
society like the United States in which there is free and easy movement from state to state
residents of state B might go to state A – which probably had a short residence period
for divorce – to take advantage of its divorce-friendly laws. Usually the divorced parties
returned to their original state of residence. This type of divorce was labelled migratory
divorce. It was one of the reasons for the establishment of the National Conference of
Commissioners on Uniform State Laws in 1892 – although the Conference did not produce a proposed Uniform Law until 1970. According to Rheinstein, 'It was New York's special interest in the problem of migratory divorce that prompted Governor David B. Hill
in 1889 and 1890 to exhort the legislature to take the initiative in organizing coordin-
ated state action on marriage and divorce. The initiative resulted in the creation of the
National Conference of Commissioners on Uniform State Laws.' See Max Rheinstein,
Marriage Stability, Divorce and the Law (University of Chicago Press, 1972), p. 47.

[97] Lawrence M. Friedman, *American Law in the Twentieth Century* (New Haven: Yale
University Press, 2002), p. 434.

[98] Herma Hill Kay, 'Equality and Difference: A Perspective on No Fault Divorce and Its
Aftermath' (1987) 56 *University of Cincinnati Law Review* 1.

American states adopted some form of no-fault divorce. About one-third of the states repealed their traditional divorce statute and enacted 'pure' no-fault ones based on proof that the marriage was no longer viable. But most states just added 'no fault' as an additional ground to their divorce statute.

14.65   No-fault divorce is a good solution for couples where the desire to divorce is mutual. But no-fault divorce also allows unilateral divorce and the partner who does not want to divorce is powerless. This problem is exacerbated for women by the fact that they have often been child-carers and homemakers and not income-producers in the marriage.[99] The reduction in their standard of living can be very problematic.[100] Post-divorce support for a former spouse – traditionally provided by alimony or maintenance – has never been a major source of income for divorced homemakers. The latest available data show only 17 per cent of divorced women reporting that they received alimony.[101]

14.66   As a result of government concern and feminist advocacy, post-divorce lives for women and children have improved, but probably the most important reason is the progress that women have made in the workplace. Women now are more able to be self-sufficient.[102]

Cohabitation and its termination

14.67   Cohabitation, an arrangement in which couples who are not married live together as a family, was once illegal in most, if not all of the states, made criminal by laws against fornication and adultery. Today, with those laws either repealed or ignored, cohabitation is a lifestyle that is growing in popularity in the United States. One source[103] estimates the

---

[99] We forget that for much of the twentieth century the work of running a household was a very time-consuming task. There were no frozen foods, no tasty quick meals, no ability to dump the clothes in the washing machine and have them ready to be dried. Keeping the family going was a full-time job, and women were not expected to be income producers in the family.

[100] One influential book on the issue of the reduced standard of living for women post divorce was Lenore Weitzman, *The Divorce Revolution: The Unexpected Social and Economic Consequences for Women and Children in America* (New York: Free Press, 1985). Although the book was criticized, it had an influential role.

[101] The last year for which alimony figures were reported was 1989. US Bureau of Census, Child Support and Alimony, *Current Population Reports*, p. 20.

[102] See Collins, *When Everything Changed*.

[103] Ira Mark Ellman, Paul M. Kurtz, Lois H. Weithorn, Brian H. Bix, Karen Czapansky and Marian Eichner, *Family Law: Cases, Text, Problems*, 5th edn (New Providence: LexisNexis, 2010), p. 920.

number of heterosexual cohabiting couples in 1960 as 439,000 and the number of married couples as 39,254,000, giving a ratio of 1.1 unmarried couples per 100 married couples. The same source estimates the number of heterosexual cohabiting couples in 2006 as 5,368,000 compared to the number of married couples as 58,179,000, giving a ratio of 9.2 unmarried couples per 100 married couples.

14.68   The legal status of cohabiting couples, their rights and obligations, particularly on termination, has been problematic.[104] A decision by the California Supreme Court in 1976, *Marvin* v. *Marvin,*[105] became a much discussed source for addressing these issues. The California Supreme Court ruled that the provisions of the California Family Code applicable to married couples on divorce did not apply when a cohabiting relationship ended. However, it concluded that the courts could examine whether the parties had an express or implied contract as to how the contributions of the parties to the relationship should be valued.

14.69   In the years since *Marvin* was decided, cohabitation has increased and a majority of courts, faced with allocating rights on the termination of the relationship, have found, like the court in *Marvin*, that the provisions of state law applying to divorcing parties did not govern the termination of a cohabiting relationship. However, also like *Marvin*, they have found a basis, usually in contract law, for allowing claims.[106] Nevertheless, the courts continue to be cautious in treating the post-separation property claims of cohabitants on the same basis as married couples.[107] In contrast to the approach of state courts, the American Law Institute Principles of Family Dissolution provide that the rules of property distribution for cohabiting couples are the same as those applied to property distribution for married couples[108] – a result that the states have been careful to avoid.

---

[104] In the past such a relationship might have developed into a common law marriage. But common law marriage as a legal status has been in decline, outlawed in a majority of states. See discussion in Clark Jr, *The Law of Domestic Relations in the United States*, §2.4. Today common law marriage is legal in eleven states: Alabama, Colorado, Iowa, Kansas, Montana, Oklahoma, Pennsylvania, Rhode Island, South Carolina, Texas and Utah. ALI Principles, 914–30.

[105] 557 P.2d 106 (1976). The case may have attracted publicity partly because Lee Marvin was a well-known movie actor.

[106] See Marsha Garrison, 'Nonmarital Cohabitation: Social Revolution and Legal Regulation' (2008) 42 *Family Law Quarterly* 209; Ann Laquer Estin, 'Unmarried Partners and the Legacy of *Marvin* v. *Marvin*: Ordinary Cohabitation' (2001) 76 *Notre Dame Law Review* 1381.

[107] *Ibid.*   [108] ALI Principles, §6.04.

Same-sex couples

14.70   As noted earlier, there is increasing tolerance of same-sex relationships as a subset of cohabiting couples. Until recently, same-sex relationships were under a legal cloud because a number of states had statutes criminalizing same-sex acts and the United States Supreme Court had upheld those statutes in *Bowers* v. *Hardwick*.[109] However, in 2003, in *Lawrence* v. *Texas*,[110] the Court struck down a Texas statute similar to the Georgia one upheld in *Bowers* v. *Hardwick*. In the following years a number of states have enacted statutes authorizing civil unions or domestic partnerships to give same-sex couples a status somewhat similar to marriage for heterosexual couples.

14.71   Same-sex couples citing their commitment to each other have pressed for equal treatment with heterosexual couples and the right to marry.[111] The reactions to this initiative have been mixed. In a few states, for example Massachusetts and Iowa, the state Supreme Court has found that same-sex couples have a constitutional right to marry.[112] Same-sex marriage has been legalized by legislation in Vermont, New Hampshire, the District of Columbia and in June 2011 in the populous state of New York.[113]

14.72   Residents of states that recognize same-sex marriage may face problems in states that do not because Congress enacted the Defense of Marriage Act 1996 (DOMA),[114] which provides, in section 2, that no state is required to treat as a marriage a same-sex marriage valid in another state. A majority of states have adopted the language of the federal statute refusing recognition of same-sex marriage. A majority have also adopted

---

[109] 478 U.S. 186 (1986).   [110] 539 U.S. 558 (2003).

[111] The conceptual difficulty for same-sex marriage is that historically marriage has been a conjugal relationship of a man and a woman and the authorization for same-sex marriage necessitates that the law redefine that relationship. See the discussion in Dan Cere, *A Report from the Council on Family Law: The Future of Family Law* (2005).

[112] The issue of same-sex marriage is very contentious. In Iowa after a unanimous Supreme Court held that same-sex marriage was a constitutional right, three of the justices were defeated in retention elections. (Iowa is one of a few states in which Supreme Court justices are appointed, but they must be approved periodically in an election.)

[113] The New York legislation, The Marriage Equality Act; see Nicholas Confessore and Michael Barbaro, 'New York Allows Same Sex Marriage, Becoming Largest State to Pass Law', *New York Times*, 24 June 2011.

[114] 28 U.S. Code §1738(c).

constitutional amendments defining marriage as between a man and a woman.[115]

14.73   Section 3 of the Defense of Marriage Act defines marriage in federal legislation as 'a legal union between one man and one woman as husband and wife' and 'spouse as a person of the opposite sex who is a husband or wife'. On 23 February 2011 the Attorney General[116] announced that, on order of the President, his office would not defend DOMA because it is unconstitutional.[117]

14.74   The issue of same-sex marriage will eventually be decided by the United States Supreme Court. A 2010 lawsuit in the federal courts in California[118] may culminate in a ruling by that Court on the constitutionality of same-sex marriage in the United States.

Consequences of adult relationships

Domestic violence

14.75   Domestic violence is a social problem with a long history. Unfortunately, until the latter part of the twentieth century, it was

---

[115]   See, for example, Wisconsin Constitution, Article XIII §13.

[116]   Charlie Savage and Cheryl Stolberg, 'In Turnabout, US Says Marriage Act Blocks Gay Rights', *New York Times*, 24 February 2011, p. 1A.

[117]   The Attorney General, Eric Holder, in a letter to John A. Boehner, Speaker of the House of Representatives, announced that the President had concluded that classifications based on sexual orientation were entitled to heightened scrutiny. 'After careful consideration, including a review of my recommendation, the President has concluded that given a number of factors, including the documented history of discrimination, classifications based on sexual orientation should be subject to a heightened standard of scrutiny. The President has also concluded that section 3 of DOMA as applied to legally married same-sex couples, fails to meet that standard and is unconstitutional. Given that conclusion, the President has instructed the Department not to defend the statute.'

[118]   *Perry* v. *Schwarzenegger*, 704 F. Supp 2d 921 (N.D.Cal. 2010). The lawsuit attacked the constitutionality of Proposition 8, a ballot initiative approved by a majority of California voters on 4 November 2008 that amended the California constitution to prohibit same-sex marriage. The Federal District Court ruled that Proposition 8 was unconstitutional because it violates the Due Process and Equal Protection Clauses of the Fourteenth Amendment of the United States Constitution. The supporters of Proposition 8 appealed to the Court of Appeals for the 9th District, which affirmed the District Court's ruling. The prediction is that this might be the first same-sex marriage case to reach the US Supreme Court. The lawsuit has attracted considerable attention. The plaintiffs are represented by two distinguished and well-known lawyers. Theodore (Ted) Olson, who represented George W. Bush in the Supreme Court litigation involving the very close 2000 Presidential election, and David Boies, who represented Al Gore.

tolerated and accepted as a part of the normal stress in domestic relationships. There were 'old wives' tales' about how a man could legally beat his wife if he used a stick no bigger than his thumb. Domestic violence[119] is a serious social problem, resulting in 2,340 deaths in 2007. Of these deaths, 70 per cent were women.[120] Unfortunately, the increase of attention to the problem has not decreased the frequency. In fact, there is evidence that the pressures of bad economic times may increase the amount of domestic violence.[121]

14.76   Traditionally, one of the problems in the domestic abuse area was that the victim – usually a woman – would complain to the police, who would arrest the abuser, only to find that the victim often dropped the charge frequently out of fear of further abuse. One of the objectives of the women's groups who are active in the domestic violence area is to make sure that the victim does not back away from prosecution of the offender. To counteract the post-arrest fear of abused women, battered women's shelters have been established to provide safe living conditions and to protect the abused women during the case processing. The Violence Against Women Act passed by congress in 1994 provided funding for these efforts.[122]

Reproductive rights

14.77   Issues of sexual and reproductive rights, both inside and outside marriage and as they affect young people and adults, have been at the forefront of the sexual revolution and a product of it in the United States. In 1965 the state of Connecticut, like some other states, prohibited the use of contraceptives even by a married couple. In *Griswold* v. *Connecticut*[123] the United States Supreme Court found this statute unconstitutional. This decision was followed by *Eisenstadt* v. *Baird*,[124] finding unconstitutional a statute that made it criminal to dispense contraceptives to anyone but a married person. Both of these decisions seemed to be in keeping with the public attitudes in the United States on these issues.

---

[119] There is an excellent review of United States legislation on domestic violence in an article comparing the United States with Ireland. See Barbara Glesner Fines, 'Approaches to Protecting Victims of Intimate Partner Violence in the United States and Ireland: People, Property and Politics' (2010) 79 *U.M.K.C. Law Review* 1.

[120] The Bureau of Justice Statistics, 2011.

[121] Peter Schworn and John M. Guilfoil, 'Rising Economic Stress Cited in Domestic Violence Increase', *Boston Globe*, 3 February 2010.

[122] 42 USC §§13925–14045d.

[123] 381 U.S. 479 (1965).   [124] 405 U.S. 438 (1972).

14.78   In 1973, in *Roe* v. *Wade*,[125] the Supreme Court found unconstitutional a Texas statute that made it criminal to perform or have an abortion unless such procedure was necessary to save the life of the mother.[126] The Court carefully spelled out the circumstances under which a law making abortion criminal would be constitutional. It held that a statute making abortion criminal, at any stage, unless to save the life of the mother, violates the Due Process Clause of the Fourteenth Amendment. Up to the end of the first trimester of pregnancy the decision must be left to the medical judgement of the woman's physician. During the second trimester the state may regulate abortion procedure in ways that are related to maternal health. In the stage subsequent to viability, the state may regulate, and even proscribe, abortion except when necessary to preserve the life or health of the mother.

14.79   In the decades following *Roe* v. *Wade* the subject of abortion has become one of the most controversial issues in United States policy. Led by conservative religious organizations – Roman Catholics and Evangelicals – the opposition has targeted medical facilities that provide abortion services – sometimes with violent results.[127] The opposition has also been very successful in obtaining legislation to limit the right to abortion.[128] As observed earlier, in the United States, where separation of church and state was a founding principle, religious organizations are very powerful on issues they care about. In 1992 in *Planned Parenthood* v. *Casey*,[129] faced with restrictive state legislation, the Court retreated from the formula in *Roe* v. *Wade* and concluded that the question was one of whether the statutory framework created an undue burden on the woman's right to abortion. In *Stenberg* v. *Carhart*[130] the Supreme Court struck

---

[125] 410 U.S. 113 (1973).

[126] The Court noted that somewhat similar statutes were in place in almost all other states. There are several histories of abortion laws. See Mary Ann Glendon, *Abortion and Divorce in Western Law* (Cambridge, MA: Harvard University Press, 1987); Laurence Tribe, *Abortion: The Clash of Absolutes* (New York: Norton, 1990).

[127] Wikipedia – http://en.wikipedia.org/wiki/anti-abortion_violence. The majority of anti-abortion violence has been committed in the United States.

[128] Congress has prohibited the use of Medicaid funds to reimburse states for the costs of abortion under Medicaid; see The Hyde Amendment, 90 Stat. 1434 (1976). States have adopted numerous statutory provisions regulating the process, for example requiring that all abortions be performed in a hospital (held unconstitutional in *Doe* v. *Bolton*, 410 U.S. 179 (1973)); that all abortions after the first trimester be performed in an accredited hospital rather than a clinic (held unconstitutional in *City of Akron* v. *Akron Center for Reproductive Health*, 462 U.S. 416 (1983)).

[129] 505 U.S. 833 (1992).   [130] 530 U.S. 914 (2000).

down a Nebraska statute that criminalized the performance of a partial birth abortion unless necessary to save the life of the mother. However, seven years later in *Gonzales* v. *Carhart*[131] the Court ruled (5–4) that a similar statute was constitutional. It found that the statute in *Gonzales* was more specific than the one in *Stenberg* as to the instances to which it applied and more precise in its coverage. In July 2011 the Associated Press reported that legislation banning almost all abortions after five months of pregnancy have been enacted in a number of states.[132]

D   Conclusions

14.80   As United States' family law begins the second decade of the twenty-first century, it deals with families that differ importantly from those of the past. The changes brought about by the Women's Movement, the Civil Rights Movement and the Gay Rights Movement have all had an impact on families.

14.81   Supported by the Women's Movement, women have made substantial economic progress. Their progress in the professions and business management is particularly visible. Women's economic progress is reflected in family organization. In this changing world, fathers have assumed more important roles as child care-givers and managers in larger amounts and in more visible ways than in the past.

14.82   In some families the principal amount of support is earned by the wife and mother – which may affect the way in which the family is organized. In a small but noticeable number of families with a wife and mother who has a successful career, the couple decide to have the husband stay home to care for the children when they are very young.

14.83   Families of lesbian and gay people have limited experience from the past – but they are managing families as successfully as heterosexual couples. Other changes include, for young people, the voting age – and of majority – has been lowered to 18; draconian criminal penalties – in some states the death penalty for people under 18 – have been declared unconstitutional by the United States Supreme Court. The stigma of illegitimacy has been lifted, both in the law and in society. The number of non-marital

---

[131]   548 U.S. 938 (2007).
[132]   David Crary, 'States Enact Record Number of Abortion Laws', (July 30, 2010) *Wisconsin State Journal* (Madison), A.10.

children has increased and their non-marital fathers have acquired rights to connect with them. The law of divorce has changed, with no-fault divorce available in all states. The process of divorce has also changed with the use of mediation and collaborative divorce on the rise.

14.84   Child support, once a little-used resource for children, has been revamped and revitalized with mathematical formulas to set the amount of child support and is vigorously enforced.

14.85   The custody of children when parents separate or have not been married has become an issue of major importance. In recent decades the problem has become more complex because modern fathers, who often regard themselves as very involved parents in the intact family, seek a substantial role in the care of children post divorce. Shared time custody is becoming a much more common post-divorce arrangement. Such parental involvement creates problems when one parent wishes to relocate to another city or state for personal, financial or business reasons.

14.86   The institution of adoption has changed from one where the objective was to conceal the identity of the birth parents to one of a more open procedure.

14.87   The area of change in family law that has generated the most discussion and public concern is the increased tolerance for different lifestyles – non-marital and same-sex couples. The future will be enriched by all these changes and developments, but the degree of change probably will not compare with that which society has seen in the last decades.

INDEX

aboriginal children, 96
abortion
  Israel, 179–180 n. 26
  Russia, 335
  South Africa, 404
  USA, 429–30, 457–9
abuse, *see* child abuse; domestic abuse;
  protection of children
access to children *see* custody of
  children
adoption
  Canada, 89–90
  China, 119
  Hague Convention, 10–11, 152, 269,
    287, 442
  India, 151–2
  Israel, 177 n. 11, 177 n. 13, 179 n. 25,
    179–180 n. 26, 188–91
  Netherlands, 13
  New Zealand, 266–7, 269, 276–8
  Norway, 306 n. 47, 314, 321, 322
  'right to know' genetic origins, 44
    n. 238, 86–8
  Russia, 342, 343–4
  Scotland, 373–4, 388–9
  South Africa, 406, 407
  UK, 10 n. 49
  USA, 439–43, 444, 450–1
adult relationships
  Australia, 62–73
  Canada, 96–110
  China, 128–41
  equality in, 23–5
  and family law, 34–41
  India, 158–71
  Israel, 196–202

Malaysia, 220–31
Netherlands, 235–6, 254–63
New Zealand, 289–94
Norway, 296–7, 298, 315–27, 329
Russia, 352–61
Scotland, 382–95, 396
South Africa, 414–26, 427
USA, 451–9
adultery, 159, 220–1
African Charter on Human and
  Peoples' Rights (the Bajul
  Charter), 11
African Charter on the Rights and
  Welfare of the Child, 11, 403
alternative dispute resolution (ADR),
  8–9, 149–50, 169–71, 178–9,
  368, 433–4 *see also* dispute
  resolution
American Convention on Human
  Rights (the Pact of San José), 11
American Law Institute (ALI)
  Principles, 433, 446–7, 454
Annas, George A., 42 n. 225
Antokolskaia, M., 334
assisted reproductive technology
  (ART)
  Australia, 52–3
  Canada, 44, 85–6
  China, 42, 120
  and family law, 41–6
  India, 152–3
  Israel, 41 n. 223, 183–7
  Netherlands, 42 n. 230, 44 n. 236,
    245
  New Zealand, 274–6
  Norway, 42 n. 230, 306–7, 321, 322

assisted reproductive technology (*cont.*)
  and parentage, 43–6, 85–6
  'right to know' genetic origins, 44–6
  Russia, 342–4
  Scotland, 42, 372–4, 388–9
  South Africa, 406–7
  UK, 41 n. 223, 42
  USA, 42, 44, 444
Atkin, Bill, ix, 5, 8 n. 38, 13
Australia
  adult relationships, 62–73
  assisted reproductive technology
      (ART), 52–3
  cases, 51, 52–4, 55–8, 60–1, 63–4,
      65–6, 67–70, 72, 73–6
  child, definition of, 51–2
  child protection, 61
  children in family setting, 51–61
  children's rights, 26 n. 149, 53–61
  dispute resolution, 49–51
  divorce, 7, 48–9, 54–61, 67–73
  Family Court of Australia, 17, 49–51
  Family Law Council, 49, 53
  family law in, 7, 47–51, 73–6
  Family Law Rules, 50
  Family Relationship Centres, 50–1
  Hague Children's Convention, 11
  intra-family disputes, 54–61
  judicial discretion, erosion of, 73–6
  law reform, 5 n. 15, 49
  marriage, 12, 48–9, 51, 62–73
  office for children's issues, 28 n. 153
  parentage, recognition of, 52–3
  parenting, 22, 53–4
  property, division of, 69–73
  same-sex relationships, 62–3, 72–3
Austria, 10 n. 49
Awal, Noor Aziah Mohd, ix, 8, 14, 38
      n. 209

Bainham, A., 43–44 n. 235
baligh, 28 n. 157, 217
Barlow, A., 39 n. 212
Bates, Frank, ix–x, 7
bigamy, 36–7, 159, 171–2, 197, 226, 289,
      355–7, 388 *see also* polygamous
      (polygynous) marriage

Blecher-Prigat, Ayelet, x, 6, 14–15
Boyd, Marion, 79–80 n. 2
Bradley, D., 1 n. 2, 39 n. 212
bride kidnapping, 340, 419–20

Canada
  adoption, 89–90
  adult relationships, 96–110
  assisted reproductive technology
      (ART), 44, 85–6
  bigamy, 36–7
  cases, 82, 83, 86, 87–8, 90, 95,
      98–100, 101–99, 106, 107,
      108–9
  child, definition of, 82–4
  child protection, 95–6
  children in family setting, 81–96
  children's rights, 81–2, 86–8
  cohabitation, 97–9, 103, 105–10
  dispute resolution, 85–6
  divorce, 92–5, 103–8
  family law in, 7, 77–81, 110–11
  financial support for children and
      partners, 92–3, 106–8
  immigration, 78
  intra-family disputes, 92–5
  law reform, 5 n. 15, 80, 86
  marriage, 12, 99–102, 103–10
  non-marital births, 83–4
  office for children's issues, 28 n. 153
  parentage, recognition of, 84–8
  parenting, delivery of, 83, 88–91
  property, division of, 105–6
  religion and family law, 15, 79–80,
      104
  same-sex marriage, 37–8, 99–100,
      106–8
  same-sex relationships, 37–8, 85–6,
      98–100
caste system, India, 161
CEDAW (United Nations Convention
      on the Elimination of
      Discrimination Against
      Women), 10, 16–17, 32–3, 127,
      145, 153–4, 206, 209–11
Central Adoption Resource Authority
      (CARA), India, 152

Charter of Fundamental Rights of the
European Union, 11
child, definition of
Australia, 51–2
Canada, 82–4
China, 117–18
India, 151
Islamic law, 28 n. 157, 217, 219
Israel, 179–80
Malaysia, 28 n. 157, 215–17
Netherlands, 239
New Zealand, 273–4
Norway, 302–4
Russia, 339–41
Scotland, 369–72
South Africa, 404–5
USA, 436–8
child abduction
China, 10 n. 47
Hague Convention, 10, 12, 154,
157–8, 269, 286–7, 348,
360, 362
India, 10 n. 47, 12, 154–8
Malaysia, 10 n. 47
New Zealand, 269, 286–7
Russia, 10, 12 n. 66, 348–9, 362
child abuse, 30–2, 279, 285, 287–8, 310,
345 *see also* child protection
child justice, 82–3, 126, 252, 273–4,
370, 414, 436–7
child labour, 125
child law *see* family law, including
child law
child protection
Australia, 61
Canada, 95–6
China, 10 n. 47, 124–8
and family law, 30–4
Hague Children's Convention, 11
India, 32 n. 185, 158
Israel, 194–6
Malaysia, 10 n. 47, 220
Netherlands, 247–54
New Zealand, 31 n. 177, 287–8
Norway, 313–15
Russia, 350–2
Scotland, 370–1, 380–2

South Africa, 32 n. 181, 412–14
USA, 448–51
Child Protection Board (CPB),
Netherlands, 247–8
child-headed households, South
Africa, 412–13
children in the family setting
Australian family law, 51–61
best interests of, 26–7
Canadian family law, 81–96
child-headed households, 412–13
Chinese family law, 116–28
equality for, 18
Indian family law, 151–8
international instruments relating
to, 9–13
Israeli family law, 177, 179–96
Malaysian family law, 215–20
Netherlands' family law, 235,
239–54
New Zealand family law, 273–88,
293
Norwegian family law, 296, 298,
300–1, 302–15, 327–8
offices for children's issues, 28, 28
n. 153, 302, 432
physical punishment, 29–30, 91,
281–2, 309, 377–8, 410, 439
Russian family law, 332, 334–5,
339–52
Scottish family law, 368–82, 396
South African family law, 403–14
USA family law, 435–51
voice of, 27–8
children's rights
adoption, 44 n. 238, 86–8
Australia, 26 n. 149, 53–61
Canada, 81–2, 86–8
China, 122–3
in family law, 25–30
India, 153–4
Israel, 177, 179–80, 189, 203
Malaysia, 215, 217–19
Netherlands, 25, 244–5
New Zealand, 280–1
Norway, 25, 302, 314–15, 327
Russia, 25, 339, 341, 360

children's rights (*cont.*)
  Scotland, 363, 366, 368–9, 373–4, 376–8, 396
  South Africa, 402–3, 406–7, 412–14, 427
  USA, 10 n. 46, 25 n. 142, 443–4
  see also 'right to know' genetic origins
China
  administrative punishments system, 126
  adoption, 119
  adult relationships, 128–41
  assisted reproductive technology (ART), 42, 120
  child, definition of, 117–18
  child abduction, 10 n. 47
  child protection, 10 n. 47, 124–8
  children in family setting, 116–28
  children's rights, 122–3
  China Association of Marriage and Family Studies, 115
  civil partnerships, 129–30
  cohabitation, 130–1, 133–4, 136, 139, 141
  dispute resolution, 8, 115–16
  divorce, 136–8
  domestic abuse, 138
  family law in, 112–16, 142–3
  illegitimacy, 18 n. 100, 117–18, 121–2
  intra-family disputes, 123–4
  law reform, 5 n. 15, 114–15
  marriage, 113, 128–9, 131–2, 134–6, 139–41
  office for children's issues, 28 n. 153
  parentage, recognition of, 118–22
  parenting, delivery of, 26 n. 146, 122–3
  population control, 126–8
  property, division of, 134–6, 139–41
  same-sex marriage, 129–30
Christians, family law relating to, 145–6, 151, 171, 175–6, 177–8, 196
circumcision, 403
civil partnerships/unions
  China, 129–30
  Netherlands, 254–7
New Zealand, 289–94
  same-sex relationships, 37–8
  Scotland, 38 n. 206, 382–4, 385–7, 388–9, 391–4
  South Africa, 414–17, 418–19, 420–1
Clive, Eric M., xv–xviii, xix, 367
cohabitation
  Canada, 97–9, 103, 105–10
  China, 130–1, 133–4, 136, 139, 141
  and family law, 38–41
  India, 159
  Israel, 198–9
  Malaysia, 220–1
  Netherlands, 242–3, 261–3
  Norway, 305, 315–18, 320–1, 322, 324, 325–6, 327
  Russia, 331–2, 334–6, 342–3, 352–3, 362
  Scotland, 374–6, 384–5, 387–8, 389–90, 393, 394–5, 396
  South Africa, 415, 417–18
  USA, 39 n. 217, 453–4
collaborative law, USA, 8–9 n. 39, 434
common law marriage, 38–9, 454 n. 104
comparativism, 1–5
concubines, 131, 133–4
Confucian ideology, 113
contraception, 457
corporal punishment *see* physical punishment
courts, 5–7
Crotty, P. McG., 17 n. 95, 23 n. 126
cultural pluralism
  children's rights, 59
  New Zealand family law, 13, 266, 267–8, 272–3, 275, 277–8, 279, 283–4, 285, 287–8, 289, 295
custody of children
  Australia, 54–61
  Canada, 93–5
  India, 154–8
  interpretations of, 21
  Israel, 192–3
  Netherlands, 248–52
  Norway, 309–13
  Russia, 341
  USA, 445–8

custom-made adult relationships
  Canada, 108–10
  China, 141
  in family law, 40–1
  India, 169–71
  Netherlands, 261–3
  New Zealand, 293–4
  Norway, 326–7
  Scotland, 395
  South Africa, 425–6
customary law
  Chinese family law, 129
  and family law, 15–16
  Indian family law, 148–9, 163–4
  Malaysian family law, 206–14, 221
  New Zealand family law, 15, 266,
    267–8, 272–3, 275, 278, 279,
    283–4, 285, 287–8, 289, 295
  South African family law, 16,
    398–400, 406
customary marriages
  and family law, 36
  New Zealand, 289
  South Africa, 34 n. 193, 414–15,
    419–20, 421–3, 424, 425–6

de facto relationships, New Zealand,
    289–94
Defence for Children International
    (DCI), 253, 254
Dewar, J., 74
discipline, see physical punishment
dispute resolution
  Australia, 49–51
  Canada, 85–6
  China, 8, 115–16
  in family law, 7–9
  India, 8, 147–50, 169–71
  Israel, 177–9
  Malaysia, 8, 211–14
  Netherlands, 237–9
  New Zealand, 8, 8 n. 38, 270–3
  Norway, 300–2
  Russia, 9, 337–9
  Scotland, 367–8
  South Africa, 401–3, 428
  systems of, 7–9
  USA, 433–5

divorce
  Australia, 7, 48–9, 54–61, 67–73
  Canada, 83, 92–5, 103–8
  China, 136–8
  collaborative law, 8–9 n. 39, 434
  dispute resolution techniques, 8–9
  equality in, 21, 24
  India, 8, 12, 163–71
  Israel, 201–2
  Malaysia, 8, 211–14, 223–31
  Netherlands, 259–61
  New Zealand, 267, 290–4
  Norway, 302, 323, 324–5, 326–7
  pro se divorce, 434–5
  Russia, 8 n. 33, 331–2, 334–6, 347–8,
    358–61
  Scotland, 391–4
  South Africa, 24 n. 138, 423–5, 426
  USA, 8–9 n. 39, 429, 433–5, 445–8,
    452–3 see also property,
    division of
Dolgin, J. L., 42–43 n. 232
domestic abuse
  China, 138
  family law relating to, 30–1, 32–4
  Israel, 195
  Netherlands, 258–9
  New Zealand, 285
  Norway, 323
  Scotland, 390–1, 397
  USA, 33–4, 456–7
dowry and the law, India, 161–2, 167–8
Druze, family law relating to, 175–6

Eichner, Maxine, 448–9 n. 80
elderly people, 116 n. 11, 295
equality
  in adult relationships, 23–5
  Australian family law, 22, 58–61
  Canadian family law, 84
  for children, 18
  and family law, 16–25
  Indian family law, 161
  in marriage, 24
  Norwegian family law, 17, 19–20,
    296–7, 311–12, 328, 329
  in parenting, 19–22, 58–61
  Russian family law, 17, 20, 357

equality (*cont.*)
  South African family law, 428
  USA family law, 16–17
Eskridge, William N., 37 n. 204
ethnicity, 13, 96
European Commission, xvii–xviii
European Convention for the
      Protection of Human Rights
      and Fundamental Freedoms
      (ECHR)
  impact on family law, 11
  Netherlands, 236, 242, 263–4
  Norway, 298, 307
  Russia, 330, 331–2, 336–7
  Scotland, 363, 366
European Convention on the Exercise
      of Children's Rights, 11
European Court of Human Rights
  Netherlands, 236
  non-marital fathers, 375
  Norway, 314
  'right to know' genetic origins, 373
  Russia, 352, 353, 362
  Scotland, 366, 370, 381, 383, 384
European Union (EU), 3, 11 n. 55, 299,
      366–7

family courts
  Australia, 47, 49–51
  India, 146
  Israel, 177–8, 182–3, 192–3
  New Zealand, 267, 270–3, 277,
      279–80, 283–4
family group conference model, New
      Zealand, 268, 273–4, 287–8
family law, including child law
  adult relationships, 34–41
  assisted reproductive technology
      (ART), 41–6
  in Australia, 7, 47–51, 73–6
  in Canada, 7, 77–81, 110–11
  challenges, 13–46
  child protection, 30–4
  children's rights, 25–30
  in China, 112–16, 142–3
  comparative analysis, 1–5
  customary law, 15–16
  dispute resolution, 7–9

diversity between jurisdictions, 4–5
and equality, 16–25
Eric Clive's work, xv–xvii
goals of this volume, xviii–xix, 1–5
in India, 6, 144–50, 171–4
international instruments, 9–13
in Israel, 6, 175–9, 202–4
law making, 5–7
law reform, 5–6
legal advice, access to, 7
in Malaysia, 205–14, 231–4
marriage, 35–7
methodology of this volume,
      xviii–xix, 1–5
and migration, 9–13
in the Netherlands, 6–7, 235–9,
      263–4
in New Zealand, 5, 265–73, 294–5
in Norway, 296–302, 327–9
and personal law, 14–15
and religion, 13–15
in Russia, 330–9, 362
same-sex marriage, 37–8
in Scotland, 16, 363–8, 396–7
in South Africa, 398–403, 427–8
in the UK, 16
in the USA, 6, 10 n. 45, 16, 429–35,
      459–60
family planning, 404
Family Support Unit (Malaysia), 214
family trusts, New Zealand, 292
fasakh (dissolution of marriage), 229
fathers, 4–5, 19–22, 404–5, 407–9
      see also parenting, delivery of
fertility treatment *see* assisted
      reproductive technology (ART)
financial support for children and
      partners
  Canada, 83, 92–3, 106–8
  India, 166
  Israel, 191
  Malaysia, 230
  Netherlands, 246
  New Zealand, 266–7, 282–3, 291–2
  Norway, 313
  Russia, 361
  Scotland, 368 n. 25, 389–90
  South Africa, 410–11, 425

USA, 444–5, 453
forced marriage
    Australia, 65–6
    Canada, 102
    China, 132
    and migration, 12
    Norway, 12 n. 63, 319–20, 323
    Russia, 340
    Scotland, 12 n. 62, 386–7
    South Africa, 419–20

Gautier, A., 23 n. 125
gender equality, 428
get (bill of divorce), 24, 200, 201, 391
    n. 183
Glendon, M.A., 23 n. 127, 35 n. 194
Golombok, Susan, 45 n. 245
grandparents, 90, 191–2, 279, 346,
    376–7, 381, 447
guardianship, 153–4, 248–52, 278–81,
    341

Hacker, Dafna, 178–9
Hague Convention on Civil Aspects of
    Child Abduction
    India, 12, 154, 157–8
    New Zealand, 269, 286–7
    purpose of, 10
    Russia, 348, 360, 362
Hague Convention on Jurisdiction,
    Applicable Law, Recognition,
    Enforcement and Co-operation
    in Respect of Parental
    Responsibility and Measures
    for the Protection of Children
    ('the Hague Children's
    Convention'), 11
Hague Convention on the Protection
    of Children and Co-operation
    in Respect of Intercountry
    Adoption, 10–11, 152, 269, 287,
    442
harmonisation, 3–4
Heaton, Jacqueline, x, 6, 16
Hindus, family law relating to, 145–6,
    171–2, 417
Holder, Eric, 456 n. 117
homosexuality, 159

illegitimacy of children, xvi n. 2, 18, 18
    n. 100, 52, 84, 98, 267, 334, 372,
    459, *see also* non-marital births
immigration, 78, *see also* migration
in loco parentis, 84–6, 89–90
India
    adoption, 151–2
    adult relationships, 158–71
    alternative dispute resolution
        (ADR), 149–50, 169–71
    assisted reproductive technology
        (ART), 152–3
    cases, 148, 150, 152, 154 n. 35, 154–5
        n. 37, 155 n. 38, 155–7, 159, 160,
        161, 162, 163, 164, 167 n. 69,
        167–70, 168–9 n. 72, 169 n. 73,
        171–2
    child, definition of, 151
    child abduction, 10 n. 47, 12, 154–8
    child protection, 32 n. 185, 158
    children in family setting, 151–8
    children's rights, 153–4
    cohabitation, 159
    dispute resolution, 8, 147–50, 169–71
    divorce, 8, 12, 163–71
    extra-judicial courts, 14 n. 75, 148–9
    family law in, 6, 144–50, 171–4
    financial support for children and
        partners, 166
    intra-family disputes, 154–8
    law reform, 5 n. 15, 144–5
    marriage, 5, 34 n. 193, 35 n. 195, 38
        n. 210, 158–62
    migration, effects of, 12–13, 166–9
    office for children's issues, 28 n. 153
    panchayats, 147, 148–9
    parentage, recognition of, 151–3
    parenting, delivery of, 153–4
    personal law, 145–7, 158–61, 166,
        171–3
    property, division of, 166
    religion and family law, 14–15,
        145–7, 148–9, 160, 171–3
    surrogacy, 152–3
    uniform civil code, need for, 171–3
International Covenant on Civil and
    Political Rights (ICCPR), 10,
    126, 268, 357–8

international instruments, 9–13
international mobility *see* migration
intra-family disputes
    Australia, 54–61
    Canada, 92–5
    China, 123–4
    India, 154–8
    Israel, 21 n. 111, 192–3
    Malaysia, 218–19
    Netherlands, 246
    New Zealand, 28 n. 156, 283–7
    Norway, 309–13
    Russia, 346–9
    Scotland, 378–80
    South Africa, 411–12
    USA, 445–8
Islamic law
    child, definition of, 28 n. 157, 217,
        219
    children's rights, 215
    divorce, 211–14, 224–9
    fasakh, 229
    intra-family disputes, 219
    khul, 229
    li'an, 229, 230
    Malaysian family law, 205–14,
        220–1, 231–4
    marriage, 222–3, 233
    talaq, 24, 171, 213, 229, 230
    taliq, 229
Israel
    abortion, 179–180 n. 26
    adoption, 177 n. 11, 177 n. 13, 179
        n. 25, 179–180 n. 26, 188–91
    adult relationships, 196–202
    alternative dispute resolution
        (ADR), 178–9
    assisted reproductive technology
        (ART), 41 n. 223, 183–7
    cases, 183–4, 190–1, 194, 198
    child, definition of, 179–80
    child protection, 194–6
    children in family setting, 177,
        179–96
    children's rights, 177, 179–80, 189,
        203
    cohabitation, 198–9
    dispute resolution, 177–9

divorce, 201–2
Family Court system, 177–8, 182–3,
    192–3
family law in, 6, 175–9, 202–4
financial support for children and
    partners, 191
intra-family disputes, 21 n. 111,
    192–3
law reform, 5 n. 15, 176–7
marriage, 196–8, 202–4
office for children's issues, 28 n. 153
parentage, recognition of, 20 n. 105,
    181–91, 203
parenting, 191–2, 203
personal law, 175–6, 196–8
property, division of, 200–1
religion and family law, 14–15,
    175–6, 177–8, 179 n. 25, 181–3,
    184 n. 45, 188 n. 63, 192–3,
    196–8, 200, 201–4
same-sex marriage, 197–8
same-sex relationships, 190–1,
    199–200, 203–4
surrogacy, 177 n. 11, 186–7, 203

Jewish law, 18, 184 n. 45
Jews, family law relating to, 145–6, 151,
    175–6, 181–3, 196–8, 201

Kahn-Freud, Otto, 3–4
Khazova, Olga A., x–xi, 8 n. 33, 9, 38
    n. 209
khul (dissolution of marriage), 229
Kornhausert, L., 20
Krause, H.D., 2 n. 3
Kronborg, Anette, 312

law reform
    Australia, 5 n. 15, 49
    Canada, 5 n. 15, 80, 86
    China, 5 n. 15, 114–15
    of family law, 5–6
    India, 5 n. 15, 144–5
    Israel, 5 n. 15, 176–7
    Malaysia, 208–11
    Netherlands, 5 n. 15, 237
    New Zealand, 5 n. 15, 269
    Norway, 5 n. 15, 299–300

Russia, 5 n. 15, 337
Scotland, 5 n. 15, 367
South Africa, 5 n. 15, 6, 400–1
USA, 5 n. 15, 432–3
legal services, access to
    Australia, 7, 49–51
    Canada, 85–6
    China, 115–16
    India, 147–50
    Israel, 177–9
    Malaysia, 213–14
    nature of, 7
    Netherlands, 237–9
    New Zealand, 272
    Norway, 7, 300–2
    Russia, 337–9
    Scotland, 7, 367–8
    South Africa, 401–3
    USA, 434–5
legal systems
    dispute resolution, 7–9
    international instruments, 9–13
    law making, 5–7
    legal advice, access to, 7
    and migration, 9–13
legislation, origins of, 5–7
legislature, and courts, 6–7
Lewis, J., 39 n. 213
Li Yinhe, 130
li'an (dissolution of marriage), 229, 230
'living apart together', 40–1

maintenance see financial support for
        children and partners
Malaysia
    adult relationships, 220–31
    adultery, 220–1
    cases, 216, 218, 219, 221, 222–3,
        225–9, 230, 232–3
    child, definition of, 28 n. 157, 215–17
    child abduction, 10 n. 47
    child protection, 10 n. 47, 220
    children in family setting, 215–20
    children's rights, 215, 217–19
    cohabitation, 220–1
    dispute resolution, 8, 211–14
    divorce, 8, 211–14, 223–31
    family law in, 205–14, 231–4

Family Support Unit, 214
    financial support for children and
        partners, 230
    intra-family disputes, 218–19
    law reform, 208–11
    marriage, 14 n. 77, 35 n. 195, 207–8,
        220–31, 233
    office for children's issues, 28 n. 153
    parentage, recognition of, 217–18
    parenting, 217–19
    personal law, 206–8
    polygamous marriage, 207–8, 221,
        222–3, 226
    property, division of, 230–1
    religion and family law, 14–15,
        205–14, 217–18, 231–4
    same-sex marriage, 38 n. 209, 220–1,
        233
    same-sex relationships, 38 n. 209,
        220–1, 233
Malhotra, Anil, xi, 5, 6, 12, 14
Malhotra, Ranjit, xi–xii, 5, 6, 12, 14
mamzerim, 18, 181–3, 183 n. 42, 203
Maori culture
    adoption, 278
    ancestry, 275
    cultural pluralism in New Zealand,
        13, 295
    family group conference, 8, 15,
        267–8, 272–3, 287–8
    family law in New Zealand, 266,
        283
    marriage, 289
    parenting, 279, 283–4, 285
marriage
    Australia, 12, 48–9, 51, 62–73
    Canada, 12, 99–102, 103–10
    China, 113, 128–9, 131–2, 134–6,
        139–41
    common law marriage, 38–9, 454
        n. 104
    concept of, -10035 n. 2
    equality in, 24
    and family law, 35–7
    India, 5, 34 n. 193, 35 n. 195, 38
        n. 210, 158–62
    Islamic law, 222–3, 233
    Israel, 196–8, 202–4

marriage (*cont.*)
  Malaysia, 14 n. 77, 35 n. 195, 207–8,
    220–31, 233
  Maori culture, 289
  minimum age, 64–5, 101, 131–2,
    159–61, 197, 255–6, 289, 318,
    339–40, 403
  Netherlands, 254–9
  New Zealand, 36 n. 199, 289–94
  Norway, 315–17, 318–20, 321–2,
    326–7, 329
  and religion, 15
  Russia, 332, 334–6, 352–9
  Scotland, 38 n. 211, 382–4, 385–7,
    388–9, 391–4
  sham marriages, 12, 102, 256, 385
    n. 139
  South Africa, 24, 36 n. 199, 403,
    414–17, 418–23
  USA, 24, 38 n. 211, 451–3
    see also forced marriage; same-
    sex marriage
mediation
  China, 115–16, 123–4
  India, 169–71
  Israel, 178–9
  Netherlands, 237–9
  New Zealand, 271–2
  Norway, 300–2, 323
  Russia, 337–9
  Scotland, 368
  South Africa, 401, 428
  USA, 433–4
Melli, Marygold (Margo), xii, 6, 15
migration
  challenges for family law, 12–13
  China, 117
  India, 12–13, 166–9
  Netherlands, 252–3
  Russia, 332, 362
  Scotland, 13, 364 n. 4
  USA, relocation within, 12, 447–8,
    452 n. 96
Miles, J., 23 n. 130
Mnookin, R. H., 20
mokopuna (Maori), 279
mothers, 19–22 *see also* parenting,
    delivery of

Müller-Freienfels, W., 1 n. 2
mumaiyiz (Islamic law), 28 n. 157, 219
Muslims, family law relating to
  Indian family law, 145–6, 148, 151,
    159, 160, 163, 171
  Israeli family law, 181 n. 32, 196,
    201–2
  Israeli personal law, 175–6, 177–8
  Malaysian family law, 205–14, 215,
    217–18, 219, 220–1, 222–3,
    224–9, 230, 231–4
  polygamous marriage in Russia,
    355–7
  South African family law, 417
  talaq, 24, 171 *see also* Islamic law

Netherlands
  adoption, 13
  adult relationships, 235–6, 254–63
  assisted reproductive technology
    (ART), 42 n. 230, 44 n. 236, 245
  cases, 245
  child, definition of, 239
  child protection, 247–54
  children in family setting, 235,
    239–54
  children's rights, 25, 244–5
  cohabitation, 242–3, 261–3
  dispute resolution, 237–9
  divorce, 259–61
  domestic abuse, 258–9
  family law in, 6–7, 235–9, 263–4
  financial support for children and
    partners, 246
  Hague Children's Convention, 11
  intra-family disputes, 246
  law reform, 5 n. 15, 237
  marriage, 254–9
  migration, effects of, 252–3
  office for children's issues, 28 n. 153
  parentage, recognition of, 240–2
  parenting, 242–5, 246
  property, division of, 257–8, 260–3
  registered partnerships, 254–61
  same-sex marriage, 37–8, 254–7
  same-sex relationships, 241–2,
    243–4, 254–7
  sham marriages, 12

New Zealand
  adoption, 266–7, 269, 276–8
  adult relationships, 289–94
  assisted reproductive technology
      (ART), 274–6
  cases, 286–7
  child, definition of, 273–4
  child abduction, 269, 286–7
  child protection, 31 n. 177, 287–8
  children in family setting, 273–88,
      293
  children's rights, 280–1
  cultural pluralism, 13, 266, 267–8,
      272–3, 275, 277–8, 279, 283–4,
      285, 287–8, 289, 295
  customary law, 15, 266, 267–8,
      272–3, 275, 278, 279, 283–4,
      285, 287–8, 289, 295
  dispute resolution, 8, 8 n. 38, 270–3
  divorce, 267, 290–4
  Family Court, 267, 270–3, 277,
      279–80, 283–4
  family law in, 5, 265–73, 294–5
  financial support for children and
      partners, 266–7, 282–3, 291–2
  intra-family disputes, 28 n. 156,
      283–7
  law reform, 5 n. 15, 269
  marriage, 36 n. 199, 289–94
  office for children's issues, 28 n. 153
  parentage, recognition of, 274–8,
      290
  parenting, 278–83
  property, division of, 267, 269, 270,
      290–4
  religion and family law, 268
  same-sex relationships, 274–5, 277,
      289
  surrogacy, 275–6
Nicola, F., 2 n. 3
non-marital births
  Australia, 52
  Canada, 83–4
  China, 18 n. 100, 117–18, 121–2
  illegitimacy, xvi n. 2, 18
  New Zealand, 267
  Norway, 297
  Russia, 331–2, 341

  Scotland, -10035 n. 2, 371–2, 374–6
  South Africa, 404–5, 406, 407–9
  USA, 438, 439–40
non-marital fathers, 4–5, 19–22,
    404–5, 407–9
Norway
  adoption, 306 n. 47, 314, 321, 322
  adult relationships, 296–7, 298,
      315–27, 329
  assisted reproductive technology
      (ART), 42 n. 230, 306–7, 321, 322
  cases, 326
  child, definition of, 302–4
  child protection, 313–15
  children in family setting, 296, 298,
      300–1, 302–15, 327–8
  children's rights, 25, 302, 314–15,
      327
  cohabitation, 305, 315–18, 320–1,
      322, 324, 325–6, 327
  dispute resolution, 300–2
  divorce, 302, 323, 324–5, 326–7
  equality, 17, 19–20, 296–7, 311–12,
      328, 329
  and the EU, 11 n. 55, 299
  family law in, 296–302, 327–9
  financial support for children and
      partners, 313
  forced marriage, 12 n. 63, 319–20,
      323
  intra-family disputes, 309–13
  law reform, 5 n. 15, 299–300
  marriage, 315–17, 318–20, 321–2,
      326–7, 329
  office for children's issues, 28, 302
  parentage, recognition of, 304–7
  parenting, 302, 308–9
  property, division of, 297–8, 316,
      321–2, 324–7, 329
  religion and family law, 318–19
  same-sex marriage, 298, 305, 316–17,
      318–20, 321–2, 326–7, 329
  same-sex relationships, 37 n. 205,
      37–8, 321
  surrogacy, 307

Palmer, Michael, xii, 8
panchayats, India, 147, 148–9

parentage, recognition of
  assisted reproductive technology
      (ART), 43–6, 85–6
  Australia, 52–3
  Canada, 84–8
  China, 118–22
  India, 151–3
  Israel, 20 n. 105, 181–91, 203
  Malaysia, 217–18
  Netherlands, 240–2
  New Zealand, 274–8, 290
  Norway, 304–7
  Russia, 341–4
  Scotland, 372–6, 396
  South Africa, 405–9
  USA, 438–44
parenting, delivery of
  Australia, 22, 53–4
  Canada, 83, 88–91
  China, 26 n. 146, 122–3
  equality in, 19–22, 58–61
  India, 153–4
  Israel, 191–2, 203
  Malaysia, 217–19
  Netherlands, 242–5, 246
  New Zealand, 278–83
  Norway, 302, 308–9
  Russia, 345–6
  Scotland, 376–8
  South Africa, 409–11
  USA, 20, 22, 444–5
parents' rights, 54–61, 86–8, 93–5,
      314–15, 404–5, 410–11
Parkinson, Patrick, 21 n. 112
Parsis, family law relating to, 145–6,
      151, 163, 171
paternity, establishment of, 374–6,
      406–7
personal law
  and family law, 14–15
  in India, 145–7, 158–61, 166, 171–3
  in Israel, 175–6, 196–8
  in Malaysia, 206–8
physical punishment, 29–30, 91, 281–2,
      309, 377–8, 410, 439
polygamous (polygynous) marriage
  Canada, 101
  family law relating to, 36

  India, 159
  Israel, 197
  Malaysia, 207–8, 221, 222–3, 226
  Netherlands, 256
  Norway, 321
  Russia, 355–7
  Scotland, 388
  South Africa, 414–15, 421–3, 425–6
      see also bigamy
population control in China, 126–8
pre-nuptial agreements, 108–10, 395,
      426
pro se divorce, USA, 434–5
Probert, R., 23 n. 130, 39 n. 212
property, division of
  Australia, 69–73
  Canada, 105–6
  China, 134–6, 139–41
  India, 166
  Israel, 200–1
  Malaysia, 230–1
  Netherlands, 257–8, 260–3
  New Zealand, 267, 269, 270, 290–4
  Norway, 297–8, 316, 321–2, 324–7,
      329
  Russia, 358–9, 360–1
  Scotland, 389–90, 393–5
  South Africa, 420–1, 424–6
  USA, 430–1
protection of children, see child
      protection
punishment see physical punishment

Quebec, 79

race and ethnicity, 13
registered partnerships, Netherlands,
      254–61
religion
  Canadian family law, 15, 79–80, 104
  court structure, 6
  and family law, 13–15
  Indian family law, 14–15, 145–7,
      148–9, 160, 171–3
  Israeli family law, 14–15, 175–6,
      177–8, 179 n. 25, 181–3, 184
      n. 45, 188 n. 63, 192–3, 196–8,
      200, 201–4

Malaysian family law, 14–15,
205–14, 217–18, 231–4
and marriage, 15
New Zealand family law, 268
Norwegian family law, 318–19
Russian family law, 332–3, 354
same-sex marriage, 15
Scottish family law, 383, 386
South African family law, 399–400,
417
USA family law, 15, 430, 458–9
see also Christians; Hindus;
Islamic law; Jews; Muslims
relocation, 447–8, 452 n. 96
see also migration
Richards, M., 43–44 n. 235
'right to know' genetic origins
and adoption, 44 n. 238, 86–8
assisted reproductive technology
(ART), 44–6
Canada, 86–8
China, 120–1
family law relating to, 41–6
Israel, 189
Netherlands, 244–5
Norway, 306–7
Scotland, 373–4
South Africa, 406–7
rights of the child see children's rights
Rogerson, Carol J., xii–xiii, 7
Russia
abortion, 335
adoption, 342, 343–4
adult relationships, 352–61
assisted reproductive technology
(ART), 342–4
Bolshevik October Revolution,
effects of, 333–6
cases, 331–2
child, definition of, 339–41
child abduction, 10, 12 n. 66, 348–9,
362
child protection, 350–2
children in family setting, 332,
334–5, 339–52
children's rights, 25, 339, 341, 360
cohabitation, 331–2, 334–6, 342–3,
352–3, 362

dispute resolution, 9, 337–9
divorce, 8 n. 33, 331–2, 334–6, 347–8,
358–61
equality in family law, 17, 20, 357
family law in, 330–9, 362
financial support for children and
partners, 361
intra-family disputes, 346–9
law reform, 5 n. 15, 337
marriage, 332, 334–6, 352–9
migration, effects of, 332, 362
office for children's
issues, 28 n. 153
parentage, recognition of, 341–4
parenting, 345–6
polygamous marriage, 355–7
property, division of, 358–9, 360–1
religion and family law, 332–3, 354
same-sex marriage, 38 n. 209, 355
surrogacy, 342

same-sex marriage
Canada, 37–8, 99–100, 106–8
China, 129–30
and family law, 37–8
Israel, 197–8
Malaysia, 38 n. 209, 220–1, 233
Netherlands, 37–8, 254–7
Norway, 298, 305, 316–17, 318–20,
321–2, 326–7, 329
and religion, 15
Russia, 38 n. 209, 355
Scotland, 38 n. 208, 382–4
South Africa, 414–17, 418–19, 420–1
UK, 38 n. 208
USA, 455–6
same-sex relationships
Australia, 62–3, 72–3
Canada, 37–8, 85–6, 98–100
and family law, 37–8
Israel, 190–1, 199–200, 203–4
Malaysia, 38 n. 209, 220–1, 233
Netherlands, 241–2, 243–4, 254–7
New Zealand, 274–5, 277, 289
Norway, 37 n. 205, 37–8, 321
parentage, recognition of, 85–6,
241–2
parenting, 243–4

same-sex relationships (*cont.*)
  Scotland, 382–4, 385–7, 388–9,
        391–4
  South Africa, 37–8
  USA, 37–8, 429–30, 443, 455–6
Schuz, Rhona, xiii, 6, 14–15
Schwenzer, Ingeborg, 3–2 n. 9
Sclater, S. D., 43–44 n. 235
Scotland
  adoption, 373–4, 388–9
  adult relationships, 382–95, 396
  alternative dispute resolution
        (ADR), 368
  assisted reproductive technology
        (ART), 42, 372–4, 388–9
  child, definition of, 369–72
  child protection, 370–1, 380–2
  children in family setting, 368–82,
        396
  children's rights, 363, 366, 368–9,
        373–4, 376–8, 396
  civil partnerships, 38 n. 206, 382–4,
        385–9, 388–9, 391–4
  cohabitation, 374–6, 384–5, 387–8,
        389–90, 393, 394–5, 396
  dispute resolution, 367–8
  divorce, 391–4
  domestic abuse, 390–1, 397
  Eric Clive's work, xv–xviii
  family law in, 16, 363–8, 396–7
  financial support for children and
        partners, 368 n. 25, 389–90
  forced marriage, 12 n. 62, 386–7
  intra-family disputes, 378–80
  law making, 6, 365–7
  law reform, 5 n. 15, 367
  marriage, 38 n. 211, 382–4, 385–7,
        388–9, 391–4
  migration, effects of, 13
  non-marital fathers, 19–20
  office for children's issues, 28 n. 153
  parentage, recognition of, 372–6,
        396
  parenting, 376–8
  property, division of, 389–90, 393–5
  religion, 383, 386
  same-sex marriage, 38 n. 208, 382–4
  same-sex relationships, 382–4,
        385–7, 388–9, 391–4

surrogacy, 373
UK Parliament's role, 365–7
self-regulation of adult relationships,
        108–10, 141, 169–71, 261–3,
        293–4, 326–7, 395, 425–6
sex-change, 221, 233
sham marriages, 12, 102, 256, 385
        n. 139
Sharia law, 333, *see also* Islamic law;
        Syariah courts (Malaysia)
Singer, Anna, 307
Smart, C., 43–44 n. 235
South Africa
  abortion, 404
  adoption, 406, 407
  adult relationships, 414–26, 427
  assisted reproductive technology
        (ART), 406–7
  child, definition of, 404–5
  child protection, 32 n. 181, 412–14
  children in family setting, 403–14
  children's rights, 402–3, 406–7,
        412–14, 427
  civil unions, 414–17, 418–19, 420–1
  cohabitation, 415, 417–18
  customary law, 16, 398–400, 406
  customary marriages, 34 n. 193,
        414–15, 419–20, 421–3, 424,
        425–6
  dispute resolution, 401–3, 428
  divorce, 24 n. 138, 423–5, 426
  family law in, 398–403, 427–8
  financial support for children and
        partners, 410–11, 425
  intra-family disputes, 411–12
  law reform, 5 n. 15, 6, 400–1
  marriage, 24, 36 n. 199, 403, 414–17,
        418–23
  non-marital fathers, 4–5
  office for children's issues, 28 n. 153
  parentage, recognition of, 405–9
  parenting, 409–11
  polygynous marriage, 414–15,
        421–3, 425–6
  property, division of, 420–1, 424–6
  religion and family law, 399–400,
        417
  same-sex marriage, 414–17, 418–19,
        420–1

same-sex relationships, 37–8
spousal support, *see* financial support
    for children and partners
state intervention for child protection
    Australia, 61
    Canada, 95–6
    China, 124–8
    India, 158
    Israel, 194–6
    Malaysia, 220
    Netherlands, 247–54
    New Zealand, 287–8
    Norway, 313–15
    Russia, 350–2
    Scotland, 380–2
    South Africa, 412–14
    USA, 448–51
step-parents, 89–90, 119, 192, 279,
    376–7, 405, 409–10, 443
Straus, Murray A., 33 n. 191
Sulh procedure, Malaysia, 213
surrogacy
    and family law, 41–6
    India, 152–3
    Israel, 177 n. 11, 186–7, 203
    New Zealand, 275–6
    Norway, 307
    Russia, 342
    Scotland, 373 *see also* assisted
        reproductive technology (ART)
Sutherland, Elaine E., xiii, 7, 29
Sverdrup, Tone, xiii–xiv
Sweden, 29, 30–31 n. 173
Switzerland, 10 n. 49
Syariah courts (Malaysia), 205, 209,
    213, 214, 221, 222–3, 224–9
    see also Islamic law
talaq (dissolution of marriage), 24, 171,
    213, 229, 230
ta'liq (dissolution of marriage), 229

ukuthwala (bride kidnapping),
    419–20
United Kingdom (UK)
    adoption, 10 n. 49
    assisted reproductive technology
        (ART), 41 n. 223, 42
    civil partnerships, 38 n. 206
    equality for children, 18

equality of parental rights, 19 n. 101,
    22
family law in, 16
office for children's issues, 28 n. 153
physical punishment, 377–8
same-sex marriage, 38 n. 208
United Nations Commission on
    Human Rights (Human Rights
    Council), 33
United Nations Committee on the
    Rights of the Child, 314, 369,
    370, 377–8
United Nations Convention on the
    Elimination of Discrimination
    Against Women (CEDAW), 10,
    16–17, 32–3, 127, 145, 153–4,
    206, 209–11
United Nations Convention on the
    Rights of the Child
    assisted reproductive technology
        (ART), 44
    basis for other charters, 11
    Canada, 77–8, 81–2, 84, 91, 94
    child abuse, 31
    and child law, 25–30
    China, population control in, 127
    equality under, 16–17
    India, 145, 153–4
    Israel, 177, 189
    Malaysia, 205, 216, 217–18, 220
    Netherlands, 236, 252
    New Zealand, 269, 273, 283
    Norway, 296, 298–9, 302, 303, 307
    purpose of, 10
    'right to know' genetic origins, 86,
        373
    Russia, 336–7, 339, 341
    Scotland, 363, 366, 369, 370
    South Africa, 403
    USA, 435–6, 437, 442
United States of America (USA)
    abortion, 429–30, 457–9
    abuse among dating partners, 33–4
    adoption, 439–43, 444, 450–1
    adult relationships, 451–9
    alternative dispute resolution
        (ADR), 433–4
    assisted reproductive technology
        (ART), 42, 44, 444

United States of America (*cont.*)
  bigamy, 36–7
  cases, 437, 438, 438 n. 30, 439–40,
      447, 449–50, 451, 454, 455,
      457–9
  child, definition of, 436–8
  child protection, 448–51
  children in family setting, 435–51
  children's rights, 10 n. 46, 25 n. 142,
      443–4
  citizen-initiated legislation, 6
  cohabitation, 39 n. 217, 453–4
  collaborative law, 8–9 n. 39, 434
  dispute resolution, 433–5
  divorce, 8–9 n. 39, 429, 433–5,
      445–8, 452–3
  domestic abuse, 33–4, 456–7
  equality, 16–17
  family law in, 6, 10 n. 45, 16, 429–35,
      459–60
  financial support for children and
      partners, 444–5, 453
  intra-family disputes, 445–8
  law reform, 5 n. 15, 432–3
  marriage, 24, 38 n. 211, 451–3

  migration, internal, 12, 447–8, 452
      n. 96
  office for children's issues, 28 n. 153,
      432
  parentage, recognition of, 438–44
  parenting, 20, 22, 444–5
  property, division of, 430–1
  religion and family law, 15, 430,
      458–9
  same-sex marriage, 455–6
  same-sex relationships, 37–8,
      429–30, 443, 455–6
Universal Declaration of Human
    Rights, 10

Vlaardingerbroek, Paul, xiv, 6–7, 13

Wardle, Lynne, 35–36 n. 198
whanau (Maori), 267–8, 283–4, 285,
    287–8
whangai (Maori), 278
women, 10, 209–11
World Health Organization (WHO), 33

Zuma, Jacob, 422–3